DON'T THROW THIS CARD AWAY!
THIS MAY BE REQUIRED FOR YOUR COURSE!

THOMSON ONE | Business School Edition

Congratulations!

Your purchase of this NEW textbook includes complimentary access to THOMSON ONE – Business School Edition for Finance. THOMSON ONE – Business School Edition is a Web-based portal product that provides integrated access to Thomson Financial content for the purpose of financial analysis. This is an educational version of the same financial resources used by Wall Street analysts on a daily basis!

For hundreds of companies, this online resource provides seamless access to:

- **Current and Past Company Data:** Worldscope which includes company profiles, financials and accounting results, market per-share data, annual information, and monthly prices going back to 1980.

- **Financial Analyst Data and Forecasts:** I/B/E/S Consensus Estimates which provides consensus estimates, analyst-by-analyst earnings coverage, and analysts' forecasts.

- **SEC Disclosure Statements:** Disclosure SEC Database which includes company profiles, annual and quarterly company financials, pricing information, and earnings.

- **And More!**

THOMSON
SOUTH-WESTERN

THOMSON ONE | Business School Edition

SERIAL NUMBER

PP1SV8VPP4XWWK

HOW TO REGISTER YOUR SERIAL NUMBER

1. Launch a web browser and go to **http://tobsefin.swlearning.com**

2. Click the "Register" button to enter your serial number.

3. Enter your serial number **exactly** as it appears here and create a unique User ID, or enter an existing User ID if you have previously registered for a different South-Western product via a serial number.

4. When prompted, create a password (or enter an existing password, if you have previously registered for a different product via a serial number.) Submit the necessary information when prompted. **Record your User ID and password in a secure location.**

5. Once registered, return to the URL above and select the "Enter" button; have your User ID and password handy.

For technical support, contact 1-800-423-0563 or email **tl.support@thomson.com**

- Navigable review of Indices Performance with results downloadable to Excel

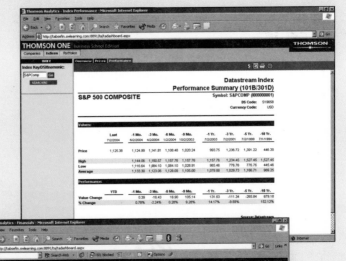

THOMSON ONE: BUSINESS SCHOOL EDITION'S UNIQUE KEY FEATURES ARE:

- Includes both Domestic and International companies

- Historical Financial Statements that can be downloaded to Excel

- Peer Set analysis with results downloadable to Excel

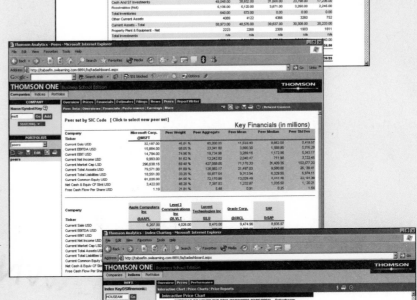

- Indices comparison available

For more information, see the animated demo at http://tobsefin.swlearning.com *or contact your local South-Western rep.*

New in 2005! Ehrhardt/Brigham; Corporate Finance: A Focused Approach, 2e, Pubs 3/15/2005

New in 2005! Hawawini/Viallet; Finance for Executives: Managing for Value Creation, 3e, Pubs 7/15/2005

Smart/Megginson/Gitman; Corporate Finance, 1e, 2004

MBA/Grad Corporate Finance/ Supplemental Products

New in 2005! Brigham/Buzzard; Cases for Topics in Financial Management Year One, Pubs 1/3/2005 Visit **http://www.textchoice. com** for more information.

Brigham/Klein; Finance Online Case Library Visit **http://www.textchoice.com** for more information.

Mayes/Shank; Financial Analysis with Microsoft® Excel 2002, 3e, 2004

INVESTMENTS COURSES

Investments—Undergraduate

Hearth/Zaima; Contemporary Investments: Security and Portfolio Analysis, 4e, 2004

Hirschey; Investments: Theory and Applications, 1e, 2001

New in 2005! Mayo; Basic Investments, 1e, Pubs 1/10/2005

New in 2005! Mayo; Investments: An Introduction, 8e, Pubs 1/10/2005

New in 2005! Reilly/Norton; Investments, 7e, Pubs 2/15/2005

StockNavigator; Online Stock Simulation visit **http://stocknavigator.swlearning.com** for more information.

Strong; Practical Investment Management, 3e, 2004

Derivatives/Futures and Options

Chance; An Introduction to Derivatives and Risk Management, 6e, 2004

Strong; Derivatives: An Introduction, 2e, 2005

Stulz; Risk Management and Derivatives, 1e, 2003

Fixed Income

New in 2005! Grieves/Griffiths; A Fixed Income Internship: Volume 1: Introduction to Fixed Income Analytics, 1e, Pubs 1/28/2005

New in 2005! Sundaresan; Fixed Income Markets and Their Derivatives, 3e, Pubs 7/15/2005

Real Options

New in 2005! Shockley; An Applied Course in Real Options Valuation, 1e, Pubs 3/15/2005

MBA/Grad Investments

New in 2005! Reilly/Brown; Investment Analysis and Portfolio Management, 8e, Pubs 10/1/2005

New in 2005! Strong; Portfolio Construction, Management, and Protection, 4e, Pubs 7/15/2005

FINANCIAL INSTITUTIONS COURSES

Financial Institutions and Markets

New in 2005! Madura; Financial Markets and Institutions, 7e, Pubs 2/15/2005

Financial Institutions Management

Gardner/Mills/Cooperman; Managing Financial Institutions, 5e, 2005

Money & Capital Markets

Liaw; Capital Markets, 1e, 2004

Commercial Banking/Bank Management

New in 2005! Koch/MacDonald; Bank Management, 6e, Pubs 3/15/2005

INSURANCE

Risk Management and Insurance/Intro to Insurance

Trieschmann/Hoyt/Sommer; Risk Management and Insurance, 12e, 2005

CERTIFICATION

NASD—National Association of Securities Dealers

Thomson South-Western; NASD Exam for Series 6: Preparation Guide, 1e, 2004

Thomson South-Western; NASD Stockbroker Series 7 Exam: Preparation Guide, 1e, 2004

PREFACE

e-resource

For more information about the text, visit the Web site at **http://crum. swlearning.com.**

The past several decades have seen dramatic transformations in the business environment. Today, most large companies have operations that extend well beyond their home country's borders, and markets continue to open in countries that were once closed. Also, changing technology is making it possible to transfer instantaneously both funds and information throughout the world. Indeed, we now recognize that events halfway around the globe can have a profound effect on our jobs, the price we pay for goods and services, and our investment portfolios.

In this changing environment, it is increasingly important for students to have a solid understanding of international finance and the role played by the finance function in broadly-defined global business operations of companies. Students recognize this need, and over the past few years the University of Florida has seen a sharp increase in students' interest in international business in general, and international finance in particular. Accordingly, we have developed new programs and courses focusing on global aspects of finance and have taken other steps to "internationalize" all areas of our finance curriculum.

While there are many international finance textbooks, we believe that they tend to be strong on the "international" component but weak in the "finance" component. These texts typically go into great depth on exchange rates and international institutions, which many students also see in their economics courses. However, the texts do not do a good job of explaining how key financial concepts such as stock and bond valuation, financial structure, and capital budgeting are applied in a global setting. Thus, finance students end up better prepared for jobs as international economists than as financial managers in multinational firms, where there are far more good jobs. And international business students, who need a good international finance course but lack a strong background in the basics of finance, usually have a difficult time understanding and appreciating the proper role of finance in a multinational company.

The absence of a book that provides what we believe students need motivated us to create Fundamentals of International Finance (FIF). Our target audience is the student who wants to work for a multinational firm or to understand how multinational competitors impact domestic companies' operations. Such students may desire to work either inside or outside the United States, but what all of them have in common is a need to learn things that would be useful to managers of companies whose vision extends beyond the border of their own home country. In putting the text together, we blended the materials that Gene Brigham and Joel Houston developed over the years for Fundamentals of Financial Management with Roy Crum's extensive experience in teaching international finance to undergraduate, graduate, and MBA students; in working with the World Bank in eastern Europe and the former Soviet Union; and in writing articles, teaching materials, and a book for the World Bank to use for private sector development *training. FIF is intended for use with upper-level undergraduate, specialized masters, and MBA students.*

We are excited about this project, and we believe FIF will be both interesting and useful to all students who need to understand international finance. The book and its accompanying ancillaries should also find a receptive audience among professors in finance departments who are interested in teaching an international finance class that builds upon the key ideas that are taught throughout the traditional finance curriculum. Professors who are not personally well-trained in international finance and economics are sometimes required to teach an international finance course, and this can be a difficult assignment. Like their students, these professors will find our book a welcome relief from those currently on the market.

In developing FIF, we borrowed many of the features that have made Fundamentals of Financial Management so successful. We also strived to provide the same general look and notation, which will minimize confusion for both students and instructors who have used one of our other books.

Also, experience has taught us that optimal student learning requires more than just a textbook—it requires a fully integrated ancillary package both to facilitate student learning and to help instructors prepare and conduct their classes. Therefore, we provide a set of ancillary materials that is similar to the set available for our other books. We list below the book's key pedagogical features and ancillaries.

PEDAGOGICAL FEATURES

e-resource

The Fundamentals of International Finance *Web site is **http:// crum.swlearning. com.***

- Value maximization is the chief financial objective of both international and domestic businesses, and for investors, hence the text has a strong emphasis on valuation. Each chapter begins by presenting the basic valuation equation, along with a brief discussion of how the ideas covered in the chapter tie in with the elements of the equation and thus affect companies' values.

- Throughout the text, we include many real world examples to help students understand how the various concepts are applied in practice. In addition, we include boxes that provide detailed descriptions of how the ideas in the chapter apply to specific companies, countries, or regions.

- We provide a number of useful Web links throughout the text to help students access additional sources of information about the ideas, companies, government agencies, and countries profiled in the chapter. These Web addresses will be updated on the text's companion Web site, **http://crum.swlearning.com.**

- Following each major section of the chapter, we provide a series of Self-Test Questions. These questions help students test their understanding of what they just read and help keep them pointed in the right direction.

- At the end of each chapter, we have added a wide range of Questions, Self-Test Problems, Starter Problems, and Exam-Type Problems to help students gauge their performance and to give them practice for their exams. These problems cover all of the key ideas discussed in the chapter and vary in level of difficulty.

- At the end of many of the chapters we have also included a short series of problems that are based on the *Thomson One: Business School Edition* database that accompanies the text (for more details about *Thomson One: Business School Edi-*

tion see the discussion of the ancillary package below). These problems expose students to the current concerns of real world companies throughout the world, and also help reinforce many of the key concepts covered throughout the chapter.

- Each chapter concludes with an integrated case that systematically covers the major concepts discussed in the chapter and shows how these concepts are applied in practice. The integrated cases can be used either as comprehensive chapter problems assigned to students to work individually or as lecture vehicles that instructors can use to demonstrate the relevance of the material. Data presented in each integrated case are coordinated with the chapter's electronic lecture slide show and *Excel*® spreadsheet model. The integrated case spreadsheet model can be used in lectures to illustrate sensitivity and scenario analyses, as well as to demonstrate specific modeling tools. The case models can also be used to help make lectures more dynamic.

A BRIEF DESCRIPTION OF THE MAJOR ELEMENTS OF THE ANCILLARY PACKAGE

- *Thomson One: Business School Edition*—Students can use the *Thomson One: Business School Edition* online database to conduct up-to-date research on a vast number of multinational companies. This database can also be used to work the *Thomson One: Business School Edition* problems provided at the end of many chapters. *Thomson One: Business School Edition*, a product of Thomson Financial's Investment Banking Group, combines a full range of fundamental financials, earning estimates, market data, and source documents for hundreds of real world companies throughout the globe. Thus, it gives students an opportunity to access and apply the most reliable information available to answer discussion questions and to work through group projects.

- **Spreadsheet Models**—Each chapter includes two spreadsheet models. The first shows how all the calculations required for the chapter can be done using *Microsoft Excel*®. The second is a modified version of the first, but it is applied to the integrated case. Both models provide extensive tutorial aids, including pictures of the dialog boxes used in the calculations. These models both help students develop their modeling skills and illustrate how *Excel* can be used to solve a wide range of real life financial problems. Interested students can go through the spreadsheets on their own and do things like test various "what if" scenarios, and instructors can use them as a component of their classroom lectures. The spreadsheet models are included on the Instructor's Resource CD-ROM and the instructor's portion of the text's Web site. Instructors are free to post the files on their own password protected site or to hand out to their students.

- **Instructor's Manual**—This comprehensive manual contains answers to all text questions and problems. A computerized version in *Microsoft Word*® is also available on the Instructor's Resource CD-ROM and the text's Web site.

- *PowerPoint* **Lecture Presentations**—Prepared in *Microsoft PowerPoint*®, this computer graphics slide show covers all essential issues presented in the chapter. Each chapter's slide show is designed so that instructors can easily modify or delete slides, or add some of their own. The slides use illustrations taken from the integrated cases, but they can be used either to facilitate a discussion of the cases or used separately from the cases. The electronic slide shows are included on both the Instructor's Resource CD-ROM and the instructor's portion of the text's Web site. Instructors are free to post the files on their own password protected site or to hand out to their students.

e-resource

The Fundamentals of International Finance *Web site is* **http://crum.swlearning.com.**

- **Test Bank**—We have put together a number of questions differing in degree of difficulty with a variety of formats: conceptual multiple choice, problem multiple choice, short-answer essay, and short-answer problems. The test bank is available in both printed and electronic forms.

- **Comprehensive Web Site**—Our extensive Web site, available at **http://crum. swlearning.com,** is designed to be a teaching and learning tool, and therefore it includes separate resources for both students and instructors.

ACKNOWLEDGMENTS

This textbook reflects the efforts of a great many people. First, we would like to thank Dana Aberwald Clark, who worked closely with us at every stage of the book's production—her assistance was absolutely invaluable. Second, Christopher Buzzard did an outstanding job helping us develop and proof manuscript, and develop the *Excel* models, the Web site, and the *PowerPoint* presentations. Susan Whitman typed and helped proof the manuscript, while Sue Nodine copyedited the manuscript. Finally, the South-Western Publishing staff, especially Mike Reynolds, Elizabeth Thomson, Dan Plofchan, Heather MacMaster, Vicky True, John Barans, Karen Schaffer, and Sandee Milewski, helped greatly with all phases of the textbook's development and production.

ERRORS IN THE TEXTBOOK

At this point, most authors make a statement like this: "We appreciate all the help we received from the people listed above, but any remaining errors are, of course, our own responsibility." And generally there are more than enough remaining errors! Having experienced difficulties with errors ourselves, both as students and instructors, we resolved to avoid this problem in *FIF*. As a result of our detection procedures, we are convinced that this book is relatively free of significant errors, meaning those that either confuse or distract readers.

Partly because of our confidence that few such errors remain, but primarily because we want very much to detect any errors that may have slipped by to correct them in subsequent printings, we decided to offer a reward of $10 per error to the first person who reports it to us. For purpose of this reward, errors are defined as misspelled words, non-rounding numerical errors, incorrect statements, and any other error that inhibits comprehension. Typesetting problems such as irregular spacing and differences of opinion regarding style, grammatical, or punctuation conventions do not qualify for this reward. Given the ever-changing nature of the World Wide Web, changes in Web addresses also do not qualify as errors, although we would like to learn about them. Finally, any qualifying error that has follow-through effects is counted as two errors only. Please report any errors to Joel Houston either through e-mail at **international@joelhouston.com** or by regular mail at the address below.

CONCLUSION

We are excited about this first edition of *Fundamentals of International Finance,* and we believe that we have put together a clear and concise text that summarizes the key topics in international finance today. In today's world, it is increasingly important for students to have a solid understanding of how finance works in an international setting. As we all know, international finance is relatively complex, and it is continually changing. This makes the subject stimulating and exciting, but also challenging and sometimes perplexing. We sincerely hope that this first edition of *FIF* will meet its own challenge by contributing to a better understanding of our global financial system.

Roy L. Crum
Eugene F. Brigham
Joel F. Houston
4723 N.W. 53rd Ave. Suite A
Gainesville, FL 32606

September 2004

Brief Contents

CONTENTS

PART 2   International Analysis and Securities   117

PART 3   International Corporate Finance   285

PART 4   International Corporate Strategy   463

International Financial Environment

Part One

CHAPTER 1

An Introduction to International Financial Management

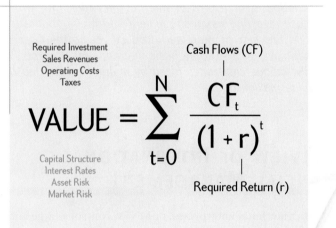

Required Investment
Sales Revenues
Operating Costs
Taxes

Cash Flows (CF)

$$\text{VALUE} = \sum_{t=0}^{N} \frac{CF_t}{(1+r)^t}$$

Capital Structure
Interest Rates
Asset Risk
Market Risk

Required Return (r)

e-resource

Visit *http://crum. swlearning.com* to see the Web site accompanying this text. This ever-evolving site, for both students and instructors, is a tool for teaching and learning, and contains Excel chapter models and PowerPoint slides.

In today's global economy, raw materials, finished goods, services, and money flow freely across most national boundaries, as do innovative ideas and new technologies. For example, world-class American companies and others around the world are making breakthroughs in foreign laboratories, obtaining capital from foreign investors, and putting foreign employees on the fast track to top management. Dozens of top U.S. manufacturers, including Dow Chemical, Colgate-Palmolive, Gillette, Hewlett-Packard, and Xerox, sell more of their products outside the United States than they do at home. Service firms are not far behind as Citigroup, Disney, McDonald's, and Time Warner all receive more than 20 percent of their revenues from foreign sales. Other multinational enterprises, or MNEs, from around the world are also experiencing similar sales and revenue growth in foreign markets, including the United States.

The trend is even more pronounced regarding profits. In recent years, Coca-Cola and many other companies have made more money in the Pacific Rim and western Europe than in the United States. However, like other companies, Coke has found that global investing also presents unique challenges and risks. Managers of multinational companies must deal with a wide range of issues that are not present when a company operates in a single country. Successful global companies such as Coca-Cola must conduct business in different countries, and they must be sensitive to the many subtleties of different cultures as well as political, legal, and economic systems.

This text is designed to help managers understand the global financial environment. We explain what "international financial management" is, and we *explore the implications of globalization for firms' values. Why is it important for people to understand international financial management? Because it explains both how managers can increase their firm's value and why it is essential for them to do so. Today more than ever before, investors are forcing managers to focus on value maximization. Similarly, that is our focus in this text. Shown on the previous page is the basic valuation equation that we will use throughout the book.*

In Part One of this text, we show that both the numerator and denominator of the valuation equation can be influenced by fluctuating economic conditions and associated changes in exchange rates. In Part Two, we use this equation to find the values of bonds, stocks, and other securities. We will also see how, given a security's price, we can use the equation to find its required rate of return. In Part Three, we discuss how managers use the valuation equation to make investment decisions within the firm. Finally, in Part Four, we show how the valuation equation is influenced by international corporate strategic decisions, including those involving risk management and multinational tax management.

In this first chapter, we introduce you to the international financial environment. We discuss some basic international concepts, reasons firms expand globally, unique challenges faced by multinationals, and the logic behind shareholder value maximization.

OVERVIEW OF INTERNATIONAL FINANCIAL MANAGEMENT

Multinational Enterprise (MNE)
A firm that operates in an integrated fashion in a number of countries.

Multinational enterprises, or **MNEs**, control a large and growing share of the world's technological, marketing, and productive resources. Rather than merely buying resources from and selling goods to foreign nations, MNEs make direct investments in fully integrated operations—from the extraction of raw materials, through the manufacturing process, and on to distribution to consumers throughout the world. The traditional aspects of international commerce—namely, sourcing inputs from and selling goods and services to other countries (*importing* and *exporting*)—are also vitally important to MNEs, but their international involvement goes far beyond these traditional functions.

The emergence of "world companies" raises a host of questions for governments. Should domestic firms be favored, or does it make no difference what a company's nationality is as long as it provides domestic jobs? Should foreign companies be permitted to acquire domestic firms (*cross-border acquisitions*), or should the independence of local companies from foreign control be maintained? Should a company make an effort to keep jobs in its home country, or should it produce where the total costs of serving its markets are lowest? Clearly, even businesses that operate exclusively in the United States or in other countries are not immune to the effects of **globalization**. Increasing globalization creates additional competition from around the world, which then affects both local jobs and company profits. Globalization also has the potential to raise our standard of living by allowing us greater access to a wider range of products and services at more competitive prices. At the same time, though, it can challenge long-held cultural values about the role of businesses in society and the regulation of company practices, and it can even threaten local control of the country's economic destiny.

Globalization
The increasing interconnectedness of economies, markets, and people across countries.

As you go through this book, you should gain a better appreciation of the problems facing governments and local societies as globalization trends advance and of the difficult, but profitable, challenges and opportunities facing managers of companies that seek to capitalize on this trend. Some of these firms will fit the definition of an MNE given earlier, but others will be more difficult to categorize. Even companies that consider themselves to be "domestic" are faced with many of the same issues as MNEs for at least three reasons:

1. Foreign competitors may enter these firms' traditional markets and use the benefits of their global scope to out-compete the domestic firms.
2. Some of the inputs used by domestic firms may be imported and/or some of their outputs may be sold to foreign customers, so changes in exchange rates can affect their costs and revenues, hence profits.
3. Even if all of a firm's inputs are domestic and all of its sales are to local customers, the globalization of capital markets will still affect the availability and cost of capital to both it and its customers.

Managers who ignore the implications of globalization for their companies do so at their own peril, so at a minimum, they need to understand how to protect themselves from adverse impacts of foreign competition and capital cost shifts, and then to take advantage of new opportunities that are created by such trends.

SELF-TEST QUESTIONS

Briefly explain whether the following statement is true or false: "MNEs' international involvement doesn't extend past importing and exporting goods and services."

What is a cross-border acquisition?

How does increased globalization raise our standard of living?

How might the trend toward globalization affect even a small, local homebuilder?

MAJOR DEVELOPMENTS IN INTERNATIONAL FINANCE

The world economy is quite fluid, so changes in one sector often have dramatic effects on economies throughout the world. Here we list a few of the major events that have shaped the current international financial environment:

1. The collapse of communism in eastern Europe and the former Soviet Union and the movement toward market economies (i.e., the privatization of state-run enterprises) throughout the world has created vast new markets for international commerce and foreign investment.
2. The European Community and the European Free Trade Association have created a "borderless" region where people, capital, goods, and services move freely among the European Union (EU) nations without the burden of tariffs. This consolidation has led to the creation of a single European currency called the "euro," and an increased militancy and clout regarding issues such as antitrust policy, product standards, and the protection of information.
3. The North American Free Trade Agreement (NAFTA) has moved the economies of the United States, Canada, and Mexico much closer together and made them more interdependent.
4. U.S., foreign bank, and capital market regulations have been loosened dramatically. One key deregulatory feature in the United States was the removal of interest rate ceilings, allowing banks to attract foreign deposits by raising rates. Another key feature was the removal of barriers to entry by foreign banks, which resulted in more cross-border banking transactions. At the same time, several foreign countries have significantly deregulated and liberalized

their foreign exchange and capital markets. All this has increased global competition in the financial services industry.

5. With the continuing reduction in trade and financial barriers, as well as advances in communication and computer technology, financial markets have become increasingly integrated (or at least less segmented), resulting in the increased globalization of these markets.

6. The emergence of China as an economic powerhouse in Asia has supplanted Japan somewhat in terms of influence and market interest. In addition to Hong Kong, with its separate economic system, new trading zones along the southeast China coast are hotbeds of investment growth and the focus of many foreign direct investments.

7. The rise of cross-border mergers and acquisitions are challenging domestic practices in many countries and causing governments to consider restrictions on the traditional flexibility of MNEs to integrate their global operations to their own benefit.

8. The ease with which imports can be brought into the United States, combined with low overseas production costs, especially in China, has led to a dramatic increase in the U.S. balance of trade deficit. This means that foreigners hold a large and increasing amount of U.S. debt securities. That, in turn, has implications for Federal Reserve monetary policy and thus the level of interest rates in the United States, which of course affects the U.S. economy.

SELF-TEST QUESTION   What are some major events that have affected the international financial environment?

WHY FIRMS "GO GLOBAL"

In response to the events just described, U.S. corporations have significantly increased their direct investments in other nations over the past two decades, and foreign corporations have mirrored the pattern and invested more in the United States. This trend is shown in Figure 1-1. These developments suggest an increasing degree of mutual interdependence among business enterprises and nations, what we have called "globalization." Table 1-1 demonstrates this trend on a country-by-country basis for 25 nations. The general trend from 1998 to 2000 shows an increase in foreign direct investment (FDI), followed by a steep drop-off that coincided with the bursting of the Internet bubble and the 2001 recession. However, this is not true of all countries, as China, France, Italy, and Mexico did not have huge declines and show almost no signs of the economic events that transpired. Notice that many nations maintained a relatively stable flow of FDI, and in some cases negative FDI even existed. An important question underlying this trend is, why do firms invest in foreign production facilities and related ventures? Various reasons have been put forth to explain why U.S. and foreign firms "go global." Some of the more important ones include the following:

1. *To seek production efficiency.* As competition increases in their domestic marketplace, and as demand increases in other markets, companies often reassess where it is best to produce their products. Depending on the nature of the production process, the availability of labor with the requisite skills, and the adequacy of transportation infrastructure, companies that operate in high-cost countries have strong incentives to shift production to lower-cost regions. For example, GE has production and assembly plants in Mexico, South Korea, and Singapore, and even Japanese manufacturers have started to shift some of

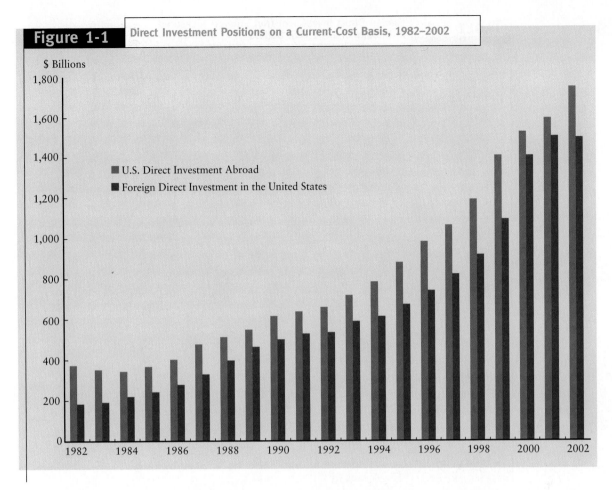

Figure 1-1   Direct Investment Positions on a Current-Cost Basis, 1982–2002

Source: Elena L. Nguyen, "The International Investment Position of the United States at Yearend 2002," *Survey of Current Business,* July 2003, 12–21.

their production to lower-cost countries in the Pacific Rim and the Americas. BMW, in response to high production costs in Germany, built assembly plants in the United States, among other countries. These examples illustrate how companies strive to remain competitive by locating manufacturing facilities wherever in the world they can produce and transport their products to meet the demand in their major markets at the lowest total unit landed costs.

Labor costs are one of the most important components in location decisions. Looking at Table 1-2, we see that labor costs vary considerably across countries. For instance, they are as high as $26.18 in Germany, $21.33 in the United States, and $18.83 in Japan, but only $2.38 in Mexico. Because labor is often immobile, particularly across countries, labor services in a country can be underpriced relative to its productivity for extended periods. This labor market imperfection makes it advantageous for firms to locate production abroad to benefit from lower-cost labor services. The ability to shift production from country to country also has important implications for labor costs in other countries. For example, when Xerox threatened to move its copier rebuilding work to Mexico, its union in Rochester agreed to work-rule changes and productivity improvements that kept the operation in the United States. In addition, transportation costs often play a vital role in the location decision.

TABLE 1-1 | Foreign Direct Investment (Net Inflows) Measured in Billions of 2001 U.S. Dollars

Country	1998	1999	2000	2001
Argentina	$ 7.29	$ 23.99	$ 11.66	$ 3.21
Australia	6.05	5.70	11.51	4.39
Belgium	22.69	142.70	214.43	73.63
Brazil	31.91	28.58	32.78	22.64
Canada	22.74	24.49	66.02	27.44
Chile	4.81	8.99	3.64	4.48
China	43.75	38.75	38.40	44.24
Costa Rica	0.61	0.62	0.41	0.45
France	29.52	46.63	43.17	52.50
Germany	23.64	54.58	207.72	31.53
Hong Kong, China	14.77	24.58	61.92	22.83
Indonesia	−0.36	−2.75	−4.55	−3.28
Israel	1.74	2.87	4.52	3.22
Italy	2.63	6.94	13.18	14.87
Japan	3.27	12.31	8.23	6.19
Kazakhstan	1.15	1.59	1.28	2.76
Kuwait	0.06	0.07	0.02	−0.04
Mexico	11.90	12.48	14.19	24.73
Morocco	0.33	0.85	0.20	2.66
Russian Federation	2.76	3.31	2.71	2.47
Singapore	6.39	11.80	5.41	8.61
South Africa	0.55	1.50	0.97	7.16
Sweden	19.413	59.386	22.125	13.085
United Kingdom	74.65	89.53	119.93	63.11
United States	179.03	289.44	307.74	130.80
Totals	$2,509.29	$2,887.94	$3,187.62	$2,564.69

Note: Net inflows represent new investments less withdrawals during the year.

Source: "Balance of Payments Statistics," *International Monetary Fund, Yearbook 2002.*

2. *To avoid political, trade, and regulatory hurdles.* Governments sometimes impose tariffs, quotas, and other restrictions on imported goods and services. They often do so to raise revenue, protect domestic industries, and pursue various political and economic policy objectives. To circumvent these government hurdles, firms often develop production facilities abroad. For instance, the primary reason Japanese auto companies moved production to the United States was to get around U.S. import quotas. Now, Honda, Nissan, Toyota, Mazda, and Mitsubishi are all assembling vehicles in the United States. This was also the situation with India in the 1970s when it was following a development strategy to compete domestically with imported products. One of the factors that prompted U.S. pharmaceutical maker SmithKline and Britain's Beecham to merge was that they wanted to avoid licensing and regulatory delays in their largest markets, western Europe and the United States. GlaxoSmith-Kline (the result of a 2000 merger between Glaxo Wellcome and SmithKline

TABLE 1-2 | Hourly Compensation Costs for Manufacturing Production Workers Measured in U.S. Dollars

	1982	1987	1992	1997	2002
Canada	$10.45	$ 12.02	$17.17	$16.47	$16.02
France	7.85	12.29	17.47	17.24	17.42
Germany (former West Germany)	10.25	16.85	25.30	27.52	26.18
Japan	5.60	10.79	16.35	19.40	18.83
Mexico	1.97	1.04	2.17	1.70	2.38
Spain	5.28	7.63	13.50	12.16	12.04
Sweden	10.07	15.12	24.59	22.22	20.18
Taiwan	1.24	2.25	5.05	5.80	5.41
United Kingdom	6.92	9.09	14.37	15.57	17.47
United States	11.68	13.52	16.09	18.79	21.33

Source: "International Comparisons of Hourly Compensation Costs for Production Workers in Manufacturing, 1975–2002," U.S. Department of Labor, Bureau of Labor Statistics, Office of Productivity and Technology, September 2003.

Beecham) now identifies itself as an inside player in both Europe and the United States.

3. *To broaden their markets.* After a company's home market matures and competition becomes more intense, growth opportunities are often better in foreign markets. According to Vernon's product life-cycle theory, a firm first produces in its home market, where it can better develop its product and satisfy local customers.[1] This attracts competitors, but when the home market is expanding rapidly, new customers provide the sales growth desired. However, as the home market matures and the growth of total demand slows, competition becomes more intense. At the same time, demand for the product develops abroad, and this creates conditions favoring production in foreign countries both to satisfy foreign demand and to cut production and transportation costs so that the company can remain competitive. Thus, such homegrown firms as IBM, Coca-Cola, and McDonald's are aggressively expanding into overseas markets, and foreign firms such as Sony and Toshiba now dominate the U.S. consumer electronics market. Also, as products become more complex and development becomes more expensive, it is necessary to sell more units to cover overhead costs, so larger markets are critical. Thus, movie companies have "gone global" to get the volume necessary to support pictures such as *Titanic.*

4. *To seek raw materials and new technology.* Supplies of many raw materials that are important for industrial societies are geographically dispersed, so companies must go where the materials are found, no matter how challenging it may be to operate in some of the locations. For example, major deposits of oil are located on the northern coast of Alaska, in Siberia, and in the deserts

[1]Raymond Vernon, "International Investment and International Trade in the Product Cycle," *Quarterly Journal of Economics* 80, 1966, 190–207.

GOING GLOBAL AND YOUR JOB

We have all heard of the blue-collar American jobs lost because manufacturers have shifted production to low-cost countries such as Mexico, Taiwan, and Singapore. However, job losses are now moving up the food chain to relatively high-paying white-collar jobs in tech support, back-office operations, architecture, and even financial analysis. Why has this change occurred? In one word, *telecommunications*.

Most of us have bought a computer, printer, or software and then called an 800 number to ask a tech support person how to do something. Or, we have called a credit card company or a bank to find out about a charge or a check, or a catalog company to order something, or an airline to purchase a ticket. We or our parents may have hired an architect to design a house using architectural software, and we all use software that has millions of lines of code telling the computer how to perform different functions. In all of these situations, we are dealing with an American company, and we assume that Americans are on the other end of the line. But increasingly, the man or woman on the other end is Indian, Irish, Chinese, or some other foreign national.

Today, virtually the entire developed world is wired (or "wireless"), and the developing world is rapidly moving toward that goal. Moreover, information such as bank account and credit card records, catalog information, and airline flight schedules, along with design details on software or products under development, are kept in huge electronic databases. Those databases can be accessed from anywhere on earth—it's just as easy to access a database from Bombay as it is from Boston via satellite links. So, the people handling your catalog order, or flight reservation, or insurance claim, or who are programming the software for your next cell phone, can be physically located anywhere. Provided they are well educated and competent, you can be served from anywhere.[†]

In the past, men and women from India, China, and elsewhere would come to the United States for an education, then stay on and work in Silicon Valley, Wall Street, and the like. Now, though, many of those people are receiving an American education, returning home, and working for American, European, Japanese, and other multinational companies in their home countries. They may be employed by the multinational, but they often establish independent contracting companies, train their countrymen in the relevant technology, and then work under contract with the multinational.

Telecommunications makes this possible, and costs drive companies to use offshore service providers. For example, Microsoft managers were urged to "pick something to move offshore today . . . [because you can get] quality work at 50 percent to 60 percent of the cost. That's two heads for the price of one." Even Wall Street firms such as Lehman and Bear Stearns are eliminating $80,000-and-up financial analyst jobs and outsourcing them to Indian analysts, who can get constantly updated data from Thomson Analytics and other sources and analyze it just as well in Bombay as in New York, but at a fraction of the cost.

Globalization will produce winners and losers. Developing nations will certainly be winners, and this trend will lower costs for companies in some developed countries and also lower inflation rates. Moreover, worldwide efficiency and productivity will improve; developing nations will have higher incomes and thus can import more from developed nations—leading to gains for developed nations. However, at least some individual Americans who lose their jobs will be losers. Regardless of the final outcome, globalization of services and technology will affect all of us, and people, companies, and nations will have to deal with it.

[†]If you need to talk to someone, then spoken English is a requirement if you are American or British, or French for a French national, and so on. Note, though, that companies in Calcutta, Shanghai, and elsewhere literally have language schools that teach foreign nationals how to speak English with an American accent!

Source: Pete Engardio, Aaron Bernstein, and Manjeet Kripalani with Frederik Balfour, Brian Grow, and Jay Greene, "The New Global Job Shift," *BusinessWeek,* February 3, 2003, 50–60.

Vertically Integrated Investment
Occurs when a firm undertakes investment to secure its input supply at stable prices.

of the Middle East, all of which present unique challenges. This is why many U.S. oil companies, such as ExxonMobil, have major production facilities around the world to ensure access to the basic input resources needed to sustain the companies' primary business line. Because ExxonMobil has refineries, distribution facilities, and oil production fields, this type of investment is referred to as a **vertically integrated investment**, whereby the firm undertakes an investment to secure its supply of inputs at stable prices.

Natural Trade Barriers
Trade barriers that are not governmentally imposed.

Additionally, high transportation costs for raw materials can create **"natural" trade barriers** that are not governmentally imposed. To reduce transportation costs, firms often invest abroad. For example, cranberry grower Cran Chile invested in concentrate facilities because it is much cheaper to ship cranberry concentrate to the United States, its primary market, than it is to ship the raw berries. Furthermore, because no single nation holds a commanding advantage in all technologies, companies scour the globe for leading scientific and design ideas. By diversifying their production facilities around the world, firms gain better access to new technologies. For example, Xerox has introduced more than 80 different office copiers in the United States that were engineered and built by its Japanese joint venture, Fuji Xerox. Similarly, versions of the super concentrated detergent that Procter & Gamble first formulated in Japan in response to a rival's product are now being marketed in Europe and the United States.

5. *To protect the secrecy of their processes and products.* Firms often possess special intangible assets such as brand names, technological and marketing know-how, managerial expertise, and superior research and development (R&D) capabilities among others. Unfortunately, property rights in intangible assets are often difficult to protect, particularly in foreign markets. Firms sometimes invest abroad rather than license local foreign firms in order to protect the secrecy of their production process, distribution system, or the product itself. Once a firm's formula or production process is revealed to other local firms, they may then more easily develop similar products or processes, which will hurt firm sales.[2] For example, to protect their formula, Coke builds bottling plants and distribution networks in foreign markets but imports the concentrate or syrup required to make the product from the United States. In the 1960s, Coke faced strong pressure from the Indian government to reveal its formula in order to continue its operations in India. Rather than reveal its formula, Coke withdrew its operations from India until the foreign investment climate improved.

6. *To diversify.* By establishing worldwide production facilities and markets, firms can cushion the impact of adverse economic trends in any single country. For example, General Motors softened the blow of poor sales in the United States during a recent recession with strong sales by its European subsidiaries. Also, oil companies were able to weather the recent disruption in Venezuelan oil production by increasing production in Mexico and elsewhere in the world. In general, geographic diversification of inputs and outputs works because the economic fluctuations or political vagaries of different countries are not perfectly correlated. Therefore, companies investing overseas can benefit from diversification in the same way that individuals benefit from investing in a broad portfolio of stocks. However, because individual shareholders can diversify their investments internationally on their own, it makes less sense for firms to undertake foreign investments solely for diversification purposes. Note, though, that in countries that place constraints on foreign stock ownership or that do not have internationally traded companies, corporate diversification might make sense because then companies can do something that shareholders cannot duplicate easily in their individual portfolios.

7. *To retain customers.* If a company goes abroad and establishes production or distribution operations, it will need inputs and services at these new locations. If it can obtain what it needs from a single supplier that also operates

[2]According to the internalization theory of foreign direct investment, firms that have intangible assets often invest directly in foreign countries to avoid potential usage problems that may occur with their intangible assets and to also take advantage of potential economies of scale. We discuss FDI in more detail in Chapter 4.

in the same set of countries, then managing the relationship is much easier, and it is likely that economies of scale and other synergies will be obtained. Therefore, from the perspective of the supplier of inputs or services, it makes good business sense to follow customers abroad to retain the business. Large U.S. banks, such as Citibank and Chase, initially expanded abroad to supply banking services to their long-time customers, although they quickly capitalized on their global network to develop new customer relationships. The same history is also true for accounting, law, and advertising firms and other similar service providers.

SELF-TEST QUESTION   Why do companies "go global"?

MULTINATIONAL VERSUS DOMESTIC FINANCIAL MANAGEMENT

Managers of multinational companies must deal with a wide range of issues that either are not present or are not as complex when a company operates in a single country. In theory, the concepts and procedures covered in your previous financial management courses are valid for both domestic and multinational operations. However, the following five major factors distinguish financial management in firms operating entirely within a single country from firms that operate globally:

1. *Different currency denominations.* Cash flows in various parts of a multinational corporate system will be denominated in different currencies. Hence, an analysis of exchange rates must be included in all financial analyses.
2. *Political risk.* Nations are free to place constraints on the transfer or use of corporate resources, and they can change regulations and tax rules at any time. At one extreme, they can even expropriate assets within their boundaries. Therefore, political risk can take on many subtle to more extreme forms. Of course, political risk is also present for companies operating in a single country, but the important reality for a multinational enterprise is that political risk not only exists but also varies from country to country, and it must be addressed explicitly in any financial analysis.
3. *Economic and legal ramifications.* Each country has its own unique economic and legal systems, and these differences can cause significant problems when a corporation tries to coordinate its worldwide operations. For example, differences in tax laws among countries cause a given economic transaction to have strikingly different after-tax consequences, depending on where the transaction occurs. Similarly, differences in legal systems of host nations, such as the Common Law of Great Britain versus the French Civil Law, complicate matters ranging from the simple recording of business transactions to the role played by the judiciary in resolving conflicts. Such differences can restrict multinational corporations' flexibility in deploying resources and make procedures that are required in one part of the company illegal in others. These differences also make it difficult for executives trained in one country to move easily to another.
4. *Role of governments.* Most financial models developed in the United States assume the existence of a competitive marketplace in which the participants determine the terms of trade. The government, through its power to establish basic ground rules, is involved in the process, but other than taxes, its role is minimal. Thus, the market provides the primary barometer of success, and it

gives the best clues about what must be done to remain competitive. This view of the process is reasonably correct for the United States and western Europe, but it does not accurately describe the situation in the rest of the world. Although market imperfections can complicate the decision process, they can also be valuable to the extent that they can be overcome by one firm but still serve as barriers to entry by competitors. Frequently, the terms under which companies compete, the actions that must be taken or avoided, and the terms of trade on various transactions are not determined in the marketplace but by direct negotiation between host governments and multinational enterprises. This is essentially a political process, and it must be treated as such. Thus, our traditional financial models have to be recast to include political and other noneconomic aspects of the decision. The ultimate outcome of such negotiations can provide access to additional profitable opportunities for the firm.

5. *Language and cultural differences.* The ability to communicate is critical in all business transactions. In this regard, U.S. citizens are often at a disadvantage because they are generally fluent only in English, while European and Japanese businesspeople are usually fluent in several languages, including English, hence they can operate in U.S. markets more easily than Americans can operate in their countries. At the same time, even within geographic regions that are considered relatively homogeneous, different countries have unique cultural heritages that shape values and influence the conduct of business. Multinational corporations find that matters such as defining the appropriate goals of the firm, attitudes toward risk, decision processes, performance evaluation and compensation system design, interactions with employees, and the ability to curtail unprofitable operations vary dramatically from one country to the next.

These five factors complicate financial management, and they increase the risks faced by multinational firms. However, the prospects for high returns and other factors make it worthwhile for firms to accept these risks and learn how to manage them.

SELF-TEST QUESTION   Identify and briefly discuss five major factors that complicate financial management in multinational firms.

THE BASIC GOAL: CREATING STOCKHOLDER VALUE

Throughout this book we assume that management's basic overriding goal is to create value for stockholders. Stockholders own the firm—it legally belongs to them. As a result, they elect the directors, who then hire the managing executives. The directors, as representatives of the stockholders, monitor the actions of the managers, set the strategic direction of the company, and determine managers' compensation, rewarding them if performance is superior or replacing them if performance is poor.

To better understand the primary goal of creating stockholder value, we use the basic valuation equation given earlier as a key tool throughout this text. The basic valuation equation is

$$\text{Value} = \sum_{t=0}^{N} \frac{CF_t}{(1 + r)^t},$$

where CF_t represents the expected cash flows at time t and r is the corresponding discount rate for the cash flows. In valuing a capital budgeting project, the valuation equation becomes

$$\text{Value} = \text{NPV} = \frac{CF_0}{(1 + r)^0} + \frac{CF_1}{(1 + r)^1} + \frac{CF_2}{(1 + r)^2} + \cdots + \frac{CF_n}{(1 + r)^n}$$

$$= \sum_{t=0}^{n} \frac{CF_t}{(1 + \text{WACC})^t}. \tag{1-1}$$

Note that Equation 1-1 is a special application of the basic valuation equation, where WACC is the project's risk-adjusted cost of capital and n is the project's life. To find a project's net present value (NPV), we estimate its relevant after-tax cash flows (CFs), its WACC, and n, after which we enter the data and solve the equation with a financial calculator or a computer spreadsheet. If a project has a positive NPV, it is generating more cash flow than is needed to cover its cost of capital, and the excess cash flow accrues to the firm's stockholders and thus raises company value. Therefore, if a firm takes on a project with a positive NPV, stockholder wealth increases by the amount of the NPV.

Societal Considerations

People with limited experience in business and economics, and sometimes even those with extensive experience, often argue that stock price maximization results in short-sighted decisions that are bad for employees, bad for consumers, and ultimately bad for society. They argue that firms should pursue nobler goals, such as the maximization of social well-being. Although such criticism makes for good press, and the lofty goals sound good, in practice the criticism is not warranted and the goals are not operational—people can't even agree how to define, much less measure, social well-being. Also, many of the activities that are criticized most often as being detrimental to social well-being (such as worker layoffs, plant closings, and similar restructuring activities) are based on the appropriate company objective of maintaining (or regaining) competitiveness. Companies that are not competitive in the global marketplace will not survive, and social well-being, however measured, will not be well served if companies go out of business.

There is another way to look at the issue. Of all the groups that have a direct stake in the continued health and prosperity of a company, only stockholders lack a contract that specifies the returns they are to receive. Virtually every other group has such a contractual relationship, and if the company does not honor the contract, they have recourse to the legal system to enforce it. This is why common stock is known as a "residual claimant"—only after all other claimants are fully satisfied do stockholders receive anything. Thus, maximizing the returns accruing to stockholders implies that all other groups with a direct stake in the fortunes of the firm have already received full and fair compensation. Also, we should always remember that in the real world, stock price maximization is constrained—we have laws that prevent managers from forming monopolies, from operating in an unsafe manner, from polluting the environment, and so forth. Stock prices respond positively to managerial actions that enhance the ability of firms to prosper in the long run, not to short-sighted actions. This means that the actions that managers legally take to maximize stock price, including restructuring when required to remain competitive, tend to provide long-run benefits to consumers as well as to stockholders.

Business students should understand why the goal of stock price maximization is indeed the proper foundation for our economic system, and why the same actions that maximize stock prices also benefit society. The economic logic behind this goal is spelled out here:

1. *Benefits to consumers.* Stock price maximization requires that corporations be efficient and produce goods and services with the required level of quality demanded by their target customer group at the lowest possible cost. They must also do this better than competitors in the minds of their customers. Moreover, the world is dynamic, so companies must continuously focus attention on producing products and services that consumers want and need, which leads to new and improved products in order to stay ahead of the competition. A competitive global economy also keeps their prices in check. For companies to maximize their stock prices, they must generate growth in sales by creating value for customers in the form of products that meet the needs of the customer, competitive prices, efficient and courteous service, adequate stocks of merchandise, and well-located business establishments.

2. *Benefits to employees.* There are cases in which a company's stock price increases when it announces plans to lay off employees. Properly interpreted, this is a signal from the market that some employees are redundant because of either bad management decisions in the past or changes in the business environment and that competitive advantage has shifted to other firms. In other words, it is a restructuring operation to regain competitive advantage, but viewed over time it is the exception rather than the rule for well-managed companies.[3] In general, companies that successfully increase stock prices also grow and add more employees, thus benefiting society. Note too that many governments across the world—including U.S. federal, state, and local governments—are privatizing some government-owned activities by selling these operations to investors. Perhaps not surprisingly, the sales and cash flows of recently privatized companies generally improve. Moreover, studies show that these newly privatized companies tend to grow at a higher rate and are more profitable than they were as state-owned enterprises, and their goods and/or services do not deteriorate in quality. When they are managed properly with the goal of stock price maximization, they require more employees, and society benefits.

3. *Other benefits.* Stockholders obviously benefit if the prices of their shares increase—it is better to be wealthier than poorer. Moreover, today many individuals around the world are stockholders, either directly or indirectly through retirement plans. Indeed, 45 percent of U.S. adults own stocks directly, and 80 percent own stocks through retirement programs. Thus, many members of society have an important stake in the stock market. Finally, strong stock prices benefit even those who have no direct or indirect ownership interest in the market, because strong markets stimulate both individual spending (through the "wealth effect") and corporate investment (because of lower capital costs and higher consumer spending). Obviously, all of this stimulates employment and economic growth.

Stockholder versus Stakeholder Wealth Maximization

Stockholder wealth maximization is generally accepted as the ultimate goal of financial management in many countries such as Australia, Canada, the United Kingdom, and the United States. However, it is not as widely accepted in many other parts of the world such as Asia and Europe. For instance, French and German firms often

---

[3]Maintaining employment is a public good and is socially desirable. However, if companies are forced to retain redundant workers, the cost of maintaining the public good is borne by the shareholders, not the public. When groups such as employees are hurt by company actions such as layoffs, government mechanisms should be available to mitigate the negative effects on the ex-employees—for example, unemployment insurance payments, job search assistance, and even retraining when necessary. These mechanisms transfer the cost of the public good to the general population so that it is not borne disproportionably by the shareholders.

Stakeholders
Include a firm's employees, customers, banks, suppliers, and community, as well as its stockholders.

focus on maximizing the overall welfare of firms' **stakeholders**, with stockholders a subset of this group. Other stakeholders include the firm's employees, customers, banks, suppliers, and community. In Japan and Korea, managers often focus on increasing the prosperity of their interlocking business groups (called *keiretsu* and *chaebol*) by focusing on increasing their market share.

While stakeholder or business group maximization goals may sound noble, they often create long-run competitiveness problems and/or monopolistic behavior on the part of the business groups. In practice, these other goals are also very difficult to implement consistently and fairly. These problems, along with the increasing integration of world markets, have caused firms throughout the world to shift their focus more and more toward stockholder wealth maximization. Businesspeople throughout the world now realize that stockholder wealth maximization is a long-run goal and that firms cannot stay in business if they do not treat appropriately their employees, customers, and the environment in which they operate. When managers take actions to maximize the prices of their companies' stock, these same actions improve the quality of life for millions of ordinary citizens.

Agency Relationship Considerations

While stockholder wealth maximization provides strong business and societal benefits, in certain situations it can go awry. Managers are empowered by the owners of the firm—the shareholders—to make decisions. However, managers may have personal goals that compete with shareholder wealth maximization, and such potential conflicts of interest are addressed by *agency theory*.

An *agency relationship* arises whenever one individual (or more), called a *principal*, (1) hires another individual or organization, called an *agent*, to perform some service and then (2) delegates decision-making authority to that agent. Within the financial management context, the primary agency relationships are those (1) between stockholders and managers; (2) between managers and debtholders; and (3) among managers, stockholders, and debtholders in times of financial distress.[4]

Agency Problem
A potential conflict of interest between the agent (manager) and (1) the outside stockholders, (2) the creditors (debtholders), and (3) stockholders and debtholders in times of financial distress.

A potential **agency problem** can arise whenever the manager of a firm owns less than 100 percent of the firm's common stock. If the firm is a proprietorship managed by its owner, the owner-manager will presumably operate so as to maximize his or her own welfare, with welfare measured in the form of increased personal wealth, more leisure, or perquisites.[5] However, if the owner-manager incorporates and then sells some of the stock to outsiders, a potential conflict of interest immediately arises. Now the owner-manager may decide to lead a more relaxed lifestyle and to work less strenuously to maximize shareholder wealth, because less of this wealth will accrue to him or her. Also, the owner-manager may decide to consume more perquisites, because some of these costs will be borne by the outside shareholders. In essence, the fact that the owner-manager will neither gain all the benefits of the wealth created by his or her efforts nor bear all of the costs of perquisites will increase the incentive to take actions that are not in the best interests of other shareholders. Agency conflicts are particularly important in large corporations because large firms' managers generally own only a small percentage of the stock. In this situation, shareholder wealth maximization could take a back seat to any number of conflicting managerial goals.

There are two extreme positions regarding how to deal with shareholder-manager agency conflicts. At one extreme, if a firm's managers were compensated solely on

[4]The classic work on the application of agency theory to financial management is Michael C. Jensen and William H. Meckling, "Theory of the Firm, Managerial Behavior, Agency Costs, and Ownership Structure," *Journal of Financial Economics,* October 1976, 305–360.

[5]*Perquisites* are executive fringe benefits such as luxurious offices, executive assistants, expense accounts, limousines, corporate jets, generous retirement plans, and the like.

the basis of stock price changes, agency costs would be low because managers would have a great deal of incentive to maximize shareholder wealth. However, it would be difficult if not impossible to hire competent managers under these terms, because the firm's earnings stream, and hence managers' compensation, would be affected by economic events that were not under managerial control. At the other extreme, stockholders could monitor every managerial action, but this would be costly and inefficient. The optimal solution lies somewhere in the middle, where executive compensation is tied to performance but some monitoring is also done.

In addition to conflicts between stockholders and managers, there can also be conflicts between stockholders (through managers) and creditors. Creditors have a contractual claim on part of the firm's earnings stream for payment of interest and principal on the debt, and they have a claim on the firm's assets in the event of bankruptcy. However, stockholders have control (through the managers) of decisions that affect the riskiness of the firm. Creditors lend funds at rates that are based on the firm's risk, which in turn is based on (1) the riskiness of the firm's existing assets, (2) expectations concerning the riskiness of future asset additions, (3) the existing capital structure, and (4) expectations concerning future capital structure decisions. These are the primary determinants of the riskiness of a firm's cash flows, hence the safety of its debt.

Now suppose stockholders, acting through management, cause a firm to sell some relatively safe assets and invest the proceeds in a large new project that is far riskier than the firm's old assets. This increased risk will cause the required rate of return on the firm's debt to increase, and that will cause the value of the outstanding debt to fall. If the risky project is successful, most of the benefits go to the stockholders, because creditors' returns are fixed at the old, low-risk rate. However, if the project is unsuccessful, the bondholders may have to share in the losses.

Can and should stockholders, through their managers/agents, try to expropriate wealth from creditors? The answer is no. First, creditors attempt to protect themselves from these types of actions by including restrictive covenants in debt agreements; so many times these actions are specifically prohibited. Second, even in the absence of covenants it does not make sense for a firm to deal unfairly with its creditors. Unethical behavior has no place in business, and if creditors perceive that a firm's managers are trying to take advantage of them, they will either refuse to deal further with the firm or will charge higher interest rates to compensate for the risk of possible exploitation. These higher interest rates, or the potential loss of access to capital markets, are detrimental to shareholders.

Corporate Governance System Provides the financial and legal framework for regulating the relationship between a company's management and its shareholders.

Ultimately, it is important that firms have a strong **corporate governance system** in place to better monitor and address the various agency conflicts that arise within firms. Corporate governance mechanisms provide the financial and legal framework for regulating the relationship between a company's management and its shareholders. These mechanisms are particularly important when operating across countries where there is a wide variation in the legal protection of shareholders.[6] Some specific mechanisms used in the United States to motivate managers to act in shareholders' best interests include (1) managerial compensation plans, (2) direct intervention by shareholders, (3) the threat of firing, and (4) the threat of takeover. Promoting good

---

[6]There are two different philosophies of corporate governance corresponding roughly to the same division that we discussed in reference to the proper goals of management. The corporate governance system used in the United States is "outsider" or stockholder-based. Most of the literature available in the United States on corporate governance focuses on mechanisms that outsiders—stockholders—can use to make managers' welfare congruent with that of the stockholders. The other philosophy of corporate governance is "insider" or bank-based. In Europe, Japan, and other countries, banks are both creditors and stockholders. They have access to inside information and use their position to ensure that managers operate in the banks' best interest. Often this means that the companies take positions that protect the creditors at the expense of the stockholders.

DOES SOCIAL CAPITAL ADD TO A NATION'S WEALTH?

What factors cause one nation to be wealthy and another poor? Obviously, an abundance of natural resources creates wealth. In addition, economists have documented that geography, institutions, and a market economy matter. Other things equal, countries closer to the equator tend to be poorer than those located in moderate climates. Institutions such as law and democracy contribute to wealth, but economists believe that "the market guides selfish human actions to serve the common good." According to sociologists, there may be a factor missing from this list.

For the past decade, sociologists have considered one additional factor: social capital. What is social capital? Researchers do not always agree on the definition, much less on its effect on a nation's wealth.

One definition of social capital is trust or community. What is its relationship to a nation's wealth? The general concept is that the more people trust one another, the better off their society. Trust causes people to work together more efficiently. Consequently, we might conclude that the United States, with a successful economy, has an abundance of social capital. Studies have shown that this may or may not be the case.

A significant paper in this field, "Bowling Alone," by Robert Putnam of Harvard University, points out that Americans were far less likely to join organizations in the 1990s than they were in the 1950s. He proved this by showing the decline of bowling leagues. We might conclude from this paper that social capital (defined in these terms) is declining in the United States.

The idea that trust or community matters in determining a nation's wealth is not consistent with a basic assumption of traditional economic theory: Humans are self-interested beings. Some behavioral economists believe that this assumption has been accepted all too readily. Samuel Bowles and Herbert Gintis, both of the University of Massachusetts, argue that this assumption is flawed because people donate their time to all sorts of activities whose costs outweigh the benefits. They argue humans are social animals. On the other hand, others argue that these activities can be explained because people derive utility from helping others. However, the authors disagree. Through experi-

ments they demonstrate how groups encourage individuals to act in the interests of the group as a whole. Many subjects punished free-riders, who then responded to the shame by cooperating. Thus, selfish preferences cannot explain the incentives of people in a village, school, or parish. They conclude that communities are the missing element, alongside markets and government, in understanding an economy.

Edward Glaeser and David Laibson of Harvard and Bruce Sacerdote of Dartmouth define social capital as an individual's social skills, including a long list of contacts, charisma, or popularity. They measure social capital by the number of organizations an individual belongs to and believe that social capital, like financial wealth, can be built by individuals. They argue that the more people invest in social capital the more likely they are to remain living in the same place. So, they attribute part of the "bowling alone" phenomenon to our society's rising mobility. In addition, they argue that as individuals invest more in social capital they are more likely to gain from that investment. If there is nothing in it for them, they will neglect their neighbors. From their analysis, the assumption of traditional economic theory is still alive—humans are self-interested beings.

How does this definition of social capital affect a nation's wealth? Decisions to invest in social capital affect everyone, not just the individuals making these decisions. If social capital is defined in terms of community or trust, it is tempting to say that the impact is only positive—but this may not be so. People can act in the interests of a group to the exclusion of others. (Entry barriers to the group may be kept high—excluding outsiders.)

So, what are we to conclude? Steven Durlauf of Wisconsin writes that conclusions about social capital are too far reaching. He argues that social capital cannot be precisely defined and that too much has been invested in its explanation of why nations become wealthy. It looks as if the verdict is out on social capital and its impact on the wealth of nations. Surely, though, more will be written about the subject on both sides.

Source: "A Question of Trust," *The Economist*, February 20, 2003.

Business Ethics
A company's attitude and conduct toward its employees, customers, community, and stockholders.

ethical behavior in the firm can also help induce managers to act appropriately with regard to shareholders. **Business ethics** can be thought of as a company's attitude and conduct toward its employees, customers, community, and shareholders. It is important to remember that the shareholders own the firm and hence their capital is at risk. Therefore, it is only equitable that they receive a fair return on their investments.

SELF-TEST QUESTIONS

What is management's primary goal?

Why is common stock said to have a residual claim on assets and income?

How does the goal of stock price maximization benefit society at large?

What are agency costs, and who bears them?

What are some mechanisms that encourage managers to act in the best interests of stockholders? To not take advantage of bondholders?

Why should managers avoid taking actions that are unfair to any of the firm's stakeholders?

How might agency considerations arise in foreign operations?

ORGANIZATION OF THE BOOK

An important aspect of operating in an international environment is the ability to understand and work with foreign exchange rates, markets, and international institutions. Part One of this text covers these important elements. Following this introductory chapter, we discuss exchange rates, currency markets, and related institutions in Chapter 2, while Chapter 3 covers exchange rate analysis. Chapter 4 concludes Part One by examining the decision to invest abroad and the process of international expansion.

In Part Two, we cover fundamental financial concepts and analysis as well as international fixed-income and equity securities. This section provides students with financial tools and concepts that can be used to make financial decisions. Chapter 5 covers the fundamentals of risk and return in an international environment, while Chapters 6 and 7 discuss financial statement analysis from an international perspective. The remaining two chapters in this section, Chapters 8 and 9, cover debt and equity markets and provide students with an understanding of the various bond and equity-related instruments that are available in international securities markets, where debt and equity capital can be raised.

Part Three deals with corporate investment decisions. Firms normally finance using a mix of capital sources—short-term bank debt, long-term bonds, preferred stock, convertible bonds, retained earnings, and common stock. If, and only if, the firm invests in assets that return more than the cost of the capital used to acquire them will investments enhance stockholders' value. Therefore, for effective capital budgeting, it is essential to have a reasonably good estimate of projects' costs of capital, which is covered in Chapter 10. Chapter 11 goes on to discuss capital budgeting methodology, using projected cash flows and the cost of capital to determine projects' values. It examines the primary methods used to evaluate projects, and it brings in important international variations. Chapter 12 addresses additional risk considerations in capital budgeting and "real options" that might be embedded in a capital project. Real options are opportunities that arise as the result of making particular investments, and such an option can turn what appears at first glance to be a negative NPV project into a home run. In Chapter 13 we take up some strategic corporate financial decisions. We discuss target capital structures, international variations in those structures, and policies for distributing corporate income to shareholders. The decisions about how much debt or equity to use to finance a firm's growth, and the level of dividends to pay, are all interrelated and can substantially affect the firm's riskiness and value. In Chapter 14, we cover working capital, defined as current assets minus current liabilities. Here, we consider the management and financing of current assets and mechanisms for globally repositioning funds among operating units of the MNE.

Finally, Part Four covers international corporate financial strategy. Chapter 15 reviews risk management issues, including the use of derivatives in risk management, along with a discussion of foreign exchange and interest rate risk management. We conclude, in Chapter 16, with a discussion of international tax systems and multinational tax management.

It is worth noting that some instructors may choose to cover the chapters in a different sequence from their order in the book. The chapters are written to a large extent in a modular, self-contained manner, so such reordering should present no major difficulties.

SUMMARY

Over the past few decades, the global economy has become increasingly integrated, and a growing number of companies generate an increasing share of their profits from overseas operations. While multinational companies have more opportunities, they also face more risks and obstacles than do companies that operate only in their home country. However, even firms that do not expand beyond their home market are affected by the globalization of world markets. This chapter introduced the international financial environment. We discussed basic international concepts, key trends affecting global financial markets today, reasons firms expand globally, unique challenges multinationals face along with important differences between multinational and domestic financial management, and shareholder value maximization. The key concepts discussed in this chapter are listed below.

- International operations are becoming increasingly important to individual firms and to the national economy. A **multinational enterprise (MNE)** is a business organization that operates in an integrated fashion in a number of countries.
- **Globalization** refers to the increasing interconnectedness of economies, markets, and people across countries.
- The movement toward **market economies** throughout the world (i.e., privatization of state-run enterprises), the **creation of currency and free trade areas**, **deregulation of financial markets**, and the **increasing globalization of markets** are some major developments in the international financial environment.
- Companies "go global" for seven primary reasons: (1) **to seek production efficiency**; (2) **to avoid political, trade, and regulatory hurdles**; (3) **to broaden markets**; (4) **to seek raw materials and new technology**; (5) **to protect the secrecy of their processes and products**; (6) **to diversify**; and (7) **to retain customers**.
- Five major factors distinguish financial management as practiced by domestic firms relative to multinational firms: (1) **different currency denominations**, (2) **political risk**, (3) **economic and legal ramifications**, (4) **role of governments**, and (5) **language and cultural differences**.
- The goal of financial management is to **maximize shareholder value** by maximizing the value of a firm's stock.
- The value of a firm's stock is determined by the **cash flows** a firm produces, the **riskiness** of those cash flows, and the **timing** of the cash flows.

- The economic logic behind stock price maximization can be shown in three ways: (1) **benefits to consumers**, (2) **benefits to employees**, and (3) other benefits such as the **stimulation of employment and economic growth.**
- Efforts to maximize stock prices benefit society in several ways. These efforts help to **make business operations more efficient.** To maximize stock prices, managers offer goods and services that consumers desire; they price those goods and services as low as possible; and low prices require efficient, low-cost operations. The quest for stock price maximization also leads to **innovation, new products and services**, and **improved productivity.**
- Firms in some European and Asian countries seek to maximize the value contributed to the firm's **stakeholders**, including its employees, customers, suppliers, community, and business groups, in addition to stockholders. However, these approaches are not always operational and can be detrimental to competition. Recently, more firms in these countries are emphasizing shareholder wealth maximization due to the realization that this is a better long-run goal.
- An **agency relationship** arises whenever an individual or group, called a **principal**, hires someone called an **agent** to perform some service, and then the principal delegates decision-making power to the agent.
- Important agency relationships exist between **shareholders and managers**; between **managers and debtholders**; and among **managers, shareholders, and debtholders** during times of financial distress.
- An **agency problem** refers to a conflict between principals and agents. For example, managers, as agents, may pay themselves excessive salaries, obtain unreasonably large stock options, and the like, at the expense of the principals, the stockholders.
- **Corporate governance systems** provide the financial and legal framework for regulating the relationship between a company's management and its shareholders. These mechanisms are particularly important when operating across countries where there is a wide variation in the legal protection of shareholders.
- To mitigate agency problems, firms should have strong **corporate governance systems** in place, better **align managers' incentives** with corporate performance, and **promote good ethical behavior** in the firm.
- **Business ethics** refers to a company's attitudes and conduct toward its employees, customers, community, and shareholders.

QUESTIONS

(1-1) What is a multinational enterprise?

(1-2) Briefly explain the following statement, "MNEs' international involvement goes far beyond traditional mechanisms of international commerce."

(1-3) What are some of the questions that arise for governments due to the emergence of "world companies"?

(1-4) Briefly identify some of the effects of globalization for businesses.

(1-5) List three reasons even companies that consider themselves to be domestic are faced with many of the same issues as MNEs.

(1-6) What must managers know with respect to globalization?

(1-7) Is stock price maximization an appropriate goal for financial managers—even those whose companies operate worldwide?

(1-8) Briefly explain the following statement, "In the real world, stock price maximization is constrained."

(1-9) Is stockholder wealth maximization generally accepted as the ultimate goal of financial management throughout the world? Explain your answer.

(1-10) Is globalization a good or bad trend? Explain your answer.

(1-11) If a firm is considering overseas operations, what benefits would a firm expect if it operated in Mexico? South Korea? Spain? Brazil? Latvia?

(1-12) How is multinational financial management different from domestic financial management?

(1-13) Explain the basic valuation equation with respect to maximizing a firm's value.

(1-14) How can the basic valuation equation be applied to financial assets (such as stocks and bonds) and capital budgeting projects?

(1-15) How can information asymmetries (through agency problems) affect individual perceptions of the basic value equation?

(1-16) Explain whether the goal of shareholder wealth maximization is a short-term or long-term goal. Can shareholder wealth maximization be distorted if considered along the wrong time dimension?

SELF-TEST PROBLEM   Solutions Appear in Appendix B

(ST-1) Define each of the following terms:
Key Terms a. Multinational enterprise; globalization; cross-border acquisition
   b. Vertically integrated investment; natural trade barriers
   c. Stakeholders
   d. Agency theory; agency relationship; agency problem
   e. Corporate governance system; business ethics

THOMSON ONE Business School Edition QUESTIONS

EXAMINING COMPENSATION STRUCTURE

Overview

The Securities and Exchange Commission (SEC) requires public corporations to regularly provide annual reports, key financial statements, and other important information to their shareholders. For a description of the SEC and the various reports it requires, you can visit the SEC's web site: **http://www.sec.gov**. The SEC also has an online service entitled Edgar, which provides the public with easy access to the various SEC filings. You can find this information at **http://www.edgar-online.com**.

Thomson Financial has developed a tool that puts together a wide range of useful information from these various filings. This database, entitled *Thomson One: Business School Edition*, is particularly useful because it is easy to navigate, and it provides a way for investors to download relevant information to an *Excel* spreadsheet. Thomson Financial has made it possible for users of this textbook to have full access to the full range of this database for many leading companies. Throughout the textbook, we will highlight areas where students can use the database to learn more about illustrative companies. We begin below by considering the compensation plan ExxonMobil has established for its key executives.

ExxonMobil's Executive Compensation Plan

While managers run companies on a day-to-day basis, several key issues require shareholder approval. These issues include the election of board members, changes in the corporate charter, and approval of significant corporate events such as mergers. With this in mind, corporations are required to provide an annual proxy statement, which summarizes the information that shareholders need to consider when voting. These proxy statements also provide a great deal of useful information about the board of directors, the amount of stock held by officers and directors of the corporation, and details regarding executive compensation.

ExxonMobil has a performance share plan under which executive compensation is tied directly to certain thresholds, or hurdles, established by the Board's Compensation Committee. You can use *Thomson One: Business School Edition* to obtain this information. From the *Thomson One: Business School Edition* home page, enter ExxonMobil's ticker symbol (XOM) and click on "GO."

- Click on the tab labeled "Filings," and notice that a second line of tabs appears.
- On your screen you should see a category heading titled "Filings" with a list of filings and date filed. Click on "Proxy."
- At this point you can find information regarding ExxonMobil's election of directors, their compensation, its principal shareholders, and the details regarding its executive compensation.
- To see details of its executive compensation plan, click on "Executive Compensation."
- To see the details regarding the long-term incentive plan, select "Other Benefit Plans."

Discussion Questions

1. Briefly describe the details regarding ExxonMobil's compensation plan, including short-term and long-term incentives.
2. What other types of compensation does ExxonMobil provide to its executives?
3. Identify some of ExxonMobil's key executives, and outline their compensation.

INTEGRATED CASE

After Amanda (Mandy) Wu graduated from USC with a degree in finance two years ago, she took a job as assistant to Rick Schmidt, Medical Reports International's chief financial officer. MRI produces electronic diagnostic equipment that is used in hospitals, nursing homes, acute care facilities, and, increasingly, in private homes. The company began in 1981 as Medical Reports Inc., a manufacturer of heat-sensing devices that used a digital transmission system to report on acute care patients in large hospitals. It was based in southern California, where its founders resided, but over time the company broadened its line of diagnostic equipment and developed into an international leader in the medical equipment field. Most of its design work—much of which involves developing software and computer chips—is done in California, but most of its manufacturing is done in the Far East and Mexico, and it has sales offices throughout the world. To reflect its international presence, the company changed its name to Medical Reports International in 1995.

Table IC1-1 gives a list of the people involved in the case. One of MRI's founders, Mike Diaz, was an engineer, and the other, Bob Conti, was a sales representative for a medical supply distributor. Diaz developed a heat-sensing device that showed "hot spots" on patients, transmitted this information to hospital control stations, and thus alerted the medical staff to developing problems. Conti used his contacts with hospitals to sell the system. They were successful from the start, and the company was profitable enough to finance its early growth with internal funds plus bank loans supported by a strong cash flow. However, in 1985 Diaz and Conti realized that additional capital was needed if the company was to realize its full potential, so they sold a minority interest to Southern California Ventures (SCV), a leading venture capital company. By 1990, MRI was highly profitable. The firm clearly had a high value even though it was not publicly traded, hence there was no way to actually measure that value. Also, it had become clear that the company should expand internationally, and that would require additional capital.

At that point, the principals decided that MRI should go public and raise the required capital by issuing new stock. Also, SCV wanted to "harvest" some of its gains; Diaz and Conti wanted to diversify their personal holdings; and a number of key employees wanted to cash in on their stock options and

TABLE IC1-1 | **People Involved in the Case**

Amanda (Mandy) Wu	Assistant to the CFO
Rick Schmidt	Vice president, CFO
Mike Diaz	Director, founder, chairman; engineering background
Bob Conti	Director, founder, president; medical products background
Vince Fuller	Director, officer of venture capital firm
Eduardo Suarez	Director, international marketing expert
Sally Williams	Director, college president; expert on adult education
Ellen Warren	Director, scientist; expert on medical equipment
John Costello	Consultant, finance professor

buy long-delayed homes and other things. So, MRI had a stock offering in which the company sold new stock to bring in additional capital, and Diaz, Conti, and SCV sold some of their shares to diversify their holdings. As a result of this offering, and of additional sales in the secondary market over the years, Diaz, Conti, and SVC each own 15 percent of the outstanding stock and public stockholders own the remaining 55 percent. Key employees hold options on 10 percent of the stock, which, when exercised, will reduce those percentages slightly.

Neither Diaz nor Conti, nor Vince Fuller, the SCV representative on the board, has had formal finance training. Fuller has an MBA, but he majored in marketing and avoided finance and accounting courses as much as possible. The other three members of the board, Sally Williams, Ellen Warren, and Eduardo Suarez, also lack financial training. Williams is the president of Foothills Community College, Warren is a respected scientist and medical equipment expert, and Suarez is an international marketing expert. After passage of the Sarbanes-Oxley Act in 2003, under which the boards of public companies can be held accountable for improper reporting, board members expressed a concern about their lack of financial expertise. Also, Schmidt thought that the board might be able to make better policy decisions if the members were better grounded in the fundamentals of financial management.

At a recent board meeting, Suarez suggested that Schmidt organize an educational program. One of his friends, a director of an aerospace company, told Suarez about such a program his company had set up and how valuable the board felt it had been. Suarez's suggestion was then discussed, and Schmidt was asked to establish an educational program for MRI's directors. The discussion then turned to the program's format—what should be its content, and who should conduct it? Williams, the college president, had been involved with various corporate training programs and suggested the best results would be obtained if the program was organized and conducted by a team consisting of a college finance professor, a senior MRI financial executive, and a sharp junior member of the company's finance staff. The team would construct a program, with *PowerPoint* slides and other exhibits, and practice their presentation on a group of company representatives who would (1) benefit from knowing more finance and (2) be able to provide feedback on what worked and did not work in terms of getting important concepts across. After that, there would be a 2-hour session before each monthly board meeting devoted to finance topics. Williams laughingly said, "At the end, we'll be awarded with a degree from MRI University." Diaz liked the idea but suggested that the six operating VPs be included, because he sensed that they too needed a stronger background in financial management. Suarez suggested that international finance topics should be covered, because international markets have the best growth potential and provide unique challenges. The remaining board members agreed with these suggestions, and Schmidt was asked to implement the idea, starting with the next monthly board meeting.

Schmidt has long felt uncomfortable because few board members had a good understanding of fundamentally important concepts like the cost of capital and capital budgeting. He thinks board discussions of key policy matters will produce better results if members know more about financial management. For several years, Schmidt has used John Costello, a brilliant finance professor at the local university, as a consultant and advisor on various financial issues. Costello is also an award-winning teacher, so he is a natural choice for the academic on the team. Schmidt himself is the logical choice for the MRI executive, and he quickly decided to ask Mandy Wu to serve as the junior MRI person. Wu is on the fast track for promotion within the company, and work on the project will give her valuable insights into the thoughts of senior executives and board members.

Immediately after the board meeting, Schmidt called Costello and Wu, explained the situation, and secured their participation in the program. At a meeting the next morning, they decided to divide the course into 16 sessions, each covering an important issue, following the organization of a leading text-book on international financial management. Costello suggested that each session be organized around a series of questions that would take participants through the fundamentals of the topic. Facts and issues relating to MRI itself would be used, so each session will teach fundamental analysis and apply the analysis to current issues facing MRI. Thus, the sessions will serve both educational and policy-making functions. The board members and executives are all quite intelligent, so they should pick things up quickly, but they are not conversant with many finance terms and concepts. Therefore, even elementary topics should at least be mentioned. Schmidt and Costello, with Wu looking on, prepared the following questions for the introductory session. Wu's task is to prepare answers for use during the session. Put yourself in Wu's position and prepare answers for the following questions.

QUESTIONS

a. What should be the primary goal of the firm? How is this goal achieved? Is this the firm's only goal? How does this goal relate to those who interact with the company (customers, employees, etc.)? How does this goal relate to other company goals? In your responses, consider the implications of international operations.

b. How will increased globalization affect MRI's financial decision making?

c. What major factors have helped shape the current international financial environment, and what business opportunities have they created?

d. MRI's first foray into international operations was selling to overseas customers, and later this expanded to overseas production. List and explain some examples of why firms "go global."

e. MRI's transition into becoming a multinational enterprise (MNE) was a rough one. Specifically, MRI's managers had trouble identifying the unique challenges that operating in an international environment presents. Identify some factors that distinguish multinational financial management from domestic financial management.

f. Define agency relationships. What agency problems can develop as a firm expands and decides to operate internationally?

g. Explain the importance of corporate governance and the need for managers to behave ethically.

CHAPTER 2

The Global Financial Environment: Markets, Institutions, Interest Rates, and Exchange Rates

Required Investment
Sales Revenues
Operating Costs
Taxes

Cash Flows (CF)

$$\text{VALUE} = \sum_{t=0}^{N} \frac{CF_t}{(1+r)^t}$$

Capital Structure
Interest Rates
Asset Risk
Market Risk

Required Return (r)

FIF

e-resource

Visit http://crum. swlearning.com to see the Web site accompanying this text. This ever-evolving site, for both students and instructors, is a tool for teaching and learning, and contains Excel chapter models and PowerPoint slides.

Managers and investors do not operate in a vacuum; rather, they make decisions within a global financial environment. Even if their decisions deal directly with only a small part of the global environment, such as a single country, the larger marketplace still influences its individual parts. The global environment includes local financial markets and institutions within specific countries as well as truly international markets and institutions that span many countries. It also includes the diverse spectrum of national tax and regulatory policies plus macroeconomic conditions within each country. This entire set of factors determines the financial alternatives, and it affects the outcomes of decisions made by both managers and investors. For all these reasons, it is important to understand the global environment and to anticipate the consequences of decisions in this context.

Sound financial decisions require an understanding of the economies, interest rates, exchange rates, and capital markets in all the countries in which a company operates. This makes sound financial decision making a difficult task. However, in recent years advances in information and transportation technologies, along with the global integration of banking and other organizational infrastructure, have helped ease this challenge. The Internet is a key factor here—indeed, the way people communicate and firms conduct business have literally been redefined by the Internet. Electronic commerce represents a paradigm shift from *the traditional business model—not only in finance but also in other business fields, as the long-promised benefits of electronic transfers of funds and data are being realized. Suddenly, capital markets in other countries are opening to foreign firms, and many companies are beginning to understand the value of dealing in the so-called euromarkets.*

In this chapter, we introduce the basic characteristics of U.S. and foreign financial markets. We show that different national economies are really global networks tied together by exchange rates, and that global investment and financing opportunities, while more complicated, are much less constrained and thus potentially much more profitable than strictly local operations. In terms of the valuation equation, this chapter's central focus is on the required return in the denominator—specifically, on how it is determined and how changes in risk and inflation lead to changes in the required return, r, over time.

FINANCIAL MARKETS

Physical Asset Markets
Also known as tangible, or real, asset markets. Capital budgeting decisions are important to these markets.

Financial Asset Markets
Marketplaces that deal with financial instruments such as stocks, bonds, notes, mortgages, currencies, and so on.

Financial Instruments
Pieces of paper or electronic entries in account ledgers with contractual provisions that spell out their owners' claims on specific real assets. Their value is defined in terms of a fixed number of money units.

Monetary
Relating to a unit of currency; value defined in terms of a fixed number of money units.

Businesses, individuals, and governments often need to raise capital. For example, suppose ChevronTexaco wants to develop a new oil field in western Kazakhstan. Because development costs are estimated at more than $3 billion, which is more cash than the company presently has available, ChevronTexaco will have to go to the financial markets to raise the money. Or suppose that Gilberto Sanchez, a Mexico City restaurateur, wants to add an outdoor patio to his restaurant. Where will he get the money to finance the addition and installation of the equipment? At the same time, some individuals and companies have incomes that are greater than their current expenditures, so they have funds available to invest. For example, Microsoft had roughly $52.8 billion of cash and marketable securities in December 2003 available for future investments.

Thus, there are many individuals, companies, and governments who need capital for investments, and another set of people, businesses, and governments that have excess funds to invest. Financial marketplaces bring these two groups together, and the more efficient financial markets are, the better off the world is.

Types of Markets

When we think of a "market," many different images may come to mind. Perhaps it conjures up a picture of a "farmers market," where you go to buy fresh vegetables, or a used car market, where you go to buy a car. You talk about "being in the market for a new computer system," or even a new job. These are all examples of **physical asset markets** (also called "tangible" or "real" asset markets), including the market for human capital. These markets are important, but so are financial markets, because borrowers often need capital to make investments in the physical asset markets. We will look closely at the decision process for acquiring physical assets later, in Chapters 11 and 12, where we discuss capital budgeting, but here we concentrate on **financial asset markets**, which deal with stocks, bonds, notes, mortgages, currencies, and other **financial instruments**. All of these assets (or liabilities if you are the borrower) are **monetary** in nature, and their values are defined in terms of money units. They are simply pieces of paper or, increasingly, electronic entries in account ledgers, and their contractual provisions spell out their owners' claims on specific real assets. For example, a corporate bond issued by Nestlé entitles its owner to a specific claim on the cash flows produced by Nestlé's physical assets, while a share of Nestlé stock entitles its owner to a different set of claims on

Derivative Security
Any asset whose value is derived from the value of some other "underlying" real or financial asset.

Spot Markets
The markets in which assets are bought or sold for "on-the-spot" delivery.

Futures Markets
The markets in which participants agree today to buy or sell an asset at some future date.

Money Markets
The financial markets in which funds are borrowed or loaned for short periods (less than one year).

Capital Markets
The financial markets for equity and for intermediate- or long-term debt (one year or longer).

Mortgage Markets
Markets that deal with loans on residential, commercial, and industrial real estate.

Consumer Credit Markets
Markets that involve loans on autos, appliances, education, vacations, and the like.

Currency Markets
Markets in which transactions for foreign exchange occur.

Physical Markets
Formal organizations having tangible physical locations that conduct auction markets in designated ("listed") securities.

those cash flows. Unlike these conventional financial instruments, **derivative securities** are not direct claims on either real assets or their cash flows. Instead, a derivative is a contractual claim whose value depends on the value of some other "underlying" asset. *Futures* and *options* are two important types of financial derivatives, and their values depend on the values of other assets, such as Japanese yen, pork bellies, or IBM stock. Therefore, the value of a derivative security is *derived* from the value of an underlying real or financial asset. The following list identifies the major types of financial markets:

1. **Spot markets** and **futures markets** are terms that refer to whether assets are being bought or sold for "on-the-spot" delivery (literally, within a few business days) or for delivery at some more distant future date.

2. **Money markets** are the markets for short-term, highly liquid debt securities. The New York and London money markets have long been the world's largest, but Tokyo and Singapore are growing rapidly. **Capital markets** are the markets for intermediate- or long-term corporate debt, and for equity securities. The New York Stock Exchange (NYSE), where stocks of the largest U.S. corporations are traded, is a prime example of a capital market. There is no hard and fast rule about this, but when describing debt markets, "short-term" generally means less than one year, "intermediate-term" means one to five years, and "long-term" means more than five years. Most equity securities never mature, so by definition equity markets are "long term."

3. **Mortgage markets** deal with loans on residential, commercial, and industrial real estate, while **consumer credit markets** involve loans on autos, appliances, education, vacations, and so on.

4. *Global, national, regional*, and *local markets* also exist. For example, the Eurobond market (headquartered mainly in London but with participants throughout the world) is a global market for long-term debt, while the Tokyo Stock Exchange is a national market for Japanese equities. Euronext is a regional market embracing Amsterdam, Brussels, Lisbon, and Paris, while the Jamaica Stock Exchange illustrates a strictly local market. Depending on an organization's size and operational scope, it may be able to acquire capital from sources all around the world, or it may be confined to a local market.

5. **Currency markets** deal with buying and selling different nations' currencies, or *foreign exchange*. There is a retail component of this market in which individuals interact globally and exchange one currency for another, but there is also a much larger commercial side in which companies engage in foreign exchange transactions as a part of their business operations.

6. **Physical markets** are those that have a trading floor and a physical presence, such as the New York Stock Exchange. **Electronic markets** do not have a physical location but rather exist as a computerized trading system such as the Nasdaq. As technology advances, electronic markets are replacing more and more physical markets. *The Wall Street Journal* and other financial publications have speculated for years that the NYSE will eventually be forced by competitive pressures to evolve into a mostly electronic market.

7. **Primary markets** are those in which corporations raise new capital. If Intel issued newly created common stock, this would be a primary market transaction because the company receives the cash proceeds from the sale.

8. **Secondary markets** are markets in which existing securities are traded among investors. Thus, if an investor bought 100 shares of Intel stock from another person, the purchase would occur in the secondary market. The NYSE is a secondary market since it deals in outstanding shares as opposed to newly issued shares. Secondary markets also exist for bonds, mortgages, various

other types of loans, and other financial assets. The corporation whose securities are being traded in a secondary market is not involved in the transaction and, thus, does not receive any funds from the sale.

9. The **initial public offering (IPO) market** is a subset of the primary market. Here firms "go public" by offering shares to the general public for the first time. Microsoft had its IPO in 1986. Prior to that time, Bill Gates and other insiders owned all the firm's shares. In many IPOs, the insiders sell some of their shares to diversify, and the company sells newly created shares to raise additional capital.

10. **Private markets**, where transactions are negotiated between two parties, are differentiated from **public markets**, where standardized contracts are traded on organized exchanges. Bank loans and private debt placed with insurance companies are examples of private market transactions. Because these transactions are private, they may be structured in any manner that is legal and agreeable to both parties. By contrast, securities issued in public markets (e.g., common stock and corporate bonds) are ultimately held by a large number of individuals. Public securities must have fairly standardized contractual features that appeal to a broad range of investors. Their standardized features and diverse ownership also make public securities relatively liquid. Private market securities are, in contrast, more tailor-made but less liquid.

An almost unlimited number of market classifications could be developed, but this breakdown is sufficient to illustrate that there are many types of financial markets and that a diverse mix of financial assets is traded. Note also that precise classifications are more useful for pedagogic than practical purposes, because people dealing in these markets focus on the nature of the contract rather than its market classification.

A healthy, free-market economy is dependent on the efficient transfer of funds from net savers to individuals and companies who need capital. Without efficient financial markets, the broader economy will not be efficient, and it cannot reach its potential. For example, in the former Soviet Union, many promising businesses are held back because capital is not readily available. Without business expansion, employment, productivity, and the standard of living will be lower than the achievable level. Similarly, financial markets in developing nations must be nurtured by governments if those markets are to function efficiently. Indeed, economic efficiency is simply impossible without a good system for allocating capital within the economy.

Recent Trends

Financial markets have been evolving at an increasing rate during the past two decades. Advances in information technology have made the globalization of banking and commerce more feasible, and that, in turn, has led to deregulation and increased global competition. The result is a much more efficient, internationally integrated market, but one that is far more complex than existed a few years ago. While globalization has been largely positive, it has also created problems for policy makers. U.S. Federal Reserve Board Chairman Alan Greenspan has stated that modern financial markets "expose national economies to shocks from new and unexpected sources, and with little if any lag." He has also stated that central banks must develop new ways to evaluate and limit risks to the financial system. Large amounts of capital can move quickly around the world in response to interest and exchange rate changes, and those capital movements can disrupt local institutions and economies, much like your personal economy would be disrupted if someone suddenly made a large withdrawal from your bank account.

Globalization has accented the need for greater cooperation among international regulators. Various committees are currently addressing the following issues: (1) the integration of different national banking and securities industry structures, (2) the trend in Europe and North America toward financial service conglomerates, and (3) the reluctance of individual countries to relinquish national monetary policy control. Still, regulators agree that gaps in global market supervision need to be closed.

Derivatives markets have played a vital role in global risk management. As noted earlier, a derivative is any security whose value is *derived* from the value of some other "underlying" asset. An option to buy IBM stock at a fixed price is a derivative as is a contract to buy Japanese yen six months from now at a fixed exchange rate. The derivatives market has grown faster than any other market in recent years, providing corporations with new opportunities but also exposing them to new risks, some of which are not visible to investors because of the complexity of the transactions and accounting rules that do not require their disclosure.

Derivatives can be used either for risk reduction or for speculation. Suppose an importer's net income falls whenever the dollar weakens against the yen, as it did throughout much of 2003. That company could reduce its risk by purchasing derivatives that increase in value whenever the dollar declines. This is called a *hedging operation*, and its purpose is to reduce risk exposure. We will look at this in detail in Chapter 15. Speculation, on the other hand, is done in the hope of earning a high return, but it raises a firm's risk exposure. For example, in the late 1990s, Procter & Gamble disclosed that it lost $150 million on derivative investments, and Nick Leeson, a currency trader working for Barings Bank in Singapore, lost more than $4.5 billion in yen-dollar speculation activities that caused the bank to go bankrupt.[1] The size and complexity of derivatives transactions concern regulators, academics, and lawmakers. U.S. Fed Chairman Greenspan noted that, in theory, derivatives should allow companies to manage risk better but that it is not clear whether recent innovations have increased or decreased the inherent stability of the financial system.

Another recent trend has been the development of new financial instruments that allow a firm's shares to be traded in prices based on local currencies in many national markets, or in global equity markets. As companies become increasingly global in perspective, they are listing shares on multiple exchanges. **Cross-listing** and **around-the-clock trading** have resulted in greater global market integration, which can mean lower shareholder risk through globally diversified portfolios and lower financing costs for companies. However, it also challenges traditional notions of nationality as companies move their headquarters from one country to another to obtain more favorable taxation and other regulations.

For example, there has been a recent trend for U.S. companies to incorporate in Bermuda to lower their corporate taxes. Ingersoll Rand, Global Crossing, and Tyco International are a few of the American companies with their "official" headquarters in Bermuda.[2] Global Crossing and Tyco have been there since 1997, while Ingersoll Rand (a manufacturer of locks, golf carts and utility vehicles, refrigeration equipment, and industrial and construction equipment) recently reincorporated in Bermuda. Similarly, in 2002 Stanley Works, makers of Stanley tools, won a shareholder vote to reincorporate in Bermuda, but after a fight with the state of Connecticut and the

Cross-Listing
Occurs when a company lists shares of stock on multiple exchanges to increase its global recognition.

Around-the-Clock Trading
Global financial institutions maintain offices in different time zones around the world and thus offer anytime trading.

---

[1]Barings was one of the world's oldest banks, and its clients included the Queen of England. There are several published books detailing the events that led up to the Barings collapse, including Nicholas William Leeson and Edward Whitley, *Rogue Trader: How I Brought Down Barings Bank and Shook the Financial World* (Little Brown & Company, New York, NY, 1996); and Judith H. Rawnsley and Nicholas William Leeson, *Total Risk: Nick Leeson and the Fall of Barings Bank* (HarperCollins, London, U.K., 1995). In addition, a movie titled *Rogue Trader* starring Ewan McGregor was released in 1999.

[2]Generally, the "real" headquarters, along with most actual operations, remains wherever it was; the main thing that changes is the location stated on some legal papers. Companies with headquarters in Bermuda or the Bahamas may have only a postal box in a lawyer's office, with no real tie to the "headquarters country." Obviously, this is considered by many to be an abuse, but it is often difficult to draw the line between a "legitimate" and an "illegitimate" decision to change the country of incorporation.

AFL-CIO, Stanley abandoned its plan to move to Bermuda. Still, the trend for U.S. companies to reincorporate in countries with more favorable tax treatment is likely to continue, given increasing pressures from competition in the global marketplace.

SELF-TEST QUESTIONS

What is the purpose of financial marketplaces?
What are some major types of financial markets?
What is a financial instrument? Give some examples.
What is a derivative security?
What recent trends have affected the global financial environment?

FINANCIAL INSTITUTIONS

Transfers of capital between savers and borrowers take place in the three different ways diagrammed in Figure 2-1:

1. *Direct transfers* of money and securities, as shown in the top section, occur when a business sells its shares or bonds directly to savers, without using a financial institution. The business delivers its securities to savers, who in turn give the firm the money it needs.

Investment Banking House
An organization that underwrites and distributes new investment securities and helps businesses obtain financing.

2. As shown in the middle section, transfers may also go through an **investment banking house** such as Merrill Lynch, which *underwrites* the issue. An underwriter serves as a middleman and facilitates the issuance of securities. If more than one underwriter is involved, there is an *underwriting consortium,* or *syndicate,* of several institutions, and one serves as the *lead underwriter.* The company sells its shares or bonds to the investment bank, which in turn sells these same securities to savers. The firms' securities and the savers' money merely "pass through" the investment banking house. However, the investment bank does hold the securities for a period of time, so it is taking a risk— it may not be able to resell them to savers for as much as it paid. Because new

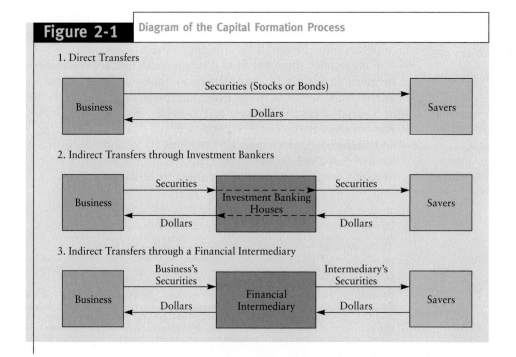

Figure 2-1   Diagram of the Capital Formation Process

1. Direct Transfers

Business → Securities (Stocks or Bonds) → Savers
Business ← Dollars ← Savers

2. Indirect Transfers through Investment Bankers

Business → Securities → Investment Banking Houses → Securities → Savers
Business ← Dollars ← Investment Banking Houses ← Dollars ← Savers

3. Indirect Transfers through a Financial Intermediary

Business → Business's Securities → Financial Intermediary → Intermediary's Securities → Savers
Business ← Dollars ← Financial Intermediary ← Dollars ← Savers

securities are involved and the company receives the proceeds of the sale, this is a primary market transaction.

3. Transfers can also be made through a **financial intermediary**, such as a bank or mutual fund. Here the intermediary first obtains funds from savers in exchange for its own securities, and then it uses this money to purchase and hold other assets (stocks, bonds, mortgages). For example, a saver might deposit funds in a bank, receiving from it a certificate of deposit, and the bank then lends the money to a small business to help it acquire working capital. Thus, intermediaries literally create new forms of capital—in this case, certificates of deposit, which are both safer and more liquid than small business loans and thus are better securities for most savers to hold. Financial intermediaries greatly increase the efficiency of money and capital markets.

Financial Intermediary
A specialized financial firm that facilitates the transfer of funds from savers to demanders of capital.

In our examples, we have assumed that the borrower is a business, but it is easy to visualize the demander of capital as a home purchaser, a government unit, or a student wanting to borrow funds for college. Of the three capital transfer mechanisms, direct transfers are the least important in developed nations, and larger firms generally employ investment banking houses to directly place securities with investors rather than acquiring capital through financial intermediaries.

Panel A of Table 2-1 lists the 10 largest U.S. bank and thrift holding companies, Panel B shows the leading world banking companies, and Panel C lists the ten leading global debt underwriters in terms of dollar volume of new issues (although many of the issues are in currencies other than dollars). Among the ten largest banks, only two (Citigroup and J. P. Morgan Chase) are based in the United States. Thus, while mergers have dramatically increased the size of U.S. banks, they are still small by

TABLE 2-1 | 10 Largest U.S. Bank and Thrift Holding Compaies, World Banking Companies, and Top 10 Leading Underwriters

Panel A U.S. Bank and Thrift Holding Companies[a]	Panel B World Banking Companies[b]	Panel C Leading Global Debt Underwriters[c]
Citigroup Inc.	Mizuho Holdings (Tokyo)	Citigroup
J. P. Morgan Chase & Co.	Citigroup (New York)	Morgan Stanley
Bank of America Corp.[d]	Sumitomo Mitsui Financial Group (Tokyo)	Merrill Lynch
Wells Fargo & Co.	UBS AG (Zurich)	Lehman Brothers
Wachovia Corp.	Allianz AG (Munich)	J. P. Morgan
MetLife Inc.	Deutsche Bank (Frankfurt)	Credit Suisse First Boston
Bank One Corp.	J. P. Morgan Chase & Co. (New York)	Deutsche Bank
Washington Mutual Inc.	HSBC Holdings PLC (London)	UBS
FleetBoston Financial Corp.[d]	ING Group NV (Amsterdam)	Goldman Sachs
U.S. Bancorp	BNP Paribas (Paris)	Banc of America

Notes:
[a]Ranked by total assets as of September 30, 2003. *Source:* "Top Bank and Thrift Holding Companies by Assets," *AmericanBanker.com,* September 30, 2003.
[b]Ranked by total assets as of December 31, 2002. *Source:* "World's Top Banking Companies by Assets," *AmericanBanker.com,* September 17, 2003.
[c]Ranked by dollar amount raised through new issues in 2003. For this ranking, the lead underwriter (manager) is given credit for the entire issue. *Source:* Adapted from *The Wall Street Journal,* January 2, 2004, R17.
[d]On March 17, 2004, Bank of America's acquisition of FleetBoston was approved by both firms' shareholders.

global standards. Note too that 6 of the top 10 underwriters are also major commercial banks or are part of bank holding companies, which demonstrates the blurring of distinctions among types of financial institutions.[3]

In what three ways do transfers of capital between savers and borrowers take place?

Differentiate between an investment banking house and a financial intermediary.

THE COST OF MONEY

Interest Rate
The price paid to borrow debt capital.

Required Return
The minimum rate of return on a common stock that will induce a stockholder to purchase the stock.

Exchange Rate
The number of units of a given currency that can be purchased for one unit of another currency.

Time Preferences for Consumption
Consumer preferences for current consumption as opposed to saving for future consumption.

Expected Rate of Inflation
The amount by which prices are expected to increase over time.

Risk
In a financial market context, the chance that an investment will provide a low or negative return.

Production Opportunities
The returns available within an economy from investments in productive real assets.

Now that we have introduced the various types of financial markets and institutions, we discuss the market mechanics used to allocate capital between lenders and borrowers. In a market economy, capital is allocated through the price system. For debt securities, the cost of borrowed money is called the **interest rate**. Equity funds also have a cost—the investors must expect a return in the form of dividends and/or capital gains, and the minimum expectation that will get the investor to provide equity capital is called the investor's **required return**. Finally, if we want to purchase another country's currency, the price we pay is called an **exchange rate**.

Supply and demand determine the price (or cost) of capital, and four fundamental factors interact to determine this cost. On the supply side are three factors: **time preferences for consumption**, the **expected rate of inflation**, and **risk**. On the demand side there is one primary factor, the amount of and returns on **production opportunities**. To see how these factors determine the cost of money, visualize the preferences of business students as they go through school, get a job, and finally retire. While they are in school, most students' expenses exceed their incomes, so they have a strong preference to consume more than they are currently earning. By borrowing today and promising to repay loans out of future earnings, students can consume more than their incomes. After graduation and entering the workforce, they hold their consumption to a level below their incomes while they pay off their student loans, and perhaps save for a down payment on a house. If they marry and have children, they may begin saving for the children's education, and when the kids go off to college, they may borrow again to cover tuition. Then, they must pay off any loans and save in earnest for their eventual retirement. Thus, as their careers progress, they shift between consumption and saving, perhaps several times. There are many students (and parents) who need capital, and also people who are saving for retirement and thus supplying capital. The market system serves to allocate capital, and in the process it determines an equilibrium price for money.

The erosion of purchasing power is called *inflation,* and it is the second factor that influences the price of money. If inflation is expected, borrowers must pay a premium to enable savers to maintain the purchasing power of the money they lend.

Savers also worry about the *risk factor* inherent in their investments. Borrowers may, of course, not repay loans as specified in the contracts, but if savings are invested in a foreign-currency investment, there is additional risk because the exchange rate between the foreign currency and the home currency may change. Even if a saver earns a high rate of return on the foreign currency, wealth can be lost

---

[3]As a result of experience during the Great Depression of the 1930s, the federal government tried to make U.S. banks safer by restricting them to commercial banking and preventing them from engaging in investment banking. However, Japanese and European banks could engage in both commercial and investment banking. Thus, they could bid on a stock or bond underwriting and also offer to make short-term credit available, which gave them an advantage over U.S. banks. The banks then lobbied successfully to have their restrictions lifted, and today giant financial service firms own both huge banks and major investment banking businesses. For example, Citigroup owns the world's second largest bank, Citibank, and one of the largest investment banking firms, Smith Barney, along with many other financial businesses. The trend toward financial consolidations is going strong in 2004, with large global mergers occurring weekly.

when proceeds from the investment are converted back into the home currency. Most people prefer to minimize their risk, whether from default or exchange rates, so to overcome savers' reluctance to accept risks, borrowers must offer a rate sufficiently high to mitigate lenders' anxieties.

On the demand side, we must look at what borrowers intend to do with the money. Some money is borrowed to finance consumption (e.g., vacations), but the majority of all loans taken out are based on expectations regarding how profitably the borrowed funds can be invested. If many people conclude that it will be profitable to return to school for a graduate degree, or if many companies decide that new plants will provide high returns, then there will be a strong demand for money, and that will lead to higher interest rates. On the other hand, if prospective students conclude that they do not need graduate degrees, or companies have sufficient capacity, the demand for money will be weak and rates will be low.

Borrowers' expected rates of return on investments set the upper limit on what they will pay to acquire capital, while savers' time preferences for consumption establish how much consumption they are willing to defer and thus the lower limit on the cost for capital. Those two factors, along with inflation and risk, determine the market-clearing rate on different types of capital.

SELF-TEST QUESTIONS

What is the price paid to borrow money called?

What do investors expect companies to provide on equity securities as the price of that capital?

Name some factors that have a substantial impact on the cost of money. Which affect the supply side? The demand side?

What determines the upper and lower limits on the price of capital used for investment purposes? How is the market-clearing interest rate determined?

INTEREST AND EXCHANGE RATE DETERMINATION

Assume initially that there is no inflation, no risk, all transactions are in dollars, and you have $1,000 that you can invest or spend. If you decide not to spend the money now, you will lend it to the federal government and receive $1,030 at the end of the year. Your choices are diagrammed here:

Now	Next Year
Spend the $1,000 today	Have none of the money next year
Invest the $1,000 at 3% today	Receive and spend $1,030 next year

Marginal Investor The investor who operates at the margin and whose decisions determine the market interest rate.

Real Risk-Free Rate of Return (r*) The interest rate that would exist on default-free U.S. Treasury securities if no inflation were expected.

Now assume that you are typical of all potential savers, so your preferences reflect those of the **marginal investor**, whose actions determine interest rates in the economy. Assume also that you are indifferent between these alternatives. If you were offered slightly more than 3 percent, then you would defer consumption and invest the $1,000, while if you were offered slightly less you would spend the $1,000 now. Thus, 3 percent is the indifference, or breakeven, rate, and it is defined as your *required rate of return*. Furthermore, because you are the marginal investor, then 3 percent will represent the cost of funds for investments of this type. Also, because the investment is riskless and no inflation is expected, the 3 percent return is also the **real, risk-free rate of return (r*)**. The term "real" means that this is the return if no inflation were expected. (Inflation is zero in this example.)

Potential borrowers make similar calculations. Depending on how profitably they think they can invest funds, they will offer more or less than 3 percent. In our example, we are implicitly assuming that borrowers at the margin have concluded

THE DANGERS OF A GLOBAL ECONOMY

An integrated global economy conjures images of new product markets and resources, but there is a dark side to this development. The United States has long been the driving force in the world economy, resulting in a highly correlated global economy. As of 2003, U.S. savings rates were at all-time lows, and government deficits (budget and current account deficits) were reaching record highs. Meanwhile, the rest of the world seemed to be sitting idly by, despite standing on the brink of a downward spiral. With no measures taken, the stage may have been set for a massive global recession. Similar conditions have existed before, but a fortunate string of events staved off disaster. Can luck hit twice?

In the last quarter of 2003, leading economic indicators suggested that the U.S. economy may be climbing out of its slump, prompting the world to sigh in relief. For decades, the United States has been the driving economic force for the rest of the world. However, overreliance on America is a serious problem facing the global economy, prompting former Treasury secretary Lawrence Summers to say, "The world economy is flying on one engine."

Since 1995 nearly 60 percent of the cumulative growth in world output has come from the United States, compared to the United States's 30 percent share of world gross domestic product (GDP). An extraordinary rise in U.S. spending is partly responsible, as U.S. domestic demand has risen 3.7 percent per year since 1995, nearly twice the rate of the rest of the world. And just as a one-engine plane is more likely to crash, a highly correlated global economy is more likely to collapse if only one of its engines is working properly. A significant drop in U.S. spending would have disastrous consequences for the rest of the world. Not an encouraging thought, as Americans have been spending beyond their means for many years and the American saving rate is at an all-time record low. Meanwhile, the U.S. current account deficit (the amount it must borrow from foreigners to spend more than it produces per year) has raced to more than 5 percent of national GDP. In the 1980s, the United States was the biggest creditor country in the world, but now it stands as the biggest debtor country in history.

The 1990s witnessed American firms using debt-financed investments to power the world economy. A decade and a stock market crash later, investment spending has collapsed as firms try to strengthen their balance sheets. Meanwhile, U.S. households have been slow to do the same. Sharp cuts in interest rates allowed households to borrow against their homes, and as of 2003 U.S. consumers' indebtedness was growing twice as fast as their income. The U.S. government has also exhibited increased spending—a large budget surplus in 2000 had turned into an even larger deficit by 2003.

The debt escalation can only go on for so long, because at some point creditors will refuse to continue lending money to the United States. Japan and China have been assuming a greater and greater share of U.S. government debt, which further ties the United States to the global economy. Their motives are to weaken their own currencies, thus buoying their exports to the United States.

There are some ways to ease the world off U.S. spending without causing it to tumble into a worldwide recession. Economic theory provides the most basic answer: Americans should spend less, foreigners should spend more, and the dollar should be weakened to allow for a U.S. shift away from importing and toward exporting. Such actions corrected a similar situation in the late 1980s, when the current account deficit was 3 percent. Then, the booming economies of Germany and Japan combined with a large drop in the value of the dollar to stave off recession. The odds of a repeat performance are slim.

With the Japanese and European economies in turmoil and their populations aging, dramatic improvement from somewhere is needed to provide support for the United States. The largest factor in easing this situation is likely to be the U.S. dollar. In the late 1980s, it fell 55 percent against the deutsche mark and 56 percent against the yen. By late 2003, the dollar had fallen 8 percent off its peak against the euro and yen. Without a dramatic shift in global demand, economists predict that the dollar will need to fall by at least 40 percent to make a significant impact on the U.S. current account deficit. However, if the dollar falls too fast the global economy is likely to roll back into a recession. Roadblocks exist. Japan has been actively keeping its currency weak, and China's economy would likely collapse if its currency (the yuan) strengthened too quickly.

Thus, the global economy is facing some serious problems. While the risk of a crash in the U.S. dollar or a serious global recession is real, sluggish growth and currency volatility seem more likely. The first step is recognizing how big the problem is.

Source: "Flying on One Engine," *The Economist,* September 18, 2003, **http://www.economist.com.**

that they will borrow if they can obtain funds for 3 percent. Millions of potential lenders and borrowers in the economy are making such decisions all the time, for thousands of different types of loans and investments, and this is the process that determines interest rates on different types of securities. Moreover, as conditions change—and they change daily, sometimes by large amounts—preferences, and thus the level of interest rates, will also change.

Further Analysis of Inflation

Inflation
The amount by which prices increase over time.

Now we can bring in inflation. Suppose a basket of goods and services that costs $1,000 today is expected to cost $1,035 in one year. This increase, expressed in percentage terms, is **inflation**, and it is given the symbol I and calculated as follows:

$$I = \text{Change in price/Initial price}$$
$$= (\$1,035 - \$1,000)/\$1,000 = 0.035 = 3.5\%.$$

Just to preserve our real purchasing power—that is, to break even—we must earn enough to increase the initial investment by I, or 3.5 percent, and to the 3.0 percent required real rate, we must earn still more. The rate of interest that both offsets inflation and provides the required real return on a riskless investment is defined as the **nominal, risk-free rate, r_{RF}**.

Nominal, Risk-Free Rate (r_{RF})
The rate of interest that both offsets inflation and provides the required real return on a riskless investment.

It is tempting to estimate r_{RF} by simply adding the expected inflation rate to the required real rate, getting a rate of 6.5 percent, but that underestimates the correct r_{RF}:[4]

$$\text{Incorrect: } r_{RF} \neq r^* + I.$$

$$\text{Correct: } r_{RF} = r^* + I + r^*I. \qquad (2\text{-}1)$$

The nominal, risk-free required rate of return in our example is thus

$$r_{RF} = 0.03000 + 0.03050 + 0.00105 = 0.06605 = 6.605\%.$$

Inflation Premium (IP)
A premium that must be added to the real risk-free rate to adjust for inflation; calculated as I + r*I.

The value that must be added to the real risk-free rate is called the **inflation premium (IP)**, and its formula is given here:

$$IP = I + r^*I. \qquad (2\text{-}2)$$

Based on our example, IP is 3.605 percent, which is higher than the expected inflation rate, 3.5 percent, because of the interaction term r^*I.

If both the real rate and expected inflation are low, as in our example, the interaction term included in the inflation premium will be very low, and the error that results from omitting it will be small. However, if inflation is high, as it often is in

---

[4] In our example with $r^* = 3\%$, $I = 3.5\%$, and $1,000 to spend or invest, we need to end up with enough money to buy goods with an initial cost of $1,000(1.03) = $1,030 if we are to earn the 3 percent real return. However, $1,000 of Year 0 goods will have a cost of $1,035 given the 3.5 percent inflation rate, so we need $1,035 just to break even in real terms. Moreover, that $1,035 must be increased by 3 percent to provide the 3 percent required real return; that is, we must end up with $1,035(1.03) = $1,066.05 if we are to earn a 3 percent real rate of return. Putting all this together, we obtain this formula for r_{RF}:

$$(1 + r_{RF}) = (1 + r^*)(1 + I) - 1$$
$$r_{RF} = r^* + I + r^*I.$$

Substituting our illustrative numbers into this equation, we obtain the following result:

$$r_{RF} = 0.0300 + 0.0350 + 0.00105 = 0.06605.$$

If we earn this nominal return, we will end up with $1,000(1.06605) = $1,066.05, which will provide us with the required 3 percent real rate of return and protect the purchasing power of the initial $1,000.

developing nations, then it is very important to use the correct formula, which means including the term r*I. Also, note that if the term "risk-free rate" is used without the modifiers "real" or "nominal," you should assume that it refers to the *quoted, or nominal, rate*, which includes the inflation adjustment. We approximate the risk-free rate by the quoted return on U.S. Treasury securities or equivalent foreign government securities with similar maturities.

Risk

Risk Premium (RP)
A premium that reflects the difference between the expected rate of return on a given risky asset and that on a less risky asset.

Investors dislike risk, so they add a **risk premium (RP)** when establishing the required rate on a risky security. To illustrate, assume that a student needs $1,000 for tuition, and because student loans are more risky than government loans, the corresponding rate is 10 percent. The difference between this risky loan rate and the nominal, risk-free rate calculated earlier is $10.000\% - 6.605\% = 3.395\%$, which compensates investors for bearing the risk inherent in the student loan.

The Nominal, Risk-Adjusted Rate (r)

Nominal, Risk-Adjusted Rate of Return (r)
The actual rate charged on a loan; it compensates investors for postponing consumption, inflation, and risk.

The 10 percent student loan rate is a **nominal, risk-adjusted rate of return (r)**, and it compensates investors for postponing consumption (r*), inflation (I), and risk (RP). It is also known as a **quoted**, or **stated**, **rate**, and it is the rate that would be given as the rate on a student loan. Quoted rates on many widely traded securities are reported in *The Wall Street Journal* or other financial publications, and they can be obtained from online sources.

Quoted (Stated) Rate
The nominal, risk-adjusted rate of return, which is actually published in financial publications.

General Formula

The general formula used for the nominal risk-adjusted required rate of return is shown here:

$$r = r^* + IP + RP = r_{RF} + RP. \tag{2-3}$$

Default Risk Premium (DRP)
A premium that reflects the difference between the interest rate on a U.S. Treasury bond and a corporate bond of equal maturity and marketability.

Here, r is the nominal risk-adjusted rate, r* is the real risk-free rate, IP and RP are the inflation and risk premiums, respectively, and $r_{RF} = r^* + IP$.

The risk premium, RP, actually consists of at least five different components:[5]

1. *Default risk premium.* Default risk reflects the probability that a borrower will not pay the interest and principal on a loan when it comes due. The higher the probability of nonpayment, the greater the default risk and thus the higher the **default risk premium (DRP)**. U.S. Treasury securities have no

[5]We adjusted the inflation premium, IP, to account for the interaction between inflation and the real rate, r*. It would be possible to make similar adjustments for the risk premium and identify interactions among r*, I, and RP. However, this is not normally done. An exception is when the Capital Asset Pricing Model (CAPM), which we discuss in Chapter 5, is used to find local costs of capital in a country that is experiencing high inflation and the U.S. market risk premium (RP_M) is not an adequate proxy for the required risk premium in the local market. The reason for this is that the RP_M consists of a real required return to compensate for risk in the market plus an inflation adjustment to preserve the value of the real risk premium. When local inflation rates are significantly higher than U.S. inflation, this second adjustment must be made to the local RP_M. To see how this should be done, assume that r* = 3% in both countries but IP_{US} = 3%, $IP_{Indonesia}$ = 30%, and $RP_{M, US}$ = 7%. r_{RF} = 3% + 3% = 6% in the United States and 3% + 30% = 33% in Indonesia. The return on the market (r_M) = 6% + 7% = 13% in the United States, but it is wrong to say that r_M = 33% + 7% = 40% in Indonesia (as some books do) because of the difference in inflation in the two countries. To find the inflation-adjusted RP_M for Indonesia, we need to find the real risk rate, r_{RSK}, for the United States and then apply this to the Indonesia case: $(1 + r^* + IP_{US})(1 + r_{RSK}) = (1 + r_{US})$; $(1 + 0.03 + 0.03)(1 + r_{RSK}) = (1 + 0.13)$; r_{RSK} = 0.066038 or 6.6038%. Then, the RP_M for Indonesia = $r_{RSK}(1 + r^* + IP_{Indonesia})$ = 0.066038(1 + 0.03 + 0.30) = 0.08783 or 8.783%. Thus, r_M for Indonesia = 33% + 8.783% = 41.783% instead of the 40 percent calculated (incorrectly) earlier. Some may wish to suggest that the risk aversion of Indonesian investors is different from that of U.S. investors so that the real risk rate should also differ for the two markets. We find merit in this suggestion, but if a person wants to assume that the risk rates are the same (an assumption that is often made), then it is necessary to make the inflation adjustment to risk premiums and avoid biasing the CAPM estimates.

default risk for American investors, hence they offer the lowest interest rates on taxable securities. Similarly, government securities denominated in the local currency in most other countries are assumed to be free of risk in their local capital markets, but investors outside the country may still build in a default premium due to exchange rate concerns and possible expropriation.

The difference between the quoted interest rate on a U.S. Treasury bond and that on a corporate bond with similar maturity, liquidity, and other features is the bond's default risk premium. The riskier the security, the higher the DRP. One indicator of the level of default risk on a corporate bond is its rating—the default premium rises as the credit rating declines.[6] Table 2-2 provides some representative interest rates and default premiums on long-term bonds during 2003. While the table does not show it, default risk premiums vary somewhat over time, but the figures in the table are representative of recent U.S. levels. DRPs in other countries will differ from those in the United States, so be careful when dealing with foreign bonds. It is important to estimate the DRP on the basis of data for the particular country. In other words, do not assume that the U.S. premium is a reasonable proxy for those in other countries. However, eurobonds denominated in U.S. dollars trade competitively with U.S. bonds, and thus do require risk premiums similar to those on U.S. bonds.

2. *Liquidity premium.* A "liquid" asset is one that can be converted into cash quickly and at a "fair market value." By definition, cash is the most liquid asset, and financial assets are usually more liquid than real assets. The harder it is to convert an asset into cash quickly and at near its fair market value, the lower its liquidity and thus the higher the required **liquidity premium (LP)**. U.S. Treasury securities are traded in a very broad, deep, and active market, so their liquidity premium is essentially zero. Although it is difficult to measure liquidity premiums accurately, the difference in premiums between the most and the least liquid financial assets of similar default risk and maturity in the U.S. is roughly 2 to 5 percent.

Liquidity Premium (LP)
A premium added to the equilibrium interest rate on a security if that security cannot be converted to cash on short notice and at close to "fair market value."

TABLE 2-2 | Representative 2003 Default Risk Premiums

	Rate	DRP
U.S. Treasury	5.0%	—
AAA	5.7	0.7%
AA	6.1	1.1
A	6.4	1.4
BBB	6.8	1.8

Sources: U.S. Treasury data represent annual average of constant 20-year maturity, *Federal Reserve Statistical Release,* selected interest rates. Corporate yields represent long-term annual averages for maturities of 20 years or more obtained from "Moody's Corporate Bond Yield Averages," *Moody's Investors Service.*

---

[6]Sometimes the actual rate on a corporate bond is a better indicator of its risk than its rating. Institutional investors have excellent credit analysts; they may pick up changes in a bond's situation before the rating agencies change their classifications and through their buying or selling change the interest rate before the rating changes. For example, if credit analysts think that an AA-rated company's situation has deteriorated to the point where it should only have an A rating, then they will sell the bonds and drive their prices down until their yields rise to the same level as A-rated bonds.

Interest Rate Risk
The risk of capital losses to which investors are exposed due to rising interest rates.

Maturity Risk Premium (MRP)
A premium that reflects interest rate risk.

3. *Maturity risk premium.* As we shall demonstrate in Chapter 8, the prices of fixed-rate bonds fall when interest rates rise and rise when rates fall. The resulting risk of capital losses due to rising interest rates is known as **interest rate risk.** The price change associated with a given change in the interest rate is much greater for a long-term than a short-term bond. Therefore, the longer the time until maturity, the greater the price risk, hence the higher the **maturity risk premium (MRP)** that investors add when determining the required nominal interest rate. Even though U.S. Treasury bonds have no default risk and virtually no liquidity risk, long-term T-bonds are exposed to a significant maturity risk. Indeed, some long-term T-bonds lost fully half of their values during the 1980s, when interest rates rose sharply. The MRP for T-bonds has recently been in the range of 1 to 2 percent, but it varies somewhat over time depending on expectations regarding future interest rate volatility. In other countries, the same process determines their MRPs, and if interest rates in a given country have been more or less volatile than in the United States, their MRPs will reflect this difference.

Business Climate
Refers to a country's social, political, and economic environment.

Country Risk Premium (CRP)
A premium that reflects the risk that arises from investing or doing business in a particular country.

4. *Country risk premium. Country risk* refers to the risk associated with investing in a particular country, and it depends on the country's social, political, and economic environment, or its **business climate.** The more uncertain the business climate, the higher the **country risk premium (CRP).** See Table 2-3 for some recent rankings from *Euromoney* magazine. Perhaps surprisingly, this study, like most, concludes that the United States has more country risk than several other nations. This is particularly significant because even though people in the United States usually assume that our bonds have no country risk, others do not agree. Foreign investors are concerned about how changes in U.S. policies (say, tax and Federal Reserve policies) might affect their positions, so they build a country risk premium into their required rate of return on both corporate and Treasury debt. Because foreign investors are major purchasers of U.S. debt, and because the CRP is reflected in rates on all U.S. dollar-denominated bonds, perceptions about U.S. country risk affect the level of rates in this country.

Exchange Rate Risk Premium (ERP)
A premium that results from the possibility that an exchange rate change will lead to a loss in a bond's value.

5. *Exchange rate risk premium.* When a bond is *denominated* in a currency other than the investor's home-country currency, a change in the exchange rate will lead to a change in the bond's value to that investor. For example, suppose a Japanese investor buys a bond denominated in dollars, and the dollar then weakens. The dollars the investor receives will then buy fewer yen, and this will lower the bond's value to the Japanese investor. As a result, **exchange rate risk premiums (ERPs)** are built into the nominal rates of return on bonds. The size of the ERP depends on the stability of exchange rates between the two countries, and even U.S. Treasury securities have an ERP because so many of them are held by foreign investors.

We can now rewrite our equation for the nominal risk-adjusted required rate of return as shown in Equation 2-4:

$$r = r^* + IP + RP = r_{RF} + DRP + LP + MRP + CRP + ERP. \qquad (2\text{-}4)$$

Exchange Rates

Until now we have dealt with interest rates in only one country. Interest rates are generally determined in the same way in all countries, but parameters such as the

TABLE 2-3 Selected Countries Ranked by Composite (Total) Risk

Rank	Country	Political Risk (25)	Economic Performance (25)	Debt Indicators (10)	Debt in Default or Rescheduled (10)	Credit Ratings (10)	Access to Bank Financing (5)	Access to Short-Term Financing (5)	Access to Capital Markets (5)	Discount on Forfeiting (5)	Total Risk (100)
1	Luxembourg	24.67	25.00	10.00	10.00	10.00	5.00	5.00	5.00	4.69	99.36
2	Norway	24.51	23.55	10.00	10.00	10.00	5.00	5.00	5.00	4.69	97.75
3	Switzerland	24.97	22.81	10.00	10.00	10.00	5.00	5.00	5.00	4.69	97.48
4	United States	24.95	21.69	10.00	10.00	10.00	5.00	5.00	5.00	5.00	96.64
12	Canada	24.64	17.98	10.00	10.00	9.79	5.00	5.00	5.00	4.69	92.11
49	China	16.84	11.22	9.66	10.00	5.83	0.12	2.50	2.00	3.34	61.52
51	Mexico	16.87	9.68	9.05	10.00	4.69	0.77	3.33	3.00	3.74	61.14
72	Russia	11.77	8.82	9.21	9.66	3.33	0.14	1.96	1.70	2.42	49.02
89	Indonesia	8.98	6.74	8.39	9.52	0.83	0.30	1.83	1.25	2.21	40.05
162	Argentina	3.26	7.39	7.75	4.15	0.21	0.02	3.00	0.00	0.00	25.78
185	North Korea	0.00	2.09	0.00	0.00	0.00	0.00	1.17	0.00	0.00	3.26

Source: "Country Risk Rankings," *Euromoney*, September 2003, **http://www.euromoney.com.**

inflation rate and the various premiums differ from country to country. These differences are reflected in local interest rates and, through them, in the exchange rate between the two currencies. We can show these linkages by extending our earlier example. The original data apply to Country A, whose currency is the dollar, and we now bring in a second country, Country B, whose currency is the peso. Our task is to derive the equilibrium exchange rate, given data on the other parameters. We start by assuming that r^* is 3 percent in both countries, and we also assume that all the premiums are similar except for inflation. The inflation rate in Country A is 3.5 percent as given in the previous example, and it is 8 percent in Country B. With this information we can calculate r_{RF} in each country:

$$r_{RF, A} = [(1.03)(1.035) - 1] = 0.06605 \text{ or } 6.605\%.$$
$$r_{RF, B} = [(1.03)(1.08) - 1] = 0.11240 \text{ or } 11.240\%.$$

For simplicity, we assume the spot exchange rate is P1.0000/$; that is, the dollar and the peso currently have the same value.

Given this information, what should the exchange rate be in one year? Figure 2-2 shows the linkages that describe the situation. The top and bottom rows show the results from investing in each country. Given that risks are the same in both countries, an investor's position should end up the same regardless of which country he or she invests in, assuming that funds can be moved without material costs from country to country (which is true). In equilibrium, the exchange rate one year from now should be such that $1,066.05 is equivalent to P1,112.40 (i.e., we can exchange P1,112.40 for $1,066.05). If this situation does not hold, then effective rates in the two markets would be different, and investors would flock to the market with the higher effective rates. Put another way, an arbitrage opportunity would exist, and thus the market would not be in equilibrium.

We can solve for the equilibrium exchange rate one year hence as follows:

$$P1,112.40/X = \$1,066.05$$
$$X = P1.043478/\$.$$

If our expectations are borne out, a year from now it will require 1.043478 pesos to buy one dollar, meaning the dollar will have strengthened relative to the peso. The exchange rate would change because the two countries' inflation rates differed.

This example illustrates the linkages between inflation, interest rates, and exchange rates. We will discuss all this in greater depth in the next chapter where we discuss exchange rates, but for now you should simply recognize that interest rates, inflation rates, and exchange rates interact in the global marketplace, and if specific relationships do not hold, then arbitrage will occur until those relationships do hold.

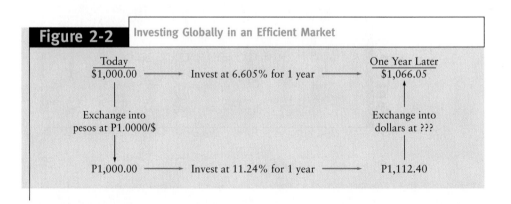

Figure 2-2   Investing Globally in an Efficient Market

	Today		One Year Later
	$1,000.00 →	Invest at 6.605% for 1 year →	$1,066.05
	Exchange into pesos at P1.0000/$		Exchange into dollars at ???
	P1,000.00 →	Invest at 11.24% for 1 year →	P1,112.40

Differentiate between the real risk-free rate and the nominal risk-free rate.
What is an inflation premium?
What is a default risk premium?
What is a liquidity premium?
What is a maturity risk premium?
What is a country risk premium?
What is an exchange rate risk premium?

INTERNATIONAL MONETARY ARRANGEMENTS

International Monetary System
The framework within which exchange rates are determined. It is the blueprint for international trade and capital flows.

In a competitive and efficient marketplace, which is characterized by an absence of government intervention to influence the exchange rate, the value of a country's currency will conform to the relationships discussed earlier. However, governments often intervene in the marketplace in an attempt to force the value of their currency to a level dictated by internal politics, so we need to look at some of the exchange rate policies and regimes in use around the world today. The **international monetary system** is the framework within which exchange rates are determined. Because exchange rates are a function of the supply and demand for various national currencies, the international monetary system is also the blueprint for international trade and capital flows. Thus, the international monetary system ties together global currency, money, capital, real estate, commodity, and real asset markets into a network of institutions and instruments, regulated by intergovernmental agreements, and driven by each country's unique political and economic objectives.[7]

International Monetary Terminology

While we will cover foreign exchange in greater detail in Chapter 3, it is useful to introduce some important concepts that will make it easier to understand the international monetary system:

1. An *exchange rate* is the price of one country's currency in terms of another currency. For example, on Wednesday, February 25, 2004, one U.S. dollar would buy 0.5348 British pound, 0.8003 euro, 1.3353 Canadian dollars, or 8.2781 Chinese yuan.[8]

2. A *spot exchange rate* is the quoted price for a unit of foreign currency to be delivered "on the spot," or within a very short period of time. The rate quoted above, £0.5348/$, is a spot rate as of the close of business on February 25, 2004.

3. A *forward exchange rate* is the quoted price for a unit of foreign currency to be delivered at a specified date in the future. If today were February 25, 2004, and we wanted to know how many pounds we could expect to receive for our dollars on August 25, 2004, we would look at the six-month forward rate,

---

[7]For a comprehensive history of the international monetary system and details of how it has evolved, consult one of the many economics books on the subject, including Robert Carbaugh, *International Economics* (Mason, OH: South-Western, 2004); Mordechai Kreinin, *International Economics: A Policy Approach*, 9th edition (Mason, OH: South-Western, 2002); and Joseph P. Daniels and David D. Van Hoose, *International Monetary and Financial Economics*, 2nd edition (Mason, OH: South-Western, 2002).

[8]The complete name for the Chinese currency is the *yuan renminbi*, but it is generally called either the yuan or the renminbi. In our experience, yuan is used more often, so we generally use that term. However, *The Wall Street Journal*, when it reports exchange rates, uses the term renminbi. Because China is becoming increasingly important in world commerce and as a U.S. trading partner, you should be familiar with both terms. Also, note that exchange rates could be, and in the past often were, defined in terms of a commodity, especially gold. In 1934, the United States defined the value of the dollar such that one ounce of gold equaled $35, but the "gold standard" was abandoned about 35 years later. If runaway inflation ever developed across the globe, countries would perhaps return to the gold standard, but if economic conditions continue to be relatively stable, that will not happen.

INSTABILITY IN THE EU

Despite early insistence on fiscal safeguards, France and Germany have become the habitual offenders of the European Union's "stability and growth" pact. The pact requires that member nations not run deficits greater than 3 percent of GDP. Successive breaches of the pact require disciplinary action, if the other member nations agree that enforcement is needed. However, there is a strong possibility that the other finance ministers would vote to let France and Germany slide on the infractions. Smaller nations are wary of making similar breaches, as there is no indication they would be given such favorable treatment if they violated the pact, and similar concerns face possible new members. Ultimately, the EU faces a tough task of coordinating the fiscal policies of its individual member nations, while having control only over the collective monetary policy of the EU.

France and Germany have been the cornerstones of the European Union since its inception. However, it is these two countries that have thrown the stability of the EU into question. Both Germany and France breached the 3 percent deficit limit in 2002 and 2003. The German deficit was 3.5 percent in 2002 and 3.8 percent in 2003, while France's deficits were 3.1 percent and 4.0 percent, respectively. Ironically, it was due to German insistence that the EU adopted the pact. In 2003, German finance minister Hans Eichel insisted that Germany would aim to comply with the pact in 2004, while French prime minister Jean-Pierre Raffarin had already given up on that goal. However, financial economists had little faith that either nation would reach the target, especially when Eichel was campaigning for a €16 billion ($17.4 billion) tax cut and Raffarin was adamant that finding jobs for the unemployed was his first priority.

If France and Germany fail to comply in 2004, protocol requires the EU to collect an interest-free deposit of between 0.2 and 0.5 percent of national GDP. Further breaches in 2005 would result in the loss of those deposits, amounting to more than €4 billion for Germany and €3 billion for France. Strict adherence to the measure would surely result in penalties for France and Germany, but if the countries are making an effort and deficits don't run out of control, fellow EU finance ministers are unlikely to vote to impose the sanctions.

French president Jacques Chirac has asked for a "temporary softening" of the stability pact, and German chancellor Gerhard Schröder has asked for leniency and more emphasis on the "growth" part of the "stability and growth" pact. Both leaders seem to suggest that the rules be applied only when no one is breaking them, and ignored when there are infractions. Together with Italy and Britain, the two offenders originally spearheaded the reform effort, much to the dismay of smaller states like Austria, Ireland, and the Netherlands, which wanted to run deficits. The smaller countries got their budgets in order, and they don't feel that the same leniency would be extended to them if they felt a need to default. Similar concerns surely plague countries that have yet to join the EU. Besides, as populations age, there will be more of a strain on annual budgetary burdens (an estimated shortfall of 2.2 percent of GDP for Germany by 2050). Turning a blind eye now could prove disastrous over the long run.

The current budgetary crises are primarily the result of economic downturns that should correct themselves in time. However, the pension problems are the result of long-term demographic trends that will take many years to play out. Proposals to quell the pension problems include postponing the retirement age and reducing benefits. These perceptions highlight the need to distinguish between cyclical and structural. The best solution to the pension problem would be a growing, vibrant economy and a workforce whose productivity is increasing; conditions that would also help solve the budget deficit problem.

The intent of the "stability and growth" pact was not to enforce the fiscal consolidation that Europe needs, but rather to safeguard the credibility of the young euro as a currency. With the euro's credibility no longer in doubt, the role of the "stability and growth" pact comes into question. French foreign minister Dominique de Villepin called for the coordination of EU member nations' fiscal policies. According to his argument, Europe needs coordination of the different countries' fiscal policies with the single monetary policy set by the European Central Bank (ECB). Obvious problems arise when the ECB sets monetary policy for all EU member nations, but has no ability to lower interest rates in response to a single country's efforts to repair its finances.

Source: "Deficits and Defiance," *The Economist,* September 2, 2003, **http://www.economist.com**.

which was £0.5434/$. Note that a *forward exchange contract* on February 25 would lock in this exchange rate, but no currency would change hands until August 25. The spot rate on August 25 might be quite different from £0.5434, in which case we would have a profit or a loss on the forward purchase.

4. A *fixed exchange rate* for a currency is set by the government and allowed to fluctuate only slightly (if at all) around the desired rate, called the *par value*. For example, China has fixed the exchange rate for the yuan at CNY 8.2781/$, and it has maintained this fixed rate for the past few years. Because the rate is fixed, only the spot rate is quoted in *The Wall Street Journal* and other publications.

5. A *floating* or *flexible exchange rate* is one that is not regulated by the government, so supply and demand in the market determine the currency's value. The U.S. dollar and the euro are examples of free-floating currencies. Note, though, that central banks do from time to time intervene in the market to nudge exchange rates up or down, even though they basically float.[9]

6. *Devaluation* or *revaluation of a currency* is the technical term referring to the decrease or increase in the par value of a currency whose value is fixed. This decision is made by the government, usually without warning.

7. *Depreciation* or *appreciation of a currency* refers to a decrease or increase in the foreign exchange value of a floating currency. These changes are caused by market forces rather than by governments.

8. A *soft* or *weak currency* is one that is expected to depreciate against most other currencies or else is being artificially maintained at an unrealistically high fixed rate by the government through open market purchases. A *hard* or *strong currency* is expected to appreciate against most other currencies or else is being artificially maintained by the government at an unrealistically low fixed rate. Many economists suggest the Chinese yuan is significantly undervalued, so it is a strong currency.[10]

The "Perfect" Currency

Before looking at currency arrangements, it might be instructive to summarize the characteristics of a "perfect," or ideal, currency. Most economists list three characteristics that are highly desirable in a money unit:

1. The currency's value should be fixed with respect to the currency used by the country's trading partners and other important nations; that is, its exchange rate should be stable. This would allow investors and businesses to plan with greater certainty regarding the future value of receipts and payments.

2. Each country would set its own domestic monetary and fiscal policy solely on the basis of its own economic situation. This would include policies regarding interest rates, managing inflation, fostering full employment, and ensuring economic prosperity for all.

3. Complete and unrestricted monetary flows should be permitted, allowing investors and businesses to move their wealth as they choose.

Many economists call these three characteristics "The Impossible Trinity" because it is impossible to achieve all three objectives together. For example, the United States has a floating-exchange-rate regime, no capital or exchange controls, and its monetary and fiscal policies are driven by domestic considerations. However, the

---

[9] Governments quite often buy or sell currencies in the open market to influence the floating rate, but they are simply changing supply or demand to influence the rate rather than using some nonmarket mandated adjustment.

[10] If the value of the yuan were allowed to rise, then a dollar would buy fewer than 8.2781 yuan, which would increase the dollar cost of Chinese goods imported into the United States; in turn it would reduce Chinese exports to the United States. The Chinese government wants to maintain export levels, so it has resisted revaluing the yuan.

U.S. dollar has not been stable against the currencies of such major trading partners as Canada, Europe, and Japan. In 2003, the dollar depreciated significantly against both the euro and the Japanese yen. China, on the other hand, maintains a fixed exchange rate with the U.S. dollar and independent monetary and fiscal policies, but the only way it can keep these policies intact is to impose strict capital and exchange controls. We see, then, that a country can maintain two of the three characteristics, but allowing all three to operate is impossible.

If we return to the problem diagrammed in Figure 2-2 we can illustrate this phenomenon. In that scenario, which mirrors the situation in the United States today, we assumed monetary independence and free capital movement, but the result was a change in the equilibrium exchange rate between the two countries. If we wanted to keep the exchange rate constant at P1.00/$, we could do so in the short run by preventing arbitrageurs from acquiring the foreign exchange needed to complete transactions. This is what China and some other countries do to maintain their fixed exchange rates. We could also maintain the exchange rate by keeping interest rates artificially low, but that would eventually overstimulate the economy and lead to inflation. If inflation in Country B was 8 percent and we wanted to keep the nominal rate at 6.605 percent, then the real rate would have to be negative! Thus, we see that countries have to make decisions about which leg of the trinity they want to abandon in order to maintain the other two. This decision is at the heart of a country's decision as to which currency arrangement to use.

Current Monetary Arrangements

At the most basic level, we can divide currency regimes into two broad groups: floating rates and fixed rates. Within the two regimes, there are gradations among sub-regimes in terms of how rigidly they adhere to the basic positions. Looking first at the floating-rate category, the two main subgroups are

Freely Floating
Occurs when the exchange rate is determined by supply and demand for the currency.

1. *Freely floating.* Here the exchange rate is determined by the supply and demand for the currency. Under a **freely-floating** regime, governments may occasionally intervene in the market to buy or sell their currency in order to stabilize fluctuations, but they do not attempt to alter the absolute level of the rate. This policy exists at one end of the continuum of exchange rate regimes. For example, the currencies of Australia, Brazil, and the Philippines are allowed to float.

Managed Float
Occurs when there is significant government intervention to control the exchange rate via manipulation of the currency's supply and demand.

2. *Managed floating.* Here there is significant government intervention to manage the exchange rate by manipulating the currency's supply and demand. The government rarely reveals its target exchange rate levels if it uses a **managed float** because this would make it too easy for currency speculators to profit. For example, the governments of Colombia, Israel, and Poland manage their respective currency's float.

Most developed countries follow either a freely floating or a managed floating regime. A few developing countries do as well, often reluctantly and as a result of a market that forces them to abandon a fixed-rate regime.

Types of fixed-exchange-rate regimes include the following:

1. *No local currency.* The most extreme position is for the country to have no local currency of its own. The country either uses another country's currency as its legal tender (such as the U.S. dollar in Panama and Ecuador) or else belongs to a group of countries that share a common currency (such as the euro). With this arrangement, the local government surrenders economic regulation.
2. *Currency board arrangement.* Under a variation of the first subregime, a country technically has its own currency but commits to exchange it for a specified foreign money unit at a fixed exchange rate. This requires it to impose domes-

Currency Board Arrangement
Occurs when a country has its own currency but commits to exchange it for a specified foreign money unit at a fixed exchange rate and legislates domestic currency restrictions, unless it has the foreign currency reserves to cover requested exchanges.

Fixed Peg Arrangement
Occurs when a country locks its currency to a specific currency or basket of currencies at a fixed exchange rate. The exchange rate is allowed to vary only within ±1% of the target rate.

tic currency restrictions unless it has the foreign currency reserves to cover requested exchanges. This is called a **currency board arrangement**. Argentina had a currency board arrangement before its crisis of January 2002, when it was forced to devalue the peso and default on its debt.

3. *Fixed peg arrangement.* In a **fixed peg arrangement** the country locks, or "pegs," its currency to another currency or basket of currencies at a fixed exchange rate. It allows the currency to vary only slightly from its desired rate, and if the currency moves outside specified limits (often set at ±1 percent of the target rate), it intervenes to force the currency back to within the limits. An example is China, where the yuan is pegged to the U.S. dollar at a rate of CNY 8.2781/$, and the Chinese central bank intervenes as necessary to maintain this target. Additional examples include Bhutan's ngultrum, which is pegged to the Indian rupee; the Falkland Islands' pound, which is pegged to the British pound; and Barbados's dollar, which is pegged to the U.S. dollar.

Other variations have been used, and new ones are developed from time to time. A majority of the world's countries employ some sort of fixed-exchange-rate arrangement. So, while the most important currencies (as measured by volume of transactions) are allowed to float, and the international monetary system is often called a "floating regime," most currencies are actually fixed in some manner.

Fixed or Floating: How Does a Country Choose?

Numerous arguments have been advanced over the years favoring one regime over others, and some researchers have suggested that countries tend to move to the polar extremes of freely floating or rigidly pegged rates. This is the so-called bipolar view. However, there seems to be no single answer to the question of the optimal exchange-rate regime. The exchange-rate regime should reflect national priorities regarding the relative importance of fighting inflation, holding down interest rates, combating unemployment, producing a favorable balance of payments, promoting trade flows, and so forth. Research suggests that priorities change as a nation goes through different stages of development, so it may be wise to follow one strategy in the early stages of development and then shift to another as the economy matures. In Table 2-4 we list some of the reasons advanced in favor of fixed and floating rates.

Some recent research by the International Monetary Fund suggests that for countries in a relatively early stage of economic development, the existence of a fixed regime appears to be a valuable tool for fighting inflation. Under such a regime, countries must intervene domestically to take counterinflationary actions, and knowledge of this requirement makes anti-inflation actions more credible. Of course, if people believe that inflation will be constrained, then this in and of itself helps hold down the inflation rate. Moreover, studies suggest that such actions do not constrain growth. However, as development progresses, and as a country becomes more closely integrated with its trading partners, there appear to be benefits from shifting to a more flexible regime. Thus, for developed countries, flexible or floating rates appear to offer higher growth potential without loss of credibility regarding an anti-inflationary stance.[11]

Emerging Markets and the Choice of Monetary Regime

As indicated earlier, empirical research suggests that developing countries benefit from adopting a fixed-rate regime until their economies become more integrated into the global marketplace. Also, the "bipolar view" seems to indicate that one of

---

[11]"Evolution and Performance of Exchange Rate Regimes," Working Paper no. 03/243, The International Monetary Fund, December 2003.

TABLE 2-4 | Pros and Cons for Fixed- versus Floating-Exchange Rates

Factors Favoring Fixed Rates

1. More stable and predictable exchange rates, which reduces risks in international commerce.
2. Helps in the fight against inflation because countries must intervene domestically to take counterinflationary actions to maintain the exchange rate at a fixed level.

Factors Against Fixed Rates

1. Significant international reserves must be available for use in defending the currency.
2. If the fixed rate is inconsistent with the country's fundamental economic condition, either painful adjustments must be made in the domestic economy or the target exchange rate must be changed.

Factors Favoring Floating Rates

1. The market adjusts automatically for changing economic fundamentals, and no government intervention is needed.
2. Governments can follow domestic policies to reduce unemployment or to stimulate growth without having to explicitly consider international implications of the exchange rate.
3. International reserves do not have to be used to preserve the exchange rate because it is allowed to find its own equilibrium level.

Factors Against Floating Rates

1. Future exchange rates are less stable and less predictable, which increases the risks inherent in international transactions.
2. Distortions in the domestic economy can persist for longer periods if the government is not bound to intervene to defend its currency.

the extremes of the fixed-rate regime—either using another country's currency or tying the currency closely to another currency—is preferable to a more relaxed variant. In this section, we look at the two fixed-rate extremes and explain their characteristics in more detail.

Dollarization
Occurs when a country abandons its own currency and adopts the U.S. dollar as its legal tender.

DOLLARIZATION The most extreme fixed-rate position is for a country to abandon its own currency and adopt that of another country as its legal tender. Ecuador did this in 2000, when it made the U.S. dollar its official currency. **Dollarization**, as this phenomenon is called, is touted as having several benefits to the adopting country.

1. There is complete stability with the dollar, and, at least theoretically, the possibility of future currency crisis is eliminated.
2. It is easier to become more economically integrated with the United States when the currencies are the same.
3. Monetary policy is taken out of the hands of local politicians, hence it cannot be used for political purposes that might destabilize the economy (e.g., printing money or giving public employees outsized pay raises).

However, there are several counterarguments to dollarization.

1. The country loses sovereignty over its monetary policy. This could be significant in countries that are ultranationalistic.
2. The local central bank cannot create money, so it cannot serve effectively as a lender of last resort during a financial crisis.
3. The country loses the ability to profit from printing money. Thus, if it costs $1 million to print $1 billion worth of bills, and if $1 billion of paper money is outstanding, then the government has effectively earned a profit of $999 million. Similarly, a country can coin its own money, which is called *seigniorage*, and if it costs $0.01 to mint a quarter but coin collectors will pay $0.25 for the coin to add to their collection, the government profits from seigniorage.

Ecuador abandoned its national currency, the sucre, on September 9, 2000, and replaced it with the U.S. dollar. This decision to "dollarize" came after several years of economic crises and high inflation. Interestingly, the decision was not supported by either the U.S. government or the International Monetary Fund (IMF), but the Ecuadorian government proceeded with the program anyway. Inflation has been controlled since dollarization, and residents immediately returned significant amounts of money into the banking system and put those funds to work rather than holding them in mattresses. It may be too soon to judge the success of dollarization in Ecuador, but thus far it appears to be working.

Some economists suggest that regional trading groups would benefit from a single currency, as this would facilitate trade, make it easier for countries to capitalize on their comparative advantages, and thus improve economic efficiency. (This was the thinking that led to the adoption of the euro by the European Union.) For this reason, some economists believe that alliances such as NAFTA would benefit if Canada, Mexico, and the United States all had the same currency, and that similar benefits would accrue to all members of the Free Trade Area of the Americas if that regional alliance becomes a reality. However, it is difficult to get the countries involved to give up their separate national currencies, as demonstrated by the fact that Great Britain, Switzerland, and the Scandinavian countries (except for Finland) have refused to switch to the euro.

CURRENCY BOARDS A less severe alternative is for the countries in a regional alliance to adopt a currency board. Under this alternative, each country maintains its own currency, but the value of that currency is locked to another currency (such as the dollar or the British pound). For this to work, the country's central bank must agree to back its money supply entirely with foreign currency reserves, and it cannot issue more of the local currency unless it has the reserves to support it. This 100 percent reserve requirement means that the only way the money supply can expand is if the country acquires more foreign currency reserves through trade, which effectively eliminates the possibility of fueling inflation by printing too much money.

Of course, the experience in Argentina tells us that while a currency board may solve one problem, if the government does not make sure that other economic variables are consistent with the currency value, problems will probably arise and destroy the arrangement's effectiveness. Argentina adopted a currency board and tied its peso to the U.S. dollar at a rate of P1.00/$ in 1991. They also allowed local investors to hold bank accounts in either pesos or dollars. Most Argentines were not convinced that the board would work, hence the peso-denominated accounts had to pay a risk premium—that is, offer a higher interest rate—to induce people to hold pesos. This skepticism was warranted, because in January 2002, the currency board was discontinued in the face of economic recession and political turmoil, and peso holders suffered large losses.

SELF-TEST QUESTIONS

What is an international monetary system?
What is the difference between spot and forward exchange rates?
What is the difference between floating- and fixed-exchange rates?
What is meant by a "perfect" currency?
Differentiate between devaluation/revaluation of a currency and depreciation/appreciation of a currency.
What is meant by a soft or weak currency? A hard or strong currency?
What are the two broad categories of the various currency regimes? What are the subgroups of these two broad categories?
What is dollarization?
What are currency boards?

SUMMARY

Managers and investors make decisions within a global financial environment. This includes the local financial markets and institutions in each country, as well as international markets and institutions across the globe. In addition, it includes national tax and regulatory policies across countries and the macroeconomic conditions of each country's economy. These factors impact the outcomes of financial decisions made by managers and investors. Consequently, it is important to understand the global environment in which firms operate. The key concepts discussed in this chapter are listed below.

- **Physical asset markets** are also known as tangible, or real, asset markets. Capital budgeting decisions are important to these markets.
- **Financial asset markets** are marketplaces that deal with financial instruments such as stocks, bonds, notes, mortgages, currencies, and the like.
- **Financial instruments** are pieces of paper or electronic entries in account ledgers with contractual provisions that spell out their owners' claims on specific real assets. Their value is defined in terms of a fixed number of money units.
- A **derivative security** is any asset whose value is derived from the value of some other "underlying" asset.
- **Spot markets** are the markets in which assets are bought or sold for "on-the-spot" delivery, while **futures markets** are the markets in which participants agree today to purchase or sell an asset at some future date.
- **Money markets** are the financial markets in which funds are borrowed or loaned for less than a year, while **capital markets** are the financial markets for equity and for intermediate- or long-term debt (one year or longer).
- **Mortgage markets** are markets that deal with loans on residential, commercial, and industrial real estate. **Consumer credit markets** are markets that involve loans on autos, appliances, education, vacations, and so on. **Currency markets** are the markets that transact in foreign exchange.
- **Physical markets** are formal organizations having tangible physical locations that conduct auction markets in designated ("listed") securities, while **electronic markets** are those with no physical location but that rather exist as a computerized trading system.
- **Primary markets** are markets in which corporations raise capital by issuing new securities, while **secondary markets** are those in which existing securities and other financial assets are traded among investors.
- **Initial public offering (IPO) market** is the market in which firms "go public" by offering shares to the public.
- **Private markets** are markets in which transactions are negotiated directly between two parties, while **public markets** are those in which standardized contracts are traded on organized exchanges.
- **Cross-listing** occurs when a company lists shares of stock on multiple exchanges to increase its global recognition.
- **Around-the-clock trading** occurs when global financial institutions maintain offices in different time zones around the world and thus offer anytime trading.
- **Transfers of capital** between savers and borrowers take place in three different ways: (1) **Direct transfers** occur when a business sells its shares or bonds directly to savers. (2) Transfers may go through an **investment banking house**, which *underwrites* the issue. An underwriter serves as a middleman and facilitates the issuance of securities. (3) Transfers may be made through a **financial intermediary.** Here the intermediary obtains funds from savers in exchange for its own securities and then lends the money to borrowers.
- The **interest rate** is the price paid to borrow debt capital, while the **required return** is the minimum rate of return on a common stock that will induce a stockholder to purchase the stock.
- An **exchange rate** is the number of units of a given currency that can be purchased for one unit of another currency.

- Four fundamental factors interact to determine the cost of money: (1) **time preferences for consumption**, (2) **expected inflation**, (3) **risk**, and (4) **production opportunities.**
- The **marginal investor** is the investor who operates at the margin and whose decisions determine the market interest rate.
- The **real risk-free rate of return (r*)** is the interest rate that would exist on default-free U.S. Treasury securities if no inflation were expected, while the **nominal, risk-free rate (r_{RF})** is the interest rate that both offsets inflation and provides the required real return on a riskless investment.
- An **inflation premium** is a premium that must be added to the real risk-free rate to adjust for inflation. It is calculated as $I + r^*I$, where I is the inflation rate.
- A **risk premium** is the premium that reflects the difference between the expected rate of return on a given risky asset and that on a less risky asset.
- The **nominal, risk-adjusted rate of return (r)** is the actual rate charged on a loan; it compensates investors for postponing consumption, inflation, and risk.
- The **quoted (stated) rate** is the nominal, risk-adjusted rate of return, which is actually published in financial publications.
- The **default risk premium** is the premium that reflects the difference between the interest rate on a U.S. Treasury bond and a corporate bond of equal maturity and marketability.
- The **liquidity premium** is a premium added to the equilibrium interest rate on a security if that security cannot be converted to cash on short notice and at close to "fair market value."
- **Interest rate risk** is the risk of capital losses to which investors are exposed due to rising interest rates.
- The **maturity risk premium** is a premium that reflects interest rate risk.
- The **country risk premium** is a premium that reflects the risk that arises from investing or doing business in a particular country.
- The **exchange rate risk premium** is a premium that results from the possibility that an exchange rate change will lead to a loss in a bond's value.
- **Business climate** refers to a country's social, political, and economic environment.
- The **international monetary system** is the framework in which exchange rates are determined; it is the blueprint for international trade and capital flows.
- A **spot exchange rate** is the quoted price for a unit of foreign currency to be delivered on the spot or within a very short period of time, while a **forward exchange rate** is the quoted price for a unit of foreign currency to be delivered at a specified date in the future.
- A **fixed exchange rate** is set by the government and regulated to fluctuate only slightly (if at all) around the desired rate.
- A **floating** or **flexible exchange rate** is not regulated by the government and allows supply and demand to determine the currency's value.
- **Devaluation** or **revaluation of a currency** is the technical term referring to the decrease or increase in the par value of a currency whose value is fixed.
- **Depreciation** or **appreciation of a currency** refers to a decrease or increase in the foreign exchange value of a floating currency.
- A **soft** or **weak currency** is expected to depreciate against major currencies or is being artificially maintained by the government at an unrealistically high fixed rate, while a **hard** or **strong currency** is expected to appreciate against major currencies or is being artificially maintained by the government at an unrealistically low fixed rate.
- **Freely floating** occurs when an exchange rate is determined by supply and demand for the currency, while **managed float** occurs when there is significant government intervention to control the exchange rate via manipulation of the currency's supply and demand.
- A **currency board arrangement** occurs when a country has its own currency but commits to exchange it for a specified foreign money unit at a fixed exchange rate and legislates domestic currency restrictions, unless it has the foreign currency reserves to back it up.

- A **fixed peg arrangement** occurs when a country locks its currency to a specific currency or basket of currencies at a fixed exchange rate. The exchange rate is allowed to vary only within ±1 percent of the central rate.
- **Dollarization** occurs when a country abandons its own currency and adopts the U.S. dollar as its legal tender.

QUESTIONS

(2-1) Differentiate between the following markets: (1) Spot versus futures markets, (2) money versus capital markets, (3) mortgage versus consumer credit markets, (4) physical versus electronic markets, (5) primary versus secondary markets, and (6) private versus public markets.

(2-2) Identify and briefly explain the four fundamental factors that interact to determine the cost of money.

(2-3) Identify and briefly explain the five different components that comprise the risk premium that make up the nominal, risk-adjusted required rate of return.

(2-4) How does inflation affect a country's exchange rate?

(2-5) What is "the impossible trinity," and why is it so named?

(2-6) Briefly identify and differentiate between the two subgroups of the floating-rate category.

(2-7) Briefly identify and differentiate among the different fixed-exchange-rate regimes.

(2-8) Briefly explain whether the following statement is true or false: "The international monetary system is often called a 'floating regime,' and that designation is generally descriptive for most currencies."

(2-9) What is meant by the "bipolar view" with respect to exchange-rate regimes?

(2-10) What must be considered in selecting an exchange-rate regime?

(2-11) What are the pros and cons for fixed-exchange rates? Floating-exchange rates?

(2-12) What are the advantages and disadvantages of dollarization? Give an example. Has it worked?

SELF-TEST PROBLEMS   Solutions Appear in Appendix B

(ST-1) Define each of the following terms:
Key Terms
a. Physical asset markets; financial asset markets
b. Financial instruments; derivative security; monetary
c. Spot markets; futures markets; money markets; capital markets
d. Mortgage markets; consumer credit markets; currency markets
e. Physical markets; electronic markets; primary markets; secondary markets
f. Initial public offering (IPO) market; private markets; public markets
g. Cross-listing; around-the-clock trading
h. Investment banking house; financial intermediary
i. Interest rate; required return; exchange rate
j. Time preferences for consumption; expected inflation; risk; production opportunities
k. Real risk-free rate of return (r^*); nominal, risk-free required rate of return (r_{RF})
l. Inflation premium; risk premium; nominal, risk-adjusted rate of return (r)
m. Quoted (stated) rate; marginal investor; business climate
n. Default risk premium (DRP); liquidity premium (LP); interest rate risk

 o. Maturity risk premium (MRP); country risk premium (CRP); exchange rate risk premium (ERP)

 p. International monetary system; freely floating; managed float

 q. Currency board arrangement; fixed peg arrangement

 r. Dollarization

(ST-2)
Inflation and Real Risk-Free Rate

Suppose a basket of goods and services that costs $2,500 today is expected to cost $2,600 in one year. In addition, assume that the nominal, risk-free rate as approximated by a 1-year Treasury security is 7.64 percent.

 a. What is the expected inflation rate, I?

 b. What is the real risk-free rate of return, r*?

 c. What is the inflation premium, IP?

(ST-3)
Inflation Premium

If the real risk-free rate of return is 2.5 percent and the expected inflation rate is 3 percent, what is the calculated inflation premium?

(ST-4)
Nominal, Risk-Adjusted Rate

A Japanese investor would like to purchase a long-term (20-year maturity) U.S. corporate, BBB-rated bond. You are given the following data:

- Default risk premium: 0.4 percent.
- Liquidity premium: 0.5 percent.
- Maturity risk premium: 1.2 percent.
- Country risk premium: 0.1 percent.
- Exchange rate risk premium: 0.2 percent.
- Nominal, risk-free rate of return (20-year Treasury): 5.7 percent.
- Real risk-free rate of return: 2.5 percent.
- Inflation premium (calculated over 20 years): 3.2 percent.

The corporation is not considered to be a "blue-chip" company, so small default risk and liquidity premiums should be added when calculating the estimated yield for the BBB-rated bond. What would be your estimate of this bond's yield?

(ST-5)
Exchange Rate

You are given the following data:

	United States	Country X
r*	3.2%	3.2%
I	4.0	10.0

Country X's currency is the LC and today's spot exchange rate is LC 2.000/$.

 a. In equilibrium, what should be the exchange rate 1 year from now?

 b. Has the dollar strengthened or weakened against LC? Explain.

STARTER PROBLEMS

(2-1)
Inflation and Nominal, Risk-Free Rate

You are given the following data:
- Inflation premium, IP: 3.75 percent.
- Real risk-free rate, r*: 2.25 percent.

 a. What is the expected inflation rate, I?

 b. What is the nominal, risk-free rate, r_{RF}?

(2-2)
Nominal, Risk-Free Rate and Risk Premium

You are given the following data:
- Inflation premium, IP: 3.5 percent.
- Real risk-free rate, r*: 2.2 percent.
- Nominal, risk-adjusted rate of return, r: 8.5 percent.

 a. What is the nominal, risk-free rate, r_{RF}?

 b. What is the risk premium, RP?

(2-3)
Exchange Rate Risk Premium

A British investor recently purchased a U.S. blue-chip, AA-rated corporate bond with a 20-year maturity. The yield on the bond is 7.5 percent, and the default risk and liquidity premiums on this bond are zero. The real risk-free rate of return is

2.4 percent and the inflation premium (calculated over 20 years) is 3 percent. The maturity risk premium is 1.6 percent, and the country risk premium is 0.2 percent. The nominal risk-free rate of return is 5.4 percent. Given these data, what was the exchange rate risk premium on the bond?

(2-4)
Exchange Rate

You are given the following data:

	United States	Foreign Country C
r*	2.3%	2.3%
I	2.5	12.5

Foreign Country C's currency is the LC and today's spot exchange rate is LC 3.75/$.
a. In equilibrium, what should be the exchange rate 1 year from now?
b. Has the dollar strengthened or weakened against LC? Explain.

EXAM-TYPE PROBLEMS

(2-5)
Nominal Interest Rate

A U.S. investor recently purchased a U.S. Treasury bond with a 20-year maturity to earn a yield of 5.5 percent. A Mexican investor just purchased a U.S. AAA-rated, "blue-chip" corporate bond with a 20-year maturity for 6.2 percent. This bond can be converted to cash very quickly, so its liquidity premium is small, 0.1 percent. The spread between U.S. Treasury bonds and AAA-rated bonds with similar maturity and liquidity is 0.2 percent. Another Mexican investor purchased a U.S. BBB-rated, corporate bond with a 20-year maturity. The liquidity premium for this BBB-rated bond is 0.8 percent, and the spread between U.S. Treasury bonds and BBB-rated bonds with similar maturity and liquidity is 1.8 percent.
a. When comparing the corporate bonds to the U.S. Treasury bond, what are the implications about country and exchange rate risks faced by Mexicans when investing in U.S. Treasury securities?
b. What yield will the Mexican investor earn on the U.S. BBB-rated, corporate bond?

(2-6)
Exchange Rate

You are given the following data:

	United States	Foreign Country D
r*	2.75%	2.75%
I	3.50	7.00

Country D's currency is the LC and the 1-year forward exchange rate is LC 2.75/$.
a. In equilibrium, what should be the spot exchange rate today?
b. During the year, has the dollar strengthened or weakened against LC? Explain.

(2-7)
Nominal, Risk-Free Rate

If the real risk-free rate is 2.4 percent and the expected inflation rate is 2.8 percent, what is the nominal, risk-free rate, r_{RF}?

(2-8)
Inflation Premium and
Nominal, Risk-Free Rate

You have the following information: the expected inflation rate, I, is 3.2 percent, and the real risk-free rate, r*, is 2.1 percent.
a. What is the inflation premium, IP?
b. What is the nominal, risk-free rate, r_{RF}?

(2-9)
Nominal, Risk-Free and
Risk-Adjusted Rates

Assume that the real risk-free rate is 2.75 percent, the expected inflation rate is 2.433 percent, and the risk premium is 3.75 percent.
a. What is the inflation premium, IP?
b. What is the nominal, risk-free rate, r_{RF}?
c. What is the nominal, risk-adjusted rate, r?

INTEGRATED CASE

Rick Schmidt, MRI's CFO, along with Mandy Wu, Schmidt's assistant, and John Costello, a consultant and college finance professor, comprise a team established to teach the firm's directors and senior managers the basics of international financial management. The program includes 16 sessions, each lasting about 2 hours, with the sessions scheduled immediately before the monthly board meetings. One session has been completed, and the team is now preparing Session 2, which will deal with global financial markets and institutions, interest rates, and exchange rates. The prior session provided an overview of international finance.

For the financial environment session, the team will identify the major types of financial markets, discuss how capital flows through the economy from savers to borrowers, and identify the factors that determine interest rates. MRI is a multinational medical supply company, headquartered in southern California. MRI has customers in Europe and South America, and is beginning to branch out to Asia. As MRI has grown, it has looked for operating opportunities in these new foreign markets. MRI's most dynamic market continues to be Europe. While a majority of MRI's development and production has remained in the southwestern United States, there has been a growing trend to move these operations abroad. The foreign unit management teams, once dominated by MRI-USA executives, have also taken on a new look as local employees have risen to the managerial ranks.

Schmidt has invited a number of these executives from different units to the program sessions. There are several benefits Schmidt expects to generate by involving them in the education process. First, Wu has met with the foreign executives in the process of organizing the session, as their input and perspective on the global financial environment is invaluable. Wu has incorporated a number of their suggestions into her presentation and has encouraged these executives to be vocal at the sessions. Second, involving foreign executives forces MRI-USA directors to be aware of the implications of their actions on global operations. On firm-wide strategic matters, they often have the strongest voice and have been accused in the past of ignoring the effect on foreign operations. Third, it allows foreign executives to learn about the perspective of other foreign executives and the MRI-USA directors. A common complaint by the board of directors has been that foreign executives suffer from myopia in only seeing how actions affect themselves. Schmidt recognizes that everyone can benefit from stepping back and seeing the picture from all perspectives.

With those thoughts in mind, the three compiled the following set of questions, which they plan to discuss during the session. In other sessions, they plan to use an *Excel* model to answer quantitative questions, but because this session is entirely qualitative, no model has been developed. Assume that you are Mandy Wu, and that you must prepare answers for use during the session.

QUESTIONS

a. Differentiate between physical and financial asset markets and identify some of the assets that trade in each. Identify some major types of financial markets.

b. What trends have shaped the landscape of the current financial environment?

c. Describe the different ways in which capital is transferred.

d. What is the cost of money? What factors affect it?

e. Differentiate between the real risk-free rate and the nominal risk-free rate.

f. What is the difference between the inflation rate and the inflation premium? What causes them to be different?

g. Define the terms default risk premium (DRP), liquidity premium (LP), maturity risk premium (MRP), country risk premium (CRP), and exchange rate risk premium (ERP). Identify which kinds of securities carry these premiums (short-term versus long-term securities and corporate versus Treasury securities).

h. How does inflation affect the exchange rate between two countries? Provide an example.

i. Describe the international monetary system.

j. What is meant by the "perfect currency"?

k. What is the difference between a depreciation/appreciation of a currency and a devaluation/revaluation of a currency?

l. Identify the major floating- and fixed-exchange-rate systems. How does a country choose a system?

m. What is dollarization? Identify some benefits and drawbacks of dollarization.

CHAPTER 3

Exchange Rate Analysis

$$\text{VALUE} = \sum_{t=0}^{N} \frac{CF_t}{(1+r)^t}$$

Required Investment
Sales Revenues
Operating Costs
Taxes

Cash Flows (CF)

Capital Structure
Interest Rates
Asset Risk
Market Risk

Required Return (r)

Foreign Exchange, FX
The money of a foreign country.

Exchange Rate
The number of units of a given currency that can be purchased for one unit of another currency.

e-resource

The textbook's Web site, http://crum. swlearning.com, contains an Excel file that will guide you through the chapter's calculations. The file for this chapter is FIFC03-model.xls, and we encourage you to open the file and follow along as you read the chapter.

For a global company to compete effectively, its managers must operate with many different currencies. In Chapter 2 we discussed at a conceptual level how exchange rates are established. We now carry those ideas further, delving into foreign exchange markets and their operations. The term *foreign exchange,* often shortened to **FX,** means the currency of a foreign country, while the **exchange rate** is simply the price of one currency in terms of another currency. Examples of foreign exchange would include the euros a U.S. citizen buys when visiting Italy, the dollars an Italian corporation needs when conducting business in the United States, or any other currency not normally used in a person's or corporation's home country. Foreign exchange transactions are essential for any firm engaged in international business. The volume of foreign exchange transactions has grown tremendously in recent years, increasing from a daily average of $590 billion in 1989 to $1,210 billion in 2001.[1]

Efficient operations for a global firm require access to foreign exchange markets 24 hours a day, 365 days a year. To meet this need, global markets and institutions have been established in which currency trading can occur whenever and wherever such trading is needed. A typical "global" business day begins in Tokyo and Sydney, just west of the International Date Line. As the day progresses, markets open in Hong Kong and Singapore, then in Bombay, on to Saudi Arabia and Bahrain, then in Frankfurt, Zurich, Paris, and London. Before the European markets close, U.S. markets have opened in New York and Chicago, and then in Los Angeles and San Francisco. Finally, before the West Coast U.S. markets close,

---

[1]See "Central Bank Survey of Foreign Exchange and Derivatives Market Activity in April 2001: Preliminary Global Data," Bank of International Settlements, October 9, 2001, **http://www. bis.org/press/p011009.htm.**

the next day has begun in Tokyo and Sydney. Moreover, many things happen over the weekend, so financial markets truly operate on a 24/7 basis.

In terms of the valuation equation, exchange rates affect cash flows directly, and they affect the required rate of return through their relationship with interest rates. Multinational enterprises generate cash flows in many different currencies, and they must translate foreign cash flows into their home currency for financial reporting purposes. They must also convert currencies physically before transferring funds from locations with excess cash to those where cash is needed. Foreign exchange markets facilitate these actions—again on a 24/7 basis.

THE FOREIGN EXCHANGE MARKETS

Foreign Exchange Markets
Range from local cab drivers to sophisticated telecommunications and global computer networks that connect banks, professional dealers, brokers, central banks, and the treasury departments of many MNEs.

Foreign exchange markets range from local cab drivers to global computer networks that connect banks, professional dealers, brokers, central banks, and the treasury departments of many multinational enterprises (MNEs). Providers of financial information such as Reuters, Telerate, and Bloomberg can be accessed for instantaneous foreign exchange quotations, either over the Internet or through specialized trading systems linked together by telephone, computer, fax, and telex. Elaborate computer programs allow market participants to buy and sell currencies for spot or future (forward) delivery quickly and at a very low cost. Computerized trading systems can also instantaneously identify disequilibria between different currencies or markets, enabling nimble traders to earn arbitrage profits, which keeps the markets in almost perfect equilibrium. These automated "matching" systems are rapidly replacing traditional trading operations, where traders operated with a phone at each ear.

Participants in the Foreign Exchange Markets

A diverse group of firms, institutions, governments, and individuals participates in foreign exchange transactions. Banks and some nonbank foreign exchange dealers are major participants in what is called the *interbank,* or *commercial, market.* Other institutions deal in the *retail market,* which serves individuals who require different currencies as they travel or purchase goods and services from abroad. Profits in the interbank market come primarily from the spread between the rate at which the traders buy currencies (the **bid rate**) and the rate at which they sell the same currencies (the **offer rate**). Spreads also generate profits at the retail level, but here spreads are usually larger, and a fixed commission is usually added to the transaction.

Bid Rate
In a foreign exchange context, the rate at which traders buy currencies.

Offer Rate
In a foreign exchange context, the rate at which traders sell currencies.

Foreign exchange brokers, who act as agents to facilitate trading among dealers but who do not take a direct position in the transactions, are also involved. They are like stock or real estate brokers who help bring buyers and sellers together but do not own the stocks or houses that are bought and sold. The brokers earn a small fee, and they help the principals find counterparties for transactions quickly while maintaining anonymity until the opposite side of the contract is in place. This anonymity is often important because knowledge of the other party might affect the quote if it were revealed before the exact terms had been agreed upon.

Governments, through their central banks, also participate in the foreign exchange market, attempting to stabilize or otherwise influence the values of their currencies. They are often willing to accept losses in order to produce a desired outcome because they are motivated more by political considerations and national policy than profits.

Any and all of these entities can participate in the market, executing commercial transactions for their own or their clients' accounts. They can also act as arbitrageurs, taking advantage of market disequilibria to earn a profit, or they can engage in outright speculation if they believe they know the future direction of exchange rates. While most banks and dealers deny that they speculate in foreign exchange, many of their trading operations are organized as profit centers, and their traders are compensated on the basis of the profits they earn. This obviously makes them susceptible to the lure of speculative profits. As we mentioned in Chapter 2, inappropriate speculation by a low-level and loosely supervised trader, Nick Leeson, resulted in the bankruptcy of Barings Bank, one of England's oldest financial institutions. This is an extreme example, but taking aggressive positions is part of normal operating procedures in many bank and foreign exchange dealer trading rooms. Note, though, that such speculation worries both central bankers and commercial banks' top managers, so they employ the kinds of risk management procedures discussed in Chapter 15.

Functions of the Foreign Exchange Markets

Multinational companies need foreign exchange to conduct day-to-day business operations, to finance worldwide operations, and to reduce the profit volatility that can arise from exchange rate fluctuations. Global markets and instruments have been developed to satisfy all these needs.

If a U.S. firm that has dollars buys something from a German firm that deals in euros, a mechanism is needed to transfer purchasing power denominated in dollars into purchasing power denominated in euros. If the price is set in euros but the dollar weakens before payment is made, then the actual dollar price will be higher than was expected. Thus, exchange rate shifts can lead to unfavorable results even if operating conditions turn out just as expected. Companies that are uncomfortable with such exchange rate risks can pay others to assume those risks. This is called *hedging*, and the foreign exchange market is where hedging transactions occur. We will discuss hedging in greater detail in Chapter 15.

Note too that when a firm expands its operations in another country, it may acquire the needed foreign-denominated capital from banks or other capital market institutions. Alternatively, if adequate home country currency is available, it may go to the foreign exchange market to trade currencies. Forward transactions, currency swaps, and other specialized instruments are examples of the credit functions embedded in the foreign exchange market, and they will be discussed in greater detail in Chapter 15, where we discuss risk management.

SELF-TEST QUESTIONS What are the foreign exchange markets?
Who participates in the foreign exchange markets?
What are the functions of the foreign exchange market?

FOREIGN EXCHANGE RATE QUOTATIONS

Foreign exchange rate quotations given in such publications as *The Wall Street Journal* are given in two different ways. As shown in Table 3-1, Column 1, they are quoted as "USD equivalent" and in Column 2 as "Currency per USD." For example, one Canadian dollar is worth (or can be exchanged for) 0.7614 U.S. dollar, or one U.S. dollar could buy 1.3134 Canadian dollars.[2]

---

[2]The quotations in Column 1 are said to be in *American terms* because they represent the number of "American" dollars that can be bought with one unit of local currency, while those in Column 2 are called "European terms." The quotations in Column 2, or the *European terms*, represent the units of local currency that can be bought with one U.S. dollar. "European" is intended as a generic term that applies globally.

TABLE 3-1 | Sample Exchange Rates: Friday, January 23, 2004

	USD Equivalent (American Terms) (1)	Currency per USD (European Terms) (2)
Australia (dollar)	0.7728	1.2940
Canada (dollar)	0.76138	1.31340
China (renminbi)	0.1208	8.2781
Indonesia (rupiah)	0.0001190	8403
Japan (yen)	0.009390	106.50
United Kingdom (pound)	1.8271	0.5473
Euro	1.2589	0.7943

Note: Column 1 shows the dollars required to purchase one unit of the foreign currency, while Column 2 shows the number of units of the foreign currency required to purchase one U.S. dollar. If you divide the numbers in Column 1 into 1 you will get the Column 2 numbers, and, similarly, dividing Column 2 into 1 yields the Column 1 numbers. The data in Column 1 are often designated "American Terms" because, if you looked at something that cost 1 Australian dollar you would ask, "What does it cost in U.S. dollars?" and the answer is in Column 1. Similarly, the data in Column 2 are called "European Terms" even when applied to non-European currencies.

Source: "Exchange Rates," *The Wall Street Journal,* January 26, 2004, C11.

Note that if the foreign exchange markets are in equilibrium, which is usually the case for the major traded currencies, then the two quotations must be reciprocals of one another as shown below for the Canadian dollar:

$$\text{Canadian dollar: } 1/1.31340 = 0.76138.$$
$$1/0.76138 = 1.31340.$$

Cross Rates

Cross Rate
The exchange rate between any two currencies.

All of the exchange rates given in Table 3-1 are relative to the U.S. dollar. Suppose, though, that a German executive is flying to Tokyo on business. The exchange rate of interest is not euros or yen per dollar—rather, he or she wants to know how many yen can be purchased with euros. This is called a **cross rate**, and it can be calculated from the following data in Column 2 of Table 3-1:

	Spot Rate
Euro	€0.7943/$1
Yen	¥106.50/$1

Because the quotations have the same denominator—one U.S. dollar—we can calculate the cross rate between these (and other) currencies by using the Column 2 quotations. For our German national, the cross rates are found as follows:

$$\text{Euro/yen exchange rate} = \frac{\text{Euro/\$}}{\text{Yen/\$}}$$

and when we cancel the dollar signs, we are left with the number of euros 1 yen would cost:

$$€0.7943/¥106.50 = €0.00746/¥.$$

Alternatively, we could find the number of yen 1 euro would buy:

TABLE 3-2 | Key Currency Cross Rates for Friday, January 23, 2004

	Dollar	Euro	Pound	SFranc	Peso	Yen	CDollar
Canada	1.3134	1.6534	2.3997	1.0573	0.12055	0.01233	
Japan	106.50	134.08	194.58	85.729	9.775		81.086
Mexico	10.8944	13.7150	19.905	8.770		0.10230	8.2950
Switzerland	1.2422	1.5639	2.2697		0.11402	0.01166	0.9458
United Kingdom	0.54730	0.6890		0.4406	0.05024	0.00514	0.41673
Euro	0.79430		1.4513	0.63945	0.07291	0.00746	0.60481
United States		1.2589	1.8271	0.80500	0.09179	0.00939	0.76140

Source: "Key Currency Cross Rates," *The Wall Street Journal,* January 26, 2004, C11.

$$\text{Yen/euro exchange rate} = \frac{\text{Yen/\$}}{\text{Euro/\$}}$$

$$\yen 106.50/€0.7943 = \yen 134.08/€.$$

Again, note that these two cross rates are reciprocals of one another.

Financial publications such as *The Wall Street Journal* publish tables of Key Currency Cross Rates; the one for January 23, 2004, is reproduced in Table 3-2. Notice that there may be slight rounding differences when you calculate cross rates due to the rounding of individual quotations. Currency traders carry quotations out to 12 decimal places.

To facilitate worldwide currency trading through electronic media, the interbank foreign exchange market has adopted a system under which all quotations are given in European (Column 2) terms with a few exceptions. The exceptions—the euro, British pound, Australian dollar, and New Zealand dollar—are quoted in American terms. Because of this convention, traders throughout the world see similar quotations on their computer screens, making it easy for them (and their computers) to compare rates quoted in different markets and to earn arbitrage profits if differences exist.

Interbank Foreign Currency Quotations

The quotations from *The Wall Street Journal* given in Tables 3-1 and 3-2 are sufficient for many purposes. For other purposes, however, additional terminology and conventions are useful. Because there are two ways to state the exchange rate between two currencies, formulas used to calculate the magnitude of rate changes over time and the premiums and discounts on currencies that are appreciating or depreciating in value will not be the same for **American** versus **European** terms. Accordingly, we first need to designate one of the currencies as the "home" currency and the other as the "foreign" currency. This designation is arbitrary, and we reach the same conclusion with either if we use the right formula. However, different traders prefer one formula over the other. The *home* currency price of one unit of the *foreign* currency is called a **direct quotation**. Thus, to a person who considers the United States to be "home," American terms represent a direct quotation. On the other hand, the *foreign* currency price of one unit of the *home* currency is called an **indirect quotation**. European terms represent indirect quotations to people in the U.S. Note that if the perspective changes and the "home" currency is no longer the U.S. dollar, then the designation of direct and indirect changes. For the remainder of this book, we will assume that the U.S. is the "home" country, unless specifically stated otherwise.

American Terms
The foreign exchange rate quotation that represents the number of American dollars that can be bought with one unit of local currency.

European Terms
The foreign exchange rate quotation that represents the units of local currency that can be bought with one U.S. dollar. "European" is intended as a generic term that applies globally.

Direct Quotation
The home currency price of one unit of the foreign currency.

Indirect Quotation
The foreign currency price of one unit of the home currency.

TABLE 3-3	Spot and Three-Month Forward Quotations for the Euro on January 22, 2004	
	American Terms USD/EUR	European Terms EUR/USD
Spot rate	1.270400	0.787154
3-month forward rate	1.267240	0.789117

Source: "Spot and Forward Rates," January 22, 2004, 2004 Bloomberg LP, **http://www.bloomberg.com.**

We can illustrate why it is useful to designate one country as "home" by looking at some interbank market quotations (for January 22, 2004). Table 3-3 gives the spot and three-month forward quotations for the U.S. dollar and euro in both American and European terms. Looking first at the quotations in American terms, notice that we can buy euros for delivery in three months at a lower price than euros delivered today, so the dollar is expected to appreciate against the euro. The same information comes from an examination of the quotes given in European terms—it takes more euros to buy dollars for delivery in three months than to buy them for delivery today, so the dollar is expected to appreciate. Of course, another way to say the same thing is to say that the euro is depreciating against the dollar. Thus, there are two alternative ways to consider this situation: (1) By how much is the dollar expected to appreciate against the euro? (2) By how much is the euro expected to depreciate against the dollar?

Percentage Change in Exchange Rate

We sometimes need to know how much the spot rate for a particular currency changed between two dates. For instance, if a subsidiary has financial statements recorded in euros but the parent company uses dollars for reporting purposes, we need to know by how much the euro changed relative to the dollar from the beginning to the end of the period. Assume that the exchange rates for the euro at year-end 2002 and 2003 are as follows:

	Year-End 2002	Year-End 2003
Dollars per euro (direct quotation)	$1.048500/€	$1.289700/€
Euros per dollar (indirect quotation)	€0.953743/$	€0.775374/$

Because it took more dollars to purchase one euro at the end of the period than at the beginning, the euro appreciated against the dollar. Said another way, the dollar depreciated against the euro.

We can find the percentage change in the foreign currency based on either the direct or indirect quotes using the formulas given here:

Direct Quotations

$$\%\Delta\text{FX} = \left(\frac{\text{Ending rate} - \text{Beginning rate}}{\text{Beginning rate}} \right) \times 100 \qquad (3\text{-}1)$$

$\%\Delta\text{FX} = [(1.289700 - 1.048500)/1.048500] \times 100 = 23.0043\% \approx 23\%.$

This means that during 2003, the euro appreciated against the dollar by 23 percent.

Indirect Quotations

$$\%\Delta\text{FX} = \left(\frac{\text{Beginning rate} - \text{Ending rate}}{\text{Ending rate}}\right) \times 100 \qquad \text{(3-1a)}$$

$$\%\Delta\text{FX} = [(0.953743 - 0.775374)/0.775374] \times 100 = 23.0043\% \approx 23\%.$$

Again, we see that the euro appreciated against the dollar by 23 percent.

Premium/Discount on Forward Rates

The following formulas give the percentage premium or discount on a foreign currency at any point in time:

Direct Quotations

$$\begin{array}{l}\text{Forward premium} \\ \text{or discount }\%\end{array} = \left(\frac{\text{Forward rate} - \text{Spot rate}}{\text{Spot rate}}\right) \times 360/n \times 100. \qquad \text{(3-2)}$$

Based on the Table 3-3 data, with n the number of days forward, we have:

$$\begin{aligned}\text{Forward discount }\% &= [(1.26724 - 1.2704)/1.2704] \times 360/90 \times 100 \\ &= -0.994962\% \approx -0.995\%.\end{aligned}$$

Thus, the three-month euro was selling at a 0.995 percent discount to the dollar as of January 22, 2004. Note that a 360-day year is used by convention.

Indirect Quotations

$$\begin{array}{l}\text{Forward premium} \\ \text{or discount }\%\end{array} = \left(\frac{\text{Spot rate} - \text{Forward rate}}{\text{Forward rate}}\right) \times 360/n \times 100. \qquad \text{(3-2a)}$$

$$\begin{aligned}\text{Forward discount }\% &= [(0.787154 - 0.789117)/0.789117] \times 360/90 \times 100 \\ &= -0.995036\% \approx -0.995\%.\end{aligned}$$

Equations 3-2 and 3-2a are reciprocals of one another, and they give the same result except for a slight rounding difference.[3]

Bid Rates and Offer Rates

There is a bid (or buy) rate and an offer (or sell) rate for each currency, and for both spot and forward deliveries. For instance, from another source we know that the interbank spot rate for euros on January 22, 2004, was quoted at

---

[3]What would happen if you used the formula for an indirect quotation but entered exchange rates for the direct quote?

$$\begin{array}{l}\text{Forward premium} \\ \text{or discount }\%\end{array} = \left(\frac{\text{Spot rate} - \text{Forward rate}}{\text{Forward rate}}\right) \times 360/n \times 100.$$

$$\text{Forward premium }\% = [(1.2704 - 1.26724)/1.26724] \times 360/90 \times 100$$

$$= 0.997443 \approx 0.997\%.$$

The positive sign indicates that the "foreign" currency is selling at a premium over the "home" currency. However, we know that the euro is actually depreciating, so we must have calculated a three-month forward premium on the dollar. We used the formula for an indirect quotation, but the rates used in the calculation were direct quotations in our previous examples. This is why we must designate the "home" currency from the beginning of our analysis—so we know which formula to use for the calculation; and it is why we need to look at the outright spot and forward quotations to see if we expect a premium or discount before doing the calculation. This is a quick check to ensure that we are calculating the premium or discount correctly.

Bid	Offer
$1.270293/€	$1.270294/€

Thus, dealers were willing to buy euros for $1.270293 per euro or to sell euros at the slightly higher rate of $1.270294/€. Assuming that a dealer buys €10,000,000 and pays with U.S. dollars, then the dollar cost of the transaction would be

$$€10,000,000 \times \$1.270293/€ = \$12,702,930.00.$$

Now if the dealer sold the €10,000,000 to another customer, he or she would receive

$$€10,000,000 \times \$1.270294/€ = \$12,702,940.00.$$

The $10 difference represents the dealer's profit from buying and selling euros, and it is called the **spread**.[4]

Spread
Profit from buying and selling currency.

Forward Quotations in Points

Up until now, we have stated all forward rates as outright quotations. In fact, in the interbank market it is customary to state forward quotations in terms of differences between the outright forward rate and the outright spot rate. For example, for the three-month forward euro, the differences in points between the outright spot and forward quotations for both the bid and offer rates are shown here:

	Bid	Offer
Outright spot	$1.270400	$1.270400
3-month forward (points)	− 31.70	− 31.50
3-month forward (outright)	$1.267230	$1.267250

Similarly, the differences in points for the bid and offer rates are shown below for the Japanese yen:

	Bid	Offer
Outright spot	$0.009404684	$0.009404684
3-month forward (points)	+ 26.832	+ 27.010
3-month forward (outright)	$0.009431516	$0.009431694

The leading zeros are dropped in calculating the points, but the trader understands that they must be added back if there is a need to calculate the outright forward quotation. Notice also that the number of leading zeros is different for the euro and the yen. Traders know how many leading zeros to add if and when they need to calculate the outright quotations.

In the first case, the euro is weakening against the dollar (it takes fewer dollars to buy 1 euro in the future), and the points are subtracted from the outright spot rate to obtain the outright forward rate. In the second case, the yen is strengthening against the dollar (it takes more dollars to buy 1 yen for future delivery), so the points are added to the outright spot rate to obtain the outright forward rate. Notice also that in the situation where the points are subtracted from the outright spot rate, the bid in points is larger than the offer in points, but in the situation where the points are added to the outright spot rate, the offer in points is larger than the bid in points. For rates that are forward by two years or more, the points quotation is called a "swap rate." Examples of interbank quotations for January 22, 2004, from Bloomberg are given in Table 3-4.

---

[4]In the interbank market, the euro-to-dollar exchange rate is always stated in American terms. The reciprocal of a bid rate is an offer rate, and the reciprocal of an offer rate is a bid rate.

TABLE 3-4 | Interbank Quotations for January 22, 2004

	EMU euro[a]			Japanese yen[b]			Canadian dollar[b]			British pound[a]		
	Midrate	Bid	Offer	Midrate	Bid	Offer	Midrate	Bid	Offer	Midrate	Bid	Offer
Spot	1.270400			106.329995			1.297800			1.841600		
1-day	1.270370	−0.40	−0.20	106.326897	−0.26	−0.36	1.297855	0.56	0.54	1.841460	−1.45	−1.35
4-day	1.270294	−1.07	−1.06	106.320792	−0.92	−0.92	1.297968	1.70	1.65	1.841232	−3.70	−3.66
1-week	1.270147	−2.56	−2.51	106.306992	−2.25	−2.35	1.298190	3.99	3.81	1.840640	−9.65	−9.55
1-month	1.269288	−11.18	−11.07	106.227593	−10.17	−10.31	1.299511	17.36	16.85	1.837200	−44.10	−43.90
2-month	1.268272	−21.38	−21.18	106.131492	−19.70	−20.00	1.300876	31.12	30.38	1.832925	−86.85	−86.65
3-month	1.267240	−31.70	−31.50	106.026493	−30.25	−30.45	1.302297	45.41	44.53	1.828295	−133.20	−132.90
4-month	1.266295	−41.20	−40.90	105.923995	−40.50	−40.70	1.303631	59.01	57.60	1.823805	−178.30	−177.60
5-month	1.265288	−51.30	−50.95	105.810997	−51.80	−52.00	1.304791	70.70	69.11	1.818818	−228.20	−227.45
6-month	1.264475	−59.40	−59.10	105.711748	−61.80	−61.85	1.305875	81.50	79.99	1.814580	−270.48	−269.75
9-month	1.262015	−84.00	−83.71	105.354245	−97.50	−97.65	1.309100	115.00	110.99	1.800863	−408.00	−406.75
1-year	1.260013	−104.25	−103.50	104.919244	−140.75	−141.40	1.311700	141.49	136.50	1.787888	−538.00	−536.25
15-month	1.258500	−120.00	−118.00	104.422987	−188.20	−193.20	1.313750	163.00	155.99	1.776350	−655.00	−650.00
18-month	1.257450	−131.00	−128.00	103.823988	−248.10	−253.10	1.315800	185.00	174.99	1.765850	−761.00	−754.00
2-year	1.256525	−140.50	−137.00	102.453983	−384.00	−391.20	1.318100	212.00	193.99	1.748200	−936.00	−932.00
3-year	1.257300	−136.00	−126.00	99.270412	−697.00	−714.90	1.324800	269.99	270.00	1.725350	−1175.00	−1150.00
4-year	1.259500	−128.00	−90.00	95.759763	−1042.00	−1072.00	1.332000	379.99	304.00	1.713500	−1301.00	−1261.00
5-year	1.264100	−86.00	−40.00	92.379564	−1375.00	−1415.00	1.338251	452.00	357.01	1.710100	−1345.00	−1285.00

Notes:
[a]American terms according to the 1978 convention.
[b]European terms according to the 1978 convention.

Source: "Spot and Forward Rates," January 22, 2004, 2004 Bloomberg LP, http://www.bloomberg.com.

Differentiate between indirect and direct quotations and American and European terms.

What are cross rates?

How do you calculate the forward premium or discount for direct quotations? For indirect quotations?

What is the bid rate? The offer rate? Does it matter whether you have a direct quotation or indirect quotation?

EXCHANGE RATE DETERMINANTS

Thus far we have looked at market exchange rates and discussed the terminology and methods used to interpret exchange rate data. Now we explore the determinants of exchange rates, why these rates change over time, and what companies need to know about the underlying dynamics if they are to manage their foreign exchange operations properly. An *exchange rate* is nothing more than the price of one currency in terms of another currency, and the equilibrium price is determined by the demand for a particular currency by foreigners versus the supply made available by holders of that currency. Imports and exports, along with decisions to make investments in foreign countries and several other factors, determine supply and demand conditions. Because of this focus on external trade flows, the *balance of payments* for a country is a valuable source of information about the future movement of exchange rates. Also, we know that the underlying prices of import and export goods are affected by inflation, interest rates, companies' ability to pass through cost increases to customers, and changing productivity. All of these factors interact in the market to determine the exchange rate. Economists have developed several theories, called *parity conditions*, that help explain how these underlying factors affect exchange rates.

Balance of Payments Report

Balance of Payments (BOP) Report
A statistical summary of all transactions during a given time period between the residents of one country and the rest of the world.

A **balance of payments (BOP) report** is a statistical summary of all transactions during a given time period between the residents of one country and the rest of the world. It is recorded using the rules of double-entry bookkeeping, but it is not like a balance sheet or an income statement. Rather, it is more similar to a flow of funds statement. Recorded in the balance of payments report are all external economic transactions, including the country's exports and imports of goods and services, income flows, capital and other financial flows, and all other transactions meeting the formal definition just given. All flows into the country (receipts) are recorded as credits, all outflows (payments) are recorded as debits, and the net flow (total credits minus total debits) shows the effect of international transactions on the country's monetary reserves.

Current Account (Group A)
Records all inflows and outflows of income derived from exporting and importing goods and services, net income from investment and employee compensation, and net unilateral transfers.

As shown in Table 3-5, the balance of payments is divided into five sections. The first section, called the **current account (Group A)**, records all inflows and outflows of income derived from exporting and importing goods and services, net income from investment and employee compensation (inflows minus outflows), and net unilateral transfers (gifts, grants, pensions, and money sent home by guest workers). These income flows do not lead to future claims, are generally not reversible, and are not made with the expectation of future payments. For instance, if a German consumer purchases a Chevrolet Corvette, the automobile is exported from the United States to Germany (where it is recorded as an import), and the money to pay for it is sent from Germany to the United States. If the buyer subsequently decides she does not want the car, Chevrolet will not take it back—the transaction is not reversible—so she will have to sell it to someone else to recover her money.

TABLE 3-5 | U.S. Balance of Payments (Billions of Dollars)

	1995	2000	2001	2002
A. Current Account[a]	**−105.19**	**−411.46**	**−393.74**	**−480.86**
Goods: exports freight on board	577.04	774.63	721.84	685.38
Goods: imports freight on board	−749.37	−1,224.43	−1,145.95	−1,164.76
Balance on goods	*−172.33*	*−449.79*	*−424.11*	*−479.38*
Services: credit	216.69	295.42	285.74	288.72
Services: debit	−139.43	−221.01	−219.44	−227.38
Balance on goods and services	*−95.07*	*−375.38*	*−357.82*	*−418.04*
Income: credit	211.96	346.86	277.36	255.54
Income: debit	−186.89	−327.25	−266.67	−259.51
Balance on goods, services, and income	*−70.00*	*−355.78*	*−347.13*	*−422.01*
Current transfers: credit	8.64	10.78	8.56	11.50
Current transfers: debit	−43.82	−66.46	−55.18	−70.35
B. Capital Account[a]	**−0.93**	**−0.80**	**−1.06**	**−1.29**
Capital account: credit	1.03	1.08	1.05	1.11
Capital account: debit	−1.96	−1.87	−2.11	−2.39
Total, Groups A plus B	*−106.12*	*−412.26*	*−394.80*	*−482.14*
C. Financial Account[a]	**95.91**	**456.63**	**420.50**	**531.68**
Direct investment abroad	−98.78	−159.21	−119.96	−137.84
Direct investment in United States	57.80	321.27	151.58	39.63
Portfolio investment assets	−122.51	−121.91	−84.64	15.80
Equity securities	−65.41	−106.71	−109.10	−17.68
Debt securities	−57.10	−15.19	24.47	33.48
Portfolio investment liabilities	210.35	420.00	425.08	421.44
Equity securities	16.52	193.60	121.42	53.20
Debt securities	193.83	226.40	303.66	368.24
Financial derivatives	.....	.....	.....	.....
Financial derivatives assets	.....	.....	.....	.....
Financial derivatives liabilities	.....	.....	.....	.....
Other investment assets	−121.38	−288.39	−140.43	−53.27
Monetary authorities	.....	.....	.....	.....
General government	−0.98	−0.94	−0.49	−0.03
Banks	−75.11	−148.66	−134.95	−21.36
Other sectors	−45.29	−138.79	−5.00	−31.88
Other investment liabilities	170.43	284.86	188.87	245.91
Monetary authorities	46.72	−6.70	35.29	64.91
General government	0.90	−0.39	4.78	2.66
Banks	64.18	122.72	88.40	108.72
Other sectors	58.63	169.24	69.96	69.62
Total, Groups A through C	*−10.21*	*44.37*	*25.70*	*49.54*
D. Net Errors and Omissions	**19.96**	**−44.08**	**−20.77**	**−45.84**
Overall balance: Total, Groups A through D	*9.75*	*0.29*	*4.93*	*3.69*
E. Reserves and Related Items	**−9.75**	**−0.29**	**−4.93**	**−3.69**
Reserve assets	−9.75	−0.29	−4.93	−3.69
Use of Fund credit and loans	.....	.....	.....	.....
Exceptional financing	.....	....	.....	.....

[a]Excludes components that have been classified in the categories of Group E.

Source: Excerpted from "Balance of Payments Statistics, Part I: Country Tables," *International Monetary Fund, Yearbook 2003.*

AN APPETITE FOR DOLLARS

How big is Japan's appetite for U.S. dollars? In recent years there has been a huge movement by Asian investors into U.S. Treasuries. This appetite for U.S. government securities has been fed by American consumers' insatiable demand for low-cost Asian imports. America has been importing more goods and services than it exports, and the resulting huge deficit in the U.S. current account has been financed by foreigners.

However, when in March 2004, the Bank of Japan announced it wanted to scale back its U.S. Treasury holdings, the currency and Treasury markets trembled. Market participants had to consider seriously the effect that Japanese sales of Treasury bonds would have on U.S. interest rates.

A newspaper report suggested that it was a sign of a changing foreign exchange policy, an account quickly refuted by Tokyo officials. For years, Asian countries have been able to fuel their economic growth and boost their exports to the United States by keeping their currencies weak. However, if talk of protectionism in the United States stifled the demand for Asian goods, the result would be less capital for Asian banks to invest in dollar-denominated assets (such as United States Treasuries and those issued by Fannie Mae and Freddie Mac). Even if threats of protectionist policies do not pan out, Asian central banks may soon decide that their prosperity is best served by stimulating their own economies rather than exporting to the United States. Such policies would narrow the trade surpluses and leave Asian nations with fewer dollars to invest in U.S. bonds.

Either way, U.S. interest rates may be poised to rise. According to David Bowers, a global strategist for Merrill Lynch, "In order to attract new investment capital, the United States may have to pay higher rates on its bonds."

In early 2004, Japan held $777 billion in foreign reserves and was selling yen (mostly for dollars) at a rate of 10 trillion yen ($92 billion) per month. The bulk of those dollars were invested in U.S. Treasuries, and Asian central banks now hold about $1 trillion. However, holding all these U.S. government bonds is risky because rates in March 2004 were near their 40-year lows and a rebound of U.S. interest rates would lead to huge losses for the Asian central banks.

Opinions on the effects of Asian intervention are mixed. Some suggest that the dollar would dip below 100 Japanese yen (from its current level of about 110 yen) and the Chinese yuan would be 20 percent stronger.

Some Asian central banks have taken steps to diversify their large dollar holdings. However, economists are still concerned about whether Japan will be able to unload U.S. debt whenever it decides to cut back. This could result in a crash in U.S. Treasury prices that would tarnish the U.S. economy on which the Japanese recovery is so dependent. This fear prompted economist Kunji Okue of Dresdner Kleinwort Wasserstein to say, "Japan is hard at work importing the U.S. deficit. That could be dangerous, since it may be impossible to unwind."

Source: Craig Karmin, "Japan Pays for Low U.S. Interest Rates," *The Wall Street Journal,* March 18, 2004, C1–C2.

Capital Account (Group B)
Includes all capital transfers into and out of a country related to the purchase and sale of fixed assets, including real estate.

Financial Account (Group C)
Includes all foreign direct investment, portfolio investment, and external flows of other financial assets and liabilities.

The second section, called the **capital account (Group B)**, includes all capital transfers into and out of a country related to the purchase and sale of fixed assets, including real estate. The third section, called the **financial account (Group C)**, includes all foreign direct investment, portfolio investment, and external flows of other financial assets and liabilities. These two accounts (Groups B and C) do not indicate income. Rather, they represent a repositioning of a part of residents' wealth geographically. These transactions are reversible, and they are made in the expectation of future gains. For instance, if you purchase shares of Toyota, there is a transfer of part of your wealth to Japan, and it is likely that you made the investment hoping to earn future profits. If your expectations are not realized, or you think you can earn more elsewhere, you can subsequently sell your Toyota stock and buy shares of Nestlé, shifting your wealth from Japan to Switzerland. The important distinction of transactions in these accounts is that the wealth is still yours—only the physical location changes. With a current account transaction (Group A), though, part of your wealth passes to someone else.

The fourth section of the BOP **(Group D)** is **net errors and omissions**. First, data for the balance of payments are collected at ports of entry, but much of the data

Net Errors and Omissions (Group D)
An adjustment made to force total debits to equal total credits.

Reserves and Related Items (Group E)
These are changes in official monetary reserves held by the government, including monetary metals, foreign exchange, and the position of the country with the International Monetary Fund (IMF).

Overall Balance
All debits and credits recorded in Groups A through D are netted out and represent the net inflow (credit balance) or outflow (debit balance) of private sector transactions.

Deficit (Surplus)
Represents a net debit (credit) balance in the overall balance of payments.

involve statistical sampling and thus are subject to errors. Second, some transactions cross borders without the government being aware of them—in fact, some exporters and importers take great pains to ensure that no one knows about their activities. Thus, for these two reasons, total debit entries do not equal total credit entries. To force total debits to equal total credits, the net errors and omissions adjustment is made.

The final section of the balance of payments **(Group E)** is **reserves and related items**. These are changes in official monetary reserves held by the government, including monetary metals (mainly gold but also some silver), foreign exchange, and the position of the country (deposits in or loans from) with the International Monetary Fund (IMF). Note that all debits and credits recorded in Groups A through D are netted out and represent the net inflow (credit balance) or outflow (debit balance) of private sector transactions.[5] This is called the **overall balance** in the BOP report, and it is of particular significance because of its affect on official reserves. If there is a net credit balance, the demand for the home currency is strong, so this currency's value will rise if the government does not intervene to supply additional currency. Likewise, if there is a net debit balance, there will be downward pressure on the currency. Depending on its exchange rate policy (as discussed in Chapter 2), the government may or may not be willing to step in and manage the supply and demand for the currency and thus influence the exchange rate.

Managerial Significance of the Balance of Payments

Interpretation of balance of payments data depends greatly on the exchange rate policy of the country. If total debit entries equal total credit entries and the overall balance nets out to zero, there will be no adjustment to the reserves. In this situation, the exchange rate will be in equilibrium. However, if there is a net debit balance—that is, a **deficit** in the overall balance—or a net credit balance—a **surplus** in the overall balance—the country's reserves will rise or fall. Note, though, that if the monetary authorities decide not to change the reserve position, then several things could happen. First, if there would otherwise be a deficit, then the currency might weaken, which would lower the prices foreigners pay for the country's export goods and raise the prices of imported goods, and these price movements would tend to lower the deficits. Alternatively, foreigners might use their surpluses (if one country has a deficit, someone else must have a surplus) to buy securities of the country, thus helping it to finance its deficit. Foreigners might also make direct investments in the country, which would again provide foreign capital and help finance the deficit. The same thing would hold in reverse if the trend were toward a surplus.

Note, though, that if a country has sufficient reserves, or is willing to add to its reserves, it can intervene in the currency markets so as to stabilize the exchange rate and thus permit the surplus or deficit to build up, at least for a time. Currently, the United States is running a deficit in the current account, and that deficit is being financed by foreigners via the capital and financial accounts.

OBLIGATIONS OF THE GOVERNMENT UNDER A FIXED EXCHANGE RATE SYSTEM

If the country operates under a fixed exchange rate system, then the government must intervene in the market, supplying foreign currency from reserves if there is a deficit and absorbing the currency if there is a surplus.[6] The supply and demand for the local currency is maintained in balance, so there is no pressure for a change in

---

[5]There are some government transactions included in Groups A through D, but they are not part of the country's reserves.

[6]Countries are, of course, sovereign, so they can set their own currency regulation rules. However, if a country wants to draw on the resources of international institutions such as the International Monetary Fund, the World Bank, and major commercial banks, it must be consistent in its regulations. Thus, if it agrees to operate under a fixed exchange rate system, it must take whatever actions are necessary to maintain that fixed rate.

the exchange rate. Of course, if a country is running a deficit, the government will have only a finite supply of foreign currency reserves to defend the exchange rate, so it must try to reduce the demand for imports, usually by increasing interest rates (which will draw in foreign capital) or instituting foreign exchange controls (which will slow imports by making it hard to pay for them). A third action is to devalue its currency, which will drastically increase the price of imports and lower the cost of exports, thereby lowering the deficit through impacts on supply and demand.

The balance of payments report for a country that uses fixed exchange rates gives three valuable pieces of information to global corporate managers:

1. If the country is running an overall deficit and the official reserves are dwindling, it will probably be forced to increase interest rates, impose foreign exchange controls, or devalue the currency to reestablish equilibrium. If it is running a surplus, interest rates may decline.
2. A country running a balance of payments deficit will want to discourage imports, so companies planning to increase exports to that country may need to rethink their growth strategies due to market realities. On the other hand, imports from the country should be favored.
3. If the company does not think that government intervention to manage the currency will be successful, then the currency will likely be devalued (or revalued if the pressure is in the other direction, but this is much less frequent). Devaluation or revaluation means that operations of MNEs in that country will experience foreign exchange gains or losses if they do not take appropriate steps to manage their currency exposure. (We will discuss this topic in more detail in Chapters 14 and 15.)

In Chapter 2, we suggested that countries in a relatively early stage of economic development might want to adopt a fixed-rate regime to help fight inflation. This means the external stability of the currency is deemed to be the primary economic policy goal, and it gives statements about an anti-inflation stance, such as increasing interest rates and discouraging imports, credibility. This enhanced credibility lowers corporations' risk of doing business in the country, which enhances its growth prospects.

OBLIGATIONS OF THE GOVERNMENT UNDER A FLOATING EXCHANGE RATE REGIME If a country is operating under a completely "free to floating" rate regime, the government has no obligation to intervene in the marketplace to control the currency. Instead, the price of the currency (the exchange rate) will change in response to changes in supply or demand, which, in turn, are determined largely by imports and exports. However, if the policy is the more usual one of a "managed float," then the government will "guide" or "tweak" the value of the currency gradually so as to maintain it within a defined, and generally narrow, range. Thus, under a managed-float system, companies will normally have time to anticipate changes and adjust their own operations to likely changes.

Exchange rates are usually guided in the desired direction through interest rate policy. Raising the interest rate will attract foreign capital, thus strengthening the currency. That, in turn, will tend to increase imports, lower exports, and thus "cool" the economy and reduce potential inflation. Of course, this policy also imposes higher borrowing costs on local companies, adding to the cooling effect. Thus, monetary intervention has good and bad implications for different clienteles. Note too that more highly developed countries have historically had the discipline to manage inflation reasonably well, so they have the credibility to use this more flexible currency regime. The European Monetary Union (EMU) is an example of a successful managed floating system. When it adopted a single currency to capture the benefits of a large currency area without having to worry about changing exchange rates, the euro was allowed to float against the currencies of its major trading partners.

What is an exchange rate?

Briefly identify some of the factors that interact to determine the exchange rate.

What is the balance of payments? How do you interpret this statement?

Why must the government intervene under a fixed exchange rate regime if the balance of payments would not otherwise net to zero?

PARITY CONDITIONS

Parity Conditions
Economic theories that interact with each other to determine national interest rates and exchange rates.

In Chapter 2, we introduced some basic principles underlying interest rates and exchange rates determination. We now explore these ideas in greater detail, beginning with five economic theories, or **parity conditions**, that interact with each other to determine interest and exchange rates. This set of relationships is shown graphically in Figure 3-1 and is explained in the following sections.

We start by assuming that the real, risk-free required rate of return, r*, which we discussed in Chapter 2, is constant and equal in all countries.[7] Given the constant real rate assumption, the basic interest and exchange rate driver is the rate of inflation in different countries. For simplicity, assume that we have two countries, one whose currency is the dollar and the other the peso. Figure 3-1 presents the five parity relationships as an integrated, mutually codetermined system. If markets in both

| **Figure 3-1** | Graphical Representation of the Five Parity Relationships as an Integrated System (Expected Inflation 4 Percent Greater in Peso Area) |

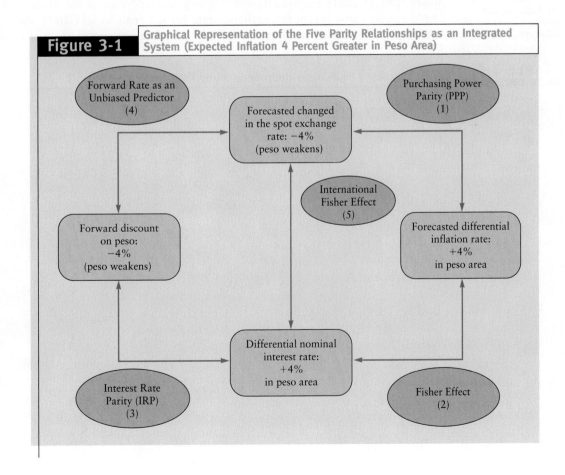

---

[7]The effect of different real rates of return is covered later in the chapter under what is called the "asset market approach" to forecasting exchange rates.

countries are in equilibrium, then the relationships among the five parity conditions will ensure that

1. The inflation rate differential between the two countries is exactly equal to the interest rate differential between those same countries.[8]
2. The currency of the country with the higher inflation rate will sell at a discount to the other currency.
3. The discount will exactly cancel out the inflation differential.
4. If the information about future inflation is unbiased and the markets are in equilibrium, then the forward rate will be an unbiased predictor of the expected future spot rate.

In the sections that follow we discuss these five parity conditions in greater detail, using the data and calculations in Table 3-6 for illustrative purposes.

Purchasing Power Parity (PPP)

Also known as the law of one price. Asserts that in the absence of transactions costs, the ratio of prices of identical products in two countries determines the exchange rate between the two currencies.

Purchasing Power Parity

Purchasing power parity (PPP), also known as the *law of one price*, asserts that in the absence of transactions costs, the ratio of the prices of identical products in two countries must be consistent with the exchange rate between the two currencies. If this parity does not exist, then economic forces will, over time, operate to force a consistency. One illustration of this concept is the *hamburger standard* created by *The Economist*. (See the "Hungry for a Big Mac?" box.) The standard commodity chosen is McDonald's Big Mac hamburger, which is sold around the world. On the date the survey was taken, the exchange rate for the euro was $1.10/€, and a Big Mac cost $2.71 in the United States and €2.71 in the euro area. Thus, the ratio of

TABLE 3-6 | Data for Calculating Equilibrium International Parity Relationships

Inputs:

1. Forecasted inflation for the next year in the dollar area = $I_\$$ = 3.68%
2. Forecasted inflation for the next year in the peso area = I_p =   8.00%
3. Forecasted real interest rate globally = r^* = 3.00%
4. Current spot exchange rate =   P2.5000/$
5. 1-year forward exchange rate =   P2.6042/$
6. Expected spot exchange rate in 1 year =   P2.6042/$

Calculations:

7. Inflation *differential* between the two countries = $[(1 + I_p) - (1 + I_\$)]/(1 + I_p) \times 100 =$
   (Inflation is higher in the peso area) $(1.08 - 1.0368)/1.08 \times 100 = + 4.00\%$.
8. 1-year nominal interest rate in the dollar area ($r_\$$) = $[(1 + r^*)(1 + I_\$) - 1] \times 100 =$
   $[(1.03)(1.0368) - 1] \times 100 = 6.790\%$.
9. 1-year nominal interest rate in the peso area (r_p) = $[(1 + r^*)(1 + I_p) - 1] \times 100 =$
   $[(1.03)(1.0800) - 1] \times 100 = 11.240\%$.
10. Interest rate *differential* between the two countries = $[(1 + r_p) - (1 + r_\$)]/(1 + r_p) \times 100 =$
    (Interest rates are higher in the peso area) $(1.1124 - 1.0679)/1.1124 \times 100 = + 4.00\%$.
11. Forward discount on the peso = $[(Spot - Forward)/Forward] \times 100 =$
    (Indirect quotation) $[(2.5000 - 2.6042)/2.6042] \times 100 = - 4.00\%$.
12. Forecasted change in the spot rate = $[(Spot - E(Future spot))/E(Future spot)] \times 100 =$
    (Indirect quotation) $[(2.5000 - 2.6042)/2.6042] \times 100 = - 4.00\%$.

---

[8]Notice that we are working here with differentials, not just the numerical difference between the two rates. It is the *relative* differences, not the absolute differences, that are factored into the exchange rates.

the price of a Big Mac in the United States divided by the price of a Big Mac in the euro area was

$$\$2.71/€2.71 = \$1.00/€.$$

For purchasing power parity to exist, the price ratio should have been $\$1.10/€$, not $\$1.00/€$. This implies that the euro was 10 percent overvalued (or the dollar was undervalued), because the burger's effective cost was higher in the euro area. *The Economist* created the hamburger standard in 1986 to make exchange rate theory more understandable, and it has done a reasonably good job of predicting the over- or undervalued currencies.[9]

Usually, PPP applications use price indices calculated on a market basket of goods and services (such as used for the Consumer Price Index, Producer Price Index, and similar indices) instead of a single product like the Big Mac. For example, assume that the U.S. CPI is 185.2 and the CPI for the Euro Zone is 168.4. In this case, the spot exchange rate between the euro and the dollar would be

$$\text{Spot rate} = PI_\$/PI_€ = 185.2/168.4 = \$1.10/€,$$

where $PI_\$$ and $PI_€$ are price indices. This version of PPP, based on relative prices of similar baskets of goods and services, is called **absolute PPP**. It is intended to estimate the equilibrium exchange rate at any given point in time.

Absolute PPP
A PPP theory based on relative prices of similar baskets of goods and services estimating the equilibrium exchange rate at any given point in time.

Relative PPP
A PPP theory stating that the spot exchange rate should change in an equal, but opposite, manner to the inflation differential between two countries.

RELATIVE PURCHASING POWER PARITY Another version of the theory, **relative PPP**, asks how much the exchange rate for two currencies should change between two points in time. Assuming that the exchange rate is in equilibrium at the start of the evaluation period, relative PPP theorizes that the spot exchange rate should change in an equal, but opposite, manner to the inflation differential between the two countries. From Table 3-6 and relationship (1) in Figure 3-1, we calculate inflation to be 4 percent higher in the peso area (in Table 3-6, line 7), so relative PPP hypothesizes that the expected future spot exchange rate for the peso should fall by this same 4 percent over the same period (in our example, one year). This is the calculation made in line 12 of Table 3-6.

EMPIRICAL TESTS OF PPP Purchasing power parity has been tested using both the absolute and relative versions. Although the theory is logical, the tests have been inconclusive; that is, it is not clear whether or not either version of PPP is a good predictor of future exchange rates. Some of the problems with both the model and the tests of PPP are indicated here:

1. PPP assumes that price changes are strictly monetary phenomena, but the goods purchased might change over time or differ between countries because of productivity or technological factors.
2. The market basket of goods and services almost certainly differs from country to country, and it includes items that are substitutable and nontraded.
3. It is not possible to observe either real interest rates or expected future inflation rates; hence, the estimated differentials are subject to error.
4. The model assumes that goods can be moved from country to country in a costless, frictionless manner.
5. The model assumes that governments do not interfere with the market process, but this is almost never true. Also, speculation distorts supply and demand and causes biases.

[9]Note that PPP would work perfectly if goods could be transported instantly and without cost around the world. Since these conditions do not hold, we cannot expect PPP to work perfectly. Note too that there has even been a book about PPP written by an IMF economist: Li Lian Ong, *The Big Mac Index: Applications of Purchasing Power Parity* (New York, NY: Palgrave Macmillan, 2003).

HUNGRY FOR A BIG MAC? GO TO CHINA!

Purchasing power parity (PPP) implies that the same product will sell for the same price in every country after adjusting for current exchange rates. One problem when testing to see if PPP holds is that it assumes that goods consumed in different countries are of the same quality. For example, if you find that a product is more expensive in Switzerland than it is in Canada, one explanation is that PPP fails to hold, but another explanation is that the product sold in Switzerland is of a higher quality and therefore deserves a higher price.

One way to test for PPP is to find goods that have the same quality worldwide. With this in mind, *The Economist* magazine occasionally compares the prices of a well-known good whose quality is the same in 118 different countries: the McDonald's Big Mac hamburger.

The table on the next page provides information collected during 2003. The first column shows the price of a Big Mac in the local currency. Column 2 calculates the price of the Big Mac in terms of the U.S. dollar—this is obtained by dividing the local price by the actual exchange rate at that time. For example, a Big Mac costs 6.30 Swiss francs in Zurich. Given an exchange rate of 1.37 Swiss francs per dollar, this implies that the dollar price of a Big Mac is 6.30 Swiss francs/1.37 Swiss francs per dollar ≈ $4.52.

The third column backs out the implied exchange rate that would hold under PPP. This is obtained by dividing the price of the Big Mac in each local currency by its U.S. price. For example, a Big Mac costs 41 rubles in Russia and $2.71 in the United States. If PPP holds, the exchange rate should be 15.13 ≈ 15.1 rubles per dollar (41 rubles/$2.71).

Comparing the implied exchange rate to the actual exchange rate in Column 4, we see the extent to which the local currency is under- or overvalued relative to the dollar. Given that the actual exchange rate at the time was 31.1 rubles per dollar, this implies that the ruble was 51 percent undervalued.

The evidence suggests that strict PPP does not hold, but recent research suggests that the Big Mac test may shed some insights about where exchange rates are headed. The average price of a Big Mac within the EMU is 2.71 euros. This implies that the euro's PPP is exactly $1.00, so at its current rate of $1.10 the euro is overvalued by 10 percent.

England, Sweden, Switzerland, and Denmark—four European countries that are not part of the EMU—have currencies that are significantly overvalued against the dollar. The British pound is overvalued by 16 percent, the Swedish krona is overvalued by 33 percent, the Swiss franc is overvalued by 69 percent, and the Danish krone is overvalued by 51 percent. In contrast, the Australian dollar is the most undervalued rich-world currency—by 31 percent.

According to the Big Mac Index, the U.S. dollar is no longer overvalued against the euro. However, the dollar may decline in value because of the increasing difficulty in financing the U.S. government's huge current account deficit. In addition, the Index indicates that the Australian dollar is likely to see a large gain, the British pound will continue to fall against the euro, and China will continue to be pressured to revalue the yuan.

One last benefit of the Big Mac test is that it tells us the cheapest places to find a Big Mac. According to the data, if you are looking for a Big Mac, head to China, and avoid Switzerland. In other words, the Chinese yuan is the most undervalued currency and the Swiss franc is the most overvalued.

Sources: Adapted from "McCurrencies," *The Economist*, Vol. 367, April 26, 2003, 68; and Li Lian Ong, "Burgernomics: the Economics of the Big Mac Standard," *Journal of International Money and Finance*, 1997, Vol. 16, no. 6, 867–878.

Despite these problems, observers generally conclude that PPP holds reasonably well over the very long run, especially for countries with relatively high rates of inflation and inefficient capital markets, where the differentials are greatest.

The Fisher Effect

Fisher Equation
Shows how the nominal risk-free rate, r_{RF}, is a function of the real risk-free rate, r^*, and the inflation rate, I.

Equation 2-1 in Chapter 2 showed how the nominal risk-free rate, r_{RF}, is a function of the real risk-free rate, r^*, and the inflation rate, I. This equation is called the **Fisher equation** after Irving Fisher, an early developer of interest rate theory. In Chapter 2 we also demonstrated that this equation must hold for any two countries

	BIG MAC PRICES		Implied PPP[a] of the Dollar	Actual Dollar Exchange Rate 26/04/03	Under(−)/ Over(+) Valuation against the Dollar, %
	In Local Currency	In Dollars			
United States[b]	$2.71	2.71	—	—	—
Argentina	Peso 4.10	1.40	1.51	2.88	−47
Australia	A$3.00	1.80	1.11	1.61	−31
Brazil	Real 4.55	1.44	1.68	3.07	−45
Britain	£1.99	3.08	1.36[c]	1.58[c]	+16
Canada	C$3.20	2.17	1.18	1.45	−18
Chile	Peso 1,400	1.95	517	716	−28
China	Yuan 9.90	1.20	3.65	8.28	−56
Czech Republic	Koruna 56.57	1.91	20.9	28.9	−28
Denmark	DKr27.75	3.99	10.2	6.78	+51
Egypt	Pound 8.00	1.38	2.95	5.92	−50
Euro area	€2.71	2.89	1.00[d]	1.10[d]	+10
Hong Kong	HK$11.50	1.47	4.24	7.80	−46
Hungary	Forint 490	2.14	181	224	−19
Indonesia	Rupiah 16,100	1.81	5,941	8,740	−32
Japan	¥262	2.18	96.7	120	−19
Malaysia	M$5.04	1.33	1.86	3.80	−51
Mexico	Peso 23.00	2.14	8.49	10.53	−19
New Zealand	NZ$3.95	2.15	1.46	1.78	−18
Peru	New Sol 7.90	2.28	2.92	3.46	−16
Philippines	Peso 65.00	1.23	24.0	52.5	−54
Poland	Zloty 6.30	1.56	2.32	3.89	−40
Russia	Rouble 41.00	1.31	15.1	31.1	−51
Singapore	S$3.30	1.85	1.22	1.78	−31
South Africa	Rand 13.95	1.74	5.15	7.56	−32
South Korea	Won 3,300	2.63	1,218	1,220	—
Sweden	SKr30.00	3.50	11.1	8.34	+33
Switzerland	SFr6.30	4.52	2.32	1.37	+69
Taiwan	NT$70.00	2.01	25.8	34.8	−26
Thailand	Baht 59.00	1.37	21.8	42.7	−49
Turkey	Lira 3,750,000	2.28	1,383,764	1,600,500	−14
Venezuela	Bolivar 3,700	2.32	1,365	1,598	−15

Notes:
[a]Purchasing power parity: local price divided by price in the United States.
[b]Average of New York, Chicago, San Francisco, and Atlanta.
[c]Dollars per pound.
[d]Dollars per euro.

Sources: McDonald's; and *The Economist*, Vol. 367, April 26, 2003, 68. Reprinted by permission from *The Economist*.

if their exchange rates are to be in equilibrium. [We illustrate this again on lines 8 and 9 of Table 3-6, and it is portrayed in Relationship (2) in Figure 3-1.] If the real, risk-free interest rate is the same in both countries, then it must be true that the differential interest rate between the two countries is equal in magnitude and has the same sign as the expected inflation rate differential. We demonstrate this in Table 3-6 for the two countries, where the calculated interest rate differential is +4 percent (line 10), which is the same as the inflation rate differential (line 7).

EMPIRICAL TESTS OF THE FISHER EFFECT The Fisher equation has as its key input *expected* inflation, and in the short run this model holds up well in empirical tests using *expected* inflation rates. However, the results are not strong based on ex-post inflation rates, because expectations are not generalized. In tests of long-term rates, the results are even poorer because expectations deviate further from realizations and also because maturity risk premiums complicate the analysis. In general, most theorists believe that the Fisher Effect is valid, but that inflation is not the only determinant of interest rates. Liquidity premia and other factors also come into play, but inflation differentials are probably the prime driver of interest rate differentials.

Interest Rate Parity

Interest Rate Parity (IRP)
A theory that shows that the forward premium or discount on the foreign currency is equal in magnitude but opposite in sign to the interest rate differential.

Interest rate parity (IRP) posits that the forward premium or discount on a foreign currency is equal in magnitude but opposite in sign to the interest rate differential. In other words, IRP relates the spot and forward exchange rates and the interest rates in any two countries in a very specific manner, shown here as Figure 3-2.[10] If both paths to the dollar amount shown in the upper right corner do not produce the same result, an arbitrage opportunity would exist and arbitrage would force a convergence. We begin with a $1,000 investment, and the top line shows the ending return on a U.S. investment that pays a 6.79 percent nominal interest rate. The down-across-and-up path shows the return on a peso investment. Starting with $1,000 and using the spot exchange rate ($S_{P/\$}$), P2.5/$, the dollars are converted to pesos. To arrive at the value of the investment one year later, the original peso-denominated investment is multiplied by $1 + r_P$, where r_P is the nominal peso interest rate. Finally, the peso investment is converted back into dollars by multiplying by $1/F_{P/\$}$, where $F_{P/\$}$ is the forward rate. Because the two paths must give the same result, we can set them equal to each other:

$$(1 + r_\$) = S_{P/\$} \times (1 + r_P) \times 1/F_{P/\$}.$$

The left side of the equation is the total return earned on a dollar investment, while the right side is the total return if the sum were converted into pesos, invested at the peso rate, and then converted back into dollars. Assuming that we can obtain a forward contract today locking in the forward rate, then if the equation holds, the spot and forward rates are said to be "at interest rate parity." Rearranging the terms, we obtain the following equation, which shows the relationship between the forward and spot exchange rates and the nominal interest rates in the two countries:

$$S_{P/\$}/F_{P/\$} = (1 + r_\$)/(1 + r_P)$$
$$F_{P/\$} = S_{P/\$} \times [(1 + r_P)/(1 + r_\$)].$$

(3-3)

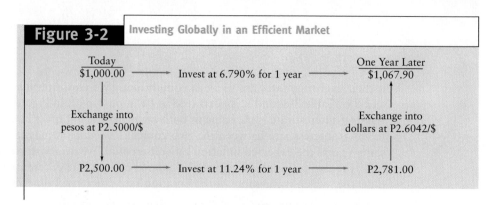

Figure 3-2 Investing Globally in an Efficient Market

Today
$1,000.00 ⟶ Invest at 6.790% for 1 year ⟶ One Year Later $1,067.90

Exchange into pesos at P2.5000/$

Exchange into dollars at P2.6042/$

P2,500.00 ⟶ Invest at 11.24% for 1 year ⟶ P2,781.00

---

[10]Note that we used a similar figure in Chapter 2, but the data in the two figures are different.

Thus, the forward rate equals the spot rate times the ratio of (1 + Peso interest rate) to (1 + Dollar interest rate).[11] Using the numbers given in Table 3-6, we obtain the following forward rate for our example:

$$F_{P/\$} = P2.5000/\$ \times [1.1124/1.06790] = P2.6042/\$.$$

COVERED INTEREST ARBITRAGE Interest rate parity defines the theoretical equilibrium conditions between interest rates and exchange rates, but market values sometimes diverge from their theoretical levels. When divergences occur, astute traders can invest in the currency that offers the highest return on a covered basis and make a riskless profit. To show how this is done, assume that the conditions in Table 3-6 hold except that the forward rate is now P2.615/\$ rather than P2.6042/\$. This is not an equilibrium rate, so an arbitrageur can profit on the disequilibrium by engaging in the transactions shown in Table 3-7. This process is known as **covered interest arbitrage.**

The profit opportunity caused by any disequilibrium can, given computers and telecommunications technology, exist only momentarily. As arbitrageurs discover the disequilibrium and take the actions in Table 3-7, the buy and sell transactions will rapidly move exchange rates into an equilibrium. Thus, markets normally tend to be in equilibrium and to be consistent with interest rate parity.

Forward Rates as Unbiased Predictors of Future Spot Rates

The fourth parity condition shown in Figure 3-1 is called the **unbiased predictor** condition. If foreign exchange markets are efficient and reflect all known information about future conditions, then the forward rate we observe today is the best unbiased estimate of what the spot rate will be in the future. Note that this statement does not imply that the forward rate is an accurate estimate of what the spot rate will be in the future. Rather, it merely says that the future spot rate is equally likely to be higher or lower than the forward rate. This condition makes intuitive sense, because if some investors had better information about the future spot rate, they could act on that information and make an arbitrage profit. However, their

Covered Interest Arbitrage
A riskless transaction in which an individual earns a profit on borrowed money due to a disequilibrium condition in the forward rate.

Unbiased Predictor
States that if foreign exchange markets are efficient and reflect all relevant information about future conditions, then the forward rate we observe today is the best unbiased estimate of what the spot rate will be in the future.

TABLE 3-7	**Covered Interest Arbitrage**

1. Borrow P10,000 at the peso interest rate of 11.240 percent for 1 year. At the end of the year, the arbitrageur will owe P10,000 × 1.11240 = P11,124.

2. Convert the pesos into dollars at the spot rate of P2.5000/\$. This will yield P10,000/P2.5000/\$ = \$4,000.

3. Invest the \$4,000 at the dollar interest rate of 6.790 percent for 1 year. At the end of the year, the arbitrageur will receive \$4,000 × 1.06790 = \$4,271.60.

4. Sell the \$4,271.60 forward 1 year at the forward rate of P2.6150/\$. At the end of the year, when the transaction is consummated, the arbitrageur will receive \$4,271.60 × P2.6150/\$ = P11,170.23.

5. In one year, the arbitrageur will: Receive P11,170.23 from the forward contract

                                          Repay   P11,124.00 principal and interest on the loan

                           Earn a profit of   P46.23 on the entire transaction

Note: This is a *covered transaction*, so there is no risk. Also, the arbitrageur does not have to commit his or her own capital, so the rate of return on the transaction is infinity.

---

[11]In the example we analyzed indirect rates. For direct rates, the formula is

$$F_{\$/P} = S_{\$/P} \times [(1 + r_\$)/(1 + r_P)].$$

trading activities would drive exchange rates into a new equilibrium, and the forward rate would again be an unbiased estimate of future spot rates.

Empirical tests of the unbiased predictor hypothesis have yielded conflicting results. Some evidence suggests that the forward rate is a good unbiased indicator of future spot rates, but other evidence finds to the contrary. Also, many foreign exchange forecasting services sell forecasts of future spot rates, and the fact that companies are willing to pay for these forecasts indicates that many managers believe that the services provide better insight into future exchange rates than a simple parity analysis. Our conclusion is that the foreign exchange market is not completely efficient, hence that the forward rate is probably not the very best predictor of future spot rates. However, unless we are dealing with very large sums, it probably does not pay to buy an expensive forecast, because fairly good results can be obtained by assuming that the parity hypothesis is true.

The International Fisher Effect

International Fisher Effect, Fisher-Open
The theory that states in equilibrium the expected change in the spot exchange rate should be equal in magnitude but opposite in sign to the interest rate differential.

Now that the four corners of the diamond in Figure 3-1 have been linked by purchasing power parity, the Fisher effect, interest rate parity, and the unbiased predictor conditions, all that is left is to link together the interest rate differential and the expected change in the spot rate. Here we use the **international Fisher effect**, or **Fisher-Open**. Fisher-Open states that, in equilibrium, the expected change in the spot exchange rate should be equal in magnitude but opposite in sign to the interest rate differential. In terms of the entries in Table 3-6, this implies that the relationship on line 12 must be equal to, but opposite in sign, to the relationship on line 10:

$$[S_{P/\$} - EFS_{P/\$}]/EFS_{P/\$} = -[(1 + r_P) - (1 + r_\$)]/(1 + r_P)$$
$$= -[r_P - r_\$]/(1 + r_P) = [r_\$ - r_P]/(1 + r_P)$$
$$[P2.5000 - P2.6042]/P2.6042 = -0.0400 = [0.06790 - 0.11240]/1.11240$$
$$= -0.0400.$$

The rationale for Fisher-Open is that before investors can be induced to invest in dollar-denominated securities earning only 6.79 percent rather than the 11.24 percent on peso-denominated securities, they have to be convinced that they will be equally well off after adjusting for the change in the spot exchange rate. Otherwise, they might be inclined to invest in peso-denominated securities with their higher nominal rates. Empirical tests of Fisher-open appear to be reasonably descriptive of market conditions, although many short-run deviations are observed. These deviations probably result from foreign exchange risk premiums that exist for most currencies.

SELF-TEST QUESTIONS

Identify the five parity conditions that interact with each other to determine national interest rates and exchange rates.
What is PPP, and differentiate between absolute and relative PPP.
What is the Fisher effect?
What is interest rate parity?

OTHER APPROACHES TO EXCHANGE RATE FORECASTING

The balance of payments approach and applications of parity theories are the most prevalent techniques used to predict future exchange rates. However, another theoretical approach, called the *asset market approach*, has gained recent popularity. Also, technical analysis using charts has been used because some researchers believe that exchange rate movements often follow long-term "waves."

The Asset Market Approach to Exchange Rate Forecasting

Asset Market Approach
The hypothesis that investors decide whether to hold monetary assets denominated in a foreign currency by looking at the country's real interest rates and its economic outlook for future growth and profitability. This theory implies that in the short run, exchange rate movements are driven by interest rates, expectations for future growth and profitability, and opportunities in the asset markets.

The **asset market approach** hypothesizes that in deciding whether to hold monetary assets denominated in a foreign currency, investors look at real interest rates in the country plus its economic outlook. For example, in 2003 the U.S. dollar fell against other major currencies. Economic prospects in the United States were not very bright at the time, and the Federal Reserve Board reduced nominal interest rates to historically low levels. The real interest rate was also very low. In this environment, investors could earn higher real rates in Europe and elsewhere, so they sold dollars to buy foreign securities, which then put downward pressure on the dollar. In early 2004, economic indicators suggested that the U.S. economy was starting to pick up and grow at a respectable rate, and the Fed hinted that it might consider raising interest rates in the future. These announcements were greeted by a slight strengthening of the dollar against other major currencies. As we write this, the market appears to be waiting for new signals about the U.S. economy and further guidance from the Fed about the future direction of monetary policy.

The asset market approach implies that, in the short run, exchange rate movements are probably driven by real and nominal interest rates, expectations for future growth and profitability, and opportunities in the asset markets. In the long term, though, more fundamental relationships such as purchasing power parity probably drive exchange rates.

Technical Analysis

Technical Analysis
Involves looking at patterns in price and volume data to assess the likely movements of future exchange rates.

Chartists who believe in **technical analysis** do not base their exchange rate forecasts on underlying economic theories but look only at patterns in price and volume data to assess the likely movements of future exchange rates. This approach is based on the belief that trends persist in the market and that patterns observed in the past will be repeated. If this is true, then we can forecast the movement of exchange rates by finding the underlying patterns, or "waves," and predicting how and when they will recur. The chartists seek to ride these waves with their forecasts. Because there is no specified causal relationship, the only empirical tests are in terms of how well the chartists can actually predict. As we might suspect, the results are mixed. Some managers swear by chart-based forecasts, while others swear at them!

SELF-TEST QUESTION   What are some other approaches used to predict future exchange rates?

SUMMARY

For a global company to compete effectively, its managers must operate with many different currencies. Foreign exchange means the currency of a foreign country, while the exchange rate is simply the price of one currency in terms of another currency. In Chapter 2 we discussed conceptually how exchange rates are established, while in this chapter we discussed foreign exchange markets and their operations.

Exchange rates affect cash flows directly, and they affect the required rate of return through their relationship with interest rates. Multinational enterprises generate cash flows in many different currencies, and they must translate foreign cash flows into their home currency for financial reporting purposes. They must also convert currencies physically before transferring funds from locations with excess cash to those where cash is needed. Foreign exchange markets facilitate these actions, and on a 24/7 basis. The key concepts discussed in this chapter are listed below.

- **Foreign exchange markets** range from local cab drivers to global computer networks that connect banks, professional dealers, brokers, central banks, and the treasury departments of many multinational enterprises.
- A diverse group of **firms, institutions, governments**, and **individuals** participates in foreign exchange transactions.
- In a foreign exchange context, the **bid rate** is the rate at which traders buy currencies, while the **offer rate** is the rate at which traders sell currencies.
- Multinational companies need foreign exchange to **conduct day-to-day business operations**, to **finance worldwide operations**, and to **reduce the profit volatility** that can arise from **exchange rate fluctuations**.
- A **cross rate** is the exchange rate between any two currencies.
- The phrase **American terms** means the foreign exchange rate quotation that represents the number of American dollars that can be bought with one unit of local currency.
- The phrase **European terms** means the foreign exchange rate quotation that represents the units of local currency that can be bought with one U.S. dollar. "European" is intended as a generic term that applies globally.
- To facilitate worldwide currency trading through electronic media, the interbank foreign exchange market has adopted a system under which all quotations are given in **European terms** with a few exceptions. The exceptions—the **euro, British pound, Australian dollar**, and **New Zealand dollar**—are quoted in **American terms**.
- A **direct quotation** is the home currency price of one unit of the foreign currency.
- An **indirect quotation** is the foreign currency price of one unit of the home currency.
- To find the **percentage change in exchange rates (direct quotation)**, the formula is

$$\% \Delta FX = \frac{\text{Ending rate} - \text{Beginning rate}}{\text{Beginning rate}} \times 100.$$

- To find the **percentage change in exchange rates (indirect quotation)**, the formula is

$$\% \Delta FX = \frac{\text{Beginning rate} - \text{Ending rate}}{\text{Ending rate}} \times 100.$$

- To find the **percentage premium or discount on a foreign currency (direct quotation)**, the formula is

$$\text{Forward premium or discount \%} = \left(\frac{\text{Forward rate} - \text{Spot rate}}{\text{Spot rate}} \right) \times 360/n \times 100.$$

- To find the **percentage premium or discount on a foreign currency (indirect quotation)**, the formula is

$$\text{Forward premium or discount\%} = \left(\frac{\text{Spot rate} - \text{Forward rate}}{\text{Forward rate}} \right) \times 360/n \times 100.$$

- The **spread** is the profit from buying and selling currency.
- In the **interbank market** it is customary to **state forward quotations in terms of differences** between the outright forward rate and the outright spot rate.
- The **equilibrium exchange rate** is determined by the **demand** for a particular currency by foreigners versus the **supply** made available by holders of that currency.
- The **balance of payments (BOP) report** is a statistical summary of all transactions during a given time period between the residents of one country and the rest of the world. It is divided into five sections: current account (Group A), capital account (Group B), financial account (Group C), net errors and omissions (Group D), and reserves and related items (Group E).

- The **current account (Group A)** records all inflows and outflows of income derived from exporting and importing goods and services, net income from investment and employee compensation, and net unilateral transfers.
- The **capital account (Group B)** includes all capital transfers into and out of a country related to the purchase and sale of fixed assets, including real estate.
- The **financial account (Group C)** includes all foreign direct investment, portfolio investment, and external flows of other financial assets and liabilities.
- **Net errors and omissions (Group D)** is an adjustment made to force total debits to equal total credits.
- **Reserves and related items (Group E)** are changes in official monetary reserves held by the government, including monetary metals, foreign exchange, and the position of the country with the International Monetary Fund (IMF).
- **Overall balance** is the net amount of all debits and credits recorded in Groups A through D, which represents the net inflow (credit balance) or outflow (debit balance) of private sector transactions.
- A **deficit (surplus)** represents a net debit (credit) balance in the overall balance of payments.
- **Parity conditions** are economic theories that interact with each other to determine national interest rates and exchange rates.
- **Purchasing power parity (PPP)**, also known as the law of one price, asserts that in the absence of transactions costs, the ratio of prices of identical products in two countries determines the exchange rate between the two currencies.
- **Absolute PPP** is a purchasing power parity theory based on relative prices of similar baskets of goods and services, estimating the equilibrium exchange rate at any given point in time.
- **Relative PPP** is a purchasing power parity theory stating that the spot exchange rate should change in an equal, but opposite, manner to the inflation differential between two countries.
- **The Fisher equation** shows how the nominal risk-free rate, r_{RF}, is a function of the real risk-free rate, r^*, and the inflation rate, I.
- **Interest rate parity (IRP)** is a theory that shows that the forward premium or discount on the foreign currency is equal in magnitude but opposite in sign to the interest rate differential.
- **Covered interest arbitrage** is a riskless transaction in which an individual earns a profit on borrowed money due to a disequilibrium condition in the forward rate.
- The **unbiased predictor** condition states that, if foreign exchange markets are efficient and they reflect all relevant information about future conditions, then the forward rate we observe today is the best unbiased estimate of what the spot rate will be in the future.
- The **international Fisher effect (Fisher-Open)** states that in equilibrium the expected change in the spot rate should be equal in magnitude but opposite in sign to the interest differential.
- The **asset market approach** is the hypothesis under which investors decide whether to hold monetary assets denominated in a foreign currency by looking at the country's real interest rates and its economic outlook for future growth and profitability. This theory implies that, in the short run, exchange rate movements are driven by real interest rates, expectations for future growth and profitability, and opportunities in the asset markets.
- **Technical analysis** involves looking at patterns in price and volume data to assess the likely movements of future exchange rates.

QUESTIONS

(3-1) Differentiate between foreign exchange and the exchange rate.

(3-2) How do exchange rates affect the valuation equation?

(3-3) How do multinational companies use foreign exchange?

(3-4) Explain why you might need to determine a cross rate and how it is calculated.

(3-5) What quotation convention has been established to facilitate worldwide currency trading? Are there any exceptions to this convention?

(3-6) Give the general formula you would use to calculate the percentage change in the yen during the year. Would the formula used be different if you wanted to calculate the percentage change in the euro? If so, give the general formula used, and explain why it is different.

(3-7) Give the general formula you would use to calculate the percentage change between the spot rate and a 6-month forward rate for the Mexican peso. Would the formula used be different if you wanted to calculate the percentage change between the spot rate and a 9-month forward rate for the British pound? If so, give the general formula used, and explain why it is different.

(3-8) How is the equilibrium exchange rate determined, and what factors affect that equilibrium exchange rate?

(3-9) What is the balance of payments report? Identify each section of the report and the information each section provides. How do you interpret this statement? Does exchange rate policy have any affect on its interpretation? Explain.

(3-10) What valuable information does the balance of payments report for a country with a fixed exchange rate regime provide global corporate managers?

(3-11) What is the obligation of the government under a floating exchange rate regime if the balance of payments does not net to zero? Explain your answer.

(3-12) What do the relationships among the five parity conditions tell us? Use Figure 3-1 as a reference, and assume that the markets in two countries are in equilibrium.

(3-13) What major assumption is made when testing PPP? Other than telling us the most and least expensive places to purchase a Big Mac, what other information does the "Big Mac index" provide? According to the Big Mac Index, is the euro under- or overvalued relative to the dollar? What about the yuan? The pound? The Swiss franc? The Canadian dollar?

(3-14) What are some of the problems with the model and tests of the PPP as given in your text?

(3-15) What information is given by the Fisher equation?

(3-16) Give the interest rate parity equation, and explain what information it provides.

(3-17) What is a covered interest arbitrage, and why is this transaction so important?

(3-18) What is the unbiased predictor condition? Has it been proven with empirical tests? Should you pay for an expensive forecast of the future spot rate? Explain your answer.

(3-19) What is the international Fisher effect? What is the rationale for it?

(3-20) Besides the balance of payments approach and the parity conditions, what other techniques are used to forecast exchange rates? Explain each technique.

SELF-TEST PROBLEMS   Solutions Appear in Appendix B

(ST-1) Define each of the following terms:
Key Terms a. Foreign exchange; exchange rate; foreign exchange markets
 b. Bid rate; offer rate; spread; cross rate
 c. American terms; European terms; direct quotation; indirect quotation
 d. Balance of payments (BOP) report
 e. Current account; capital account; financial account; net errors and omissions

f. Reserves and related items; overall balance; deficit; surplus
g. Parity conditions; purchasing power parity (PPP); absolute PPP; relative PPP
h. Fisher equation; international Fisher effect (Fisher-Open); unbiased predictor condition
i. Interest rate parity (IRP); covered interest arbitrage
j. Asset market approach; technical analysis

(ST-2) Tom Smitherson, a British executive for TMN Industries International, is flying to
Cross Rates Beijing on a business trip. Smitherson will be spending a few days in Beijing scouting out different locations for a manufacturing plant that the company would like to build, so he needs to know the exchange rate between the yuan and the pound. Smitherson cannot find this rate published anywhere; however, he has found the following spot rate quotations:

| Pound: | $1.8271/£ |
| Yuan: | CNY8.2781/$ |

a. Given this information, how many Chinese yuan can be purchased with 1 British pound?
b. Given this information, how many British pounds can be purchased with 1 Chinese yuan?

(ST-3) For purposes of answering this question, use the information given in Table 3-4.
Interbank Quotations, a. Assume that the 1-year midrate for the euro given in Table 3-4 is its actual
Forward Premium or spot rate on January 22, 2005. During the year, what was the percentage
Discount, and Spread change in the euro relative to the dollar? During the year, did the euro appreciate or depreciate against the dollar?
b. What are the outright 3-month forward offer rates for the British pound and Canadian dollar?
c. Calculate the forward premium or discount percentage between the spot rates and the forward rates (calculated in part b) for the British pound and Canadian dollar.
d. Calculate the dollar profit a dealer would make if he purchases 100,000,000 pounds 1 month from today (where today is January 22, 2004), and then sells those pounds on that very same day.

(ST-4) A television costs $425 in the United States. Today, in the currency markets, you
Purchasing Power Parity observe the following exchange rates:

| Japanese yen: | ¥106.63/$ |
| EMU euro: | €0.00785/¥ |

Assume that the currency markets are efficient and that purchasing power parity holds worldwide. What should be the price of the same television in Italy?

(ST-5) You are given the following exchange rate quotations between the U.S. dollar and
Interest Rate Parity British pound:

| Spot rate: | $1.8192/£ |
| 1-year forward rate: | $1.7606/£ |

The 1-year U.S. Treasury rate in the United States is 1.35 percent. If interest rate parity holds, what is the yield today on 1-year risk-free British securities?

STARTER PROBLEMS

(3-1) Stated in European terms (an indirect quotation), the spot rate for the Danish
Exchange Rates krone is Dkr 6.2305/$. What is the spot rate for the Danish krone in American terms (a direct quotation)?

(3-2) You are given the following spot exchange rate data:
Cross Rates

Swiss franc:	SwF1.2997/$
Swedish krona:	kr7.6746/$

    a. Given this information, how many Swedish kronor can be purchased with 1 Swiss franc?

    b. Given this information, how many Swiss francs can be purchased with 1 Swedish krona?

(3-3) A stereo costs $750 in the United States. The same stereo in Jordan costs 532
Purchasing Power Parity dinar.

    a. In European terms (an indirect quote), what is the exchange rate between these two currencies?

    b. In American terms (a direct quote), what is the exchange rate between these two currencies?

(3-4) You are given the following exchange rate quotations between the U.S. dollar and
Interest Rate Parity Japanese yen:

Spot rate:	¥106.63/$
1-year forward rate:	¥105.31/$

The 1-year risk-free rate in Japan is 1.23 percent. If interest rate parity holds, what is the yield today on 1-year U.S. Treasury securities?

EXAM-TYPE PROBLEMS

(3-5) Anne Winters, an Australian tourist, is planning a trip to Moscow. Winters is a
Cross Rates very meticulous planner, and she is trying to estimate how much her trip will cost. To do this, she needs to know the exchange rate between the ruble and the Australian dollar. (She realizes that exchange rates fluctuate over time; however, right now she is just trying to determine a ballpark figure, so spot rates will suffice.) Winters cannot find this rate published anywhere; however, she has found the following spot rate quotations:

Australian dollar:	$0.7548/A$
Russian ruble:	R28.637/$

    a. Given this information, how many Russian rubles can be purchased with 1 Australian dollar?

    b. Given this information, how many Australian dollars can be purchased with 1 Russian ruble?

(3-6) For purposes of answering this question, use the information given in Table 3-4.
Interbank Quotations, Forward Premium or Discount, and Spread

    a. Assume that the 1-year midrate for the pound given in Table 3-4 is its actual spot rate on January 22, 2005. During the year, what was the percentage change in the pound relative to the dollar? During the year, did the pound appreciate or depreciate against the dollar?

    b. What are the outright 6-month forward offer rates for the EMU euro and Japanese yen?

    c. Calculate the forward premium or discount percentage between the spot rates and the forward rates (calculated in part b) for the EMU euro and Japanese yen.

    d. Calculate the dollar profit a dealer would make if he purchases 50,000,000 Canadian dollars 2 months from today (where today is January 22, 2004), and then sells those pounds on that very same day.

(3-7)
Purchasing Power Parity

You are given the following exchange rate data:

New Zealand dollar:	$0.6539/NZ$
South African rand:	R6.5445/$
Mexican peso:	Mex$11.2524/$

A pair of Nike tennis shoes costs $85.00 in the United States. Assume that purchasing power parity holds.
a. How much would that same pair of Nike tennis shoes cost in New Zealand?
b. How much would that same pair of Nike tennis shoes cost in South Africa?
c. How much would that same pair of Nike tennis shoes cost in Mexico?

(3-8)
Interest Rate Parity

You are given the following information:

Swiss franc, 1-year forward rate:	SwF1.3376/$
1-year U.S. Treasury yield:	3%
1-year risk-free Swiss yield:	6%

Assume that interest rate parity holds. In European terms (an indirect quotation), what is the spot exchange rate between Swiss francs and U.S. dollars?

(3-9)
International Parity
Relationships

You are given the following data:

Forecasted inflation for next year in dollar area ($I_\$$)	2.5%
Forecasted inflation for next year in local currency area (I_{LC})	6.0%
Forecasted real interest rate globally (r^*)	3.5%
Current spot exchange rate	LC1.75/$
1-year forward exchange rate	LC1.8098/$
Expected spot exchange rate in 1 year	LC1.8098/$

Use the data provided to construct a table similar to Table 3-6 by answering the questions below.
a. What is the inflation differential between the two countries?
b. What is the 1-year nominal interest rate in the dollar area ($r_\$$)?
c. What is the 1-year nominal interest rate in the local currency area (r_{LC})?
d. What is the interest rate differential between the two countries?
e. What is the forward discount on LC?
f. What is the forecasted change in the spot rate?

INTEGRATED CASE

Rick Schmidt, MRI's CFO, along with Mandy Wu, Schmidt's assistant, and John Costello, a consultant and college finance professor, comprise a team set up to teach the firm's directors and senior managers the basics of international financial management. The program includes 16 sessions, each lasting about 2 hours, and they are scheduled immediately before the monthly board meetings. Two sessions have been completed, and the team is now preparing Session 3, which will deal with exchange rate analysis. Prior sessions have provided an overview of international finance and interest rate determination.

For the exchange rate analysis session, the team will explain how multinational enterprises and international investors handle the uncertainties presented by exchange rate fluctuations. They plan to go through the types of quotations seen in foreign exchange markets, the calculations required in currency trading, and the parity conditions that govern the foreign exchange and interest rate system. One of MRI's executives had once commented to Schmidt that the dollar was strengthening against the other major currencies that week and that it was good news for the company. Schmidt reminded this executive that MRI generates a lot of sales and profits overseas, and the stronger dollar means these cash flows are smaller when converted to U.S. dollars. This episode reinforced Schmidt's belief that MRI's directors must be more astute regarding the foreign exchange environment. Anyone can read quotes from *The Wall Street Journal*, but it takes a lot of work to understand how rates interact and affect commerce.

Wu expressed concern about addressing controversial issues, where the proper analysis is in question. She recalled that in college some students simply "tuned out" when the instructor raised a question for which there was no definitive answer, and she was concerned that the directors might react similarly. Schmidt and Costello agree that this could be a problem, but they felt strongly that it would not be appropriate to "sweep problems under the carpet." So, they want to bring up relevant unresolved issues, discuss alternative ways of dealing with them, and point out the implications of different decisions. The directors are all intelligent, experienced in dealing with complex situations, and would rather know about potential problems than be kept in the dark.

With those thoughts in mind, the three compiled the following set of questions, which they plan to discuss during the session. Assume that you are Mandy Wu, and that you must prepare answers for use during the session.

QUESTIONS

a. Describe the inter-bank foreign and retail exchange markets. How do foreign exchange dealers generate profits?

b. Why might a government or central bank engage in foreign exchange transactions?

c. Consider the following exchange rates:

	USD per 1 unit of foreign currency
Chinese yuan	0.1208
Canadian dollar	0.76138

(1) Are these currency quotations direct or indirect quotations (from an American investor's perspective)? Calculate the alternative direct or indirect quotation.

(2) Differentiate between American and European term quotations.

(3) What is a cross rate? Calculate the cross rate between the yuan and Canadian dollar.

(4) Assume Hip Couture Inc. produces sweaters and ships them to China and Canada for a total cost of $20.75. (Assume the product can be shipped for the same price to each country.) The firm wants a 50 percent markup on the sweater. Assuming that purchasing power parity holds, what should the product sell for in China and Canada?

(5) Now, assume that Hip Couture Inc. begins producing the same sweater in China. The product costs CNY60 to produce and shipping to Canada costs only CNY1.50 per unit. If Hip Couture wants to sell the sweater at the same prices as before in China and Canada, what are the markups Hip Couture enjoys now in these two countries?

d. Suppose 1 year ago, the spot quotation for the Canadian dollar was $0.7400. Currently, the 3-month forward rate on the Canadian dollar is $0.77125 and the current spot rate is given in part c. Calculate the percentage change in exchange rates over the last year and the current premium/discount on the forward exchange rate.

e. One of MRI's executives recently heard a currency trader remark, "The 2-year Canadian dollar is selling at 196.6 to 210.5." Briefly discuss foreign quotations in points, and explain what the currency trader was actually saying. (Hint: The first number is the bid price.)

f. Describe the balance of payments and the information it conveys.

g. What is purchasing power parity? If a stereo costs $80 in the United States, how much should it cost in Canada, if purchasing power parity holds?

h. What is interest rate parity? If the current risk-free rate on a 3-month security in Canada is 7 percent, what is the risk-free rate on a 3-month security in the United States? Use the 3-month forward rate given in part d.

i. What is covered interest arbitrage?

j. What is the Fisher effect?

k. What is the unbiased predictor condition?

l. What is the asset market approach?

CHAPTER 4

International Trade and Foreign Direct Investment

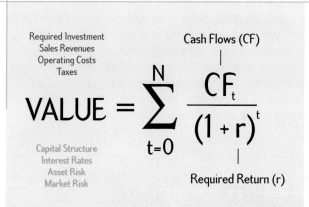

Required Investment
Sales Revenues
Operating Costs
Taxes

Cash Flows (CF)

$$\text{VALUE} = \sum_{t=0}^{N} \frac{CF_t}{(1+r)^t}$$

Capital Structure
Interest Rates
Asset Risk
Market Risk

Required Return (r)

e-resource

The textbook's Web site, **http://crum. swlearning.com,** *contains an Excel file that will guide you through the chapter's calculations. The file for this chapter is* **FIFC04-model.xls,** *and we encourage you to open the file and follow along as you read the chapter.*

Hundreds of years ago, international commerce in the form of importing and exporting flourished, using sea and land trade routes throughout the known world. Traders acquired locally produced merchandise, packed it, traveled to a foreign country or region, and exchanged it for other goods that were unavailable in their home country. When these products were brought home, they could be sold to provide the trader with a handsome profit. Over time, outposts in foreign lands served as bases of operations for traders, and formal payment arrangements were developed to make trade more efficient. Cities, such as Venice, became trading centers, and their merchants became extremely wealthy.

Trade is still extremely important today, but it has been supplemented with new mechanisms that promote global commerce. Most importantly, the rapid expansion of private companies that span multiple countries has given rise to a new and different player in international commerce, the multinational enterprise (MNE). While MNEs have existed in some areas for many years, their real growth came after World War II. Indeed, MNEs are currently the preeminent industrial organization in global commerce. Those who place primary value on economic efficiency and wealth expansion celebrate this development, but those whose central focus is on protecting local companies, national sovereignty, and social structures in the developing world condemn it.

When most people think about MNEs, they think of huge, impersonal, monolithic companies with physical presences in many countries and loyalty to none. There is an element of truth to this vision, but MNEs are far more complex and *diverse than most people imagine, and their contribution to host economies can spark rapid improvements in local societies. MNEs still engage extensively in international trade, both with other companies and among subsidiaries in their corporate network. However, they differ from the old merchant companies in that today they also make extensive investments, called "foreign direct investments (FDIs)," outside their home countries. Innovations in information technology are facilitating this process, making real-time control of global corporations increasingly feasible, but all this presents major challenges to traditional political and economic structures.*

This chapter examines MNEs and the way they do business around the world. We begin with traditional theories of international trade and focus on answering this question: "Why, when, and how should we go abroad?" In terms of the valuation equation, it is first important to understand that for many companies today, international investments represent a large and increasing portion of firm value. In many respects, these international investments will have a profound effect on both the firm's cash flows and risk. More specifically, the discussion in this chapter focuses on the cash flows that are generated in many countries by FDI and flow from and to all parts of the MNE where they can best be employed to create value. Because these cash flows are generated in many countries with differing degrees of uncertainty, the material also has implications for risk and the required rate of return.

WHY COUNTRIES TRADE

Mercantilism
An economic and military system developed to gain and retain national power and wealth.

Prior to the late 18th century, the international trade policy practiced by virtually all industrial powers was **mercantilism**. Mercantile theory found that gaining and retaining national power and prestige required large armies and navies, which, in turn, required massive amounts of capital. Moreover, the national wealth needed to support the military establishment could be acquired through trade with less powerful countries or, better yet, with colonies. Payments for trade were usually made with gold, and successful mercantilist nations exported goods and services to the rest of the world, receiving payments in gold but rarely importing products from other countries. This policy tended to preserve a nation's wealth because outflows of gold to pay for trade were minimized. Trade, to a mercantilist, was a zero-sum game. Some countries won while others lost, and the mercantilists stacked the deck to ensure that they were on the winning side. Of course, if every country wanted to export but none wanted to import, the system would not work. This is one reason powerful nations amassed colonial empires: Wealth flowed from the colonies to the home country, which grew ever richer and more powerful.

Absolute Advantage
Adam Smith's theory that all countries can gain from specialization and trade, thus resulting in a positive-sum game.

In 1776, Scottish economist Adam Smith published *An Inquiry into the Nature and Causes of the Wealth of Nations.* His work questioned mercantilism and endorsed economic specialization and trade, based on what is called the theory of **absolute advantage**. Its greatest impact was the notion that all countries can gain from specialization and trade; hence, trade can be a positive-sum game. For example, assume that a Country C is very efficient in producing coffee but inefficient in producing wheat. Assume at the same time that, for Country W, this situation is reversed—it is efficient in producing wheat but inefficient in producing coffee. Smith's theory suggests that rather than having each country produce both wheat and coffee, it makes sense for Country C to specialize in producing coffee and for Country W to specialize in producing wheat.

Comparative Advantage
David Ricardo's theory that all countries could still gain from specialization and trade if they produced those goods in which they were relatively more efficient than others.

While Smith's theory suggested an important role for trade, if any single country held an absolute advantage in the production of most goods and services, the theory would not hold. This issue was addressed in 1817 by British economist David Ricardo in his book, *Principles of Political Economy and Taxation*. Ricardo developed the theory of **comparative advantage**, which showed that all countries could still gain from specialization and trade if they produced those goods in which they were *relatively* more efficient than others. The comparative advantage model is the intellectual basis for the work of the World Trade Organization (WTO) today, and it is still useful for explaining many decisions made by MNEs. For these reasons, we begin our discussion of international commerce with this theory.

SELF-TEST QUESTIONS   What is mercantilism? Why was trade a zero-sum game in this system?
Differentiate between absolute and comparative advantage.

THE THEORY OF COMPARATIVE ADVANTAGE

For simplicity, we focus on just two products, coffee and wheat, and on two countries, Country A and Country B. Country A has an absolute advantage in the production of both products, so, under Adam Smith's theory, trade would not occur. However, Ricardo showed that there would be an advantage to trade. Now assume that both countries have an available production capacity of 1,000 units, where "units" consist of labor, land, and other materials, and those productive units can be used to produce either coffee or wheat. If the two countries were isolated and did not trade, they would consume what they produced. However, the countries have different production efficiencies, as shown in Table 4-1. Also, assume that both countries initially use their factor inputs as shown in Panel B of the table.

Although both countries have 1,000 production units, Country A is more efficient and can produce more coffee and also more wheat per unit of input than Country B. Thus, A has an absolute advantage in the production of both coffee and wheat, and it is the richer nation. However, its *relative advantage* is not the same for the two products. Its advantage over B in coffee production is 6 to 3, or $6/3 = 2.00$, while its advantage in wheat is only 4 to 3, or $4/3 = 1.33$. Thus, A has a *larger absolute advantage* in the production of coffee, which means that it has a *comparative advantage* in the production of coffee. Thus A should specialize in coffee, B in

TABLE 4-1 | Production Possibilities for Coffee and Wheat

Panel A. Production Capacity and Output

Country	Available Production Units	OUTPUT PER UNIT OF INPUT	
		Bags of Coffee	Bushels of Wheat
A	1,000 units	6	4
B	1,000 units	3	3

Panel B. Initial Production, Assuming No Trade

Country	Units Used to Produce Coffee	Units Used to Produce Wheat
A	600 units × 6 = 3,600 bags of coffee	400 units × 4 = 1,600 bushels of wheat
B	600 units × 3 = 1,800 bags of coffee	400 units × 3 = 1,200 bushels of wheat
	Total output = 5,400 bags of coffee	Total output = 2,800 bushels of wheat

wheat, and the two countries should trade with each other to obtain the proper mix of products.[1]

Given the resources required to produce bags of coffee and bushels of wheat, the opportunity cost of a bushel of wheat in Country A is 6/4, or 1.5 bags of coffee, while in B it would be 3/3, or 1 bag of coffee per bushel of wheat.[2] Using coffee as the medium of exchange, or "currency," a bushel of wheat would cost 1.5 in A but only 1.0 in B. These would be the domestic prices, measured in bags of coffee, in each country in the absence of trade.[3]

The existence of comparative advantages makes trade between the two countries beneficial, but the prices at which goods are exchanged determine how those benefits are allocated. Under one set of prices, A would receive all the benefits, under a second set B would get all the benefits, while under a third set the benefits would be shared between the two countries. These situations are set forth in Table 4-2. Obviously, each country would prefer to maximize its own position, and the final result will probably be a middle position, where the benefits are shared in some manner.

Base Case: No Trade between A and B

The top panel of Table 4-2 shows production and consumption as given in Table 4-1. This establishes the minimum acceptable situation for the two countries.

Case I. Trade Occurs at A's Pretrade Price

As noted earlier, in Country A one bushel of wheat is worth 1.5 bags of coffee. (In B, where the production of wheat is relatively more efficient than coffee, a bushel of wheat would cost only 1.0 bag of coffee.) Thus, 1.5 bags of coffee is the price of wheat in A. If trade occurred at this price, then production, trade, and consumption would be as given in Case I of the table. Country A would produce only coffee, where its comparative advantage is greatest, consume 3,600 units of its production, and sell the remaining 2,400 units to B in exchange for 1,600 bushels of wheat. Country B would produce only wheat, sell 1,600 bushels to A for 2,400 bags of coffee, and consume the remaining 1,400 bushels of wheat. Consumption in A would end up exactly the same as in the no-trade case, but B would be better off because it would now have 600 more bags of coffee and 200 more bushels of wheat than before. Thus, having production occur in a situation where a comparative advantage exists causes **gross world product (GWP)** to increase by [6,000 − 5,400] = 600 bags of coffee and [3,000 − 2,800] = 200 bushels of wheat. Note, though, that all of the benefits from trade would be captured by B if A's pricing structure were used. This occurs because the price of A's export good, coffee, is being priced at its low domestic price while B's export good, wheat, is being priced at its high value in A. Thus, B is selling at a high price and buying at a low price, and this causes it to receive all the benefits from the trade.

Gross World Product (GWP) The aggregate value of all goods and services produced worldwide in a given year.

---

[1]We may also say that B has the least absolute disadvantage—which means a comparative advantage—in the production of wheat, so we come to the same conclusion.

[2]The opportunity cost of a product is the amount of a second product that must be given up to produce a unit of the first product. In Country A, 1.5 bags of coffee must be given up to produce a bushel of wheat, so the opportunity cost of wheat is 1.5 bags of coffee.

[3]For the sake of simplicity, we assume barter instead of introducing money into this example. The outcome is the same with this assumption, and the explanation is significantly streamlined, so we assume that the countries trade coffee directly for wheat without using money. Also, note that we couched the discussion in terms of opportunity costs. Originally the theories were based on another concept called the *labor theory of value*, under which the value of a product was assessed by looking at the labor cost it took to make the product. In modern production this assumption is not valid, so *opportunity cost theory* replaced the labor theory of value. The theories of Smith and Ricardo were confirmed in the late 19th century in the new context. However, it is interesting to note that the work of another prominent 19th-century economist, Karl Marx, could not be proved using the opportunity cost theory, which is why the former Soviet Union clung to the labor theory of value until its collapse.

TABLE 4-2 | Relationship between Production Efficiency, Prices, and Trade

		Coffee		Wheat
Base Case: No Trading				
Country A	(1 bushel of wheat "costs" 1.5 bags of coffee)			
	Produces and consumes	**3,600**	Produces and consumes	**1,600**
Country B	(1 bushel of wheat "costs" 1.0 bag of coffee)			
	Produces and consumes	**1,800**	Produces and consumes	**1,200**
Case I.	*Trade at A's Domestic Price (1 bushel wheat = 1.5 bags coffee)*			
Country A	Produces	6,000	Produces	0
	Exports	2,400	Imports	1,600
	Consumes	**3,600**	Consumes	**1,600**
Country B	Produces	0	Produces	3,000
	Imports	2,400	Exports	1,600
	Consumes	**2,400**	Consumes	**1,400**
Case II.	*Trade at B's Domestic Price (1 bushel wheat = 1.0 bag coffee)*			
Country A	Produces	6,000	Produces	0
	Exports	1,800	Imports	1,800
	Consumes	**4,200**	Consumes	**1,800**
Country B	Produces	0	Produces	3,000
	Imports	1,800	Exports	1,800
	Consumes	**1,800**	Consumes	**1,200**
Case III.	*Trade at Market-Determined Price (1 bushel wheat = 1.25 bags coffee)*			
Country A	Produces	6,000	Produces	0
	Exports	2,100	Imports	1,680
	Consumes	**3,900**	Consumes	**1,680**
Country B	Produces	0	Produces	3,000
	Imports	2,100	Exports	1,680
	Consumes	**2,100**	Consumes	**1,320**

Note: Coffee serves as the medium of exchange, so wheat is priced in terms of units of coffee.

Case II. Trade Occurs at B's Pretrade Price

In B, where wheat is relatively inexpensive because it is produced relatively more efficiently than coffee, each bushel of wheat is worth only 1.0 bag of coffee. If trade were based on this price, then, as shown in Case II, B would end up exactly as well off as in the no-trade situation, but A would have 600 more bags of coffee and 200 more bushels of wheat. Thus, if B's prices were used, then A receives all of the production benefits based on comparative advantages. Again, this shows that if a country's export prices are high and its import prices are low, then the country will gain from trade.

Case III. Trade Occurs at a Price Determined in the Marketplace

In Case I, A exports coffee at a low price and buys wheat at a high price, causing all the gains to accrue to B, and in Case II the prices are reversed and thus A is the winner. These two cases represent the extreme prices, or end points, of the feasible range of potential prices. If prices were such that wheat cost less than 1 bag of coffee, then B would be worse off than before (hence no trade would occur), and A would refuse to trade if it took more than 1.5 bags of coffee to buy a bushel of wheat. The actual prices at which trade occurs are determined by bargaining in the marketplace. Let us assume that a price of 1.25 bags of coffee for 1 bushel of wheat is established in the market. Case III in the table shows the results under this scenario. Country A is better off than in the no-trade case by 300 bags of coffee and 80 bushels of wheat. Country B is also better off, by 300 bags of coffee and 120 bushels of wheat. Finding the most likely set of prices as determined in the market is a complicated process that goes beyond the scope of this book. However, it is clear that there is some set of prices—or, if money were used, some exchange ratio—that would cause both countries to be better off if they specialized in the product where they have a comparative advantage and then traded for the other product.[4]

Shortcomings of the Classical Theories of Trade

While the intellectual foundation of free trade rests upon Smith's and Ricardo's classical theories of specialization, the world today is very different, and more complex, than it was in the late 18th and early 19th centuries. The changes do not invalidate the basic principles, but those principles are now less helpful in assessing the global trading and investment situation. Here are some problems with the classical theories when they are applied today:

1. Countries do not behave in the manner indicated by the theory of comparative advantage—they continue producing items for which they have no comparative advantage. This may be to support full employment (Japan), for reasons of "national defense" (Russia), to preserve the cultural identity of the population (France), or to protect inefficient but politically favored industries (United States).
2. Smith and Ricardo assumed that the prices charged for internationally traded goods are set in a free and competitive market, but in fact they are often established by administrative processes, not market forces.
3. The factors of production (land, labor, and capital) were assumed to be fully employed at a constant average cost, homogeneous, and fungible (interchangeable). However, economies of scale and scope, varying skill requirements, and unequal quality violate these assumptions.
4. The factors of production were assumed to be mobile within a country but not between countries, so only goods could cross international borders. However, capital, technology, and labor are today globally mobile, and, as they move among countries, comparative advantages change.
5. Important issues such as transaction costs, the effect of uncertainty on trade, segmented markets, and differentiated products were not considered.
6. The comparative advantage model does not explain how such advantages are gained and lost over time as economic development progresses, nor does it consider the effects of trade on people in each country.

In spite of these shortcomings, the concept of comparative advantage is useful for considering both why countries trade and why multinational enterprises have developed into such effective vehicles for fostering international commerce.

---

[4]Each country would, of course, like to sell its products at high prices and buy at low prices, subject to the limits discussed here. The process of determining the equilibrium price (or the terms of trade) is covered in textbooks on international trade such as Robert Carbaugh, *International Economics* (Mason, OH: South-Western Publishing, 2004); and Beth V. Yarbrough and Robert M. Yarbrough, *The World Economy: Trade and Finance*, 6th edition (Mason, OH: South-Western Publishing, 2003).

Briefly explain the concept of comparative advantage, and then indicate how trade based on this concept affects gross world product, that is, the collective wealth of the world.

How do the prices used in international trade affect the allocation of gains from this trade?

WHY COMPANIES TRADE

The classical theories of international trade give virtually no consideration to the business enterprises that make the goods and conduct the trading that occurs internationally. In today's world, most business enterprises are value-maximizing private entities that make decisions considering factors not covered in the classical theories. Indeed, the kind of exporting and importing described in Table 4-2 constitutes only a small fraction of the actions multinational firms take as they engage in international commerce. What motivates a domestic company to consider exporting or importing, and why might these firms want to deepen their global involvement with more active forms of international commerce, such as building plants in foreign countries?

Motivations for Exporting and Importing

EXCESS DOMESTIC CAPACITY If a company has excess productive capacity, this means that it can produce additional output at a relatively low marginal cost. If goods can be exported at any price above marginal cost, then the export sales will increase the firm's profits. Of course, this raises the issue of "dumping," where foreign producers sell at prices that are below the full costs of domestic firms, which helps the foreign firms but hurts the domestic ones. Restrictions are imposed to prevent "unfair" dumping, but this is a murky and controversial issue.

ECONOMIES OF SCALE Economies of scale are significant in many industries, and in these cases high levels of production are crucial to maintaining a competitive cost structure. Overseas operations can increase sales and help a company reach the level needed to maximize scale economies. Again, pricing can be an issue. If a firm expands overseas, pricing low to gain economies of scale, producers in the importing country can be harmed. Thus, pricing policies can affect the comparative advantage of firms and nations, and this raises political issues.

DIVERSIFICATION AND FLEXIBILITY Firms that sell in many different markets, or that source inputs from different countries, can shift between markets and countries as economic conditions change. This reduces risk because all markets are unlikely to experience good or bad conditions at the same time. For example, makers of clothing and sports shoes often outsource production to several different low-labor-cost countries and then trade them off against each other as cost structures and relative productivity change over time. Similarly, producers of oil, steel, and microchips can shift sales to the markets where demand is strongest and prices highest.

MATURE DOMESTIC PRODUCTS Companies with products in the mature or declining phases of the product life cycle in their home country may find that these same products are still in the growth stage in other countries. Then, by selling in these markets, more profits can be squeezed out of an aging product line. For example, U.S. personal computer sales tend to be based on the latest microprocessor technology. Developing countries, though, are good markets for older, less expensive technologies. Intel sells large quantities of earlier generation chips abroad even when domestic demand is declining, thereby spreading its development costs over a larger volume of sales.

GLOBALISM IS NOT THE ENEMY

Relocating plants and outsourcing jobs to other countries have become a searing political issue in the United States, especially during the 2004 presidential election. However, with some of the presidential candidates wanting to rewrite or rescind NAFTA, President Bush's chief economic adviser had stated on the record that if a service or good could be produced more cheaply abroad, Americans were better off importing it than producing it. This is the basic tenet of comparative advantage; however, the adviser's remarks have rankled many in Congress. Many politicians have blamed corporate greed for relocating U.S. plants and jobs overseas, boosting returns for investors at the expense of American workers.

Over the years, Americans have seen U.S. plants close and technical jobs leave the United States, only to have them go abroad. Recently, Levi Strauss & Co. closed its last two U.S. factories in San Antonio. While its headquarters in San Francisco will remain open, most of the production of its jeans (considered to be an American classic and icon) is divided among 50 foreign countries. Maytag, the third largest U.S. home appliance maker, announced plans to close a refrigeration plant in Galesburg, Illinois, by December 2004 and to build a new one in Mexico. Maytag's move south of the border marks the first time that it will produce a product completely outside the United States. American candy makers are also moving abroad. Mints are now produced in Argentina, candy canes in Mexico, and soon, LifeSavers will be produced in Quebec. The list of companies relocating abroad goes on and on.

So, what is actually happening? There are three main explanations:

1. Although America's economy has suffered net job loss since the start of the decade, the vast majority of these job losses are cyclical rather than structural. As the economy recovers from the recent recession, the job picture should improve.

2. Outsourcing has occurred for centuries, but it still only accounts for a small proportion of jobs continually being created and destroyed in our economy. Even during the best of times, our economy has a tremendous rate of "churn"—over 2 million jobs a month. This churning process creates many more jobs than it destroys. For example, during the 1990s, 24 million jobs were created. This is just part of the process of reallocating resources—money and human capital—to where they can be most productive. It is a natural result of competition, and the outcome is lower prices. Higher productivity creates a higher standard of living for all of us.

3. The growing globalization of information technology (IT) services should have a major effect on productivity in the service sector. Even though some IT will be done abroad, many more higher-paying jobs will be created in America. During the 1990s, American factories became much more efficient from IT; during this decade retailers, banks, and hospitals should cash in on this efficiency.

While recent job growth predictions have been overestimated, there are reasons to believe that growth will be more robust. Productivity growth has been running at twice the long-run average; this will have to slow down eventually. In the face

OUTSOURCING ABROAD Companies facing shortages of key inputs, including skilled labor, can "import" the necessary skills from abroad by outsourcing routine tasks and releasing scarce local talent to perform higher value-added jobs at home. Harris Corporation has benefited by outsourcing much of its routine software development to Russia and elsewhere and then using its domestic software engineers to work on innovative new products.

These illustrations show how importing and exporting can lead to more efficient and profitable operations. Virtually all MNEs engage in exporting and importing operations, but eventually, most migrate from relatively passive participation to more active global operations.

SELF-TEST QUESTION   What motivates companies, as opposed to nations, to export or import?

of rising orders, businesses will have to hire more workers.

The creation of new jobs always outnumbers the destruction of old jobs—by a huge margin. Between 1980 and 2002, our population grew by 23.9 percent, while the number of employed Americans grew by 37.4 percent. Today 138.6 million Americans work—this is a near record, both in absolute number and as a proportion of the population. Of course, the workforce in certain industries did shrink; however, new jobs created outnumbered these reductions.

What about the "threats" from China and India taking over American jobs? China competes with some labor-intensive industries that have long been in decline, such as the textile industry. However, most Chinese imports are consumer goods, competing with imports from other poor countries, while America manufactures mainly capital goods. The Indian "outsourcing" threat has had an effect on some white-collar jobs that until now had been safe from foreign competition. Forrester Research, a consulting agency, estimates that 3.3 million American service-industry jobs will move overseas by 2015—which is a very small number when you consider the 7 to 8 million jobs lost every quarter through churning. And the bulk of these jobs will not be high-end IT consulting jobs, but rather jobs writing computer code.

Does globalization have the power to reduce prices, thus spreading new technology and job-creating investment throughout the economy? Yes—consider cheap IT hardware during the 1990s. Most of the reduction in personal computer and mainframe prices was caused by technology advances; however, trade and globalized production were responsible for 10 to 30 percent of the price decline. Lower prices led to increased American productivity, principally in manufacturing, and added $230 billion of extra gross domestic product between 1995 and 2002. Today, software spending is increasing at twice the rate for hardware. If IT software sees price reductions similar to those seen in hardware, partly due to globalization, then productivity gains could be even greater than what happened in the 1990s. Construction and health-care services (with low efficient use of IT) could benefit the most.

Will this productivity lead to more jobs going overseas? Yes; however, this shouldn't be seen as a disaster. America runs a large surplus in services with the rest of the world. The jobs lost would be low-paying ones—trade protection will not save them. And, even if these jobs did not go overseas, they would still be at risk from automation. By contrast, the jobs created in the United States will demand high-end IT skills, and the pay for these jobs will be high. Examples include computer-support specialists and software engineers.

What does all this mean? Americans need to ensure that they have the education to match these new jobs. The belief that globalism is the enemy does more harm to the U.S. worker than any foreign software programmer ever could.

Sources: "The Great Hollowing-Out Myth; Jobs in America," *The Economist,* February 19, 2004, **http://www.economist.com**; L. A. Lorek, "End of a U.S. Manufacturing Era," *San Antonio Express-News,* December 14, 2003, 1L; Matt Adrian and Rachel Cohen, "Maytag to Close Plant, Cut 1,600 Jobs," *Reuters,* **http://www.SiliconValley.com**; and Lauren Belsie, "Bitter Reality: Candy Less Likely to Be 'Made in the U.S.'," *The Christian Science Monitor,* April 8, 2002, **http://www.csmonitor.com**.

WHY COMPANIES SHIFT TO MORE DIRECT INVOLVEMENT ABROAD

As MNEs mature, they tend to employ more active strategies in foreign countries as a result of considerations covered in this section. At first, the idea of dealing in foreign markets with different languages, currencies, and cultures is daunting to most managers. New challenges arise and the rules of the game are uncertain, so it is not surprising that many companies ignore potentially profitable overseas operations. Eventually, though, circumstances may force a company to engage in foreign operations if it is to remain competitive, or even survive. Foreign operations usually begin in countries where the shock is not too great, but as a company acquires knowledge about foreign operations and becomes more comfortable, it may expand into other regions. Thus, experience reduces uncertainty, and, as the perceived risk diminishes, the prospect of larger profits becomes the driving force.

Exporting and importing usually involves working with a foreign contractor or distributor in an arms-length transaction. These relationships may work well, but it may be difficult to ensure that the foreign partner will uphold its end of the agreement. Frictions are common, and they can intensify if left unchecked. When such conflicts develop, the company might decide that its own personnel could do a better job and at a lower cost. At this point, the company might open its own office in the country.

Another source of concern with arms-length foreign partners is the need to share information the partner needs to do its job properly. For example, a U.S. computer manufacturer might hire a Chinese firm to make computers to the U.S. firm's specifications for sale in China. This would obviously require the U.S. firm to turn over design and manufacturing details to its Chinese partner. This might not be a problem in the early stages of the relationship, when activity is low. However, as the local market increases, the U.S. company would have to worry about creating a potential competitor. This might lead it to decide to set up shop in China and build the next-generation computer itself.

As a foreign operation grows, a point may be reached where direct foreign involvement would be more profitable and efficient. Importing and exporting tend to involve low fixed costs but relatively high variable costs. More ambitious plans, such as building distribution warehouses or production facilities, involve higher fixed but lower variable costs. As output increases, the least cost method for foreign participation will shift from the passive mode to more intensive direct involvement.

SELF-TEST QUESTION   What are some considerations that cause companies to increase their direct presence in foreign countries?

HOW COMPANIES DECIDE WHERE TO GO ABROAD

The decision to establish a more active international presence is a goal-oriented decision, so it is important to identify the motives and goals for going abroad. Some motives are listed below.

1. *Market seekers.* These companies want to increase their sales by going to countries with strong market potential, particularly before competition becomes intense or if a failure to gain a market share would put the company at a competitive disadvantage elsewhere. For an example, cell phone providers are moving into China in hopes of gaining market share in the world's largest marketplace.
2. *Input resource seekers.* These firms go abroad to obtain the resources necessary to be competitive. Oil and mining companies were among the first industries to move abroad in search of input resources.
3. *Production efficiency seekers.* Firms want to serve their markets at the lowest possible cost, so they look for locations where needed inputs are available at the lowest costs. Labor-intensive production operations that require semi-skilled workers often fall into this category, and examples include textile plants and electronics assembly operations.
4. *Political safety seekers.* Some companies locate facilities in countries that are politically stable and amenable to private enterprise, and other companies move their headquarters to avoid a threatening business environment. An early example of a company that moved to escape a threatening business environment is the Bata Shoe Organization. After the Nazi invasion of Czecho-

AN AMERICAN ICON GONE ABROAD

On January 8, 2004, Levi Strauss & Co. closed its last two sewing plants in the United States. The financially troubled clothing manufacturer's jeans have long been a world-renowned symbol of America. Poor financial results have forced the manufacturer to gradually shift its production overseas. The final closing, announced in September 2003, marked the end of an era for the company that once had 63 manufacturing plants in the United States.

Levi Strauss was founded in San Francisco during the 1850 California Gold Rush. Originally made for miners and other workers, Levi's became popular in the 1950s and its popularity grew. As it grew, Levi Strauss resisted the temptation to move its manufacturing overseas. But in recent years, changing fashion trends and competition spelled trouble for Levi Strauss. Harry Bernard, a San Francisco–based apparel marketing consultant, said, "there are two sets of dynamics at work here. One is the real sense of fashion that was lost, and the other is operating style and operating capabilities." There was a time when Levi Strauss faced no market time constraints and enjoyed unending demand.

Levi's financial peak occurred in 1996 when it reported earnings of $7.1 billion. However, profits had declined each year since, with 2002 sales of $4.1 billion and 2003 sales expected to be 2 to 3 percent lower. Levi's global workforce has been shrinking along with its profits. In 1996, Levi had 37,000 employees, but by the end of 2003 that number had declined to 12,000, with only half of its workforce in the United States. Levi will continue to run its design and sales departments in the United States, and its headquarters will remain in San Francisco.

A Levi spokesman said that the company was making a delayed, but necessary, business decision. He said, "We tried to do our best to maintain manufacturing in the United States, but we have to be competitive to survive as a company." Indeed, most of Levi's competitors had long since made the move abroad. The spokesman went on to say, "We're still an American brand, but we're also a brand and a company whose products have been adopted by consumers around the world. We have to operate as a global company." According to retail analyst Walter Loeb, Levi's symbolic presence in the United States is worth less than the increased profitability of moving abroad.

This process of moving abroad has slowly developed since the late 1990s. In a 1999 discussion on PBS's Online NewsHour, Carol Emert, a retail reporter for the *San Francisco Chronicle*, offered this view on Levi Strauss moving manufacturing abroad:

> It doesn't really have as much to do with their softness at retail. They closed 13 plants last year, and fired about 7,000 people, and that was because of softness at retail. The plant closings that were announced this week are really a long-term strategic decision by the company, that they have to give up their humanitarian goal of manufacturing in the United States. They simply can't compete.

Five years before the final plant closings, the course appeared to be set toward foreign manufacturing.

Moving manufacturing abroad is a matter of survival for some firms. Levi Strauss must fear that the move abroad will only slow the bleeding. Low foreign labor costs may allow Levi to engage more in price competition, but tense brand competition, declining sales, and changing fashion tastes may provide Levi a hurdle that it cannot jump with low labor costs alone.

Sources: "Levi Strauss Closes Last Two U.S. Plants," *CNN.com*, January 8, 2004, **http://www.cnn.com**, and "Leaving Levi's," Online NewsHour with Jim Lehrer, February 23, 1999.

slovakia in 1939, Bata moved to Canada rather than face the uncertainties of operating under German occupation. Likewise, Jardine Matheson, a Hong Kong company, moved its headquarters to Bermuda prior to the transfer of Hong Kong from Britain to China because of the uncertainties of what the communist officials would do once they assumed control.

Choosing a Country

Once a company decides to go abroad, it must answer two questions: Where should we produce, and where should we sell? At times it makes sense to produce and sell in the same country, but at other times it is prudent to separate the two decisions.

This separation is especially useful if a country gives special tax, financing, and/or labor rule concessions to companies that locate manufacturing facilities in special economic zones and produce only for export. Headlines of companies closing U.S. facilities and moving production abroad because of the competitive pressures have become common. Companies are also moving customer services or routine software development operations abroad because the same service or expertise can be obtained at a fraction of the domestic cost. For a company contemplating a move abroad, the following four factors should be considered:

1. *Target market size.* The size of the potential market is obviously an important consideration, as is the possibility of gaining economies of scale through growth.
2. *Compatibility with existing operations.* Countries that share a border with the home country, have existing successful operations, and have the same language and cultural characteristics are preferred candidates for expansion. Familiarity is probably more important to companies early in their international operations than later.
3. *Costs of producing in or serving a market.* Most news articles about companies that close U.S. factories and move production overseas focus on jobs because wage rates are lower in developing countries. Wage rates are certainly lower in many foreign countries, but low wages are not necessarily a sufficient reason for a move overseas. Low-cost workers in other countries may require costly training, foreign production may require the use of less efficient technology, quality may suffer, and transportation costs may absorb most of the potential savings. The total costs of an overseas move must be taken into account.
4. *Risks.* The risks associated with producing or selling varies widely across countries, and they must be factored into foreign investment decisions. Many different risks could be identified, and many classifications could be used, but the key ones include (a) **business risk**, which is the risk of doing business in the new environment, and (b) **country risk**, which is the additional risk, on top of the usual business risk, incurred when operating in a foreign country. Business risk exists in all countries (whether home or foreign), but it varies across countries. Country risk arises mainly out of indigenous factors such as the host country's resource endowment, religion, culture, currency reserves, political stability, value system, administrative procedures, likelihood of expropriation, and so on.

Business Risk
The risk of doing business in the new environment. It exists in all countries but varies across countries.

Country Risk
The additional risk, on top of the usual business risk, when operating in a foreign country. It arises mainly out of indigenous factors.

Country Attractiveness Scorecard
A system used to consolidate information and compare the attractiveness of different countries.

Country Attractiveness Scorecard

Once a company has evaluated alternative production and distribution facilities, it needs a system to consolidate information and compare the attractiveness of different countries. Many different methods have been suggested, but we can summarize these approaches in what is called a **country attractiveness scorecard**. The scorecard starts with two broad classes of information: *trade-off variables*, sometimes called *compensatory variables*, and *go/no-go variables*, or *noncompensatory variables*. Trade-off variables are those where a poor value for one variable can be offset by a good value for another. For instance, Country A may appear to be riskier than Country B, but if the expected return in A is significantly higher than that in B, the higher return might compensate for the higher risk. However, the go/no-go variables are either acceptable or unacceptable, and if they are unacceptable, the country is dropped from further consideration regardless of its potential profitability.

Thus, the first step in the analysis is to list the go/no-go variables and screen possible countries on that basis. Assume that a company has identified four go/no-go variables:

1. 100 percent foreign ownership must be allowed.
2. The subsidiary must be allowed to pay license and management fees.
3. It must be possible to repatriate at least 50 percent of local earnings.
4. The subsidiary must be allowed to sell in the country's domestic market.

Many other factors could, of course, be considered. Note too that the go/no go criteria are rather arbitrary, and they would at times prevent a value-maximizing decision. Still, they do serve as an initial screen that many companies find useful for planning purposes.

In addition to the go/no-go criteria, companies identify two sets of variables, those relating to potential profitability and those relating to risk. The variables in each list are somewhat subjective, and they will differ across companies. Table 4-3 illustrates a country attractiveness scorecard. The first column lists the variables, while the second column shows each variable's "weight," or importance, as determined by management. The last four columns show management's assessment of Countries A through D for each variable.

The last line of the scorecard gives the overall score for each country, calculated as the total return minus the total risk for the country. In Table 4-3, Country A has the lowest return potential, but it also has the lowest risk score; and overall, it dominates the other countries. Remember, countries that fail to jump the go/no-go hurdle have already been eliminated, so this analysis ranks the countries in terms of attractiveness. This analysis suggests that Country A is a good candidate, but it should not be interpreted as the unambiguous preferred location. A more in-depth analysis would be used to flesh out the characteristics of the top few locations, and this might lead to a change in the rankings.

TABLE 4-3 | Country Attractiveness Scorecard

		COUNTRIES			
	Weight	A	B	C	D
Return Variables (Higher is Better)					
1. Potential market size in first 2 years	0-3	3	2	3	1
2. Potential market size in 5 years	0-5	4	4	3	5
3. Expected market share in 2 years	0-3	1	2	3	2
4. Expected market share in 5 years	0-5	3	3	4	4
5. Expected profit margin	0-5	4	4	3	4
6. Amount of investment required	0-4	2	3	3	2
7. Fairness of the tax system	0-4	3	3	4	3
Total for return		20	21	23	21
Risk Variables (Lower Is Better)					
1. Strength of competitors in local market	5-0	1	3	3	2
2. Extent of government red tape	3-0	1	2	2	3
3. Potential for political unrest	3-0	1	1	2	1
4. Quality and transparency of accounting rules	4-0	2	2	2	3
5. Enforcement and effectiveness of legal code	5-0	2	2	3	2
6. Availability of foreign exchange	5-0	1	2	2	1
7. Compatibility with global network	5-0	3	3	4	3
Total for risk		11	15	18	15
Overall country score (Return − Risk)		9	6	5	6

Identify and briefly explain some motives for a firm going abroad.
At a minimum, what four factors should be considered when a firm
contemplates a move abroad?
What is the country attractiveness scorecard? How is it used?

DETERMINING HOW TO ENTER THE CHOSEN COUNTRIES

As noted earlier, for most companies the first step in "going global" involves importing and exporting. Beyond that, companies can take several different steps. Some are relatively active, involving foreign direct investments, while others are more passive, such as licensing technology to a foreign producer or franchising to a local owner. Some other strategies include contracting production, having a plant built as a "turnkey operation," and joint ventures. How does a company choose which strategy to use? While there is no single best answer to this question, the **OLI paradigm**, developed by Peter Buckley and Mark Casson, is often used to help determine if a foreign direct investment (FDI) makes sense.

OLI Paradigm
A tool used for evaluating foreign direct investments. It considers three dimensions: owner-specific advantages, location-specific advantages, and internalization advantages.

The OLI Paradigm

According to Buckley and Casson, companies need to consider three dimensions when evaluating potential foreign direct investments: **O**wner-specific advantages, **L**ocation-specific advantages, and **I**nternalization, hence the name OLI paradigm.[5] **Owner-specific advantages** are competitive advantages in its home market that a company can transfer to another country. This would include patents, copyrights, trademarks, and process technology.

Owner-Specific Advantages
Competitive advantages in its home market that a company can transfer to another country.

Location-specific advantages are local attributes or resources that can be used by the firm to enhance its global competitiveness. They include scarce input resources such as oil or minerals, a highly educated and productive workforce, and a large domestic market for the company's products.

Location-Specific Advantages
Local attributes or resources that can be used by the firm to enhance its global competitiveness.

Internalization advantages refer to the use of nonpatentable intangible assets such as "know-how," product designs, research skills, customer lists, and the like. Companies need to keep this information confidential, and multinational firms can utilize such information throughout their global organizations without having to share it with potential competitors. In any event, the ability to use this type of valuable information, which is costly and time consuming to develop, on a broad scale gives multinational firms a significant advantage.

Internalization Advantages
Valuable assets usually associated with "know-how," product designs, research skills, and customer lists. Information that the company needs to keep confidential to maintain its competitive advantage.

Entry Methods for Foreign Direct Investment

If all of the OLI advantages exist, then companies should seriously consider making foreign direct investments in countries identified as good candidates for such investments. The two primary procedures are (1) acquire an existing company in the host country and (2) start from scratch and build the necessary facilities and infrastructure, called a *greenfield investment*. Sometimes both options are available; sometimes only one possibility exists. Assuming that both options are possible, we now discuss some factors the company should consider.

ACQUISITION OF AN EXISTING COMPANY This is often the most efficient and cost-effective way to expand overseas. Some of the advantages are listed here.

---

[5]Peter J. Buckley and Mark Casson, *The Future of the Multinational Enterprise* (London: McMillan, 1976). John Dunning has also contributed to this theory.

1. Purchasing an existing company does not add productive capacity to the market. If overcapacity exists, this can be a critical consideration, and it is why most FDIs in industries such as steel, tires, and other "old-economy" sectors are usually accomplished through acquisitions rather than building new facilities.
2. Purchasing an existing company also eliminates a competitor. The realignment and consolidation of the global publishing industry has been driven in part by this consideration. Also, buying a company prevents another competitor from acquiring it, thus protecting the acquiring company's position.
3. Purchasing a facility as a "going concern" allows the acquirer to avoid startup problems often associated with new facilities.
4. It is often easier to obtain financing for an acquisition because the lender can rely on historical information about the target company when assessing loan risk.
5. If an existing operation is purchased, then revenues begin immediately, and competitors do not have time to plan countermeasures.

Greenfield Investment
The name given when companies expand internationally by building operations de novo rather than through acquisitions.

GREENFIELD INVESTMENT Companies that expand internationally by building operations de novo through a **greenfield investment** usually do so for three reasons:

1. There are no attractive acquisition candidates available.
2. Acquiring an existing company means that existing problems and liabilities are acquired as well. For example, many potential Russian acquisitions were unattractive because the government had not clarified the liability of new owners for environmental problems underneath the existing industrial facilities.
3. Acquisitions can be more difficult to finance because of the liability issue. Also, it is often difficult to conduct a proper "due diligence" analysis of an acquisition target because accounting and production data are either not available or not reliable. If the proper price cannot be determined, it may be better to just start the business from scratch.

Alternatives to Foreign Direct Investment

By far the most important reason companies choose FDI over licensing and other procedures has to do with control. A company must often maintain absolute control over key information to keep it from competitors. This is difficult if the company must deal with other parties that have different objectives. However, if control is not the dominant issue and the company does not have the advantages described in the OLI paradigm, it may choose to increase its global activities through collaborative arrangements with other companies. Arrangements that place most of the operating burden on foreign partners are most common when the company has little experience with foreign operations or when it is trying to locate in a country that is very different from its home country. Companies that find themselves in this position usually cite the following reasons for considering collaboration:

1. *Expense.* It may be expensive to build a factory from the ground up in another country, so it may be less expensive to contract with another firm to handle work for the company. This is an important consideration for companies that outsource most of their production overseas, such as clothing manufacturers.
2. *Maintain focus at home.* Licensing and other forms of collaboration can allow a company to obtain additional revenues from its assets without having to divert attention to problems abroad. This is particularly important for products that are not part of the strategic core, where licensing is generally impractical.
3. *Reduce competition.* The company may be able to avoid competing directly with a foreign company and instead can work with it for the benefit of both.

4. *Gain knowledge.* Collaborative arrangements with foreign companies can be used to gain experience and knowledge, putting the firm in a better position to make an FDI at a later date.

5. *Governmental and political considerations.* Some countries do not permit foreign companies to own 100 percent of the equity of a local operation, so if the company wants to establish a presence in that country, it must enter a partnership with a local firm. In other situations, "local" companies may have an advantage in contract bidding or using local resources.

SELF-TEST QUESTIONS What are the three legs of the OLI paradigm?

What are the two primary methods for entering a foreign country through direct investment? What are the reasons for choosing one method over the other?

Why might a company consider collaboration rather than FDI?

TYPES OF COLLABORATIVE ARRANGEMENTS

Collaborative Arrangements
Arrangements that allow a company to participate in global commerce without incurring the full cost or the total risk of the venture.

There are six **collaborative arrangements** that allow a company to participate in global commerce without incurring the full cost or the total risk that comes from such ventures: (1) *licensing*, (2) *franchising*, (3) *management contracts*, (4) *turnkey operations*, (5) *joint ventures*, and (6) *equity alliances*. All of these arrangements should be analyzed using the same tools that are employed to evaluate foreign direct investments. Thus, a company must forecast the cash flows that would accrue if it participates in the arrangement, estimate the risk entailed, and then discount the cash flows at the appropriate required rate of return. If the net present value of the cash flows is positive, then the proposed arrangement is economically viable.

Licensing

Licensing
Allows a company to earn a return from an intangible asset by granting permission for another firm to use the asset in its own production and marketing operations.

Licensing allows companies to earn returns from intangible assets by granting permission for another firm to use an asset in its own production and marketing operations. Patents, copyrights, trademarks, and other forms of intangible property can be licensed, and the company can write the contract in a manner that protects its interests. The license can be *exclusive*, which grants the licensee a monopoly in a particular region or for a fixed period of time. It can also be *nonexclusive* in the sense that other companies in the same area can also be granted similar licenses. If the asset is vital to the granting company's operations, it can structure the contract so that the licensee is precluded from competing with the licensor in specified markets.

There are two circumstances under which licensing can generate controversy. First, many MNEs insist on using a formal license agreement with their foreign subsidiaries, where the license defines the property rights that have been transferred and specifies the cash flows that must be sent to the parent. License fees are a tax-deductible expense for the subsidiary, thus reducing taxable income and local taxes paid, but they are taxable income for the parent, so some taxes are paid in the home country rather than in the host country. Second, if the host country has a balance of payments problem, then license fees can be used to get around restrictions on capital transfers. These two factors make host countries wary of licensing fees, and that makes it important that such fees be negotiated before capital is invested in a foreign operation.

The second controversial issue is the complaint that license fees are often unreasonably high for developing countries that need intangible assets but do not have the resources to pay the fees. Developed industrial countries have a near monopoly on research and development; hence, they may be able to extract monopoly rents via licensing. A prime example is the licensing of pharmaceuticals to combat

HIV/AIDS in Sub-Saharan Africa, where millions of people are dying every year because they cannot afford the medications. Even if you do not agree with the African nations' position, there is an understandable logic to it, and this example reinforces our suggestion that license fees be negotiated early.

Franchising

Franchising
A collaborative arrangement that involves the transfer of a trademark and its business processes to a foreign entity and the continual infusion of required assets for the franchisee to operate.

Franchising involves the transfer of a trademark and its business processes to a foreign entity, along with a continual infusion of assets the franchisee needs to operate. Examples of franchisers include McDonald's, Kentucky Fried Chicken, 7-Eleven, and Jiffy Lube. The best franchises are characterized by close cooperation between the franchiser and franchisees so that a customer receives the same product at every location. A Big Mac in Atlanta, Paris, Munich, Tokyo, or Moscow is virtually the same product, and, to a very great extent, the restaurants look the same everywhere. However, you can buy a beer with your Big Mac in Munich and wine in Paris, but not in Atlanta. Thus, some adjustments to cultural differences are necessary, but the more adjustments made, the less the franchise is recognizable to customers from other countries, and the less the franchiser is needed.

Management Contracts

Management Contracts
Occur when a foreign company is hired by the owner of the asset to run the operation for a contracted payment; used when the foreign company manages better than the owners.

Management contracts are useful if a foreign company can manage an operation better than its owners. Specialized management companies provide expertise, and some of them combine the management contract with a type of franchise as part of the deal. Such arrangements are often seen in the hotel industry, where a hotel in a foreign country has the name of a familiar international chain but is actually owned by local nationals. The hotel chain franchises the name and certain services, such as reservations, and it also trains the local staff and provides expatriate managers. Also, in regions where governments have nationalized foreign companies, it is not unusual for the former owners to be retained as managers via a management contract.

Turnkey Operations

Turnkey Operations
Ownership is transferred after the facility is built and tested, so the owner only runs the operations.

Turnkey operations are usually performed by international construction companies with expertise in the design and construction of complex industrial plants. The company is hired to design, build, and test the facility and to ensure that it operates as intended. It is then transferred to the owner, who only has to "turn the key" to place the facility into production. Halliburton, Fluor-Daniel, and Bechtel are examples of companies that engage in these activities. The turnkey contract may be with a foreign government, and it is not unusual for the company to run the operation after it is completed. In this case, the builder would also sign a management contract.

Joint Ventures

Joint Ventures
Business ventures formed by two or more companies to achieve a specific, but limited, objective.

Joint ventures are business ventures formed by two or more companies to achieve a specific, but limited, objective. An example would be the development of an offshore oil field, where a group of companies combines to build and operate a drilling platform and related pipeline. The project is owned equally by the affiliated enterprises, and its management could be controlled either by one of the partners or by a separate management organization established just for the project. The venture may be organized as a partnership, a corporation, a joint-stock company, or some other legal form, and it can continue indefinitely. The rationale for a joint venture is usually to diversify risk among the members and/or to combine expertise and assets that none of the participants provide alone. Companies that are new to foreign operations may start by establishing a joint venture with a local company. The local company provides local knowledge, and the foreign partner brings technology, capital, and other types of knowledge to the table. Control is usually shared among the participants, so companies that are comfortable with decentralized operations are more likely to use joint ventures than highly centralized firms.

Many joint ventures are dissolved because they have completed their limited objective, but many others break down because of dissension among the members. Some of the factors that lead to dissension are listed here:

1. Over time, joint venture participants may come to have different objectives for the operation, or see it as becoming more or less important for their core business. Circumstances change, as do overall corporate strategies, causing one partner to want to expand the venture while the other wants to scale it back and withdraw investment from it.
2. Over time, participants can disagree on control issues. Specifying in detail the rights and responsibilities of all the participants is critical in avoiding such disputes.
3. Many breakdowns are caused by some participants perceiving that others are not contributing their "fair share." This is a problem especially when things are not going well.
4. If companies participating in the joint venture have very different corporate cultures and disagree about issues such as compensation and the decision-making process, then problems are likely to arise.

Equity Alliances

Equity Alliances
Collaborative arrangements that involve independent companies in related or supporting fields that band together to solidify a collaboration contract and make it harder to break.

Equity alliances exist when companies in related or supporting fields band together to make a collaboration contract harder to break. Cross ownership of equity is common in such arrangements. The most successful models for equity alliances are the *keiretsu* in Japan and the *chaebol* in Korea. These are large groupings of industrial and financial companies under one umbrella that are controlled by a single family or company. Western equity alliances differ from their Asian counterparts because, generally, the independent companies are not all controlled by a single person or group, so their cooperation continues only as long as it is in the best interests of all the individual companies. Equity alliances are quite common in the airline industry, where they link together airlines with good international route systems and those with good domestic systems.

SELF-TEST QUESTIONS
What are some different types of collaborative arrangements that companies can employ? How do they differ from one another?
How can licensing generate controversy?
What are some problems that can occur over time with a joint venture?

SUMMARY

In this chapter we examined the ways in which an MNE may conduct business around the world. We began with a discussion of traditional trade theories and focused on answering the question, "Why, when, and how should companies go abroad?" Companies begin international trade through exports and imports; however, as they mature they increase their direct presence in foreign countries and employ more active strategies in those markets. We discussed how an MNE decides where to go abroad and what factors it must consider when making this decision. Once it has decided where to go, it then must decide how to enter that market. While there is no single criterion that answers this question, the OLI paradigm helps MNEs decide when foreign direct investment makes sense. This chapter laid out the basic foundation of this framework. Of course, the MNE can decide on a presence in which it maintains full control of global operations, or it can decide on a more collaborative arrangement. This chapter detailed the different types of collaborative arrangements available. The key concepts discussed in this chapter are listed below.

- **Mercantilism** is an economic and military system developed prior to the late 18th century to gain and retain national power and wealth. Trade, to a mercantilist, was a zero-sum game.
- **Absolute advantage** was Adam Smith's theory that all countries can gain from specialization and trade, thus resulting in a positive-sum game. This theory failed if any single country held an absolute advantage in the production of most goods and services.
- **Comparative advantage** was David Ricardo's theory that all countries could still gain from specialization and trade if they produced those goods in which they were relatively more efficient than others. The comparative advantage model is the intellectual basis for the World Trade Organization's (WTO) work today, and it is still useful for explaining many decisions made by MNEs today.
- **Gross world product** is the aggregate value of all goods and services produced worldwide in a given year.
- There are some **shortcomings of the classical trade theories** when applied today: (1) Countries do not behave in the manner indicated by the theory of comparative advantage. They continue producing items for which they have no comparative advantage. (2) Prices charged for internationally traded goods are assumed to be set in a free and competitive market; however, they are often determined by administrative processes, not market forces. (3) Factors of production (land, labor, and capital) are assumed to be fully employed at a constant average cost, homogeneous, and interchangeable; however, economies of scale and scope, varying skill requirements, and unequal quality violate these assumptions. (4) Factors of production are assumed to be mobile within a country but not between countries; however, capital, technology, and labor are globally mobile, so, as they move between countries comparative advantages change. (5) The classical trade theories do not consider transaction costs, impact of uncertainty on trade, segmented markets, and differentiated products. (6) Comparative advantage is a static model. It does not explain how such advantages are gained and lost over time, nor does it consider the effects of trade on people in each country.
- The **motivations for** a company to consider **exporting and importing** are (1) excess domestic capacity, (2) economies of scale, (3) diversification and flexibility, (4) mature domestic products are growth products abroad, and (5) outsourcing abroad.
- Seeking a more active international presence involves identifying a company's motives/goals for going abroad: (1) **market seekers**, (2) **input resource seekers**, (3) **production efficiency seekers**, and (4) **political safety seekers**.
- Four factors should be considered when contemplating a move abroad: (1) **target market size**, (2) **compatibility with existing operations**, (3) **costs of producing in or serving a market**, and (4) **risk**.
- Many different risks could be identified, and many classifications could be used, but the key ones include business and country risk. **Business risk** is the risk of doing business in the new environment, while **country risk** is the additional risk, on top of the usual business risk, incurred when operating in a foreign country. It arises mainly out of indigenous factors such as the host country's resource endowment, religion, culture, currency reserves, political stability, value system, administrative procedures, likelihood of expropriation, and so on.
- The **country attractiveness scorecard** is a system used to consolidate information and compare the attractiveness of different countries. The scorecard starts with trade-off variables and go/no-go variables. Trade-off variables are those where a poor value for one variable can be offset by a good value for another. The go/no-go variables are either acceptable or unacceptable, and if they are

unacceptable, the country is dropped from further consideration regardless of its potential profitability.

- The **OLI paradigm** is a tool used to help a company decide when foreign direct investment makes sense. It considers **owner-specific advantages**, **location-specific advantages**, and **internalization advantages**.

- **Owner-specific advantages** include competitive advantages in its home market that a company can transfer to another country.

- **Location-specific advantages** are local attributes or resources that can be used by the firm to enhance its global competitiveness.

- **Internalization advantages** are valuable assets usually associated with "know-how," product design, research skills, and customer lists. They are information that the company needs to keep confidential to maintain its competitive advantage.

- If a company decides to enter a particular country through direct investment in productive facilities, it must determine the optimal strategy for investment. The two primary procedures are **acquisitions** and **greenfield investments**. Greenfield investments involve a company expanding internationally by building operations de novo.

- Companies that expand through greenfield investments do so for three reasons: (1) There are **no attractive acquisition candidates available**, (2) acquiring an existing company means that **existing problems and liabilities are acquired** as well, and (3) **acquisitions can be more difficult to finance** due to liability.

- Companies cite the following reasons for increasing their global activities through collaboration: (1) **expense**, (2) **maintain focus at home**, (3) **reduce competition**, (4) **gain knowledge**, and (5) **governmental and political considerations**.

- A **collaborative arrangement** is the general name given to arrangements that allow a company to participate in global commerce without incurring the full cost or the total risk that comes from such ventures. Different collaborative arrangements include licensing, franchising, management contracts, turnkey operations, joint ventures, and equity alliances.

- **Licensing** is a collaborative arrangement that allows companies to earn returns from intangible assets by granting permission for other firms to use the assets in its own production and marketing operations.

- **Franchising** is a collaborative arrangement that involves the transfer of a trademark and business processes to a foreign entity and the continual infusion of required assets needed for the franchisee to operate.

- **Management contracts** occur when a foreign company is hired by the owner of the asset to run the operation for a contracted payment. These are used when the foreign company is a better manager than the owner.

- **Turnkey operations** occur when ownership is transferred after the facility is built and tested, so the owner only runs the operations.

- **Joint ventures** are business ventures formed by two or more companies to achieve a specific, but limited, objective. The rationale for a joint venture is usually to diversify risk among the members and/or to combine expertise and assets that none of the participants provide alone.

- **Equity alliances** are collaborative arrangements that involve independent companies in related or supporting fields that band together to solidify a collaboration contract and make it harder to break. Cross ownership of equity is common in such arrangements. The most successful models for equity alliances are the *keiretsu* in Japan and the *chaebol* in Korea.

QUESTIONS

(4-1) How do international trade and foreign direct investment affect the valuation equation?

(4-2) Why is the theory of comparative advantage still important today?

(4-3) Briefly explain whether the following statement is true or false: "The additional complexities faced today invalidate the basic principles of the classic theories of international trade, and they are less helpful in explaining global trading and investment."

(4-4) Briefly explain whether the following statement is true or false: "The classic theories of international trade take into consideration the business enterprises that make the goods and conduct the trading that occurs internationally."

(4-5) When would you classify a company as a "political safety seeker"?

(4-6) When might a company separate out the decision of selling and producing in a country?

(4-7) Why would you expect U.S. companies to have a greater presence in Canada than in Mexico?

(4-8) Explain whether the following statement is true or false: "U.S. companies close their factories here and locate them abroad for the sole reason that wage rates are lower in developing countries."

(4-9) Differentiate between business and country risk.

(4-10) When would a company use a country attractiveness scorecard? How does this tool work?

(4-11) What are compensatory variables? Noncompensatory variables? How do they enter into a company's decision to locate abroad? How are they used in the country attractiveness scorecard?

(4-12) What is the OLI paradigm and for what purpose is it used?

(4-13) Differentiate among owner-specific, location-specific, and internalization advantages. Give an example of each.

(4-14) What is a greenfield investment?

(4-15) Why might a company decide to acquire a company abroad? Why might a company choose to use a greenfield investment?

(4-16) Why would a firm choose FDI over a collaborative arrangement? Why might it choose a collaborative arrangement over FDI?

(4-17) When might a firm choose licensing as a collaborative arrangement? What are exclusive and nonexclusive licenses? What are two controversial issues related to licensing?

(4-18) When might a firm choose franchising as a collaborative arrangement? What dilemma does a franchiser face?

(4-19) What are joint ventures, and what is the rationale behind their formation? How can they be organized?

(4-20) How do Western equity alliances differ from their Asian counterparts?

SELF-TEST PROBLEMS   Solutions Appear in Appendix B

(ST-1) Define each of the following terms:
Key Terms a. Mercantilism; absolute advantage; comparative advantage
b. Gross world product (GWP)
c. Business risk; country risk
d. Country attractiveness scorecard

e. OLI paradigm
f. Owner-specific advantages; location-specific advantages; internalization advantages
g. Greenfield investment
h. Collaborative arrangements; licensing; franchising; management contracts
i. Turnkey operations; joint ventures; equity alliances

(ST-2) You are given the following data:

Trade Theory

Production Capacity and Output

| Country | Available Production Units | OUTPUT PER UNIT OF INPUT | |
		Barrels of Tea	Bushels of Corn
F	2,500	7.5	7.5
G	2,500	15.0	10.0

Initial Production, Assuming No Trade (65 percent Tea, 35 percent Corn)

Country	Barrels of Tea	Bushels of Corn
F	12,187.5	6,562.5
G	24,375.0	8,750.0
Total	36,562.5 barrels	15,312.5 bushels

Use the data to answer the following questions; however, before answering them you may want to develop a table similar to Table 4-2.
a. Does one of the countries have an absolute advantage over the other? If so, which one?
b. Which country has the least absolute disadvantage in harvesting corn?
c. Which country should specialize in producing tea? Which country should specialize in harvesting corn?
d. What is the domestic price for a bushel of corn (in terms of barrels of tea) in Country G?
e. Assume that trade between the two nations occurs at the domestic price for a bushel of corn (in terms of barrels of tea) in Country G, and Country G consumes exactly the same quantities of both products as it did with no trade. Is Country F better or worse off? Explain. Has GWP improved or worsened? Explain.
f. What is the domestic price for a bushel of corn (in terms of barrels of tea) in Country F?
g. Assume now that trade between the two nations occurs at the domestic price for a bushel of corn (in terms of barrels of tea) in Country F, and Country F consumes exactly the same quantities of both products as it did with no trade. Is Country G better or worse off? Explain. Has GWP improved or worsened? Explain.
h. Assume that the price for a bushel of corn is 1.43 barrels of tea, and Country G consumes exactly the same number of bushels of corn as it did in the no-trade case. Which country is better off? Explain. Has GWP improved or worsened? Explain.

STARTER PROBLEMS

(4-1) Management for Daniel Smitherson Inc. is considering building a manufacturing plant abroad. They have developed the following scorecard to help them decide in which country the plant should be built.

Country Attractiveness
Scorecard

Country Attractiveness Scorecard

			COUNTRIES		
	Weight	A	B	C	D
Return Variables (Higher Is Better)					
1. Potential market size in first 2 years	0-3	2	1	3	3
2. Potential market size in 5 years	0-5	3	4	3	2
3. Expected market share in 2 years	0-3	1	1	2	1
4. Expected market share in 5 years	0-5	3	3	2	1
5. Expected profit margin	0-5	2	4	5	3
6. Amount of investment required	0-4	1	3	3	4
7. Fairness of the tax system	0-4	2	1	4	3
Risk Variables (Lower Is Better)					
1. Strength of competitors in local market	5-0	4	1	3	2
2. Extent of government red tape	3-0	3	2	2	1
3. Potential for political unrest	3-0	3	1	1	2
4. Quality and transparency of accounting rules	4-0	1	2	3	2
5. Enforcement and effectiveness of legal code	5-0	1	2	4	2
6. Availability of foreign exchange	5-0	3	1	2	2
7. Compatibility with global network	5-0	1	1	2	2

a. Complete the Country Attractiveness Scorecard.
b. Which country has the best return ranking? (Hint: highest score = best.)
c. Which country has the best risk ranking? (Hint: lowest score = best.)
d. From the scores shown on the scorecard, which country ranks the highest? Ranks the lowest? Rank the countries from highest to lowest on the basis of their overall rankings.
e. Assume that management considers the following variables as requirements before they will enter a particular country: (1) There must be 100 percent foreign ownership, and (2) the local subsidiary must pay license and management fees. It has just been discovered that Country B will not allow 100 percent foreign ownership. Does this change your answer to part d? How do the countries now rank in terms of their overall rankings? Which country now ranks the highest?

(4-2) You are given the following data:

Trade Theory

Production Capacity and Output

		OUTPUT PER UNIT OF INPUT	
Country	Available Production Units	Bushels of Wheat	Crates of Widgets
X	5,000	19.0	28.5
Y	5,000	18.0	13.0

Initial Production, Assuming No Trade
(48 percent Wheat, 52 percent Widgets)

Country	Bushels of Wheat	Crates of Widgets
X	45,600	74,100
Y	43,200	33,800
Total	88,800 bushels	107,900 crates

Use the data to answer the following questions; however, before answering them you may want to develop a table similar to Table 4-2.

a. Does one of the countries have an absolute advantage over the other? If so, which one?

b. Which country has the least absolute disadvantage in wheat production?

c. Which country should specialize in producing wheat? Which country should specialize in producing widgets?

d. What is the domestic price for a bushel of wheat (in terms of crates of widgets) in Country X?

e. Assume that trade between the two nations occurs at the domestic price for a bushel of wheat (in terms of crates of widgets) in Country X, and Country X consumes exactly the same quantities of both products as it did with no trade. Is Country Y better or worse off? Explain. Has GWP improved or worsened? Explain.

f. What is the domestic price for a bushel of wheat (in terms of crates of widgets) in Country Y?

g. Assume now that trade between the two nations occurs at the domestic price for a bushel of wheat (in terms of crates of widgets) in Country Y, and Country Y consumes exactly the same quantities of both products as it did with no trade. Is Country X better or worse off? Explain. Has GWP improved or worsened? Explain.

h. Assume that the price for a bushel of wheat is 0.95 crate of widgets, and Country X consumes 46,500 bushels of wheat. Which country is better off? Explain. Has GWP improved or worsened? Explain.

EXAM-TYPE PROBLEMS

(4-3) CuervoRodriguez International is considering undertaking a new project abroad.
Country Attractiveness Scorecard Management must decide where to locate the new project's production facilities. They have developed the following scorecard to help them with their decision.

a. Complete the Country Attractiveness Scorecard below.

b. Which country has the best return ranking? (Hint: highest score = best.)

c. Which country has the best risk ranking? (Hint: lowest score = best.)

d. From the scores shown on the scorecard, which country ranks the highest? Ranks the lowest? Rank the countries from highest to lowest overall ranking.

e. Assume that CuervoRodriguez considers the following variables as requirements before they will enter a particular country: (1) There must be 100 percent foreign ownership, and (2) the local subsidiary must pay license and management fees. It has just been discovered that Country N will not allow the local subsidiary to pay license and management fees. Does this change your answer to part d? How do the countries now rank in terms of overall rankings? Which country now ranks the highest?

Country Attractiveness Scorecard

		COUNTRIES			
	Weight	M	N	O	P
Return Variables (Higher Is Better)					
1. Potential market size	0-4	3	3	2	3
2. Potential market share	0-4	2	2	3	4
3. Expected profit margin	0-5	2	3	2	4
4. Amount of investment required	0-3	2	1	3	3
5. Fairness of the tax system	0-5	1	3	4	2

		COUNTRIES			
	Weight	M	N	O	P
Risk Variables (Lower Is Better)					
1. Strength of local competitors	5-0	1	1	2	4
2. Government red tape	4-0	1	2	3	3
3. Potential for political unrest	3-0	1	1	3	3
4. Accounting and legal systems	5-0	2	2	5	4
5. Availability of foreign exchange	3-0	2	2	3	3

(4-4) You are given the following data:

Trade Theory

Production Capacity and Output

Country	Available Production Units	OUTPUT PER UNIT OF INPUT	
		Bushels of Corn	Bags of Coffee
M	7,500	5.0	4.5
N	7,500	8.0	6.0

Initial Production, Assuming No Trade
(60 percent Corn, 40 percent Coffee)

Country	Bushels of Corn	Bags of Coffee
M	22,500	13,500
N	36,000	18,000
Total	58,500 bushels	31,500 bags

Use the data to answer the following questions; however, before answering them you may want to develop a table similar to Table 4-2.

a. Does one of the countries have an absolute advantage over the other? If so, which one?

b. Which country has the least absolute disadvantage in the production of coffee?

c. Which country should specialize in producing coffee? Which country should specialize in producing corn?

d. What is the domestic price for a bag of coffee (in terms of bushels of corn) in Country N?

e. Assume that trade between the two nations occurs at the domestic price for a bag of coffee (in terms of bushels of corn) in Country N, and Country N consumes exactly the same quantities of both products as it did with no trade. Is Country M better or worse off? Explain. Has GWP improved or worsened? Explain.

f. What is the domestic price for a bag of coffee (in terms of bushels of corn) in Country M?

g. Assume now that trade between the two nations occurs at the domestic price for a bag of coffee (in terms of bushels of corn) in Country M, and Country M consumes exactly the same quantities of both products as it did with no trade. Is Country N better or worse off? Explain. Has GWP improved or worsened? Explain.

h. Assume that the price for a bag of coffee is 1.2 bushels of corn, and Country N consumes 19,000 bags of coffee. Which country is better off? Explain. Has GWP improved or worsened? Explain.

THOMSON ONE
Business School Edition   QUESTIONS

ANALYZING FOREIGN DIRECT INVESTMENT

Overview

In this chapter we described international trade and how companies decide to invest abroad. The decision to go global is not an easy one, but you would be surprised to learn that many companies you thought were domestic are actually global companies. Today, nearly every major corporation has a strong international presence. In this *Thomson One: Business School Edition* exercise, we look at an American icon, McDonald's (MCD). While symbolizing the United States around the world, McDonald's has taken on an international flavor in every country in which it operates.

Discussion Questions

1. Access McDonald's geographic segment financial statements from *Thomson One: Business School Edition*. To gain access, enter the ticker symbol and select "GO". Then, click on "FINANCIALS > MORE > WORLDSCOPE REPORTS & CHARTS > GEOGRAPHIC SEGMENT REVIEW." On this page you will find a 5-year review of McDonald's financial statements. Which geographic segment is growing the fastest? Which segment provides the greatest sales per asset investment? Have any trends developed in McDonald's capital expenditures?

2. Now see if there is anything in the recent news headlines affecting McDonald's international operations. Click on "NEWS" to obtain a list of recent newswire articles regarding McDonald's. Have there been any recent international developments affecting McDonald's or its industry?

3. Like many companies, McDonald's generates an International Annual Report to accompany its standard Shareholder's Annual Report. Click on "FILINGS" to obtain a full list of recent filing categories. Access McDonald's most recent "Int'l Annual Report." The report is long, so you would not be expected to read it all, but you can highlight some of McDonald's international operations (key financial results or new investments).

INTEGRATED CASE

Rick Schmidt, MRI's CFO, along with Mandy Wu, Schmidt's assistant, and John Costello, a consultant and college finance professor, comprise a team set up to teach the firm's directors and senior managers the basics of international financial management. The program includes 16 sessions, each lasting about 2 hours, and they are scheduled immediately before the monthly board meetings. Three sessions have been completed, and the team is now preparing Session 4, which will deal with international trade and the global investment decision. Prior sessions have provided an overview of international finance, exchange rates, and the global financial environment.

For this session, the team will explain the classical theories of trade and how they relate to countries and companies engaging in international trade. Some members of MRI's board don't like the idea of creating or moving operations abroad. Their ethnocentric view is shared by many of the company's employees and has been a hot political topic in recent years. For this reason, Schmidt thinks it is important to communicate to its board members exactly what it means to engage in international trade and how the firm can go about expanding internationally. Schmidt feels this is important for three reasons: (1) Board members will be better educated in making decisions that affect firm operations, (2) board members will be able to disseminate this information to managers and to lower-level workers, and (3) MRI's public relations department will be better able to communicate with the media and protect MRI's public image as it makes tough decisions.

To further illustrate the notion of comparative advantages, Wu created a fictional two-country, two-product economy shown in Table IC4-1. In this two-country world, Countries X and Y produce only two goods (P and Q). The production possibilities are shown in the table, and they indicate how many units of resources are being allocated to the production of each good and how many units of output can be created per unit of input.

This session comes at a perfect time for MRI because it is considering a few locations for future investment. Thus far, MRI has been quite successful in choosing foreign ventures and locations. However, some directors fear that this has been more luck than anything else. Schmidt wants to use all that MRI has learned in its global operations to make more informed decisions. Table IC4-2 shows estimates for a country attractiveness scorecard. Schmidt wants to use this as a basis for making the foreign investment decision.

Wu expressed concern about addressing controversial issues, where the proper analysis is in question. She recalled that in college some students simply "tuned out" when the instructor raised a question for which there was no definitive answer, and she was concerned that the directors might react similarly. Schmidt and Costello agree that this could be a problem, but they felt strongly that it would not be appropriate to "sweep problems under the carpet." So, they want to bring up relevant unresolved issues, discuss alternative ways of dealing with them, and point out the implications of different decisions. The directors are all intelligent, experienced in dealing with complex situations, and would rather know about potential problems than be kept in the dark.

With those thoughts in mind, the three compiled the following set of questions, which they plan to discuss during the session. Assume that you are Mandy Wu, and that you must prepare answers for use during the session.

QUESTIONS

a. Explain the difference between absolute and comparative advantage. How does this distinction illustrate the motivation for international trade? What is the key contribution of comparative advantage theory and how does it apply to the world's current economic issues?

b. To further illustrate the theory of comparative advantage consider the two-country, two-product economy described in Table IC4-1. Which country holds absolute and comparative advantages in which products?

(1) If there is no trade, what is the price of P in terms of Q in each country? How many units of each product will be produced? What is the GWP if there is no trade?

(2) If trade occurs at X's pretrade price for P, how many units would be produced, consumed, and imported/exported of each product in each country? What is the GWP if trade does occur?

(3) If trade occurs at Y's pretrade price for P, how many units would be produced, consumed, and imported/exported of each product in each country? What is the GWP if trade does occur?

TABLE IC4-1 **Production Possibilities for Goods P and Q**

Panel A. Production Capacity and Output

Country	Available Production Units	Units of P	Units of Q
X	1,000 units	6	3
Y	1,000 units	2	2

Panel B. Allocation of Inputs

Country	Units Used to Produce P	Units Used to Produce Q
X	600 units	400 units
Y	600 units	400 units

TABLE IC4-2 | Country Attractiveness Scorecard

		COUNTRIES			
	Weight	A	B	C	D
Return Variables (Higher Is Better)					
1. Potential market size	0-8	7	7	3	8
2. Expected market share	0-7	5	5	7	2
3. Expected profit margin	0-6	4	2	5	5
4. Required investment	0-8	7	7	4	3
5. Favorable tax system	0-7	3	3	4	6
Risk Variables (Lower Is Better)					
1. Competition	7-0	3	3	4	6
2. Bureaucratic problems	8-0	6	3	4	3
3. Political risk	5-0	4	4	4	2
4. Accounting and legal system	5-0	3	4	5	2
5. Compatibility with corporation	6-0	6	4	5	2

(4) If trade occurs at a market-determined price where the price of P is 1.5 units of Q, and consumption of Q remains the same for both countries, how many units would be produced, consumed, and imported/exported of each product in each country? What is the GWP at this market-determined price?

c. What are the major deficiencies of the classical theories of trade?

d. What are the primary motives that drive companies to trade globally?

e. Identify some reasons countries might want to shift more direct investment abroad.

f. Identify some of the motives MNEs have for going abroad.

g. What are the key factors MNEs consider in choosing a foreign country in which to operate?

h. What is a country attractiveness scorecard? Evaluate MRI's country attractiveness scorecard in Table IC4-2. Give a brief appraisal of each location.

i. What is the OLI paradigm? If all of the OLI advantages exist, what are the primary procedures an MNE can use to make a foreign direct investment?

j. Identify some of the reasons an MNE might choose to collaborate with a foreign partner rather than make a foreign direct investment.

k. Describe the six major types of collaborative arrangements.

International Analysis and Securities

Part Two

CHAPTER 5

Risk and Return

Required Investment
Sales Revenues
Operating Costs
Taxes

Cash Flows (CF)

$$\text{VALUE} = \sum_{t=0}^{N} \frac{CF_t}{(1+r)^t}$$

Capital Structure
Interest Rates
Asset Risk
Market Risk

Required Return (r)

Finance involves a trade-off between risk and return. To induce investors to invest in riskier assets, they must be compensated with higher returns. So, to understand financial markets and optimal investment strategies, we must define the concept of risk and return and develop specific metrics to evaluate it. Having done this, we can develop a framework that specifies how investors are compensated for bearing risk. In later chapters, we incorporate these concepts when we value bonds, stocks, capital budgeting projects, and firms.

As you will see, risk can be measured along several dimensions. Risk analysis can be confusing, but it helps to remember the following:

1. All business assets are expected to produce cash flows, and an asset's risk is judged in terms of the riskiness of its expected future cash flows.
2. An asset's risk can be considered in two ways: (a) on a stand-alone basis, where cash flows from different assets are analyzed independently, or (b) in a portfolio context, where several assets are combined to form a portfolio and their consolidated cash flows are analyzed.[1] There is an important dif- ference between stand-alone and portfolio risk, and an asset with a great deal of stand-alone risk may not be very risky if it is held in a portfolio.
3. An asset's total risk can be divided into two components: (a) diversifiable risk, which can be eliminated by holding the asset in a large, widely diver- sified portfolio, and (b) market risk, which reflects the risk that results from the possibility of a general market decline that affects (almost) all stocks.

---

[1]A *portfolio* is a collection of investment securities. If you owned some General Motors stock, some ExxonMobil stock, and some IBM stock, you would be holding a three-stock portfolio. Because diversification lowers risk, most stocks are held in portfolios.

Rational investors will diversify and eliminate diversifiable risks, hence they are of little concern to most investors. Market risk, however, cannot be eliminated; hence, it is relevant to most investors.

4. *In general, investors are risk averse; hence, they will not buy risky assets unless they provide sufficiently high expected returns. An asset with above-average market risk must provide an above-average expected return to offset that risk and thus attract investors.*

In the general valuation equation, risk is reflected in the asset's cash flows (the numerator) as well as the required return (the denominator). If a competitor introduces a new and potentially better product to the market, investors will be fearful that the firm's cash flows will decline. That increase in risk will cause the required rate of return to increase. Of course, if favorable developments occur, investors may become convinced that the firm's cash flows are likely to continue, causing its risk and thus its required rate of return to decline. So, the riskiness of an asset's cash flows is an important determinant of its value. In this chapter, we focus on financial assets (such as stocks and bonds), but we later apply the concepts developed here to all types of physical assets.

INVESTMENT RISK AND RETURN BASICS

With most investments, an investor spends money today with the expectation of earning additional money in the future. To illustrate, suppose you purchase 10 shares of a stock for $1,000. The stock pays no dividends, but at the end of one year, you sell the stock for $1,100. What rate of return do you receive on your $1,000 investment?

The annualized rate of return, or holding period return, is:

$$\text{Holding period rate of return} = \frac{\text{Total proceeds} - \text{Amount invested}}{\text{Amount invested}}$$

$$= \frac{\text{Dollar return}}{\text{Amount invested}} = \frac{\$100}{\$1,000}$$

$$= 0.10 = 10\%.$$

The rate of return "standardizes" the dollar return by the unit of investment. In this example, the 10 percent return indicates that each dollar invested will earn $0.10(\$1.00) = \$0.10$. If the return is negative, then the original investment is not recovered.

Although we illustrated the return concept with one outflow and one inflow, rate of return concepts can easily be applied when multiple cash flows occur over time. For example, when Intel invests in new chip-making technology, the investment is made over several years, and the resulting inflows occur over even more years. Also, holding periods other than a year can be used, but in such cases we generally convert to annualized returns.[2]

---

[2]It is easy to convert nonannual rates of return to annualized rates. For instance, in the example above if the holding period had been six months rather than a year, then the 10 percent rate would have been for six months, and it would be converted to an annualized rate as follows:

$$\text{Annualized rate} = (1 + 6\text{-month rate})^2 - 1 = (1.10)^2 - 1 = 0.21 = 21\%.$$

Nonannual return concepts are discussed in detail in Eugene F. Brigham and Joel F. Houston's *Fundamentals of Financial Management*, 10th edition (Mason, OH: South-Western Publishers, 2004), Chapter 6, and most other corporate finance textbooks. We introduce rate of return concepts in this text as they are needed.

**Probability
Distribution**
A listing of all
possible out-
comes, or events,
with a probability
(chance of occur-
rence) assigned to
each outcome.

*Wilshire Associates
provides a download
site for various
returns series for
indexes such as the
Wilshire 5000 and
the Wilshire 4500 at*
**http://www.wilshire.
com** *in Microsoft
Excel format.*

**Expected Rate
of Return, r̂**
The rate of return
expected to be
realized from an
investment; the
weighted average
of the probability
distribution of
possible results.

Probability Distributions

An event's *probability* is defined as the chance that the event will occur. For example, a weather forecaster might state, "There is a 40 percent chance of rain today and a 60 percent chance that it will not rain." If all possible outcomes are listed, and if a probability is assigned to each outcome, the listing is called a **probability distribution.** For the stock investment shown above, assume that the probability distribution of returns is as shown in Table 5-1. The possible states of the economy are listed in Column 1, the probabilities of these outcomes are given in Column 2, and the returns under each state are given in Column 3. Notice that the probabilities must sum to 1.0, or 100 percent.

If you purchase a bond, the possible outcomes are that the issuer will (1) make the required payments or (2) default on some or all of the payments. The higher the probability of default, the riskier the bond, and the higher the risk, the higher the required return. If you invest in a stock, you will again expect to earn a return on your money. Stock returns come from dividends and the capital gains when the stocks are sold. Again, the riskier a stock—which means the higher the probability that the stock will not provide the cash flows that were expected—the higher the expected return must be to induce investors to invest in the stock.

Expected Rate of Return

If we multiply each possible outcome by its probability of occurrence and then sum these products, we have a *weighted average* of outcomes. The weights are the probabilities, and the weighted average is the **expected rate of return**, r̂, called "r-hat."[3] The expected return for our investment is shown in Table 5-2.

TABLE 5-1 | Probability Distribution Listing

State of the Economy (1)	Probability (2)	Return (3)
Poor	0.25	−5%
Average	0.50	10
Good	0.25	25
	1.00	

TABLE 5-2 | Calculation of Expected Rate of Return

State of the Economy (1)	Probability (2)	Return (3)	Product (2) × (3) = (4)
Poor	0.25	−5%	−1.25%
Average	0.50	10	5.00%
Good	0.25	25	6.25%
	1.00		r̂ = 10.00%

[3]In Chapters 8 and 9, we will use r_d and r_s to signify the returns on bonds and stocks, respectively. However, this distinction is unnecessary in this chapter, so we just use the general term, r̂, to signify an investment's expected return.

The expected rate of return calculation can also be expressed as an equation:

$$\text{Expected rate of return} = \hat{r} = P_1 r_1 + P_2 r_2 + \cdots + P_n r_n$$

$$= \sum_{i=1}^{n} P_i r_i. \qquad (5\text{-}1)$$

Here r_i is the ith possible outcome, P_i is the probability of the ith outcome, and n is the number of possible outcomes. Thus, $\hat{r}$ is a weighted average of the possible outcomes, with each outcome's weight being its probability of occurrence. The expected return for our stock investment is calculated as

$$\hat{r} = P_1(r_1) + P_2(r_2) + P_3(r_3)$$
$$= 0.25(-5\%) + 0.5(10\%) + 0.25(25\%)$$
$$= 10\%.$$

We can graph the returns to obtain a picture of the variability of possible outcomes; this is shown in Figure 5-1, panel A. The height of each bar signifies the probability that a given outcome will occur. The range of probable returns is from -5 to $+25$ percent, with an expected return of 10 percent.

Thus far, we have assumed that only three outcomes can exist: poor, average, and good conditions. Of course, actual conditions could take on a great number of outcomes. Suppose we had the time and patience to assign a probability to each possible outcome (with the sum of the probabilities still equaling 1.0) and to assign a return for each outcome. The result would be the curve in Figure 5-1, panel B, which assumes that the returns probability distribution is approximately normal with a mean of 10 percent. Here we have also changed the assumptions so that there is essentially a zero probability that the return will be less than -5 percent or more than 25 percent, but virtually any return within these limits is possible.

The tighter the probability distribution, the more likely it is that the actual outcome will be close to the expected value, and, consequently, the less likely it is that

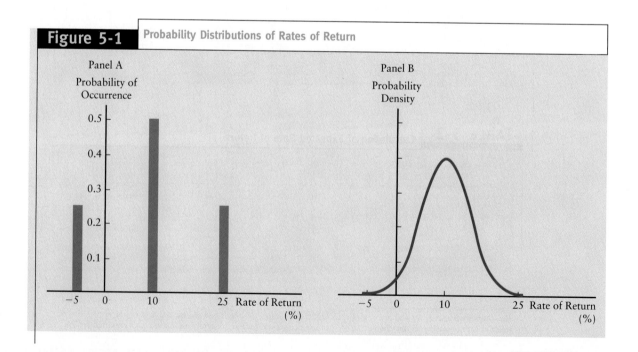

Figure 5-1 Probability Distributions of Rates of Return

the actual return will end up far below the expected return. Thus, the tighter the probability distribution, the lower the investment risk. Note, though, that here we are considering only one asset, hence we are measuring *stand-alone risk*. The asset's risk in a portfolio context could be quite different from its stand-alone risk.

Measuring Risk: The Standard Deviation with Probability Data

Risk is a difficult concept to grasp, and a great deal of controversy surrounds attempts to define and measure it. However, a common definition is stated in terms of probability distributions such as the curve shown in Figure 5-1, panel B: *The tighter the probability distribution of expected returns, the smaller the risk of a given investment.*

To be most useful, any risk measure should have a definite value—we need a measure of the tightness of the probability distribution. One such measure is the **standard deviation**, σ, pronounced "sigma." The smaller the standard deviation, the tighter the probability distribution and thus the less risky the investment. To calculate the standard deviation, we proceed as follows:

1. Calculate the expected rate of return.
2. Subtract the expected rate of return ($\hat{r}$) from each possible outcome (r_i) to obtain a set of deviations about $\hat{r}$, ($r_i - \hat{r}$).
3. Square each deviation, then multiply the result by the probability of occurrence for its related outcome, and then sum these products to obtain the **variance**, σ^2:

$$\text{Variance} = \sigma^2 = \sum_{i=1}^{n} (r_i - \hat{r})^2 \, P_i. \tag{5-2}$$

4. Finally, take the square root of the variance to obtain the standard deviation:

$$\text{Standard deviation} = \sigma = \sqrt{\sum_{i=1}^{n} (r_i - \hat{r})^2 \, P_i}. \tag{5-3}$$

Thus, the standard deviation is essentially a weighted average of the deviations from the expected value, and it provides an idea of how far above or below the expected value the actual value is likely to be.

If a probability distribution is normal, the *actual* return will be within ± 1 standard deviation of the *expected* return 68.26 percent of the time. Figure 5-2 illustrates this point, and it also shows the situation for $\pm 2\sigma$ and $\pm 3\sigma$. For the average firm listed on the New York Stock Exchange, σ has generally been in the range of 35 to 40 percent in recent years.

Using Historical Data to Measure Risk

In the example just given, we described the procedure for finding the mean and standard deviation when the data are in the form of a known probability distribution. If only sample returns data over some past period are available, the standard deviation of returns should be estimated using this formula:

$$\text{Estimated } \sigma = S = \sqrt{\frac{\sum_{t=1}^{n} (\bar{r}_t - \bar{r}_{Avg})^2}{n-1}}. \tag{5-3a}$$

Standard Deviation, σ
A statistical measure of the variability of a set of observations.

Variance, σ^2
The square of the standard deviation.

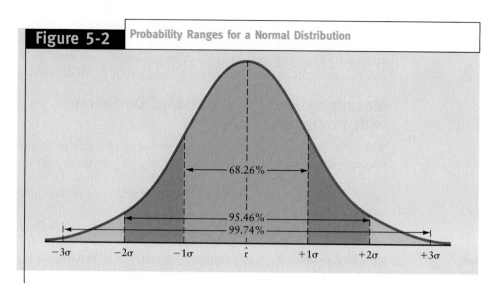

Figure 5-2   Probability Ranges for a Normal Distribution

68.26%

95.46%
99.74%

-3σ -2σ -1σ $\hat{r}$ $+1\sigma$ $+2\sigma$ $+3\sigma$

Notes:
a. The area under the normal curve always equals 1.0, or 100 percent. *Thus, the areas under any pair of normal curves drawn on the same scale, whether they are peaked or flat, must be equal.*
b. Half of the area under a normal curve is to the left of the mean, indicating that there is a 50 percent probability that the actual outcome will be less than the mean, and half is to the right of $\hat{r}$, indicating a 50 percent probability that it will be greater than the mean.
c. Of the area under the curve, 68.26 percent is within $\pm 1\sigma$ of the mean, indicating that the probability is 68.26 percent that the actual outcome will be within the range $\hat{r} - 1\sigma$ to $\hat{r} + 1\sigma$.
d. Procedures exist for finding the probability of other ranges. These procedures are covered in statistics courses.
e. For a normal distribution, the larger the value of σ, the greater the probability that the actual outcome will vary widely from, and hence perhaps be far below, the expected, or most likely, outcome. *Because the probability of having the actual result turn out to be far below the expected result is one definition of risk, and because σ measures this probability, we can use σ as a measure of risk.* This definition may not be a good one, however, if we are dealing with an asset held in a diversified portfolio. This point is covered later in the chapter.

Here $\bar{r}_t$ ("r bar t") denotes the past realized rate of return in period t, and $\bar{r}_{Avg}$ is the average annual return earned during the last n years. Here is an example:

Year	$\bar{r}_t$
2002	15%
2003	−5
2004	20

$$\bar{r}_{Avg} = \frac{(15\% - 5\% + 20\%)}{3} = 10.0\%.$$

$$\text{Estimated } \sigma \text{ (or S)} = \sqrt{\frac{(15\% - 10\%)^2 + (-5\% - 10\%)^2 + (20\% - 10\%)^2}{3 - 1}}$$

$$= \sqrt{\frac{350\%}{2}} = 13.2\%.$$

The historical σ is often used as an estimate of the future σ. Much less often, and generally incorrectly, $\bar{r}_{Avg}$ for some past period is used as an estimate of $\hat{r}$, the expected future return. Because past variability is likely to be repeated, σ may be a good estimate of future risk. However, it is much less reasonable to expect that the average return during any particular past period is the best estimate of what investors think will happen in the future. For instance, between 2000 and 2002 the historical average return on the S&P 500 index was negative, but it is not reasonable to assume

TABLE 5-3	**Calculation of Standard Deviation**		
P_i (1)	$r_i - \hat{r}$ (2)	$(r_i - \hat{r})^2$ (3)	$(r_i - \hat{r})^2 P_i$ (4)
0.25	$-0.05 - 0.10 = -0.15$	0.0225	0.005625
0.50	$0.10 - 0.10 = \ \ \ 0.00$	0.0000	0.000000
0.25	$0.25 - 0.10 = \ \ \ 0.15$	0.0225	0.005625
		Variance $= \sigma^2 =$	0.011250
		Standard deviation $= \sigma =$	0.106066

that investors expect returns to continue to be negative in the future; if they did, they would hold cash rather than buy stocks.

Equation 5-3a is built into all financial calculators, and it is easy to use. We simply enter the rates of return and press the key marked S (or S_x) to obtain the standard deviation. However, calculators have no built-in formula for finding σ where probabilistic data are involved; there you must go through the process outlined in Table 5-3 and Equation 5-3. The same situation holds for *Excel* and other computer spreadsheet programs. Note also that both versions of the standard deviation are interpreted and used in the same manner—the only difference is in the way they are calculated.

Measuring Risk: The Coefficient of Variation

If a choice must be made between two investments that have the same expected returns but different standard deviations, most people would choose the one with the lower standard deviation and, therefore, the lower risk. Similarly, given a choice between two investments with the same risk (standard deviation) but different expected returns, investors would generally prefer the one with the higher expected return. To most people, this is common sense—return is "good," risk is "bad," and consequently investors want as much return and as little risk as possible. But how do we choose between two investments if one has a higher expected return while the other has a lower standard deviation? To help answer this question, we often use another measure of risk, the **coefficient of variation (CV)**, which is the standard deviation (calculated either way) divided by the expected return:

Coefficient of Variation (CV)
A standardized measure of the risk per unit of return; calculated as the standard deviation divided by the expected return.

$$\text{Coefficient of variation} = \text{CV} = \frac{\sigma}{\hat{r}}. \qquad (5\text{-}4)$$

The coefficient of variation shows the risk per unit of return, and it provides a more meaningful basis for comparison when the expected returns on two alternatives are not the same. The coefficient of variation for our investment is $0.106066/0.10 = 1.06066$.

Complications in an International Setting

So far we have assumed that investors put money into investments that return cash flows in the investor's home currency. However, calculating the return for an investor whose investment generates cash flows in another currency is more complex. Assume that on January 1, 2003, a French investor bought a one-year $1,000 U.S. corporate bond. At the end of 2003, the investor received $1,100. The dollar rate of return on this investment was ($1,100 − $1,000)/$1,000 = 10 percent.

However, the French investor is interested in his or her euro return. On January 1, 2003, the exchange rate was $1.0500/€, so the investment cost $1,000/$1.0500/€ = €952.381. The $1,100 return at the end of 2003, when translated into euros at the then-applicable spot exchange rate, was $1,100/$1.2579/€ = €874.4733, producing a rate of return of (€874.47 − €952.38)/€952.38 = −8.18%, well below the dollar rate of return. The lower euro return resulted because the dollar weakened against the euro, meaning that each dollar received bought fewer euros at the end than at the start of the year. If the dollar had strengthened against the euro, then the earned euro return would have been greater than 10 percent.

The potential for exchange rate fluctuations also affects the required returns on investments. For example, a U.S. Treasury security that is risk free to U.S. investors would, because of potential exchange rate fluctuations, be regarded as having some risk by French investors. We cover the effects of currency volatility in more detail in Chapter 12, but you should always remember that additional risk is introduced when investments are made in currencies other than the investor's home currency.

SELF-TEST QUESTIONS

Differentiate between dollar returns and rates of return.

Explain the logic for using the standard deviation as a measure of risk.

How is the standard deviation calculated (a) when a probability distribution for the data is available and (b) when only historical data are available?

Which is a better measure of risk if assets have different expected returns: (1) the standard deviation or (2) the coefficient of variation? Why?

How do exchange rates affect assets' risk and returns?

STAND-ALONE RISK AND RISK AVERSION

Risk is defined in *Webster's* as "a hazard; a peril; exposure to loss or injury." Thus, risk refers to the chance that some unfavorable event will occur. An asset's risk can be analyzed in two ways: (1) on a stand-alone basis, where the asset is considered in isolation, or (2) on a portfolio basis, where the asset is held as one of a number of different assets in a portfolio. The **stand-alone risk** of an asset is the risk an investor would face if he or she held only this one asset, and it is generally measured by the standard deviation of the asset as calculated earlier. Although most investors hold financial assets in portfolios (e.g., mutual funds), it is necessary to understand stand-alone risk first in order to understand risk in a portfolio context.

Stand-Alone Risk
The risk an investor would face if he or she held only one asset.

As we stated earlier, *no investment should be undertaken unless the expected rate of return is high enough to compensate for the risk inherent in the investment.* Except for high-grade bonds held until they mature, risky assets rarely produce their expected rates of return—generally, risky assets earn either more or less than was expected when they were purchased. Indeed, if assets always produced their expected returns, they would not be risky! **Investment risk**, then, is related to the likelihood of actually achieving a low or negative return—the higher the probability that the actual return will be low or negative, the riskier the investment.

Investment Risk
The likelihood of actually earning a low or negative return on an investment.

Risk Aversion and Required Returns

Suppose you worked hard and saved $1 million, which you now plan to invest. You can buy a 5 percent U.S. Treasury security, and at the end of one year you will have a certain $1.05 million, which is your original investment plus $50,000 in interest. Alternatively, you can buy stock in Genetic Advances. If Genetic Advances' research programs are successful, your stock will increase in value to $2.1 million. However, if the research is a failure, the value of your stock will go to zero, and you will be penniless. You regard Genetic Advances' chances of success or failure as being 50-50,

THE TRADE-OFF BETWEEN RISK AND RETURN

The accompanying table summarizes the historical trade-off between risk and return for different classes of investments from 1926 through 2003. As the table shows, those assets that produced the highest average returns also had the highest standard deviations and the widest ranges of returns. For example, small-company stocks had the highest average annual return, 17.5 percent, but their standard deviation of returns, 33.3 percent, was also the highest. By contrast, U.S. Treasury bills had the lowest standard deviation, 3.1 percent, but they also had the lowest average return, 3.8 percent.

When deciding among alternative investments, we need to be aware of the trade-off between risk and return. While there is certainly no guarantee that history will repeat itself, returns observed over a long period in the past are a good starting point for estimating investments' future returns. Likewise, the standard deviations of past returns provide useful insights into the risks of different investments. For T-bills, however, the standard deviation needs to be interpreted carefully. Note that the table shows that Treasury bills have a positive standard deviation, which indicates some risk. However, if you invested in a one-year Treasury bill and held it for the full year, your realized return would be the same regardless of what happened to the economy that year, and thus the standard deviation of your return would be zero. So, why does the table show a 3.1 percent standard deviation for T-bills, which indicates some risk? In fact, a T-bill is riskless *if you hold it for one year*, but if you invest in a rolling portfolio of one-year T-bills and hold the portfolio for a number of years, your investment income will vary depending on what happens to interest rates in each year. So, while you can be sure of the return you will earn on a T-bill in a given year, you cannot be sure of the return you will earn on a portfolio of T-bills over a number of years.

Distribution of Realized Returns, 1926–2003

	Small-Company Stocks	Large-Company Stocks	Long-Term Corporate Bonds	Long-Term Government Bonds	U.S. Treasury Bills	Inflation
Average return	17.5%	12.4%	6.2%	5.8%	3.8%	3.1%
Standard deviation	33.3	20.4	8.6	9.4	3.1	4.3
Excess return over T-bonds[a]	11.7	6.6	0.4			

[a]The excess return over T-bonds is called the "historical risk premium." If and only if investors expect returns in the future to be similar to returns earned in the past, the excess return will also be the current risk premium that is reflected in security prices.

Source: Based on *Stocks, Bonds, Bills, and Inflation: Valuation Edition 2004 Yearbook* (Chicago: Ibbotson Associates, 2004).

so the expected value of the investment is 0.5($0) + 0.5($2,100,000) = $1,050,000. Subtracting the cost of the stock leaves an expected profit of $50,000, producing an expected but risky 5 percent rate of return. Thus, you have a choice between a certain $50,000 profit (5 percent return) on the Treasury security and a risky expected $50,000 profit (5 percent return) on the Genetic Advances stock. Which one would you choose? *If you choose the less risky investment, you are risk averse. Most investors are risk averse, and certainly the average investor is risk averse with regard to his or her "serious money."*[4] *Because this is a well-documented fact, we shall assume* **risk aversion** *throughout the remainder of the book.*

What are the implications of risk aversion for security prices and returns? Other things held constant, the higher a security's risk, the higher its required return and the lower its price. Most investors are risk averse, so under these conditions there would be a general preference for investments with less risk and more return. In fact, investors will require additional compensation, in the form of a *risk premium*, *RP*, to compensate them for bearing additional risk. If a risky investment has an

Risk Aversion
Risk-averse investors dislike risk and require higher rates of return as an inducement to buy riskier securities.

---

[4]Even risk-averse people who are careful to protect their serious money may play the lottery or go to a casino, although they know that the odds of winning are against them. Most people gamble for recreation rather than for wealth management, so this does not violate our definition of risk aversion.

expected return of 10 percent when the risk-free return is 5 percent, then the risky investment carries a 10% − 5% = 5% risk premium.

In a market dominated by risk-averse investors, riskier securities must have higher expected returns, as estimated by the marginal investor, than less risky securities. If this situation does not exist, buying and selling in the market will force it to occur. We consider the question of how much higher the returns on risky securities must be later in the chapter, but first we explain how diversification affects the way risk should be measured.

SELF-TEST QUESTIONS

What is stand-alone risk?

Explain the following statement: "Most investors are risk averse."

How does risk aversion affect rates of return?

Briefly explain whether the following statement is true or false: "The fact that risk-averse people play the lottery or gamble at a casino indicates that risk aversion is not a valid principle."

PORTFOLIO RISK AND RETURN

In the preceding section, we considered the risk of assets held in isolation, or stand-alone risk. Now we analyze the risk of assets when they are held in portfolios. As we shall see, an asset held as part of a portfolio is usually less risky than the same asset held in isolation. Accordingly, most financial assets are actually held in portfolios. Banks, pension funds, insurance companies, mutual funds, and other financial institutions are required by law to hold diversified portfolios. Even individuals—at least those whose security holdings constitute a significant part of their total wealth—generally hold portfolios, not the stock of only one firm. Thus, the fact that a particular stock's return increases or decreases is not very important; *what is important is the return on his or her portfolio, and the portfolio's overall risk. Logically, then, the risk and return of an individual security should be analyzed in terms of how that security affects the risk and return of an investor's portfolio.*

Portfolio Returns

Expected Return on a Portfolio, $\hat{r}_p$
The weighted average of the expected returns of the individual assets held in the portfolio.

The **expected return on a portfolio, $\hat{r}_p$,** is simply the weighted average of the expected returns of the individual assets in the portfolio:

$$\hat{r}_p = w_1\hat{r}_1 + w_2\hat{r}_2 + \cdots + w_n\hat{r}_n$$

$$= \sum_{i=1}^{n} w_i\hat{r}_i. \tag{5-5}$$

Here, the $\hat{r}_i$'s are the expected returns on the individual stocks, the w_i's are the weights, and there are n stocks in the portfolio. Note (1) that w_i is the fraction of the portfolio's dollar value invested in Stock i and (2) that the w_i's must sum to 1.0.

Assume that in August 2004, a security analyst estimated the following returns on the stocks of four companies:

	Expected Return, $\hat{r}$
Microsoft	12.0%
General Electric	11.5
Pfizer	10.0
Coca-Cola	9.5

If we formed a $100,000 portfolio by investing $25,000 in each stock, the expected portfolio return would be 10.75 percent:

$$\hat{r}_p = w_1\hat{r}_1 + w_2\hat{r}_2 + w_3\hat{r}_3 + w_4\hat{r}_4$$
$$= 0.25(12\%) + 0.25(11.5\%) + 0.25(10\%) + 0.25(9.5\%)$$
$$= 10.75\%.$$

Realized Rate of Return, r̄
The return that was actually earned during some past period. The actual return ($\bar{r}$) usually turns out to be different from the expected return ($\hat{r}$) except for riskless assets.

Of course, the actual **realized rates of return, r̄,** on the individual stocks will almost certainly be different from their expected values, so $\bar{r}_p$ will be different from $\hat{r}_p = 10.75\%$. For example, Coca-Cola might double and provide a return of $+100$ percent, whereas Microsoft might have a terrible year, fall sharply, and have a return of -75 percent. Note, though, that those two events would be somewhat offsetting, so the portfolio's return might still be close to its expected return, even though the individual stocks' actual returns were far from their expected returns.

Portfolio Risk

As we just saw, the expected portfolio return is simply the weighted average of the expected returns on the individual assets in the portfolio. However, unlike returns, the portfolio standard deviation, σ_p, which is the measure of its risk, is generally *not* the weighted average of the standard deviations of the individual assets in the portfolio; the portfolio's risk will almost always be *less* than the weighted average of the assets' σ's. In theory, it is possible to combine very risky stocks to form a portfolio that is completely riskless, with $\sigma_p = 0$.

Correlation
The tendency of two variables to move together.

The key to benefiting from diversification is to combine assets that are not highly correlated with one another. In doing so, if a particular stock in the portfolio performs badly, the other stocks, since they are not perfectly correlated, should provide returns that offset, to a degree, that poor return. The tendency of two variables to move together is called **correlation**, and the **correlation coefficient**, ρ, pronounced "rho," measures this tendency.[5] If $\rho = -1.0$, *perfect negative correlation* exists, and if $\rho = +1.0$, *perfect positive correlation* exists. Diversification would be most beneficial for reducing risk if stocks had perfect negative correlations, and would do nothing to reduce risk if the portfolio consisted of perfectly positively correlated stocks.

Correlation Coefficient, ρ
A measure of the degree of relationship between two variables.

In the real world, most stocks are positively correlated, but not perfectly so. On average, studies have shown the correlation coefficient for the returns on two randomly selected stocks to lie in the range of $+0.3$ to $+0.7$.[6] *Under such conditions, forming stock portfolios reduces risk but does not completely eliminate it.*

What would happen if we include more stocks in the portfolio? *As a rule, portfolio risk declines as the number of stocks in the portfolio increases.* If we added enough partially correlated stocks, could we completely eliminate risk? In general, the answer is no, but the extent to which adding stocks to a portfolio reduces its risk depends on the *degree of correlation* among the stocks: The smaller the positive

---

[5]The *correlation coefficient*, ρ, can range from $+1.0$, denoting that the two variables move up and down exactly together, to -1.0, denoting that the variables always move in exactly opposite directions. A correlation coefficient of zero indicates that changes in one variable are *independent* of changes in the other.

The correlation coefficient is called R when it is estimated using historical data. Here is the formula to estimate the correlation between stocks i and j ($\bar{r}_t$ is the actual return in period t and $\bar{r}_{Avg}$ is the average return during the period; similar notation is used for stock j):

$$R = \frac{\sum_{t=1}^{n}(\bar{r}_{i,t} - \bar{r}_{Avg,i})(\bar{r}_{j,t} - \bar{r}_{Avg,j})}{\sqrt{\sum_{t=1}^{n}(\bar{r}_{i,t} - \bar{r}_{Avg,i})^2 \sum_{t=1}^{n}(\bar{r}_{j,t} - \bar{r}_{Avg,j})^2}}.$$

Fortunately, it is easy to calculate correlation coefficients with a financial calculator. Simply enter the returns on the two stocks and then press a key labeled "r." In *Excel*, use the CORREL function.

[6]See Louis K. C. Chan, Jason Karceski, and Josef Lakonishok, "On Portfolio Optimization: Forecasting Covariances and Choosing the Risk Model," *Review of Financial Studies*, Winter 1999, 937–974.

correlation coefficients, the lower the risk in a large portfolio. If we could find a set of stocks whose correlations were −1.0, all risk could be eliminated. *In the real world, however, where the correlations among the individual stocks are generally positive but less than +1.0, some, but not all, risk can be eliminated.*

Diversifiable Risk versus Market Risk

As noted earlier, it is difficult if not impossible to find stocks whose expected returns are negatively correlated—most stocks tend to do well when the national economy is strong and badly when it is weak.[7] Thus, even very large portfolios end up with substantial risk, but not as nearly as much risk as if all the money were invested in only one stock.

To see more precisely how portfolio size affects portfolio risk, consider Figure 5-3, which shows how portfolio risk is affected by forming larger and larger portfolios of randomly selected New York Stock Exchange (NYSE) stocks. Standard deviations

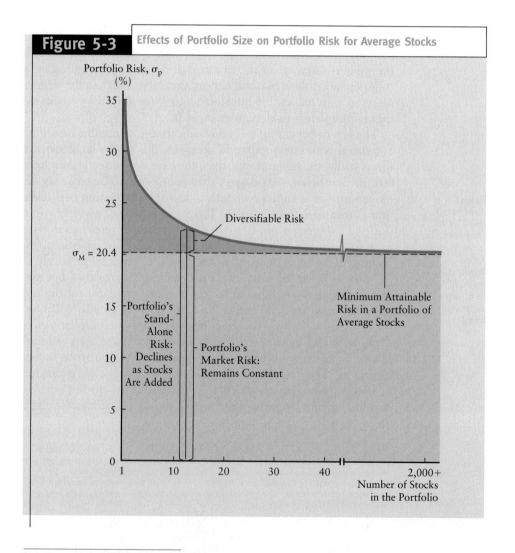

Figure 5-3   Effects of Portfolio Size on Portfolio Risk for Average Stocks

---

[7]It is not too hard to find a few stocks that happened to have risen because of a particular set of circumstances in the past while most other stocks were declining, but it is much harder to find stocks that could logically be *expected* to go up in the future when other stocks are falling.

However, note that derivative securities (options) having correlations close to −1.0 with stocks can be created. Such derivatives can be bought and used as "portfolio insurance." Derivatives are discussed in Chapter 15.

are plotted for an average one-stock portfolio, a two-stock portfolio, and so on, up to a portfolio consisting of all 2,000-plus common stocks that were listed on the NYSE at the time the data were graphed. The graph illustrates that, in general, portfolio risk tends to decline and to approach some limit as the number of different companies in the portfolio increases. According to data accumulated in recent years, σ_1, the standard deviation of a one-stock portfolio (or an average stock), is approximately 35 percent. A portfolio consisting of all stocks, which is called the **market portfolio**, would have a standard deviation, σ_M, of about 20.4 percent, which is shown as the horizontal dashed line in Figure 5-3.

Thus, almost half of the riskiness inherent in an average individual stock can be eliminated if the stock is held in a well-diversified portfolio, which is one containing 40 or more stocks in a number of different industries. Some risk will always remain, however, so it is virtually impossible to form stock portfolios that diversify away the effects of the broad stock market movements that affect almost all stocks.

The part of a stock's risk that *can* be eliminated is called *diversifiable risk*, while the part that *cannot* be eliminated is called *market risk*.[8] The fact that much of a stock's risk can be eliminated is vitally important, because rational investors *will* eliminate it and thus render it irrelevant.

A stock's **diversifiable risk** is caused by random events such as lawsuits, strikes, successful and unsuccessful marketing programs, winning or losing a major contract, and other events that are unique to the particular firm. Because these events are random, their effects on a portfolio can be eliminated by diversification—bad events in one firm will be offset by good events in another. **Market risk**, on the other hand, stems from factors that systematically affect most firms, including war, inflation, recessions, and high interest rates. Because most stocks are negatively affected by these factors, market risk cannot be eliminated by diversification.

Capital Asset Pricing Model (CAPM)

Investors demand a premium for bearing risk—the higher a security's risk, the higher its expected return must be to induce investors to buy (or to hold) it. However, if investors are concerned primarily with portfolio risk, not stand-alone risk, how should the risk of an individual stock be measured? One answer is provided by the **Capital Asset Pricing Model (CAPM)**, an important tool used to analyze the relationship between risk and return.[9] The primary conclusion of the CAPM is this: *The **relevant risk** of an individual stock is the stock's contribution to the risk of a well-diversified portfolio, which is its market risk; hence, investors require compensation only for market risk.*

A simple example will help make this point clear. Suppose you were offered the chance to flip a coin once. If a head comes up, you win $20,000, but if a tail comes up, you lose $16,000. This is a good bet—the expected return is 0.5($20,000) + 0.5(−$16,000) = $2,000. However, it is a highly risky proposition, because you have a 50 percent chance of losing $16,000. Thus, you might well refuse to make the bet. Alternatively, suppose you were offered the chance to flip a coin 100 times, and you would win $200 for each head but lose $160 for each tail. It is theoretically

Market Portfolio A portfolio consisting of all stocks.

Diversifiable Risk That part of a stock's risk associated with random events; it can be eliminated by proper diversification.

Market Risk That part of a security's risk that cannot be eliminated by diversification.

Capital Asset Pricing Model (CAPM) A model based on the proposition that any stock's required rate of return is equal to the risk-free rate of return plus a risk premium that reflects only the risk remaining after diversification.

Relevant Risk The risk of a security that cannot be diversified away, or its market risk. This reflects a security's contribution to the riskiness of a portfolio.

[8]Diversifiable risk is also known as *company-specific,* or *unsystematic,* risk. Market risk is also known as *nondiversifiable,* or *systematic,* or *beta,* risk; it is the risk that remains after diversification.

[9]The 1990 Nobel Prize was awarded to the developers of the CAPM, Professors Harry Markowitz and William F. Sharpe. The CAPM is a relatively complex theory, and only its basic elements are presented in this chapter. In Chapter 10 we introduce the global CAPM, an extension of the original model applicable to firms with access to global capital markets.

The basic concepts of the CAPM were developed specifically for common stocks, and, therefore, the theory is examined first in this context. However, it has become common practice to extend CAPM concepts to capital budgeting and to speak of firms as having "portfolios of tangible assets and projects."

possible that you would flip all heads and win $20,000, and it is also theoretically possible that you would flip all tails and lose $16,000, but the chances are very high that you would actually flip about 50 heads and about 50 tails, winning a net of about $2,000. Although each individual flip is a risky bet, collectively you have a low-risk proposition because most of the risk has been diversified away. This is the idea behind holding portfolios rather than just a single stock, except that with stocks all of the risk cannot be eliminated by diversification—those risks related to broad, systematic changes in the stock market will remain.

Are all stocks equally risky in the sense that adding them to a well-diversified portfolio would have the same effect on the portfolio's riskiness? The answer is no. Different stocks will affect the portfolio differently, so different securities have different relevant risk. How can the relevant risk of an individual stock be measured? As we have seen, all risk except that related to broad market movements can, and presumably will, be diversified away. After all, no rational investor will accept risk that can be easily eliminated. *The risk that remains after diversifying is market risk, or the risk that is inherent in the market, and it can be measured by the degree to which a given stock tends to move up or down with the market.* In the next section, we develop a measure of a stock's market risk (called the "beta coefficient") and then, in a later section, we introduce an equation for determining the required return on a stock, given its market risk.

CONCEPT OF BETA As we noted earlier, the primary conclusion of the CAPM is that the relevant risk of an individual stock is the risk the stock contributes to a well-diversified portfolio. The benchmark for a well-diversified stock portfolio is the market portfolio, which is a portfolio that contains all stocks. The ith stock's relevant risk is measured by its **beta coefficient**, denoted as b_i, which is calculated as follows:

Beta Coefficient, b_i
A measure of market risk, which is the extent to which the returns on a given stock move with the stock market.

$$b_i = \left(\frac{\sigma_i}{\sigma_M}\right)\rho_{iM}. \tag{5-6}$$

Here, σ_i is the standard deviation of the ith stock's return, σ_M is the standard deviation of the market's return, and ρ_{iM} is the correlation between the stock's return and that on the market portfolio. Thus, a company's beta depends on its stand-alone risk as measured by σ_i, the market's risk as measured by σ_M, and its correlation with the market as measured by ρ_{iM}. The higher σ_i and ρ_{iM}, the higher the stock's beta. Note, though, that it is possible for a company to have a high standard deviation and thus a great deal of risk if it were held alone, but a low beta and thus little relevant risk if its correlation with the market is low.

Equation 5-6 is programmed into all financial calculators and spreadsheets, and we can input returns data for a stock and the market and quickly obtain the stock's beta. If $b_i = 1.0$, then the stock is defined as an **average-risk stock**. Such a stock tends to move up and down in sync with the market, and a large portfolio of such stocks has exactly the same risk as the market. If the market moves up (down) by 10 percent, the stock will, in general, also move up (down) by 10 percent. If beta is less than 1.0, say 0.5, the stock is half as risky as an average stock, while if beta were 2.0, the stock would be twice as risky as average.[10] If a stock whose beta is greater than 1.0 is added to an average-risk portfolio, then the portfolio's beta, and

Average-Risk Stock
A stock with $b = 1.0$.

---

[10]The concept of betas is described in most introductory textbooks in terms of a scatter diagram, where the stock's returns are plotted on the y-axis and the market's returns are shown on the x-axis. The regression line indicates the tendency of the stock to move up and down with the market, and its slope measures the company's beta coefficient. Equation 5-6 is an efficient way to find this slope, and thus the stock's beta.

THE BENEFITS OF DIVERSIFYING OVERSEAS

The global stock market has grown steadily over the last several decades, and it passed the $15 trillion mark during 1995. U.S. stocks accounted for approximately 41 percent of this total, whereas the Japanese and European markets constituted roughly 25 and 26 percent, respectively. The rest of the world accounted for the remaining 8 percent. Although the U.S. equity market has long been the world's biggest, its share of the world total has decreased over time.

The expanding universe of international securities suggests the possibility of achieving a better risk-return trade-off than could be obtained by investing solely in U.S. securities. In other words, investing overseas might lower risk and simultaneously increase expected returns. The potential diversification benefits are due to relatively low correlations between U.S. and international stocks and relatively high returns on stocks in developing nations.

Figure 5-3, presented earlier, demonstrated that an investor can significantly reduce his or her portfolio risk by holding a large number of stocks. The figure accompanying this box suggests that investors may be able to reduce risk even further by holding a large global portfolio.

Despite the apparent benefits from investing overseas, the typical U.S. investor still dedicates less than 10 percent of his or her portfolio to foreign stocks—even though foreign stocks represent roughly 60 percent of the worldwide equity mar-

ket. Researchers and practitioners alike have struggled to understand this reluctance to invest overseas. One explanation is that investors prefer domestic stocks because they have lower transaction costs. However, this explanation is not completely convincing, given that recent studies have found that investors buy and sell their overseas stocks more frequently than they trade their domestic stocks. Other explanations for the domestic bias focus on the additional risks from investing overseas (for example, exchange rate risk) or suggest that the typical U.S. investor is uninformed about international investments and views international investments as being more risky than the data suggest. More recently, other analysts have argued that as world capital markets have become more integrated, the correlations of returns between different countries has increased, and international diversification benefits have declined. A third explanation is that U.S. corporations are themselves investing more internationally, hence U.S. investors de facto obtain international diversification even though they invest only in U.S. firms.

Whatever the reason for the general reluctance to hold international assets, it is a safe bet that in the years ahead U.S. investors will shift more and more of their assets to overseas investments.

Source: Kenneth Kasa, "Measuring the Gains from International Portfolio Diversification," *Federal Reserve Bank of San Francisco Weekly Letter,* Number 94-14, April 8, 1994.

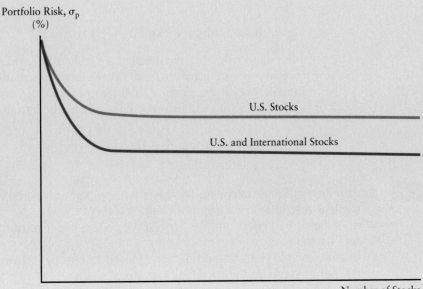

consequently its risk, will increase, and the reverse would hold if a low-beta stock were added. Most stocks have betas in the range of 0.50 to 1.50.

The preceding analysis of portfolio risk is part of the Capital Asset Pricing Model (CAPM), and we can summarize our discussion as follows:

1. A stock's risk consists of two components, *market risk* and *diversifiable risk*.
2. Diversifiable risk can be eliminated by diversification, and most investors do indeed diversify, either by holding large portfolios or by purchasing shares in a mutual fund. We are left, then, with market risk, which is caused by general movements in the stock market and reflects that most stocks are systematically affected by events such as war, recession, and inflation. Market risk is the only *relevant risk* to a rational, diversified investor because such an investor would eliminate diversifiable risk.
3. Investors must be compensated for bearing risk—the greater a stock's risk, the higher its required return. However, compensation is required only for risk that cannot be eliminated by diversification. If risk premiums existed on stocks to reflect diversifiable risk, then well-diversified investors would start buying those securities (which would not be especially risky to such investors) and bid up their prices, and the stocks' final (equilibrium) expected returns would reflect only nondiversifiable market risk.
4. A stock's market risk is measured by its beta coefficient, which is an index of its relative volatility.
5. The beta of a portfolio is a weighted average of its individual securities' betas.

$$b_p = w_1b_1 + w_2b_2 + \cdots + w_nb_n$$

$$= \sum_{i=1}^{n} w_ib_i. \tag{5-7}$$

Here b_p is the beta of the portfolio, and it shows how volatile the portfolio is relative to the market; w_i is the fraction of the portfolio invested in the *i*th stock; and b_i is the beta coefficient of the *i*th stock. For example, if an investor holds a $100,000 portfolio invested equally in three stocks, and if each stock has a beta of 0.7, then the portfolio's beta will be $b_p = 0.7$:

$$b_p = 1/3(0.7) + 1/3(0.7) + 1/3(0.7) = 0.7.$$

This portfolio is less risky than the market, and it should experience relatively narrow price swings and relatively small rate-of-return fluctuations.

Now suppose one of the existing stocks is sold and replaced by a stock with $b_i = 2.0$. This action will increase the portfolio's beta from $b_{p1} = 0.7$ to $b_{p2} = 1.13$:

$$b_{p2} = 1/3(0.7) + 1/3(0.7) + 1/3(2.0)$$
$$= 1.13.$$

SELF-TEST QUESTIONS

Explain the following statement: "An asset held as part of a portfolio is generally less risky than the same asset held in isolation."

What is meant by *perfect positive correlation, perfect negative correlation,* and *zero correlation*?

In general, can the risk of a portfolio be reduced to zero by increasing the number of stocks in the portfolio? Explain.

What is the definition of an average-risk stock? What is its beta?

Why is beta the theoretically correct measure of a stock's risk?

Describe how portfolio returns and standard deviations are determined.

THE RELATIONSHIP BETWEEN RISK AND RETURN

In the preceding section, we saw that according to CAPM theory, beta should be used to measure a stock's risk. The CAPM also goes on to answer this question: For a given level of risk as measured by beta, what rate of return should investors require on the security? To begin, we define the following terms:

$$\hat{r}_i = \textit{expected} \text{ rate of return on the } i\text{th stock.}$$
$$r_i = \textit{required} \text{ rate of return on the } i\text{th stock.}$$
$$\bar{r} = \text{realized return.}$$
$$r_{RF} = \text{risk-free rate of return.}$$
$$b_i = \text{beta coefficient of the } i\text{th stock.}$$
$$r_M = \text{required return on the market portfolio.}$$
$$RP_M = (r_M - r_{RF}) = \text{risk premium on the market. } RP_M \text{ is the additional return over and above the risk-free rate required to compensate investors for assuming the risk of an average stock.}$$

Market Risk Premium, RP_M
The additional return over the risk-free rate needed to compensate investors for assuming an average amount of risk.

The **market risk premium** depends on the marginal investor's aversion to risk.[11] To illustrate, assume that Treasury bonds yield $r_{RF} = 6\%$ and an average stock has a required return of $r_M = 11\%$. Therefore, the market risk premium is 5 percent:

$$RP_M = r_M - r_{RF} = 11\% - 6\% = 5\%.$$

If one stock were twice as risky as another, its risk premium would be twice as high, while if its risk were only half as much, its risk premium would be half as large.

The required return for any investment can be expressed as follows:

$$\text{Required return}_i = \text{Risk-free return} + \text{Risk premium}_i.$$

Here the risk-free return includes a premium for expected inflation, and we assume that the assets under consideration have similar maturities and liquidity. Under these conditions, the relationship between the required return and risk is called the **Security Market Line (SML)**, although it is also frequently referred to as the CAPM equation.

Security Market Line (SML)
The line on a graph that shows the relationship between risk as measured by beta and the required rate of return for individual securities. Equation 5-8 is the equation for the SML.

SML Equation:

$$\begin{array}{c}\text{Required return} \\ \text{on Stock i}\end{array} = \begin{array}{c}\text{Risk-free} \\ \text{rate}\end{array} + \left(\begin{array}{c}\text{Market risk} \\ \text{premium}\end{array}\right)\left(\begin{array}{c}\text{Stock i's} \\ \text{beta}\end{array}\right)$$

$$r_i = r_{RF} + (r_M - r_{RF})b_i$$
$$= r_{RF} + (RP_M)b_i.$$

(5-8)

The required return for Stock i with a $b_i = 0.5$ and the market data just given is

$$r_i = 6\% + (11\% - 6\%)(0.5)$$
$$= 6\% + 5\%(0.5)$$
$$= 8.5\%.$$

---

[11]It should be noted that the risk premium of an average stock, $r_M - r_{RF}$, cannot be measured with great precision because it is impossible to obtain precise values for the expected future return on the market, r_M. However, empirical studies suggest that where long-term U.S. Treasury bonds are used to measure r_{RF} and where r_M is an estimate of the expected (not historical) return on the S&P 500, the market risk premium varies somewhat from year to year, and it has generally ranged from 4 to 6 percent during the past 20 years.

Equation 5-8 is called the Security Market Line (SML) equation, and it is often expressed graphically, as in Figure 5-4, which shows the SML when $r_{RF} = 6\%$ and $r_M = 11\%$. Note the following points:

1. Required returns are shown on the vertical axis, while risk is measured by beta and is shown on the horizontal axis.
2. Riskless securities have $b_i = 0$. Therefore, r_{RF} is the vertical axis intercept in Figure 5-4. If we could construct a zero-beta portfolio, its expected return would be equal to the risk-free rate.
3. The slope of the SML (5% in Figure 5-4) reflects the risk aversion of the economy—the greater the average investor's risk aversion, then (a) the steeper the slope of the line, (b) the greater the risk premium for all stocks, and (c) the higher the required return on all stocks.[12] If investors become more averse to risk, then the market risk premium increases, as does the slope of the SML.

Note that both the Security Market Line and a company's position on it will change over time as a result of changes in the risk-free interest rate, investors' risk aversion and thus the slope of the line, and the individual company's beta.

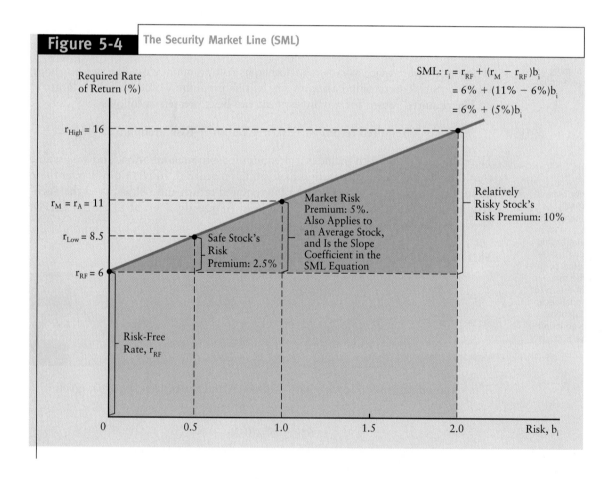

Figure 5-4 The Security Market Line (SML)

Required Rate of Return (%)

$$\text{SML: } r_i = r_{RF} + (r_M - r_{RF})b_i$$
$$= 6\% + (11\% - 6\%)b_i$$
$$= 6\% + (5\%)b_i$$

$r_{High} = 16$

$r_M = r_A = 11$

Market Risk Premium: 5%. Also Applies to an Average Stock, and Is the Slope Coefficient in the SML Equation

Relatively Risky Stock's Risk Premium: 10%

$r_{Low} = 8.5$

Safe Stock's Risk Premium: 2.5%

$r_{RF} = 6$

Risk-Free Rate, r_{RF}

0   0.5   1.0   1.5   2.0   Risk, b_i

---

[12]The slope of a line is measured by the "rise" divided by the "run," or the vertical distance divided by the corresponding horizontal distance. The vertical distance from $r_{RF} = 6\%$ to $r_M = 11\%$ is 5%. The corresponding horizontal distance, or the change in beta, is from 0 to 1.0, or 1. Therefore, the slope of the SML is 5%/1 = 5%.

The Impact of Inflation

Interest on debt amounts to "rent" on borrowed money, or the price of money. Thus, r_{RF} is the price of money to a riskless borrower. The risk-free rate, as measured by the rate on U.S. Treasury securities, is called the *nominal, or quoted, rate,* and it consists of two elements: (1) a *real inflation-free rate of return, r*,* and (2) an *inflation premium, IP*.[13] In the United States, it is common to make the simplifying assumption that the inflation premium is equal to the inflation rate, I, so $r_{RF} \approx r^* + I$ in most textbook presentations. However, this approximation may not be adequate when we deal with interest rates in countries where inflation is high. Recall, from Chapter 2, that 3.5 percent inflation combined with a 3 percent real rate would result in an inflation premium of 3.605 percent. The difference, or downward bias, increases with inflation, and for countries with high inflation, ignoring the interaction term, Ir^*, can bias the r_{RF} estimate downward by as much as a whole percent.

Another effect of inflation is its impact on the market risk premium.[14] However, for small changes in the inflation rate, it is reasonable to assume that the RP_M is stable. We have made this assumption in Figure 5-5, which shows the shift in the SML caused by an increase in inflation from 3 to 5 percent.

Changes in Risk Aversion

The slope of the Security Market Line reflects investor's risk aversion—the steeper the line's slope, the greater the average investor's risk aversion. Suppose investors were risk neutral; that is, they do not care about risk. If r_{RF} were 6 percent, then risky assets would also provide an expected return of 6 percent, because if there were no risk aversion, r_{RSK} would equal zero and there would be no risk premium. In this situation, the SML would be horizontal. As risk aversion increases, r_{RSK} increases, thereby increasing the market risk premium, and causing the slope of the SML to become steeper.

Figure 5-6 illustrates an increase in risk aversion. The market risk premium rises from 5 to 7.5 percent, causing r_M to rise from $r_{M1} = 11\%$ to $r_{M2} = 13.5\%$. (The risk-free rate, r_{RF}, remains constant at 6 percent—it is not affected by risk aversion because this is the riskless rate.) The returns on other risky assets also rise, and the effect of this shift in risk aversion is more pronounced on riskier securities. For example, the required return on a stock with $b_i = 0.5$ increases by only 1.25 percentage points, while a stock with $b_i = 1.5$ increases by 3.75 percentage points.

Changes in a Stock's Beta Coefficient

As we shall see later in the book, a firm can influence its market risk, hence its beta, through changes in the composition of its assets and its use of debt. A company's

[13]As we saw in Chapter 2, long-term Treasury bonds also contain a maturity risk premium, MRP. Here we include the MRP in r^* to simplify the discussion.

Also, recall that the inflation premium for any asset is equal to the average expected rate of inflation over the asset's life adjusted as given earlier. Thus, in this analysis we must assume either that all securities plotted on the SML graph have the same life or else that the expected rate of future inflation is constant.

Finally, it should be noted that r_{RF} in a CAPM analysis can be proxied by either a long-term rate (the T-bond rate) or a short-term rate (the T-bill rate). Traditionally, the T-bill rate was used, but in recent years there has been a movement toward use of the T-bond rate because there is a closer relationship between T-bond yields and stocks than between T-bill yields and stocks.

[14]In a recent article, it has been shown that inflation also affects the market risk premium. Inflation's effect on the market risk premium is given by the following equation: $RP_M = (1 + I)[(1 + r^*)(r_{RSK})]$. Theoretically, in a hyperinflationary environment an adjustment should be made to the market risk premium; however, in such an environment obtaining accurate data to make this adjustment is questionable. This discussion goes beyond the scope of our textbook; however, the interested student is referred to Roy L. Crum and Itzhak Goldberg, *Restructuring and Managing the Enterprise in Transition* (Washington, DC: Economic Development Institute of the World Bank, 1998); and Roy L. Crum, "Managing the Enterprise in Transition While Coping with Inflation," Dan Mozes, ed., *Uncertainty, Risk, and Capital Market Signals under Inflation* (Economic Development Institute, IBRD, 1993).

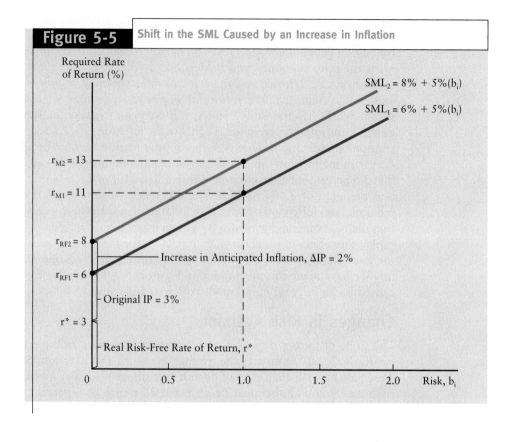

Figure 5-5   Shift in the SML Caused by an Increase in Inflation

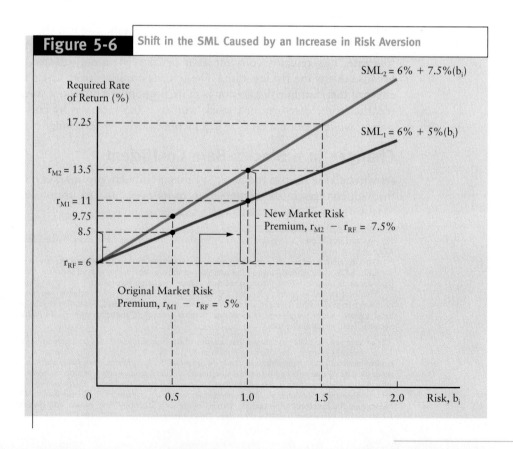

Figure 5-6   Shift in the SML Caused by an Increase in Risk Aversion

beta can also change as a result of external factors such as increased industry competition, the expiration of basic patents, and the like. When such factors cause beta to change, the stock's required return changes, which affects its price. Within the context of the SML, changes in beta show up as movements along the SML.

The CAPM in Practice

The CAPM approach is useful for valuing stocks, making capital budgeting decisions, and other applications. The three key parameters required for applications are the risk-free rate (r_{RF}), market risk premium (RP_M), and the asset's beta coefficient (b_i). We discuss those parameters next.

ESTIMATING THE RISK-FREE RATE   Technically, r_{RF} is the return on a riskless security. However, there is no truly riskless asset in the U.S. or global economy. Nonindexed U.S. Treasury securities are subject to inflation, a portfolio of short-term Treasuries will provide a volatile earnings stream as the T-bill rate changes over time, and inflation-indexed securities have risk because the real risk-free rate of interest can change. A recent survey of highly regarded companies showed that about two-thirds of the companies responding use the long-term U.S. Treasury bond yield as an estimate of the risk-free rate.[15] We agree with this strategy for the following reasons:

1. Common stocks are long-term securities, and most stockholders invest on a long-term basis. Therefore, it is reasonable to assume that stock returns have similar long-term inflation expectations as long-term bonds.
2. Treasury bond rates are less volatile than Treasury bill rates.
3. Many practical applications of the CAPM (capital budgeting) pertain to long-term investments, so it makes sense to use a risk-free rate with a long-term maturity.

ESTIMATING THE MARKET RISK PREMIUM   The RP_M is the expected market return minus the risk-free rate, and it can be estimated using either (1) historical or (2) forward-looking data. Theoretically, all of the CAPM's parameters should be based on expected future data, but because such data are difficult to obtain, people often use historical data and assume that investors expect future data to resemble that of the past.

The most common approach to estimating the forward-looking risk premium is based on the discounted cash flow model as we will discuss in Chapter 9. In its short form, the expected rate of return on a stock is simply the expected dividend yield and the expected growth rate, which results in capital gains:

Expected return = $\hat{r}$ = Expected dividend/Current price + Expected growth rate.

The expected returns for a large sample of stocks such as the S&P 500 are estimated, and their average is taken to be the expected return on the market. The yield in the market on a Treasury bond is used to represent the expected return on a risk-free asset. Subtracting the T-bond yield from the expected market return produces the estimated forward-looking market risk premium. It is difficult enough to profile the marginal investor, let alone what he or she anticipates about the dividends and growth rate of a particular stock.

---

[15]See Robert E. Bruner, Kenneth M. Eades, Robert S. Harris, and Robert C. Higgins, "Best Practices in Estimating the Cost of Capital: Survey and Synthesis," *Financial Practice and Education*, Spring/Summer 1998, 13–28.

There are a number of problems with this approach: (1) Different analysts project different growth rates for any given stock, so it is difficult to decide which growth rate to use. (2) Investors do not necessarily rely on analysts' forecasts, especially in view of recent criticisms of analysts' work and their possible biases. (3) Points 1 and 2 make it difficult to have a lot of confidence in the estimated market return, but there are also issues with the determination of the risk-free rate. The rate on short-term or long-term Treasury securities can be used—and the choice makes a difference. Still, in recent years most analysts have obtained estimates of the forward-looking market risk premium in the range of 4.5 to 6.5 percent.

As an alternative to the forward-looking premium, we can base the estimate on historical data, and such a historical premium is available annually for a fee from Ibbotson Associates. Ibbotson has collected market data over a long period of time and found the average annual returns on stocks, T-bonds, T-bills, and high-grade corporate bonds. The historical market risk premium is then estimated by subtracting the historical return on bonds from the average historical return on stocks. Ibbotson finds that stocks' historical risk premium over long-term T-bonds is about 7.0 percent using an arithmetic average and 5.0 percent using a geometric average. The historical premium over short-term T-bills is higher because bills generally return less than bonds.

There are several problems with historical risk premiums: (1) It is not clear that investors expect the future to be like the past. (2) The choice of the time period used for the average returns can result in very different estimates of the risk premium. Ibbotson uses data from 1926 to the most current year because this is the data set available to them. That encompasses the Great Depression of the 1930s, World War II, the market bubble of the late 1990s, and all the years in between. It is not clear that investors base their future expectations on such distant returns, but we really do not know what the marginal investor is thinking. We do know that Ibbotson's historical risk premium was 7.2 percent based on data from 1926 to 2003, but we also know that very different numbers result depending on the period studied. Here are some historical premiums for several different periods:

1926–1999	8.1%	1982–1999	10.7%
1926–2000	7.8%	1982–2000	8.1%
1926–2001	7.4%	1982–2001	8.0%
1926–2002	7.0%	1982–2002	6.3%

The dramatic decline in the historical premium from 1999 to 2002 was caused by the sharp decline in stock prices during those years. However, it is logical to think that a declining market would be accompanied by an increasing risk premium, just the opposite from what we observe. In any event, it is clear that market risk premiums based on historical data are unstable, and they may or may not reflect the "true" premiums that the marginal investor uses to determine his or her required rate of return.

Recently, some academics have argued that the "true" risk premium is lower than those found using either forward-looking or historical data. Eugene Fama of the University of Chicago and Kenneth French of Dartmouth used earnings and dividend growth rates for the period 1951–2000 to suggest a risk premium of 2.55 percent. Jay Ritter of the University of Florida argues that the true risk premium should be based on inflation-adjusted expected returns, and he concluded that the proper rate is about 1 percent.[16]

[16]See Eugene Fama and Kenneth R. French, "The Equity Premium," *Journal of Finance*, Vol. 27, no. 2, April 2002, 637–659; and Jay Ritter, "The Biggest Mistakes We Teach," *Journal of Financial Research*, Summer 2002, 159–168.

Given all this conflicting evidence, what should we use for the market risk premium? Investors are probably less risk averse than they were 50, or even 20, years ago, so the historical premium of 7.2 percent would seem to overestimate the current premium. In our own work, we typically use a risk premium of about 5 percent, or a range of 4 to 6 percent. While some academic research has suggested using far lower estimates, this thinking does not at this time represent the mainstream view.

ESTIMATING BETA   Beta coefficients are calculated by running regressions of stock returns on market returns. However, this procedure is necessarily based on historical data, so it is subject to the same problems as encountered with efforts to estimate the market risk premium. There is no guarantee that investors expect past trends to continue on into the future. Also, there has been considerable debate about what a stock's return should be regressed against. We normally use a market index such as the S&P 500, but other indexes could be used. Also, the market return should, theoretically, include all assets, including human capital, and such an index is not available. Furthermore, as global markets become more integrated, it is becoming ever more important to use an index that reflects the entire world's equity markets. We will take this step in Chapter 10, when we discuss a global CAPM model.

Two final points should be made. First, betas can be based on daily, weekly, monthly, or annual returns. Most organizations use monthly data, but other periods could be justified just as easily, and the period used can have a significant effect on the calculated beta. Second, once a stock's beta has been estimated, its statistical significance should be considered. An estimated beta might be 1.0, but a statistical analysis might lead us to conclude that the true beta could easily lie anywhere in the range of 0.6 to 1.4.

In view of all these potential problems, managers and financial analysts should use betas, and the CAPM in general, with caution.

SELF-TEST QUESTIONS

Differentiate among the expected rate of return ($\hat{r}$), the required rate of return (r), and the realized, after-the-fact return ($\bar{r}$) on a stock. Which would have to be larger to get you to purchase the stock, $\hat{r}$ or r? Would $\hat{r}$, r, and $\bar{r}$ typically be the same or different for a given company?

What happens to the SML graph when inflation increases or decreases?

What happens to the SML graph when risk aversion increases or decreases? What would the SML look like if investors were indifferent to risk, that is, if they were not risk averse?

How can a firm influence its market risk as reflected in its beta?

Discuss some of the problems that arise when applying the CAPM equation.

INTERNATIONAL EXTENSIONS

To apply the CAPM in a global setting, several additional factors should be considered:

1. Adding securities traded in markets outside the United States provides additional diversification benefits because foreign markets are not perfectly positively correlated with U.S. markets. In fact, empirical studies have found that even markets close to the United States, such as in Canada, have a correlation of only approximately +0.8, and more distant markets, such as in Japan, can have a correlation as low as +0.2. Of course, these correlations change over time, and they have also been increasing as markets have become more integrated, but there are still a lot of potential benefits from international diversification.

2. If foreign securities denominated in a currency other than the investor's home currency are added to a portfolio, then exchange rate risk should be considered. Some experts believe that holding assets denominated in many currencies provides sufficient protection against any single currency losing value. However, others believe that currency risk should be managed through hedging to keep the benefits of foreign diversification from being diluted. Regardless of the strategy taken, you should keep in mind that fluctuating exchange rates have the potential for either hurting or helping a portfolio's returns.

3. The CAPM assumes that a risk-free asset can be specified. While this assumption is questionable in the domestic setting, it is even more problematic for global investors, as there is no single risk-free rate that applies to investors everywhere. Also, the CAPM assumes that investors can select from the entire universe of risky assets, that information is freely available about the future risk and return potential of each company, and that capital is internationally mobile without barriers. In reality, though, these conditions are not completely accurate in international markets.

SELF-TEST QUESTION   What additional considerations exist when the CAPM is applied internationally?

SOME CONCERNS ABOUT BETA AND THE CAPM

Kenneth French's Web site http://mba. tuck.dartmouth.edu/ pages/faculty/ken. french/index.html is an excellent resource for data and information regarding factors related to stock returns.

The Capital Asset Pricing Model (CAPM) is more than just an abstract theory—it is widely used by analysts, investors, and corporations. However, despite the CAPM's intuitive appeal, a number of studies have raised concerns about its validity. First, note that under the CAPM a stock's return depends entirely on the risk-free rate, the market risk premium, and the stock's beta. Other factors such as the size of the company, its industry, and the like are not reflected in the CAPM except to the extent that those factors affect its beta. However, numerous studies have cast doubt on the CAPM. For example, a study by Fama and French found that two variables, the firm's size and its market/book ratio, are consistently related to stock returns, but returns are not related to betas.[17] After adjusting for other factors, smaller firms have provided relatively high returns, and returns are also relatively high on stocks with low market/book ratios. At the same time, and contrary to the CAPM, they found virtually no relationship between a stock's beta and its return.

Studies such as Fama-French have led researchers to seek an alternative to the traditional CAPM. Thus, "multi-beta" models that relate returns to a number of factors such as Fama-French's size and market/book ratio, as well as the traditional beta, have been developed. Multi-beta models are thought of as being more general than the traditional CAPM. In the multi-beta models, market risk is measured relative to a number of risk factors that are thought to determine asset returns, whereas the CAPM gauges risk only relative to the market return.[18] This research is ongoing, but it appears that several risk factors, including bond default premiums and maturities, and inflation, are important.

SELF-TEST QUESTION   Are there any reasons to question the validity of the CAPM? Explain.

---

[17]See Eugene F. Fama and Kenneth R. French, "The Cross-Section of Expected Stock Returns," *Journal of Finance*, Vol. 47, 1992, 427–465; and Eugene F. Fama and Kenneth R. French, "Common Risk Factors in the Returns on Stocks and Bonds," *Journal of Financial Economics*, Vol. 33, 1993, 3–56.

[18]One such model is the Arbitrage Pricing Theory (APT) developed by Stephen Ross. Refer to Chapter 3 of Eugene F. Brigham and Phillip R. Daves, *Intermediate Financial Management*, 8th edition (Mason, OH: South-Western Publishing, 2004) for additional information.

Summary

In this chapter, we described the trade-off between risk and return. We began by discussing how to measure risk and return for both individual assets and portfolios. In particular, we differentiated between stand-alone and portfolio risk, and explained the benefits of diversification. Finally, we developed the CAPM, which explains how risk affects rates of return. In the chapters that follow, we will give you the tools to estimate the required rates of return for bonds, preferred stock, and common stock, and we will explain how firms use these returns to develop their costs of capital. As you will see, the cost of capital is an important element in the firm's capital budgeting process. The key concepts discussed in this chapter are listed below.

- **Risk** can be defined as the chance that some unfavorable event will occur.
- The **expected rate of return** on an investment is the rate of return expected to be realized from an investment; the weighted average of the probability distribution of possible results.
- The **tighter the probability distribution**, the more likely it is that the actual outcome will be close to the expected value, and, consequently, the less likely it is that the actual return will end up far below the expected return. Thus, the tighter the probability distribution, the **lower the investment's stand-alone risk.**
- When investing in foreign currencies, it is best to invest in those that are increasing in value. Additional risk is introduced when investments are made in currencies other than the home currency. **Exchange rate fluctuations** will not just **affect** the **expected returns** on investments, but also their **risk.**
- The risk of an asset's cash flows can be considered on a **stand-alone basis** (each asset by itself) or in a **portfolio context,** where the investment is combined with other assets and its risk is reduced through **diversification.**
- The average investor is **risk averse,** which means that he or she must be compensated for holding risky assets. Therefore, riskier assets have higher required returns than less risky assets.
- Most rational investors hold **portfolios of assets,** and they are more concerned with the riskiness of their portfolios than with the risk of individual assets.
- An asset's risk consists of (1) **diversifiable risk,** which can be eliminated by diversification, plus (2) **market risk,** which cannot be eliminated by diversification.
- The **relevant risk** of an individual asset is its contribution to the riskiness of a well-diversified portfolio, which is the asset's **market risk.** Because market risk cannot be eliminated by diversification, investors must be compensated for bearing it.
- The **Capital Asset Pricing Model (CAPM)** describes the relationship between market risk and required rates of return. A stock's required rate of return is equal to the risk-free rate plus a risk premium that reflects only the risk remaining after diversification.
- A stock's **beta coefficient, b,** is a measure of its market risk. Beta measures the extent to which the stock's returns move relative to the market.
- A **high-beta stock** is more volatile than an average stock, while a **low-beta stock** is less volatile than an average stock. An **average stock** has b = 1.0.
- The **beta of a portfolio** is a **weighted average** of the betas of the individual securities in the portfolio.
- The **market risk premium (RP$_M$)** is the additional return over the risk-free rate needed to compensate investors for assuming an average amount of risk.
- The **Security Market Line (SML)** equation shows the relationship between a security's market risk as measured by beta and the required rate of return for individual securities.
- Even though the expected rate of return on a stock is generally equal to its required return, a number of things can happen to cause the required rate of return to change: (1) the **risk-free rate can change** because of changes in either

real rates or anticipated inflation, (2) a **stock's beta can change**, and (3) **investors' aversion to risk can change.**
- Because returns on assets in different countries are not perfectly correlated, **global diversification** may result in lower risk for multinational companies and globally diversified portfolios.
- Although the CAPM provides a convenient framework for thinking about risk and return issues, a number of studies have raised concerns about its validity. A study by **Fama and French** has cast doubt on the CAPM. They found that firm size and the market/book ratio are consistently related to stock returns, and they found no relationship between a stock's beta and its return.
- As an alternative to the traditional CAPM, researchers and practitioners have begun to look for more general **multi-beta models** that expand on the CAPM and address its shortcomings. In the multi-beta model, market risk is measured relative to a set of risk factors that determine the behavior of asset return, whereas the CAPM gauges risk only relative to the market return. One such multi-beta model is the **Arbitrage Pricing Theory (APT)**.

QUESTIONS

(5-1) The probability distribution of a less risky expected return is more peaked than that of a riskier return. What shape would the probability distribution have for (a) completely certain returns and (b) completely uncertain returns?

(5-2) Security A has an expected return of 8.5 percent, a standard deviation of expected returns of 30 percent, a correlation coefficient with the market of −0.35, and a beta coefficient of −0.4. Security B has an expected return of 14 percent, a standard deviation of returns of 15 percent, a correlation with the market of 0.6, and a beta coefficient of 1.05. Which security is riskier? Why? Would your answer be different if each security were held in isolation rather than as part of a portfolio? Explain.

(5-3) If investors' risk aversion increased, would the risk premium on a high-beta stock increase more or less than that on a low-beta stock? Explain.

(5-4) If a stock's beta were cut in half, would its expected return be halved? Explain.

(5-5) A stock had a 15 percent return last year, a year in which the overall stock market declined in value. Does this mean that the stock has a negative beta? Explain.

(5-6) Briefly explain whether the following statement is true or false: "No additional risk is introduced when investments are made in currencies other than the home currency."

(5-7) In a market dominated by risk-averse investors, why must riskier securities have higher expected returns, as estimated by the marginal investor, than less risky securities?

(5-8) Briefly explain whether the following statement is true or false: "Much like the portfolio return calculation, the portfolio risk, σ_p, is the weighted average of the standard deviations of the individual assets in the portfolio."

(5-9) Briefly explain whether the following statement is true or false: "As a general rule, if we added enough partially correlated stocks to a portfolio, we could completely eliminate risk."

(5-10) Differentiate between diversifiable and market risk.

(5-11) Why does it make sense to use a long-term U.S. Treasury bond yield as an estimate of the risk-free rate used in the CAPM?

(5-12) What are the additional considerations for applying CAPM in a global setting?

(5-13) What would happen in the market if an investor were compensated for diversifiable risk in addition to market risk?

SELF-TEST PROBLEMS   Solutions Appear in Appendix B

(ST-1) Define the following terms, using graphs or equations to illustrate your answers
Key Terms   wherever feasible:
   a. Probability distribution; expected rate of return, $\hat{r}$
   b. Standard deviation, σ; variance, σ^2; coefficient of variation, CV
   c. Stand-alone risk; investment risk; risk aversion
   d. Expected return on a portfolio, $\hat{r}_p$; realized rate of return, $\bar{r}$
   e. Correlation; correlation coefficient, ρ
   f. Market portfolio; diversifiable risk; market risk
   g. Capital Asset Pricing Model (CAPM); relevant risk; beta coefficient, b
   h. Market risk premium, RP_M
   i. Security Market Line (SML)

(ST-2) An analyst has estimated SmytheHanratty Inc.'s returns under various economic
Expected Return, Standard   states as given below:
Deviation, and Coefficient
of Variation

State of the Economy	Probability of State Occurring	Stock's Expected Return if This State Occurs
Recession	0.05	−20%
Below average	0.25	−5
Average	0.40	10
Above average	0.25	25
Boom	0.05	40

   a. What is the stock's expected return, $\hat{r}$?
   b. What is the stock's standard deviation, σ?
   c. What is the stock's coefficient of variation, CV?

(ST-3) You are an equity analyst who is reviewing information regarding the stock of
Required Rate of Return   Valdez Inc. You have the following data:

   • Real risk-free rate, $r^* = 2.5\%$
   • Inflation $= I = 4.25\%$
   • Market risk premium $= 5.75\%$

   Valdez has a beta of 1.50, and its realized rate of return has averaged 12 percent over the last 5 years.
   a. What is the inflation premium, IP?
   b. What is the nominal, risk-free rate, r_{RF}?
   c. What is the return on the market, r_M?
   d. What is Valdez's required rate of return?
   e. If an investor expected to earn a return of 16 percent on Valdez's stock, would the investor purchase Valdez stock? Explain.

(ST-4) You hold a diversified portfolio consisting of a $25,000 investment in each of 20
Portfolio Beta   different common stocks. Your total investment is $500,000, and the portfolio beta is equal to 1.1. You have decided to sell one of your stocks that has a beta equal to 0.6 for $25,000, and you plan to use the proceeds to purchase another stock that has a beta equal to 1.5. What will be the beta of the new portfolio?

STARTER PROBLEMS

(5-1)
CAPM and Portfolio Betas
and Returns

Consider the following information for three stocks, A, B, and C. The returns on each of the three stocks are positively correlated, but they are not perfectly correlated. (That is, all of the correlation coefficients are between 0 and 1.)

Stock	Expected Return	Standard Deviation	Beta
A	9.85%	20%	0.8
B	11.00	20	1.0
C	12.15	20	1.2

Portfolio 1 has half of its funds invested in Stock A and half invested in Stock B. Portfolio 2 has one-third of its funds invested in each of the three stocks. The risk-free rate is 5.25 percent, and the market is in equilibrium (that is, required returns equal expected returns).
a. What is the market risk premium (RP_M)?
b. What is the beta of Portfolio 1? Portfolio 2?
c. What is Portfolio 1's required return? Portfolio 2?
d. In part c, you should have found that Portfolio 2's required return is 11 percent. This is the same as Stock B's expected return. Should it make a difference to you whether you own Portfolio 2 or just Stock B? Explain.

(5-2)
Portfolio Return and Beta

You are a common stock investor, and you currently hold a well-diversified portfolio with an expected return of 11.8 percent, a beta of 1.05, and a total value of $100,000. You plan to add to your portfolio by purchasing 1,000 shares of Biogen Inc. at $20 a share. Biogen has an expected return of 19 percent and a beta of 2.25. What will be the portfolio's required return and beta after you purchase the Biogen stock?

(5-3)
Expected Return, Standard
Deviation, and Coefficient
of Variation

An analyst has estimated HMC International's stock returns under various economic states as given below:

State of the Economy	Probability of State Occurring	Stock's Expected Return if This State Occurs
Recession	0.15	−25%
Below average	0.20	−7
Average	0.30	12
Above average	0.20	30
Boom	0.15	50

a. What is the stock's expected return, $\hat{r}$?
b. What is the stock's standard deviation, σ?
c. What is the stock's coefficient of variation, CV?

(5-4)
Required Rate of Return

You are a financial analyst for Worldwide Publications Inc. (WPI) and are reviewing the following market data:

- $r^* = 2.0\%$
- Inflation $= I = 3.0\%$
- Market risk premium $= 5.4\%$

Worldwide has a beta of 0.85, and because of recent problems in the publishing industry its realized rate of return has averaged only 8 percent over the last 5 years, which is significantly lower than its 12 percent average over the past 10 years.
a. What is the inflation premium, IP?
b. What is the nominal, risk-free rate, r_{RF}?
c. What is the return on the market, r_M?

    d. What is Worldwide's required rate of return?

    e. If an investor expected to earn a return of 9 percent on Worldwide's stock, would the investor purchase WPI stock? Explain.

EXAM-TYPE PROBLEMS

(5-5)
Portfolio Return
Assume that Stocks X and Y and the market have had the following returns over the past five years.

Year	Market	X	Y
2000	25%	15%	30%
2001	15	10	18
2002	-12	-9	-15
2003	-5	-3	-10
2004	8	9	2

The risk-free rate is 5.25 percent, and the market risk premium is 5.60 percent. What is the required rate of return for a portfolio that consists of 60 percent invested in Stock X and 40 percent invested in Stock Y? (Hint: Use your calculator to determine each stock's beta.)

(5-6)
CAPM and Portfolio Return
A money manager is holding a $2 million portfolio that consists of the following five stocks:

Stock	Amount Invested	Beta
A	$800,000	1.0
B	400,000	0.6
C	400,000	0.8
D	200,000	1.5
E	200,000	1.2

The portfolio has a required return of 10.5 percent, and the market risk premium, RP_M, is 6 percent.

    a. What is the portfolio's beta, b_p?

    b. What is the nominal, risk-free rate, r_{RF}?

    c. What is the required rate of return on Stock D?

    d. Which stock in the portfolio is expected to earn the same return as the market? Explain. What is r_M?

(5-7)
Portfolio Return and Beta
A money manager is holding the following portfolio:

Stock	Amount Invested	Beta
1	$1.0 million	0.50
2	1.5 million	0.75
3	1.5 million	1.10
4	1.0 million	1.60

Currently, the risk-free rate is 5.1125 percent, and the portfolio has an expected return of 9.50 percent. Assume that the market is in equilibrium so that expected returns equal required returns. The manager would like to take on additional risk so that the portfolio's expected return is 11 percent. Her plan is to sell Stock 1 and use the proceeds to purchase another stock. To reach her goal, what should be the beta of the stock that the manager selects to replace Stock 1?

(5-8) A money manager is holding the following portfolio:

Portfolio Return and Beta

Stock	Amount Invested	Beta
1	$500,000	1.75
2	500,000	1.35
3	250,000	0.95
4	250,000	0.65

The risk-free rate is 5.3 percent, and the portfolio's required rate of return is 13.1 percent. The manager would like to sell all of her holdings of Stock 4 and use the proceeds to purchase more shares of Stock 1. What would be the portfolio's new required return and beta following this change?

THOMSON ONE
Business School Edition — QUESTIONS

ESTIMATING REQUIRED RETURNS

Overview

In this chapter, we discussed the basic trade-off between risk and return. In our discussion of the Capital Asset Pricing Model (CAPM), we stressed that beta is the correct measure of risk for diversified shareholders. Recall that beta measures the extent to which the returns of a given stock move with the stock market. When using the CAPM to estimate required returns, we would ideally like to know how the stock will move with the market in the future, but because we don't have a crystal ball, we generally use historical data to estimate beta. We can estimate beta by regressing the individual stock's returns against the returns of the overall market. As an alternative to running our own regressions, we can instead rely on reported betas from a variety of sources. These published sources make it easy for us to readily obtain beta estimates for most large publicly traded corporations. However, a word of caution is in order. Beta estimates can often be quite sensitive to the time period in which the data are estimated; the market index used; and whether or not we use daily, weekly, or monthly data. Therefore, it is not uncommon to find a wide range of beta estimates among the various published sources. Indeed, *Thomson One: Business School Edition* reports multiple estimates of beta. These multiple estimates reflect the fact that *Thomson One: Business School Edition* assembles data from a variety of different sources.

Discussion Questions

1. Begin by taking a look at the historical performance of the overall stock market. If you want to see, for example, the performance of the S&P 500, select "INDICES," type "S&PCOMP," and then click on "GO." Click on "PERFORMANCE," and you will immediately see a quick summary of the market's performance in recent months and years. How has the market performed over the past year? The past 3 years? The past 10 years? Compare the S&P 500 Composite performance to the FTSE 100 (FTSE100) and to the Tokyo SE (TOKYOSE).

2. Now take a closer look at the stocks of three wireless telecommunications companies: Vodafone Group PLC (VOD), AT&T Wireless (AWE), and NTT Docomo Inc. (9437-TO). Before looking at the data, which of these companies would you expect to have a relatively high beta (greater than 1.0), and which of these companies would you expect to have a relatively low beta (less than 1.0)?

3. Return to the overview page for the stock you selected. If you scroll down the page, you should see an estimate of the company's beta. What is the company's beta? What was the source of the estimated beta? (Note: These betas are calculated relative to the appropriate domestic stock index, so direct comparison of betas is not possible because they are from different countries.)

4. Click on the tab labeled "PRICES." What is the company's current dividend yield (stated in its local currency)? What has been its total return to investors over the past 6 months? Over the past 3 years? (Remember that total return includes the dividend yield plus any capital gains or losses.)

5. What is the estimated beta on this page? What is the source of the estimated beta? Why might different sources produce different estimates of beta?

6. Select a beta estimate that you think is best. (If you are not sure, you may want to consider an average of the given estimates.) Assume that the risk-free rate is 5 percent and the market risk premium is 6 percent. What is the required return on the company's stock?

7. Repeat the same exercise for each of the two remaining companies. Do the reported betas confirm your earlier intuition? In general, do you find that the higher-beta stocks tend to do better in up markets and worse in down markets?

INTEGRATED CASE

Rick Schmidt, MRI's CFO, along with Mandy Wu, Schmidt's assistant, and John Costello, a consultant and college finance professor, comprise a team set up to teach the firm's directors and senior managers the basics of international financial management. The program includes 16 sessions, each lasting about 2 hours, and they are scheduled immediately before the monthly board meetings. Four sessions have been completed, and the team is now preparing Session 5, which will deal with risk and return. Prior sessions have provided an overview of international finance, exchange rates, the global environment, and foreign investment.

For the risk and return session, the team will explain the fundamental trade-off between risk and return and how it drives financial decision making. They plan to go through some basic terminology and calculations to make sure all the directors have the same "vocabulary" when discussing risk and return. Then, Schmidt wants to turn to more detailed discussions of risk and compensation for that risk, including asset pricing theories.

The risk and return session is important for three reasons: (1) The company wants to maximize its stock value, and risk is a major determinant of a stock's value. If the stock's risk can be reduced, other things held constant, then its required rate of return will decline and its value will rise. Thus, the directors need to know how investors evaluate risk and relate it to required returns so that they can judge better how their actions will affect the stock's risk and therefore its price. (2) The rate of return investors require on different types of securities depends on their risks. MRI needs to know the required return (cost) of its different types of capital so it can determine if potential capital budgeting projects are likely to earn their costs of capital. (3) The company's retirement program is based on a 401(k) plan in which individual employees direct their own pension asset allocations between common and preferred stocks, bonds, mutual funds, and MRI's own stock. There is a danger that some employees will lose money, become unhappy, and sue the company for not providing adequate investment advice. Rick wants to make sure the directors and managers—who may be asked for investment advice—are knowledgeable about the risks inherent in various types of investments; in the benefits of creating diversified portfolios of bonds, stocks, and other assets; and in how optimal portfolios can differ among different investors depending on their age, tolerance to risk, and other characteristics.

All of the directors invest in the stock and bond markets and know that different types of securities have different risk. However, the individual directors' knowledge varies considerably, and that makes it difficult to decide what to cover and how in-depth the coverage should be. After much discussion, the team concluded that they should concentrate on the difference between stand-alone risk and risk in a portfolio context; on how those two types of risk can be measured; on the differences between expected, required, and realized returns; and on how the different types of risk affect the different types of returns. As in the other sessions, they plan to use an *Excel* model both to illustrate the discussion and to help the directors become more familiar with *Excel*.

Schmidt also noted that several of the directors have expressed concern about the relationship between inflation and interest rates, and the risks posed by sharp changes in these rates. He plans to discuss the effects of interest rates on bond prices and income in a later session.

Wu expressed concern about addressing controversial issues, where the proper analysis is in question. She recalled that in college some students simply "tuned out" when the instructor raised a question for which there was no definitive answer, and she was concerned that the directors might react similarly. Schmidt and Costello agree that this could be a problem, but they feel strongly that it would not be appropriate to "sweep problems under the carpet." So, they want to bring up relevant unresolved issues, discuss alternative ways of dealing with them, and point out the implications of different decisions. The directors are all intelligent, experienced in dealing with complex situations, and would rather know about potential problems than be kept in the dark.

With those thoughts in mind, the three compiled the following set of questions, which they plan to discuss during the session. As with the other sessions, they plan to use an *Excel* model to answer the quantitative questions. Assume that you are Mandy Wu, and that you must prepare answers for use during the session.

QUESTIONS

a. Find the expected returns, standard deviations (σ), and coefficients of variation (CV) for the assets in Table IC5-1, then rank the assets from least risky to most risky based on σ and CV, and discuss the pros and cons of using σ and/or CV as a measure of investment risk. Note that Bruner Inc. does well when the economy is weak and companies are laying off employees but badly when the economy is strong. If data were shown for an index fund designed to mirror the market, would it have approximately the same expected return and σ as the market?

b. Now use the data in Table IC5-2 to calculate the returns and standard deviations on portfolios consisting of 50 percent each of Bruner and Kaufman for the period 2000–2004. Also, calculate the correlation coefficient between Bruner and Kaufman. Then discuss the implications of your results for the investment risks of these securities.

c. Now, suppose a Japanese investor held a portfolio of 50 percent Kaufman and 50 percent Bruner from the beginning of 2000 through the end of 2004. Use the JPY/USD exchange rate data given in Table IC5-3 to calculate the average portfolio return and standard deviation from a Japanese investor's perspective. What does this imply about international investments?

TABLE IC5-1 | Probability Distribution of Returns

| Economy | Probability | RATES OF RETURN | | | |
		T-Bills	Market	Kaufman Inc.	Bruner Inc.
Strong	0.25	4.75%	25.00%	65.00%	−15.00%
Normal	0.50	4.75	11.50	15.00	10.00
Weak	0.25	4.75	−5.00	−45.00	35.00

TABLE IC5-2 | Historical Returns, 2000–2004

Year	Kaufman	Bruner	Market
2000	40.0%	−6.0%	13.0%
2001	−5.0	41.0	−6.0
2002	−10.0	7.0	−2.0
2003	−15.0	20.0	20.0
2004	50.0	−11.0	25.0

TABLE IC5-3 | Exchange Rates, 1999–2004

Date	JPY/USD
12/31/99	105.30
12/31/00	116.67
12/31/01	132.68
12/31/02	118.81
12/31/03	106.27
12/31/04	107.20

d. Now use the historical returns data in Table IC5-2 to calculate the market's, Kaufman's, and Bruner's standard deviation, beta coefficient, correlation coefficient with the market, and R^2 value. Why are returns data for T-Bills not provided and analyzed? Discuss the roles of these statistics to assess assets' risks, and rank the assets from least risky to most risky.

e. Are the probability data given in Table IC5-1 consistent with the time series data given in Table IC5-2? If securities' expected values and standard deviations as shown in the two sets of data are different, does this prove that something is wrong with the data, that is, that one or the other set of data must be incorrect?

f. The real risk-free rate is 2.75 percent, expected inflation is 2.00 percent, and the expected market risk premium is 6.00 percent. Use these data to establish parameters for the SML equation, and construct a graph of the SML. Calculate the required rates of return for the various securities, and then (based on the data in Table IC5-1) indicate where each security lies in relation to the SML. Do the different securities appear to be in equilibrium? If they do not appear to be in equilibrium, might the problem be with the data (that is, might the stocks actually be in equilibrium, but the data we provided do not reflect the marginal investor's expectations)? (Note that we are explicitly assuming that the data in Table IC5-1 reflect investor expectations, and we are also implicitly assuming that investors form expectations on the basis of historical data such as that in Table IC5-2.)

g. Would an increase in (1) expected inflation to 4.0 percent and (2) the market risk premium to 8.0 percent have the same effect on the required returns of all the securities in Table IC5-1?

h. Suppose you formed a one-stock portfolio, and then added one randomly picked stock at a time to the portfolio, continuing until the portfolio contained every publicly traded stock. Draw a "reasonable" graph that shows the effects of adding stocks to the portfolio's standard deviation. If you had divided all traded stocks into four groups, ranked from the 25 percent with the highest betas to the 25 percent with the lowest betas, and then formed portfolios by picking stocks from each group, how would that affect the graph?

CHAPTER 6

Financial Statement Analysis

Financial Statements
Ratio Analysis
Reliable Reporting

Cash Flows (CF)

$$\text{VALUE} = \sum_{t=0}^{N} \frac{CF_t}{(1+r)^t}$$

e-resource

*The textbook's Web site, **http://crum. swlearning.com,** contains an Excel file that will guide you through the chapter's calculations. The file for this chapter is **FIFC06-model.xls,** and we encourage you to open the file and follow along as you read the chapter.*

A manager's primary financial goal is to maximize the value of the firm's common stock. The value of any business asset—whether a financial asset such as a stock or a bond, or a real (physical) asset such as land, buildings, and equipment—depends on the usable after-tax cash flows the asset is expected to produce over its life. Therefore, to maximize stock value, a manager must take actions that increase the firm's after-tax cash flows. Similarly, investors generally get good results if they buy stocks of firms whose cash flows are increasing. But how do managers predict how their actions will affect cash flows, and how do investors predict how successful managers will be? The answers to both questions can be found in firms' financial statements. However, accounting statements tend to focus on net income, while value depends on cash flows, so we must translate from income to cash flows. This chapter clarifies the differences between accounting income and cash flow and the adjustments that must be made to go from one to the other, while the next chapter explores in greater depth the consolidated financial statements of a multinational enterprise (MNE) and discusses several issues that are important from the global perspective but tend to be ignored for purely domestic U.S. firms.

Financial statements record past financial performance and also provide valuable glimpses into a firm's overall health and future direction. When assessing a firm's performance, managers, creditors, investors, and analysts combine quantitative information from financial statements with qualitative information about the firm, its competitors, and the market. Consequently, outsiders rely heavily on the validity of financial statement information when they make assessments and predictions about the firm. If outsiders do not trust the financial statements or *find the information hard to interpret—that is, not "transparent"—they tend to lower the firm's perceived value. Responsible financial reporting and auditing are imperative if markets are to function properly, prices are to be efficient, and firms are to successfully attract investor capital at attractive rates.*

This chapter begins with a brief overview of the basic financial statements, thus providing a quick review of the concepts covered in basic accounting and finance classes. We also provide a brief overview of ratio analysis and explain the connection between accounting statements and various cash flow measures. These cash flow measures are used heavily in future chapters, where we discuss the valuation of international stocks, bonds, and corporate projects. Along the way, we will highlight some of the unique aspects that arise when evaluating multinational firms. Looking closely at a multinational firm's annual report and financial statements, we can gauge the importance of its various investments around the world and their effects on its bottom line and overall risk. While accounting guidelines are becoming increasingly standardized throughout the world, some accounting guidelines still vary from country to country. Managers, outside investors, and analysts need to be aware of these differences when assessing international investments.

FINANCIAL STATEMENTS AND REPORTS

Annual Report
Issued annually by a corporation to its stockholders. It contains basic financial statements, management's analysis of the past year's operations, and opinions about the firm's future prospects.

Of the various reports corporations issue to their stockholders, the **annual report** is probably the most important. Two types of information are given in this report. First, a verbal section, often including a letter from the chairman, describes the firm's operating results during the past year and discusses new developments that will affect future operations. Second, the annual report presents four basic financial statements—the *income statement*, the *balance sheet*, the *statement of retained earnings*, and the *statement of cash flows*.[1] Together, these statements give an accounting picture of the firm's operating and financial positions. Detailed data are provided for the two or three most recent years, along with historical summaries of key operating statistics for the past 5 or 10 years.[2]

The quantitative and verbal sections are equally important. The financial statements report *what has happened* to assets, earnings, and dividends over the past few years, whereas the verbal statements attempt to explain *why* things turned out as they did and make forward-looking statements about the direction the firm is heading.

For illustrative purposes, we shall focus on a California-based company called Sound Systems International. Formed in 1970 under the name Sound Systems for America, the company began by producing top-of-the-line speaker systems for large auditoriums and outdoor stadiums, primarily in the California market. Over the past 35 years, the company has grown steadily and developed new products such as home stereo systems and personal audio products. Throughout the years, the company has also expanded geographically. Today its products are sold in all 50 states and in 21 countries worldwide. While the majority of the products are developed and produced

---

[1] The statement of retained earnings and statement of cash flows are not covered in detail here. For further information about these financial statements, refer to Eugene F. Brigham and Phillip R. Daves, *Intermediate Financial Management*, 8th edition (Mason, OH: South-Western Publishing, 2004), Chapter 6.

[2] Firms also provide quarterly reports, but these are much less comprehensive. In addition, larger firms file even more detailed statements, giving breakdowns for each major division or subsidiary, with the Securities and Exchange Commission (SEC). These reports, called 10-K reports, are made available to stockholders upon request to a company's corporate secretary. They are also available on the SEC's Web site at **http://www.sec.gov** under the heading "EDGAR."

Are you interested in learning about the history of accounting? If so, take a tour through the "History of Accounting" organized by the Association of Chartered Accountants in the United States and located at *http://www.acaus. org/acc_his.html*. For an excellent example of a multinational's annual report, take a look at 3M's annual report found at *http://www.mmm. com/about3M/index. jhtml*. Click on "Investor Relations," "Quarterly Earnings & Annual Reports," "2004 Proxy Materials," and "2003 Annual Report." A source for links to the annual reports of many companies is *http://www.annual reportservice.com*.

Income Statement
Summarizes the firm's revenues and expenses over an accounting period, generally a quarter or year.

in the United States, the company also has production plants in Mexico as well as production and distribution facilities in Germany and Argentina. It is also currently in negotiations with government officials in China to locate a production facility in the Pudong free trade area of Shanghai in order to better serve the growing Asian market. Recognizing the growing importance of its international operations, in 1997 the company changed its name to Sound Systems International (SSI).

While SSI has done well over the years, it has struggled somewhat recently. A quick look at SSI's 2004 annual report indicates that SSI's earnings have decreased from $297.7 million to $294.4 million, a decrease of 1.11 percent. However, the annual report further reveals that sales fell from $7,740 million to $6,912 million over the same period, a decrease of 10.70 percent. The "Management Discussion" section of the annual report blamed macroeconomic conditions such as a slowing economy, exchange rate conditions, and declining consumer confidence for the sharp downturn in sales, but it pointed to cost-cutting measures that mitigated the effect on earnings. The discussion continued to suggest that the economic recovery, an aggressive global investment policy, and continued cost-cutting measures will help SSI's future earnings recovery. Detailed data from SSI's income statement and balance sheet are used in this chapter to analyze its financial position. The financial statements presented in this chapter are consolidated financial statements. In the next chapter, we present detailed subsidiary statements denominated in local currencies and use those statements to explain the processes of foreign currency translation and very basic consolidation. We abstract from those details in this chapter.

The Income Statement

Table 6-1 gives the 2003 and 2004 consolidated **income statements** for SSI, which show its financial performance over each of the last two years. Income statements can cover any period of time, but they are usually prepared monthly, quarterly, and annually.

The income statement reflects financial performance over a specified period of time. It is the sum of all inflows of assets (called revenues) during the period less the sum of all outflows of assets (called expenses) during the period. The income available to common shareholders, which is revenues less expenses, taxes, and preferred stock dividends but before common stock dividends, is generally referred to as *net income*. SSI's *earnings per share (EPS)*, commonly called "the bottom line," was $0.654 per share in 2004, down from $0.662 in 2003. Throughout this book, unless otherwise indicated, we use the term "net income" to mean *net income available to common stockholders*. (Note that when accountants use the term "net income," they mean the item that we refer to as net income before preferred dividends.)[3]

EBITDA
Earnings before interest, taxes, depreciation, and amortization. It represents a better measure of cash flow than net income.

Another important accounting measure that is widely used by managers, analysts, and bank loan officers is **EBITDA**, which stands for earnings before interest, taxes, depreciation, and amortization. Because neither depreciation nor amortization is paid in cash, EBITDA is a better measure of cash flow than is net income.[4] SSI's 2004 EBITDA was $1,159 million, and this gives an idea of the cash flow generated from operations.

---

[3]Beginning December 15, 1997, companies are required to report "comprehensive income" as well as net income; however, comprehensive income does not have to be displayed directly below the income statement. Comprehensive income is equal to net income plus several comprehensive income items. Examples of comprehensive income include the unrealized gain or loss that occurs when a marketable security, classified as available for sale, is marked-to-market, and foreign currency translation adjustments, which we discuss in Chapter 7. For our purposes, we assume that comprehensive income is displayed on a separate statement, which we leave for advanced accounting courses to cover. It is interesting to note that the FASB is currently (2004) considering an overhaul of the income statement with a focus on comprehensive income.

[4]FASB Opinion 95 defines an even more comprehensive measure of cash flow, called *cash flows from operations*.

Table 6-1 also lists SSI's stock price at the end of 2003 and 2004. Despite its decline in earnings per share, SSI's stock price increased from $19.25 to $20.00 per share during 2004. The company's 3.90 percent realized return in 2004 was roughly in line with the returns of its key competitors but was well below the returns of the overall market in 2004. SSI's underperformance relative to the market reflects continued concerns about its ability to generate solid earnings growth in the years ahead.

TABLE 6-1 | **Sound Systems International: December 31 Income Statements (Millions of Dollars)**

	2004	2003
Net sales revenue	$6,912.0	$7,740.0
Cost of goods sold	4,545.0	5,270.0
General and administrative costs	1,208.0	1,278.5
Total operating costs	5,753.0	6,548.5
EBITDA	$1,159.0	$1,191.5
Depreciation and amortization	466.5	484.0
EBIT	$ 692.5	$ 707.5
Interest expense	143.5	153.0
EBT	$ 549.0	$ 554.5
Taxes	219.6	221.8
Net income before preferred dividends[a]	$ 329.4	$ 332.7
Preferred dividends	35.0	35.0
Net income	$ 294.4	$ 297.7
Common dividends	$ 0.0	$ 0.0
Additions to retained earnings	$ 294.4	$ 297.7
Per-Share Data		
Common stock price	$ 20.00	$ 19.25
Earnings per share (EPS)[b]	$ 0.654	$ 0.662
Dividends per share (DPS)[b]	$ 0.00	$ 0.00
Book value per share (BVPS)[b]	$ 8.64	$ 7.98
Cash flow per share (CFPS)[b]	$ 1.69	$ 1.74
Other Data		
Lease payments	$ 10.00	$ 10.00
Principal payments	$ 50.00	$ 50.00

[a]On a typical firm's income statement, this line would be labeled "net income" rather than "net income before preferred dividends." However, when we use the term "net income" in this text, we mean "net income available to common shareholders." To simplify the terminology, we refer to net income available to common shareholders as simply net income. Students should understand that when they review annual reports, accountants use the term "net income" to mean "income after taxes but before preferred and common dividends."

[b]There are 450 million shares of common stock outstanding. Note that EPS is based on earnings after preferred dividends—that is, on net income available to common stockholders. Calculation of EPS, DPS, BVPS, and CFPS for 2004 are as follows:

$$\text{Earnings per share} = \text{EPS} = \frac{\text{Net income}}{\text{Common shares outstanding}} = \frac{\$294,400,000}{450,000,000} = \$0.654.$$

$$\text{Dividends per share} = \text{DPS} = \frac{\text{Dividends paid to common stockholders}}{\text{Common shares outstanding}} = \frac{\$0}{450,000,000} = \$0.$$

$$\text{Book value per share} = \text{BVPS} = \frac{\text{Total common equity}}{\text{Common shares outstanding}} = \frac{\$3,887,400,000}{450,000,000} = \$8.639.$$

$$\frac{\text{Cash flow}}{\text{per share}} = \text{CFPS} = \frac{\text{Net income} + \text{Depreciation and amortization}}{\text{Common shares outstanding}} = \frac{\$760,900,000}{450,000,000} = \$1.691.$$

GLOBAL ACCOUNTING STANDARDS: CAN ONE SIZE FIT ALL?

These days you must be a good financial detective to analyze financial statements, especially if the company operates overseas. Despite attempts to standardize accounting practices, there are still many differences in financial reporting in different countries, and these differences create headaches for investors making cross-border company comparisons. However, the writing is on the wall regarding accounting standards, and at least some of these accounting differences may disappear beginning in 2005. As businesses become more global and more foreign companies list on U.S. stock exchanges, accountants and regulators are realizing the need for a global convergence of accounting standards.

The accounting profession has long recognized international accounting differences. In fact, the effort to internationalize accounting standards began in 1973 with the formation of the International Accounting Standards Committee. However, in 1998 it became apparent that a full-time rule-making body with global representation was necessary. Consequently, the International Accounting Standards Board (IASB) was established with members representing nine countries.

The IASB has been charged with the responsibility of creating a set of International Financial Reporting Standards (IFRS) for EU companies to adopt by January 1, 2005. This means that by 2005 more than 7,000 publicly listed European companies will have to conform to these standards. In contrast, only 350 of these companies are using international standards that are now in place. In addition a number of other countries, including Australia and other Pacific Rim countries, South Africa, Canada, Russia, Japan, and China, are interested in adopting IFRS.

As if the IASB's task wasn't daunting enough, in September 2002 the IASB and the U.S. Financial Accounting Standards Board (FASB) agreed to "formalize their commitment to the convergence" of U.S. and international standards. Convergence between the two standards is needed to level the playing field for U.S. companies and the thousands of European and Australian companies that will be using IFRS in 2005. The reconciliation of U.S. GAAP with IFRS has been divided into two separate tracks: a short-term convergence project to resolve minor issues separating the two different standards and a longer-term project to resolve larger issues. The FASB has set September 30, 2004, as the target date for issuing a final statement or statements covering some, if not all, of the differences identified in the short-term convergence project.

Convergence between the two standards is already taking place. In June 2001, the FASB issued Statement of Financial Accounting Standards (SFAS) 141 banning the pooling method for acquisitions and allowing only the purchase method, which is consistent with international standards. In February 2004, the IASB issued IFRS 2, which requires companies to reflect in its profit or loss and financial position the effects of share-based transactions, including expenses associated with transactions in which share options are granted to employees. FASB's SFAS 123 encourages companies to use a fair-value-based accounting method for reporting stock options as compensation, and in December 2002 it issued SFAS 148 to aid in the transition for companies voluntarily changing to this method. The FASB is expected to release an exposure draft during the first quarter 2004 that will bring several other U.S. accounting rules in line with international standards. One of the more significant changes expected is the requirement for companies to apply accounting changes retroactively (where statements are restated) rather than the current use of a cumulative "catch-up" adjustment in the year of change. In addition, the FASB is looking to overhaul the income statement with a focus on comprehensive income rather than net income. (Comprehensive income includes items such as unrealized gains or losses on securities held for sale that affect stockholders' equity but that don't currently flow through the income statement.) The FASB expects an exposure draft on comprehensive income during the second quarter 2005. The IASB is also looking at comprehensive income and an exposure draft is due out during the second quarter 2005. One area where convergence is not expected any time soon is the accounting treatment for derivatives.

Unfortunately, there is an additional complexity to reconciling the two standards—neither the IASB nor the FASB has any actual statutory power. They can create and reconcile standards, but only government agencies such as the SEC and the European Commission can actually decide what is legal. So, the question remains as to which agency will oversee the unified standards.

A survey of senior executives from 85 financial institutions worldwide found that 92 percent of those responding favored a single set of international standards but only 55 percent thought that

(continued on next page)

adoption of the single set of standards was achievable. Obviously, the globalization of accounting standards is a huge endeavor—one that will involve compromises between the IASB and FASB. U.S. GAAP has developed from a rules-based approach, while the IASB insists on using a principles-based approach to standards.

A global accounting structure would enable investors and practitioners around the world to read and understand financial reports produced anywhere in the world. In addition, it would enhance all companies' access to all capital markets, which would improve investor diversifica-

tion, reduce risk, and lower the cost of capital. However, it remains to be seen whether the IASB's lofty goal can be achieved.

Sources: "All Accountants Soon May Speak the Same Language," *The Wall Street Journal,* August 29, 1995, A15; Jim Cole, "Global Standards Loom for Accounting," *East Bay Business Times,* November 12, 2001; "Accountants Struggle to Reconcile Rules," *BestWire,* April 28, 2003; "For and Against; Standards Need Time to Work," *Accountancy Age,* June 5, 2003, 16; Larry Schlesinger, "Overview; Bringing about a New Dawn," *Accountancy Age,* September 4, 2003, 18; Cassell Bryan-Low, "Deals & Deal Makers: Accounting Changes Are in Store," *The Wall Street Journal,* September 10, 2003, C4; and Fay Hansen, "Get Ready for New Global Accounting Standards," January 2004, **http://www.BusinessFinanceMag.com.**

The income statements shown in Table 6-1 are actually consolidated statements representing the financial results of all SSI's separate subsidiaries located in the United States and abroad. The financial results of foreign subsidiaries are first reported in that country's local currency. Then, those results are translated into a reporting currency, which for U.S. multinationals, and any other multinationals required to file with the SEC, is the U.S. dollar. Once all statements are in dollars, intracompany accounts are cancelled out and the statements are summed to get the consolidated statements shown in Table 6-1. In the next chapter, we present SSI's 2003 subsidiary income statements and show the translation process from each subsidiary's local currency to the U.S. dollar and their resulting consolidation.

There are two permitted methods for translating financial statements: the *current rate method* and the *temporal method*. The appropriate method is determined by the subsidiary's operations and its relationship with the parent. While there are some complicated situations, in this overview we will give you a simplified explanation of when each method should be used. We defer to the next chapter for more detailed explanations.

A *self-sustaining foreign entity* is an operating unit located in another country that functions as a separate going concern and is largely independent of the parent. This type of subsidiary must use the current rate method to translate financial statements. For SSI, the German subsidiary falls into this category.

An *integrated foreign entity* is an operating unit located in another country that functions as an extension of the parent and whose cash flows are interrelated with those of the parent. This type of subsidiary must use the temporal method to translate foreign statements. For SSI, the Mexican subsidiary is considered to be an integrated foreign entity.

The current rate method uses the average exchange rate for income statement items (other than dividend payments), and the spot exchange rate on the payment date for distributions such as dividend payments. Any translation gains or losses do not flow through the income statement but rather are recorded in an account titled cumulative translation adjustment (CTA). This account is in the equity section of the balance sheet, and amounts in this account represent unrealized gains or losses resulting only from the need to prepare consolidated financial statements. There are no tax implications with the CTA adjustment.

The temporal method distinguishes between monetary and nonmonetary items. Nonmonetary items include inventories and fixed assets. The temporal method uses the average exchange rate for income statement items (other than items linked to nonmonetary items and dividend payments) and the spot exchange rate on the payment date for distributions such as dividend payments. Income statement items linked to nonmonetary items, such as depreciation, would use the same historical exchange rate used for that item in the balance sheet. Any translation gains or losses flow directly through the income statement.

The Balance Sheet

Balance Sheet
A statement of the firm's financial position at a specific point in time.

Table 6-2 shows SSI's 2003 and 2004 consolidated **balance sheets**.[5] Unlike the income statement, which reflects performance over time, the balance sheet represents a "snapshot" of the firm's financial position at a specific point in time (in this case, the last day of 2003 and 2004). Balance sheet accounts change continuously as inventories are stocked or sold, as fixed assets are purchased or retired, and as bank loans are borrowed or repaid, but only the amounts in the various accounts as of the balance sheet dates are shown. The upper section, sometimes called the "active" section, lists assets in order of "liquidity," or the length of time it typically would take to convert them to cash. The current assets (cash, accounts receivable, inventories, and prepaid expenses) are followed by net fixed assets (gross fixed assets less accumulated depreciation). The lower section, sometimes called the "passive" section, lists liabilities and equity, which are claims against the assets, in the order in which they must be paid: Accounts payable must generally be paid off within 30 days, notes payable within 90 days, and so on, down to the stockholders' equity accounts, which represent ownership and need never be "paid off." The easiest way to think of a balance sheet is that the assets section shows what the company has, and the passive section shows how they acquired assets, either from spontaneous liabilities (accounts payable and accrued liabilities), investor-supplied debt (notes payable and long-term debt), preferred stock, or common equity capital (retained earnings and common stock).

Taking a closer look at Table 6-2, we see that SSI's total assets remained relatively constant between 2003 and 2004—the company's decline in current assets was roughly offset by its increase in net fixed assets. Looking at the passive section of the balance sheet, we see that while the company did not issue any new preferred or common stock in 2004, the total common equity increased because of additions to retained earnings. While the company's current liabilities showed little change in 2004, SSI did reduce the amount of long-term debt on its balance sheet. Responding to lower interest rates, the company decided in 2004 to call in some of its outstanding long-term bonds.

The balance sheets shown in Table 6-2 are actually consolidated statements representing the year-end financial position of all SSI's separate subsidiaries located in the United States and abroad. Each foreign subsidiary's financial position will first be reported in that country's local currency. As before, that statement will be translated into the reporting currency, which for U.S. multinationals, and any other multinationals required to file with the SEC, is the U.S. dollar. In the next chapter, we present SSI's 2003 subsidiary balance sheets and show their translation from each subsidiary's local currency to the U.S. dollar and their resulting consolidation.

The current rate method of translation, described earlier, uses the current spot exchange rate for monetary and nonmonetary assets and liabilities and uses historical rates for equity accounts. Retained earnings represent beginning-of-year retained earnings plus the year's earnings after dividend payments. The temporal method uses the current spot exchange rate for monetary assets and liabilities and appropriate historical exchange rates for nonmonetary assets and equity accounts.

---

[5]There are other permitted formats for presenting balance sheets, but the one used here is far and away the most commonly encountered.

TABLE 6-2	Sound Systems International: December 31 Balance Sheets (Millions of Dollars)		
		2004	2003
Cash and equivalents		$ 579.0	$ 703.0
Accounts receivable		1,581.5	1,575.5
Inventories		1,208.5	1,271.5
Prepaid expenses		11.5	10.0
Total current assets		$3,380.5	$3,560.0
Net plant and equipment		4,724.5	4,563.0
Total assets		$8,105.0	$8,123.0
Accounts payable		$ 556.6	$ 463.5
Accrued liabilities		894.5	923.5
Notes payable		452.6	458.5
Current maturities of long-term debt		164.9	194.0
Total current liabilities		$2,068.6	$2,039.5
Long-term bonds		1,649.0	1,990.5
Total liabilities		$3,717.6	$4,030.0
Preferred stock (5,000,000 shares)		500.0	500.0
Common stock (450,000,000 shares)		2,000.0	2,000.0
Retained earnings		1,887.4	1,593.0
Total common equity		$3,887.4	$3,593.0
Total liabilities and equity		$8,105.0	$8,123.0

Retained earnings represent beginning-of-year retained earnings plus the year's earnings after dividend payments plus or minus currency translation gains or losses.

Other Information in the Annual Reports

SSI's annual report contains a lot of important information beyond just a qualitative discussion of the company's performance and its key financial statements. Toward the end of its report, SSI has a section labeled, "Notes to Financial Statements." In this section the company provides details on a number of important issues, including its pension plan, its bank loan agreements, the sources and terms of its long-term debt, and the strategies employed to hedge interest rate and exchange rate risk. Currently, all of SSI's debt is dollar-denominated and issued in the United States, but the company mentions that it would consider issuing bonds in the overseas markets if the terms were favorable. Similarly, SSI states that it has a fair amount of exchange rate risk because of its foreign sales, and despite not having used the derivative markets (or other techniques) to hedge this currency risk in the past, it is seriously considering using derivatives in the future. (See Chapter 15 for a more detailed discussion of derivatives.)

In another section of the annual report, SSI presents details about the performance of its various product lines and geographical segments. Table 6-3 summarizes the information that SSI provides concerning its international operations. (Note that all of these numbers are presented in terms of U.S. dollars.) While a majority of the company's sales, assets, and employees are in the United States, its international operations have become increasingly important in recent years. Figure 6-1 illustrates the dramatic increase in the proportion of international sales since 1990. Because Asia is

TABLE 6-3 | Summary of SSI's International Operations

2004

	United States	Mexico and Canada	South America	Europe	Asia	Total
Net sales ($M)	$3,679.4	$426.5	$423.5	$1,812.0	$570.6	$6,912.0
Total assets ($M)	$4,650.5	$717.5	$689.5	$2,047.5	$ 0.0	$8,105.0
Number of employees	46,155	3,785	7,340	11,945	0	69,225

	United States	Mexico and Canada	South America	Europe	Asia	Foreign Totals as % of Corporate Total
Percentage of Totals						
Sales	53.23%	6.17%	6.13%	26.22%	8.26%	46.77%
Assets	57.38	8.85	8.51	25.26	0.00	42.62
Employees	66.67	5.47	10.60	17.26	0.00	33.33

	United States	Mexico and Canada	South America	Europe	Asia	Total
Year to Year Growth Rates						
Sales growth	-22.52%	3.28%	4.31%	10.32%	7.76%	-10.70%
Asset growth	-0.81	6.30	0.86	-1.37	NA	-0.22
Employee growth	0.25	9.22	16.60	14.91	NA	4.58

2003

	United States	Mexico and Canada	South America	Europe	Asia	Total
Net sales ($M)	$4,749.0	$413.0	$406.0	$1,642.5	$529.5	$7,740.0
Total assets ($M)	$4,688.4	$675.0	$683.6	$2,076.0	$ 0.0	$8,123.0
Number of employees	46,040	3,465	6,295	10,395	0	66,195

	United States	Mexico and Canada	South America	Europe	Asia	Foreign Totals as % of Corporate Total
Sales	61.36%	5.34%	5.25%	21.22%	6.84%	38.64%
Assets	57.72	8.31	8.42	25.56	0.00	42.28
Employees	69.55	5.24	9.51	15.70	0.00	30.45

Note: The company currently has no production location in Asia; it serves the market only through exports.

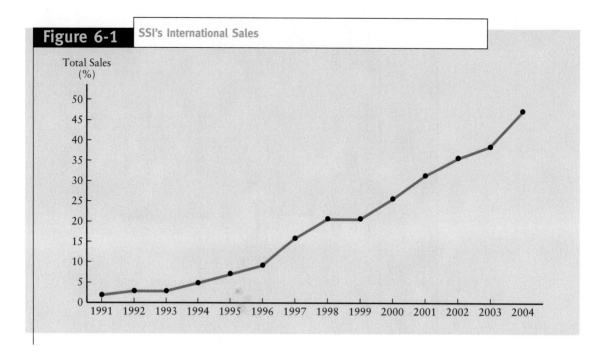

Figure 6-1 SSI's International Sales

a big part of potential future growth, SSI would like to locate a production facility in China; hence, it has been conducting negotiations with the Chinese government.[6]

SSI's international operations were particularly important in 2004. While total sales fell by 10.7 percent, U.S. sales fell by more than 22 percent. Looking at Table 6-3, we see that higher international sales helped partially offset some of the decline in the U.S. market. Sales were particularly strong in Europe and South America. The higher dollar-equivalent sales in these markets can be largely attributed to changing exchange rates. For example, in 2004, SSI actually sold fewer units in Brazil than it did in 2003, which resulted in less real-denominated revenue. However, because the Brazilian real appreciated relative to the dollar in 2004, SSI's Brazilian sales (measured in terms of U.S. dollars) increased. Likewise, the increase in European sales was due in large part to the relative strength of the euro in 2004.

While currency movements helped SSI's bottom line in 2004, there have been times in the past when changing exchange rates have hurt the company's performance. Most notably, in 1999, the company's yen-denominated sales in Japan were down only slightly from 1998, but the dollar-denominated sales plummeted because of the decline in the yen during the second half of 1999. Similar events occurred in SSI's other Asian markets—which explains why we see a leveling off in Figure 6-1 of the company's percentage of international sales in 1999. (Asian market sales were only a small percentage of total sales but have rapidly grown over the last five years.) These recent events forced SSI's financial managers to take a closer look at the risks of its international operations, and they are currently considering using derivatives (hedging) to reduce the company's risk exposure to changing exchange rates.

SELF-TEST QUESTIONS

What is the annual report, and what two types of information are given in it?
Why is the annual report of great interest to investors?
What is an income statement, and what information does it provide?

[6]Currently, the Asian market is served through exports. However, due to the increasing importance of this market, SSI is very interested in establishing a production site in Shanghai.

What is the balance sheet, and what information does it provide?

How is the order of the information on the balance sheet determined?

Regarding the time period reported, how does the income statement differ from the balance sheet?

Briefly describe the translation process used by a multinational firm from which it transforms its subsidiary statements into one consolidated financial statement. Does the subsidiary's relationship with the parent impact the process? Explain.

FINANCIAL STATEMENT ANALYSIS

Financial statements report both a firm's position at a point in time (the balance sheet) and its operations over some past period (the income statement). However, the real value of financial statements lies in helping predict future earnings, dividends, and free cash flow. From an investor's standpoint *predicting the future is what financial statement analysis is all about*, while from management's standpoint *financial statement analysis is useful both to help anticipate future conditions and, more important, as a starting point for planning actions that will improve the firm's future performance.*[7]

As we showed earlier, financial statements provide considerable information about a company's performance over the past few years. With a quick look at a company's income statements and balance sheets, we can immediately answer a number of important questions, such as, How big is the company? Is the company growing or shrinking? Is the company profitable? What sources of capital does the company use to finance its assets? At the same time, if we want to take a more detailed look at a company's financial performance, it is useful to construct financial ratios. For example, if we are told that a company has $25 million in inventory, it is hard to know if this is a large or small amount unless we compare it with other information such as the company's sales or assets. Likewise, to determine the financial risk of a company that has $1 million in debt, it is important to compare its total debt to its total assets. One million dollars of debt is highly significant for a company with $1.2 million in total assets but insignificant for a company with $500 million in total assets.

Even after constructing financial ratios, it is often hard to interpret the firm's performance without making further comparisons. For example, if we find that a company's days sales outstanding (DSO) is 39 days, it is hard to know if this is good or bad without comparing this ratio to past performance, to the company's credit terms, or to other firms in the same industry. Consequently, when conducting ratio analysis, analysts evaluate a company's ratios relative to their peers and to their own past record.

Categories of Financial Ratios

As you may recall from your introductory accounting and finance classes, financial analysts routinely calculate a wide range of financial ratios. A summary of SSI's key ratios, based on data from the income statements and balance sheets in Tables 6-1 and 6-2, is provided in Table 6-4. To put SSI's ratios in perspective, we also compare them with industry averages.

---

[7]Widespread accounting fraud has cast doubt on whether all firms' published financial statements can be trusted. New regulations by the SEC and the exchanges, and new laws enacted by Congress, have both improved accounting industry oversight and increased management's criminal penalties for fraudulent reporting. These measures should improve published accounting statements and restore investors' confidence in them.

TABLE 6-4 | SSI: Summary of 2004 Financial Ratios (Millions of Dollars)

Ratio	Formula for Calculation	Calculation	Ratio	Industry Average	Comment
Solvency					
Current	$\dfrac{\text{Current assets}}{\text{Current liabilities}}$	$\dfrac{\$3,380.5}{\$2,068.6}$	= 1.63×	1.91×	Poor
Quick	$\dfrac{\text{Current assets} - \text{Inventories}}{\text{Current liabilities}}$	$\dfrac{\$3,380.5 - \$1,208.5}{\$2,068.6}$	= 1.05×	1.30×	Poor
Assets Management					
Days inventory held (DIH)	$\dfrac{\text{Inventory}}{\text{Cost of goods sold}/365}$	$\dfrac{\$1,208.5}{\$4,545/365}$	= 97.05 days	65.84 days	Poor
Days sales outstanding (DSO)	$\dfrac{\text{Receivables}}{\text{Annual sales}/365}$	$\dfrac{\$1,581.5}{\$6,912/365}$	= 83.51 days	44 days	Poor
Fixed assets turnover	$\dfrac{\text{Sales}}{\text{Net fixed assets}}$	$\dfrac{\$6,912.0}{\$4,724.5}$	= 1.46×	1.49×	OK
Total assets turnover	$\dfrac{\text{Sales}}{\text{Total assets}}$	$\dfrac{\$6,912.0}{\$8,105.0}$	= 0.85×	1.05×	Low
Debt Management					
Days payables outstanding (DPO)	$\dfrac{\text{Accounts payable}}{\text{Cost of goods sold}/365}$	$\dfrac{\$556.6}{\$4,545/365}$	= 44.70 days	30.25 days	Good
Total debt to total assets	$\dfrac{\text{Total debt}}{\text{Total assets}}$	$\dfrac{\$3,717.6}{\$8,105.0}$	= 45.87%	57.82%	Low (good)
Times-interest-earned (TIE)	$\dfrac{\text{Earnings before interest and taxes (EBIT)}}{\text{Interest charges}}$	$\dfrac{\$692.5}{\$143.5}$	= 4.83×	3.11×	High (good)
EBITDA coverage	$\dfrac{\text{EBITDA} + \text{Lease payments}}{\text{Interest} + \text{Principal payments} + \text{Lease payments}}$	$\dfrac{\$1,169.0}{\$203.5}$	= 5.74×	5.0×	Good
Cash conversion period (CCP)	DSO + DIH − DPO	$\dfrac{83.51 + 97.05}{- 44.70}$	= 135.86 days	79.59 days	Poor
Profitability					
Profit margin on sales	$\dfrac{\text{Net income available to common stockholders}}{\text{Sales}}$	$\dfrac{\$294.4}{\$6,912.0}$	= 4.26%	5.00%	Poor
Basic earning power (BEP)	$\dfrac{\text{Earnings before interest and taxes (EBIT)}}{\text{Total assets}}$	$\dfrac{\$692.5}{\$8,105.0}$	= 8.54%	10.03%	Poor
Return on total assets (ROA)	$\dfrac{\text{Net income available to common stockholders}}{\text{Total assets}}$	$\dfrac{\$294.4}{\$8,105.0}$	= 3.63%	5.25%	Poor
Return on common equity (ROE)	$\dfrac{\text{Net income available to common stockholders}}{\text{Common equity}}$	$\dfrac{\$294.4}{\$3,887.4}$	= 7.57%	13.61%	Poor
Market Value					
Price/earnings (P/E)	$\dfrac{\text{Price per share}}{\text{Earnings per share}}$	$\dfrac{\$20.00}{\$0.654}$	= 30.58×	44.0×	Low
Price/cash flow	$\dfrac{\text{Price per share}}{\text{Cash flow per share}}$	$\dfrac{\$20.00}{\$1.691}$	= 11.83×	16.68×	Low
Market/book (M/B)	$\dfrac{\text{Market price per share}}{\text{Book value per share}}$	$\dfrac{\$20.00}{\$8.639}$	= 2.32×	3.20×	Low

FINANCIAL ANALYSIS ON THE INTERNET

A wide range of valuable financial information is available on the Internet. With just a couple of clicks, an investor can easily find the key financial statements for most publicly traded companies. Most sites also have detailed ratio analysis and comparison to industry peers and the S&P 500.

Say, for example, you are thinking about purchasing a company's stock, and you are looking for financial information regarding its recent performance. Here's a partial (but by no means a complete) list of places you can go to get started:

- One source is Yahoo's finance Web site, **http://finance.yahoo.com**. Here you will find updated market information along with links to a variety of interesting research sites. Enter a stock's ticker symbol, click on Go, and you will see the stock's current price, along with recent news about the company. Click on Key Statistics (under Company on the left-hand side of the screen) and you will find a report on the company's key financial ratios. Links to the company's income statement, balance sheet, and statement of cash flows can also be found. The Yahoo site also has a list of insider transactions, so you can tell if a company's CEO and other key insiders are buying or selling their company's stock. In addition, there is a message board where investors share opinions about the company, and there is a link to the company's filings with the Securities and Exchange Commission (SEC). Note that, in most cases, a more complete list of the SEC filings can be found at **http://www.sec.gov**.

- Other sources for up-to-date market information are **http://money.cnn.com**, **http://www.bloomberg.com**, and **http://www.cbs.marketwatch.com**. Each also has an area where you can obtain stock quotes along with company financials, links to Wall Street research, and links to SEC filings.

- Another good source is **http://www.quicken.com**. Enter the ticker symbol in the area labeled quotes and research. The site will take you to an area where you can find a link to analysts' earnings estimates and SEC filings. This site also has a section where you can estimate the stock's intrinsic value. (In Chapter 9 we discuss various methods for calculating intrinsic value.)

- If you are looking for charts of key accounting variables (e.g., sales, inventory, depreciation and amortization, and reported earnings), along with the financial statements, take a look at **http://www.smartmoney.com**.

- Another good place to look is **http://www.morningstar.com**. Here you find links to analysts' research reports along with the key financial statements.

- Two other places to consider: **http://www.hoovers.com** and **http://www.zacks.com**. Each has free research available along with more detailed information provided to subscribers.

Once you have accumulated all this information, you may be looking for sites that provide opinions regarding the direction of the overall market and views regarding individual stocks. Two popular sites in this category are The Motley Fool's Web site, **http://www.fool.com**, and the Web site for The Street.com, **http://www.thestreet.com**.

Keep in mind that this list is just a small subset of the information available online. You should also realize that a lot of these sites change their format and content over time, and new and interesting sites are always being added to the Internet.

Liquid Asset
An asset that can be converted to cash quickly without having to reduce the asset's price very much.

Solvency
Condition where the firm has sufficient assets to cover all claims of creditors on the assets.

The ratios in Table 6-4 are divided into five major categories that focus on solvency and liquidity, assets management, debt management, profitability, and market values. Each category addresses different issues related to overall firm performance. Next, we briefly review each category and provide a quick summary of SSI's performance along each dimension.

SOLVENCY AND LIQUIDITY RATIOS.   A **liquid asset** is one that trades in an active market and can be quickly converted to cash at the going market price. **Solvency** is the condition in which the firm has sufficient assets to cover all claims of creditors on the assets. **Solvency** and **liquidity ratios** answer the question, Will the firm be able to pay off its debts as they come due in the near future? The most common solvency ratios are the **current ratio** and the **quick ratio**.

Solvency and Liquidity Ratios
Ratios that show the relationship of a firm's cash and other current assets to its current liabilities.

Current Ratio
This ratio is calculated by dividing current assets by current liabilities. It indicates the extent to which current liabilities are covered by those assets expected to be converted to cash in the near future.

Quick Ratio
This ratio is calculated by deducting inventories from current assets and then dividing the remainder by current liabilities. It is a measure of the firm's ability to pay off short-term obligations without relying on the sale of inventories.

Assets Management Ratios
A set of ratios that measure how effectively a firm is managing its assets.

Fixed Assets Turnover Ratio
The ratio of sales to net fixed assets.

Total Assets Turnover Ratio
The ratio of sales to total assets.

Days Inventory Held (DIH)
This ratio is calculated by dividing inventories by average cost of goods sold per day; it indicates the average length of time between receipt of raw materials until they are moved into accounts receivable upon being sold.

Looking at Table 6-4, we see that SSI's solvency ratios are slightly below the industry averages, so its solvency and liquidity position is relatively weak. Still, because current assets are scheduled to be converted to cash in the near future, it is likely that they will be converted into cash flows through the company's operations, or, in a crunch, they could be liquidated at close to their stated values. With a current ratio of 1.63, SSI could liquidate its current assets at only 61 percent of book value and still pay off its current creditors in full.[8]

ASSETS MANAGEMENT RATIOS   The **assets management ratios** measure how effectively the firm manages its assets. Excessive investments in assets cause operating assets and capital to be unnecessarily high, and this leads to a reduction in free cash flow and thus the stock price. On the other hand, if a company does not have enough assets, it loses sales, thus hurting profitability, free cash flow, and its stock price. Therefore, it is important to invest the *right* amount in assets.

Assets management ratios include turnover ratios like **fixed assets turnover** and **total assets turnover**. These ratios measure the efficiency of the company's fixed assets and total assets, respectively. **Days inventory held (DIH)** measures the length of time between receipt of items placed in inventory and when they are sold. **Days sales outstanding (DSO)** measures the average time it takes the company to collect its accounts receivable. The sum of DIH and DSO is the length of time that these current assets must be financed, either by spontaneous liabilities or by investor-supplied capital.

With the exception of fixed assets turnover, SSI's assets management ratios generally indicate below-average performance relative to its peers. Of particular concern are the company's DSO of 83.51 days, which is well above the 44-day industry average, and the DIH of 97.05 days, which is also well above the 65.84-day industry average.

The DSO can also be compared with the company's terms of sale. For example, SSI's sales terms call for payment within 45 days, so the fact that 83.51 days' sales, not 45 days', are outstanding indicates that customers, on average, are not paying their bills on time. This deprives SSI of funds that it could use to reduce debts, return to stockholders, or invest in productive assets. In some instances, customers paying late may signal that they are in financial trouble. Therefore, if the trend in DSO over the past few years has been rising but SSI's credit policy has not changed, the company should take steps to expedite the collection of its accounts receivable. Similarly, the company holds more inventory than the industry norm, thus diverting funds away from more productive investments and possibly indicating that it is holding obsolete inventory.

DEBT MANAGEMENT RATIOS   The extent to which a firm uses debt financing, or **financial leverage**, has three important implications: (1) By raising funds through debt, stockholders maintain control of an expanding firm without increasing their investment. (2) If the firm earns more on investments financed with borrowed funds than it pays in interest, then shareholder returns are magnified, or "leveraged," but shareholder risks are also magnified. (3) Creditors look to the equity, or owner-supplied funds, to provide a margin of safety, so the higher the proportion of funds supplied by stockholders, the less risk creditors face.

Examples of debt management ratios include the **debt ratio**, which measures the proportion of debt on the company's balance sheet, and the **times-interest-earned (TIE)** and the **EBITDA coverage ratios**, which consider the amount of income or cash flow the company generates to service its debt obligations. **Days payables outstanding (DPO)** represents supplier credit that usually has no explicit cost, so the longer the company has to pay its accounts payable (while still paying on time), the

---

[8] $1/1.6342 = 0.6119$, or 61.19 percent. Note that $0.6119(\$3,380.5) = \$2,068.6$, the amount of current liabilities.

less it must rely on costly investor-supplied debt. Finally, the **cash conversion period (CCP)** reveals the extent to which the company uses costly investor-supplied debt to finance working capital. Looking at Table 6-4, we see that SSI's debt ratio is below the industry average while its TIE and EBITDA coverage ratios are both above the industry average. Its accounts payable are outstanding for significantly longer than the average for the industry and, if the company is not simply paying late, this is a positive sign. However, in spite of the long payment period, the cash conversion period indicates that SSI must depend on interest-bearing debt to finance its working capital for a much longer period than the average firm in the industry. The debt management ratios generally suggest that SSI is financed fairly conservatively, and that it would not face difficulties if it attempted to borrow additional funds. However, it would not need to borrow so much if it could reduce its investment in working capital.

PROFITABILITY RATIOS Profitability is the net result of a number of policies and decisions, hence the **profitability ratios** show the combined effects of liquidity, assets management, and debt on operating results.

Profitability ratios include **basic earning power (BEP)**, **profit margin on sales**, **return on total assets (ROA)**, and **return on common equity (ROE)**. We see from Table 6-4 that SSI's profitability ratios are all below the industry averages. This poor performance is an obvious source of concern. As we mentioned, the 2004 ratios would have looked even worse if not for the relatively strong performance of SSI's international operations and the appreciation of the euro and Brazilian real.

MARKET VALUE RATIOS The **market value ratios** relate the firm's stock price to its earnings, cash flow, and book value per share. These ratios give management an indication of investors' perceptions of the company's past performance and future prospects. If the liquidity, assets management, debt management, and profitability ratios all look good, then the stock price and market value ratios will likely be high.

The **price/earnings (P/E) ratio** shows how much investors are willing to pay per dollar of reported profits. SSI's stock sells for $20, and its EPS is $0.65, so its P/E ratio is 30.58. P/E ratios are higher for firms with strong growth prospects, other things held constant, but they are lower for riskier firms. Because SSI's P/E ratio is below the industry average of 44.0, this suggests that the company is regarded as being somewhat riskier than most, as having poorer growth prospects, or both. However, it is worth noting that SSI's P/E ratio is still significantly greater than that of the average S&P 500 firm.

In some industries, stock price is tied more closely to cash flow rather than net income. Consequently, investors often look at the **price/cash flow ratio**, which is the stock price divided by the net cash flow per share, or net cash flow divided by common shares outstanding. SSI's price/cash flow ratio of 11.83 is also below the industry average of 16.68, once again suggesting its growth prospects are below average, its risk is above average, or both. Depending on the industry, some analysts also look at other multiples such as price/sales, price/customers, or price/EBITDA per share. Ultimately, though, value depends on free cash flows, so if these "exotic" ratios do not forecast future free cash flow they may turn out to be misleading. This was true in the case of the dot-com retailers before they crashed and burned in 2000, costing investors many billions of dollars.

The ratio of a stock's market price to its book value gives another indication of how investors regard the company. Companies with relatively high rates of return on equity generally sell at higher multiples of book value than those with low returns. SSI's book value per share (total common equity divided by shares outstanding) is $8.64. If we divide the market price by the book value we obtain a **market/book (M/B) ratio** of 2.32 times. The industry average M/B ratio is 3.20 times. This suggests

Basic Earning Power (BEP) Ratio
This ratio indicates the ability of the firm's assets to generate operating income; calculated by dividing EBIT by total assets.

Profit Margin on Sales
This ratio measures net income per dollar of sales; it is calculated by dividing net income by sales.

Return on Total Assets (ROA)
The ratio of net income to total assets.

Return on Common Equity (ROE)
The ratio of net income to common equity; measures the rate of return on common stockholders' investment.

Market Value Ratios
A set of ratios that relate the firm's stock price to its earnings, cash flow, and book value per share.

Price/Earnings (P/E) Ratio
The ratio of the price per share to earnings per share; shows the dollar amount investors will pay for $1 of current earnings.

Price/Cash Flow Ratio
The ratio of price per share divided by cash flow per share; shows the dollar amount investors will pay for $1 of cash flow.

that investors are willing to pay slightly less for a dollar of SSI's book value than for a dollar of its peers' book values.

The average company in the S&P 500 had a market/book ratio of about 3.68 in the summer of 2004. Because M/B ratios typically exceed 1.0, this means that investors are willing to pay more for stocks than their accounting book values. The book value is a record of the past, showing cumulative stockholder investment. In contrast, the market price is forward-looking, incorporating investors' expectations of future cash flows.

Comparative Ratios and "Benchmarking"

Ratio analysis involves comparisons—a company's ratios are compared with those of other firms in the same industry, that is, with industry averages. Like most firms, SSI's managers go one step further and compare their ratios with those of a smaller set of the leading electronic equipment companies. This technique is called **benchmarking**, and the companies used for the comparison are called **benchmark companies**. This procedure allows management to see, on a company-by-company basis, how it stacks up against its major competitors and the best companies in the industry.[9]

Many companies benchmark various parts of their overall operation against top companies, whether they are in the same industry or not. For example, SSI has a division that sells stereo components directly to consumers through catalogs and the Internet. This division's shipping department benchmarks against L.L. Bean, even though they are in different industries, because L.L. Bean's shipping department is one of the best. SSI wants its own shippers to strive to match L.L. Bean's record for on-time shipments.

Benchmarking is complicated for multinational firms. Operating units in foreign countries are best compared with similar units in the same country or region. However, multinational firms will often have units that operate in many different regions, making it difficult to determine the most appropriate benchmark firms. Another complication arises because of clashing corporate cultures. Different regions have different attitudes about the role of debt and about leasing rather than purchasing equipment, so country-by-country comparisons are often the best that can be achieved. Even then, interpreting the meaning of the data is challenging.

Comparative ratios for U.S. firms are available from a number of sources, including *Value Line*, Dun and Bradstreet (D&B), and the *Annual Statement Studies* published by Robert Morris Associates, which is the national association of bank loan officers. One must be careful, though, because each data-supplying organization uses a somewhat different set of ratios designed for its own purposes. Additionally, there are often definitional differences in the ratios presented by different sources.

Evaluating Trends in Financial Ratios

To this point we have focused attention on external comparisons. It is also important to examine trends in the company's ratios over time to see if it is moving in the right direction. While the data in this chapter provide only two observations, most trend analyses are based on a minimum of three observations, and preferably at least five, so that unusual events will not bias the conclusions. However, even with two data points for each ratio we can see some important trends developing.

SOLVENCY AND LIQUIDITY Both the current ratio and the quick ratio declined in 2004 from their 2003 levels, and in both years the company's ratios were lower than the industry's. Unless we had other information to the contrary, we would conclude

---

[9]Companies that use industry averages as their gauge of good performance instead of benchmarking on the industry leaders have been said to be "managing for mediocrity."

A great link for comparative ratios is http://www.quicken.com. Here you can find stock quotes, company ratios, and comparative ratios.

Market/Book (M/B) Ratio
The ratio of a stock's market price to its book value.

Benchmarking
The process of comparing a particular company with a smaller group of similar companies within the same industry, otherwise known as "benchmark" companies.

Benchmark Companies
A selection of a small subset of similar companies within the same industry as the company to which comparisons are made.

that the company has been becoming less liquid and thus less solvent. However, because of the reduction in debt over the period, this trend might not be as worrisome as it would be if debt had been increasing.

ASSETS MANAGEMENT All four of SSI's assets management ratios declined in 2004 from their 2003 levels. In both years, the company's days inventory held and days' sales outstanding ratios were higher than industry averages, which is bad. In 2003, its fixed assets turnover was also higher than the industry average, although its total assets turnover was the same as the industry average. These statistics indicate that the firm is not managing its assets very efficiently—asset levels are too high given the level of sales. SSI needs to increase sales for the assets it currently has or else reduce its assets. In addition, it should be aware that some inventory items may be obsolete and some receivables uncollectible.

DEBT MANAGEMENT SSI has reduced its debt from 49.61 percent of assets to 45.87 percent over the period. Because its debt level is lower than the industry average (57.82 percent), it has less than average risk on this count. This observation is borne out by looking at the TIE and EBITDA coverage ratios. Both ratios increased over the period and are well above the industry average. However, even as interest-bearing debt has declined, the DPO ratio shows that spontaneous liabilities (accounts payable) have been increasing. The industry average for this ratio is 30.25 days, but SSI has stretched its ratio to 44.7 days in 2004. Assuming that the company has negotiated a longer credit payment period than other firms in the industry and is not simply paying late, this is a good trend. On the other hand, if SSI is delaying payments past the due date, this would be a dangerous practice that should not continue. Even with the longer DPO, the company's cash conversion period is much higher than the industry average and is increasing. As a result, the cash conversion period indicates that SSI must finance its working capital with interest-bearing debt for more than 4.5 months before it receives payment for the money it has invested. The previously noted problems with accounts receivable and inventory, and the company's depressed profitability, reinforce the negative implications of this situation.

PROFITABILITY While all of the profitability ratios are below the industry averages, there is a positive trend in the profit margin on sales. This demonstrates that the cost-reduction program instituted in 2004 is taking hold. The other profitability ratios are all trending downward, although only slightly. Because these ratios all depend on asset levels, the overinvestment in current assets is probably causing this negative trend. Also, the reduction in debt caused the equity multiplier to decline, and this caused ROE to trend downward the most.

MARKET VALUE The trend in market value ratios is almost flat. The P/E and P/CF ratios increased slightly, but the market-to-book ratio fell slightly. The market seems to be reacting positively to management's efforts to control costs and reduce financial leverage, but it is still worried that other problems have not been addressed, especially the overinvestment in assets.

SELF-TEST QUESTIONS

Identify and describe the five major ratio categories.
What are the implications regarding the extent to which a firm uses debt?
How do market value ratios reflect what investors think about a stock's risk and expected return?
What does the P/E ratio show? If one firm's P/E ratio is lower than another, what are some factors that might explain the difference?
What is benchmarking?
What is the importance of trend analysis?

USES AND LIMITATIONS OF RATIO ANALYSIS

As noted earlier, ratio analysis is used by three main groups: (1) *managers*, who employ ratios to help analyze, control, and thus improve their firms' operations; (2) *credit analysts*, who analyze ratios to assess a company's ability to pay its debts; and (3) *stock analysts*, who are interested in a company's efficiency, risk, and growth prospects. Note, though, that while ratio analysis can provide useful information concerning a company's operations and financial condition, it has limitations that necessitate care and judgment. Some potential problems are listed here:

1. Many large firms operate different divisions in different industries and countries (or regions), and for these companies it is difficult to develop a meaningful set of benchmarks (industry averages or comparison firms). Therefore, ratio analysis is more useful for small, narrowly focused firms than for large, multidivisional ones. Large, multidivisional companies should rely more on trend analysis to ensure that they are moving in the right direction.

2. Firms can employ **"window dressing" techniques** to make their financial statements look stronger. To illustrate, a Chicago builder borrowed on a two-year basis in late December. Because the loan was for more than one year, it was not included in current liabilities. The builder held the loan proceeds as cash, which improved his current and quick ratios and made his year-end balance sheet look stronger. However, the improvement was strictly window dressing; on the third of January the builder paid off the loan and the balance sheet was back at its old level.

3. Different accounting practices can distort comparisons. Inventory valuation, depreciation methods, and revenue reporting vary greatly across countries, and this can affect financial statements and distort comparisons between firms.

4. It is difficult to generalize about whether a particular ratio is "good" or "bad." For example, a high current ratio may indicate a strong liquidity position, which is good, or excessive cash, which is bad. Different countries also have different impressions of what is important in terms of financial health. For example, a firm's debt ratio could be reasonable by U.S. standards, excessive by Asian standards, and overly conservative by European standards.

5. Effective use of financial ratios requires accurate financial statements. Revelations in 2001 and 2002 of accounting fraud by WorldCom, Enron, and others showed that financial statements are not always accurate, even if they are "blessed" by accounting firms; hence information based on reported data can be misleading.

Window Dressing Techniques
Techniques employed by firms to make their financial statements look better than they really are.

Ratio analysis is useful, but analysts should be aware of these problems and make necessary adjustments. Ratio analysis conducted in a mechanical manner is dangerous, but when used intelligently and with good judgment, it provides useful insights into a firm's operations.

Looking Beyond the Numbers

Sound financial analysis involves more than just calculating numbers—good analysis requires that certain qualitative factors be considered when evaluating a company. These factors, as summarized by the American Association of Individual Investors (AAII), include the following:

1. Are a company's revenues or costs tied to one key customer or supplier?
2. To what extent are the company's revenues tied to one key product?

Students might want to refer to AAII's educational Web site at *http://www.aaii. com*. The site provides information on investing basics, financial planning, portfolio management, and the like, so individuals can manage their own assets more effectively.

3. What percentage of the company's business is generated in other countries?
4. What role do new and existing competitors play in the firm's future?
5. Does the firm invest enough in research and development to ensure good future prospects?
6. How do different legal and regulatory environments affect the firm's decision-making process?

List three types of analysts who use ratio analysis in their work. Would the different users emphasize exactly the same or somewhat different ratios?

List several potential problems with ratio analysis.

What are some qualitative factors an analyst should consider when evaluating a company's likely future financial performance?

MODIFYING ACCOUNTING DATA FOR MANAGERIAL DECISIONS

Thus far, we have focused on financial statements as they are presented in the annual report. However, these statements are designed more for use by stock analysts, creditors, and tax collectors than for managers. Therefore, certain modifications are needed for use in corporate decision making. In the following sections we discuss how financial analysts combine stock prices, taxes, and accounting data to make the statements more useful.

Operating Assets and Total Net Operating Capital

Different firms have different financial structures, tax situations, and amounts of nonoperating assets. These differences affect traditional accounting measures like the rate of return on equity. They can cause two firms, or two divisions within a single firm, that actually have identical operations to appear to be operated with different efficiency. This is important, because if managerial compensation systems are to function properly, operating managers must be judged and compensated for those factors under their control. Therefore, to judge managerial performance, we need to compare managers' ability to generate *operating income* (or *EBIT*) with the *operating assets* under their control.

Operating Assets
The cash and marketable securities, accounts receivable, inventories, and fixed assets necessary to operate a business.

The first step in modifying traditional accounting data is to divide total assets into two categories: **operating assets**, consisting of those assets necessary to operate the business, and **nonoperating assets**, which include short-term investments and cash above the level required for normal operations, investments in subsidiaries, land held for future use, and other assets not used in operations. Moreover, operating assets are further divided into *operating current assets*, such as inventory and accounts receivable, and *operating long-term assets*, such as plant and equipment. Obviously, if a manager generates a given amount of profit and cash flow with a relatively small investment in operating assets, then the amount of capital investors must provide declines, and that causes the rate of return on capital to increase.

Nonoperating Assets
Cash and marketable securities above the level required for normal operations, investments in subsidiaries, land held for future use, and other nonessential assets.

Investors—stockholders, bondholders, and other lenders—supply most of the capital used by a business. Investors must be paid for the use of their money, with payment coming as interest in the case of debt and as dividends plus capital gains for stock. So, if a company raises more capital than it needs for investment, then its capital costs will be unnecessarily high.

Does all of the capital used to acquire assets have to be obtained from investors? The answer is no, because some of the funds are provided in the normal course of operations. For example, some funds used to acquire inventories will come from suppliers and be reported as accounts payable, while other funds will come as accrued liabilities, which include short-term "loans" from workers and tax authorities. Such funds are called *operating current liabilities*. Therefore, if a firm needs $100 million of assets, but has $10 million of accounts payable and another $10 million of accrued liabilities, then its *investor-supplied capital* needed is only $80 million. Each dollar of operating current liabilities is a dollar that the company does not have to raise from investors to acquire operating assets and hence has no stated cost.

Operating Working Capital
Current assets used in operations.

Net Operating Working Capital (NOWC)
Operating working capital less accounts payable and accrued liabilities. It is the working capital acquired with investor-supplied funds.

Operating current assets are called **operating working capital**, and operating working capital less operating current liabilities is called **net operating working capital (NOWC)**.[10] Therefore, net operating working capital is the working capital acquired with investor-supplied funds. Here is the definition in equation form:

$$\text{Net operating working capital} = \text{Operating current assets} - \text{Operating current liabilities}. \tag{6-1}$$

We can apply these definitions to SSI, using the balance sheet data given in Table 6-2. Here is the net operating working capital for 2004:

$$\begin{aligned}
\text{Net operating working capital} &= \left(\text{Cash} + \text{Accounts receivable} + \text{Inventories}\right) - \left(\text{Accounts payable} + \text{Accrued liabilities}\right) \\
&= (\$579.0 + \$1,581.5 + \$1,208.5) - (\$556.6 + \$894.5) \\
&= \$1,917.9 \text{ million.}
\end{aligned}$$

SSI's total net operating capital at year-end 2004 is the sum of its net operating working capital and operating long-term assets:

$$\text{Total net operating capital} = \left(\text{Net operating working capital}\right) + \left(\text{Operating long-term assets}\right). \tag{6-2}$$

$$\begin{aligned}
&= \$1,917.9 + \$4,724.5 \\
&= \$6,642.4 \text{ million.}
\end{aligned}$$

Note that SSI's only operating long-term assets are net fixed assets. Also note that SSI's total operating capital at year-end 2003 was:

$$\begin{aligned}
\text{Total net operating capital} &= \$2,163.0 + \$4,563.0 \\
&= \$6,726.0 \text{ million.}
\end{aligned}$$

Thus, SSI decreased its operating capital from $6,726 million to $6,642.4 million, or by $83.6 million, during 2004. This decline in operating capital occurred even though net fixed assets increased, from $4,563.0 million to $4,724.5 million, because of a decline in current assets, from $3,560.0 million to $3,380.5 million. The 3.5 percent increase in net fixed assets versus a sales decrease of 10.7 percent raises this question: Why did SSI tie up additional cash in operating capital even as sales were declining? Is the company gearing up for a big increase in sales, are inventories not moving, are receivables not being collected, or is management not as efficient as it

---

[10]Prepaid expenses, which are a creation of the "accrual" basis of accounting, are not included in operating current assets. They represent money the firm has paid for services (expenses) in advance. An example would be prepaid insurance. On the other hand, customer deposits (which are a current liability) do not represent investor-supplied capital. Therefore, they should not be deducted from operating current assets to arrive at net operating working capital.

should be? While we have some hints about the reasons from our ratio analysis, we will address these questions more directly later in the chapter.

Net Cash Flow

Net Cash Flow
The actual net cash, as opposed to accounting income, that a firm generates during some specified period.

Accounting Profit
A firm's net income as reported on its income statement.

Many financial analysts focus on **net cash flow**. A business's *net cash flow* generally differs from its **accounting profit** because some of the revenues and expenses on the income statement were not received or paid in cash during the year. Formally, net cash flow is net income plus noncash expenses less noncash revenues, although typically depreciation and amortization are by far the largest noncash items, and in many cases the other noncash items roughly net out to zero. For this reason, many analysts assume that net cash flow equals net income plus depreciation and amortization:

$$\text{Net cash flow} = \text{Net income} + \text{Depreciation and amortization.} \qquad (6\text{-}3)$$

To keep things simple, we generally assume that Equation 6-3 holds, but remember that Equation 6-3 will not accurately reflect net cash flow in those instances where there are significant noncash items beyond depreciation and amortization.

We can illustrate Equation 6-3 with 2004 data from Table 6-1:

$$\text{Net cash flow} = \$294.4 + \$466.5 = \$760.9 \text{ million.}$$

SSI's net cash flow declined by $20.8 million from its 2003 level of $781.7 million, which is not good.

Net Operating Profit after Taxes (NOPAT)

Net Operating Profit After Taxes (NOPAT)
The profit a company would generate if it had no debt and held no nonoperating assets.

Net income is certainly important, but it does not always reflect the true performance of a company's operations and hence the effectiveness of its operating managers. A better measurement for comparing managers' performance is **net operating profit after taxes**, or **NOPAT**, which is the amount of profit the company would generate if it had no debt and held no financial assets. NOPAT is defined as follows:[11]

$$\text{NOPAT} = \text{EBIT} (1 - \text{Tax rate}). \qquad (6\text{-}4)$$

Using data from the income statements in Table 6-1, SSI's 2004 NOPAT is found to be

$$\text{NOPAT}_{2004} = \$692.5(1 - 0.4) = \$692.5(0.6) = \$415.5 \text{ million.}$$

This was actually $9 million lower than NOPAT_{2003} of $707.5(0.6) = $424.5 million. However, SSI's financial statements indicate that net income fell by only $3.3 million. This difference arose mainly from a reduction in interest on long-term debt.

Free Cash Flow

We defined net cash flow as net income plus noncash adjustments, which typically means net income plus depreciation and amortization. Note, though, that cash flows cannot be maintained over time unless depreciating fixed assets are replaced,

---

[11]For firms with a more complicated tax situation, it is better to define NOPAT as follows: NOPAT = (Net income before preferred dividends) + (Net interest expense)(1 − Tax rate). Also, if firms are able to defer paying some of their taxes, perhaps by the use of accelerated depreciation, then NOPAT should be adjusted to reflect the taxes that the company actually paid on its operating income. For additional information see Tom Copeland, Tim Koller, and Jack Murrin, *Valuation: Measuring and Managing the Value of Companies*, 3rd edition (New York: John Wiley & Sons, Inc., 2000); and G. Bennett Stewart III, *The Quest for Value* (New York: HarperCollins Publishers, Inc., 1991).

so management is not completely free to use its cash flows as it chooses. Therefore, the concept of **free cash flow (FCF)**, which is the cash flow actually available for distribution to investors or deployed elsewhere in the enterprise, has been developed: *FCF is the cash flow after taxes and after the company has made all the investments in fixed assets and working capital necessary to sustain ongoing operations.* FCF can be calculated for the entire firm or for divisions within the firm.

When you studied income statements in accounting, the emphasis was probably on the firm's net income, which is its *accounting profit*. However, the value of a company's operations is determined by the stream of free cash flows that it is expected to generate now and in the future, because this is the cash that is actually available for distribution to investors.

CALCULATING FREE CASH FLOW As shown earlier in the chapter, SSI had $6,642.4 million of operating capital at the end of 2004, and $6,726 million at the end of 2003. Therefore, during 2004, it made this *net new investment in operating capital*: Net new investment in operating $capital_{2004}$ = $6,642.4 − $6,726.0 = −$83.6 million. In 2004, SSI had a NOPAT of $415.5 million. Therefore, its 2004 free cash flow was

$$\text{FCF} = \text{NOPAT} - \text{Net new investment in operating capital} \qquad (6\text{-}5)$$

$$= \$415.5 - (-\$83.6)$$
$$= \$499.1 \text{ million.}$$

USES OF FCF. Recall that free cash flow (FCF) is the amount of cash available for distribution to all investors, including shareholders and debtholders. There are five "reasonable" uses for FCF:

1. Pay interest to debtholders. This is a priority item.
2. Repay debtholders.
3. Pay dividends to shareholders.
4. Repurchase stock from shareholders.
5. Buy marketable securities or other nonoperating assets pending permanent deployment of the funds. (This is more of a short-term strategy until the firm can invest in other more productive assets with higher rates of return.)

Recall that the company does not have to use FCF to acquire operating assets since, by definition, FCF already takes into account the purchase of operating assets needed to support growth. Unfortunately, there is evidence suggesting that some companies with high FCF tend to make unnecessary investments that do not add value, such as overpaying for acquisitions. Thus, a high FCF can be wasted if managers fail to act in the best interests of shareholders.

In practice, most companies combine these five uses in such a way that the net total is equal to FCF. For example, a company might pay interest and dividends, issue new debt, and also sell some of its marketable securities. Some of these activities are cash outflows (paying interest and dividends) and some are cash inflows (issuing debt and selling marketable securities), but the aggregate cash flow from these five activities is equal to FCF.

FCF AND CORPORATE VALUE FCF is the amount of cash available for distribution to investors, hence a firm's value depends on its expected future FCFs. Chapter 9 develops a valuation model to calculate SSI's value by forecasting its FCFs and evaluating their risk. It is important to understand this basic concept: *FCF is the cash available for distribution to investors; hence, the firm's value depends primarily on its expected future FCFs.*

Evaluating FCF, NOPAT, and Operating Capital

In 2004 SSI generated a positive NOPAT and positive FCF, despite a 10.7 percent decline in sales. This resulted from an effective cost-cutting plan (reducing operating costs by over 12 percent from the previous year) and a decline in the investment in operating capital. SSI's decision to decrease its operating capital investment seems to be a smart move considering the economy was still relatively slow. However, SSI's managers are aware that reducing the investment in productive assets in 2004 will require greater future investment, for otherwise SSI will lose ground to its competitors over the long run. Therefore, even if SSI's projected sales growth and additional cost-cutting measures are realized, there is no guarantee that FCF will be higher in the next few years because required investment in operating capital might outweigh future NOPAT. Also, SSI must be careful that its cost-cutting plans do not hinder operations by cutting bone and muscle as well as fat.

SSI's free cash flow is positive, at $499.1 million, but would a negative FCF be a bad sign? Not necessarily—it all depends on *why* the FCF is negative. If FCF is negative because NOPAT is negative, that is a bad sign, and it probably indicates operating problems. However, many high-growth companies have positive NOPAT but negative FCF because they are making large but profitable investments in operating assets to support growth. There is nothing wrong with profitable growth, even if it causes negative free cash flows during a period of high growth. However, those free cash flows do need to turn positive somewhere down the road.

What is net operating working capital? Why are accounts payable and accrued liabilities deducted in its calculation?

What is total net operating capital, and how is it used in a financial analysis?

Differentiate between net cash flow and accounting profit. Which is emphasized in finance? Why?

What is NOPAT? Why might it be a better performance measure than net income?

What is free cash flow (FCF)? Why is FCF the most important determinant of a firm's value?

MVA AND EVA

Neither traditional accounting data nor the modified data discussed in the preceding section incorporates stock prices. However, management's primary goal is to maximize the firm's stock price, hence financial analysts have developed two additional performance measures, MVA, or Market Value Added, and EVA, or Economic Value Added.[12]

Market Value Added (MVA)

Market Value Added (MVA)
The difference between the market value of the firm's stock and the amount of equity capital investors have supplied.

The primary goal of most firms is to maximize shareholders' wealth. This goal is obviously good from the standpoint of shareholders, but it also helps to ensure that scarce resources are allocated efficiently, which is good for the economy. Shareholder wealth is maximized by maximizing the *difference* between the stock's market value and the amount of equity capital supplied by shareholders.[13] This difference is called the **Market Value Added (MVA):**

[12]The concepts of EVA and MVA were developed by Joel Stern and Bennett Stewart, co-founders of the consulting firm Stern Stewart & Company. Stern Stewart copyrighted the terms "EVA" and "MVA," so other consulting firms have given other names to these values. Still, EVA and MVA are the terms most commonly used in practice.

[13]Equity includes the proceeds of stock sales by the company and its retained earnings since its inception.

$$MVA = \text{Market value of stock} - \text{Equity capital supplied by shareholders} \quad (6\text{-}6)$$
$$= (\text{Shares outstanding})(\text{Stock price}) - \text{Total common equity.}$$

To illustrate, SSI's balance sheet shows that it has 450 million shares of common stock currently outstanding, with a par value of $2,000 million. Combined with retained earnings of $1,887.4 million, SSI has a book value of common equity equal to $3,887.4 million (BVPS = $8.64). At a current stock price of $20 per share, SSI's market value of common equity is $9 billion. Therefore, SSI's MVA, as of December 31, 2004, is

$$MVA = \$9,000.0 - \$3,887.4 = \$5,112.6 \text{ million.}$$

This $5,112.6 million represents the difference between the money that SSI's common stockholders have invested in the corporation since its founding—including retained earnings—versus the cash they could receive if they sold the business at December 31, 2004. The higher its MVA, the better the job management has done over the years for the firm's shareholders. SSI's MVA, as of December 31, 2003, was $8,662.5 − $3,593.0 = $5,069.5 million, so MVA increased by $43.1 million during 2004. Note, though, that this increase could have come more from a higher stock market than from management's good performance, so it must be investigated further.

Economic Value Added (EVA)

Economic Value Added (EVA)
Value added to shareholders by management during a given year.

Whereas MVA measures the effects of managerial actions since the inception of a company, **Economic Value Added (EVA)** focuses on managerial effectiveness in a given year. The basic EVA formula is as follows:

$$EVA = NOPAT - (\text{Operating capital})(WACC). \quad (6\text{-}7)$$

Operating capital is the sum of the interest-bearing debt, preferred stock, and common equity used to acquire the company's net operating assets, that is, its net operating working capital plus net plant and equipment. Notice that this is really the same as our earlier definition of operating capital—we just added up the sources of financing rather than taking operating assets and subtracting operating liabilities. When operating capital is multiplied by the firm's weighted average cost of capital (WACC), the result is the after-tax dollar cost of the capital used to support operations.

EVA is an estimate of a business's true economic profit for the year, and it differs sharply from accounting profit.[14] EVA represents the income remaining after *the cost of all capital*, including equity capital, has been deducted, whereas accounting profit is determined without imposing a charge for equity capital. As we discuss in Chapter 10, equity capital does have a cost—an *opportunity cost*—because funds provided by shareholders could have been invested elsewhere where they would have earned a return.

EVA measures the extent to which the firm has increased shareholder value during the year. Therefore, if managers focus on EVA, this will help to ensure that they operate in a manner that is consistent with maximizing shareholder wealth. Note too that EVA can be determined for divisions as well as for the company as a whole,

If you want to read more about EVA and MVA, surf over to http://www.sternstewart.com. and read about it from the people that invented it, Stern Stewart & Co.

---

[14]The most important reason EVA differs from accounting profit is that the cost of equity capital is deducted when calculating EVA. Other factors that could lead to differences include adjustments that might be made to depreciation, to research and development costs, to inventory valuations, and so on. These other adjustments also can affect the calculation of investor-supplied capital, which affects both EVA and MVA. See Stewart, *The Quest for Value.*

so it provides a useful basis for determining managerial performance at all levels. Consequently, EVA is used by many firms as a primary basis for determining managerial compensation.

During the course of 2004, managerial actions led to a decline in SSI's economic value:

$$EVA = \$415.5 - (\$6,642.4 \times 0.0876) = -\$166.4 \text{ million.}$$

This negative EVA in 2004, combined with the $-\$164.7$ million of EVA in 2003, suggests that SSI has been unable to generate sufficient profits to compensate investors for the capital they have provided. The company earned an accounting profit, but that profit failed to account for the cost of the equity capital stockholders have provided. Also, remember that we previously indicated that SSI's increase in fixed assets was troubling in light of its decline in revenue and profits. These additional fixed assets had to be financed, and that meant additional capital, which has a cost. So, while net income fell in 2004, it did so at a much slower rate than EVA, because net income did not reflect the cost of all capital. Because EVA accounts for the cost of all capital, it is a better measure of managerial performance than net income.

SELF-TEST QUESTIONS

Define the terms "Market Value Added (MVA)" and "Economic Value Added (EVA)."

How does EVA differ from accounting profit?

SUMMARY

The primary purposes of this chapter were (1) to describe the basic financial statements, (2) to analyze those statements, and (3) to present some background information on cash flows. In the next chapter we focus on foreign subsidiary statements and the complications that arise when translating those statements from local currencies to a single reporting currency. The key concepts discussed in this chapter are listed below.

- The four basic statements contained in the **annual report** are the balance sheet, the income statement, the statement of retained earnings, and the statement of cash flows.
- The **income statement** reports the results of operations over a period of time, and it shows earnings per share as its "bottom line."
- The **balance sheet** shows assets on the top and liabilities and equity, or claims against assets, on the bottom. The balance sheet may be thought of as a snapshot of the firm's financial position at a particular point in time.
- **Financial statement analysis** generally begins by calculating a set of **financial ratios** designed to reveal a company's strengths and weaknesses as compared with other companies in the same industry. Ratios also show whether the firm's financial position has been improving or deteriorating over time.
- **Solvency and liquidity ratios** show the relationship between a firm's current assets and its current liabilities, and thus its ability to meet maturing debts. Two commonly used solvency and liquidity ratios are the **current** and **quick ratios**.
- **Assets management ratios** measure how effectively a firm is managing its assets. These ratios include **days inventory held, days sales outstanding, fixed assets turnover**, and **total assets turnover**.
- **Debt management ratios** reveal (1) the extent to which the firm is financed with debt and (2) its likelihood of defaulting on its debt obligations. They include the **debt, times-interest-earned**, and **EBITDA coverage ratios**.

- **Days payables outstanding (DPO)** represents supplier credit that usually has no explicit cost, so the longer the company has to pay its accounts payable (while still paying on time) the less it must rely on costly investor-supplied debt.
- **Cash conversion period (CCP)** reveals the extent to which the company uses costly investor-supplied debt to finance working capital.
- **Profitability ratios** show the combined effects of liquidity, assets management, and debt management policies on operating results. They include **profit margin on sales**, **basic earning power**, **return on total assets**, and **return on common equity ratios**.
- **Market value ratios** relate the firm's stock price to its earnings, cash flow, and book value per share, thus giving management an indication of what investors think of the company's past performance and future prospects. These include **price/earnings**, **price/cash flow**, and **market/book ratios**.
- **Trend analysis**, where ratios are looked at over time, is important, because it reveals whether the firm's condition has been improving or deteriorating over the period analyzed.
- **Benchmarking** is the process of comparing a particular company with a group of **benchmark companies**.
- **Window dressing** is any action a firm takes to make its year-end financial statements look stronger than they really are.
- **Operating current assets** are the current assets that are used to support operations and they include cash, inventory, and accounts receivable. Short-term investments and prepaid expenses are not operating current assets.
- **Operating current liabilities** are the current liabilities that occur as a natural consequence of operations, such as accounts payable and accrued liabilities. They do not include customer deposits and notes payable or any other short-term debts that charge interest.
- **Net operating working capital (NOWC)** is the difference between operating current assets and operating current liabilities. Thus, it is the amount of working capital acquired with investor-supplied funds.
- **Operating long-term assets** are the long-term assets used to support operations, such as net plant and equipment. They do not include long-term securities that pay interest or dividends.
- **Total operating assets** (or **capital**), or just **operating assets**, is the sum of net operating working capital and operating long-term assets. It is the total amount of capital needed to run the business.
- **Net cash flow** differs from **accounting profit** because some of the revenues and expenses reflected in accounting profit may not have been received or paid out in cash during the year. Depreciation and amortization expense is typically the largest noncash item, so net cash flow is often expressed as net income plus depreciation and amortization. Investors are at least as interested in a firm's projected net cash flow as in reported earnings because it is cash, not paper profit, that is paid out as dividends and plowed back into the business to produce growth.
- **NOPAT** is net operating profit after taxes. It is the after-tax profit a company would have if it had no debt and no investments in nonoperating assets. Because it excludes the effects of financial decisions, NOPAT is a better measure of operating performance than is net income.
- **Free cash flow (FCF)** is the amount of cash flow remaining after a company makes the asset investments necessary to support operations. In other words, FCF is the amount of cash flow available for distribution to investors, and it is defined as NOPAT minus the net new investment in operating capital. *The value of a company is directly related to its ability to generate free cash flow.*
- **Market Value Added (MVA)** represents the difference between the market value of common stock and the amount of common equity its shareholders have supplied.

- **Economic Value Added (EVA)** is the difference between after-tax operating profit and the total dollar cost of capital, including the cost of equity capital. EVA is an estimate of the value created by management during the year, and it differs substantially from accounting profit, which reflects no charge for the use of equity capital.

Questions

(6-1) Explain the relevance of the firm's accounting statements to the maximization of shareholder value.

(6-2) What would be some of the advantages to having global accounting standards? Have there been any recent accounting standards issued by either the FASB or IASB that suggest convergence between the two?

(6-3) What is EBITDA, and why has its usage become so popular among managers, analysts, and bank loan officers?

(6-4) Differentiate between the objective of financial statement analysis from an investor's perspective and management's perspective.

(6-5) Name a few Web sites where you might go for financial information regarding a specific company. What information would you expect to find at each of these Web sites?

(6-6) List the five categories of financial ratios discussed in this chapter, and briefly explain what each category is intended to measure.

(6-7) Is a high current ratio always good? Explain.

(6-8) Differentiate among the following ratios, and explain how each affects a firm's cash conversion period: days inventory held (DIH), days sales outstanding (DSO), and days payables outstanding (DPO).

(6-9) What information does the cash conversion period provide, and how is it calculated?

(6-10) Why is it important for a firm to have the "right" amount of assets?

(6-11) Why would you want to compare a firm's DSO with its terms of sale?

(6-12) Explain whether the following statement is true or false: "P/E ratios are lower for firms with strong growth prospects, other things held constant, but are higher for riskier firms."

(6-13) Why would a firm want to compare itself with "benchmark" companies rather than just to industry averages?

(6-14) How is benchmarking complicated for multinational firms?

(6-15) Why might accounting income not equal net cash flow?

(6-16) Why might operating cash flow not equal net cash flow?

(6-17) To judge managerial performance, why should you compare managers' ability to generate operating income with the operating assets under their control?

(6-18) Must all of the capital used to acquire assets be supplied by investors—stockholders, bondholders, and lenders? Explain.

(6-19) What are five good uses for a firm's free cash flow?

(6-20) Why might a high FCF be detrimental to shareholders?

(6-21) If a firm's free cash flow is negative, is this necessarily bad? Explain.

(6-22) What does a firm's MVA represent?

(6-23) How does MVA differ from EVA?

(6-24) How is focusing on EVA consistent with maximizing shareholder value?

(6-25) Why is EVA a better measure of managerial performance than net income?

(6-26) Provide a brief overview of how subsidiary financial statements denominated in local currencies are translated to a single reporting currency. (Note: This process will be explained in greater detail in Chapter 7.)

SELF-TEST PROBLEMS   Solutions Appear in Appendix B

(ST-1)   Define each of the following terms:
Key Terms
a.   Annual report; income statement; balance sheet
b.   EBITDA
c.   Liquid asset; solvency; solvency and liquidity ratios
d.   Current ratio; quick ratio
e.   Assets management ratios; fixed assets turnover ratio; total assets turnover ratio
f.   Days inventory held; days sales outstanding
g.   Financial leverage; debt ratio; times-interest-earned ratio; EBITDA coverage ratio
h.   Days payables outstanding; cash conversion period
i.   Profitability ratios; basic earning power ratio; profit margin on sales; return on total assets; return on common equity
j.   Market value ratios; price/earnings ratio; price/cash flow ratio; market/book ratio
k.   Benchmarking; benchmark companies
l.   Window dressing techniques
m.   Operating assets; nonoperating assets; operating working capital; net operating working capital
n.   Net cash flow; accounting profit; net operating profit after taxes; free cash flow
o.   Market value added; economic value added

(ST-2)   Last year, CGI International had net operating profit after-taxes (NOPAT) of $14
Income Statement,   million. Its EBITDA was $30 million and net income amounted to $8.5 million.
FCF, and EVA   During the year, CGI made $10 million in net capital expenditures (that is, capital expenditures net of depreciation). Finally, CGI's finance staff has concluded that the firm's total after-tax capital costs were $11.5 million and its tax rate was 40 percent.
a.   What is CGI's depreciation and amortization expense?
b.   What is CGI's interest expense?
c.   What is CGI's free cash flow?
d.   What is CGI's EVA?

(ST-3)   Global Electronics Inc. has the following data:
EBIT

Assets	$250,000,000
Profit margin	8.0%
Tax rate	40.0%
Debt ratio	45.0%
Interest rate	7.5%
Total assets turnover	3.6×

What is Global's EBIT?

STARTER PROBLEMS

(6-1) Global Technologies Inc. recently reported an EBITDA of $48 million and $20
Income Statement million of net income. The company has $8.75 million interest expense and the
corporate tax rate is 35 percent. What was the company's depreciation and amortization expense?

(6-2) Worldwide Communications Corp. has $75 million in total investor-supplied oper-
EVA ating capital. The company's WACC is 8.25 percent. The company has the following income statement:

Sales	$40,000,000
Operating costs	24,000,000
Operating income (EBIT)	$16,000,000
Interest expense	8,000,000
Earnings before taxes (EBT)	$ 8,000,000
Taxes (40%)	3,200,000
Net income	$ 4,800,000

What is Worldwide's EVA?

(6-3) Global Pharmaceuticals Inc. has $3,000 million of common equity on its balance
MVA and Stock Price sheet and 80 million shares of common stock outstanding. The company's Market
Value Added (MVA) is $1,000 million. What is the company's stock price?

(6-4) Restaurant Supplies International (RSI) has the following data (dollars in millions):
ROE

Net income	$ 1,000
Sales	$40,000
Total assets	$25,000
Debt ratio	53.5%
TIE ratio	3.5×
Current ratio	1.7×
BEP ratio	15.0%

If RSI could streamline operations, cut operating costs, and raise net income to
$1,250 million without affecting sales or the balance sheet (the additional profits
will be paid out as dividends), by how much would its ROE increase? Assume
that RSI has no preferred stock.

(6-5) International Manufacturing Inc. (IMI) had the following balance sheet and
Profit Margin income statement information for 2004 (dollars are in millions):

Balance Sheet

Cash	$ 10		
Accounts receivable	5,090		
Inventories	25,000		
Total current assets	$30,100	Debt	$18,000
Net fixed assets	14,900	Equity	27,000
Total assets	$45,000	Total claims	$45,000

Income Statement

Sales	$50,000
Cost of goods sold (75%)	37,500
EBIT	$12,500
Interest (8%)	1,440
EBT	$11,060
Taxes (35%)	3,871
Net income	$ 7,189

The industry average inventory turnover is 6.25×. Management plans to change the firm's inventory control system so IMI's turnover will equal the industry average, and this change is expected to have no effect on either sales or cost of goods sold. The cash generated from reducing inventories will be used to buy U.S. tax-exempt securities that have a 4 percent rate of return. What will your profit margin be after the change in inventories is reflected in the income statement?

EXAM-TYPE PROBLEMS

(6-6) You have just obtained financial information for the past 2 years for Worldwide Publishing Inc.

NOPAT, NOWC, and FCF

Worldwide Publishing Inc.: Income Statements for Year Ending December 31 (Millions of Dollars)

	2004	2003
Sales	$9,000.0	$7,500.0
Operating costs (excluding depreciation and amortization)	7,650.0	6,375.0
EBITDA	$1,350.0	$1,125.0
Depreciation and amortization	225.0	187.5
Earnings before interest and taxes	$1,125.0	$ 937.5
Interest	162.5	150.0
Earnings before taxes	$ 962.5	$ 787.5
Taxes (35%)	336.9	275.6
Net income available to common stockholders	$ 625.6	$ 511.9
Common dividends	$ 437.9	$ 256.0

Worldwide Publishing Inc.: Balance Sheets on December 31 (Millions of Dollars)

	2004	2003
Assets		
Cash and marketable securities	$ 90.0	$ 75.0
Accounts receivable	1,350.0	1,125.0
Inventories	1,350.0	1,500.0
Total current assets	$2,790.0	$2,700.0
Net plant and equipment	2,250.0	1,875.0
Total assets	$5,040.0	$4,575.0
Liabilities and Equity		
Accounts payable	$ 810.0	$ 680.0
Notes payable	502.5	408.0
Accrued liabilities	540.0	487.2
Total current liabilities	$1,852.5	$1,575.2
Long-term bonds	1,125.0	1,125.0
Total debt	$2,977.5	$2,700.2
Common stock (50 million shares)	375.0	375.0
Retained earnings	1,687.5	1,499.8
Total common equity	$2,062.5	$1,874.8
Total liabilities and equity	$5,040.0	$4,575.0

a. What is WPI's net operating profit after taxes (NOPAT) for 2004?
b. What is WPI's net operating working capital for 2004?

c. What is WPI's amount of total investor-supplied operating capital for 2004?

d. What is WPI's free cash flow for 2004?

(6-7) Dan's Club Stores' current financial statements (in millions of dollars) are shown
ROE and Financing below:

Balance Sheet

Inventories	$1,625	Accounts payable	$ 325
Other current assets	1,300	Short-term notes payable	1,005
Fixed assets	1,202	Common equity	2,797
Total assets	$4,127	Total liabilities and equity	$4,127

Income Statement

Sales	$6,500.0
Operating costs	5,525.0
EBIT	$ 975.0
Interest	95.5
EBT	$ 879.5
Taxes (40%)	351.8
Net income	$ 527.7

A recently released report indicates that Dan's Club's current ratio of 2.2× is in
line with the industry average. However, its accounts payable, which have no
interest cost and are due entirely to purchases of inventories, amount to only 20
percent of inventories versus an industry average of 52 percent. Suppose Dan's
Club took actions to increase its accounts-payable-to-inventories ratio to the 52
percent industry average, but it (a) kept all of its assets at their present levels (that
is, the assets side of the balance sheet remains constant) and (b) also held its current ratio constant at 2.2×. Assume that Dan's Club's tax rate is 40 percent, that
its cost of short-term debt is 9.5 percent, and that the change in payments will not
affect operations. In addition, common equity will not change. With the changes,
what will be Dan's Club's new ROE?

(6-8) Alfresco Imported Tile Company has the following data (dollars are in thousands):
TIE Ratio

Assets	$27,500
Profit margin	4.25%
Tax rate	35%
Debt ratio	52.5%
Interest rate	8.5%
Total assets turnover	2.5×

What is the firm's TIE ratio? Assume that the firm has no preferred stock.

(6-9) Victoria Enterprises has $2.4 million of accounts receivable on its balance sheet.
Current Ratio The company's DSO is 45 (based on a 365-day year), its current assets are $3.75
million, and its current ratio is 1.6. The company plans to reduce its DSO from
45 to the industry average of 30 without affecting sales. The resulting decrease in
accounts receivable will free up cash that will be used to reduce current liabilities.
If the company succeeds in its plan, what will Victoria's new current ratio be?

(6-10) FEI Inc.'s balance sheet and income statement (dollars are in millions) are given
P/E Ratio and Stock Price below:

Balance Sheet

Cash	$ 250	Accounts payable	$ 375
Accounts receivable	750	Notes payable	125
Inventories	1,500	Long-term debt	3,500
Fixed assets	2,500	Common equity	1,000
Total assets	$5,000	Total liabilities and equity	$5,000

Income Statement

Sales	$5,000
Cost of goods sold	4,000
EBIT	$1,000
Interest	323
EBT	$ 677
Taxes (35%)	237
Net income	$ 440

The industry average inventory turnover is 4×, the interest rate on the firm's notes payable is 5.5 percent, and on its long-term debt it is 10 percent. The firm has 44,000,000 shares outstanding and the stock sells at a P/E of 5.0×. If FEI changed its inventory methods so as to operate at the industry average inventory turnover, if it used the funds generated by this change to buy back common stock at the current market price and thus to reduce common equity, and if sales, the cost of goods sold, and the P/E ratio remained constant, by what dollar amount would its stock price increase?

THOMSON ONE
Business School Edition **QUESTIONS**

EXPLORING FINANCIAL STATEMENTS

Overview

Pepsico Inc. manufactures, markets, and sells a variety of snack, food, and beverage products around the world. Pepsico operates in four divisions: Frito-Lay North America (manufactures, markets, and sells branded snacks, which includes Lay's potato chips, Doritos, and Cheetos); PepsiCo Beverages North America (manufactures and sells beverage concentrates, fountain syrups, and finished goods for the Pepsi brands); PepsiCo International (manufactures a variety of snack foods); and Quaker Foods North America (manufactures, markets, and sells cereals, rice, pasta, and other branded products). Pepsico operates in the United States, Canada, the United Kingdom, Mexico, and other countries.

We can use *Thomson One: Business School Edition* to obtain a wide variety of financial information for companies such as Pepsico Inc. To find some background information, begin by entering the company's ticker symbol, PEP, and then selecting "GO." On the opening screen, you will see a great deal of useful information, including a summary of what Pepsico does, a chart of its recent stock price, EPS estimates, some recent news stories, and a list of key financial data and ratios.

In researching a company's operating performance, a good place to start is the recent stock price performance. Click on "PRICES" for data on Pepsico's recent stock performance over a variety of time horizons, as well as estimates of the stock price's momentum.

As you can see, Pepsico has had its ups and downs, but the company's overall performance has been quite strong, and it has beaten the overall market during this period.

Looking at Pepsico's Financial Statements

We can also find Pepsico's recent financial statements. Near the top of your screen, click on "FINANCIALS." Here you will find the company's balance sheet, income statement, and statement of cash flows for the past 5 years. You can click on the *Excel* icon and then download these statements to a spreadsheet.

Discussion Questions

1. Looking at the most recent year available, what is the value of Pepsico's total assets? What percentage is fixed assets such as plant and equipment, and what percentage is current assets? How much has the company grown over the years that are shown?

2. Does Pepsico have a lot of long-term debt? What are the chief ways in which Pepsico has financed assets?

3. Looking at the statement of cash flows, what factors can explain the change in the company's cash position over the last couple of years?

4. Looking at the income statement, what are the company's most recent sales and net income? Over the past several years, what has been the sales growth rate? What has been the growth rate in net income?

5. Over the past few years, has there been a strong correlation between stock price performance and reported earnings?

6. Click on the tab labeled "PEERS" near the top of the screen; you will see some summary financial information for Pepsico and a few of its peers. If you click on "PEER SETS" on the second line of tabs, you can modify the list of peer firms. The default setup is "Peers set by SIC Code." To obtain a comparison of many of the key ratios presented in the text, just click on "FINANCIALS" (on the second line of tabs) and then click on "KEY FINANCIAL RATIOS" that appears on the drop-down menu. Additionally, clicking on "PERFORMANCE" allows you to access a tool to run peer comparisons regarding performance, profitability, liquidity, and growth. What has happened to Pepsico's liquidity position over the past 3 years? How does Pepsico's liquidity compare with its peers? (Hint: You may use both the peer key financial ratios and liquidity comparison to answer this question.)

7. Take a look at Pepsico's assets turnover ratio. How does this ratio compare with its peers? Have there been any interesting changes over time in this measure? Do you consider Pepsico's assets management to be a strength or a weakness?

8. Look at the list of peers listed for Pepsico. Does this seem like a good set of competitors to compare Pepsico with? Can you think of any company that might make a better comparison? What conclusions can you draw about this peer comparison?

INTEGRATED CASE

Rick Schmidt, MRI's CFO, along with Mandy Wu, Schmidt's assistant, and John Costello, a consultant and college finance professor, comprise a team established to teach the firm's directors and senior managers the basics of international financial management. The program includes 16 sessions, each lasting about 2 hours, and they are scheduled immediately before the monthly board meetings. Five sessions have been completed, and the team is now preparing Session 6, which will deal with financial statement analysis. Prior sessions have provided an overview of international finance, foreign exchange markets and international institutions, exchange rate analysis, foreign direct investment, and risk and return.

In the financial statement session, the team will discuss the role of financial reporting, the importance of accurate reporting, ratio analysis, and modifying accounting data for managerial decisions. MRI has foreign subsidiaries in Italy, Japan, and Indonesia. The Italian and Japanese subsidiaries are self-sustaining operating units, while the Indonesian subsidiary is an integrated foreign entity. The cash flows of the Indonesian subsidiary are integrally tied to the operations in Japan. Tables IC6-1 and IC6-2 display MRI's consolidated income statements and balance sheets, respectively. Data for 2004 and 2003 are taken from this year's annual report, which will soon be sent to shareholders. The purpose of this session will be to discuss the financial health of the whole firm, while the next session will discuss the role of international operations. Schmidt is primarily concerned with communicating MRI's true financial position to shareholders. He has witnessed some of the recent accounting scandals and the resulting lawsuits, and he is determined to honestly report to shareholders and keep MRI's financial results as transparent

TABLE IC6-1 | Medical Records International: General Company Data (Thousands of Dollars except Stock Price)

	2004	2003
Stock price	$21.00	$19.00
Tax rate	40%	40%
WACC	8.50%	8.50%
Shares outstanding (in thousands)		
Common stock shares	40,000	40,000
Preferred stock shares	600	600
Lease payments	$10.00	$10.00
Principal payments	$50.00	$50.00

TABLE IC6-2 | Medical Records International: December 31 Income Statements (Thousands of Dollars)

	2004	2003
Net sales revenue	$1,003,137.0	$917,789.0
Cost of goods sold	660,681.0	618,374.0
General and administrative costs	226,496.0	199,344.0
Total operating costs	$ 887,177.0	$817,718.0
EBITDA	$ 115,960.0	$100,071.0
Depreciation and amortization	25,063.0	21,951.0
EBIT	$ 90,897.0	$ 78,120.0
Interest expense	14,716.0	14,280.0
EBT	$ 76,181.0	$ 63,840.0
Taxes	30,472.4	25,536.0
Net income before preferred dividends	$ 45,708.6	$ 38,304.0
Preferred dividends	3,600.0	3,600.0
Net income	$ 42,108.6	$ 34,704.0
Common dividends	$ 0.0	$ 0.0
Additions to retained earnings	$ 42,108.6	$ 34,704.0
Per-Share Data		
Common stock price	$21.00	$19.00
Earnings per share (EPS)	$1.053	$0.868
Dividends per share (DPS)	$ 0.00	$ 0.00
Book value per share (BVPS)	$ 8.31	$ 7.25
Cash flow per share (CFPS)	$ 1.68	$ 1.42

as possible. A majority of the company's stock is held by either institutional or inside investors; however, there is still a substantial portion of the stock traded publicly.

Most of the directors have a basic understanding of financial statements, but obviously some know more than others, and it is difficult deciding what to cover and how in-depth the analysis should be. After much discussion, the team concluded that they should briefly cover the annual report and basic financial statements, emphasizing their role in shareholder communications. The session will also include ratio analysis and converting accounting information to cash flow measures, for which the team plans to use an *Excel* model both to ease the burden of calculations and to help the directors become more familiar with *Excel*.

TABLE IC6-3	Medical Records International: December 31 Balance Sheets (Thousands of Dollars)		
		2004	2003
Cash and equivalents		$ 57,595.3	$ 50,825.1
Accounts receivable		122,255.2	107,609.7
Inventories		179,131.0	152,409.7
Prepaid expenses		—	—
Total current assets		$358,981.5	$310,844.5
Net plant and equipment		559,027.5	460,725.0
Total assets		$918,009.0	$771,569.5
Accounts payable		$ 93,363.1	$ 82,444.8
Accrued liabilities		11,815.9	10,574.5
Notes payable		59,281.9	44,650.4
Current maturities of long-term debt		16,119.1	10,500.4
Total current liabilities		$180,580.0	$148,170.1
Long-term bonds		345,170.4	273,249.4
Total liabilities		$525,750.4	$421,419.5
Preferred stock (600,000 shares)		60,000.0	60,000.0
Common stock (40,000,000 shares)		79,500.0	79,500.0
Retained earnings		252,758.6	210,650.0
Total common equity		$332,258.6	$290,150.0
Total liabilities and equity		$918,009.0	$771,569.5

With those thoughts in mind, the three compiled the following set of questions, which they plan to discuss during the session. As with the other sessions, they plan to use an *Excel* model to answer the quantitative questions. Assume that you are Mandy Wu, and that you must prepare answers for use during the session.

QUESTIONS

a. What is the annual report? Identify and describe its principal financial statements. What do MRI's statements say about the company?

b. In last year's annual report, there was a forward-looking statement in the "Management Discussion" section that said:

MRI continues to pursue its mission to be a global leader in medical equipment product innovation. MRI has embraced an aggressive investment policy and taken advantage of favorable conditions in world debt markets to bolster MRI's future. Responsible cost management has allowed MRI to generate greater profitability out of its sales.

Has MRI moved in the direction suggested by the statement? How should Schmidt address this issue in the current annual statement?

c. Conduct a full ratio analysis for MRI's two most recent years of financial statements. Assess MRI's ratios along the dimensions discussed in the chapter. From the data in Table IC6-4, how does MRI fare against its competitors? Are any significant trends evident?

d. Why are ratios useful? What problems/limitations do ratio analyses suffer from?

e. What effect did MRI's cost management program have on net operating working capital, total investor-supplied capital, and net operating profit?

f. What effect did the company's activities have on net cash flow, operating cash flow, and free cash flow?

g. How have MRI's actions over the past couple years benefited shareholders? Use Economic Value Added and Market Value Added to explain your answer.

TABLE IC6-4 | Medical Records International: Industry Average Ratios

	Industry Average			Industry Average
Solvency Ratios			*Profitability Ratios*	
Current ratio	2.3		Profit margin (PM)	4.75%
Quick ratio	1.7		Basic earning power (BEP)	10.03%
			Return on assets (ROA)	6.65%
Assets Management Ratios			Return on equity (ROE)	15.77%
Days inventory held (DIH)	58			
Days sales outstanding	41		*Market Value Ratios*	
Fixed assets turnover	1.9		Price-to-earnings	16.5
Total assets turnover	1.4		Price-to-cash flow	9.1
			Book value per share (BVPS)	$8.2
Debt Management Ratios			Market-to-book	2.4
Days payables outstanding	43			
Total debt ratio	56.00%			
Times interest earned	5.1			
EBITDA coverage ratio	7.2			
Cash conversion period	56			

CHAPTER 7

Translating and Consolidating Subsidiary Financial Statements

Financial Statements
Currency Translation
Inflation

Cash Flows (CF)
|

$$\text{VALUE} = \sum_{t=0}^{N} \frac{CF_t}{(1+r)^t}$$

e-resource

*The textbook's Web site, **http://crum. swlearning.com,** contains an Excel file that will guide you through the chapter's calculations. The file for this chapter is **FIFC07-model.xls,** and we encourage you to open the file and follow along as you read the chapter.*

A manager's primary financial goal is to maximize the value of the firm's common stock. The value of any business asset depends on the usable after-tax cash flows the asset is expected to produce over its life. As we discussed in Chapter 6, managers use financial statements to help predict how their actions will affect cash flows, while investors use them to predict how successful managers will be. But financial statements focus on net income, so to concentrate on value we must translate from income to cash flow. While the last chapter reviewed financial statement concepts, this chapter outlines some of the intricacies of multinational reporting.

In Chapter 6 we abstracted from reporting complications that arise for a U.S. multinational with subsidiaries located abroad by presenting the final consolidated statements denominated in U.S dollars. In this chapter, we address the basics of foreign currency translation, discussing both the current rate and temporal methods and when each method should be used. Next we address hyperinflation and the implications for translating financial statements in that environment. Finally, we actually demonstrate the translation of SSI's 2003 subsidiary statements into its consolidated financial statements. We leave the translation of SSI's 2004 consolidated financial statements as an exercise for the student in Problem 7-5.

OVERVIEW

Consolidated Financial Statements
Aggregated financial statements for parent and subsidiary organizations presented in annual reports and required in SEC filings that exclude intracompany transactions.

Reporting Currency
The currency into which a subsidiary's financial statements are ultimately recast from its local currency. For U.S. multinationals, and other multinationals required to submit financials to the SEC, the reporting currency is the U.S. dollar.

SSI's financial statements shown in Tables 6-1 and 6-2 are consolidated totals for the entire company, including its U.S. parent and its subsidiaries in Mexico, Germany, and Argentina. **Consolidated financial statements** are presented in annual reports and are required in SEC filings, and they are what most investors use to assess the company's performance and value. Table 6-3 categorized the firm's financial results geographically, but it did not show where the company has physical facilities and investments. This information exists, though, as each operating segment maintains separate financial records that are used to develop the consolidated statements. These records are maintained in local currencies, as required by local law, and follow the generally accepted accounting practices of the host country. Some of the subsidiary operations may be completely self-sufficient, while others may be closely integrated with the parent's operations (or even with other subsidiaries). Periodically (quarterly for U.S. public companies), the parent must prepare and file consolidated financial statements. This reporting requirement means that subsidiaries' financial statements must be recast into equivalent U.S. dollars (the **reporting currency** for a U.S. company such as SSI) and aggregated in a manner that avoids double counting of transactions between related entities. This chapter explains this process and discusses some problems that arise.

Since these are technical accounting issues, why is it necessary to delve into the mechanics of preparing an MNE's consolidated financial statements in a finance book? While we do not go into an exhaustive discussion of the accounting process of translating and aggregating subsidiary financial statements, it is necessary for financial managers to have a basic understanding of the underlying principles for at least three different reasons:

1. Depending on the nature of the subsidiaries' operations, the translation process can have direct implications for the amount and volatility of reported earnings. Even when earnings are not affected directly, the book value of owners' equity can change as a function of the macroeconomic environment and exchange rates.

2. The process of evaluating and compensating managerial performance in the various operating subsidiaries is quite complex. Different subsidiaries often base their records in different currencies as governed by different commercial laws and practices, and they face different competitive environments. These differences can affect various ratios and other performance measures, and they can be magnified in the translation process. Diverse operating conditions make it difficult to use the same measurement tools in every country, but comparability is sacrificed when different metrics are used. Factors that are beyond management's control should be recognized when evaluating and rewarding managerial performance.

3. Most of the gains and losses that arise from the quarterly reporting requirement are unrealized in economic terms, and they could reverse before the next reporting date. They are almost never subjected to taxation because they are unrealized, but most managers believe they still have a bearing on firm value. Thus, they become a concern of the company's integrated risk management system. Is it best to manage unrealized gains and losses as they occur, or to wait until they are converted into realized economic gains or losses?

This chapter presents the basic ideas underlying foreign currency translation, discusses the consolidation of subsidiary statements, and outlines some issues that arise during implementation. In particular, inflation can be a significant problem for some subsidiaries, so we explain how it is handled in the translation process and its effect on taxes and fixed assets valuation.

Differentiate between local currencies and reporting currencies.

Why must financial managers have a basic understanding of the accounting process for translating and aggregating subsidiary financial statements to form consolidated statements?

BASICS OF FOREIGN CURRENCY TRANSLATION

Companies with equity securities traded in the United States are required to report the results of their operations periodically (quarterly) provided they have 500 or more shareholders of record. Purely domestic companies maintain their accounting records in U.S. dollars and find this requirement fairly easy to meet. However, MNEs maintain accounting records in different currencies and face a far more complex task. Before MNEs can prepare consolidated statements, they must translate their foreign currency accounting information into financially equivalent U.S. dollar values. While this sounds like a straightforward process using exchange rates, there are several issues that must be addressed:

1. Should all balance sheet entries (and associated income statement items) be translated using the same exchange rate, or should different rates be used for different line items?
2. If the exchange rate between the local and reporting currency fluctuates over time, should the translation rate be based on the spot exchange rate on the statement date, on the exchange rate on the day the accounting entry was made, or on some sort of average?
3. Is the relationship between the two company entities (parent-subsidiary or two subsidiaries) of relevance in answering the first two questions? That is, would the answers be different if the two entities were independent of each other?
4. Does the translation methodology require an inflation adjustment? If inflation is high, the money in that country may not be a good basis for measuring values.

We explore these issues and indicate how the accounting profession, as represented by the Financial Accounting Standards Board (FASB) in the United States and the International Accounting Standards Board (IASB) elsewhere, answers these questions.

Choosing Exchange Rates

Monetary Item
Includes both financial assets and liabilities whose values are based on a fixed number of nominal money units.

Denominated
Expressed or designated in nominal money units.

Before we discuss translation methodologies, we need to understand the difference between monetary and nonmonetary items. **Monetary items**, both financial assets and liabilities, are accounts whose values are based on a fixed number of nominal money units. For instance, a U.S. $20 bill was worth $20 when it was issued in 1999, it is worth $20 today, and it will be worth $20 in 10 years. We say that its value is **denominated** in nominal money units. As exchange rates change, the nominal value of the $20 bill remains constant in U.S. dollar terms, even if the purchasing power of the dollar changes. However, if we had wanted to purchase euros, we could have exchanged the $20 for €22.42 at the end of 2001, for €19.64 at the end of 2002, and for €17.15 at the end of 2003. In other words, when we *measure* the value of our U.S. $20 bill in another money unit (for example, the euro), its value changes over time.

Nonmonetary Item
Items such as inventory and fixed assets whose values are not equivalent to a fixed number of nominal money units.

Values of **nonmonetary items**, which include inventory, fixed assets, and all other items in the financial statements not considered monetary items, are not locked in to a fixed number of nominal money units. Values of nonmonetary items are *measured* in money units, and these values will change as the purchasing power of the money unit changes. For example, speakers held in inventory by SSI are recorded at their historical costs. We then add a markup to determine today's selling price, or "value." Next year, though, the selling price (value) may change if SSI's costs change or if competition dictates a change. We can also measure the values of the speakers in other currencies, and even if costs and competition are constant, these values will change if exchange rates change. So, nonmonetary items whose real values are constant will still change over time in nominal terms if exchange rates change.

This situation means that the values of assets and liabilities can change as we translate their values from one currency to another, which implies that even if accounting statements maintained in a local currency are in balance, the balance sheet may no longer be in balance after translation if exchange rates have shifted. For instance, assume that at year-end 2002 a firm had assets of €1,000 and liabilities of €500. At an exchange rate of $1.01835/€, the assets would be worth $1,018.35 and the liabilities would be $509.18, for a net value of $509.17. If we remeasure their value at year-end 2003, when the exchange rate is $1.16639/€, the assets would have increased in value to $1,166.39 and the liabilities to $583.20. Thus, the firm's net value would have also increased to $583.19, up $74.02 from the 2002 value. On the other hand, suppose the firm has assets of €500 and liabilities of €1,000. In this situation, the firm's net value would have decreased by $74.02. Finally, if the firm has assets of €1,000 and liabilities of €1,000, the change in the assets' value would have exactly offset the change in value of the liabilities, and the firm's net value would have remained constant (at zero). This last example is particularly significant for managing exchange rate risk. It is called a *balance sheet hedge,* and it will be discussed in more detail later in the chapter. Also, note that if the U.S. dollar had strengthened against the euro, the first two scenarios would have yielded the opposite results.

Current Rate Method
One of two methods permitted in most countries for translating financial statements. Assets and liabilities are translated at the spot exchange rate on the day the financial statements are prepared, while equity accounts are translated at historical exchange rates in effect on the dates the items were recorded.

If gains and losses due to exchange rates cause the translated balance sheet to be out of balance, how do we restore its balance? *We adjust the residual equity accounts to offset the gain or loss in the asset section of the balance sheet.* In the translation methodologies discussed next, equity accounts are translated at their historical exchange rates and the gains (losses) are added (subtracted) to restore balance to the balance sheet.

METHODS FOR TRANSLATING FINANCIAL STATEMENTS   In most countries, only two methods for translating financial statements are permitted. The two translation procedures, which are explained here, are (1) the *current rate method* and (2) the *temporal method.* The choice is usually dictated by the situation, as we discuss below. In the **current rate method**, assets and liabilities (debts) are translated at the spot exchange rate on the day the financial statements are prepared, while equity accounts are translated at the historical exchange rates that were in effect on the dates the items were recorded. Thus, the effective historical rate for equity accounts is a uniquely defined average exchange rate. Translating the equity accounts at a fixed historical rate (except for new equity from issuing stock, repurchased shares, and net income reinvested in the firm) means there will be more **exposed assets** than **exposed liabilities,** or a **net asset exposure.** If the reporting currency (say, U.S. dollars) strengthens relative to the local currency in which the accounts are maintained, this results in a foreign currency translation loss because the local currency will buy fewer dollars. A weaker dollar would result in translation gains. The gain or loss on the net asset exposure is recorded in the equity account, and the entry is called a

Exposed Assets
Assets that are subject to a change in value if exchange rates change.

Exposed Liabilities
Liabilities that are subject to a change in value if exchange rates change.

Net Asset Exposure
The situation that occurs when there are more exposed assets than exposed liabilities.

Cumulative Translation Adjustment (CTA)
The entry made in the equity account to reflect the unrealized gain or loss on the net asset exposure under the current rate translation method.

Temporal Method
One of two methods permitted in most countries for translating financial statements. This method distinguishes between monetary and nonmonetary items. All monetary assets and all liabilities are translated at the spot exchange rate on the day the financial statements are prepared. However, nonmonetary items must be translated or remeasured at the historical exchange rates in effect on the dates the items were first recorded.

Net Liability Exposure
The situation that occurs when there are more exposed liabilities than exposed assets.

Monetary Balance
The situation that occurs when the gains or losses from translation on the assets side exactly match the losses or gains from translation on the liabilities side.

cumulative translation adjustment (CTA). Two characteristics of the CTA account need to be understood:

1. The gain or loss is recorded directly in the equity section without flowing it through the income statement as would normally be done when changes in equity are recorded.
2. The addition or subtraction to the CTA account represents an *unrealized* gain or loss that resulted from the periodic reporting requirement, and it could reverse by the next reporting date if exchange rates move in the opposite direction. Moreover, the CTA adjustment has no tax consequence.

The **temporal method**, on the other hand, starts by distinguishing between monetary and nonmonetary items on the balance sheet. All monetary items, including cash, marketable securities, accounts receivable, and prepaid expenses in the assets section, and all liabilities (debts) in the passive section, are translated at the spot exchange rate on the day the financial statements are prepared, just as with the current rate method. However, the temporal method requires nonmonetary items, primarily inventories and fixed assets, to be translated or *remeasured* at the historical exchange rates in effect on the dates the items were first recorded. Thus, the appropriate historical exchange rates for nonmonetary items are uniquely defined averages of historical exchange rates. Equity accounts are also translated at historical rates, just as they were in the current rate method. Because nonmonetary assets and equities are translated at historical rates, it is possible to have a net asset exposure (exposed assets greater than exposed liabilities), a **net liability exposure** (exposed liabilities greater than exposed assets), or the two may exactly offset. The last case is called a **monetary balance**, because gains on one side match losses on the other.

The other major difference between the methods is the treatment of gains and losses. Recording them in separate CTA accounts is not permitted under the temporal method. Instead, gains and losses are "flowed through" the income statement, hence they have a direct effect on reported earnings. There are no tax consequences from these gains or losses because they are unrealized, but they do change reported earnings and increase earnings variability over time. Table 7-1 summarizes the rules for translating foreign financial statements using the two methods.

TABLE 7-1 | Rules for Translating Foreign Currency Financial Statements

	Current Rate Method	Temporal Method
Monetary assets	Current rate	Current rate
Nonmonetary assets	Current rate	Historical rate
Liabilities	Current rate	Current rate
Capital stock and surplus	Historical rate	Historical rate
Retained earnings	Beginning amount plus earnings for year	Beginning amount plus earnings for year plus or minus translation gains/losses
Gains/losses	Record in CTA account	Flow through income statement
Income statement items	Average for period	Average for period except items linked to nonmonetary items such as depreciation, which uses historical rate
Distributions	Rate on payment date	Rate on payment date

Subsidiary Operations

The use of the current rate or temporal method is determined by the subsidiary's operations and its relationship with the parent. The FASB and the IASB use slightly different approaches to make the selection, but they almost always get to the same place.

The IASB classifies foreign subsidiaries depending on the extent to which they are tied in with the ongoing operations of the parent. A **self-sustaining foreign entity** is an operating unit located in another country that functions as a separate going concern and is largely independent of the parent. An **integrated foreign entity** is an operating unit located in another country that functions as an extension of the parent and whose cash flows are interrelated with those of the parent. If a subsidiary is a self-sustaining foreign entity, the current rate method must be used to translate financial statements. Gains and losses from exchange rate changes are accumulated in the CTA account and do not flow through the consolidated income statement until the gains and losses are realized. On the other hand, if a subsidiary is an integrated foreign entity, the temporal method is used. Gains and losses from exchange rate changes flow through the current income statement and thus directly affect reported earnings.

In the United States, the FASB uses a *functional currency determination* to differentiate between self-sustaining and integrated foreign entities. The **functional currency** is the currency of the primary economic environment in which the subsidiary operates. If a subsidiary is a self-sustaining foreign entity, the functional currency will be the local money unit and translation into the reporting currency (the U.S. dollar) will be done using the current rate method. This is exactly the same as the IASB regulations. Also, if the subsidiary is an integrated foreign entity, its functional currency is the money unit of the operation with which it is integrated, and translation into that currency will be done using the temporal method.

For the most part, there is consistency between the IASB and FASB requirements, but FASB diverges in one important way: If the operation is integrated with the parent, the functional currency is the parent's home currency, which is also the reporting currency. However, it is possible for a foreign entity to be integrated with another subsidiary. In this situation, the functional currency of the integrated foreign entity might be the currency of another country rather than the reporting currency. To illustrate, consider this example. Under FASB, if a European subsidiary is integrated with its U.S. parent, its functional currency is the U.S. dollar. Suppose, however, that the U.S. parent has a self-sustaining Japanese subsidiary whose functional currency is the yen, and another subsidiary in Korea that keeps its accounting records in Korean won but whose primary operating environment involves transactions in Japanese yen. Its local currency is the won, but its functional currency is the yen, and the reporting currency is the U.S. dollar. In this case, the Korean won financial statements are translated into Japanese yen (the functional currency) using the temporal method, and then translated again into U.S. dollars (the reporting currency) using the current rate method. When the translation is from a local currency into a functional currency using the temporal method, it is referred to as **remeasuring** the financial statements. When the translation is from a functional currency into a reporting currency using the current rate method, it is referred to as **restating** the financial statements. Figure 7-1 is a flow chart that illustrates how the functional currency is determined and the translation method that should be used.

Hyperinflation

The accounting profession generally assumes that the local currency maintains its real value over time and represents a storehouse of value in which people and companies can keep their wealth without fear of erosion. However, if a country is expe-

Self-Sustaining Foreign Entity
An operating unit located in another country that functions as a separate ongoing concern and is largely independent of the parent.

Integrated Foreign Entity
An operating unit located in another country that functions as an extension of the parent and whose cash flows are interrelated with those of the parent.

Functional Currency
The currency of the primary economic environment in which the subsidiary operates.

Remeasuring
The process of translating financial statements from a local currency into a functional currency using the temporal method.

Restating
The process of translating financial statements from a functional currency into a reporting currency using the current rate method.

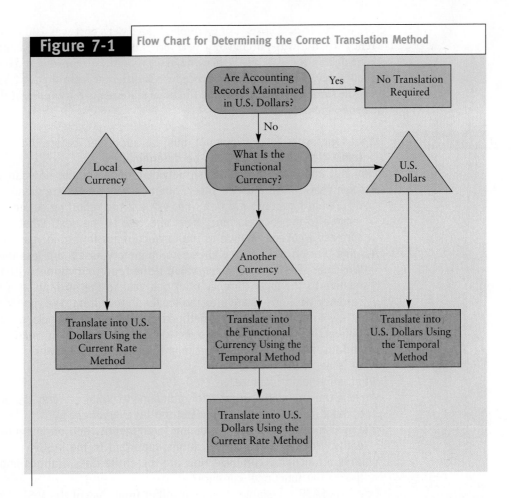

Figure 7-1   Flow Chart for Determining the Correct Translation Method

Hyperinflation
A situation in which cumulative annual inflation of approximately 100 percent occurs over three years. In this situation, currency no longer functions as a storehouse of value.

riencing **hyperinflation**, loosely defined as cumulative annual inflation of approximately 100 percent over three years, then the currency no longer functions effectively as a storehouse of value. In this situation, nonmonetary balance sheet items maintain their real value much better than monetary items, and their nominal market price skyrockets. Because they are listed on the balance sheet at historical costs, the accounting records no longer approximate their real economic value—in fact, with hyperinflation they are usually grossly undervalued.

Under this scenario, the FASB requires a translation process that tries to offset the inflation biases. The process assumes that the U.S. dollar is a stable currency that serves as a good storehouse of value. If, at the time of purchase, the local currency price of a nonmonetary asset reflects its true economic value, and if the exchange rate with the dollar is freely determined in the marketplace, then the dollar-equivalent of the historical cost should not only reflect the true value at the time of purchase but also maintain its value over time because of the dollar's stability. These ideas require (1) that the U.S. dollar be deemed the functional currency for subsidiaries operating in highly inflationary economies and (2) that the financial statements be translated using the temporal method. Monetary assets and liabilities are then translated at current exchange rates, which are appropriate, but the nonmonetary assets are remeasured into dollar equivalents using historical rates. Gains and losses flow through the income statement and are reflected in net income.

The IASB uses a different procedure to account for hyperinflation—nonmonetary assets are restated to reflect current purchasing power as measured by the local currency by applying a general price index such as the consumer price index (CPI) to "gross up" historical costs. For example, if an asset's cost was 100 units of the local currency when it was purchased a year ago, and if inflation in the country was 100 percent during the past year, then the asset would be reported at 200 units of the local currency. While the IASB's procedure is different from that of FASB, the intention is the same: To ensure that the financial statements fairly present the company's true economic position.

SELF-TEST QUESTIONS

What four issues (at a minimum) must be addressed before the appropriate translation methodology can be determined?

Why is it important to distinguish between monetary and nonmonetary items?

Assume that on the balance sheet, nonmonetary assets are greater than liabilities. What happens to a firm's net value if the reporting currency strengthens relative to the local currency from one year to the next? What if the reporting currency weakens relative to the local currency from one year to the next?

Assume that on the balance sheet, nonmonetary assets are less than liabilities. What happens to a firm's net value if the reporting currency strengthens relative to the local currency from one year to the next? What if the reporting currency weakens relative to the local currency from one year to the next?

What are the two permissible methods for translating financial statements? Differentiate between the two methods, particularly their treatment of gains and losses. (Hint: A flow chart might help with this answer.)

What is net asset exposure?

What is monetary balance?

What is the cumulative translation adjustment? What are two characteristics about CTA that should be understood by everyone?

Distinguish between a self-sustaining foreign entity and an integrated foreign entity. Why are these classifications important to the IASB?

What is a functional currency? How are the entity classifications important relative to the functional currency?

Does the FASB translation treatment differ from that of the IASB? Explain.

Distinguish between remeasuring and restating financial statements.

What is the definition for hyperinflation? How is the translation process required by FASB affected by hyperinflation? How does inflation affect the IASB's translation procedure?

TRANSLATING AND CONSOLIDATING THE SSI FINANCIAL STATEMENTS

In the previous section, we reviewed the basic provisions for translating financial statements from the local currency to the reporting currency. In this section, we demonstrate their application by translating the December 31, 2003, financial statements for SSI's three subsidiaries and combining them into a single set of consolidated statements. The data used for this example are meant to be illustrative. Translation and consolidation for the December 31, 2004, financial statements will be left for students in Problem 7-5 at the end of the chapter.

Determining Each Subsidiary's Functional Currency

To begin the translation process, we must first apply the logic of Figure 7-1 to each SSI operating unit to determine its functional currency:

1. The parent maintains its accounting records in the reporting currency, the U.S. dollar, so no translation is necessary.

2. The Mexican subsidiary maintains its accounting records in Mexican pesos. However, almost all of its transactions are with the parent and are invoiced in dollars. Therefore, it meets the definition of an integrated foreign entity, and its functional currency is that of its parent, or the U.S. dollar. To translate from the local currency (pesos) to the functional currency (dollars), we use the temporal method to remeasure the Mexican subsidiary's financial statements into the functional currency. Gains or losses from this remeasurement flow through the income statement directly to net income.

3. The German subsidiary maintains its accounting records in euros. While it coordinates its activities with the company's other operating units, it is largely independent of the other subsidiaries. It sources most of its inputs locally and sells its products primarily in Europe and Asia. Occasionally, it will sell in other markets when demand is higher than can be met in the short run by the subsidiary that normally serves that market. Consequently, it is a self-sufficient foreign entity; hence, its functional currency is the euro. Because its financial statements are already measured in its functional currency (the euro), translating them into the reporting currency (dollars) requires the current rate method. Gains or losses from this restatement are reported directly in the cumulative translation adjustment account rather than flowing through the income statement.

4. The determination of the Argentine subsidiary's functional currency is more complex. Its accounting records are kept in the local currency (pesos), and it operates largely independently of the other subsidiaries. Normally, this would indicate that the local currency should be the functional currency, and the current rate method should be used to translate from Argentine pesos into U.S. dollars. However, during the year, Argentina experienced approximately a 41 percent rate of inflation. Remember, when hyperinflation exists, the FASB dictates that the U.S. dollar be designated the functional currency and the temporal method be used to translate into dollars. The issue, then, is does the Argentine situation qualify as hyperinflation? The FASB identifies hyperinflation as when prices change by approximately 100 percent over a period of three years. However, the FASB also suggests that hyperinflation exists when the money unit no longer functions as a storehouse of value, which is the situation here, even though Argentina has experienced only one year of high inflation. Thus, we conclude that the functional currency should be the U.S. dollar, the temporal method should be used for translation, and gains or losses should flow through the income statement and affect reported net income. Note, though, that some discretion must be used. Argentina had a 41 percent inflation rate, but suppose it had been 31 percent? Rules are useful in accounting, but there will always be areas where judgment must be applied.

The Translation Process for SSI and Its Subsidiaries

Once the appropriate functional currency and the proper translation method for converting to the reporting currency (the U.S. dollar) have been determined for each operating unit, we must translate and then consolidate SSI's 2003 financial statements. The local currency balance sheets for each operating unit are shown in Table 7-2.

In Mexico, the functional currency is the U.S. dollar and that subsidiary is an integrated foreign entity. According to both the IASB and the FASB, the temporal method must be used for the translation, and gains or losses must flow through the income statement. For monetary assets and liabilities, we use the current exchange rate on the balance sheet date, which is $0.097836/peso. Nonmonetary assets are translated at historical rates. The average historical rates are as follows:

TABLE 7-2 | December 31, 2003 Balance Sheets (Local Currency)

	United States	Mexico		Germany		Argentina	
Cash	$ 534.7	MXN	32.7	EUR	155.7	ARS	22.9
Accounts receivable	870.9		38.8		636.9		184.2
Accounts receivable from intrafirm transactions	109.1		680.7		—		—
Inventories	703.7		2,209.0		290.1		31.2
Prepaid expenses	—		—		—		35.2
Current assets	$2,218.3	MXN	2,961.2	EUR	1,082.7	ARS	273.5
Net plant and equipment	2,618.1		3,898.1		1,387.7		128.1
Investment in Mexico	331.5		—		—		—
Investment in Germany	1,310.3		—		—		—
Investment in Argentina	136.7		—		—		—
Total assets	$6,615.0	MXN	6,859.3	EUR	2,470.4	ARS	401.6
Accounts payable	$ 285.2	MXN	689.9	EUR	95.5	ARS	47.9
Accounts payable from intrafirm transactions	66.6		968.0		—		50.7
Notes payable	218.6		282.1		206.6		6.8
Current maturities LTD	168.8		72.6		17.8		—
Accrued liabilities	478.3		944.4		288.6		207.3
Current liabilities	$1,217.5	MXN	2,957.0	EUR	608.5	ARS	312.7
Long-term debt	1,490.2		996.6		392.9		9.5
Total liabilities	$2,707.7	MXN	3,953.6	EUR	1,001.4	ARS	322.2
Preferred stock	500.0		—		—		—
Common stock	2,000.0		990.6		425.1		50.0
Retained earnings	1,407.3		1,915.1		1,043.9		29.4
Total equity	$3,407.3	MXN	2,905.7	EUR	1,469.0	ARS	79.4
Total capital	$6,615.0	MXN	6,859.3	EUR	2,470.4	ARS	401.6

Note: Table was created using Microsoft *Excel*, so rounding differences may occur.

$0.109190/peso for inventory items
$0.103513/peso for net fixed assets
$0.100947/peso for common stock

Each of the three historical rates is different because each represents the exchange rate on the dates the items entered the accounting records.

The translation process for the Mexican balance sheet is shown in Table 7-3. Note that there is no exchange rate given for retained earnings. Technically, the entry represents the retained earnings from the previous balance sheet (translated at the appropriate historical rate) plus current additions to retained earnings (translated at this year's rate) plus or minus exchange rate gains or losses from this accounting period.

For the German subsidiary, the functional currency is the euro, and the current rate method is used to restate the balance sheet into the reporting currency. Table 7-4 illustrates this process. The current exchange rate on the balance sheet date is $1.01835/euro, and all assets and liabilities are translated at this rate. Common stock is translated at the historical rate of $1.17613/euro, and retained earnings represents the beginning balance plus current period additions to retained earnings. Note that the gain in value from the euro's appreciation does not flow through the

TABLE 7-3 | Translation of Balance Sheet for Mexican Subsidiary Remeasured from Pesos to Dollars Using the Temporal Method

	Mexico		$/MXN	$ Equivalent
Cash	MXN	32.7	0.097836	$ 3.2
Accounts receivable		38.8	0.097836	3.8
Accounts receivable from intrafirm transactions		680.7	0.097836	66.6
Inventories		2,209.0	0.109190	241.2
Prepaid expenses		—		—
Current assets	MXN	2,961.2		$314.8
Net plant and equipment		3,898.1	0.103513	403.5
Total assets	MXN	6,859.3		$718.3
Accounts payable	MXN	689.9	0.097836	$ 67.5
Accounts payable from intrafirm transactions		968.0	0.097836	94.7
Notes payable		282.1	0.097836	27.6
Current maturities LTD		72.6	0.097836	7.1
Accrued liabilities		944.4	0.097836	92.4
Current liabilities	MXN	2,957.0		$289.3
Long-term debt		996.6	0.097836	97.5
Total liabilities	MXN	3,953.6		$386.8
Preferred stock		—		—
Common stock		990.6	0.100947	100.0
Retained earnings		1,915.1		231.5
Total equity	MXN	2,905.7		$331.5
Cumulative translation adjustment				—
Total capital	MXN	6,859.3		$718.3

Notes: The Mexican subsidiary is an integrated foreign entity, so its functional currency is the U.S. dollar. Consequently, the temporal method must be used. Table was created using Microsoft *Excel,* so rounding differences may occur.

income statement to the retained earnings balance but rather is included in the cumulative translation adjustment account, which, depending on whether there is a translation gain or loss, is added to or subtracted from equity on the balance sheet.

Due to the 41 percent inflation rate in Argentina during the year, the U.S. dollar is used as the functional currency for the Argentine subsidiary, and its balance sheet is remeasured using the temporal method. This is shown in Table 7-5. Monetary assets and liabilities are translated into equivalent U.S. dollars at the spot exchange rate, or $0.28397/ARS. The average exchange rate of inventory items is $1.00050/ARS. The rate is significantly higher than the current rate because the Argentine peso devaluated precipitously during the year. The other nonmonetary assets, net plant and equipment, are translated at the appropriate historical rate of $1.00070/ARS. Finally, common stock is translated at the historical rate of $1.00040/ARS. The historical exchange rates are very close to parity with the U.S. dollar because the Argentine peso was pegged to the dollar for a long period prior to the peso's devaluation.

The income statements for the three foreign subsidiaries are translated using the transaction-weighted average exchange rate for the year, except for those items linked to specific balance sheet accounts that are translated using historical rates. (This applies to Mexico and Argentina because they use the temporal method.) In

TABLE 7-4 | Translation of Balance Sheet for German Subsidiary Restated from Euros to Dollars Using the Current Rate Method

	Germany		$/EUR	$ Equivalent
Cash	EUR	155.7	1.01835	$ 158.6
Accounts receivable		636.9	1.01835	648.6
Accounts receivable from intrafirm transactions		—	1.01835	—
Inventories		290.1	1.01835	295.4
Prepaid expenses		—	1.01835	—
Current assets	EUR	1,082.7		$1,102.6
Net plant and equipment		1,387.7	1.01835	1,413.2
Total assets	EUR	2,470.4		$2,515.7
Accounts payable	EUR	95.5	1.01835	$ 97.3
Accounts payable from intrafirm transactions		—	1.01835	—
Notes payable		206.6	1.01835	210.4
Current maturities LTD		17.8	1.01835	18.1
Accrued liabilities		288.6	1.01835	293.9
Current liabilities	EUR	608.5		$ 619.7
Long-term debt		392.9	1.01835	400.1
Total liabilities	EUR	1,001.4		$1,019.8
Preferred stock		—		—
Common stock		425.1	1.17613	500.0
Retained earnings		1,043.9		810.3
Total equity	EUR	1,469.0		$1,310.3
Cumulative translation adjustment				185.7
Total capital	EUR	2,470.4		$2,515.7

Notes: The German subsidiary is a self-sustaining foreign entity, so its functional currency is the euro. Consequently, the current rate method must be used. Table was created using Microsoft *Excel*, so rounding differences may occur.

other words, cost of goods sold and depreciation are translated at the same rates used for inventories and net plant and equipment, respectively. Because the U.S. operation was the only one to have preferred stock outstanding, no translation is needed for the preferred dividend. If another subsidiary had preferred stock outstanding, the preferred dividend would have been translated at the exchange rate on the day the distribution was made. The same would be true for common stock dividend distributions.

Consolidating Subsidiary Financial Statements

With the subsidiary financial statements restated and remeasured into the reporting currency (U.S. dollars), we are now ready to prepare the consolidated statements. The consolidation process is quite straightforward. In Table 7-6, we show that the consolidated entry for each line item is simply the summation of the amount for each subsidiary after subtracting intracompany transactions. Intracompany transactions are those between subsidiaries and the parent, or among subsidiaries. For example, accounts receivable from intrafirm sales cancels out accounts payable from the same intracompany sales. Note that we have segregated the intracompany items from the aggregate amounts of accounts receivable and payable to demon-

TABLE 7-5	Translation of Balance Sheet for Argentine Subsidiary Remeasured from Argentinean Pesos to Dollars Using the Temporal Method		

	Argentina		$/ARS	$ Equivalent
Cash	ARS	22.9	0.28397	$ 6.5
Accounts receivable		184.2	0.28397	52.3
Accounts receivable from intrafirm transactions		—	0.28397	—
Inventories		31.2	1.00050	31.2
Prepaid expenses		35.2	0.28397	10.0
Current assets	ARS	273.5		$100.0
Net plant and equipment		128.1	1.00070	128.2
Total assets	ARS	401.6		$228.2
Accounts payable	ARS	47.9	0.28397	$ 13.6
Accounts payable from intrafirm transactions		50.7	0.28397	14.4
Notes payable		6.8	0.28397	1.9
Current maturities LTD		—	0.28397	—
Accrued liabilities		207.3	0.28397	58.9
Current liabilities	ARS	312.7		$ 88.8
Long-term debt		9.5	0.28397	2.7
Total liabilities	ARS	322.2		$ 91.5
Preferred stock		—		—
Common stock		50.0	1.00040	50.0
Retained earnings		29.4		86.7
Total equity	ARS	79.4		$136.7
Cumulative translation adjustment		—		—
Total capital	ARS	401.6		$228.2

Notes: The Argentine subsidiary is considered a self-sustaining foreign entity; however, hyperinflation exists. Therefore, its functional currency is the U.S. dollar, and the temporal method must be used. Table was created using Microsoft *Excel*, so rounding differences may occur.

strate this offset more clearly. In reality, there would usually be only a single aggregate account for receivables and one for payables. Also, on the parent's books, investments in the subsidiaries must be removed along with the corresponding common equity accounts of each foreign subsidiary, because these are also intracompany items. These are SSI's only intracompany items that must be cancelled out before consolidating the financial statements, but other items, such as intracompany loans, are often found in other companies' financial statements.

SELF-TEST QUESTIONS

Briefly explain why the temporal method was used to translate SSI's Mexican subsidiary's financial statements.

Briefly explain why the current rate method was used to translate SSI's German subsidiary's financial statements.

Briefly explain why the temporal method was used to translate SSI's Argentine subsidiary's financial statements. What method would have been used if hyperinflation had not existed?

What are "intracompany transactions," and how are they handled in consolidations?

TABLE 7-6 | SSI December 31, 2003 Financial Statements

	United States	Mexico	Germany	Argentina	Consolidated
Income Statements (USD)					
Sales	$4,367.9	$229.9	$2,668.0	$474.2	$7,740.0
Cost of goods sold	2,972.1	134.4	1,907.2	256.3	5,270.0
General and administrative	694.9	27.5	418.6	137.5	1,278.5
EBITDA	$ 700.9	$ 68.0	$ 342.2	$ 80.4	$1,191.5
Depreciation and amortization	277.7	42.8	149.9	13.6	484.0
EBIT	$ 423.2	$ 25.2	$ 192.3	$ 66.8	$ 707.5
Interest	59.5	9.5	27.8	56.2	153.0
EBT	$ 363.7	$ 15.7	$ 164.5	$ 10.6	$ 554.5
Taxes	145.5	6.3	65.8	4.2	221.8
Net income before preferred stock dividends	$ 218.2	$ 9.4	$ 98.7	$ 6.4	$ 332.7
Preferred stock dividends	35.0	—	—	—	35.0
Net income to common stockholders	$ 183.2	$ 9.4	$ 98.7	$ 6.4	$ 297.7
Balance Sheets (USD)					
Cash	$ 534.7	$ 3.2	$ 158.6	$ 6.5	$ 702.9
Accounts receivable	870.9	3.8	648.6	52.3	1,575.6
Accounts receivable from intrafirm transactions	109.1	66.6	—	—	—
Inventories	703.7	241.2	295.4	31.2	1,271.6
Prepaid expenses	—	—	—	10.0	10.0
Current assets	$2,218.3	$314.8	$1,102.6	$100.0	$3,560.0
Net plant and equipment	2,618.1	403.5	1,413.2	128.2	4,563.0
Investment in Mexico	331.5	—	—	—	—
Investment in Germany	1,310.3	—	—	—	—
Investment in Argentina	136.7	—	—	—	—
Total assets	$6,615.0	$718.3	$2,515.7	$228.2	$8,123.0
Accounts payable	$ 285.2	$ 67.5	$ 97.3	$ 13.6	$ 463.5
Accounts payable from intrafirm transactions	66.6	94.7	—	14.4	—
Notes payable	218.6	27.6	210.4	1.9	458.5
Current maturities LTD	168.8	7.1	18.1	—	194.0
Accrued liabilities	478.3	92.4	293.9	58.9	923.5
Current liabilities	$1,217.5	$289.3	$ 619.7	$ 88.8	$2,039.5
Long-term debt	1,490.2	97.5	400.1	2.7	1,990.5
Total liabilities	$2,707.7	$386.8	$1,019.8	$ 91.5	$4,030.0
Preferred stock	500.0	—	—	—	500.0
Common stock	2,000.0	100.0	500.0	50.0	2,000.0
Retained earnings	1,407.3	231.5	810.3	86.7	1,407.3
Total equity	$3,407.3	$331.5	$1,310.3	$136.7	$3,407.3
Cumulative translation adjustment	—	—	185.7	—	185.7
Total capital	$6,615.0	$718.3	$2,515.7	$228.2	$8,123.0

Note: Table was created using Microsoft *Excel*, so rounding differences may occur.

OTHER ISSUES IN FOREIGN CURRENCY ACCOUNTING

Now that we have covered the mechanics of translating and consolidating foreign currency financial statements, we can turn to several other issues that need to be addressed. The first is the effect of translation gains and losses and the need to include them in the company's risk management system.

Hedging Accounting or Translation Exposures

Earlier in the chapter we introduced the concepts of exposed assets, exposed liabilities, and the company's net exposure. We defined exposed assets and liabilities as those whose values would change when measured in the reporting currency if exchange rates changed. This means that if the company uses the current rate method, all assets and liabilities are exposed, but because equity balances are always translated at historical rates, they are never exposed. If the temporal method is used, monetary assets and liabilities are exposed, but neither equity accounts nor inventories and net plant and equipment are exposed. Is there any economic significance to a company's accounting exposure position?

To answer this question, we need to remember that gains and losses from translation into the reporting currency are *unrealized* gains and losses, and that they may reverse in the next accounting period. In addition, they do not create any tax obligation because they are unrealized, even when they flow through the income statement using the temporal method. In other words, accounting translation gains and losses have no economic effect on the firm's cash flows, and they should not reflect a change in the firm's value. However, there are several scenarios in which this conclusion may be modified:

1. If the translation gain or loss is expected to be realized soon through a specific transaction, we may want to manage the future effect of the accounting position. *Transaction* gains and losses have real economic significance because they affect tax liability and the firm's cash flow. If a subsidiary is to be sold or liquidated soon, the gains or losses would be realized upon its sale, so the translation exposure has strategic implications for the firm's value.
2. The company may have debt covenants specifying minimum accounting ratios, such as the debt ratio. Accounting gains and losses affect consolidated equity, so it is conceivable that a debt ratio covenant could be violated if a company has significant translation losses.
3. If there is hyperinflation in a country, such as was the case in Argentina for SSI, exposed assets will lose value when exchange rates change, and it is unlikely that these losses will reverse in the future (through significant deflation).

Balance Sheet Hedge
The situation that occurs when the change in assets value exactly offsets the change in value of the liabilities.

Each of these scenarios suggests that managing translation exposure might be worthwhile.[1] The technique for achieving this objective is called a **balance sheet hedge**. In a balance sheet hedge, we want exposed assets to equal exposed liabilities so that the net exposure position is zero. Gains (losses) on the assets side of the balance sheet exactly offset losses (gains) on the claims side, so there are no foreign currency

---

[1]Some authors contend that another reason translation exposure management is important is because managers may be evaluated and compensated on the basis of accounting ratios, and the performance evaluation system may become distorted because of translation gains and losses. Our view is that appropriate adjustments can be made to the evaluation metrics to cancel out such biases, and it is not appropriate to use activities that have real economic consequences to offset translation gains or losses.

gains or losses to record or to flow through the income statement. It is easy to see why and how this neutral position removes distortions in all three scenarios given above.

How does a company develop a hedged balance sheet? This is accomplished by creating new exposed asset or liability positions to offset corresponding exposures on the other side of the balance sheet. If the subsidiary's financial statements are translated using the temporal method, achieving a balance sheet hedge is fairly easy, and the required actions depend on the magnitude of nonmonetary assets in the assets section and equities in the claims section. If the company has a net asset exposure, borrowing the amount of the exposure is one way to create the needed exposed liability. However, the funds must be used to acquire additional nonmonetary assets or be kept in assets denominated in the reporting currency, so they do not increase assets exposure. If one of the preceding scenarios is relevant, or if the company needs to finance additional nonmonetary assets, a balance sheet hedge makes good economic sense. However, if reducing reported earnings volatility is the only reason for creating the balance sheet hedge, remember that it has a real economic cost in the form of increased interest payments. There is no evidence that an efficient market cannot interpret the earnings volatility correctly; that is, in an efficient market there may be no reduction in the firm's value, hence no reason to bear the additional cost of the hedge.

If the subsidiary has a net liability exposure, there are several ways to hedge the balance sheet. An easy solution is to convert some liabilities to U.S. dollar–denominated debt with no changes to the assets side of the balance sheet. If the right amount of debt is converted in this manner, the remaining exposed liabilities will equal exposed assets, and there will be a zero net exposure position.

Translation with the current rate method always creates a net asset exposure because all assets are translated at the current rate. However, if sufficient monetary assets are denominated in the reporting currency to offset the equity, it is still possible to obtain a balance sheet hedge. If denominating the monetary assets in the reporting currency makes sense from a business perspective, this strategy is worth pursuing. Otherwise, it distorts normal business operations and imposes a real economic cost on the firm.

Inflation: The Case of Disappearing Assets

Accounting principles assume that the monetary unit in which the accounting records are maintained remains essentially stable over time, serves as a unit of exchange, and functions as a storehouse of value. These premises are violated in periods of high inflation, and companies often turn to investments in nonmonetary assets as a hedge against inflation. However, as we mentioned earlier, inflation causes a distortion in the balance sheet because nonmonetary assets, which are carried at their historical cost, have substantially more purchasing power than the current money unit. Thus, if we translate the balance sheet using the current rate method, the dollar-equivalent amount does not reflect the real value of underlying assets, hence they would be seriously undervalued.

We demonstrate this situation by looking at the implications of using the current rate method rather than the temporal method to translate the Argentine subsidiary's financial statements. Table 7-7 shows this translation, and Table 7-8 compares the dollar-equivalent balance sheet obtained using the temporal method with that resulting from the current rate method. We see that nonmonetary assets decrease in value by $114.2, and thus retained earnings are reduced by the same amount. It is easy to see that if inflation is very high (approximately 41 percent in Argentina during the

TABLE 7-7 | Translation of Balance Sheet for Argentine Subsidiary: Dollar-Equivalent Statements If Current Rate Method Is Used

	Argentina		$/ARS	$ Equivalent
Cash	ARS	22.9	0.28397	$ 6.5
Accounts receivable		184.2	0.28397	52.3
Accounts receivable from intrafirm transactions		—	0.28397	—
Inventories		31.2	0.28397	8.9
Prepaid expenses		35.2	0.28397	10.0
Current assets	ARS	273.5		$ 77.7
Net plant and equipment		128.1	0.28397	36.4
Total assets	ARS	401.6		$114.0
Accounts payable	ARS	47.9	0.28397	$ 13.6
Accounts payable from intrafirm transactions		50.7	0.28397	14.4
Notes payable		6.8	0.28397	1.9
Current maturities LTD		—	0.28397	—
Accrued liabilities		207.3	0.28397	58.9
Current liabilities	ARS	312.7		$ 88.8
Long-term debt		9.5	0.28397	2.7
Total liabilities	ARS	322.2		$ 91.5
Preferred stock		—		—
Common stock		50.0	1.00040	50.0
Retained earnings		29.4		(27.5)
Total equity	ARS	79.4		$ 22.5
Total capital	ARS	401.6		$114.0

Note: Table was created using Microsoft *Excel*, so rounding differences may occur.

year), as the purchasing power of the money unit falls, the translated value of the nonmonetary assets quickly approaches zero, or at least a very small number. However, the nonmonetary assets probably retain most of their real value, so if the company were to sell them, it would receive substantially more current pesos than the historical peso amounts shown on the books.

Table 7-8 illustrates why the FASB requires the company to use the temporal method for translating financial statements when the local currency is experiencing high inflation, even if the subsidiary is self-sustaining. Another approach to this type of adjustment, and the one required by the IASB in IAS 29, is to restate the local currency beginning balance sheet into the ending money unit using a general price index such as the Consumer Price Index (CPI). In the case of Argentina, though, this approach would yield a substantially different translation than required by the FASB because the depreciation of the currency was greater than would have been implied by purchasing power parity. There is no definitive evidence indicating which approach is better for presenting operating results.

Inflation: Taxation and Erosion of Capital

High inflation distorts taxes. When calculating taxable income, we use current period revenues, but some of the historical costs deducted from revenues may have been

TABLE 7-8 | Balance Sheet for Argentine Subsidiary Using Different Translation Methods

	Argentina		Temporal $ Equivalent	Current $ Equivalent	Difference
Cash	ARS	22.9	$ 6.5	$ 6.5	$ —
Accounts receivable		184.2	52.3	52.3	—
Accounts receivable from intrafirm transactions		—	—	—	—
Inventories		31.2	31.2	8.9	(22.4)
Prepaid expenses		35.2	10.0	10.0	—
Current assets	ARS	273.5	$100.0	$ 77.7	$ (22.4)
Net plant and equipment		128.1	128.2	36.4	(91.8)
Total assets	ARS	401.6	$228.2	$114.0	$(114.2)
Accounts payable	ARS	47.9	$ 13.6	$ 13.6	$ —
Accounts payable from intrafirm transactions		50.7	14.4	14.4	—
Notes payable		6.8	1.9	1.9	—
Current maturities LTD		—	—	—	—
Accrued liabilities		207.3	58.9	58.9	—
Current liabilities	ARS	312.7	$ 88.8	$ 88.8	$ —
Long-term debt		9.5	2.7	2.7	—
Total liabilities	ARS	322.2	$ 91.5	$ 91.5	$ —
Preferred stock		—	—	—	—
Common stock		50.0	50.0	50.0	—
Retained earnings		29.4	86.7	(27.5)	(114.2)
Total equity	ARS	79.4	$136.7	$ 22.5	$(114.2)
Total capital	ARS	401.6	$228.2	$114.0	$(114.2)

Note: Table was created using Microsoft *Excel*, so rounding differences may occur.

recorded when the purchasing power of the currency was higher. Because we cannot restate the costs in terms of the current purchasing power money unit, the costs are understated, taxable income is overstated, and taxes due are overstated.

The following numerical example illustrates this effect. Assume that a new company is started in a country experiencing high inflation. At time t_0, the firm receives an order for one unit of its product at a selling price of LC 119, and it purchases raw materials at a cost of LC 100. (Here, LC represents local currency.) The production cycle is long, six months, and we assume that the raw materials represent the only cost. A second order is received three months later, so the company buys more raw materials to build the second unit, but the cost is now LC 108.95. At the end of the six-month production cycle, the company delivers the product and receives LC 119 from the customer. At this time it also receives a third order, and it buys the needed raw materials for LC 118.71. (For purposes of this example, assume the latest raw materials are not in inventory at the time funds are received from the first customer.)

How much profit will the company earn after taxes of 40 percent on the first unit sold? There are several possible answers depending on the "cost" used to calculate taxable income.

CASE 1: FIFO If the company uses the first-in-first-out or FIFO inventory method, profit is calculated as follows:

Revenue	LC	119.00
Cost		100.00
Taxable income	LC	19.00
Taxes (40%)		7.60
Net income	LC	11.40
Inflow	LC	119.00
Outflow	LC	7.60
Net inflow	LC	111.40

The company spends LC 118.71 to replace the raw materials, so it invests an additional LC 118.71 − LC 111.40 = LC 7.31 in order to continue production. If this continues over time, investors will have to invest more and more money in the business just to remain in operation because taxes are eroding the firm's capital.

CASE 2: LIFO If the company can use the last-in-first-out or LIFO inventory method, profits are calculated as follows:

Revenue	LC	119.00
Cost		108.95
Taxable income	LC	10.05
Taxes (40%)		4.02
Net income	LC	6.03
Inflow	LC	119.00
Outflow	LC	4.02
Net inflow	LC	114.98

The company must then spend LC 118.71 to replace the raw materials, so it must invest additional capital in the amount of LC 118.71 − LC 114.98 = LC 3.73 to continue production. Again, there is erosion of the company's capital position and investors are constantly being called upon to invest more money.

CASE 3: REPLACEMENT COST If the company is able to use the replacement cost inventory method, the profit is

Revenue	LC	119.00
Cost		118.71
Taxable income	LC	0.29
Taxes (40%)		0.12
Net income	LC	0.17
Inflow	LC	119.00
Outflow	LC	0.17
Net inflow	LC	118.83

The company must then spend LC 118.71 to replace the raw materials. In this case, capital is not eroded because the firm is able to use replacement cost to value the raw materials used. However, the company would not earn the profit that seemed to be built in when it made the sale. In fact, it barely broke even.

Three other points should be noted. First, no country in the world permits replacement cost accounting for tax purposes, so Case 3 is presented only for illustrative purposes. Many countries, though, do permit LIFO, and this should always be used for calculating costs if inflation exists. Second, we disregarded "inventory profits," or the increased value of inventories still on hand if replacement cost accounting were used. The balance sheet would show inventories at LC 100, but in fact those inventories would be worth LC 118.71. And third, we assumed in the example that prices were held constant even though costs were rising, which is generally not appropriate. If the company wanted to earn 11.4 percent after taxes, then it would have to set the selling price higher than LC 119 so that after taxes it would still have sufficient money to replace inventory and provide equity investors with a reasonable return on their capital. Of course, competitive pressures sometimes prevent companies from raising prices as much as they would like.

SELF-TEST QUESTIONS

Briefly identify three issues that affect the firm's translation gains and losses and the need to include them in the company's risk management system.

Do accounting translation gains and losses impact a firm's value? Briefly explain.

Identify several scenarios that might suggest that translation exposure should be managed.

How does a company achieve a balance sheet hedge?

Briefly explain why FASB requires that in periods of hyperinflation the temporal method rather than current rate method be used for translation.

How do international accounting standards differ from FASB for translation in hyperinflationary environments?

How can inflation affect taxes?

SUMMARY

The primary purpose of this chapter was to explain the process of translating and consolidating basic financial statements. We also introduced techniques designed to hedge accounting exposure and to adjust for inflation. The key concepts discussed in this chapter are listed below.

- Multinational enterprises usually maintain separate financial records, denominated in local currencies, for their different operating units. Those records are then combined to form **consolidated financial statements**, which are aggregated financial statements for parent and subsidiary organizations that exclude intracompany transactions. Consolidated statements must be filed with the SEC and are usually presented in annual reports.
- The **reporting currency** is the monetary unit of the parent company and into which the subsidiaries' financial statements are ultimately recast from their local currencies. For U.S. multinationals and other multinationals required to submit financials to the SEC, the reporting currency is the U.S. dollar.
- **Monetary items** include financial assets and liabilities whose values are fixed in terms of nominal money units. Treasury bills held as liquid reserves, accounts payable, and notes payable to banks are examples of monetary items.
- **Nonmonetary items** are items such as inventory and fixed assets whose values are not equivalent to a fixed number of nominal money units.
- Two methods are used for translating financial statements: the current rate method and the temporal method. In the **current rate method**, assets and liabilities are translated at the spot exchange rate on the day the financial statements are prepared, while equity accounts are translated at historical exchange rates in effect on the dates the items were recorded. In the **temporal method**, mone-

tary and nonmonetary items are first distinguished from one another. Next, all monetary asset items and all liabilities are translated at the spot exchange rate on the day the financial statements are prepared, while nonmonetary items must be translated or **remeasured** at the historical exchange rates in effect on the dates the items were first recorded.

- **Exposed assets** are assets that are subject to a change in value in terms of the reporting currency if exchange rates change.
- **Exposed liabilities** are liabilities that are subject to a change in value if exchange rates change.
- A **net asset exposure** is created when there are more exposed assets than exposed liabilities. A **net liability exposure** exists when exposed liabilities exceed exposed assets.
- A **cumulative translation adjustment (CTA)** is an equity account entry made to reflect the unrealized gain or loss on a net exposure under the current rate translation method. Entries made in one period may reverse in later periods if exchange rates merely fluctuate rather than move steadily in a given direction.
- **Monetary balance** is achieved when the exposure in one section of the balance sheet offsets the exposure in the other section. In other words, gains in one section will match losses in the other.
- A foreign operating unit that functions as a separate ongoing concern and is largely independent of the parent is called a **self-sustaining foreign entity**.
- An **integrated foreign entity** is an operating unit located in another country that serves as an extension of the parent and whose cash flows are correlated with those of the parent.
- **Functional currency** is the monetary unit in which the primary economic activities of the subsidiary are conducted.
- The process of translating financial statements from a local currency into a functional currency, using the temporal method, is called **remeasuring** the financial statements.
- The process of translating financial statements from a functional currency into a reporting currency, using the current rate method, is called **restating** the financial statements.
- **Hyperinflation** is a situation in which cumulative annual inflation of approximately 100 percent occurs over three years. In this situation, currency no longer functions effectively as a storehouse of value.
- The **FASB** requires that the U.S. dollar be deemed the functional currency for subsidiaries operating in **highly inflationary economies** and the financial statements be translated using the **temporal method**.
- The **IASB** uses a different procedure to account for **hyperinflation**. Nonmonetary assets are restated to reflect current purchasing power as measured by the local currency by applying a **general price index** such as the Consumer Price Index (CPI) to gross up historical costs.
- A **balance sheet hedge** occurs when the change in assets value exactly offsets the change in value of the liabilities.
- **Inflation** causes a **distortion** in the **balance sheet** because nonmonetary assets, which are carried at their historical cost, have substantially more purchasing power than the current money unit. If the balance sheet is translated using the current rate method, the dollar-equivalent amount does not reflect the real value of underlying assets, hence they would be seriously undervalued.
- High **inflation distorts taxes.** When calculating taxable income, we use current period revenues, but some of the historical costs deducted from revenues may have been recorded when the purchasing power of the currency was higher. Because costs cannot be restated in terms of the current purchasing power money unit, costs are understated, taxable income is overstated, and taxes due are overstated.

QUESTIONS

(7-1) What are the differences among local currency, reporting currency, and functional currency?

(7-2) Depending on the nature of a subsidiary's operations, how can the translation process have direct implications for the amount and volatility of reported earnings?

(7-3) Why do MNEs face a much more difficult task in complying with the SEC's periodic reporting requirements than domestic firms?

(7-4) Provide some examples of both monetary and nonmonetary items.

(7-5) Explain whether the following statement is true or false: "Nonmonetary items whose real values are constant will not change over time even when exchange rates change."

(7-6) How is "balance" restored to the balance sheet when gains and losses due to exchange rates cause the translated balance sheet to be out of balance?

(7-7) How is the correct translation method to use determined when working with foreign subsidiary financial statements? (Hint: Figure 7-1 will help in answering this question.) Do the FASB and IASB use different approaches to make the selection? If so, how are they different? Will the same result be achieved?

(7-8) What are the two translation methods, and what are the major differences between them?

(7-9) Explain whether the following statement is true or false: "Translation gains and losses have significant tax consequences but do not change reported earnings or increase earnings variability over time."

(7-10) Why is there a problem with a foreign subsidiary's accounting statements when hyperinflation exists in that foreign country and those statements need to be translated to another currency? Are there differences in the FASB and IASB procedures? What are these procedures in effect trying to do?

(7-11) Why is there a need to "consolidate" certain transactions? Give some examples of typical transactions that would be consolidated.

(7-12) Provide a brief overview of the process used by an MNE with several foreign subsidiaries to arrive at its consolidated financial statements. Assume that the MNE's reporting currency is the U.S. dollar and it has both self-sustaining and integrated foreign entities as subsidiaries.

(7-13) Why might managing translation exposure be useful? In general terms, how would this be done? Differentiate between the necessary steps depending on whether the statements were translated using the temporal and current rate methods and whether there was a net asset or net liability exposure.

(7-14) Explain whether the following statement is true or false: "There is evidence to suggest that an efficient market cannot interpret earnings volatility from translation gains and losses correctly. Therefore, it is absolutely imperative that firms hedge their balance sheets for these translation gains and losses—particularly because there is no real economic cost for them to do so."

(7-15) Why in periods of high inflation do firms tend to invest in nonmonetary assets? What happens to the balance sheet of a foreign subsidiary with high investments of nonmonetary assets if the current rate method is used to translate from the local currency to the reporting currency? If the temporal method is used? Which method should be used under hyperinflationary environments? Explain.

(7-16) How does inflation distort taxes and erode capital? Provide an example of this using FIFO, LIFO, and replacement cost inventory methods.

SELF-TEST PROBLEMS   Solutions Appear in Appendix B

(ST-1) Define each of the following terms:
Key Terms
a. Consolidated financial statements; remeasuring, restating
b. Reporting currency; local currency; functional currency
c. Monetary items; nonmonetary items; denominated; measured
d. Current rate method; temporal method
e. Exposed assets; exposed liabilities; net asset exposure; net liability exposure
f. Cumulative translation adjustment; monetary balance
g. Self-sustaining foreign entity; integrated foreign entity
h. Hyperinflation; balance sheet hedge

(ST-2) MST International is an electronics manufacturer with two subsidiaries, one
Translation and located in the United States and one located abroad. The foreign subsidiary's func-
Consolidation tional currency is the U.S. dollar, and it is an integrated foreign entity. MST's
December 31, 2004, income statements in U.S. dollars and its December 31, 2004,
subsidiary balance sheets in local currency are shown here.

Income Statements (USD) for December 31, 2004

(Thousands of Dollars)	United States	Foreign	Consolidated
Sales	$5,678.3	$517.3	$6,195.6
Cost of goods sold	3,974.8	362.1	4,336.9
General and administrative expenses	903.4	35.8	939.2
EBITDA	$ 800.1	$119.4	$ 919.5
Depreciation and amortization	361.0	55.6	416.6
EBIT	$ 439.1	$ 63.8	$ 502.9
Interest	77.4	12.4	89.8
EBT	$ 361.7	$ 51.4	$ 413.1
Taxes (40%)	144.7	20.6	165.3
Net income before preferred stock dividends	$ 217.0	$ 30.8	$ 247.8
Preferred stock dividends	45.5	—	45.5
Net Income to common stockholders	$ 171.5	$ 30.8	$ 202.3

December 31, 2004, Balance Sheets (Local Currency)

(Thousands of Dollars)	United States	Foreign	
Cash	$ 695.0	LC	42.5
Accounts receivable	1,132.1		50.4
Accounts receivable from intrafirm transactions	12.0		884.9
Inventories	914.8		2,613.8
Prepaid expenses	—		
Current assets	$2,753.9	LC	3,591.6
Net plant and equipment	3,403.6		4,467.5
Investment in foreign country	22.0		—
Total assets	$6,179.5	LC	8,059.1
Accounts payable	$ 225.3	LC	896.9
Accounts payable from intrafirm transactions	8.4		1,258.4
Notes payable	284.2		366.7
Current maturities LTD	219.4		94.4
Accrued liabilities	335.6		944.4
Current liabilities	$1,072.9	LC	3,560.8

(Thousands of Dollars)	United States	Foreign
Long-term debt	1,455.2	1,295.5
Total liabilities	$2,528.1	LC 4,856.3
Preferred stock	600.0	—
Common stock	2,050.0	1,280.0
Retained earnings	1,001.4	1,922.8
Total equity	$3,051.4	LC 3,202.8
Total capital	$6,179.5	LC 8,059.1

You have found the following exchange rate data:

December 31, 2004, exchange rate	$0.0095/LC
Average historical rate for inventory	$0.0080/LC
Average historical rate for plant and equipment	$0.0085/LC
Average historical rate for common stock	$0.0075/LC

Translate the foreign subsidiary's balance sheet and show MST's consolidated balance sheet as of December 31, 2004.

(ST-3)
Translation and
Consolidation

Hubbard International is a furniture manufacturer with two subsidiaries, one located in the United States and one located abroad. The foreign subsidiary's functional currency is the local currency, and it is a self-sustaining foreign entity. Hubbard's December 31, 2004, income statements in U.S. dollars and its December 31, 2004, subsidiary balance sheets in local currency are shown here.

Income Statements (USD) for December 31, 2004

	United States	Foreign	Consolidated
Sales	$13,977.3	$8,537.6	$22,514.9
Cost of goods sold	9,510.7	6,103.0	15,613.7
General and administrative expenses	2,223.7	1,339.6	3,563.3
EBITDA	$ 2,242.9	$1,095.0	$ 3,337.9
Depreciation and amortization	888.7	479.7	1,368.4
EBIT	$ 1,354.2	$ 615.3	$ 1,969.5
Interest	190.4	89.0	279.4
EBT	$ 1,163.8	$ 526.3	$ 1,690.1
Taxes (40%)	465.5	210.5	676.0
Net income before preferred stock dividends	$ 698.3	$ 315.8	$ 1,014.1
Preferred stock dividends	112.0	—	112.0
Net income to common stockholders	$ 586.3	$ 315.8	$ 902.1

December 31, 2004, Balance Sheets (Local Currency)

	United States	Foreign
Cash	$1,710.9	LC 498.2
Accounts receivable	2,786.8	2,038.1
Accounts receivable from intrafirm transactions	87.1	125.0
Inventories	2,251.9	803.4
Prepaid expenses	—	—
Current assets	$6,836.7	LC 3,464.7

	United States	Foreign
Net plant and equipment	8,378.0	4,440.5
Investment in foreign country	1,802.4	—
Total assets	$17,017.1	LC 7,905.2
Accounts payable	$ 600.3	LC 305.6
Accounts payable from intrafirm transactions	128.1	85.0
Notes payable	522.8	576.1
Current maturities LTD	540.2	57.0
Accrued liabilities	1,200.7	923.5
Current liabilities	$ 2,992.1	LC 1,947.2
Long-term debt	3,567.7	2,257.2
Total liabilities	$ 6,559.8	LC 4,204.4
Preferred stock	500.0	—
Common stock	5,000.0	2,205.0
Retained earnings	4,957.3	1,495.8
Total equity	$ 9,957.3	LC 3,700.8
Total capital	$17,017.1	LC 7,905.2

You have found the following exchange rate data:

December 31, 2004, exchange rate	$1.025/LC
Average historical rate for inventory	$1.250/LC
Average historical rate for plant and equipment	$1.185/LC
Average historical rate for common stock	$0.620/LC

Translate the foreign subsidiary's balance sheet and show Hubbard's consolidated balance sheet as of December 31, 2004. Assume that the December 31, 2004 retained earnings balance for the foreign subsidiary is $435.3 and the balancing item is the cumulative translation adjustment.

STARTER PROBLEMS

(7-1) Dombrowski Industries, located in Poland, is a foreign subsidiary of a U.S. multi-national. Its functional currency is the U.S. dollar, and it is an integrated foreign
Translation entity. Dombrowski's December 31, 2004, balance sheet (in thousands) is shown here.

December 31, 2004, Balance Sheet (Local Currency)

	Poland	
Cash	ZTY	2,452.5
Accounts receivable		2,910.0
Inventories		165,675.0
Current assets	ZTY	171,037.5
Net plant and equipment		270,810.0
Total assets	ZTY	441,847.5
Accounts payable	ZTY	51,742.5
Notes payable		21,157.5

	Poland
Current maturities LTD	5,445.0
Accrued liabilities	70,830.0
Current liabilities	ZTY 149,175.0
Long-term debt	74,745.0
Total liabilities	ZTY 223,920.0
Common stock	74,295.0
Retained earnings	143,632.5
Total equity	ZTY 217,927.5
Total capital	ZTY 441,847.5

Assume a review of exchange rate data shows the following:

December 31, 2004, exchange rate	$0.2750/zloty
Average historical rate for inventory	$0.2820/zloty
Average historical rate for plant and equipment	$0.4000/zloty
Average historical rate for common stock	$0.3575/zloty

a. Which translation method should be used? Explain.
b. How will translation gains and losses be treated?
c. Translate Dombrowski's balance sheet from its local currency to its reporting currency. For purposes of this problem, retained earnings will simply be the balancing item.

(7-2) Sawamuri Enterprises, located in Japan, is a foreign subsidiary of a U.S. multina-
Translation tional. Its functional currency is the Japanese yen, and it is a self-sustaining foreign entity. Sawamuri's December 31, 2004, balance sheet (in thousands) is shown below.

December 31, 2004, Balance Sheet (Local Currency)

	Japan
Cash	JPY 9,342.0
Accounts receivable	38,214.0
Inventories	17,406.0
Current assets	JPY 64,962.0
Net plant and equipment	83,262.0
Total assets	JPY 148,224.0
Accounts payable	JPY 5,730.0
Notes payable	12,396.0
Current maturities LTD	1,068.0
Accrued liabilities	17,316.0
Current liabilities	JPY 36,510.0
Long-term debt	23,574.0
Total liabilities	JPY 60,084.0
Common stock	25,506.0
Retained earnings	62,634.0
Total equity	JPY 88,140.0
Total capital	JPY 148,224.0

Assume a review of exchange rate data shows the following:

December 31, 2004, exchange rate	$0.0090/yen
Average historical rate for inventory	$0.0085/yen
Average historical rate for plant and equipment	$0.0070/yen
Average historical rate for common stock	$0.0080/yen

a. Which translation method should be used? Explain.
b. How will translation gains and losses be treated?
c. Translate Sawamuri's balance sheet from its local currency to its reporting currency. Assume that the December 31, 2004, retained earnings balance is $600,000 and the balancing item is the cumulative translation adjustment.

(7-3)

Hyperinflation

Ennis Manufacturing, located in Venezuela, is a foreign subsidiary of a U.S. multinational. Its functional currency is the bolivar, and it is a self-sustaining foreign entity. Assume that during the past three years, the country's inflation rate has been running rampant—its cumulative annual inflation is 100 percent. Ennis Manufacturing's December 31, 2004, balance sheet (in thousands) is shown here.

December 31, 2004, Balance Sheet (Local Currency)

	Venezuela	
Cash	VEB	1,259.5
Accounts receivable		10,131.0
Inventories		2,046.8
Prepaid expenses		35.2
Current assets	VEB	13,472.5
Net plant and equipment		5,553.0
Total assets	VEB	19,025.5
Accounts payable	VEB	2,634.5
Notes payable		374.0
Current maturities LTD		10.0
Accrued liabilities		7,117.5
Current liabilities	VEB	10,136.0
Long-term debt		4,522.5
Total liabilities	VEB	14,658.5
Common stock		2,750.0
Retained earnings		1,617.0
Total equity	VEB	4,367.0
Total capital	VEB	19,025.5

Assume a review of exchange rate data shows the following:

December 31, 2004, exchange rate	$0.0012/VEB
Average historical rate for inventory	$0.0008/VEB
Average historical rate for plant and equipment	$0.0020/VEB
Average historical rate for common stock	$0.0015/VEB

a. Which translation method should be used? Explain.
b. How will translation gains and losses be treated?
c. Translate Ennis Manufacturing's balance sheet from its local currency to its reporting currency. For purposes of this problem, retained earnings will simply be the balancing item.

EXAM-TYPE PROBLEMS

(7-4)
Translation and
Consolidation
International Computers Inc. (ICI) is a computer hardware manufacturer with three subsidiaries, one located in the United States and two located abroad. The first foreign subsidiary is located in Hong Kong. The Hong Kong subsidiary's functional currency is the U.S. dollar, and it is considered an integrated foreign entity. The second foreign subsidiary is located in Great Britain. The British subsidiary's functional currency is the British pound, and it is considered a self-sustaining foreign entity. ICI's December 31, 2004, income statements (in thousands of U.S. dollars) and its December 31, 2004, subsidiary balance sheets (in thousands of local currency) are shown here.

ICI Income Statements (USD) for December 31, 2004

	United States	Hong Kong	Great Britain	Consolidated
Sales	$14,414.1	$758.7	$8,804.4	$23,977.2
Cost of goods sold	9,807.9	443.5	6,293.8	16,545.2
General and administrative expenses	2,293.2	90.8	1,381.4	3,765.4
EBITDA	$ 2,313.0	$224.4	$1,129.2	$ 3,666.6
Depreciation and amortization	916.4	141.2	494.7	1,552.3
EBIT	$ 1,396.6	$ 83.2	$ 634.5	$ 2,114.3
Interest	196.4	31.4	91.7	319.5
EBT	$ 1,200.2	$ 51.8	$ 542.8	$ 1,794.8
Taxes (40%)	480.1	20.7	217.1	717.9
Net income before preferred stock dividends	$ 720.1	$ 31.1	$ 325.7	$ 1,076.9
Preferred stock dividends	115.5	—	—	115.5
Net income to common stockholders	$ 604.6	$ 31.1	$ 325.7	$ 961.4

December 31, 2004, Balance Sheets (Local Currency)

	United States	Hong Kong		Great Britain	
Cash	$ 764.3	HKD	108.0	GBP	813.8
Accounts receivable	2,073.8		128.0		2,101.8
Accounts receivable from intrafirm transactions	527.1		2,246.3		—
Inventories	2,322.3		7,289.7		1,057.3
Prepaid expenses	21.6		—		—
Current assets	$ 5,709.1	HKD	9,772.0	GBP	3,972.9
Net plant and equipment	7,500.0		12,863.7		4,279.4
Investment in Hong Kong	2,640.2		—		—
Investment in Great Britain	8,494.9		—		—
Total assets	$24,344.2	HKD	22,635.7	GBP	8,252.3
Accounts payable	$ 941.0	HKD	2,276.7	GBP	515.2
Accounts payable from intrafirm transactions	370.6		3,194.4		
Notes payable	721.4		930.9		581.8
Current maturities LTD	557.0		239.6		258.7
Accrued liabilities	1,578.4		3,116.5		1,252.3
Current liabilities	$ 4,168.4	HKD	9,758.1	GBP	2,608.0
Long-term debt	3,917.7		3,288.8		1,796.6
Total liabilities	$ 8,086.1	HKD	13,046.9	GBP	4,404.6

	United States	Hong Kong	Great Britain
Preferred stock	1,650.0	—	—
Common stock	8,782.0	3,269.0	1,402.8
Retained earnings	5,826.1	6,319.8	2,444.9
Total equity	$14,608.1	HKD 9,588.8	GBP 3,847.7
Total capital	$24,344.2	HKD 22,635.7	GBP 8,252.3

You have found the following exchange rate data:

Hong Kong

December 31, 2004, exchange rate	$0.1650/HKD
Average historical rate for inventory	$0.1875/HKD
Average historical rate for plant and equipment	$0.2345/HKD
Average historical rate for common stock	$0.2500/HKD

Great Britain

December 31, 2004, exchange rate	$1.8250/GBP
Average historical rate for inventory	$1.7980/GBP
Average historical rate for plant and equipment	$1.6500/GBP
Average historical rate for common stock	$1.6000/GBP
December 31, 2004, retained earnings (in thousands of dollars)	$6,250.4

Translate each foreign subsidiary's balance sheet and show ICI's December 31, 2004, consolidated balance sheet. For purposes of this problem, when using the temporal method, retained earnings will be the balancing item.

(7-5)
Translation and
Consolidation

Use the following information to translate and consolidate SSI's 2004 financial statements. The Mexican subsidiary is an integrated foreign entity, and its functional currency is the U.S. dollar; the German subsidiary's functional currency is the euro, and it is a self-sustaining foreign entity; and Argentina is still plagued with hyperinflation. Remember, SSI paid no common dividends in 2004. Note that the cumulative translation adjustment made in 2003 reverses itself completely in 2004, so there is no balance in this account for 2004.

SSI Income Statements (USD) for December 31, 2004

	United States	Mexico	Germany	Argentina	Consolidated
Sales	$3,900.6	$205.3	$2,382.6	$423.5	$6,912.0
Cost of goods sold	2,563.2	115.9	1,644.8	221.1	4,545.0
General and administrative expenses	656.6	26.0	395.5	129.9	1,208.0
EBITDA	$ 680.8	$ 63.4	$ 342.3	$ 72.5	$1,159.0
Depreciation and amortization	267.6	41.3	144.5	13.1	466.5
EBIT	$ 413.2	$ 22.1	$ 197.8	$ 59.4	$ 692.5
Interest	55.8	8.9	26.1	52.7	143.5
EBT	$ 357.4	$ 13.2	$ 171.7	$ 6.7	$ 549.0
Taxes (40%)	143.0	5.2	68.7	2.7	219.6
Net income before preferred stock dividends	$ 214.4	$ 8.0	$ 103.0	$ 4.0	$ 329.4
Preferred stock dividends	35.0	—	—	—	35.0
Net income to common stockholders	$ 179.4	$ 8.0	$ 103.0	$ 4.0	$ 294.4

December 31, 2004, Balance Sheets (Local Currency)

	United States	Mexico	Germany	Argentina
Cash	$ 341.4	MXN 19.0	EUR 181.7	ARS 39.6
Accounts receivable	670.1	39.0	699.5	151.7
Accounts receivable from intrafirm transactions	96.1	620.0	—	—
Inventories	542.6	2,275.0	330.5	52.1
Prepaid expenses	11.4	—	—	—
Current assets	$1,661.6	MXN 2,953.0	EUR 1,211.7	ARS 243.4
Net plant and equipment	2,510.7	3,898.1	1,387.7	110.3
Investment in Mexico	339.4	—	—	—
Investment in Germany	1,413.3	—	—	—
Investment in Argentina	140.7	—	—	—
Total assets	$6,065.7	MXN 6,851.1	EUR 2,599.4	ARS 353.7
Accounts payable	$ 335.1	MXN 798.1	EUR 106.7	ARS 49.3
Accounts payable from intrafirm transactions	57.7	839.8	—	53.6
Notes payable	144.3	315.0	225.8	7.2
Current maturities LTD	132.8	75.4	20.5	—
Accrued liabilities	396.8	850.0	324.1	64.3
Current liabilities	$1,066.7	MXN 2,878.3	EUR 677.1	ARS 174.4
Long-term debt	611.6	996.6	768.6	9.5
Total liabilities	$1,678.3	MXN 3,874.9	EUR 1,445.7	ARS 183.9
Preferred stock	500.0	—	—	—
Common stock	2,000.0	990.6	425.1	50.0
Retained earnings	1,887.4	1,985.6	728.6	119.8
Total equity	$3,887.4	MXN 2,976.2	EUR 1,153.7	ARS 169.8
Total capital	$6,065.7	MXN 6,851.1	EUR 2,599.4	ARS 353.7

Assume a review of exchange rate data shows the following:

Mexico
December 31, 2004, exchange rate	$0.093000/MXN
Average historical exchange rate for inventory	$0.102500/MXN
Average historical exchange rate for plant and equipment	$0.103513/MXN
Average historical exchange rate for common stock	$0.100947/MXN

Germany
December 31, 2004, exchange rate	$1.22500/EUR
Average historical exchange rate for inventory	$1.20000/EUR
Average historical exchange rate for plant and equipment	$1.15670/EUR
Average historical exchange rate for common stock	$1.17613/EUR

Argentina
December 31, 2004, exchange rate	$0.3357/ARS
Average historical exchange rate for inventory	$0.5351/ARS
Average historical exchange rate for plant and equipment	$1.0007/ARS
Average historical exchange rate for common stock	$1.0004/ARS

Integrated Case

Rick Schmidt, MRI's CFO, along with Mandy Wu, Schmidt's assistant, and John Costello, a consultant and college finance professor, comprise a team established to teach the firm's directors and senior managers the basics of international financial management. The program includes 16 sessions, each lasting about 2 hours, and they are scheduled immediately before the monthly board meetings. Six sessions have been completed, and the team is now preparing Session 7, which will deal with financial statement translation and consolidation. Prior sessions have provided an overview of international finance, foreign exchange markets and international institutions, exchange rate analysis, foreign direct investment, risk and return, and financial statement analysis.

In the financial statement consolidation session, the team will address accounting issues faced by multinational enterprises, with special emphasis on inflation. MRI has foreign subsidiaries in Italy, Japan, and Indonesia. The Italian and Japanese subsidiaries are self-sustaining operating units, while the Indonesian subsidiary is an integrated foreign entity. The cash flows of the Indonesian subsidiary are integrally tied to the operations in Japan. Tables IC7-1 and IC7-2 display MRI's 2003 and 2004 subsidiary income statements and balance sheets. Notice that foreign subsidiary balance sheet figures are reported in local currencies. Income statements have already been translated and are not our main concern in this exercise. Table IC7-3 provides spot and historical exchange rate data for MRI's subsidiaries. The spot rates correspond to the reporting dates of the statements. Notice that there are two sets of historical dollar-to-yen exchange rates. The first set pertains to the Japanese subsidiary, while the second pertains to the Indonesian subsidiary. MRI is not required to publicly release all of these data, but they must consolidate their statements in accordance with the appropriate accounting standards. Besides, MRI likes to highlight some of their foreign operating results in the annual report to show shareholders that it is ripe with growth.

Most of the directors have a basic understanding of financial statements, but only the accountants seem to know much about the consolidation process. One of the directors (in marketing) recently said, "What's the big deal? Just multiply the numbers by the spot exchange rate and give me the answer!" Obviously this director does not understand the nuances of international financial reporting. Schmidt would like all of the directors to become familiar with the consolidation process, so they can gain a better perspective of how managerial decisions affect the multinational firm. The session will include an *Excel* model to handle the consolidation process and to help the directors become more familiar with *Excel*.

With those thoughts in mind, the three compiled the following set of questions, which they plan to discuss during the session. As with the other sessions, they plan to use an *Excel* model to answer the quantitative questions. Assume that you are Mandy Wu, and that you must prepare answers for use during the session.

Questions

a. What is the difference between a self-sustaining entity and an integrated foreign entity?

b. What is the difference between monetary and nonmonetary items?

c. Differentiate between the current rate and temporal translation methods. When should each method be used?

d. Differentiate among reporting, functional, and local currencies.

e. What is meant when an MNE has an exposed assets or liabilities position, and what is meant by the term net asset (liability) exposure?

f. Explain the role of inflation in the consolidation process. How does hyperinflation change the process?

g. Fully translate and consolidate MRI's subsidiary statements to obtain consolidated balance sheets for 2003 and 2004. Identify the appropriate exchange rate used, and clearly identify all reporting and functional currencies, cumulative translaton adjustments, and intrafirm transactions.

h. How can a multinational entity manage any accounting or translation risk exposures?

TABLE IC7-1 | Income Statements

Panel A: December 31, 2004	United States	Japan	Italy	Indonesia	Consolidated
Sales	$475,970.0	$196,659.0	$238,127.0	$92,381.0	$1,003,137.0
Cost of goods sold	299,907.0	137,299.0	171,506.0	51,969.0	660,681.0
General and administrative expenses	144,433.0	28,937.0	30,931.0	22,195.0	226,496.0
EBITDA	$ 31,630.0	$ 30,423.0	$ 35,690.0	$18,217.0	$ 115,960.0
Depreciation and amortization	8,818.0	6,365.0	7,662.0	2,218.0	25,063.0
EBIT	$ 22,812.0	$ 24,058.0	$ 28,028.0	$15,999.0	$ 90,897.0
Interest	6,200.0	1,478.0	4,141.0	2,897.0	14,716.0
EBT	$ 16,612.0	$ 22,580.0	$ 23,887.0	$13,102.0	$ 76,181.0
Taxes	6,644.8	9,032.0	9,554.8	5,240.8	30,472.4
Net income before preferred stock dividends	$ 9,967.2	$ 13,548.0	$ 14,332.2	$ 7,861.2	$ 45,708.6
Preferred stock dividends	3,600.0	—	—	—	3,600.0
Net income to common stockholders	$ 6,367.2	$ 13,548.0	$ 14,332.2	$ 7,861.2	$ 42,108.6
Panel B: December 31, 2003	United States	Japan	Italy	Indonesia	Consolidated
Sales	$437,249.0	$180,900.0	$209,690.0	$89,950.0	$917,789.0
Cost of goods sold	290,651.0	125,825.0	151,068.0	50,830.0	618,374.0
General and administrative expenses	122,379.0	27,150.0	27,165.0	22,650.0	199,344.0
EBITDA	$ 24,219.0	$ 27,925.0	$ 31,457.0	$16,470.0	$100,071.0
Depreciation and amortization	7,664.0	5,579.0	6,682.0	2,026.0	21,951.0
EBIT	$ 16,555.0	$ 22,346.0	$ 24,775.0	$14,444.0	$ 78,120.0
Interest	4,479.0	2,082.0	3,319.0	4,400.0	14,280.0
EBT	$ 12,076.0	$ 20,264.0	$ 21,456.0	$10,044.0	$ 63,840.0
Taxes	4,830.4	8,105.6	8,582.4	4,017.6	25,536.0
Net income before preferred stock dividends	$ 7,245.6	$ 12,158.4	$ 12,873.6	$ 6,026.4	$ 38,304.0
Preferred stock dividends	3,600.0	—	—	—	3,600.0
Net income to common stockholders	$ 3,645.6	$ 12,158.4	$ 12,873.6	$ 6,026.4	$ 34,704.0

TABLE IC7-2 | Balance Sheets

Panel A: December 31, 2004	United States	Japan	Italy	Indonesia
Cash	$ 17,925.1	JPY 1,725,326.0	EUR 12,125.0	IDR 71,287,740.0
Accounts receivable	35,561.0	3,493,225.0	28,945.0	150,605,940.0
Accounts receivable from intrafirm transactions	11,900.0	622,782.0	—	211,236,344.0
Inventories	47,097.0	4,002,391.0	51,722.0	243,613,288.0
Prepaid expenses	—	—	—	—
Current assets	$112,483.1	JPY 9,843,724.0	EUR 92,792.0	IDR 676,743,312.0
Net plant and equipment	176,345.0	17,435,806.0	134,106.0	402,117,137.0
Investment in subsidiaries	279,375.4	—	—	—
Total assets	$568,203.5	JPY 27,279,530.0	EUR 226,898.0	IDR 1,078,860,449.0
Accounts payable	$ 46,554.0	JPY 1,549,220.0	EUR 19,288.0	IDR 67,156,056.0
Accounts payable from intrafirm transactions	—	2,560,163.0	9,227.0	51,385,082.0
Notes payable	15,000.0	1,025,000.0	10,125.0	192,995,649.0
Current maturities LTD	12,250.2	—	3,000.0	—
Accrued liabilities	4,462.0	280,293.0	2,454.0	14,111,414.0
Current liabilities	$ 78,266.2	JPY 5,414,676.0	EUR 44,094.0	IDR 325,648,201.0
Long-term debt	97,678.8	11,713,897.0	90,204.0	199,428,830.0
Total liabilities	$175,945.0	JPY 17,128,573.0	EUR 134,298.0	IDR 525,077,031.0
Preferred stock	60,000.0	—	—	—
Common stock	79,500.0	1,879,556.0	37,605.0	216,460,300.0
Retained earnings	252,758.5	8,271,401.0	54,995.0	337,323,118.0
Total equity	$332,258.5	JPY 10,150,957.0	EUR 92,600.0	IDR 553,783,418.0
Total capital	$568,203.5	JPY 27,279,530.0	EUR 226,898.0	IDR 1,078,860,449.0

Panel B: December 31, 2003	United States	Japan	Italy	Indonesia
Cash	$ 18,110.0	JPY 1,517,568.0	EUR 11,817.0	IDR 72,373,340.0
Accounts receivable	34,095.0	3,285,016.0	28,364.0	154,626,221.0
Accounts receivable from intrafirm transactions	9,015.0	685,648.0	—	206,689,182.0
Inventories	46,585.0	3,537,944.0	49,642.0	232,255,971.0
Prepaid expenses	—	—	—	—
Current assets	$107,805.0	JPY 9,026,176.0	EUR 89,823.0	IDR 665,944,714.0
Net plant and equipment	153,275.0	16,245,899.0	127,463.0	388,143,955.0
Investment in subsidiaries	209,170.0	—	—	—
Total assets	$470,250.0	JPY 25,272,075.0	EUR 217,286.0	IDR 1,054,088,669.0
Accounts payable	$ 43,750.0	JPY 1,479,171.0	EUR 18,512.0	IDR 65,710,427.0
Accounts payable from intrafirm transactions	—	2,741,374.0	8,598.0	51,695,254.0
Notes payable	7,000.0	975,144.0	9,204.0	183,805,380.0
Current maturities LTD	7,250.0	—	3,100.0	—
Accrued liabilities	4,375.0	274,259.0	2,360.0	13,555,633.0
Current liabilities	$ 62,375.0	JPY 5,469,948.0	EUR 41,774.0	IDR 314,766,694.0
Long-term debt	57,725.0	11,713,917.0	93,204.0	199,428,830.0
Total liabilities	$120,100.0	JPY 17,183,865.0	EUR 134,978.0	IDR 514,195,524.0
Preferred stock	60,000.0	—	—	—
Common stock	79,500.0	1,879,556.0	37,605.0	216,460,300.0
Retained earnings	210,650.0	6,208,654.0	44,703.0	323,432,845.0
Total equity	$290,150.0	JPY 8,088,210.0	EUR 82,308.0	IDR 539,893,145.0
Total capital	$470,250.0	JPY 25,272,075.0	EUR 217,286.0	IDR 1,054,088,669.0

TABLE IC7-3 | Exchange Rates

	2004	2003
Spot Exchange Rates		
$/JPY	0.009281	0.008204
$/EUR	1.289700	1.048500
JPY/IDR	0.012120	0.013263
Historical Exchange Rates		
$/JPY: common stock	0.008779	0.008779
$/JPY: retained earnings	0.008749	0.008600
$/EUR: common stock	0.917431	1.090000
$/EUR: retained earnings	0.907233	1.121022
JPY/IDR: common stock	0.011252	0.011252
JPY/IDR: retained earnings	0.013464	0.014053
JPY/IDR: inventories	0.012463	0.012989
JPY/IDR: fixed assets	0.012833	0.012726
$/JPY (Indonesia): common stock	0.009279	0.009279
$/JPY (Indonesia): retained earnings	0.008723	0.008669

CHAPTER 8

Debt Instruments and Markets

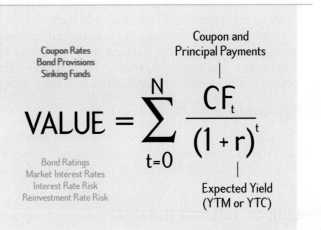

$$\text{VALUE} = \sum_{t=0}^{N} \frac{CF_t}{(1 + r)^t}$$

Coupon Rates
Bond Provisions
Sinking Funds

Coupon and
Principal Payments

Bond Ratings
Market Interest Rates
Interest Rate Risk
Reinvestment Rate Risk

Expected Yield
(YTM or YTC)

e-resource

*The textbook's Web site, http://crum. swlearning.com, contains an Excel file that will guide you through the chapter's calculations. The file for this chapter is **FIFC08-model.xls,** and we encourage you to open the file and follow along as you read the chapter.*

The basic valuation equation that we use throughout the book was developed and first applied to securities—stocks and bonds. In Chapter 8 we use it to evaluate debt instruments, while in Chapter 9 we apply it to common stock. It is important to go beyond the math, so we also consider other aspects of bond and stock valuation, including such institutional arrangements as the nature of debt and equity markets, and how corporations and investors in world markets determine the supply, demand, and, consequently, the cost of capital.

As can be seen from the valuation equation, the cost of debt capital, plus interest and principal payments, determine a bond's value. The relevant cash flows, which are contractual, include the promised principal (due at maturity) and the periodic interest payments (made during the bond's life). The relevant interest rate in determining a bond's value is its expected yield, which is influenced by the firm's financial health and ability to make required payments, the general level of interest rates, and the market's attitude about the firm's risk. In this chapter, we discuss bond characteristics, types of debt instruments (both domestic and foreign), bond valuation, and the assessment of a bond's risk. We conclude with a description of both domestic and international bond markets.

KEY CHARACTERISTICS OF BONDS

Bond
A long-term debt instrument.

An excellent site for information on many types of bonds is Bonds Online, which can be found at http:// www.bondsonline. com. The site has a great deal of information about corporates, municipals, Treasuries, and bond funds. It includes free bond searches, through which the user specifies the attributes desired in a bond and then the search returns the publicly traded bonds meeting the criteria. The site also includes a downloadable bond calculator and an excellent glossary of bond terminology.

Par Value
The face value of a bond.

Coupon Payment
The specified number of dollars of interest paid each period, generally each six months.

Coupon Interest Rate
The stated annual interest rate on a bond.

Maturity Date
A specified date on which the par value of a bond must be repaid.

Original Maturity
The number of years to maturity at the time a bond is issued.

Call Provision
Gives the issuer the right to redeem the bonds under specified terms prior to the normal maturity date.

A **bond** is a long-term contract under which a borrower agrees to make payments of interest and principal on specific dates to the holders of the bond. For example, on January 5, 2005, Sound Systems International (SSI) borrowed $50 million by issuing $50 million of bonds. For convenience, we assume that SSI sold 50,000 individual bonds with a face value of $1,000 each. SSI received the $50 million and in exchange promised to make semiannual interest payments and to repay the $50 million on a specified maturity date.

Although all bonds have some common characteristics, they do not always have the same contractual features. For example, most corporate bonds have provisions for early repayment (call features), but these provisions can be quite different for different bonds. Differences in contractual provisions, and in the underlying strength of the companies backing the bonds, lead to major differences in bonds' risks, prices, and expected returns. To understand bonds, it is important that you understand the terms discussed in the following sections.

Par Value

The **par value** is the stated face value of the bond, which is typically $1,000. The par value generally represents the amount of money the firm promises to repay on the maturity date. If the bond is issued at par, it is also the amount of money the firm borrows.

Coupon Interest Rate

SSI's bonds require the company to pay a fixed dollar amount of interest each six months. When the annual **coupon payment** is divided by the par value, the result is the **coupon interest rate**. For example, SSI's bonds have a $1,000 par value and pay $40 each six months—$80 in interest each year. The bond's annual coupon interest is $80, so its coupon interest rate is $80/$1,000 = 8%. This payment, which is fixed at the time of issue, remains in force during the life of the bond.[1] Typically, a bond's coupon payment is set at a level that will enable the bond to be issued at or near its par value.

Maturity Date

Bonds generally have a specified **maturity date** on which the par value must be repaid. SSI's bonds, which were issued on January 5, 2005, will mature on January 5, 2025; thus, they had a 20-year maturity at the time they were issued. Most bonds have **original maturities** (the maturity at the time the bond is issued) ranging from 10 to 30 years, but any maturity is legally permissible.[2] Of course, the effective maturity of a bond declines each year after it has been issued.

Provisions to Call or Redeem Bonds

Many corporate bonds contain a **call provision**, which gives the issuing corporation the right to call the bonds for redemption. The call provision generally states that the issuer must pay the bondholders an amount greater than the par value if they

---

[1]In this section of the chapter we assume that a bond's coupon interest rate is fixed. However, in some cases, a bond's coupon payment will vary over time. We will discuss these *floating-rate bonds* in more detail later in the chapter.

[2]In July 1993, Walt Disney Co., attempting to lock in a low interest rate, issued the first 100-year bonds to be sold by any borrower in modern times. Soon after, Coca-Cola became the second company to stretch the meaning of "long-term bond" by selling $150 million of 100-year bonds.

Call Premium
The additional amount that must be paid to a bondholder if a bond is called.

are called. The additional sum, which is termed a **call premium**, is often set equal to one year's interest if the bonds are called during the first year, and the premium declines at a constant rate of INT/N each year thereafter, where INT = Annual interest and N = Original maturity in years. However, bonds are often not callable until several years (generally 5 to 10) after they are issued. This is known as a *deferred call,* and the bonds are said to have *call protection.*

Suppose a company sold bonds when interest rates were relatively high. Provided the issue is callable, the company could sell a new issue of low-yielding securities if and when interest rates drop. It could then use the proceeds of the new issue to retire the high-rate issue and thus reduce its interest expense. This process is called a *refunding operation.*

A call provision is valuable to the issuer but potentially detrimental to investors. If interest rates increase, the issuer will not call the bond, and the investor will be stuck with the original coupon rate on the bond, even though interest rates in the economy have risen sharply. However, if interest rates fall, the issuer *will* call the bond and pay off investors, who then must reinvest the proceeds at the current market interest rate, which is lower than the rate they were receiving on the original bond. In other words, the investor loses when interest rates rise, but doesn't reap the gains when rates fall. To induce an investor to take on this risk, a new issue of callable bonds must provide a higher interest rate than an otherwise similar issue of noncallable bonds.

Put Provision
Protects investors against an increase in interest rates by permitting a bondholder to "put" bonds back to the issuer, who must redeem them at par.

A **put provision** allows bonds to be "put back" to the issuer at the holder's option, and the issuer must then redeem them at par. The put provision protects investors against an increase in interest rates. If rates rise, the price of a fixed-rate bond declines. However, if holders have the option of turning their bonds in and having them redeemed at par, they are protected against rising rates. This provision enables issuers to sell bonds at lower coupon rates than other similarly rated bonds, but issuers are exposed to greater risk because they may have to replace the putable bonds with others that carry higher interest rates.

Sinking Fund Provisions

Sinking Fund Provision
Requires the issuer to retire a portion of the bond issue each year. It facilitates the orderly retirement of a bond issue.

Some bonds also include a **sinking fund provision** that requires the issuer to buy back a specified percentage of the bonds each year, say, 5 percent of the initial amount issued. A failure to meet the sinking fund requirement throws the bond into default, which may force the issuer into bankruptcy. Obviously, a sinking fund can constitute a significant cash drain to a company.

In most cases, the issuer can handle the sinking fund in either of two ways:

1. The issuer can call in for redemption (at par value) a certain percentage of the bonds each year; for example, it might be able to call 5 percent of the total original amount of the issue at a price of $1,000 per bond. The bonds are numbered serially, and those called for redemption are determined by a lottery administered by the trustee.
2. The issuer may buy the required number of bonds on the open market.

The issuer will choose the least-cost method. If interest rates have risen, causing bond prices to fall, it will buy bonds in the open market at a discount; if interest rates have fallen, it will call the bonds. A sinking fund call typically requires no call premium (although it could), but only a small percentage of the issue is normally callable in any one year.

Although sinking funds are designed to protect bondholders by ensuring that an issue is retired in an orderly fashion, sinking funds can work to the detriment of bondholders if market interest rates fall. On balance, however, bonds that have a sinking fund are regarded as being safer than those without such a provision, so, at the time they are issued, sinking fund bonds typically have lower coupon rates than otherwise similar bonds without sinking funds.

SELF-TEST QUESTIONS

What is a bond?

Why is a call provision advantageous to a bond issuer? When will the issuer initiate a refunding call? Why?

What are the two ways a sinking fund can be handled? Which method will be chosen by the firm if interest rates have risen? If interest rates have fallen?

Are securities that provide for a sinking fund regarded as being riskier than those without this provision? Explain.

Briefly explain why a new issue of callable bonds must provide a higher interest rate than an otherwise similar issue of noncallable bonds.

Briefly explain whether the following statement is true or false: "At the time they are issued, sinking fund bonds typically have higher coupon rates than otherwise similar bonds without sinking funds."

WHO ISSUES BONDS?

Investors have many choices when investing in bonds, whether within the United States or abroad. The three main types of domestic bonds are: Treasury, corporate, and municipal. Each type differs with respect to expected return and degree of risk.

Treasury Bonds
Bonds issued by the U.S. federal government, sometimes referred to as government bonds.

Treasury bonds, sometimes referred to as government bonds, are issued by the U.S. federal government.[3] It is reasonable to assume that the U.S. federal government will make good on its promised payments, so these bonds have no default risk. However, Treasury bond prices decline when interest rates rise, so they are not free of all risks.

Corporate Bonds
Bonds issued by corporations.

Corporate bonds, as the name implies, are issued by corporations. Unlike Treasury bonds, corporate bonds are exposed to default risk—if the issuing company gets into trouble, it may be unable to make the promised interest and principal payments. Different corporate bonds have different levels of default risk, depending on the issuing company's characteristics and the terms of the specific bond. Default risk often is referred to as "credit risk," and the larger the default or credit risk, the higher the interest rate the issuer must pay.

Municipal Bonds
Bonds issued by state and local governments.

Municipal bonds, or "munis," are issued by state and local governments. Like corporate bonds, munis have default risk. However, munis offer one major advantage over all other bonds: The interest earned on most municipal bonds is exempt from federal taxes and also from state taxes if the holder is a resident of the issuing state. Consequently, municipal bonds have considerably lower yields than those on corporate bonds with the same default risk.

International Bonds
Bonds issued by either foreign governments or foreign corporations.

In addition to domestic bonds, we have **international bonds**, which are issued by foreign governments or corporations. International corporate bonds are, of course, exposed to default risk, and so are some international government bonds. Moreover, foreign exchange rate risk exists even on default-free bonds if the bonds are denominated in a currency other than the investor's home currency. For example, if a U.S. investor purchases a corporate bond denominated in Japanese yen and the yen subsequently falls relative to the dollar, the investor loses money, even if the company

---

[3]The U.S. Treasury actually issues three types of securities: "bills," "notes," and "bonds." A *bond* makes an equal payment every six months until it matures, at which time it makes an additional lump sum payment equal to the amount originally borrowed. If the maturity at the time of issue is less than 10 years, it is called a *note* rather than a bond. A *T-bill* has a maturity of 52 weeks or less at the time of issue, and it makes no payments at all until it matures. Thus, bills are sold initially at a discount to their face, or maturity, value.

does not default on its bonds, because the yen received will buy fewer dollars. We explore the characteristics of international bonds and distinguish between the two major classes of these bonds later in the chapter.

What are the four main types of bonds?
Why are U.S. Treasury bonds not riskless?
To what types of risk are investors of international bonds exposed?

BOND VALUATION

The value of any financial asset—a stock, bond, lease, or even a physical asset such as an apartment building or a machine—is simply the present value of the cash flows the asset is expected to produce.

The cash flows from a specific bond depend on its contractual features, which we described earlier. For a standard coupon-bearing bond such as the one issued by SSI, the cash flows consist of interest payments during the 20-year life of the bond plus the amount borrowed (generally the $1,000 par value) when the bond matures. In the case of a **floating-rate bond**, the interest payments vary over time, and in the case of a **zero coupon bond**, there are no periodic interest payments but the face amount must be paid when the bond matures. For a "regular" bond with a fixed semiannual coupon rate, here is the time line that illustrates the bond's cash flows, recognizing that the bond's interest payments are received semiannually:

Floating-Rate Bond
Its interest rate payments fluctuate with shifts in the general level of interest rates.

Zero Coupon Bond
Pays no annual interest but is sold at a discount below par, thus providing compensation to investors in the form of capital appreciation.

0	$r_d/2$	1	2	3		2N
Bond's Value		INT/2	INT/2	INT/2	• • •	INT/2 M

Here

$r_d/2 =$ the bond's market interest rate divided by 2 because interest payments are received every six months. In our example, $r_d = 8\%$ so $r_d/2 = 4\%$. This is the discount rate that is used to calculate the present value of the bond's cash flows.[4]

$2N =$ the number of semiannual periods before the bond matures. In our example, the bonds were issued for $N = 20$ years, so there are 40 semiannual periods before the bond matures. Note that 2N declines each period, so a bond that had a maturity of 20 years when it was issued (Semiannual periods $= 40$) will have $2N = 38$ semiannual periods remaining after one year, $2N = 36$ semiannual periods remaining after two years, and so on. Note also that virtually all bonds pay interest twice a year, or semiannually. Simple adjustments can accommodate any other payment pattern (annual, monthly, quarterly, and so on).

$INT/2 =$ dollars of interest paid each six months = (Coupon rate × Par value)/2 $= (0.08)(\$1,000)/2 = \$40$.

$M =$ the par, or maturity, value of the bond $= \$1,000$. This amount must be paid at maturity.[5]

---

[4]The appropriate interest rate on a bond depends on its risk, liquidity, and years to maturity, as well as supply and demand conditions in the capital markets.

[5]Actually, bonds can have any face value. Some years ago actual bond certificates were issued, and they generally were for $1,000 each. Today, paper certificates are no longer used in most developed nations—everything is done electronically—and face values can be set at any level, and they vary for different purchasers.

We can now redraw the time line to show the numerical values for all variables for our bond illustration except the bond's value:

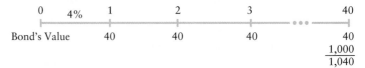

The following general equation can be used to find the value of a semiannual coupon bond:

$$\text{Bond's value} = V_B = \sum_{t=1}^{2N} \frac{INT/2}{(1 + r_d/2)^t} + \frac{M}{(1 + r_d/2)^{2N}}. \qquad (8\text{-}1)$$

Inserting values for our particular bond, we have

$$V_B = \sum_{t=1}^{40} \frac{\$40}{(1.04)^t} + \frac{\$1,000}{(1.04)^{40}}$$

$$= \$1,000.$$

The value of the bond can be calculated quite easily with a financial calculator or spreadsheet.

Changes in Bond Value over Time

At the time a coupon bond is issued, the coupon is generally set at a level that causes the bond's market price to equal its par value. If a lower coupon were set, investors would not be willing to pay $1,000 for the bond, while if a higher coupon were set, investors would bid its price up over $1,000. Investment bankers judge quite precisely the coupon rate that will cause a bond to sell at its par value.

A bond that has just been issued is known as a *new issue.* Once the bond has been on the market for a while, it is classified as an *outstanding bond,* also called a *seasoned issue.* Newly issued bonds generally sell very close to par, but the prices of seasoned bonds vary widely from par. Except for floating-rate bonds, coupon payments are constant, so when economic conditions change, a bond with a $40 semiannual coupon that sold at par when issued may sell for more or less than par in the marketplace.

SSI's bonds with an 8 percent semiannual coupon were originally issued at par. If r_d remained constant at 8 percent, what would the bond's value be one year after issue? Now the term to maturity is only 19 years—that is, $2N = 38$, and you should find that the bond's value is still $1,000. If we continued, setting $2N = 36$, $2N = 34$, and so forth, we would see that the value of the bond will remain at $1,000 *as long as the going interest rate remains at the 8 percent coupon rate.*[6]

Now suppose interest rates fall after the SSI bonds are issued, and, as a result, r_d falls *below the coupon rate,* decreasing from 8 to 5 percent. Both the coupon interest payments and the maturity value remain constant, but now 5 percent must be

[6]The bond prices quoted by brokers are calculated as described. However, if you bought a bond between interest payment dates, you would have to pay the basic price plus accrued interest. Thus, if you purchased an SSI bond three months after it was issued, your broker would send you an invoice stating that you must pay $1,000 as the basic price of the bond plus the interest that had accrued in the three months. Throughout the chapter, we assume that bonds are being evaluated immediately after an interest payment date. Note, though, that it is easy to deal with bonds between payment dates with spreadsheets or financial calculators.

substituted for r_d in Equation 8-1. The value of the bond at the end of the first year will be $1,365.23:

$$V_B = \sum_{t=1}^{38} \frac{\$40}{(1.025)} + \frac{\$1,000}{(1.025)^{38}}$$

$$= \$1,365.23.$$

Thus, if r_d falls *below* the coupon rate, the bond sells above par, or at a *premium*.

The arithmetic of the bond value increase should be clear, but what is the logic behind it? The fact that r_d has fallen to 5 percent means that if you had $1,000 to invest, you could buy new bonds like SSI's except that these new bonds would pay $25 of interest each six months rather than $40. Naturally, you would prefer $40 to $25, so you would be willing to pay more than $1,000 for an SSI bond to obtain the higher coupons. All investors would react similarly, and as a result, the bond price would be bid up to $1,365.23, at which point they would provide the same rate of return to a potential investor as the new bonds, 5 percent.

Assuming that interest rates remain constant at 5 percent for the next 19 years, what would happen to the value of the SSI bonds? It would fall gradually from $1,365.23 at present to $1,000 at maturity, when SSI will redeem each bond for $1,000. This point can be illustrated by calculating the bond value one year later, when it has 18 years remaining to maturity. The bond value will be $1,353.34, and it will have fallen by $11.89. If you were to calculate the bond's value at other future dates, the price would continue to fall as the maturity date approaches.

Note that if you purchased the bond at $1,365.23 and sold it one year later with r_d still at 5 percent, you would have a capital loss of $11.89, producing a total return of $80.00 − $11.89 = $68.11. Your percentage rate of return would consist of an *interest yield* (also called a *current yield*) plus a *capital gains yield*, calculated as follows:[7]

Current yield = $80/$1,365.23 = 0.0586 = 5.86%.
Capital gains yield = −$11.89/$1,365.23 = −0.0087 = −0.87%.

Had interest rates risen from 8 to 11 percent during the first year after issue, then the value of the bond would fall to $762.93. In this case, the bond sells at a *discount* of $237.07 below its par value. The total expected future return on the bond would again consist of a current yield and a capital gains yield, but now the capital gains yield would be *positive*. To see this, the bond's price with 18 years left to maturity, assuming that interest rates remain at 11 percent, would be $766.96. The capital gain for the year would be $766.96 − $762.93 = $4.03, and the current yield and capital gains yield would be calculated as follows:

Current yield = $80/$762.93 = 0.1049 = 10.49%.
Capital gains yield = $4.03/$762.93 = 0.0053 = 0.53%.

Figure 8-1 shows three possible lines for the bond value over time, assuming (1) that market interest rates remain constant at 8 percent, (2) that rates fall to 5 percent and then remain constant at that level, and (3) that rates rise to 11 percent and remain constant at that level. Of course, if interest rates do *not* remain constant, the price of the bond will fluctuate. However, regardless of what future interest rates do, the bond's price will approach $1,000 as it nears the maturity date (barring bankruptcy, in which case the bond's value might fall to zero).

---

[7]The total return (or yield) is equal to the current yield plus the capital gains yield. Because SSI's bond pays a semiannual coupon, there is a "rounding" difference, as the current yield plus capital gains yield equals 4.99 percent (rather than 5 percent).

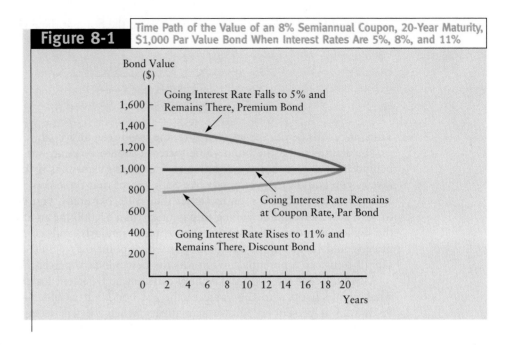

Figure 8-1 Time Path of the Value of an 8% Semiannual Coupon, 20-Year Maturity, $1,000 Par Value Bond When Interest Rates Are 5%, 8%, and 11%

Figure 8-1 illustrates the following key points:

1. Whenever the going rate of interest, r_d, equals the coupon rate, a *fixed-rate* bond will sell at its par value. Normally, the coupon rate is set equal to the going rate when a bond is issued, causing it to sell at par initially.

2. Whenever the going rate of interest *rises above* the coupon rate, a fixed-rate bond's price will *fall below* its par value. Such a bond is called a **discount bond**.

Discount Bond
Sells below its par value; occurs whenever the going rate of interest is above the coupon rate.

3. Whenever the going rate of interest *falls below* the coupon rate, a fixed-rate bond's price will *rise above* its par value. Such a bond is called a **premium bond**.

4. There is an inverse relationship between a bond's price and interest rates—rising rates lead to falling bond prices, and vice versa.

5. The market value of a bond will always approach its par value as its maturity date approaches, provided the issuer does not go bankrupt.

Premium Bond
Sells above its par value; occurs whenever the going rate of interest is below the coupon rate.

These points are very important; they show that bondholders may suffer capital losses or make capital gains, depending on whether interest rates rise or fall after the bond is purchased.

SELF-TEST QUESTIONS

Explain the following equation: $V_B = \sum_{t=1}^{2N} \dfrac{INT/2}{(1 + r_d/2)^t} + \dfrac{M}{(1 + r_d/2)^{2N}}$.

What is meant by the terms "new issue" and "seasoned issue"?

Explain what happens to the price of a fixed-rate bond if interest rates (1) rise above the bond's coupon rate or (2) fall below the coupon rate.

What is a "discount bond"? A "premium bond"?

BOND YIELDS

If you examine the bond market table of *The Wall Street Journal* or a bond dealer's price sheet, you will typically see information regarding each bond's maturity date, price, and coupon interest rate. You will also see the bond's reported yield. Table 8-1

TABLE 8-1 | Representative Corporate Bond Trades Report

Trade Date	Issue/CUSIP	Coupon	Maturity	Yield	Price/Size
12/26/2003 15:42	FORD MTR CR CO 345397TX1	6.500	01/25/2007	3.727	107.962 75K
12/26/2003 15:35	PLAYTEX APPAREL 72813PAH3	9.375	06/01/2011	8.210	105.000 10K
12/26/2003 15:33	NORWEST FINL INC 669383DX6	7.600	05/03/2005	2.259	107.000 10K
12/26/2003 15:23	FORD MOTOR CRD 345397TT0	6.125	03/20/2004	1.972	100.900 65K
12/26/2003 15:22	CITICORP 173034GK9	7.125	03/15/2004	1.600	101.125 50K
12/26/2003 15:21	GENERAL MTRS CP 370442BW4	8.250	07/15/2023	7.260	100.250 25K

Source: Corporate Bond Trades Report for December 26, 2003, from **http://www.investinginbonds.com**. The listing shown here is just a partial listing of all trades that occurred on December 26, 2003.

shows a partial listing of corporate bond trades just after 3 P.M. on December 26, 2003, from the **http://www.investinginbonds.com** Web site. This report provides additional information such as the bond's CUSIP number (which is the unique number that identifies the bond) and the size of the trade, which is displayed below the bond's price.

Unlike the coupon interest rate, which is fixed, the bond's yield varies from day to day depending on current market conditions. Moreover, the yield can be calculated in three different ways, and three "answers" can be obtained. These different yields are described in the following sections. Note that the yield shown in Table 8-1 is the YTM unless the bond is callable. If the bond is callable, then the lower of the YTC or YTM is shown.

Yield to Maturity

Yield to Maturity (YTM)
The rate of return earned on a bond if it is held to maturity.

Suppose you were offered a 19-year, 8 percent semiannual coupon, $1,000 par value bond at a price of $1,365.23. What rate of interest would you earn on your investment if you bought the bond and held it to maturity? This rate is called the bond's **yield to maturity (YTM)**. The yield to maturity is generally the same as the market rate of interest, r_d, and to find it, all you need to do is solve Equation 8-1 for r_d:

$$V_B = \$1,365.23 = \frac{\$40}{(1 + r_d/2)^1} + \cdots + \frac{\$40}{(1 + r_d/2)^{38}} + \frac{\$1,000}{(1 + r_d/2)^{38}}.$$

Realistically, you would use a financial calculator or spreadsheet to solve for r_d. Using either method, you would find that this bond has a semiannual YTM, $r_d/2$, of 2.5 percent. Therefore, the bond's nominal YTM is 2(2.5%) = 5%.

The YTM is identical to the total rate of return discussed in the preceding section. It can also be viewed as the bond's *promised rate of return*, which is the return that investors will receive if all the promised payments are made. However, the YTM equals the *expected rate of return* only if (1) the probability of default is zero and (2) the bond cannot be called, for otherwise there is some probability that the promised payments to maturity will not be received, causing the calculated yield to maturity to differ from the expected return.

Yield to Call

If you purchased a callable bond and the company called it, you would not have the option of holding the bond until maturity. Therefore, you would not earn the yield to maturity. For example, if SSI's 8 percent semiannual coupon bonds were callable, and if interest rates fell to 5 percent, then the company could call the 8 percent semi-annual coupon bonds, replace them with 5 percent semiannual coupon bonds, and save $40 − $25 = $15 interest per bond per six-month period, or $30 per year. This would be beneficial to the company, but not to its bondholders.

Yield to Call (YTC)
The rate of return earned on a bond if it is called before its maturity date.

If current interest rates are well below an outstanding bond's coupon rate, then a callable bond is likely to be called, and investors will expect to earn the **yield to call (YTC)** rather than the yield to maturity. To calculate the YTC, solve this equation for r_d:

$$\text{Price of callable bond} = \sum_{t=1}^{2N} \frac{\text{INT}/2}{(1 + r_d/2)^t} + \frac{\text{Call price}}{(1 + r_d/2)^{2N}}. \tag{8-2}$$

Here 2N is the number of six-month periods until the company can call the bond; the call price is the price the company must pay in order to call the bond; and r_d is the YTC.

To illustrate, suppose SSI's 20-year bonds had a provision that permitted the company to call the bonds 10 years after issuance at a price of $1,100. Suppose further that interest rates had fallen, and one year after issuance the going interest rate had declined to 5 percent, causing the price of the bonds to rise to $1,365.23. Solving Equation 8-2 for r_d, the YTC is 4.05 percent—this is the return you would earn if you bought the bond at $1,365.23 and it was called nine years from today.

Do you think SSI *will* call the bonds when they become callable? SSI's action would depend on what the going interest rate is when the bonds become callable. If the going rate remains at $r_d = 5\%$, then SSI could save $8\% − 5\%$, or $30 of interest per bond annually, by calling them and replacing the 8 percent semiannual coupon bonds with a new 5 percent semiannual coupon issue. SSI would incur additional administrative costs when refunding the issue, but the interest savings would probably be worth the cost, so SSI would probably refund the bonds. Therefore, you would probably earn YTC = 4.05% rather than YTM = 5%.

Current Yield

Current Yield
The annual interest payment on a bond divided by the bond's current price.

If you examine brokerage house reports on bonds, you will often see reference to a bond's **current yield**. The current yield is the annual interest payment divided by the bond's current price. For example, if SSI's bonds with an 8 percent semiannual coupon were currently selling at $1,365.23, the bond's current yield would be $80/$1,365.23 = 5.86\%$.

Except for a bond selling at its par value, the current yield does not represent the rate of return that investors expect to earn on the bonds. The current yield provides information regarding the amount of cash income that a bond will generate in a given year, but because it does not consider capital gains or losses, it does not provide an accurate measure of the bond's total expected return.

SELF-TEST QUESTIONS

Explain the difference between yield to maturity and yield to call.
How does a bond's current yield differ from its total return?

ASSESSING BOND RISK

Interest Rate Risk

Interest rates fluctuate over time, and an increase in interest rates leads to a decline in the value of outstanding bonds. The risk of a decline in bond values due to rising interest rates is called **interest rate risk**. To illustrate, suppose you bought some 8 percent semiannual coupon SSI bonds at a price of $1,000, and interest rates in the following year rose to 11 percent. As we saw earlier, the price of the bonds would fall to $762.93, so you would lose $237.07 per bond.[8] Interest rates can and do rise, so bondholders can and do suffer losses at times even on default-free bonds such as U.S. Treasury issues.

Interest Rate Risk
The risk of a decline in a bond's price due to an increase in interest rates.

Interest rate risk exposure is higher on bonds with long maturities than on those with short maturities.[9] This point can be demonstrated by showing how the value of a 1-year bond with an 8 percent semiannual coupon fluctuates with changes in r_d, and comparing these changes with those on a 20-year bond as calculated previously.

The values of the 1-year and 20-year bonds at a range of market interest rates are summarized and plotted in Figure 8-2. Note how much more sensitive the price of the 20-year bond is to interest rate changes. At an 8 percent interest rate, both the 20-year and the 1-year bonds are valued at $1,000. When rates rise to 11 percent, the 20-year bond falls to $759.31, but the 1-year bond declines only to $972.31.

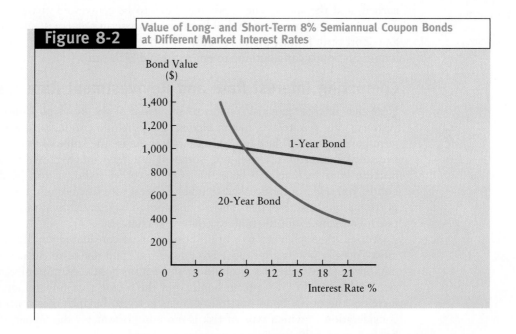

Figure 8-2 Value of Long- and Short-Term 8% Semiannual Coupon Bonds at Different Market Interest Rates

---

[8]You would have an *accounting* (and tax) loss only if you sold the bond; if you held it to maturity, you would not have such a loss. However, even if you did not sell, you would still have suffered a *real economic loss in an opportunity cost sense* because you would have lost the opportunity to invest at 11 percent and would be stuck with an 8 percent bond in an 11 percent market. In an economic sense, "paper losses" are just as bad as realized accounting losses.

[9]Actually, a bond's maturity and coupon rate both affect interest rate risk. Low coupons mean that most of the bond's return will come from repayment of principal, whereas on a high-coupon bond with the same maturity, more of the cash flows will come in during the early years due to the relatively large coupon payments. *Duration* is a calculation that finds the average number of years the bond's PV of cash flows remain outstanding, and it combines the maturity and coupon. A zero coupon bond, which has no interest payments and whose payment all comes at maturity, has a duration equal to the bond's maturity. Coupon bonds all have durations that are shorter than maturity, and the higher the coupon rate, the shorter the duration. Bonds with longer duration are exposed to more interest rate risk.

For bonds with similar coupons, this differential sensitivity to interest rate changes always holds true—the longer until maturity, the more the bond's price changes in response to a given change in interest rates. Thus, even if the default risk on two bonds is exactly the same, the one with the longer maturity is exposed to more interest rate risk.

Reinvestment Rate Risk

Reinvestment Rate Risk
The risk that a decline in interest rates will lead to a decline in income from a bond portfolio.

As we saw in the preceding section, an *increase* in interest rates hurts bondholders because it leads to a decline in the value of a bond portfolio. But can a *decrease* in interest rates also hurt bondholders? The answer is yes, because if interest rates fall, a bondholder will probably suffer a reduction in his or her income. For example, consider a retiree who has a bond portfolio and lives off the income it produces. The bonds in the portfolio, on average, have a coupon rate of 8 percent. Now suppose interest rates decline to 5 percent. Many of the bonds will be called, and as calls occur, the bondholder will have to replace 8 percent bonds with 5 percent bonds. Even bonds that are not callable will mature, and when they do, they will have to be replaced with lower-yielding bonds. Thus, our retiree will suffer a reduction of income.

The risk of an income decline due to a drop in interest rates is called **reinvestment rate risk**, and its importance has been demonstrated in recent years by sharp drops in rates since the mid-1980s. Reinvestment rate risk is obviously high on callable bonds. It is also high on short-term bonds, because the shorter the maturity of a bond, the fewer the years when the relatively high old-interest rate will be earned, and the sooner the funds will have to be reinvested at the new low rate. Thus, retirees whose primary holdings are short-term securities, such as bank CDs and short-term bonds, are hurt badly by a decline in rates, even though holders of long-term bonds can continue to enjoy the old high rates.

Comparing Interest Rate and Reinvestment Rate Risk

Note that interest rate risk relates to the *value* of the bond portfolio, while reinvestment rate risk relates to the *income* the portfolio produces. If you hold long-term bonds, you will face interest rate risk, because the value of your portfolio will decline if interest rates rise, but you will not face much reinvestment rate risk because your income will be stable. On the other hand, if you hold short-term bonds, you will not be exposed to much interest rate risk because the value of your portfolio will be stable, but you will be exposed to reinvestment rate risk, and your portfolio income will fluctuate with interest changes.

We see, then, that no fixed-rate bond can be considered totally riskless—even most Treasury bonds are exposed to interest rate and reinvestment rate risk. We can minimize interest rate risk by holding short-term bonds, or minimize reinvestment rate risk by holding long-term bonds, but the action that lowers one type of risk increases the other. Bond portfolio managers try to balance these two risks, giving consideration to which type of risk is more important for the owner of the portfolio, but some risk generally remains in any bond.

Default Risk

Default Risk
The risk that an investor will receive less than the promised return on the bond because the issuer fails to make either interest or principal payments.

Another important risk associated with bonds is **default risk**. If the issuer defaults, investors receive less than the promised return on the bond. Therefore, investors need to assess a bond's default risk before making a purchase. The quoted interest rate includes a default risk premium—the greater the default risk, the higher the bond's yield to maturity. The default risk on U.S. Treasury securities is zero, but default risk can be substantial for corporate, municipal, and some foreign government bonds.

Suppose two bonds have the same promised cash flows, coupon rate, maturity, liquidity, inflation exposure, country risk, and exchange rate risk, but one bond has more default risk than the other. Investors will naturally pay less for the bond with the greater chance of default. As a result, bonds with higher default risk will have higher interest rates:

$$r_d = r^* + IP + DRP + LP + MRP + CRP + ERP.$$

If its default risk changes, this will affect the price of a bond. For example, if the default risk of the SSI bonds increases, the bonds' price will fall and the yield to maturity (YTM = r_d) will increase.

Differentiate between interest rate and reinvestment rate risk.

To which type of risk are holders of long-term bonds more exposed? Short-term bondholders?

What is the duration of a zero coupon bond? Briefly explain the relationship of the duration of coupon bonds with their maturities.

What is the relationship of a bond's duration with its interest rate risk?

VALUING FLOATING-RATE BONDS

Reference Rate
The rate to which the coupon rate of a floating-rate bond is adjusted.

Until now we have assumed that the coupon rate is fixed at the time of issue and does not change over the life of the bond. However, many debt instruments are issued with coupon rates that can be reset at fixed intervals to the then-current market rate. Thus, because market rates change, the coupon rate on the bond can vary over time, either increasing or decreasing depending on what interest rates in the economy are doing. Valuing a floating-rate issue is more difficult than valuing a fixed-rate bond because the future coupon payments are uncertain.

We start by assuming that the floating-rate bond has a maturity of five years and no default risk, so the default risk premium equals zero. We also assume that the **reference rate** used to adjust the coupon rate is LIBOR, and that the coupon rate is equal to LIBOR and is reset every six months. At the most basic level, this floating-rate bond is equivalent to a series of 10 short-term fixed-rate bonds (each with a six-month maturity) with a guaranteed rollover and with the same zero default risk premium. On the date the coupon rate is to be reset, the bond's value will equal the par value because the new coupon rate will be the market rate, and earlier we identified this as the condition under which the bond will sell at its par value. Between reset dates, though, the value can fluctuate in exactly the same manner as described earlier for the fixed-rate bond because over that period the coupon rate is fixed.

When the bond has default risk, the analysis is more complex because the risk premium creates a fixed portion of the coupon rate that does not vary with changes in market interest rates. Assume that the floating-rate bond is priced at LIBOR (which is generally assumed to be riskless) plus 100 basis points, and the other characteristics of the issue are as given earlier. This means that the default risk premium equals 100 basis points, or 1 percent. In this situation, every six months the coupon rate is reset to LIBOR plus 100 basis points, but only the LIBOR portion is variable.[10] Thus, there are two components to the value: the floating component that is a function of LIBOR and a fixed component that is a function of the DRP. On the day the coupon rate is reset, the bond value might differ from the par value in this

---

[10]The major difference between this bond with a guaranteed rollover at a fixed default risk premium and a series of six-month issues with no guaranteed rollover is that in the latter case the default risk premium can also change as the risk perceptions of investors about the creditworthiness of the company change.

situation if the creditworthiness of the issuing company has changed (for either better or worse), because the fixed 100-point DRP would not reflect the revised market evaluation of the risk, and the adjustment in the market would cause the bond to sell at a slight discount if the creditworthiness declined, or at a slight premium if it increased.

All-In Cost
Literally, total costs explicit and implicit. As the term is used with respect to floating-rate bonds, it is equivalent to the YTM assuming the bond is a fixed-rate bond.

The yield to maturity for a floating-rate bond is also problematical because the interest income stream is uncertain until the maturity date. Analysts and investors often make assumptions about future interest rates or calculate yields assuming that LIBOR is constant over the bond's life. In other words, they treat it as if it were a fixed-rate bond and calculate the **all-in cost** in the same way that the YTM would be calculated. Sensitivity analysis can be performed with various interest rate scenarios to bracket the YTM (or the bond's value).

SELF-TEST QUESTIONS

Explain why valuing floating-rate bonds is more difficult than valuing fixed-rate bonds.

What is meant by the term "reference rate"?

Explain whether the following statement is true or false: "The value of a floating-rate bond never fluctuates since the coupon is always changing."

In what situation might a floating-rate bond's value at reset not be equal to par?

How do analysts calculate a floating-rate bond's YTM?

What is meant by the term "all-in cost"?

CREDIT MARKETS

U.S. Marketplace

In the United States, long-term corporate bonds are traded primarily in the over-the-counter market. Most bonds are owned by and traded among the large financial institutions, and it is relatively easy for the over-the-counter bond dealers to arrange the transfer of large blocks of bonds among the relatively few holders of the bonds. It would be much more difficult to conduct similar operations in the stock market, with its millions of large and small stockholders, so a higher percentage of stock trades occur on the exchanges.

Commercial Paper
An alternative to bank loans for large, financially stable borrowers that takes the form of short-term, unsecured promissory notes.

Information on bond trades in the over-the-counter market is not published, but a representative group of bonds is listed and traded on the bond division of the NYSE and is reported on the bond market page of *The Wall Street Journal*. Data on Treasury issues of all maturities are likewise reported in *The Wall Street Journal*. Bond data are also available on the Internet at sites such as **http://www.investinginbonds.com** and **http://www.bondsonline.com**.

Short-term credit for U.S. companies comes from sources like commercial banks in the form of revolving loans and investors in the commercial paper market. **Commercial paper** is an alternative to bank loans for large, financially stable borrowers and takes the form of short-term (usually 90 days or less) unsecured promissory notes. Commercial paper is the primary source of working capital financing in the United States.

Eurocredits
Floating-rate bank loans, available in most major trading currencies, that are tied to LIBOR for the issue's currency as the reference rate and issued for a fixed term with no early repayment.

International Marketplace

There are three major types of credit markets in the international marketplace that mirror equivalent U.S. markets in many ways. Floating-rate bank loans, called **eurocredits**, are tied to LIBOR for the issue's currency as the reference rate and tend to

Too Big?

In May 2003, better than expected economic news triggered a sell-off of Japanese government bonds. Further rumors that Japanese banks (the major holders of Japanese bonds) were selling caused an even greater sell-off. Prices plunged and 10-year government bond yields rose to 1.4 percent, up from a recent all-time low of 0.43 percent. Then, in July, yields began to fall again as signs remained that Japan's economic slump was still far from over. One of the greatest bond rallies in history had resumed.

The sporadic behavior of Japan's bond market reflected the uncertainty pervading world bond markets. Around the globe, bond prices had soared while stock prices floundered, and record low yields in global markets signaled an inevitable bond sell-off. At the same time Japanese bond yields were stabilizing, U.S. bond prices continued to fall as yields moved from 3.11 percent in mid-June to 3.93 percent by mid-July. Investors, taking their cue from the continued slide in U.S. bonds, worried that the resurgence of the Japanese bond market might not last. Indeed, a major factor in the bullish Japanese bond market had been concern about Japan's prolonged economic slump. However, some day the Japanese economy has to recover, and when it does, Japan might run into a wall if the bond market collapses.

Economists have warned that the Japanese bond market is far too big (as large as the combined markets of Germany and France), and unless the government seeks to stabilize it, Japan could be headed for financial trouble. It also shows no signs of slowing down, having grown at double-digit rates over the previous five years. The greatest problem is that too much money has been invested by too few investors, compounded by banks moving more and more of their cash into bonds. Japanese banks and other financial institutions control more than 60 percent of the Japanese bonds. So, if the bond market begins to falter, the major players in Japan's financial health will be hurt the most. It was estimated that Japan's eight major banks would collectively lose one trillion yen for each percentage point rise in 10-year bond yields. If these large bond positions are predicated upon Japan's economic sluggishness, what happens when the economy begins to recover?

Japanese recovery could hold negative global implications, too. Japanese investors also hold large foreign investments (U.S. Treasuries and corporates) that would be sold off in a financial pinch. Japanese regulators are looking for ways to stabilize the Japanese markets and have launched ambitious advertisements, featuring popular Japanese figures, aimed at encouraging people to purchase bonds. The bond advertising campaign for fiscal year 2004 was budgeted at ¥713 million. In addition, the Japanese government has started selling bonds through banks, securities firms, and post offices (in varying denominations) and is looking to offer bonds online and in convenience stores. Regulators contend that ordinary savers are more likely to be long-term investors, and thus have targeted the ordinary investor. This strategy seems advisable in light of the fact that individual investors account for only 2 percent of the Japanese government bond market, compared with 10 percent in the United States.

Source: "Japan's Bond Market: Too Big?" *The Wall Street Journal,* July 16, 2003, **http://www.wsj.com**.

---

be issued for a fixed term with no early repayment. The oldest of these eurocredits is eurodollar bank loans tied to U.S. dollar LIBOR, but today eurocredits come in most major trading currencies. As in the United States, there is no secondary market for eurocredit bank loans. For very large eurocredits beyond the capacity of a single lender, there are syndicated credits organized by a lead bank and spread over a consortium of banks. These floating-rate loans usually involve an up-front commitment fee of approximately 1.5 percent.

The eurobond market is the medium- to long-term international market for both fixed- and floating-rate debt. It is almost as old as the eurodollar market and is a natural extension of it. A **eurobond** is an international bond underwritten by an international bank syndicate and sold to investors in countries other than the one in whose money unit the bond is denominated. Thus, U.S. dollar–denominated eurobonds cannot be sold in the United States, sterling eurobonds cannot be sold in the United Kingdom, and yen eurobonds cannot be sold in Japan. This is a true

Eurobond
An international bond underwritten by an international syndicate of banks and sold to investors in countries other than the one in whose money unit the bond is denominated.

Floating-Rate Notes (FRNs)
Eurobonds with floating-rate coupons.

Foreign Bond
A type of international bond issued in the domestic capital market of the country in whose currency the bond is denominated, and underwritten by investment banks from the same country.

international debt instrument and is usually issued in bearer form, which means that the owner's identity is not registered and known; in order to receive the interest payments the owner must clip a coupon and present it for payment at one of the designated payor banks. Most eurobonds are not rated by one of the rating agencies such as S&P or Moody's, although an increasing number of them are starting to be rated. Eurobonds can be issued with either a fixed coupon rate or a floating rate depending on the preferences of the issuer, and they have medium- or long-term maturities. Eurobonds with floating rates are called **floating-rate notes (FRNs)** and are valued as we discussed earlier. Recently, several FRNs have been issued as perpetuities, so they have characteristics akin to equities.

Another type of international bond is a **foreign bond**. A foreign bond is issued in the domestic capital market of the country in whose currency the bond is denominated and is underwritten by investment banks from the same country. The only thing foreign about a foreign bond is the nationality of the borrower. For instance, Canadian companies often issue U.S. dollar–denominated foreign bonds in New York to fund their U.S. operations. Foreign bonds issued in the United States are sometimes called "Yankee bonds." Similarly, "bulldogs" are foreign bonds issued in London, and "samurai bonds" are foreign bonds issued in Tokyo. Foreign bonds can be either fixed or floating and have the same maturities as the purely domestic bonds with which they must compete for funding.

Recent Developments

The most recently developed international credit market is the short-to-medium-term Euronote market. This category includes the Euro commercial paper market at the very short end of the maturity spectrum. Also at the short-term end are negotiable promissory notes placed with public investors at a lower cost than is incurred with eurocredits or syndicated credits. These promissory notes can be issued through a note issuance facility (NIF), a standby note issuance facility (SNIF), or as a revolving underwriting facility (RUF). One of the more recent innovations in the euronote market is the euro medium-term note (EMTN). Medium-term notes can be issued over a period of time in a manner similar to shelf registration in the United States under SEC Rule 415. Interest on EMTNs is paid semiannually on set calendar dates instead of being tied to the exact date of issuance because they are issued continuously and usually in small denominations (under $5 million). Thus, they fill in the maturity gap between euro commercial paper and eurobonds, and the relatively small denominations increase the liquidity of the secondary market.

SELF-TEST QUESTIONS

Why do most bond trades occur in the over-the-counter market?
What are some sources of short-term credit for U.S. companies?
What is commercial paper, and what is its primary usage?
Differentiate between eurobonds and foreign bonds.
Differentiate between eurocredits and floating-rate notes (FRNs).
What is the most recently developed international credit market? What instruments make up this market?

SUMMARY

This chapter described different debt instruments, bond valuation, and how investors estimate their expected rates of return. We also discussed the various types of risks that investors face and described debt markets.

It is important to remember when an investor purchases a company's bonds that the investor is providing the company with capital. Therefore, when a firm issues bonds, *the return that investors receive represents the cost of debt financing for the issuing company.* This point is emphasized in Chapter 10, where the ideas developed in this chapter are used to help determine a company's overall cost of capital, which is a basic component in the capital budgeting process.

The key concepts discussed in this chapter are listed below.

- A **bond** is a long-term promissory note issued by a business or governmental unit. The issuer receives money in exchange for promising to make interest payments and to repay the principal on a specified future date.
- Some key characteristics of bonds are **par value**, **coupon payment**, **coupon interest rate**, and **maturity date.**
- A **call provision** gives the issuing corporation the right to redeem the bonds prior to maturity under specified terms, usually at a price greater than the maturity value. The difference between the call price and the maturity value is a **call premium.** A firm will typically call a bond if interest rates fall substantially below the coupon rate because it can reissue bonds at a lower interest rate.
- A **put provision** allows bonds to be redeemed at par at the holder's option; it protects investors against an increase in interest rates.
- A **sinking fund** is a provision that requires the corporation to retire a portion of the bond issue each year. The purpose of the sinking fund is to provide for the orderly retirement of the issue. A sinking fund typically requires no call premium. On balance, however, bonds that have a sinking fund are regarded as being safer than those without such a provision, so at the time they are issued sinking fund bonds have lower coupon rates than otherwise similar bonds without sinking funds.
- Three main types of domestic bonds are **Treasury, corporate,** and **municipal bonds. International bonds** are issued by foreign governments or foreign corporations.
- Some recent innovations in long-term financing include **zero coupon bonds**, which pay no annual interest, but are issued at a discount; and **floating-rate debt**, whose interest payments fluctuate with changes in interest rates.
- The **value of a bond** is found as the present value of an annuity (the **interest payments**) plus the present value of a lump sum (the **principal**). The bond is evaluated at the appropriate periodic market interest rate over the number of periods for which interest payments are made.
- The equation used to find the value of a semiannual bond is

$$V_B = \sum_{t=1}^{2N} \frac{\text{INT}/2}{(1 + r_d/2)^t} + \frac{M}{(1 + r_d/2)^{2N}}.$$

- A **discount bond** is one that sells below its par value. This occurs whenever the market interest rate is above the coupon rate.
- A **premium bond** is one that sells above its par value. This occurs whenever the market interest rate is below the coupon rate.
- The return earned on a bond held to maturity is defined as the bond's **yield to maturity (YTM).** If the bond can be redeemed before maturity, it is **callable,** and the return investors receive if it is called is defined as the **yield to call (YTC).** The YTC is found as the present value of the interest payments received while the bond is outstanding plus the present value of the **call price** (the par value plus a call premium).
- The **current yield** is the annual interest payment on a bond divided by the bond's current price.
- The longer the maturity of a bond, the more its price will change in response to a given change in interest rates; this is called **interest rate risk.** However, short-term bonds expose investors to high **reinvestment rate risk,** which is the risk that income from a bond portfolio will decline because cash flows received from bonds will roll over at lower interest rates.

- **Default risk** is the risk that an investor will receive less than the promised return on the bond because the issuer fails to make either interest or principal payments.
- The **reference rate** is the rate to which the coupon rate of a floating-rate bond is adjusted.
- At the most basic level, and assuming no default risk, a **floating-rate bond** is equivalent to a series of short-term, fixed-rate bonds with a guaranteed rollover with the same default risk premium.
- **Commercial paper** is an alternative to bank loans for large, financially stable borrowers that takes the form of short-term, unsecured promissory notes.
- **Eurocredits** are floating-rate bank loans, available in most major trading currencies, tied to LIBOR for the issue's currency as the reference rate and issued for a fixed term with no early repayment.
- A **eurobond** is an international bond underwritten by an international syndicate of banks and sold to investors in countries other than the one in whose money unit the bond is denominated.
- **Floating-rate notes (FRNs)** are eurobonds with floating-rate coupons.
- A **foreign bond** is a type of international bond issued by a foreign borrower in the domestic capital market of the country in whose currency the bond is denominated, and it is underwritten by investment banks from the same country.

QUESTIONS

(8-1) Briefly explain whether the following statement is true or false: "The values of outstanding bonds change whenever the going rate of interest changes. In general, short-term interest rates are more volatile than long-term interest rates. Therefore, short-term bond prices are more sensitive to interest rate changes than are long-term bond prices."

(8-2) Briefly explain the factors that determine a bond's value.

(8-3) What is a call provision? Does an issuer have to pay an additional sum when a bond is called? Explain. What are meant by the terms deferred call and call protection?

(8-4) Why would an issuer have a put provision feature in their bond issue?

(8-5) What are the advantages and disadvantages for issuers and investors of the two methods that can be used to handle sinking fund provisions?

(8-6) Briefly explain the differences in valuation methodology for regular coupon bonds, zero coupon bonds, and floating-rate bonds.

(8-7) How is it possible to distinguish between a new issue bond versus a seasoned issue bond without knowledge of the issue date?

(8-8) Under what conditions would an investor expect to earn the YTC on a bond? To earn the YTM?

(8-9) Under what conditions does the YTM equal the bond's expected rate of return?

(8-10) Differentiate among interest rate risk, reinvestment rate risk, and default risk.

(8-11) How does the international credit market mirror the U.S. market?

SELF-TEST PROBLEMS   Solutions Appear in Appendix B

(ST-1) Define each of the following terms:
Key Terms a. Bond; par value; coupon payment; coupon interest rate
b. Maturity date; original maturity; call provision; call premium

c. Put provision; sinking fund provision
d. Treasury bonds; corporate bonds; municipal bonds; international bonds
e. Floating-rate bond; zero coupon bond
f. Discount bond; premium bond
g. Yield to maturity (YTM); yield to call (YTC); current yield
h. Interest rate risk; reinvestment rate risk; default risk
i. Reference rate; all-in cost
j. Commercial paper; eurocredits; eurobond
k. Floating-rate notes (FRNs); foreign bond

(ST-2)
Bond Valuation
International Beverage Corporation (IBC) recently issued 15-year bonds at a price of $1,000. These bonds pay $50 in interest each 6 months. Their price has remained stable since they were issued; that is, they still sell for $1,000. Due to additional financing needs, the firm wishes to issue new bonds that would have a maturity of 15 years, a par value of $1,000, and pay $30 in interest every 6 months. If both bonds have the same yield, how many new bonds must IBC issue to raise $5,000,000?

(ST-3)
Floating-Rate Bond
ABC Foods International recently issued 2-year floating-rate notes. The security was originally issued at its par (or maturity) value, $1,000, which will be received at the end of the second year. The notes paid $50 each 6-month period for the first year, and then the semiannual coupon would be reset the following year so the security's price will equal its par value. If an investor desires a nominal annual return of 9.04 percent, what would be the amount received in dollars each six-month period during the second year? Round your answer to the nearest whole dollar.

STARTER PROBLEMS

(8-1)
YTM and YTC
A corporate bond matures in 10 years. The bond has a 6 percent semiannual coupon and a par value of $1,000. The bond is callable in 5 years at a call price of $1,020. The price of the bond today is $1,050. What are the bond's yield to maturity and yield to call?

(8-2)
Current and Capital Gains Yields
Consider a $1,000 par value bond with an 8 percent semiannual coupon (i.e., $40 coupons every 6 months). There are 9 years remaining until maturity.
a. What is the current yield on the bond assuming that the required annual return on the bond is 12 percent?
b. What is the capital gains yield?

(8-3)
Bond Valuation
A bond with a face value of $1,000 matures in 20 years. The bond has a 6 percent semiannual coupon and a yield to maturity of 8 percent. If market interest rates remain at 8 percent, what will be the price of the bond two years from today?

EXAM-TYPE PROBLEMS

(8-4)
Current Yield, YTM, and Bond Value
A bond that matures in 10 years sells for $850. The bond has a face value of $1,000 and a 9 percent semiannual coupon.
a. What is the bond's current yield?
b. What is the bond's yield to maturity?
c. Assume that the yield to maturity remains constant for the next 3 years. What will be the price of the bond 3 years from today?

(8-5)
Bond Valuation
To accurately assess the firm's capital structure, it is necessary to convert its balance sheet figures to a market value basis. ABC International Foods Inc.'s balance sheet as of today, January 1, 2005, is as follows:

Long-term debt (bonds, at par)	$25,000,000
Preferred stock	5,000,000
Common stock ($10 par)	25,000,000
Retained earnings	10,000,000
Total debt and equity	$65,000,000

The bonds have a 6 percent coupon rate, payable semiannually, and a par value of $1,000. They mature on January 1, 2015. The yield to maturity is 10 percent, so the bonds now sell below par. What is the current market value of the firm's debt?

(8-6)
Bond Valuation
You just purchased a 20-year bond with a 12 percent semiannual coupon (i.e., $60 payable every 6 months). The bond has a face value of $1,000 and a current yield of 9 percent. Assuming that the yield to maturity of 8.5043 percent remains constant, what will be the price of the bond 1 year from now?

(8-7)
Sinking Fund
Global Electronics Inc. (GEI) sold $1,000,000 of 10 percent, 30-year, semiannual coupon bonds 15 years ago. The bonds are not callable, but they do have a sinking fund that requires GEI to redeem 5 percent of the original face value of the issue each year ($50,000), beginning in Year 11. To date, 25 percent of the issue has been retired. The company can either call bonds at par for sinking-fund purposes or purchase bonds on the open market, spending sufficient money to redeem 5 percent of the original face value each year. If the nominal yield to maturity (15 years remaining) on the bonds is currently 12 percent, what is the least amount of money GEI must put up to satisfy the sinking fund provision?

(8-8)
Coupon Payment
Worldwide Broad Band Services (WBBS) has two bond issues outstanding, and both sell for $712.37. The first issue has an annual coupon rate of 7 percent and 15 years to maturity. The second has an identical yield to maturity as the first bond, but only 8 years remain until maturity. Both issues pay interest annually. What is the annual interest payment on the second issue?

INTEGRATED CASE

Rick Schmidt, MRI's CFO, along with Mandy Wu, Schmidt's assistant, and John Costello, a consultant and college finance professor, comprise a team assigned to teach the firm's directors and senior managers the basics of international financial management. The program includes 16 sessions, each lasting about 2 hours, with the sessions scheduled immediately before the monthly board meetings. Seven sessions have been completed, and the team is now preparing Session 8, which will deal with bonds and bond markets. Prior sessions have provided an overview of international finance plus discussions of foreign exchange markets, international institutions, exchange rate analysis, foreign direct investment, risk and return, and financial statements.

For the bond session, the team will identify the major types of bonds, procedures used to value them, and the markets in which they trade. The debt session is important for three reasons. First, MRI uses debt in its capital structure, and the board needs to understand the different types of debt securities that can be issued. Second, the principles of fixed-income analysis are important when estimating the cost of capital, a topic that will be addressed in an upcoming session. Finally, the company's retirement program is based on a 401(k) plan under which individual employees direct their own pension asset allocations among common and preferred stocks, bonds, mutual funds, and MRI's own stock. There is a danger that some employees will lose money, become unhappy, and want to sue someone for not providing adequate investment advice. Schmidt has asked the directors and managers not to give investment advice, but they sometimes do anyway, and he wants to make sure that they are knowledgeable about debt securities.

All of the directors invest in the stock and bond markets and keep up with them to at least some extent, but the individual directors' knowledge varies considerably. This makes it difficult to decide what to cover and how deep the analysis should go. After much discussion, the team concluded that they should cover the different types of bonds, procedures for estimating the values and expected returns on these securities, factors that affect bonds' risk, and the markets in which bonds trade. Schmidt specifically wants to cover interest rate and reinvestment rate risks and to explain how a bond's term to maturity affects those risks. He also wants to consider how credit risk affects the rate of return on debt, and what determines credit risk. As in the other sessions, the team plans to use an *Excel* model both to illustrate the concepts and to help the directors become more familiar with *Excel*.

Schmidt also noted that several of the directors are concerned about whether the low interest rates in 2004 are likely to continue and what will happen if rates rise sharply. This topic has surfaced in two different situations. First, the director of human resources wonders whether to advise employees to invest their 401(k) funds primarily in common stocks, in fixed-income securities, or a combination of the two, and if a combination, whether the percentage allocation should vary systematically with the characteristics of the employee.[11] Second, the potential for an increase in interest rates has been mentioned in discussions as to whether MRI should use debt or equity when raising capital during the coming year.

Yet another issue is whether MRI should call one of its bond issues and pay it off before its maturity date. The company's investment bankers have suggested that it should call the issue and refund it with new, lower-cost debt. However, there is a substantial cost to the refunding—which means revenues to the investment bankers—and Schmidt wants to consider the wisdom of that action. Because the directors will have to vote on the refunding, Schmidt asked Wu to work up some numbers for use during the session. To simplify the analysis and keep the focus on the big issue, Rick wants to disregard taxes in this discussion.

To begin the discussion of bond value and expected yields, Wu gathered the information shown in Table IC8-1 to illustrate the process. Next, information specific to MRI is contained in Table IC8-2. She chose the first set of bonds so that a desired result was reached. The rationale for her decision was to discuss valuation abstractly and then discuss MRI's particular situation.

With those thoughts in mind, the three compiled the following set of questions, which they plan to discuss during the session. As with the other sessions, they plan to use an *Excel* model to answer the quantitative questions. Assume that you are Mandy Wu and that you must prepare answers for use during the session.

Questions

a. What is a bond? Identify the key characteristics of a bond and then explain how its value is determined. What are some provisions that can be included in a bond contract?

b. Who are the major issuers of bonds?

c. On the basis of data in Table IC8-1, find the yield an investor is most likely to earn on Bonds 1 and 2, and explain your answer. What do these results suggest about the shape of the yield curve? How might economic conditions shift and cause the prices of Bonds 1 and 2 to change from $903 and $1,088, respectively, to $1,075 and $1,165.50, and what would the bonds' expected yields be under those conditions? (Hint: To answer this last question using the model, replace the old bond prices with the new ones. Note that the model requires the prices to be entered as percentages of par.) If investment bankers suggested modifications to the data, could the model be adapted for use with the new data?

d. On the basis of data in Table IC8-1, find the most likely market prices for Bonds 3 and 4. If you were to buy these bonds in the marketplace, would you pay these amounts? If not, why not? Do the credit risks of these bonds appear to be similar to or quite different from those of Bonds 1 and 2? Rank the desirability of these four bonds as holdings in a pension plan portfolio, and also rank them from the standpoint of a corporate borrower.

e. Using the data in Table IC8-1, find the most likely prices and lives in years for Bonds 5, 6, and 7. Rank them from highest to lowest in terms of interest rate (or price) risk and of reinvestment rate risk. On the basis of your analysis, do the bonds appear to be priced in a reasonable manner? If not, how might their prices be expected to change?

f. Zero coupon bonds illustrate an interesting scenario because no payments are actually received by investors until maturity. Consider a zero coupon bond where the lender is in the 35 percent tax bracket and the corporate borrower is in the 40 percent federal-plus-state bracket. How would taxes be handled for these bonds, and how would the tax situation affect the desirability of zeros to a purchaser or an issuer?

---

[11]Company officials are discouraged from giving investment advice, but the investment firms who manage the employee retirement funds do give advice, and if that advice turns out to be incorrect, the employees will not be happy. So, management wants to do whatever it can to ensure that employees receive good advice.

TABLE IC8-1 — Data on Non-MRI Bonds to Be Analyzed

Panel A. Analysis between Payment Dates

	Bond 1	Bond 2	Bond 3	Bond 4
Issue date	1/1/04	1/1/04	1/1/04	1/1/04
First interest date	7/1/04	7/1/04	7/1/04	7/1/04
Settlement date (today)	11/15/04	11/15/04	11/15/04	11/15/04
Maturity date	1/1/24	1/1/24	1/1/24	1/1/24
First call date	1/1/09	1/1/09	1/1/14	1/1/14
Coupon interest rate	7.00%	9.50%	6.75%	9.25%
Rate: broker quote	To be calculated		8.00%	
Maturity value (% of par)	100	100	100	100
Price (% of par)	90.30	108.80	To be calculated	
Call price (% of par)	105.0	105.0	105.0	105.0
Payments per year	2	2	2	2

Panel B. Analysis on a Payment Date

	Bond 5	Bond 6	Bond 7
Issue date	11/15/03	11/15/00	11/15/00
First interest date	5/15/04	5/15/01	5/15/01
Settlement date (today)	11/15/04	11/15/04	11/15/04
Maturity date	11/15/05	11/15/25	11/15/25
First call date	Not callable	Not callable	11/15/07
Coupon interest rate	8.00%	8.00%	8.00%
Rate: broker quote	6.00%	6.00%	6.00%
Maturity value (% of par)	100	100	100
Price (% of par)	To be calculated		
Call price (% of par)	N/A	N/A	103.0
Payments per year	2	2	2

TABLE IC8-2 — MRI Bonds to Be Analyzed

	MRI − 1	MRI − 2
Years to maturity	20	20
Maturity value	$1,000	$1,000
Price	$926.29	$1,121.00
Coupon interest rate	6.00%	8.50%
Call price	$1,075	$1,075
Years to call	4	4
Payments per year	2	2

g. Floating-rate debt—which could be bonds, bank loans, or other loans—have a stated interest rate (the "coupon rate") that changes over time as some market rate such as the T-bill rate or LIBOR changes. Some bonds are indexed against inflation as measured by the CPI. An example is the Treasury inflation protected security, or TIPS, an inflation-indexed bond that pays a relatively low fixed amount plus an additional amount equal to inflation during the last year, which means that the fixed rate is a real, or inflation-free, rate. How do these two types of bonds compare with regular coupon bonds in terms of interest rate price risk and reinvestment rate risk?

h. MRI has two bond issues outstanding. Data for those bond issues are shown in Table IC8-2. Determine the expected yield for each bond and calculate the current and capital gains yields. Should MRI call either issue at this time, assuming it could do so? Are there any additional factors that should be considered before deciding to call the bonds?

i. Describe the major credit markets in the United States and internationally.

CHAPTER 9

Stocks and Stock Markets

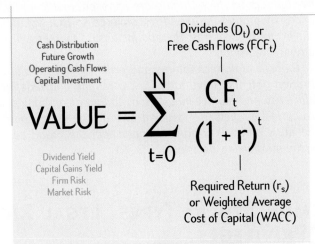

$$\text{VALUE} = \sum_{t=0}^{N} \frac{CF_t}{(1+r)^t}$$

Cash Distribution
Future Growth
Operating Cash Flows
Capital Investment

Dividends (D_t) or
Free Cash Flows (FCF_t)

Dividend Yield
Capital Gains Yield
Firm Risk
Market Risk

Required Return (r_s)
or Weighted Average
Cost of Capital (WACC)

FIF

e-resource

*The textbook's Web site, **http://crum. swlearning.com,** contains an Excel file that will guide you through the chapter's calculations. The file for this chapter is **FIFC09-model.xls,** and we encourage you to open the file and follow along as you read the chapter.*

Like all financial assets, the value of a share of stock is the present value of its expected future cash flows. Those cash flows depend on how effectively management runs the business, on economic conditions, and on the firm's cash distribution policies. The rate used to discount the cash flows depends on market interest rates, the firm's business risk, and its capital structure. Again, the basic valuation equation provides a framework for analyzing stocks.

Two alternative approaches can be taken to stock valuation. Under one we forecast future dividends and then discount them at the required return on equity, r_s, given the company's risk and capital market conditions. Under the other approach we forecast the firm's free cash flows and then discount them at the weighted average cost of capital (WACC) as calculated using procedures discussed in Chapter 10. We explain both approaches in this chapter.

It is important to note that the firm's operating efficiency, product market conditions, and management's policies determine its free cash flows, which are the primary determinant of value. As the global economy evolves, potential markets grow almost without limit, and opportunities to improve operating efficiency are expanded as firms look overseas. However, it is especially difficult to estimate multinational firms' free cash flows, as a host of new concerns enter the free cash flow estimation process: exchange rate fluctuations, natural disasters, famine, political risk, and so on. Note too that management can retain and reinvest cash flows locally or reallocate them to another subsidiary, or it can distribute them to stockholders as dividends or by repurchasing stock in the open market. Whatever management does with cash flows generated by the worldwide operations, the resulting distribution policy determines the actual cash flows received by stockholders, and those cash flows largely determine the firm's value.

Management's goal is to maximize the stock price, so managers should recognize the effects their decisions have on this price. This requires them to understand the principles of stock price valuation. Note too that stock prices are not determined in a vacuum—they are determined in the marketplace by investors, and increasingly, the marketplace includes a broad range of global capital markets and participants. If the markets in which shares trade are "efficient," then the actual stock price will be "correct" in the sense that it reflects, as closely as possible, the company's true prospects for providing future cash flows to investors. However, if a market is "inefficient," then stock prices in that market could be radically different from their true, or intrinsic, values. Still, unless artificial barriers to stock trading are imposed, multicountry arbitrage will cause stock prices all around the world to converge so that risk-adjusted rates of return are similar in all locations, thereby increasing market efficiency and the extent of global integration.

Globalization, technology, and ordinary investors looking for enhanced diversification potential have forced us to rethink and redefine how we look at market efficiency and market integration. Today, a company's shares may trade in many countries' markets, so focusing only on the home-country market may not tell the full story and will not give management the broad perspective it needs to make value-maximizing decisions.

COMMON STOCK: TYPES, LEGAL RIGHTS, AND PRIVILEGES

Types of Common Stock

Classified Stock
Common stock given a special designation, such as Class A, Class B, and so forth, to meet special needs of the company.

Although most firms have only one type of common stock, some companies use **classified stock** to meet their specific needs. Generally, when special classifications are used, one type is designated *Class A*, another *Class B*, and so on. Small, new companies seeking funds from outside sources frequently use different types of common stock. For example, when Genetic Concepts recently went public, its Class A paid a dividend but had no voting rights for five years. Its Class B stock, which was retained by the organizers of the company, had full voting rights, but the legal terms stated that dividends could not be paid on the Class B stock until the company had established its earning power by increasing retained earnings to a designated level. The use of classified stock enabled the public to take a position in a conservatively financed growth company without sacrificing income, while the founders retained absolute control during the crucial early stages of the firm's development. At the same time, outside investors were protected against excessive withdrawals of funds by the original owners. As is often the case in such situations, the Class B shares were called **founders' shares.** Founders' shares were used extensively in the privatization programs in Eastern Europe and the former Soviet Union to ensure that company control remained with the local shareholders, even when substantial amounts of new investment capital were contributed by western partners.

Founders' Shares
Stock owned by the firm's founders with sole voting rights but restricted dividends for a specified number of years.

In some countries, foreigners are legally restricted from holding an equity stake in local companies. Sometimes these limitations affect all companies in the country, but more commonly they apply only to firms in certain "strategic" industries, such as natural resources producers, financial institutions, transportation companies, and public utilities. For instance, in the United States, foreigners are prohibited from owning a majority of the shares of domestic air transportation companies (passenger and cargo). This restriction recently caused a political stir when the ownership of the express mail company DHL was questioned by its competitors and the U.S. government. (Refer to the box, "The Shipping News," on the next page.) While the usual way these restrictions are imposed is to limit transfers in the firm's stock book (listing of ownership), it is also possible that they could be enforced by issuing classified stock (Class A shares) that can be legally owned only by citizens of the country. For example, Class B shares could be owned by anyone, foreign or domestic. Then Class A shares, or **citizens' shares**, could have superior voting rights so as to enable local citizens to maintain control over the company. These so-called **golden shares** are found in many parts of the world, including Europe and the United States.

Citizens' (Golden) Shares
Class of common stock that may be issued by a company for investors in the company's home country in order to maintain local control of the company.

Legal Rights and Privileges

The common stockholders are the *owners* of the corporation and as such they have certain rights and privileges. Although there are slight differences among countries, some of which are noted next, the major developed markets have similar rules regarding common stocks, and emerging markets generally employ those same rules. Therefore, the principles set forth in this and other sections apply to most countries, both those with developed markets and those with emerging markets.

CONTROL OF THE FIRM   Its common stockholders have the right to elect a firm's directors, who, in turn, elect the officers who manage the business and set its strategic direction. In the so-called German system, the directors are not permitted to serve on the company's management board, so all are "outside" directors. This has advantages in terms of evaluating managerial performance, but because the directors are not involved in the firm's day-to-day operations, they might not have all of the information needed to make sound strategic decisions. In the "American" system, the same people are permitted to serve as both a director and as an operating manager. This system ensures that directors have insight into the company's affairs, but a nonindependent board is more likely to allow improper management self-dealings and/or leave an incompetent management team in place. Recent corporate scandals in the United States, such as the one involving Tyco and its chairman Dennis Kozlowski, emphasize the importance of the role played by outside directors in the Anglo-American governance system, and they have led the SEC and other oversight bodies to recommend changes in the composition of boards of directors of public companies to ensure independence and objectivity. Recently, General Electric appointed two new directors to bolster the independence of its board, while Disney added former U.S. Senator George Mitchell to co-chair its corporate governance committee in response to shareholder criticism for having too few independent board members. A recent survey of 300 CFOs of U.S. public companies conducted by Protiviti Inc., a leading internal audit and business and technology risk consulting firm, indicated that 40 percent of the respondents reported there have been or will likely be changes in the makeup of their boards or board committees.[1]

In small U.S. firms, the largest stockholder typically holds the positions of president and chairperson of the board of directors. In large, publicly owned firms, the managers typically have some stock, but their personal holdings are generally too small to give them voting control. Thus, stockholders (acting through the directors) can remove the managers of most publicly owned firms if the management team is judged to be ineffective.

---

[1]"CFOs Name Top Sarbanes-Oxley Challenges," *Orlando Business Journal*, September 12, 2003, **http://orlando. bizjournals.com/orlando/stories/2003/09/08/daily51.html**.

THE SHIPPING NEWS

U.S. law forbids foreign ownership of cargo and passenger transportation companies that haul freight or people between U.S. cities. However, that restriction has been tested recently in U.S. court cases. American-owned-and-headquartered transportation companies FedEx (headquartered in Memphis, TN) and UPS (headquartered in Atlanta, GA) have a lot at stake as U.S. federal courts define the parameters of the ownership restrictions.

In 2001, Department of Transportation (DOT) officials refused to launch a formal investigation into the ownership structure of DHL Airways Inc. (now called Astar Air Cargo Inc.) or to revoke a license given to the company controlled by Deutsche Post. In April 2003, Congress, hoping to resolve the matter, forced the DOT to turn over the case to an administrative judge. In December 2003, Deutsche Post received a huge boost when a DOT administrative judge ruled that Astar was owned and controlled by U.S. citizens. The ruling allowed Astar to continue transporting packages for Deutsche Post.

Astar claimed that it was independent of DHL, despite relying on the DHL network for 90 percent of its revenues and using 38 of its 40 planes to carry DHL packages. FedEx and UPS insisted that Deutsche Post had illegal control over Astar, a claim rejected by the judge. The judge further cited that Astar was free to make personnel and pay decisions and to make acquisitions when needed. An investor group, led by former Northwest Airlines CEO John Dasburg, bought the remaining 95 percent stake in Astar from Deutsche Post in July 2003, giving the group exclusive ownership of Astar. However, FedEx and UPS have alleged that this transaction was a soft deal designed to deflect scrutiny of Deutsche Post's ownership of Astar. They note that the 95 percent stake of Astar was snapped up by the Dasburg group for only $57 million.

The ruling had further reaching implications as it could allow Deutsche Post's DHL Worldwide Express unit to narrow the gap between it and market leaders FedEx and UPS. With the U.S. package delivery sector generating nearly $50 billion a year, Astar is likely to step up its expansion plans in hopes of carving out a larger industry share. A company spokesperson indicated that it intended to increase U.S. deliveries by combining its operations with recently acquired Airborne Inc. (acquired in August 2003 for $1.05 billion). However, FedEx and UPS have not surrendered the fight yet and still hope to persuade DOT officials to strip Deutsche Post (a privatized German postal agency) of its freight-forwarding license, which would cripple its ground operations. The two rival companies found themselves in new territory as they banded together to stave off what they say is foreign competition. However, they must be careful in their efforts to derail Astar so as to avoid accusations of unfair competitive practices.

Together, FedEx and UPS account for nearly 75 percent of U.S. air and ground shipments, while the United States Postal Service has a market share of about 19 percent. Astar is left with only 6 percent of the U.S. market. Dasburg has claimed that the case had "taken an enormous toll" on his company and suggested that FedEx and UPS "get on about competing and not trying to rely on a technical rationale to try to put us out of business."

Source: "Deutsche Post Wins Victory Over U.S. Rivals UPS, FedEx," *The Wall Street Journal*, December 22, 2003, **http://www.wsj.com**.

During 2002 and 2003, the number of CEOs fired for poor performance or misconduct increased to record levels. Forced exits accounted for 39 percent of CEO departures in 2002, and while data are still being collected for 2003, it appears that performance-related departures rose to another record level. Some CEOs who resigned under pressure in 2003 included those of Delta, American Airlines, Raytheon, Kmart, Spiegel, Schering-Plough, Motorola, Boeing, and Freddie Mac. The NYSE's CEO, Richard Grasso, was fired after his huge retirement package became public. All this reinforced the drive for independent boards, for the removal of problem managers and board independence go hand in hand.

Preemptive Right
A provision in the corporate charter or bylaws that gives common stockholders the right to purchase, on a pro rata basis, new issues of common stock (or convertible securities).

THE PREEMPTIVE RIGHT Common stockholders often have the right, called the **preemptive right**, to purchase any additional shares issued by the firm. In most U.S. states, the preemptive right is automatically included in firms' corporate charters, but in some it is necessary to add it specifically to the charter. Preemptive rights are also found in companies in most countries around the world, especially in de markets and for the more established and broadly-owned companies.

The preemptive right enables current stockholders to maintain contro also prevents a wealth transfer from current to new stockholders. Selling n mon stock at a price below its market value dilutes a stock's price and wealth from current stockholders to those allowed to purchase the new shares. Therefore, if it were not for this safeguard, the company's management could issue a large number of additional shares and then buy them at a steep discount, thereby seizing control and stealing value from current stockholders. The preemptive right prevents such occurrences.

THE RIGHT TO RECEIVE DIVIDENDS   Many people do not realize that the corporate (or joint stock company) form of organization creates an entity that is a legal "person" separate from its shareholders. This means that the company itself owns the enterprise's assets and controls the earnings and cash flows generated by those assets. Such separation is beneficial in terms of the company's continuity even if its individual stockholders die, and it also facilitates stockholders' ability to transfer their shares to others. However, it also means that the shareholders have no inherent right to receive cash dividends unless and until the board of directors formally declares them. The directors, as representatives of the stockholders, have a fiduciary obligation to look after stockholders' welfare, but they have the sole authority to determine whether it is in the body of stockholders' best interests to plow earnings back into the company's operations or to pay them out as cash dividends. Thus, while shareholders may *expect* to receive cash dividends, the company is under no obligation to pay one if in the directors' view the money can be used more effectively in financing the firm's operations.

SELF-TEST QUESTIONS   Why might a company use classified stock?
What are the two primary reasons for the preemptive right?

MARKETS FOR COMMON STOCK

Closely Held Corporation
Owned by a few individuals who are typically associated with the firm's management.

Publicly Owned Corporation
Owned by a relatively large number of individuals who are not actively involved in the firm's management.

Some companies are so small that their common stocks are not actively traded; they are owned by only a few people, usually their managers. Such firms are **closely held**, or *privately owned*, **corporations**, and their stock is called *closely held stock*. In contrast, the shares of most larger companies are owned by a large number of investors, most of whom are not active in management. Such companies are called **publicly owned corporations**, and their stocks are called *publicly held stocks*.

Small countries typically have relatively few publicly traded stocks and just one stock market. Larger countries often have several different stock markets. For example, the United States has the New York Stock Exchange (NYSE), where the stocks of most large companies trade, the Nasdaq market, where many of the larger technology companies trade, the AMEX, where a number of smaller stocks trade, and a number of regional exchanges. In Europe there are a number of national exchanges, but there has also been a consolidation among exchanges in Amsterdam, Brussels, and Paris into the exchange known as Euronext. Companies whose stocks are traded on these exchanges must "list" their shares with the exchange and abide by the exchange's rules. These rules pertain to company size, number of shares outstanding, and other characteristics, and the principal purpose of these rules is to provide an active, liquid market in the listed stocks. The exchanges also have rules or otherwise can put pressure on firms regarding corporate governance to ensure that stockholders are not taken advantage of by managers. For example, in 2003 the

A CHRYSLER BY ANY OTHER NAME

In November 1998, DaimlerChrysler AG launched its shares on stock markets worldwide in the form of a Global Registered Share (GRS) certificate. At the time, this move was hailed as a landmark event for financial markets. Before the merger, shares of DaimlerBenz AG traded on the Frankfurt exchange and as an American Depository Receipt on the NYSE, with about 99 percent of its $777 million a day trading volume occurring in Germany. Likewise, Chrysler's shares traded on the NYSE and the Frankfurt exchange, with an overwhelming majority of trading on the NYSE. The average daily trading value was just under $100 million.

The new global share traded in 21 markets under the ticker DCX. However, trading activity for the GRS was not nearly as robust as expected. After six months of trading, DCX share prices were weak, with only 5 percent of the trading volume on the NYSE. Right after the DCX unveiling, average trading on the NYSE dropped to about $200 million and had fallen to about $100 million per day by February 1999. Meanwhile, trading on the Frankfurt exchange rose to over $1 billion per day, and by August 1999 Frankfurt accounted for 95 percent of DCX trading. What explains the clustering of trading on the Frankfurt exchange?

According to Professor Andrew Karolyi, of Ohio State University, the "winner market takes all" phenomenon leads traders to seek out the lowest-cost market. According to Karolyi's research, DCX's share price fell 10 percent (on a risk-adjusted basis) during this period. Weak share prices contributed to Standard and Poor's decision to drop Daimler-

Chrysler AG from its S&P 500 Index. Why has DCX had such weak price performance? Karolyi speculates that risk arbitrage trading around the merger talks and the flowback of shares to the Frankfurt exchange may have contributed to its poor performance.

Why use GRSs? The GRS offers a good alternative to an American Depository Receipt (ADR), which represents an ordinary share deposited with a custodial bank. Daimler's GRS is bilingual with English text on the left side (meeting U.S. and Canadian trading requirements) and German on the right side (meeting European and Asian requirements). The GRS also offers the benefits of registration, while the ADR had a mostly bearer share ownership base in Germany. GRS issuers also gain access to detailed shareholder identity information not available to many U.S. companies.

Karolyi does not expect the GRS market to completely replace the ADR market. In particular, companies from emerging markets will continue listing and raising capital in developed markets and will likely use ADRs as long as the market does not demand more operational efficiency. The GRS makes the most sense for more established global firms trying to gain full efficiency in their shareholder and capital structures across world financial markets.

Source: "DaimlerChrysler Global Registered Shares Make Weaker Show Than Expected," *Research Today,* February 2000, **http://fisher.osu.edu/researchtoday/rt3-1-daimler.htm.**

NYSE stipulated that to be listed on the NYSE, companies must have a majority of independent outside directors—people who are not employees or who otherwise do business with the company and who thus might be reluctant to question management's decisions as closely as they should. As mentioned earlier, General Electric and Disney are just two of the companies that recently changed their boards' composition to adhere to this rule.

The shares of some companies trade only in their home countries' markets, but the stocks of a number of large multinational firms trade in several markets. For example, DaimlerChrysler's stock trades on both the NYSE and the Frankfurt exchange. Originally, DaimlerBenz was listed on the NYSE as an **American Depository Receipt,** or **ADR,** which is a negotiable certificate, is issued by a bank, is denominated in dollars, and is traded on an exchange like the NYSE. ADRs represent underlying shares of a company that are held in trust by a foreign depository institution. While there are several types of ADRs, most (including those of DaimlerBenz) require financial results be reported in accordance with U.S. GAAP, along with registration with the

American Depository Receipt (ADR) A negotiable certificate, issued by a bank, denominated in dollars, and traded on an exchange like the NYSE; represents underlying shares of a company that are held in trust by a foreign depository institution.

SEC and compliance with its rules. While many companies would like to b[...] New York, they do not want to disclose all the information required by thes[...] hence do not apply to trade as an ADR. After the merger with Chrysler (whic[...] traded on the NYSE), DaimlerChrysler decided not to list in New York as an A[...] but instead used a relatively new instrument called a **Global Registered Share (GRS** Global Registered Shares trade electronically on a number of exchanges in the local host currencies. This relieves the need for the specialized certificates and depositories that characterize ADRs, but companies must still meet full registration requirements for electronic trading. However, GRS cannot be held in bearer form because of the nature of the trading system, so many foreign companies who traditionally have shares in bearer form find them less useful.

Stocks listed on multiple exchanges often trade "after hours" in different locations all around the world. Thus, if news regarding a given company breaks after its regular exchange has closed, someone may still be able to buy or sell its shares in an overseas market, for example, in Singapore, using electronic equipment and Asian representatives of a U.S. investment bank. Strictly national markets certainly exist, but markets are becoming increasingly integrated, especially for the large multinational firms. In addition, a true international euroequities market is developing rapidly.

In terms of shareholders' characteristics, institutional investors (including pension plans, mutual funds, insurance companies, and brokerage firms) own more than 60 percent of all publicly held common stocks in the United States. These institutions buy and sell relatively actively, hence they account for about 75 percent of all transactions. Thus, in the United States, institutional investors have an especially heavy influence on the prices of individual stocks.

Types of Stock Market Transactions

Stock market transactions are classified into three distinct types:

1. *Initial public offerings by privately held firms: the IPO market.* A number of years ago, the Coors Brewing Company, which was owned by the Coors family at the time, decided to sell some stock to raise capital needed for a major expansion program.[2] This type of transaction is called **going public**—whenever stock in a closely held corporation is offered to the public for the first time, the company is said to be going public. The market for stock that is just being offered to the public is called the **initial public offering (IPO) market.**

2. *Additional shares sold by established, publicly owned companies: the primary markets.* If Sound Systems International (SSI) decides to sell (or issue) an additional one million shares to raise new equity capital, this transaction would be said to occur in the **primary market.**[3]

3. *Trading in the outstanding shares of established, publicly owned companies: the secondary market.* SSI has 450 million common shares outstanding. If the owner of 100 shares sells his or her stock, the trade is said to have occurred in the **secondary market.** Thus, the market for outstanding shares, or *used shares*, is the secondary market. SSI receives no new money when sales occur in this market.

Global Registered Share (GRS) Share not held in bearer form that trades electronically on a number of exchanges in the local host currencies.

Going Public The act of selling stock to the public at large for the first time by a closely held corporation or its principal stockholders.

Initial Public Offering (IPO) Market The market in which firms "go public" by offering shares to the public for the first time.

Primary Market The market for new equity capital. Corporations receive money when sales occur in this market.

Secondary Market The market for outstanding shares. Corporations receive no new money when sales occur in this market.

---

[2]The stock Coors offered to the public was designated Class B, and it was nonvoting. The Coors family retained the founders' shares, called Class A stock, which carried full voting privileges. The company was large enough to obtain an NYSE listing, but at that time the Exchange had a requirement that listed common stocks must have full voting rights, which precluded Coors from obtaining an NYSE listing.

[3]SSI has 500 million shares authorized but only 450 million outstanding; thus, it has 50 million authorized but unissued shares. If it had no authorized but unissued shares, management could increase the authorized shares by obtaining stockholders' approval, which would generally be granted without any arguments.

Differentiate between closely held and publicly owned corporations.
Differentiate between primary and secondary markets.
What is meant by the term "going public"?
What is an IPO?

COMMON STOCK VALUATION: THE DIVIDEND APPROACH

Market Price, P_0
The price at which a stock sells in the market.

Intrinsic (Fundamental) Value, $\hat{P}_0$
The value of an asset that, in the mind of a particular investor, is justified by the facts; $\hat{P}_0$ may be different from the asset's current market price.

Dividend Growth Rate, g
The expected rate of growth in dividends per share.

Required Rate of Return, r_s
The minimum rate of return on a common stock that a stockholder considers acceptable.

Expected Total Rate of Return, $\hat{r}_s$
The rate of return on a common stock that a stockholder expects to receive in the future. It is equal to the sum of the expected dividend yield and the expected capital gains yield.

Common stock represents an ownership interest in a corporation, but to the typical investor a share of common stock is simply a piece of paper that entitles its owner to dividends, and it may be sold at some future date at a price different from the purchase price.

Definitions of Terms Used in Stock Valuation Models

Common stocks provide an expected future cash flow stream, and a stock's value, like other financial assets, is the present value of the expected future cash flow stream. The expected cash flows consist of two elements: (1) the dividends expected in each year and (2) the price investors expect to receive when they sell the stock. The expected final stock price includes the return of the original investment plus an expected capital gain. At this point we develop some models to help show how the value of a share of stock is determined. We begin by defining the follows terms:

D_t = dividend the stockholder expects to receive at the end of Year t. Note that D_0, the dividend that has just been paid, is known with certainty. However, all future dividends are expected values, so the estimate of D_t may differ among investors.[4]

P_0 = actual **market price** of the stock today.

$\hat{P}_0$ = expected price of the stock at the end of each Year t. $\hat{P}_0$ is the **intrinsic**, or **fundamental, value** of the stock today as seen by the particular investor doing the analysis.

g = expected **dividend growth rate** as predicted by the marginal investor.

r_s = minimum acceptable, or **required, rate of return** on the stock, considering both its risk and the returns available on other investments.

$\hat{r}_s$ = **expected total rate of return** that an investor who buys the stock expects to receive in the future. It is equal to the expected dividend yield (D_1/P_0) plus expected capital gains yield $[(\hat{P}_1 - P_0)/P_0]$.

$\bar{r}_s$ = **actual**, or **realized**, *after-the-fact* **rate of return**.

D_1/P_0 = **expected dividend yield** during the coming year.

$\dfrac{\hat{P}_1 - P_0}{P_0}$ = **expected capital gains yield** during the coming year.

Expected Dividends as the Basis for Stock Values

In Chapter 8, we found a bond's value as the present value of interest payments over the life of the bond plus the present value of the bond's maturity (or par) value:

---

[4]Stocks generally pay dividends quarterly, so theoretically we should evaluate them on a quarterly basis. However, in stock valuation, most analysts work on an annual basis because the data generally are not precise enough to warrant refinement to a quarterly model. For additional information on the quarterly model, see Charles M. Linke and J. Kenton Zumwalt, "Estimation Biases in Discounted Cash Flow Analysis of Equity Capital Cost in Rate Regulation," *Financial Management*, Autumn 1984, 15–21.

Actual (Realized) Rate of Return, $\bar{r}_s$
The rate of return on a common stock actually received by stockholders in some past period; $\bar{r}_s$ may be greater or less than $\hat{r}_s$ and/or r_s.

Expected Dividend Yield
The expected dividend divided by the current stock price.

Expected Capital Gains Yield
The expected increase or decrease in share value during the coming year divided by the beginning stock price.

$$V_B = \frac{INT/2}{(1 + r_d/2)^1} + \frac{INT/2}{(1 + r_d/2)^2} + \frac{INT/2}{(1 + r_d/2)^3} + \cdots + \frac{M}{(1 + r_d/2)^{2N}}.$$

Stock prices are likewise determined as the present value of a stream of cash flows, and the basic stock valuation equation is similar to the bond valuation equation. What are the cash flows that corporations provide to their stockholders? First, think of yourself as an investor who purchases a stock with the intention of holding it in your family forever. In this case, all that you (and your heirs) will receive is the stream of dividends, and the stock's value today is calculated as the present value of an infinite stream of dividends:

$$\text{Stock} = \hat{P}_0 = \text{PV of expected future dividends}$$

$$= \frac{D_1}{(1 + r_s)^1} + \frac{D_2}{(1 + r_s)^2} + \cdots + \frac{D_\infty}{(1 + r_s)^\infty}$$

$$= \sum_{t=1}^{\infty} \frac{D_t}{(1 + r_s)^t}. \tag{9-1}$$

What about the more typical case, in which you expect to hold the stock for a finite period and then sell it—what will be the value of $\hat{P}_0$ in this case? The stock's value is again determined by Equation 9-1. To see this, recognize that for any individual investor, the expected cash flows consist of expected dividends while the stock is held plus the stock's expected future sale price. However, the future price will depend on the dividends future investors expect to receive. Put another way, unless a firm is liquidated or sold to another firm, the cash flows it provides to its stockholders will consist only of a stream of dividends; hence, the value of a share of its stock must be the present value of that expected dividend stream.

SELF-TEST QUESTIONS

Explain the following statement: "Whereas a bond contains a promise to pay interest, a share of common stock typically provides an expectation of, but no promise of, dividends plus capital gains."

What is the definitional difference between a stock's expected return and its required return? What would happen if the two were different?

What are the two components of a stock's expected total return?

How does one calculate the capital gains yield? The dividend yield?

CONSTANT GROWTH STOCKS

Equation 9-1 is a generalized stock valuation model in the sense that the time pattern of D_t can by anything: D_t can be rising, falling, fluctuating randomly, or it can even be zero for several years, and Equation 9-1 will still hold. With a computer spreadsheet we can easily use this equation to find a stock's intrinsic value for any pattern of dividends. In practice, the most difficult part is getting an accurate forecast of the future dividends. However, in some cases, the stream of dividends is expected to grow at a constant long-run rate. If this is the case, Equation 9-1 may be rewritten as follows:[5]

---

[5]Equation 9-2 is derived in the Web Extension to Eugene F. Brigham and Phillip R. Daves, *Intermediate Financial Management*, 8th edition (Mason, OH: South-Western Publishing, 2004), Chapter 5.

$$P_0 = \frac{D_0(1 + g)^1}{(1 + r_s)^1} + \frac{D_0(1 + g)^2}{(1 + r_s)^2} + \cdots + \frac{D_0(1 + g)^\infty}{(1 + r_s)^\infty}$$

$$= D_0 \sum_{t=1}^{\infty} \frac{(1 + g)^t}{(1 + r_s)^t}$$

$$= \frac{D_0(1 + g)}{r_s - g} = \frac{D_1}{r_s - g}. \qquad (9\text{-}2)$$

Constant Growth (Gordon) Model
Used to find the value of a constant growth stock.

Equation 9-2 is called the **constant growth model**, or the **Gordon model** after Myron J. Gordon, who developed and helped to popularize it.

Note that a necessary condition for the derivation of Equation 9-2 is that r_s be greater than g; otherwise, the constant growth model gives an answer that is both wrong and misleading.

Illustration of a Constant Growth Stock

Assume that Atlantic Corporation just paid a dividend of $3.00 (i.e., D_0 = $3.00). Its stock has a required rate of return, r_s, of 10 percent, and investors expect the dividend to grow at a constant 4 percent rate in the future. The estimated dividend one year from now would be D_1 = $3.00(1.04) = $3.12, which is inserted into Equation 9-2 to find the stock's intrinsic value, $52.00:

$$\hat{P}_0 = \frac{\$3.00(1.04)}{0.10 - 0.04} = \frac{\$3.12}{0.06} = \$52.00.$$

The concept underlying the valuation process for a constant growth stock is graphed in Figure 9-1. Dividends are growing at the rate g = 4%, but because r_s, the rate used for discounting the dividends to the present (10 percent), is greater than g, the growth rate, the present value of each future dividend is declining. If we summed the present values of each future dividend, this summation would be the value of the stock, $\hat{P}_0$. Therefore, if we extended the lower step function curve in Figure 9-1 on out to infinity and added up the present values of each future dividend, the summation would be identical to the value given by Equation 9-2, $52.00.[6]

Although Equation 9-2 assumes that dividends grow to infinity, most of the value is based on dividends during a relatively short time period. In our example, 75.4 percent of the value is attributed to the first 25 years, 93.9 percent to the first 50 years, and 99.6 percent to the first 100 years. So, companies don't have to exist forever for the Gordon growth model to be valid.

When Can the Constant Growth Model Be Used?

For a constant growth stock, the following conditions must hold:

1. The dividend is expected to grow forever (or at least for a long time) at a constant rate, g.
2. The stock price is expected to grow at this same rate.
3. The expected dividend yield is constant.
4. The expected capital gains yield is also constant, and it is equal to g.

---

[6]The PV of each future dividend is $D_0[(1 + g)^t/(1 + r_s)^t]$. If g = r_s, then the term in the bracket is 1.0 for all values of t, in which case D_t = D_0. Then, the value of the stock would be the summation of an infinite number of dividends, which would of course be infinity, which is nonsense. Or, if g > r_s, then the bracketed term would be greater than 1.0, which would indicate that the PV of each dividend is larger than the prior one, which again indicates a nonsensical infinite price. Only if r_s > g do the PVs of the dividends decline, resulting in a price less than infinity.

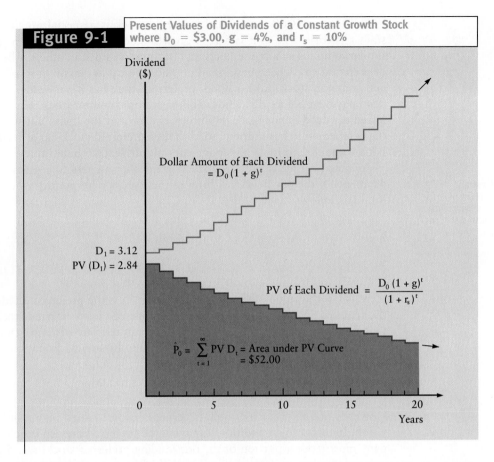

Figure 9-1 | Present Values of Dividends of a Constant Growth Stock where $D_0 = \$3.00$, $g = 4\%$, and $r_s = 10\%$

The constant growth model is often appropriate for mature companies with a history of stable growth. Growth in dividends occurs primarily as a result of growth in *earnings per share (EPS)*. Earnings growth, in turn, results from a number of factors, including (1) inflation, (2) the amount of earnings the company retains and reinvests, and (3) the rate of return the company earns on its equity (ROE).

Even though a stock's value is derived from expected dividends, this does not necessarily mean that corporations can increase their stock prices by simply raising the current dividend. Shareholders care about *all* dividends, both the current one and those expected in the future. As we will discuss in Chapter 13, there is a trade-off between current and future dividends.

Expected growth rates vary somewhat among companies and industries, but dividend growth for most mature firms is expected to continue in the future at about the same rate as nominal gross domestic product, or real GDP plus inflation. On this basis, we might expect the dividends of an average, or "normal," company to grow at a rate of 4 to 6 percent a year.

Note too that Equation 9-2 is sufficiently general to handle the case of a **zero growth stock**, where the dividend is expected to remain constant over time. If $g = 0$, Equation 9-2 reduces to Equation 9-3:

Zero Growth Stock
A common stock whose future dividends are not expected to grow at all; that is, $g = 0$.

$$\hat{P}_0 = \frac{D}{r_s}. \qquad (9\text{-}3)$$

This is the same as the equation for a *perpetuity,* and it is simply the dividend divided by the discount rate.

PREFERRED STOCK   Perpetual preferred stock is a special application of a constant growth stock, as it is a zero growth stock. Preferred stock is a *hybrid*—it is similar to bonds in some respects and to common stock in others. The hybrid nature of preferred stock becomes apparent when we try to classify it in relation to bonds and common stock. Like a bond, preferred stock has a par value and a fixed dividend payment before dividends can be paid on common stock. However, if the preferred dividend is not paid, the directors can omit (or "pass") it without throwing the company into bankruptcy. So, although preferred stock has a fixed payment like bonds, a failure to make this payment will not lead to bankruptcy.

As noted earlier, a preferred stock entitles its owners to regular, fixed dividend payments. If the payments last forever, the issue is a **perpetuity** whose value, V_{ps}, is found as follows:

Perpetuity
A stream of equal payments expected to continue forever.

$$V_{ps} = \frac{D_{ps}}{r_{ps}}. \qquad (9\text{-}4)$$

Here, V_{ps} is the value of the preferred stock, D_{ps} is the preferred dividend, and r_{ps} is the required rate of return on preferred stock. SSI has preferred stock outstanding that pays a dividend of $7 per year. If the required rate of return on this preferred stock is 7 percent, then its value is $100, found by solving Equation 9-4 as follows:

$$V_{ps} = \frac{\$7.00}{0.07} = \$100.00.$$

However, not all preferred stock is perpetual; some issues have a sinking fund provision. In this case, in addition to paying the preferred dividend each year, the company must retire a portion of the outstanding preferred stock, say, 5 percent of the original number of shares beginning in the fifth year after issue. This gives the preferred stock a finite life, and in our example the last of the preferred would be retired at the end of the 25th year. Sinking fund preferreds are valued much like bonds. Cash flows must be estimated, and they consist of dividend payments plus the periodic sinking fund payments over the security's life. By applying the appropriate required return, we can find the value of a sinking fund preferred stock. Alternatively, if we know the price, we can solve for the rate of return that investors expect on the preferred.

SELF-TEST QUESTIONS

Write out and explain the constant growth stock valuation formula.

Explain how the equation for a zero growth stock is related to the one for a constant growth stock.

Does the constant growth model assume that companies exist forever? Is this assumption necessary or might the equation give reasonably good results even if the company has a shorter life, say, 75 years, rather than infinity?

What conditions aside from a long life must hold if a stock is to be evaluated using the constant growth model?

What does the term "expected" mean when we say "expected growth rate"?

VALUING NONCONSTANT GROWTH STOCKS

For many companies, it is *not* appropriate to assume that dividends will grow at a constant rate. Firms typically go through *life cycles*. During the early part of their lives, their growth is much faster than that of the economy as a whole; then they match the economy's growth; and finally their growth drops below that of the economy.[7] Automobile manufacturers in the 1920s, computer software firms such as Microsoft in the 1990s, and biotech firms such as Genentech in the 2000s are examples of firms in the early part of the cycle; these are **nonconstant**, or **supernormal**, **growth** firms.

Because Equation 9-2 requires a constant growth rate, we obviously cannot use it to value stocks that have nonconstant growth. However, assuming that a company is currently enjoying a supernormal growth rate, g_s, but it will eventually slow down to a normal (constant) growth rate, g_n, we can combine Equations 9-1 and 9-2 to form Equation 9-5. In that equation, we assume that the dividend will grow at the nonconstant rate (generally a relatively high rate) for N periods, after which it will grow at a constant rate, g_n. N is often called the **terminal date**, or **horizon date**.

We can use a modified version of the constant growth formula, Equation 9-2a, to determine what the stock's **terminal**, or **horizon**, **value** will be N periods from today:

$$\text{Terminal value} = TV_N = \frac{D_{N+1}}{r_s - g_n} = \frac{D_N(1 + g_n)}{r_s - g_n}. \tag{9-2a}$$

The stock's intrinsic value today, $\hat{P}_0$, is the present value of the dividends during the nonconstant growth period plus the present value of the terminal value:

$$\hat{P}_0 = \frac{D_1}{(1 + r_s)^1} + \frac{D_2}{(1 + r_s)^2} + \cdots + \frac{D_N}{(1 + r_s)^N} + \frac{TV_N}{(1 + r_s)^N}. \tag{9-5}$$

To implement Equation 9-5, we go through the following four steps:

1. Find the expected dividend during each year of the nonconstant growth period. Note that growth during this period out to N could be constant, but at a rate different from the long-run normal rate, or it could vary in any manner from year to year.
2. Find the PV of the dividends during the nonconstant growth period.
3. Find the stock price at the end of the nonconstant growth period (terminal value), at which point it has become a constant growth stock, and discount this price back to the present.
4. Add these two components to find the stock's intrinsic value, $\hat{P}_0$.

Figure 9-2 illustrates the process for valuing nonconstant growth stocks using data on SSI. The company is not expected to pay a dividend until five years from now, when it is expected to pay an initial dividend of $1.10. After that time, the dividend is expected to grow at a constant rate of 7.5 percent indefinitely. If we assume that investors require an 11 percent rate of return on the stock, what is the intrinsic value of SSI's stock?

The valuation process diagrammed in Figure 9-2 is explained in the steps set forth below the time line. The value of SSI's stock, which is a nonconstant growth stock, is calculated at $20.70.

Nonconstant (Supernormal) Growth
The part of the firm's life cycle in which it grows differently from the economy as a whole.

Terminal Date (Horizon Date)
The date when the growth rate becomes constant. At this date it is no longer necessary to forecast individual dividends.

Terminal (Horizon) Value
The value at the horizon date of all dividends expected thereafter.

[7]The concept of life cycles could be broadened to *product cycle*, which would include both small startup companies and large companies such as Procter & Gamble, which periodically introduce new products that give sales and earnings a boost. We should also mention *business cycles*, which alternately depress and boost sales and profits. The growth just after a major new product has been introduced, or just after a firm emerges from the depths of a recession, is likely to be much higher than the "expected long-run average growth rate," which is the proper number for a DCF analysis.

Figure 9-2	Process for Finding the Value of SSI's Nonconstant Growth Stock

Notes to Figure 9-2:

Step 1: Calculate the dividends expected at the end of each year during the nonconstant growth period. Because the dividends during the first four years are zero, $D_1 = D_2 = D_3 = D_4 = 0$. We know that $D_5 = \$1.10$. We must also calculate D_6 because that dividend is needed to calculate the terminal value for Step 2. $D_6 = D_5(1 + g) = \$1.10(1.075) = \$1.18250$. These values are shown on the time line. Note that D_0 is used only to calculate D_1, and D_6 is used only to calculate $\widehat{TV}_5$ in the next step. Note also that we could have begun with a positive dividend and had a growth rate or rates from $t = 0$ to N.

Step 2: After D_5 has been paid, which is at $t = 5$, SSI will be a constant growth stock. Therefore, we can use the constant growth formula to find $\widehat{TV}_5$, which is the PV of the dividends from $t = 6$ to infinity as evaluated at $t = 5$. First, we determine $D_6 = \$1.10(1.075) = \$1.18250$ for use in the formula, and then we calculate $\widehat{TV}_5$ as follows:

$$\widehat{TV}_5 = \frac{D_6}{r_s - g_n} = \frac{\$1.18250}{0.11 - 0.075} = \$33.78571.$$

We show this $33.78571 on the time line as a second cash flow at $t = 5$. The $33.78571 is a $t = 5$ cash flow in the sense that the owner of the stock could sell it for $33.78571 at $t = 5$ and also in the sense that $33.78571 is the present value of the dividend cash flows from $t = 6$ to infinity. Note that the total cash flow at $t = 5$ consists of the sum of $D_5 + \widehat{TV}_5 = \$1.10000 + \$33.78571 = \$34.88571$.

Step 3: Now that the cash flows have been placed on the time line, we can discount each of them at the required rate of return, $r_s = 11\%$. We could discount each cash flow by dividing by $(1.11)^t$, where $t = 1$ for Time 1, $t = 2$ for Time 2, $t = 3$ for Time 3, and so on. This produces the PVs shown to the left below the time line, and the sum of the PVs is the value of this nonconstant growth stock, $20.70.

With a financial calculator, you can find the PV of the cash flows as shown on the time line with the cash flow (CFLO) register of your calculator. Enter 0 for CF_0 because you receive no cash flow at Time 0, $CF_1 = 0$, $CF_2 = 0$, $CF_3 = 0$, $CF_4 = 0$, and $CF_5 = 1.10000 + 33.78571 = 34.88571$. Then enter I = 11, and press the NPV key to find the value of the stock, $20.70. The calculations are even easier, and more transparent, using an *Excel* spreadsheet.

The discounted dividend model is straightforward and logical, and it is widely employed in practice. However, an alternative model that focuses on free cash flows is also available, and it is superior for some purposes. We discuss the free cash flow model in the next section.

SELF-TEST QUESTIONS

Explain how to find a nonconstant growth stock's value.

Could the nonconstant growth model be applied to both companies that currently pay dividends and companies that do not pay dividends?

What is the "terminal (horizon) value" as that term is used in stock valuation?

CORPORATE VALUATION MODEL: VALUING FREE CASH FLOWS

The dividend growth model depends on future dividend payments, whether the firm currently pays dividends or not. However, startup companies, and even many established firms, pay no dividends, and in some of these cases, the company is likely to be sold to another firm and thus never pay a dividend. Similarly, many large companies consist of many different divisions, and at times it is necessary to value these units. For example, the firm may be thinking of selling a division, or perhaps buying a division from another firm. Because divisions do not pay dividends per se and have no quoted price, the discounted dividend model cannot be used to value them. Thus, there are situations where the dividend growth model is of little practical use.

In situations such as those described, and even where dividends are paid but future payments are difficult to forecast, the **corporate valuation model**, which discounts free cash flows rather than dividends, may yield more reliable results. Moreover, even if dividends can be forecasted, it is useful to have an alternative valuation procedure, because any forecast can be wrong and more information is generally better than less. For these reasons, the corporate valuation model is an important and useful tool.

Corporate Valuation Model Discounts a firm's free cash flows rather than its dividends in order to value the firm.

Estimating the Value of Operations

The first step in implementing the model is to forecast pro forma financial statements for the next few years; five years is a commonly used period. These forecasted statements are valuable because they provide an estimate of profitability (NOPAT) and the required investment in operating capital, and they also provide information that can be used to make ratios and thus evaluate the firm's risk.[8] Table 9-1 summarizes information from SSI's pro forma statements related to expected operating

TABLE 9-1 | SSI Free Cash Flow Data

Inputs for FCF valuation

Long-run FCF growth rate g	5.75%				
WACC	8.76%				

Calculation of free cash flow

	2004	2005	2006	2007	2008
NOPAT		$ 623.7	$ 925.3	$1,180.2	$ 1,300.1
Req'd net operating working capital	$1,917.9	$2,084.8	$2,243.0	$2,471.8	$ 2,656.6
Req'd net plant and equipment	$4,724.5	$5,538.5	$6.237.5	$6,926.0	$ 7,577.0
Req'd total net operating capital*	$6,642.4	$7,623.3	$8,480.5	$9,397.8	$10,233.6
Less: Investment in operating capital		$ 980.9	$ 857.2	$ 917.3	$ 835.8
Free cash flow		−$ 357.2	$ 68.1	$ 262.9	$ 464.3

Terminal value (2008) = $16,312.6

Determining intrinsic value per share

Value of operations	$11,923.9
+ Nonoperating assets	$ 0.0
Total firm value	$11,923.9
− BV of notes payable	$ 452.6
− BV of long-term debt**	$ 1,813.9
− BV of preferred stock	$ 500.0
Value of common equity	$ 9,157.4
÷ Number of shares	450
Intrinsic value per share	$ 20.35

*Asset requirement forecasts combine quantitative data (sales forecasts, asset-to-sales ratios, etc.) with qualitative data from managers (production capacity, efficiency, etc.) to estimate required capital.

**Long-term debt here includes long-term debt plus current maturities of long-term debt on the balance sheet.

[8]For a review of financial forecasting, refer to Chapter 8 of Brigham and Daves, *Intermediate Financial Management*.

profits and required capital investment. SSI forecasts a sharp increase in NOPAT from 2005 to 2006, and substantial but less dramatic increases for the following two years. The higher NOPAT is due to a projected increase in sales, combined with continued benefits from cost-cutting measures. However, the firm will need new investments in working capital and fixed assets. Free cash flow is equal to NOPAT minus the required investment in operating assets, and the FCF forecast is summarized in Table 9-1. We see that SSI forecasts a negative FCF for 2005 but substantial positive FCFs in the following years.

Recall that free cash flow (FCF) is the cash from operations that is actually available for distribution to all investors: common and preferred stockholders and bondholders. The value of operations is defined as the present value of the forecasted future free cash flows, discounted at the WACC, and the total corporate value is the value of operations plus the value of any nonoperating assets. However, SSI's financial statements indicate that the firm does not hold any nonoperating assets.[9] Here is the equation for the value of operations, which is the firm's value as a going concern:

$$\text{Value of operations} = V_{OP} = \text{PV of expected FCFs}$$
$$= \sum_{t=1}^{\infty} \frac{FCF_t}{(1 + WACC)^t}. \tag{9-6}$$

SSI's cost of capital is 8.76 percent, so to find its value of operations we use an approach similar to the nonconstant dividend growth model, proceeding as follows:

1. The firm is expected to experience nonconstant growth in FCF for N years, after which FCF will grow at a constant rate.
2. Calculate the expected FCF for each of the N nonconstant growth years.
3. Recognize that after Year N growth will be constant, so we can use the constant growth formula to find the firm's terminal value at Year N. This is the sum of the PVs for all years past N, discounted back to Year N.
4. Find the PV of the FCF for each of the N nonconstant growth years, the PV of the terminal value, and then add those PVs to find the value of the firm's operations.

In Table 9-1 we see that SSI's long-run constant FCF growth rate is 5.75 percent and its WACC is 8.76 percent. The table also shows that SSI expects to begin 2005 with $6,642.4 million in operating capital and to have investment requirements of an additional $980.9 million. Because the company expects to generate only $623.7 million of NOPAT in 2005, the forecasted FCF for that year is −$357.2 million. This shortfall must be made up by investors in the form of debt, equity, or some combination. Negative free cash flow is obviously not good, but it is typical for young, high-growth firms and for firms in periods where they are undertaking major capital projects.

Having calculated free cash flow for the next four years, we next use Equation 9-7 to calculate the terminal value as of 2008, which is Year N in the formula:

$$\text{Terminal value} = TV_N = \frac{FCF_{N+1}}{WACC - g_n}. \tag{9-7}$$

---

[9]If the firm carried nonoperating assets such as short-term marketable securities on its balance sheet, the value of those nonoperating assets would be added to the value of operations.

With an 8.76 percent cost of capital, $464.3 million of free cash flow in 2008, and a 5.75 percent growth rate, the terminal value of SSI's operations as of December 31, 2008, is forecasted at $16,312.6 million:

$$\text{SSI's terminal value}_{(12/31/08)} = \frac{\text{FCF}_{(12/31/08)}(1 + g_n)}{\text{WACC} - g_n} = \frac{\text{FCF}_{(12/31/09)}}{\text{WACC} - g_n}$$

$$= \frac{\$464.31(1 + 0.0575)}{0.0876 - 0.0575} = \frac{\$491.01}{0.0301}$$

$$= \$16,312.55 \approx \$16,312.6.$$

This $16,312.6 million is the company's terminal, or horizon, value, because it is the firm's value at the end of the forecast period. It is the amount that SSI could expect to receive if it sold its operating assets on December 31, 2008. The terminal value is added to the $464.31 million of FCF in 2008 to obtain the imputed total cash flow in 2008.

Table 9-1 shows the free cash flow for each year of the nonconstant growth period, along with the terminal value in 2008. We next discount all of the cash flows at the 8.76 percent cost of capital. Remember, the 2008 cash flow has two components: (1) the annual free cash flow and (2) the terminal value as of 2008. The sum of the PVs is approximately $11,923.9 million, and it represents an estimate of the price SSI could expect to receive if it sold its operating assets today, in 2004.

Estimating the Intrinsic Value per Share

Since SSI has only operating assets, its total value is simply the value of its operations. To determine the value of the common equity, the sum of notes payable, long-term debt, and preferred stock must be deducted from the total firm value.[10] Referring to the 2004 balance sheet (detailed in Table 6-2 but summarized in Table 9-1), we see that SSI has $452.6 million of notes payable, $1,813.9 million of long-term debt, and $500 million of preferred stock, or $2,766.5 million in total.[11] Thus, the value of the common equity is $9,157.4 million:

$$\text{Value of SSI's equity} = \$11,923.9 - \$2,766.5 = \$9,157.4 \text{ million.}$$

SSI has 450 million shares of common stock outstanding, so the value per share as estimated by the free cash flow model is $9,157.4/450 = $20.35. This is close to the $20.70 value found using the discounted dividend model. The two valuations should be close, and they will be if the same underlying assumptions are used in both estimations, but if the assumptions are not coordinated, then wide divergences can occur. When significant differences arise, it might be best to give more weight to the FCF model's results because it is generally based on a more detailed set of assumptions and calculations, hence has greater transparency.

SELF-TEST QUESTIONS

How can stocks that do not pay dividends be valued?
Why might someone use the corporate valuation model instead of the dividend model?
What are the steps for finding a firm's total value?

---

[10]Accounts payable and accrued liabilities are not subtracted from firm value because they were deducted when we estimated the FCF. They are not investor-supplied capital and were deducted from current operating assets when we found the required investment in net operating working capital.

[11]Rather than subtracting the book values of debt and preferred stock, it would be theoretically better to subtract their market values. However, the book values of fixed-income securities are generally close to their market values, and that permits us to simplify the process and work with book values.

RELATIVE VALUATION: MARKET MULTIPLE ANALYSIS

Market Multiple Analysis
A method used for valuing companies that applies market-determined multiples to net income, earnings per share, sales, book value, and so forth.

A third procedure used to value stocks is the **market multiple analysis**, in which we apply market-determined multiples to net income, earnings per share, sales, book value, or, for businesses such as cable TV or cellular telephone systems, the number of subscribers. While the discounted dividend and free cash flow methods apply the valuation equation in a direct manner, the market multiple method assumes that some specific number is the key driver of value, that the market has somehow correctly valued a number of similar firms, and that the driver variable for the company under study can be estimated and then used in conjunction with the multiple of the other firms to find our firm's value. To illustrate, suppose the company to be valued has forecasted earnings per share of $2.00 for 2005. If the average P/E ratio for a group of similar publicly traded companies is 12, we would multiply the $2 of earnings by the 12 market multiple to obtain a value per share of $2.00(12) = $24.00.

Note that measures other than net income can be used in the market multiple approach. For example, another commonly used measure is *earnings before interest, taxes, depreciation, and amortization (EBITDA)*. The EBITDA multiple is the total value of a company (the market value of equity plus debt) divided by EBITDA. This multiple is based on total value, since EBITDA measures the entire firm's performance. Therefore, it is called an **entity multiple**. To find the company's estimated stock price per share, subtract debt from total value and then divide by the number of shares of common stock.

Entity Multiple
A multiple based on total value; it is a measure of the entire firm.

As noted earlier, some early-stage, developing businesses (including cable TV, cellular telephone, and HMOs), before they had positive cash flows or dividends, were valued on the basis of number of customers, and Internet companies were valued by the number of "eyeballs," or hits on the Web site. For example, telephone companies in the late 1990s paid about $2,000 per customer when acquiring cellular operators. This valuation procedure can make sense, but only if one has an idea about how much profit and cash flow a customer will provide once the company stabilizes. This last stage was omitted, or at least not analyzed in a reasonable manner, when some of the dot-com companies were appraised, and the result contributed to the huge tech stock bubble of the late 1990s.

The market multiple method can be useful for firms trying to value foreign operations, which are often nearly impossible to value directly. In these cases, firms can employ relative valuation techniques, such as using barrels of oil produced to value oil-drilling projects.

SELF-TEST QUESTIONS

What is market multiple analysis?
What is an entity multiple?
When are market multiple (or relative valuation) techniques most useful?

STOCK MARKET EQUILIBRIUM

Recall that r_i, the required return on Stock i, can be found using the Security Market Line (SML) equation as it was developed in the Capital Asset Pricing Model (CAPM) section of Chapter 5:

$$r_i = r_{RF} + (r_M - r_{RF})b_i.$$

The expected rate of return on Stock i is equal to its expected dividend yield plus its expected capital gains yield:

$$\hat{r}_i = \frac{D_1}{P_0} + \frac{P_1 - P_0}{P_0}.$$

Marginal Investor
A representative investor whose actions reflect the beliefs of those people who are currently trading a stock. It is the marginal investor who determines a stock's price.

Equilibrium
The condition under which the expected return on a security is just equal to its required return, $\hat{r}_i$ = r_i. Also, $\hat{P}_0$ = P_0, and the price is stable.

The **marginal investor** will be willing to buy Stock i if its expected return is greater than its required return, will want to sell it if the expected rate of return is less than the required return, and will be indifferent, hence will hold but not buy or sell, if the expected rate of return equals the required return. The third situation is defined as an **equilibrium**, and it requires that two related conditions hold:

1. The stock's expected rate of return as seen by the marginal investor must equal its required rate of return: $\hat{r}_i = r_i$.
2. The stock's actual market price must equal its intrinsic value as estimated by the marginal investor: $P_0 = \hat{P}_0$.

Of course, some individual investors may believe that $\hat{r}_i > r$ and $\hat{P}_0 > P_0$, hence they are willing to purchase the stock, while other investors with equal buying power have an opposite view and are willing to sell their shares. However, it is the marginal investor who establishes the actual market price, and for this investor, we must have $\hat{r}_i = r_i$ and $P_0 = \hat{P}_0$. If these conditions do not hold, trading will occur and the stock's price will adjust until they do hold.

Changes in Equilibrium Stock Prices

Stock prices are not constant—they undergo violent changes at times. For example, on September 17, 2001, the first day of trading after the September 11 terrorist attacks, the Dow Jones average dropped 685 points. This was the largest decline ever for the Dow, but not the largest percentage loss, which was −22.6 percent on October 19, 1987. The Dow has also had some spectacular increases. In fact, its fifth largest increase was 368 points on September 24, 2001, a few days after its largest-ever decline. The Dow's largest increase ever was 499 points on April 16, 2000, and its largest percentage gain of 15.4 percent occurred on March 15, 1933. We see, then, that the United States stock market is volatile, but volatility in the U.S. pales in comparison to that seen in developing markets, where 100 percent annual gains and 50 percent losses are commonplace.

Stock price changes are the result of changes in expected future dividends and/or the required rate of return. What might cause investors to change their expectations about future dividends, that is, the growth rate built into the valuation equation? It could be new information about the company, such as preliminary results of an R&D program, the initial sales of a new product, or the discovery of harmful side effects from the use of an existing product. Or, new information that will affect many companies could arrive, such as a tightening of interest rates by the Federal Reserve or another terrorist attack. Given the existence of computers and telecommunications networks, new information hits the market on an almost continuous basis rather than trickling in slowly, and it causes frequent and sometimes large changes in stock prices. In other words, *the increasingly rapid dissemination of information has contributed to increased stock price volatility.*[12]

If a stock's price is stable, that probably means that little new information is coming into the market. But if you think it's risky to invest in a volatile stock, imagine how risky it would be to invest in a stock that rarely released new information about its sales or operations! It may be bad to see your stock's price jump around, but it would be a lot worse to see a stable quoted price most of the time but then see huge moves on the rare days when new information was released. Fortunately, in our

---

[12]Actually, improved communications may have changed the nature rather than the absolute level of market volatility. With poorer communication of relevant information, price changes are small until pent-up news hits, and then the stock's price undergoes a very large change. Better communication can lead to many smaller fluctuations. The situation here is a bit like earthquakes, where a series of small quakes can relieve pressures and prevent a catastrophic quake.

economy timely information is readily available, and evidence suggests that stocks in developed markets, especially those of large companies, adjust rapidly to new information. Consequently, equilibrium ordinarily exists for any given stock, and required and expected returns are generally equal. Stock prices certainly change, sometimes violently and rapidly, but this simply reflects changing conditions and expectations. There are, of course, times when a stock appears to react for several months to favorable or unfavorable developments. However, this does not signify a long adjustment period; rather, it simply indicates that as new pieces of information about the situation become available, the market adjusts to them, and that investors' perceptions can evolve. The market's ability to adjust to new information is discussed in the next section.

The Efficient Markets Hypothesis

Efficient Markets Hypothesis (EMH)
The hypotheses that securities are typically in equilibrium—that they are fairly priced in the sense that the price reflects all publicly available information on each security.

A body of theory called the **efficient markets hypothesis (EMH)** asserts (1) that stocks are always in equilibrium and (2) that it is impossible for an investor to consistently "beat the market." Essentially, those who believe in the EMH note that there are 100,000 or so full-time, highly trained, professional analysts and traders operating in the market, while there are fewer than 3,000 major stocks. Therefore, if each analyst followed 30 stocks (which is about right, as analysts tend to specialize in the stocks of a specific industry), there would be, on average, 1,000 analysts following each stock. In addition, SEC disclosure requirements and electronic information networks generally allow these 1,000 analysts to receive and evaluate new information at about the same time. Therefore, a stock's price will adjust almost immediately to any new development. This being the case, stocks should always either be in equilibrium or move into equilibrium quite rapidly.

LEVELS OF MARKET EFFICIENCY   If markets are efficient, stock prices will rapidly reflect all available information. This raises an important question: What types of information are available and thus incorporated into stock prices? Financial theorists have discussed three forms, or levels, of market efficiency.

1. *Weak-form efficiency.* All information relating to past events is fully reflected in current market prices. If this were true, then information about recent trends in stock prices would be of no use in selecting stocks.
2. *Semistrong-form efficiency.* Current market prices reflect all *publicly available* information. Therefore, if semistrong-form efficiency exists, it would do no good to pore over annual reports or other published data because market prices would have adjusted to any good or bad news contained in such reports as soon as the news was released.
3. *Strong-form efficiency.* Current market prices reflect all pertinent information, whether publicly available or privately held. If strong-form efficiency holds, even insiders would find it impossible to earn consistently abnormal returns in the stock market.[13]

Implications of Market Efficiency

What bearing does the EMH have on financial decisions? Because stock prices do seem to reflect public information, most stocks appear to be fairly valued. This does not mean that new developments could not cause a stock's price to soar or to plummet, but it does mean that stocks generally are neither overvalued nor undervalued—

---

[13]Several cases of illegal insider trading have made the headlines, as well as the Enron, WorldCom, and other scandals that were reported in 2001 and 2002. These cases involved employees of several corporations and major investment banking houses, and even an employee of the SEC. In one famous case during the 1980s, Ivan Boesky admitted to making $50 million by purchasing the stocks of firms he knew were about to be acquired. He went to jail, and he had to pay a large fine, but he did help disprove the strong-form EMH.

they are fairly priced and in equilibrium. However, there are certainly situations where corporate insiders have information not known to outsiders.

If the EMH is correct, it is a waste of time for most of us to analyze stocks by looking for those that are undervalued. If stock prices already reflect all publicly available information, and hence are fairly priced, we can "beat the market" consistently only by luck, and it is difficult, if not impossible, for anyone to consistently outperform the market averages. Empirical tests have shown that the weak form of the EMH is valid, and the semistrong form is also valid, at least for the larger companies that are followed by a number of analysts. However, people such as corporate officers, who have inside information, can do better than the averages, and individuals and organizations that are especially good at digging out information on small, new companies also seem to do consistently well. Also, some investors may be able to analyze and react more quickly than others to releases of new information, and these investors may have an advantage over others. However, the buy–sell actions of those investors quickly bring market prices into equilibrium, so it is generally safe to assume that $\hat{r}_i = r$, that $\hat{P}_0 = P_0$, and that stocks plot on the SML.[14]

Is the Stock Market Efficient?

Over the past 25 years or so, many empirical studies have been conducted to test the validity of the three forms of market efficiency. Up until about 10 years ago, most of these studies suggested that the stock market was highly efficient in the weak form and reasonably efficient in the semistrong form, at least for the larger and more widely followed stocks. However, most evidence also suggested that the strong form of the EMH did not hold, because those who possessed inside information could and did (illegally) make abnormal profits.

More recently, the empirical support for the EMH has been somewhat diminished. Skeptics point to the recent stock market bubble and suggest that at the height of the boom, the prices of many companies (particularly in the technology sector) vastly exceeded their intrinsic values. These skeptics suggest that investors are not simply machines who rationally process all available information—rather, a variety of psychological and, perhaps, irrational factors also come into play. Indeed, researchers in **behavioral finance** have begun to use elements of cognitive psychology in an effort to better understand how individuals and entire markets respond to different circumstances.[15]

Behavioral Finance
Incorporates elements of cognitive psychology into finance in an effort to better understand how individuals and entire markets respond to different circumstances.

---

[14]Market efficiency also has important implications for managerial decisions, especially those pertaining to issuing and repurchasing common stock. Stocks are generally fairly valued, so decisions based on the premise that a stock is undervalued or overvalued should be approached with caution. However, managers do have better information about their own companies than outsiders, and this information can legally be used to the companies' (but not the managers') advantage.

We should also note that some Wall Street pros have beaten the market over many years, which is inconsistent with the EMH. An interesting article in the April 3, 1995, issue of *Fortune* (Terence P. Paré, "Yes, You Can Beat the Market") argued strongly against the EMH. Paré suggested that each stock has a fundamental value, but when good or bad news about it is announced, most investors fail to interpret that news correctly. As a result, stocks are generally priced above or below their long-term values.

Think of a graph with stock price on the vertical axis and years on the horizontal axis. A stock's fundamental value might be moving up steadily over time as it retains and reinvests earnings. However, its actual price might fluctuate about the intrinsic value line, overreacting to good or bad news and indicating departures from equilibrium. Successful value investors, according to the article, use fundamental analysis to identify stocks' intrinsic values and then buy stocks that are undervalued and sell those that are overvalued.

Paré's argument implies that the market is systematically out of equilibrium, and that investors can act on this knowledge to beat the market. That position may turn out to be correct, but it may also be that the superior performance Paré noted simply demonstrates that some people are better at obtaining and interpreting information than others, or have just had a run of good luck.

[15]Three noteworthy sources for students interested in behavioral finance are Richard H. Thaler, editor, *Advances in Behavioral Finance* (New York: Russell Sage Foundation, 1993); Andrei Shleifer, *Inefficient Markets: An Introduction to Behavioral Finance* (New York: Oxford University Press, 2000); and Nicholas Barberis and Richard Thaler, "A Survey of Behavioral Finance," a National Bureau of Economic Research working paper, forthcoming in *Handbook of the Economics of Finance*, George Constantinides, Milt Harris, and Rene Stulz, editors, part of the Handbooks in Economics Series (Elsevier/North-Holland). Students interested in learning more about the efficient markets hypothesis should consult Burton G. Malkiel, *A Random Walk Down Wall Street* (New York: W.W. Norton & Company, 1999).

Keep in mind that the EMH does not assume that all investors are rational. Rather, it assumes that whenever stock prices deviate from their intrinsic values due to the availability of new information, investors quickly take advantage of these mispricings by purchasing undervalued stocks and selling overvalued stocks. Thus, investors' actions work to drive prices to their equilibrium level. EMH critics stress, however, that the stock market is inherently risky and that rational investors trading in an irrational market can lose a lot of money even if they are ultimately proven to be correct. For example, a "rational" investor in mid-1999 might have concluded that the Nasdaq was overvalued when it was trading at 3,000. If that investor had acted on that assumption, he or she would have lost a lot of money the following year when the Nasdaq soared to over 5,000 as "irrational exuberance" pushed the prices of already overvalued stocks to even higher levels. Ultimately, if our "rational investor" had the courage, patience, and wherewithal to hold on, he or she would have been vindicated, because the Nasdaq later fell to about 1,300.

The events of recent years, and the studies of researchers in behavioral finance, indicate with hindsight that the stock market is not always efficient. Still, the logic behind the EMH is compelling, and most researchers believe that markets are generally efficient in the long run. Thus, for our purposes, it is generally safe to assume that $\hat{r} = r$, that $\hat{P}_0 = P_0$, and that stocks plot on the SML.

SELF-TEST QUESTIONS
For a stock to be in equilibrium, what two conditions must hold?
What is the efficient markets hypothesis (EMH)?
If a stock is not in equilibrium, explain how financial markets adjust to bring it into equilibrium.
What are the differences among the three forms of the EMH, that is, (1) weak form, (2) semistrong form, and (3) strong form?
What are the implications of the EMH for financial decisions?
What is behavioral finance?
Is the stock market efficient? Explain your answer.

STOCK MARKETS AND RETURNS

Our discussion thus far has focused on *expected* stock prices and *expected* rates of return. Anyone who has ever invested in the stock market knows that there can be, and generally are, large differences between *expected* and *realized* prices and returns.

Figure 9-3 shows how total realized portfolio returns have varied from year to year. The market trend has been strongly up, but it has gone up in some years and down in others, and the stocks of individual companies have likewise gone up and down.[16] We know from theory that expected returns, as estimated by a marginal investor, are always positive, but in some years, as Figure 9-3 shows, actual returns are negative. Of course, even in bad years some individual companies do well, so "the name of the game" in security analysis is to pick the winners. Financial managers attempt to put their companies into the winners' column, but they don't always succeed. In subsequent chapters, we will examine the decisions managers make to increase the odds of their firms performing well in the marketplace.

[16]If we constructed a graph like Figure 9-3 for individual stocks rather than for a large portfolio, far greater variability would be shown. Also, if we constructed a graph like Figure 9-3 for bonds, it would have the same general shape, but the bars would be smaller, indicating that gains and losses on bonds are generally smaller than those on stocks. Above-average bond returns occur in years when interest rates decline, losses occur when interest rates rise sharply, and interest payments further stabilize bonds' total returns.

Figure 9-3   S&P 500 Index, Total Returns: Dividend Yield + Capital Gain or Loss, 1968–2003

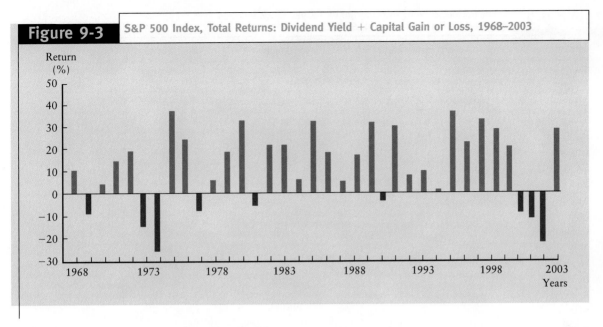

Source: Adapted from data derived from various issues of *The Wall Street Journal*, "Investment Scoreboard" section.

Investing in International Stocks

The U.S. stock market amounts to only about 40 percent of the world stock market, and most U.S. investors hold at least some foreign stocks. Analysts have for years touted the benefits of investing overseas, arguing that foreign stocks provide both diversification and solid growth opportunities. For example, after the U.S. stock market rose an average of 17.5 percent a year during the 1980s, many analysts thought that the U.S. market in the 1990s was due for a correction, and they suggested that investors increase their foreign stock holdings. To the surprise of many, however, U.S. stocks outperformed foreign stocks in the 1990s—gaining about 15 percent annually versus only 3 percent for foreign stocks.

Table 9-2 shows how stocks in different countries performed during 2003, ranked by performance in U.S. dollar terms. The numbers on the right indicate how stocks in each country performed in terms of its local currency, while the numbers on the left show how the country's stocks performed in terms of the U.S. dollar. For example, in 2003 Brazilian stocks rose by 89.01 percent, but the Brazilian real rose sharply against the U.S. dollar. Therefore, if U.S. investors had bought Brazilian stocks, they would have gained 89.01 percent in Brazilian real terms, but those reals would have bought 42.39 percent more in U.S. dollars, so the effective return would have been a whopping 131.40 percent. Thus, the results of foreign investments depend in part on what happens to the exchange rate. Indeed, whenever you invest overseas, you are making two bets: (1) that the foreign securities will increase in their local markets and (2) that the currencies in which you are paid will rise relative to the dollar.

Although U.S. stocks had outperformed foreign stocks during 2000–2002, this by no means suggests that investors should avoid foreign stocks. In fact, in 2003, global stock markets enjoyed their first rally in four years with even higher expectations for 2004. Foreign investments still improve diversification, and there will certainly be years when foreign stocks outperform domestic stocks. When this occurs, U.S. investors will be glad they put some of their money in overseas markets.

TABLE 9-2	**2003 Performance of the Dow Jones Global Stock Indexes (Ranked by Performance in U.S. Dollar Terms)**				
Country	U.S. Dollars	Local Currency	Country	U.S. Dollars	Local Currency
Thailand	+138.70%	+119.29%	France	+39.11%	+15.87%
Brazil	+131.40	+89.01	Hong Kong	+38.69	+38.07
Venezuela	+119.88	+152.70	Portugal	+38.53	+15.39
Chile	+83.53	+51.13	Italy	+38.35	+15.24
Indonesia	+65.95	+56.17	Japan	+37.61	+24.40
Greece	+65.08	+37.50	Taiwan	+36.63	+33.91
Germany	+61.33	+34.37	Singapore	+36.27	+33.43
Sweden	+60.06	+32.63	Switzerland	+33.14	+19.38
Austria	+58.26	+31.82	Mexico	+31.46	+42.50
Spain	+55.59	+29.59	South Korea	+31.45	+32.14
Canada	+51.54	+25.15	Great Britain	+28.54	+15.82
New Zealand	+50.85	+20.84	United States	+28.44	+28.44
Philippines	+49.62	+55.66	Malaysia	+26.19	+26.18
Denmark	+49.35	+25.03	Netherlands	+25.27	+4.34
Australia	+45.95	+9.07	Finland	+17.33	−2.27
Ireland	+44.26	+20.16	World, excluding		
South Africa	+41.78	+10.69	United States	+38.58	–
Belgium	+40.78	+17.26	World	+33.02	–
Norway	+40.62	+35.32			

Source: "The Year of the Bull," *The Wall Street Journal*, January 2, 2004, R6.

Stock Market Reporting

Up until a couple of years ago, the best source of stock quotations was the business section of a daily newspaper, such as *The Wall Street Journal*. One problem with newspapers, however, is that they are printed only once a day. Now it is possible to get quotes all during the day from a wide variety of Internet sources.[17] One of the best is Yahoo!, and Figure 9-4 shows a detailed quote for GlaxoSmithKline PLC

Figure 9-4	**Stock Quote for GlaxoSmithKline, January 7, 2004**

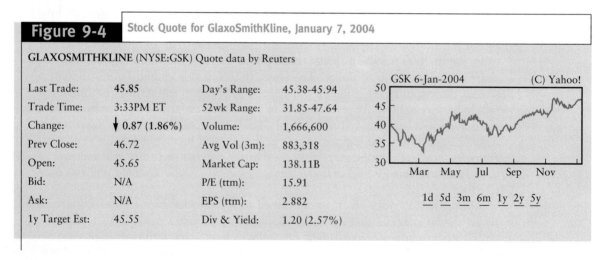

GLAXOSMITHKLINE (NYSE:GSK) Quote data by Reuters

Last Trade:	45.85	Day's Range:	45.38-45.94	
Trade Time:	3:33PM ET	52wk Range:	31.85-47.64	
Change:	↓ 0.87 (1.86%)	Volume:	1,666,600	
Prev Close:	46.72	Avg Vol (3m):	883,318	
Open:	45.65	Market Cap:	138.11B	
Bid:	N/A	P/E (ttm):	15.91	
Ask:	N/A	EPS (ttm):	2.882	
1y Target Est:	45.55	Div & Yield:	1.20 (2.57%)	

Source: **http://finance.yahoo.com.**

---

[17] Most free sources actually provide quotes that are delayed by 15 minutes.

U.S. FIRMS ARE SHOPPING FOR EUROPEAN M&A DEALS

Since 2000, when the U.S. economy slowed sharply and stocks began a long slide, mergers and acquisitions (M&A) have been in the doldrums, especially relative to M&A activity in Europe. For example, in the second quarter of 2003, $138 billion of deals were announced in Europe versus $90 billion in the United States. Somewhat surprisingly, because of the weakening dollar against the euro, American firms were active buyers of expensive European companies. Cross-ocean mergers fluctuate from quarter to quarter, but even so, in 2003 American firms were very active acquirers.

Some of the major deals included N.Y. Community Bancorp's $1.69 billion deal to purchase Roslyn Bancorp, United Technologies' $1 billion buyout of London-based electronic security firm Chubb, American Express's acquisition of money-management company Threadneedle, and Zimmer Holdings' $3.2 billion offer for Swiss orthopedics manufacturer Centerpulse AG. These acquisitions, and most of the others, were strategic ones. The U.S. acquirers were seeking to fill gaps in their product lines (United Technologies), to increase market share and gain economies of

scale (American Express), to gain access to the European market (N.Y. Community Bancorp), or to obtain all of these advantages (Zimmer).

The weak dollar–strong euro situation made all of these acquisitions more expensive for the American buyers, but strategic considerations outweighed the higher acquisition costs.

Strategic factors favoring mergers are at least as important for European companies, especially German firms, due to Europe's relatively weak economies, high unemployment, and rigid union-backed governmental regulations. Thus, European companies have been busy purchasing American companies, and as the strong euro makes such acquisitions less expensive, more and more European takeovers can be expected.

These mergers are, of course, nothing new. The economic advantages to international operations are, in many industries, simply overwhelming, so the trend toward multinational corporations is likely to continue unabated.

Source: Wall Street Journal Online, June 30, 2003.

(GSK). As the heading shows, GlaxoSmithKline is traded on the New York Stock Exchange under the symbol GSK. (The NYSE is just one of many world markets on which the stock trades.) The first two rows of information show that GSK last traded at $45.85, and the stock traded thus far during the day from as low as $45.38 and as high as $45.94. (Note that the price is reported in decimals rather than fractions, reflecting a recent change in trading conventions.) The last trade was at 3:33 P.M. ET on January 7, 2004, and its price range during the past 52 weeks was from $31.85 to $47.64.

The next three lines show that GSK opened trading on January 7 at $45.65, it closed on January 6 at $46.72, and its price fell by $0.87 (or a 1.86 percent decline) from the previous closing price to the current price. So far during the day, 1,666,600 shares had traded hands. GlaxoSmithKline's average daily trading volume (based on the past three months) is 883,318 shares, so the current trading volume of 1.66 million shares suggests a heavy trading day. The total value of all of its stock, called its Market Cap, is $138.11 billion.

The last three lines report other market information for GSK. If GlaxoSmithKline were trading on Nasdaq rather than a listed exchange, the most recent bid and ask quotes from dealers would have been shown. However, because GSK trades on the NYSE, these data are not available. GSK's P/E ratio (price per share divided by the most recent 12 months' earnings) is 15.91, and its earnings per share for the most recent 12 months was $2.882. The mean of the analysts' one-year target price for GSK is $45.55. GSK's dividend is $1.20 per share, so the quarterly dividend is $0.30 per share, and the dividend yield, which is the annual dividend divided by the price, is 2.57 percent.

GLOBAL MARKETS REBOUND

Stock markets around the world posted gains in 2003, after experiencing declines during the past three years. Gains were not limited to just a few regions—they were experienced around the globe. Emerging markets performed the best—posting a 42 percent return. Money poured into emerging markets at a rate not seen in almost a decade. Overall, the Dow Jones World Stock Index, including the United States, rose 33 percent. This is the index's highest return since its creation in 1992. Inclusion of the United States in this index actually brought the index average down, as the U.S. return was only 28 percent—compared with more than 38 percent (measured in dollars) for the remaining global markets.

Even Europe's bear market turned bullish in 2003. As shown in Table 9-2 (which shows the performance of the Dow Jones Global Indexes), in terms of local currency Germany posted a 34 percent return, Austria posted almost a 32 percent return, and even Great Britain managed approximately a 16 percent return. The Netherlands was Europe's worst-performing market with only a 4 percent return.

For Latin America, the 2003 stock market performance was its best in more than 12 years. The gains were sorely needed because the region's stock performance over the last three years makes Nasdaq's declines look mild in comparison. Cyclical conditions that favored emerging markets helped the region's markets bounce back. Rebounding economies, higher commodity prices, and China's growing demand for resources from this region helped fuel gains.

Some of the best performing markets were in Asia despite the SARS epidemic and terrorism threats. Thailand led the way with a whopping 119 percent return (measured in local currency). Even Japan's Nikkei Stock Average rose 24 percent amid signs of the country's economic recovery and company restructurings—shaking off a decade of dismal performance. As the U.S. economic recovery improves, this will aid Asian markets—the United States is Asia's biggest export market.

However, there is even better news for U.S. investors that diversified into overseas markets: During 2003 the dollar weakened against most world currencies. So, these "local" returns are even higher when expressed in terms of U.S. dollars. So for U.S. investors who invested overseas, their dollar returns were amplified because of the favorable exchange rate when converting local currencies to U.S. dollars.

What sparked this global rally? Companies cut costs and reduced debt, which strengthened their financial positions. In addition, lower interest rates, the beginning of a global economic recovery, and a decrease in investors' risk aversion fueled the rally.

What does this mean for 2004? Of course, given the gains posted in 2003, expectations now are even higher for next year. Whether those expectations will be met or not depends on whether (1) company profits can continue to grow from higher sales levels rather than continued cost-cutting measures, (2) global interest rates remain stable rather than rising, and (3) inflation remains at current levels rather than escalating to even higher levels. In addition, fluctuating exchange rates will have a dramatic impact on global markets.

Sources: Craig Karmin, "Global Stock Markets Regain Their Luster," *The Wall Street Journal*, January 2, 2004, R6–R7; Silvia Ascarelli, "Europe Goes from Bear to Bull, and Fund Managers Believe It Will Outshine U.S. in 2004," *The Wall Street Journal*, January 2, 2004, R6–R7; David Luhnow, "Latin American Stocks Get Boost from World-Wide Recovery," *The Wall Street Journal*, January 2, 2004, R6–R7; and Phillip Day, "The Year of the Bounce-Back: Asian Stock Markets Leapt Ahead in Face of SARS, Terror and War," *The Wall Street Journal*, January 2, 2004, R6–R7.

The chart to the right of the stock data plots the daily prices for the past year. The links below the chart allow a web user to pick different intervals for plotting data on the chart. As you can see, Yahoo! provides a great deal of information in its detailed quote, and even more detail is available on the screen page below the basic quote information.

Effects of Exchange Rates on Stock Returns

Exchange rates affect stock returns in two key ways. First, exchange rates influence export and import prices. This affects companies' sales and profits, and thus stock prices and earned returns. Second, exchange rates affect the home country returns investors earn on their foreign investments. For example, if a German investor bought SSI shares at $20, and at the end of the year the stock was selling for $22.22, then the investor would have a dollar rate of return of 11.1 percent. However, that German investor would want euros, not dollars, and the euro return would depend on whether the dollar had strengthened or weakened against the euro. If the dollar had strengthened, then it would buy more euros than at the start of the year, so the euro return would be higher. For example, if the dollar had strengthened by 5 percent, then the German investor's return would be $1.111(1.05) - 1 = 16.66\%$.

Suppose, on the other hand, that an American investor had purchased a German security and earned a euro rate of return of 11.1 percent. The investor would have earned a much lower dollar return due to the exchange rate change [or $1.111(0.95) - 1 = 5.55\%$], because the euros earned would buy fewer dollars. These exchange rate effects increase the risk of foreign investments, at least when viewed on a stand-alone basis. Note, though, that (1) hedging with currency futures can mitigate this risk (we will discuss this in Chapter 15) and (2) as we discussed in Chapter 5, in a portfolio context, international diversification lowers, not raises, investment risk, as long as the investments have about the same amount of variance risk as domestic investments.

SELF-TEST QUESTIONS

Explain why expected, required, and realized returns are often different.

What are the key benefits of adding foreign stocks to a portfolio?

When a U.S. investor purchases foreign stocks, what two things is he or she hoping will happen?

In what two ways do exchange rates affect stock returns?

What actions can mitigate the risk of foreign investments?

SUMMARY

The primary purposes of this chapter were (1) to identify the types and characteristics of common stock, (2) to evaluate different methods of stock valuation, (3) to introduce the concepts of market equilibrium and efficiency, and (4) to demonstrate trends in stock returns and the financial reporting of common stocks. The key concepts discussed in this chapter are listed below.

- Companies often find that issuing **classified stock** helps serve their special needs. A company's common stock may be given special designations like Class A, Class B, etc., to indicate different voting or cash flow rights.
- **Founders' shares** are shares of stock owned by the firm's founders that has sole voting rights but restricted dividends for a specified number of years.
- **Citizens' shares** (also called **golden shares**) enable local citizens to maintain control over a multinational company and would likely have different voting rights than other classes of stock.
- A **preemptive right** is a provision in the corporate charter or bylaws that gives common stockholders the right to purchase on a pro rata basis new issues of common stock (or convertible securities).
- A corporation that is owned by a few individuals who are typically associated with the firm's management is called a **closely held corporation**.
- A corporation that is owned by a relatively large number of individuals who are not actively involved in its management is called a **publicly owned corporation**.
- An **American Depository Receipt** (**ADR**) is a negotiable certificate, issued by a bank, denominated in dollars, and traded on an exchange like the NYSE. It represents underlying shares of a company that are held in trust in a foreign depository institution.

- **Global Registered Shares (GRSs)** trade electronically on a number of exchanges in the local host currencies.
- The act of selling stock to the public at large by a closely held corporation or its principal stockholders is called **going public**.
- The **initial public offering (IPO) market** is the market in which firms "go public" by offering shares to the public for the first time.
- The **primary market** is the market for additional new shares sold by established, publicly owned companies. Corporations receive money when sales occur in this market.
- The **secondary market** is the market where outstanding shares of established, publicly owned companies are traded among investors. Corporations receive no new money when sales occur in this market.
- The **market price** is the price at which a stock sells in the market; while the **intrinsic value** is the value that, in the mind of a particular investor, is justified by the data.
- The **required rate of return** is the minimum rate of return on a common stock that a stockholder considers acceptable.
- The **expected total rate of return** is equal to the sum of the expected dividend yield and the expected capital gains yield.
- The **constant growth (Gordon) model** is used to find the value of a constant growth stock.
- A **zero growth stock** is a common stock whose future dividends are not expected to grow at all; that is, $g = 0$.
- A **perpetuity** is a stream of equal payments expected to continue forever.
- Most firms experience periods of **nonconstant (supernormal) growth**, which is the part of the firm's life cycle in which it grows differently from the economy as a whole.
- The **terminal (horizon) date** is the date when a stock's growth rate becomes constant. At this date it is no longer necessary to forecast individual dividends.
- The **terminal (horizon) value** of a stock is the value at the horizon date of all dividends expected thereafter.
- **Market multiple analysis** applies market-determined multiples to net income, earnings per share, sales, book value, and so forth in an effort to determine firm value.
- An **entity multiple** is based on total value and is a measure of the entire firm.
- The actions of the **marginal investor** reflect the beliefs of those people who are currently trading a stock. It is the marginal investor who determines a stock's price.
- **Equilibrium** is a condition under which a security's expected return is just equal to its required return, $\hat{r} = r$. Also, $\hat{P}_0 = P_0$, and the price is stable.
- The **efficient markets hypothesis (EMH)** suggests that securities are typically in equilibrium—that they are fairly priced in the sense that the price reflects all publicly available information on each security. There are three levels of market efficiency: **weak form**, where all information relating to past events is fully reflected in current market prices; **semistrong form**, where current market prices reflect all publicly available information; and **strong form**, where current market prices reflect all pertinent information, whether publicly available or privately held.
- **Behavioral finance** is a discipline that suggests investors are not simply machines that rationally process all available information. Instead, it claims that a variety of psychological and perhaps irrational factors also come into play in decision making. Behavioral finance researchers try to incorporate elements of cognitive psychology to better understand how market participants respond to different circumstances.

QUESTIONS

(9-1) In the beginning of the chapter the text presents the general valuation equation and addresses factors that are important in stock valuation. What factors are shown, and how do they affect a firm's stock price? Briefly explain how these factors are complicated for a multinational firm.

(9-2) Two investors are evaluating DaimlerChrysler's stock for possible purchase. They agree on the expected value of D_1 and also on the expected future dividend growth rate. Further, they agree on the risk associated with owning the stock. However, one investor normally holds stocks for 2 years, while the other normally holds stocks for 10 years. On the basis of the dividend model analysis, they should both be willing to pay the same price for DaimlerChrysler's stock. True or false? Explain.

(9-3) It is frequently stated that the primary purpose of the preemptive right is to allow individuals to maintain their proportionate share of the ownership and control of a corporation.
   a. How important do you suppose this consideration is for the average stock-holder of a firm whose shares are traded on the New York Stock Exchange?
   b. Is the preemptive right likely to be of more importance to stockholders of publicly owned or closely held firms? Explain.

(9-4) Why might founders' shares be used in foreign companies located abroad?

(9-5) Why might foreigners be legally restricted from holding an equity stake in local companies? How might these restrictions be enforced?

(9-6) Briefly explain the following statement and its implications on dividends: "The corporate (or joint stock company) form of organization creates an entity that is a legal 'person' separate from its shareholders."

(9-7) Differentiate between an American Depository Receipt (ADR) and a Global Registered Share (GRS). Why might one be used over the other?

(9-8) Differentiate between the discounted dividend model and the free cash flow model for valuing a nonconstant growth firm. Under what circumstances might you use one model over the other?

(9-9) Why might you use market multiple analysis when valuing foreign operations? Provide an example.

(9-10) Explain the importance of the marginal investor and the concept of market equilibrium.

(9-11) Briefly explain whether the following statement is true or false: "The efficient markets hypothesis assumes that all investors are rational."

(9-12) Briefly explain whether the following statement is true or false: "The stock market is always efficient."

(9-13) Why should an investor include international stocks in his or her portfolio?

(9-14) How do exchange rates affect stock returns? Is there any way to lessen these effects? Explain.

SELF-TEST PROBLEMS   Solutions Appear in Appendix B

(ST-1) Define each of the following terms:
Key Terms   a. Classified stock; founders' shares; citizen's (golden) shares

b. Preemptive right; closely held corporation; publicly owned corporation
c. American Depository Receipt (ADR); Global Registered Share (GRS)
d. Going public; initial public offering (IPO) market; primary market; secondary market
e. market price (P_0); intrinsic (fundamental) value $(\hat{P}_0)$; dividend growth rate
f. Required rate of return (r_s); expected total rate of return $(\hat{r}_s)$; actual (realized) rate of return $(\bar{r}_s)$
g. Expected dividend yield; expected capital gains yield
h. Constant growth (Gordon) model; zero growth stock; perpetuity
i. Nonconstant (supernormal) growth; terminal date (horizon date); terminal (horizon) value
j. Corporate valuation model; market multiple analysis; entity multiple
k. Marginal investor; equilibrium; behavioral finance

(ST-2)
Stock Valuation
Today is December 31, 2004. The following information applies to International Oil:
- After-tax, operating income [EBIT$(1 - T)$] for the year 2005 is expected to be $650 million.
- The company's depreciation expense for the year 2005 is expected to be $75 million.
- The company's capital expenditures for the year 2005 are expected to be $240 million.
- The company's net operating working capital in 2005 must increase by $30 million.
- The company's free cash flow is expected to grow at a constant rate of 4 percent per year.
- The company's most recent dividend (D_0), $2.05, was paid yesterday.
- Unlike the firm's free cash flows, the company's dividends are not expected to grow at a constant rate during the next 3 years. Its dividends are expected to grow by 25 percent next year, 15 percent the following year, and 10 percent the third year. After the third year, the firm's dividends are expected to grow at a steady rate of 6 percent.
- The company's cost of equity is 12 percent.
- The company's WACC is 9 percent.
- The current market value of the company's debt is $1.75 billion.
- The company currently has 150 million shares of stock outstanding.
a. Using the dividend discount model, what should be the company's stock price today?
b. Using the free cash flow valuation method, what should be the company's stock price today?

Starter Problems

(9-1)
Constant Growth Stock
HensfordSmytheRobinson Inc.'s stock is currently trading at $40 per share. The stock's dividend is projected to increase at a constant rate of 6 percent per year. The required rate of return on the stock, r_s, is 11 percent. What is the expected price of the stock 3 years from today?

(9-2)
Nonconstant Growth Stock
Global Pharmaceuticals just paid a dividend of $1.50. The growth rate is expected to be 15 percent next year, 10 percent the following year, 8 percent for the following year, and then the growth rate is expected to be a constant 6 percent thereafter. The required rate of return on equity (r_s) is 9 percent. What is the current stock price?

(9-3)
FCF Model
An analyst estimating the intrinsic value of the Worldwide Resources Corporation stock estimates that its free cash flow at the end of the year $(t = 1)$ will be $250,000,000. The analyst estimates that the firm's free cash flow will grow at a constant rate of 5 percent a year, and that the company's weighted average cost of

capital is 8 percent. The company currently has debt and preferred stock totaling $333,333,333. There are 250 million outstanding shares of common stock. What is the intrinsic value (per share) of the company's stock?

EXAM-TYPE PROBLEMS

(9-4)
Nonconstant Growth Stock
Assume that the average firm in your company's industry is expected to grow at a constant rate of 6 percent, and its dividend yield is 2 percent. Your company is about as risky as the average firm in the industry, but it has just developed a line of innovative new products, which leads you to expect that its earnings and dividends will grow at a rate of 30 percent $[D_1 = D_0(1.30)]$ this year and 20 percent the following year after which growth should match the 6 percent industry average rate. The last dividend paid (D_0) was $1.25. What is the stock's value per share?

(9-5)
Stock Valuation
You have been given the following projections for Worldwide Electronics Inc. for the coming year.
- Sales = 10,000,000 units.
- Sales price per unit = $100.
- Variable cost per unit = $25.
- Fixed costs = $10,000,000.
- Bonds outstanding = $150,000,000.
- r_d on outstanding bonds = 7%.
- Tax rate = 40%.
- Shares of common stock outstanding = 110,000,000 shares.
- Beta = 1.2.
- r_{RF} = 5%.
- r_M = 10%.
- Dividend payout ratio = 55%.
- Growth rate = 5%.

Calculate the current price per share for Worldwide Electronics Inc.

(9-6)
Stock Valuation
The probability distribution for r_M for the coming year is as follows:

Probability	r_M
0.05	5%
0.20	6
0.30	8
0.40	11
0.05	13

If r_{RF} = 5.25% and Stock C has a beta of 1.6, an expected constant growth rate of 5 percent, and D_0 = $1.75, what market price gives the investor a return consistent with the stock's risk?

(9-7)
FCF Model
An analyst has collected the following information about International Electronics Inc.:
- Projected EBIT for the next year = $200 million.
- Projected depreciation expense for the next year = $45 million.
- Projected capital expenditures for the next year = $75 million.
- Projected increase in operating working capital next year = $25 million.
- Tax rate = 40%.
- WACC = 9.5%.
- Cost of equity = 12.5%.
- Market value of debt and preferred stock today = $300 million.
- Number of shares outstanding today = 40 million.

The company's free cash flow is expected to grow at a constant rate of 4.5 percent a year. The analyst uses the corporate value model approach to estimate the stock's intrinsic value. What is the stock's intrinsic value today?

(9-8)
Stock Valuation
Bridges & Associates' stock is expected to pay a $0.45 per-share dividend at the end of the year. The dividend is expected to grow 30 percent the next year and 15 percent the following year. After t = 3, the dividend is expected to grow at a constant rate of 8 percent a year. The company's cost of common equity is 12 percent and it is expected to remain constant.
a. What is the expected price of the stock today?
b. What is the expected price of the stock 5 years from today?

(9-9)
Nonconstant Growth Stock
An analyst has put together the following spreadsheet to estimate the intrinsic value of the stock of Kazmirski International (in millions of dollars):

	t = 1	t = 2	t = 3
Sales	$5,000	$5,500	$6,250
NOPAT	750	1,100	1,250
Net investment in operating capital*	425	575	625

*Net investment in operating capital = Capital expenditures + Changes in net operating capital − Depreciation.

After Year 3 (t = 3), assume that the company's free cash flow will grow at a constant rate of 6 percent a year and the company's WACC equals 9.75 percent. The market value of the company's debt and preferred stock is $569 million. The company has 250 million outstanding shares of common stock.
a. What is the company's free cash flow the first year (t = 1)?
b. Using the free cash flow model, what is the intrinsic value of the company's stock today?

THOMSON ONE
Business School Edition QUESTIONS

ESTIMATING INTRINSIC STOCK VALUE

Overview

In this chapter we described the various factors that influence stock prices. We also described a couple of approaches that analysts use to estimate a stock's intrinsic value. By comparing these estimates of intrinsic value to the current price, an investor can assess whether it makes sense to buy or sell a particular stock. Stocks trading at a price far below their estimated intrinsic values may be good candidates for purchase, whereas stocks trading at prices far in excess of their intrinsic value may be good stocks to avoid or sell.

While estimating a stock's intrinsic value is a complex exercise that requires a lot of reliable data and good judgment, we can use the data available in *Thomson One: Business School Edition* to determine a quick "back of the envelope" calculation of intrinsic value.

Discussion Questions:

1. For purposes of this exercise, let's take a closer look at the stock of Brady Corp. (BRC). Looking at the COMPANY OVERVIEW we can immediately see the company's current stock price and its performance relative to the over-

all market in recent months. What is Brady's current stock price? How has the stock performed relative to the market over the past few months?

2. Click on the tab labeled "NEWS" to see the recent news stories for the company. Have there been any recent events that have had a major effect on the company's stock price, or have things been relatively quiet?

3. To provide a starting point for gauging a company's relative valuation, analysts often look at a company's price-to-earnings (P/E) ratio. Returning back to the "COMPANY OVERVIEW" page, you can see BRC's current P/E ratio. To put this number in perspective, it is useful to compare this ratio with other companies in the same industry and to take a look at how this ratio has changed over time. If you want to see how BRC's P/E ratio stacks up to its peers, click on the tab labeled "PEERS". Click on "FINANCIALS" on the next row of tabs and then select "KEY FINANCIAL RATIOS". Toward the bottom of the table you should see information on the P/E ratio in the section titled "MARKET VALUE RATIOS". Toward the top, you should see an item where it says "CLICK TO SELECT NEW PEER SET"—do this if you want to compare BRC to a different set of firms. For the most part, is BRC's P/E ratio above or below that of its peers? In Chapter 6, we discussed the various factors that may influence P/E ratios. Off the top of your head, can these factors explain why BRC's P/E ratio differs from its peers?

4. Now to see how BRC's P/E ratio has varied over time, return back to the "COMPANY OVERVIEW" page. Next click "FINANCIALS—GROWTH RATIOS" and then select "WORLDSCOPE GROWTH RATIOS—INCOME STATEMENT RATIOS." Is BRC's current P/E ratio well above or well below its historical average? If so, do you have any explanation for why the current P/E deviates from its historical trend? On the basis of all this information, does BRC's current P/E suggest that the stock is under- or overvalued?

5. In the text, we discussed at some length how you can you use the dividend growth model to estimate a stock's intrinsic value. To keep things as simple as possible, first assume that BRC's dividend is expected to grow at some constant rate over time. If so, the intrinsic value equals $D_1/(r_s - g)$, where D_1 is the expected annual dividend 1 year from now, r_s is the stock's required rate of return, and g is the dividend's constant growth rate. To estimate the dividend growth rate, it is first helpful to look at BRC's dividend history. Staying on the current Web page ("WORLDSCOPE GROWTH RATIOS—INCOME STATEMENT RATIOS") you should immediately find the company's annual dividend over the past several years. On the basis of this information, what has been the average annual dividend growth rate? Another way to obtain dividend growth rate estimates is to look at analysts' forecasts for future dividends. To see these forecasts, click on the tab labeled "ESTIMATES". Under "AVAILABLE MEASURES," click on the down arrow key and select "DIVIDENDS PER SHARE (DPS)." What is the median year-end dividend forecast? You can use this as an estimate of D_1 in your measure of intrinsic value. You can also use this forecast along with the historical data to arrive at a measure of the forecasted dividend growth rate, g.

6. The required return on equity, r_s, is the final input needed to estimate intrinsic value. For our purposes you can either assume a number (say, 11 or 12 percent) or you can use the CAPM to calculate an estimate of the cost of equity using the data available in *Thomson One: Business School Edition*. (For more details take a look at the *Thomson One: Business School Edition* exercise for Chapter 5.) Having decided on your best estimates for D_1, r_s, and g, you can calculate BRC's intrinsic value. How does this estimate compare with the current stock price? Does your preliminary analysis suggest that BRC is under- or overvalued?

7. It is often useful to perform a sensitivity analysis, where you show how your estimate of intrinsic value varies according to different estimates of D_1, r_s, and g. To do so, recalculate your intrinsic value estimate for a range of different estimates for each of these key inputs. One convenient way to do this is to set up a simple data table in *Excel*. In the Chapter 5 spreadsheet model found on the text's Web site, you will find an explanation of how to set up a data table. On the basis of this analysis, what inputs does it take to justify the current stock price?

8. From the dividend history you uncovered in Question 5 and your assessment of BRC's future dividend payout policies, do you think it is reasonable to assume that the constant growth model is a good proxy for its intrinsic value? If not, how would you use the data available in *Thomson One: Business School Edition* to estimate Brady's intrinsic value using the nonconstant growth model?

Finally, note that you can also use the information in *Thomson One: Business School Edition* to value the entire corporation. This approach requires that you estimate BRC's annual free cash flows. Once you estimate the value of the entire corporation, you subtract the value of debt and preferred stock to arrive at an estimate of the company's equity value. Divide this number by the number of shares of common stock outstanding, and you calculate an alternative estimate of the stock's intrinsic value. While this approach may take some more time and involves more judgment concerning forecasts of future free cash flows, you can use the financial statements and growth forecasts in *Thomson One: Business School Edition* as useful starting points. Indeed, it turns out that if you go to Worldscope's Cash Flow Statement Ratios Report (which you find by clicking on "FINANCIALS/FUNDAMENTAL RATIOS" and "WORLDSCOPE RATIOS"), there is a calculation of "free cash flow per share." While this number is useful, please note that Worldscope's definition of free cash flow subtracts out dividends per share—therefore, in order to make it comparable to the measure in the text, you must add back dividends.

INTEGRATED CASE

Rick Schmidt, MRI's CFO, along with Mandy Wu, Schmidt's assistant, and John Costello, a consultant and college finance professor, comprise a team set up to teach the firm's directors and senior managers the basics of international financial management. The program includes 16 sessions, each lasting about 2 hours, and they are scheduled immediately before the monthly board meetings. Eight sessions have been completed, and the team is now preparing Session 9, which will deal with common stock. Prior sessions have provided an overview of international finance, international security markets, exchange rates, risk analysis, financial statements, and bond valuation.

For the common stock session, the team will identify the types of common stock, the markets in which they are traded, the valuation process, and the concept of market equilibrium. This session is important for three main reasons: (1) Management's stated goal is to maximize the firm's stock price, and to accomplish this goal management must understand how stock prices are determined in the marketplace. (2) The principles of stock valuation are important in cost of capital calculations, the topic of the next session. (3) The company's retirement program is based on a 401(k) plan under which individual employees direct their own pension asset allocations between stocks, bonds, mutual funds, and the company's own stock. There is a danger that some employees will lose money, become unhappy, and sue the company for not providing adequate investment advice. Schmidt does not want managers giving out investment advice, but he is afraid that they will do so anyway. All of the directors invest in the stock market and keep up with it to at least some extent. However, the individual directors' knowledge varies considerably, and that makes it difficult to decide what to cover and how deep the stock analysis session should go. After much discussion, the team created a game plan of topics to cover. As in the other sessions, they plan to use an *Excel* model both to illustrate the discussion and to help the directors become more familiar with *Excel*.

Wu expressed concern about addressing controversial issues, where the proper analysis is in question. She recalled that in college some students simply "tuned out" when the instructor raised a question but then had no definitive answer, and she was concerned that the directors might react similarly. Schmidt and Costello agree that this could be a problem, but they felt strongly that it would not be appropriate to "sweep problems under the carpet." So, they want to bring up relevant unresolved issues, discuss alternative ways of dealing with them, and point out the implications of different decisions. The directors are all intelligent, experienced in dealing with complex situations, and would rather know about potential problems than be kept in the dark. Wu also believes that the session should include a discussion of the different stock markets in the United States and around the world. This discussion should focus on two issues: (1) Should MRI, if it decides to issue new stock to raise capital, raise this capital in the U.S. over-the-counter market, where its stock now trades, or should it consider selling stock in some other market; and (2) should the company's 401(k) advisors encourage or discourage workers from investing their retirement funds in one or more foreign stock markets? These two questions raised several other questions: How large are the different markets? How liquid are they; that is, can large amounts of stocks be traded on those markets without driving the price up or down substantially? Is reliable information available on the stocks traded in all the markets? What have historical returns been in the different markets? What role do exchange rates play on investment results in other markets? Finally, one director raised the question of whether MRI should apply to list its stock on a national exchange—either the NYSE or the Nasdaq—and Schmidt thinks this should be discussed.

Under Schmidt's direction, Wu (who is MRI's expert on *Excel*) has been working on a corporate model that analyzes the effects of different operating decisions on sales, costs, earnings, and dividends, and thus on the stock price. The model is operational, and Schmidt plans to use it to analyze major decisions facing the firm. However, some directors think that the discounted dividend model provides a better picture of the stock valuation process. Costello noted that most textbooks focus primarily on the constant growth dividend model because of its simplicity, but since MRI and most other tech companies are not in a constant growth situation, Wu built a nonconstant version of the DCF formula into her model. Therefore, Schmidt wants to explain the nonconstant dividend model and illustrate it with MRI's own data. He also plans to explain the more complex corporate valuation model, which forecasts and then analyzes the firm's free cash flows.

Schmidt also noted that several of the directors have expressed concern about whether a new stock market "bubble" is forming, and hence whether stock prices might be "too high." That topic came up in connection with a discussion of whether or not the 401(k) advisors should suggest that employees invest their 401(k) funds in stocks or in fixed-income securities, and especially whether or not they should invest 401(k) money in MRI's own stock. The question was also raised, in the same discussion, whether MRI should issue new stock to raise capital. In view of all this, Costello suggested that it would be appropriate to devote part of the session to market equilibrium, and to introduce the directors to the efficient market hypothesis and its implications.

With those thoughts in mind, the three compiled the following set of questions, which they plan to discuss during the session. As with the other sessions, they plan to use an *Excel* model to answer the quantitative questions. Assume that you are Mandy Wu, and that you must prepare answers for use during the session.

QUESTIONS

a. Who has the power to control a firm—its stockholders, board of directors, or executives? Is there a difference between control in theory and control in practice? Most stockholders own only a very small stake in large, publicly traded companies, say, 500 shares out of a billion shares outstanding. For such stockholders, does it really matter who controls the firm? Differentiate between publicly owned companies and closely held companies. Would stock transactions by MRI's insiders have an influence on the stock price, and what, if anything, should the company do about any such influence?

b. MRI has only one class of common stock outstanding. Describe some different classifications of stock that it might have used. Do all classes of stock have the same rights and characteristics? Can you think of any circumstances under which MRI might want to use some other types of stock?

c. How does the U.S. stock market compare with other world markets in terms of size and risk? How do changes in currency exchange rates affect earned returns in different markets? Would you recommend that MRI's employees allocate some of their retirement funds to overseas investments? Should one of MRI's employees based in the United States make the same allocation as a Brazilian employee based in Brazil?

d. MRI's stock is traded in the over-the-counter market, but some directors have suggested that it should be listed on the NYSE or the Nasdaq. Should MRI list its stock on one of these exchanges at this time? Since MRI does business all around the world, should it consider listing its stock on one or more foreign exchanges?

e. Describe and give examples of the basic types of stock market transactions.

f. Brooke Power is a utility company headquartered near MRI. Brooke is a stable, established company that has enjoyed steady growth for the past decade and expects to continue that trend into the future. Brooke just today paid a dividend (D_0) of $2.75. The company's required return on equity is 10 percent, and its expected constant dividend growth rate is 4 percent. According to the dividend growth (Gordon) model, what is Brooke's intrinsic stock value today? How sensitive is the stock value to variations in the required return and growth rate?

g. MRI's stock does not currently pay a dividend. However, the directors are expected to declare a $0.50 dividend 3 years from now. That dividend is expected to grow at a rate of 20 percent during the next year, at 15 percent the following year, and at a constant 8 percent rate thereafter. MRI's required return on equity is estimated to be 10.25 percent. What is its intrinsic value; that is, at what price should the stock sell if the marginal investor knew and agreed with management's growth forecast and r_s?

h. Suppose the current market prices of Brooke Power and MRI stock are $52.25 and $21.00, respectively. What conclusions could you draw about the pricing of these stocks? Are they in equilibrium? Would you advise investors to buy or sell them? Suppose that the growth rate forecasted for Brooke Power is quite reliable; what does Brooke's market price suggest about the required return estimate that Brooke uses?

i. Using the data in Table IC9-1, assess the value of MRI's stock using the corporate valuation, or free cash flow, model. Assume the book values of debt and preferred stock equal their market values. How do the results compare with those obtained using the discounted dividend model? What are the pros and cons of the two models?

j. Could management influence the market price by changing the information it provides to investors? Is management constrained in terms of the information it gives out, including its accuracy and who it is provided to?

k. Suppose MRI's internal forecasts indicated a much lower dividend growth rate than most security analysts were forecasting, and most other companies were similarly more pessimistic than most security analysts. Would this have any implications for the question of whether a stock market bubble was developing? If indeed you concluded that a bubble was developing, what action could you take yourself, and what, if anything, would you suggest that MRI as a company do?

l. Explain how analysts might use multiples, or relative valuation, to determine the intrinsic value of MRI's stock. What are the potential dangers of using a multiples analysis?

m. Define market equilibrium. Explain the levels of market efficiency. If you observe a market inefficiency (e.g., an identical asset selling for different prices in different markets), how do you explain this event within the context of market equilibriums and efficiency?

n. Suppose you studied the situation carefully and concluded that the dollar is going to strengthen against most foreign currencies by an amount greater than "the marginal investor" expects it to strengthen. What could you personally do, and what could you recommend that MRI do to benefit the company, in the event your analysis is correct?

TABLE IC9-1

Expected FCF in 2005	$20.7 million
FCF growth rate (2006–2007)	15%
FCF growth rate (2008)	6.5%
WACC	8.5%
Book value of notes payable	$59,281,800
Book value of long-term debt	$361,289,500
Book value of preferred stock	$60,000,000
Number of shares outstanding	40 million

International Corporate Finance

Part Three

CHAPTER 10

The Cost of Capital

$$VALUE = \sum_{t=0}^{N} \frac{CF_t}{(1+r)^t}$$

Capital Structure
Component Costs
Firm Risk
Project Risk

Weighted Average Cost
of Capital (WACC)

e-resource

The textbook's Web site, http://crum. swlearning.com, contains an Excel file that will guide you through the chapter's calculations. The file for this chapter is FIFC10-model.xls, and we encourage you to open the file and follow along as you read the chapter.

In Part Two we used the basic valuation equation to find the values of bonds, stocks, and other securities. Given a security's price, we also use the equation to find the required rate of return. In Part Three, we discuss how managers use the valuation equation to make investment decisions. We begin this chapter with a discussion of the discount rate used in capital budgeting. Firms typically finance projects with a mix of debt, preferred stock, and common equity, and a weighted average of these securities' costs should be used as the discount rate, or required return. Consequently, you will notice that we have substituted WACC in the denominator of the valuation equation in place of r as the required return. Of course, discount rates are affected by the riskiness of the relevant cash flows, so the riskier a project's cash flows, the higher its cost of capital. In Chapter 11, we discuss how project cash flows are estimated and combine them with the cost of capital to determine a project's value. Chapter 12 focuses on measuring a project's risk and incorporating that risk into the capital budgeting decision and on how "real options," or decisions that managers can make after a project has gone into operation, affect cash flow, risk, and expected value.

Chapter 13 covers two important theoretical issues. The first is the optimal mix of capital (debt, preferred stock, and common equity), called the optimal capital structure. The second is the decision to distribute cash flows to investors (pay dividends or repurchase stock) versus to retain cash within the firm and reinvest for future growth.

Chapters 10, 11, 12, and 13 relate primarily to long-term assets and capital. But because long-term assets such as factories require the use of short-term assets such as inventories, Chapter 14 addresses working capital management, which includes the managing and financing of current assets.

*Steve Walsh, Assistant Treasurer of JCPenney, discusses international cost of capital issues in a video clip entitled "The Global Financial Marketplace." The video clip can be found at **http://fisher.osu.edu/fin/clips.htm**. This Ohio State University Web site contains video clips of business professionals discussing various topics of interest in finance.*

Conceptually, capital budgeting decisions are the same for both multinational and purely domestic firms. Naturally, they are more complicated for multinationals, which may raise money in several countries with more types of securities denominated in several different currencies. Additionally, different countries have different cultures, operating rules, and political risks, all of which can affect cash flow. We discuss the basic concepts applied to a purely domestic firm in an open, developed economy, after which we show how international factors impact the decision process.

OVERVIEW OF THE WEIGHTED AVERAGE COST OF CAPITAL

Capital Component
One of the types of capital used by firms to raise money.

What precisely do the terms "cost of capital" and "weighted average cost of capital" mean? To begin, note that it is possible to finance a firm entirely with common equity. However, as they grow, most firms employ several types of capital, called **capital components**, with common stock, preferred stock, and debt the three most frequently used types. All capital components have one feature in common: The investors who provide the funds expect a return on their investment at least equal to their required return.

Component Cost
The required rate of return on each capital component.

If a firm's only investors are common stockholders, then the cost of capital is the required rate of return on equity. However, most firms employ different types of capital, and, due to differences in risk, these different securities have different required rates of return. The required rate of return on each capital component is called its **component cost**, and, for the reasons we illustrate below, the cost of capital used to analyze capital budgeting decisions should be a *weighted average* of these components' costs. We call this weighted average just that, the **weighted average cost of capital**, or **WACC**.

Weighted Average Cost of Capital, WACC
A weighted average of the component costs of debt, preferred stock, and common equity.

Most firms set target percentages for the different financing sources. For example, Sound Systems International (SSI) plans to raise 30 percent of its required capital as debt, 10 percent as preferred stock, and 60 percent as common equity. This is its **target capital structure**. We discuss how targets are established in Chapter 13, but for now simply accept SSI's 30/10/60 debt, preferred, and common percentages as given.

Target Capital Structure
The mix of debt, preferred stock, and common equity with which the firm plans to raise capital over the long run and that minimizes the firm's WACC.

Although SSI and other firms try to stay close to their target capital structures, they frequently deviate for several reasons. First, market conditions may be more favorable in one market than another at a particular time. For example, if the stock market is extremely strong, a company may decide to issue more common stock than is needed to maintain its target equity ratio. The second, and probably more important, reason for deviations relates to flotation costs, which are the costs that a firm must incur to issue securities. Flotation costs are usually fixed, so they are prohibitively high if a small amount of capital is raised. Thus, it is inefficient and expensive to issue relatively small amounts of debt, preferred stock, and common stock. Therefore, a company might issue new common stock one year, debt the next couple of years, preferred stock the following year, and use only additions to retained earnings the next year, thus fluctuating around its target capital structure.

This situation causes unsophisticated managers to make serious errors in selecting projects if they do not understand the rationale behind the WACC. To illustrate, assume SSI is currently at its target capital structure and is considering how to finance next year's projects. It has internal equity in the form of current-period earnings available for reinvestment but will need more equity to finance the anticipated capital budget. SSI can raise a combination of debt and new common stock, but to minimize flotation costs it will issue either debt or common equity, but not both. Suppose SSI borrows heavily at 5 percent (after taxes) during 2005 to finance long-term projects that yield 7 percent. The next year, it has new long-term projects that yield 10 percent, well above the return on the 2005 projects. However, to return to its target capital structure, it issues new common equity, which costs 11 percent. Therefore, the company might incorrectly reject these 10 percent projects because they have to be financed with funds costing 11 percent.

However, this entire line of reasoning would be incorrect. Why would a company accept 7 percent long-term projects one year and reject 10 percent long-term projects the next? Note that if SSI had reversed the order of its financing, raising equity in 2005 and debt in 2006, it would have reversed its decisions, rejecting all projects in 2005 and accepting all projects in 2006. Does it make sense to accept or reject projects because of the more-or-less arbitrary sequence in which capital is raised? The answer is no. *To avoid such errors, managers should view companies as ongoing concerns and calculate their costs of capital as weighted averages of the various types of funds they intend to use over the long run, regardless of the specific source of financing employed in a particular year.*

The preceding discussion applies to both purely domestic and multinational firms, but complications arise with multinationals. Companies such as SSI raise capital across the globe, and component costs can be somewhat different depending on where capital is raised. Because SSI has access to local capital markets in countries that it operates in as well as international capital markets, the supply of capital at a constant interest rate is much larger than for a purely domestic company. Similarly, SSI and other multinationals often finance foreign subsidiaries with different debt/equity mixes. We defer consideration of these issues until later in the chapter.

SELF-TEST QUESTIONS

What are the three major capital components?

What is a component cost?

Why should a WACC be used when analyzing capital budgeting decisions?

What is a target capital structure?

Why should the cost of capital used in capital budgeting be calculated as a weighted average of the various types of funds the firm generally uses rather than the cost of the specific financing used to fund a particular project?

COST OF DEBT, r_d (1 − T)

The first step in estimating the cost of debt is determining the rate of return debtholders require, or r_d. Although estimating r_d is conceptually simple, some problems arise in practice. Companies use both fixed- and floating-rate debt, straight and convertible debt, and debt with and without sinking funds, and each form has a somewhat different cost. Moreover, multinational firms often borrow money all across the globe and in different currencies.

It is unlikely that the financial manager will know at the start of a planning period the exact types and amounts of debt that will be raised during the period. The type or types used will depend on the location and nature of the specific assets to be financed and on capital market conditions in various countries as they develop over time. As we will see in Chapter 15, borrowing can have a dual purpose when used to hedge currency risk. Even so, the financial manager knows which type of debt is typical for the firm. For example, SSI typically issues commercial paper, or its international equivalent, to raise short-term money to finance working capital and issues 20-year bonds to raise long-term debt to finance capital budgeting projects. Because the WACC is used primarily in capital budgeting, SSI's treasurer uses the cost of 20-year bonds in the WACC estimate.

Assume it is January 2005, and SSI's treasurer is estimating the WACC for the coming year. How should the component cost of debt be calculated? Most financial managers begin by discussing current and prospective interest rates with their investment bankers. Assume SSI's bankers forecast that a new 20-year, non-callable, straight bond issue would require an 8 percent coupon rate with semiannual payments and that it would be offered to the public at its $1,000 par value. Therefore, r_d is equal to 8 percent.[1]

New (Marginal) Debt
Debt that is not already outstanding.

Note that 8 percent is the cost of **new**, or **marginal**, **debt**, and it will probably not be the same as the average rate on SSI's previously issued debt, which is called the **historical**, or **embedded**, **rate**. The embedded cost is important for some decisions, but not for others. For example, the average cost of all the capital raised in the past and still outstanding is used by regulators when they determine the rate of return a public utility should be allowed to earn. However, in financial management, the WACC is used primarily to make investment decisions, which hinge on projects' expected future returns versus the cost of new, or marginal, capital. *Thus, for our purposes, the relevant cost is the marginal cost of new debt to be raised during the planning period.*

Historical (Embedded) Rate
The interest rate on previously issued, or currently outstanding, debt.

Suppose SSI issued debt in the past, and its bonds are publicly traded. The financial staff can use the market price of the bonds to find their yield to maturity (or yield to call if the bonds sell at a premium and are likely to be called). The YTM (or YTC) is the rate of return the existing bondholders expect to receive, and if the market is reasonably efficient, it is also a good estimate of r_d, the rate of return new bondholders require.

If SSI has no publicly traded debt, its staff can look at yields on publicly traded debt of firms with similar risks. This provides a reasonable estimate of r_d and provides a reality check on the rate estimated by the investment bankers.

The required return to debtholders, r_d, may not equal the company's cost of debt used in calculating the WACC because interest payments are tax deductible in most countries. This means that, in effect, the government pays part of the total cost. As a result, the cost of debt to the firm is less than the rate of return required by debtholders.

After-Tax Cost of Debt, $r_d(1 - T)$
The relevant cost of new debt, taking into account the tax deductibility of interest; used to calculate the WACC.

The **after-tax cost of debt**, $r_d(1 - T)$, is used to calculate the weighted average cost of capital and is the interest rate on debt, r_d, less the tax savings resulting because interest is tax deductible. This is the same as r_d multiplied by $(1 - T)$, where T is the firm's marginal tax rate:[2]

$$\text{After-tax component cost of debt} = \text{Interest rate} - \text{Tax savings}$$
$$= r_d - r_d T$$
$$= r_d (1 - T). \tag{10-1}$$

Therefore, if SSI borrows at an interest rate of 8 percent, and has a marginal federal-plus-state tax rate of 40 percent, then its after-tax cost of debt is 4.8 percent:

$$r_d (1 - T) = 8\%(1.0 - 0.4)$$
$$= 8\%(0.6)$$
$$= 4.8\%.$$

---

[1] The effective annual rate is $(1 + 0.08/2)^2 - 1 = 8.16\% \approx 8.2\%$, but SSI and most other companies use nominal rates for all component costs.

[2] The federal tax rate for most U.S. corporations is 35 percent. However, most corporations are also subject to state income taxes, so the total marginal tax rate on most corporate income is about 40 percent. For illustrative purposes, we assume that the effective federal-plus-state tax rate on marginal income is 40 percent. Note that the effective tax rate is zero for a firm with such large current or past losses that it does not pay taxes. In this situation the after-tax cost of debt is equal to the pre-tax interest rate. Tax rates and rules in other countries vary widely, as we discuss in Chapter 16.

Flotation costs are usually fairly small for debt issues, so most analysts ignore them when estimating the cost of debt.[3]

Cost of Foreign-Currency-Denominated Debt, $r_d(1 − T)(1 + \Delta FX^e) + \Delta FX^e$

Suppose SSI can borrow at a rate of 11.25 percent in Europe with one-year debt that is denominated in euros.[4] It would have to pay back the euro principal plus the 11.25 percent interest in euros. When calculating the cost of debt denominated in a foreign currency, an additional adjustment is necessary to account for foreign exchange rates. If the dollar appreciates against the euro, then it takes fewer dollars to obtain the necessary euros, and this results in a lower cost rate than if exchange rates had not changed. Conversely, the cost rate rises if the dollar depreciates. Thus, in addition to the tax adjustment, we must adjust the cost of debt for expected exchange rate changes, leading to this equation for the after-tax cost of foreign-currency-denominated debt:

$$\text{After-tax component cost of foreign-currency-denominated debt} = r_d (1 − T)(1 + \Delta FX^e) + \Delta FX^e. \qquad (10\text{-}2)$$

Here r_d is the yield to maturity on debt, T is the corporation's marginal tax rate, and ΔFX^e is the expected percentage change in the exchange rate. Also, ΔFX^e is calculated as $(FX_t − FX_{t−1})/FX_{t−1}$, where FX_t is defined as dollars per unit of the foreign currency at time t. The first term in Equation 10-2, $r_d(1 − T)(1 + \Delta FX^e)$, is the tax- and exchange-rate adjusted interest cost. The second term, ΔFX^e, is the expected percentage increase or decrease in the principal to be repaid.

For example, suppose SSI needs $115 and can borrow 100 euros for one year at 11.25 percent to obtain the funds. In addition, assume the dollar is expected to appreciate over the year from $1.15/€ to $1.13/€. Here are the calculations for determining the after-tax cost of the euro debt:

Inputs for euro-denominated loan	
Contract interest rate on euro debt	11.25%
Euros borrowed	100.00
Spot exchange rate ($/€)	1.15
Forecasted 1-year forward exchange rate ($/€)	1.13
Tax rate	40%
Calculations for euro-denominated loan	
Dollars borrowed (€100 × $1.15/€)	$115.00
Dollars required to repay principal (€100 × $1.13/€)	113.00
Dollars required to pay interest (after taxes) (€100 × 0.1125 × (1 − 0.4) × 1.13/€)	7.63
Total dollars paid as principal and interest	$120.63
After-tax cost of loan ($120.63/$115.00 − 1)	4.8935%

The same result is obtained using this formula:

$$\text{After-tax cost of loan} = r_d(1 − T)(1 + \Delta FX^e) + \Delta FX^e$$

---

[3]In perfect markets, the after-tax cost of debt should reflect the *expected* cost of debt. However, while not including the possibility of default may lead to an overstatement in the cost of debt, the exclusion of flotation costs leads to an understatement, making r_d a good approximation of the before-tax cost of debt.

[4]The SSI example uses one-year debt, but this formula can be used to accommodate any maturity.

where

$$\Delta FX^e = (FX_1 - FX_0)/FX_0$$
$$= (\$1.13 - \$1.15)/\$1.15 = -0.0173913.$$

After-tax cost of foreign debt $= 0.1125 \times 0.6 \times (1 - 0.0173913) - 0.0173913$
$$= 4.8935\%.$$

Notice, dollar appreciation against a foreign currency lowers the cost of the foreign debt. This 4.8935 percent after-tax cost rate should be compared with the after-tax cost of borrowing dollar-denominated debt, which is 4.8 percent. Since the after-tax cost of the dollar-denominated debt is slightly lower than the after-tax cost of the foreign debt, the after-tax cost of the dollar-denominated debt should be used in SSI's WACC calculation.

Why is the after-tax cost of debt rather than the before-tax cost used to calculate the weighted average cost of capital?

Is the relevant cost of debt the interest rate on *currently outstanding* debt or that on *new* debt? Why?

What adjustments are needed when calculating the cost of foreign-currency-denominated debt?

Briefly explain why the appreciation of the dollar against a foreign currency would result in a lower cost of the foreign-currency-denominated debt. What would you expect to happen if the dollar depreciated?

COST OF PREFERRED STOCK, r_{ps}

A number of firms, including SSI, use preferred stock as part of their permanent financing mix, though common shares are the most prevalent type of equity issued by most corporations around the world. Preferred dividends are not tax deductible to the issuing firm in the United States and most other countries, while interest expenses typically are.[5] Therefore, the company bears their full cost, and *no tax adjustment is made when calculating the cost of preferred stock*. Note that while some preferred stocks are issued without stated maturity dates, today most have sinking funds that effectively limit their lives. For firms that issue sinking fund preferred stock, adhering to a long-run target capital structure implies the firm will periodically reissue preferred stock, as existing preferred stock is retired. Although it is not mandatory that preferred dividends be paid, firms generally have every intention of doing so, because otherwise (1) they cannot pay common dividends, (2) they will find it difficult to raise additional funds in the capital markets, and (3) in some cases preferred stockholders can take control of the firm.

Cost of Preferred Stock, r_{ps}
The rate of return investors require on the firm's preferred stock. It is calculated as the preferred dividend, D_{ps}, divided by the net issuing price, P_n.

The component **cost of preferred stock**, r_{ps}, is the preferred dividend, D_{ps}, divided by the net issuing price, P_n, which is the price the firm receives after deducting flotation costs:

$$r_{ps} = \frac{D_{ps}}{P_n}. \tag{10-3}$$

Flotation costs are higher for preferred stock than for debt; hence, they are incorporated into the cost.

---

[5]In some countries, corporations owning shares in other corporations are only partially taxed on the dividends they receive.

To illustrate, assume SSI has perpetual preferred stock that pays a $7 dividend per share and sells for $100 per share. If SSI issued new shares of preferred, it would incur an underwriting (or flotation) cost of 2.5 percent, or $2.50 per share, so it would net $97.50 per share. Therefore, SSI's cost of preferred stock is 7.2 percent:[6]

$$ r_{ps} = \frac{\$7}{\$97.50} = 7.18\% \approx 7.2\%. $$

Does the component cost of preferred stock include or exclude flotation costs? Explain.

Why is no tax adjustment made to the cost of preferred stock for an American company? Would this same situation hold for all companies, worldwide?

How would the calculation for a firm's cost of preferred stock differ if a firm issued perpetual preferred versus preferred with a maturity?

COST OF COMMON EQUITY, r_s

Marginal Investor
A representative investor whose actions reflect the beliefs of those people who are currently lending capital. It is the marginal investor who determines the cost of capital.

As we saw in the preceding sections, debt and preferred stock capital has a cost, and the cost of each is based on the return required by a marginal investor in the marketplace. If a company wants to raise debt or preferred stock, it will shop around to find the lender that provides the capital at the lowest cost. The company and lender sign a contract requiring the company to pay a specified amount under specified conditions. The lender/investor that offers money at the lowest cost is, by definition, the **marginal investor**. For most larger companies, many investors are willing and able to provide funds at about the same cost, so there are a number of marginal investors who have approximately the same required rate of return for the firm's debt and preferred stock. It is relatively easy to measure the costs of debt and preferred stock because they have contractual costs and there are many marginal investors.

The situation is different for common equity capital. Most importantly, there is no contractually specified cost rate—investors have a required rate that is undoubtedly higher than that for debt and preferred stock because common stock is more risky. We could ask investors, but larger companies have thousands of stockholders, and we need to know the marginal investor's required return. Even if we could identify the marginal investor, it would be hard to ascertain his or her required return—most people, even professional money managers, have a hard time stating their required return, and their statements are often inconsistent, even over short time periods. Given this problem, how do we estimate the cost of common equity?

Company-Bond-Yield-Plus-Risk-Premium Approach

The first approach is to add a subjectively-determined risk premium to the firm's own bond yield. For example, we have seen proprietary studies by security analysts where portfolio managers were asked how much more they require on stocks than on bonds of selected companies, and the answers generally ranged from 2 to 4 percent. To illustrate, SSI can borrow at a rate of 8 percent, so an investor that applies a 2 percent risk premium will buy SSI's stock if his or her expected (but risky) return is 10 percent or more. A more risk-averse investor that demands a 4 percent risk premium will buy the stock only if his or her expected return is 12 percent or more. This makes sense, but it is highly subjective, and we do not know the marginal investor's risk premium.

---

[6]Note that the equation used here estimates the cost of perpetual preferred. If SSI's preferred had a maturity date, then the equation used would be similar to the one used to estimate a bond's yield to maturity.

Cost of Common Equity, r$_s$
The rate of return required by stockholders on a firm's common stock.

SSI's financial manager recognizes the limitations of the subjective risk premium method, but still calculates the firm's **cost of common equity, r$_s$**, using a 3 percent risk premium:

$$r_s = \text{Bond yield} + \text{Risk premium}$$
$$= 8\% + 3\% = 11\%.$$

The "reasonable range" for SSI's cost of equity, based on a risk premium of 2 to 4 percent, is 10 to 12 percent. This subjective risk premium method provides a useful "ballpark" estimate of the firm's cost of equity. Consequently, when using other approaches to evaluate SSI's cost of equity, any estimates for SSI outside this range should be subjected to careful scrutiny.

Discounted Cash Flow (DCF) Approach

A second approach uses the discounted cash flow (DCF) stock valuation model, or dividend approach, discussed in Chapter 9. We know investors expect cash returns consisting of dividends and capital gains. Moreover, investors evaluate stocks by forecasting dividend streams and a future stock price and discounting those cash flows at the required rate of return. If the calculated stock value exceeds the market price, an investor will buy the stock but would sell if the calculated price is less than the market price. At the margin, the expected return equals the required return, because if not, buying or selling would change the stock price and force equilibrium where the two returns are equal. Now suppose we know the current market price, the marginal investor's expectations regarding future dividends, and the stock price at a specified horizon date. Given that information, we can solve the valuation equation for that investor's expected rate of return, r$_s$.

The marginal investor's cash flow forecasts are very difficult to determine. We could ask selected investors for their views and obtain forecasts from security analysts, but different investors and analysts will have different views. Suppose a number of respected analysts following SSI indicate that they do not expect the firm to pay dividends for four years but expect a $1.10 dividend in Year 5. Thereafter, they expect the firm's dividend to grow at a constant rate of 7.5 percent a year. The firm's common stock sells at a current market price of $20.00. If the discounted cash flow approach is used, what is the estimate of the firm's cost of common equity?[7]

Figure 10-1 illustrates the DCF estimation of SSI's cost of equity. Using an *Excel* spreadsheet with the data, the firm's cost of equity is found to be approximately 11.1 percent. A realistic DCF model is best solved using a spreadsheet, so we defer further comments on this method to the chapter model.

Capital Asset Pricing Model (CAPM)

As we saw in Chapter 5, the CAPM is both logical and widely used by investors, and it provides a direct cost of equity estimate. Studies show it is clearly the most popular method among academicians, consultants, and corporations; about 85 percent of large U.S. companies use the CAPM to estimate the cost of equity. Moreover, firms operating internationally are more likely to use the CAPM than purely domestic firms.[8]

---

[7]Indeed, some years ago the DCF method was widely used for cost of equity estimates, but recent surveys indicate that it is rarely used for this purpose today. See Robert F. Bruner, Kenneth M. Eades, Robert S. Harris, and Robert C. Higgins, "Best Practices in Estimating the Cost of Capital: Survey and Synthesis," *Financial Practice and Education*, Spring/Summer 1998, 13–28; and John R. Graham and Campbell R. Harvey, "The Theory and Practice of Corporate Finance: Evidence from the Field," *Journal of Financial Economics*, 60, 2001, 187–243. Both papers reported that about 85 percent of the corporations they surveyed used either the pure, one-factor CAPM or else a multifactor version of the CAPM to estimate the cost of equity. The DCF model was used by 15 percent of respondents, and none of the respondents admitted to using the subjective risk premium approach.

[8]See Bruner et al., "Best Practices in Estimating the Cost of Capital," and Graham and Harvey, "The Theory and Practice of Corporate Finance."

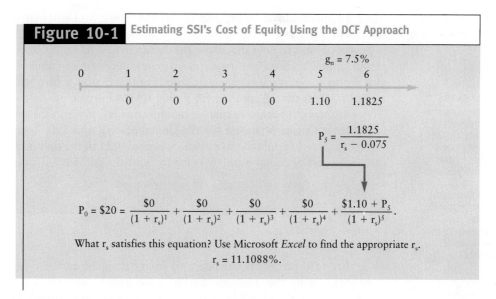

Figure 10-1   Estimating SSI's Cost of Equity Using the DCF Approach

$$g_n = 7.5\%$$

| 0 | 1 | 2 | 3 | 4 | 5 | 6 |

| 0 | 0 | 0 | 0 | 1.10 | 1.1825 |

$$P_5 = \frac{1.1825}{r_s - 0.075}$$

$$P_0 = \$20 = \frac{\$0}{(1 + r_s)^1} + \frac{\$0}{(1 + r_s)^2} + \frac{\$0}{(1 + r_s)^3} + \frac{\$0}{(1 + r_s)^4} + \frac{\$1.10 + P_5}{(1 + r_s)^5}.$$

What r_s satisfies this equation? Use Microsoft *Excel* to find the appropriate r_s.

$$r_s = 11.1088\%.$$

Recall that three parameters are necessary to find the required rate of return—the risk-free rate, r_{RF}, the firm's beta coefficient, b_i, and the market risk premium, RP_M:

$$r_s = r_{RF} + (RP_M)b_i. \tag{10-4}$$

If the current risk-free rate, as measured by the yield on 20-year T-bonds, is 5 percent, the market risk premium (RP_M) is 6 percent, and the best estimate of the firm's beta coefficient is 1.25, then we estimate SSI's CAPM cost of equity as 12.5 percent:

$$r_s = 5\% + (6\%)(1.25)$$
$$= 12.5\%.$$

Global CAPM

As countries have become more integrated, so have international capital markets.[9] Globalization results in lower costs of capital because equity risk is shared among a greater number of investors who have different risk requirements, thus magnifying the diversification effect.[10] Additionally, firms from less-developed capital markets raising capital in more developed markets often import more stringent reporting and corporate oversight guidelines (corporate governance) from those developed markets. This leads to more effective monitoring and improvement in the terms when subsequent capital is raised.

In addition to reducing risk premiums and improving corporate governance, globalization affects a company's beta and cost of equity. A firm's beta depends on its covariance with the world portfolio in an internationally integrated capital market. In this case, we use the CAPM framework shown in Equation 10-4, $r_s = r_{RF} + (RP_M)b_i$; however, the risk premium and beta for the international model are redefined in global terms. Here, RP_W is the world risk premium, which is often proxied using the return on Morgan Stanley's Capital Market International (MSCI)

---

[9]Capital market integration refers to the extent to which similar assets in different countries are priced equally.

[10]See René Stulz, "Globalization, Corporate Finance, and the Cost of Capital," *Journal of Applied Corporate Finance*, Fall 1999, 8–25. There is also some evidence that additional risks of overseas operations from agency costs, political risk, currency risk, information asymmetries, and similar things more than offset the diversification potential so that the cost of capital for an MNE is actually higher than for a purely domestic firm. See David M. Reeb, Chuck C. Y. Kwok, and H. Young Baek, "Systematic Risk of the Multinational Corporation," *Journal of International Business Studies*, Second Quarter 1998, 263–279.

value-weighted world index, and $b_{i,W}$ is the firm's beta calculated with respect to the world index.

It is important to note that using the domestic CAPM for companies with access to global capital markets can result in an overstated cost of equity because holding a global portfolio diversifies domestic risks. For this reason, a firm with access to global capital markets should consider the **global CAPM** to calculate its cost of equity.

Global CAPM
A model based on the proposition that any stock's required rate of return is equal to the risk-free rate of return plus a risk premium that reflects only the risk remaining after diversification in world markets.

For example, suppose the current risk-free rate is 5 percent, the world risk premium is 5 percent (it was 6 percent for the United States), and SSI's beta coefficient is 1.2 when calculated against the world index (versus 1.25 in the domestic analysis). In this case, SSI's cost of equity estimate using the global CAPM is 11.0 percent:

$$r_s = r_{RF} + (RP_W)b_{i,W} \tag{10-5}$$

$$= 5\% + (5\%)(1.2)$$
$$= 11.0\%.$$

Note that 11.0 percent is considerably lower than the earlier estimate of 12.5 percent obtained by the domestic CAPM. The lower estimate is reasonable because purely domestic risks have been diversified away and the correlation of returns with the world portfolio is slightly less than for the domestic market.

Summary: SSI's Cost of Common Equity

SSI's cost of common equity is calculated by each of the four methods in the chapter model. Here is a summary of the findings:

Method	Most Likely Estimate (%)	Range (%)
Subjective risk premium	11.0	10.00 – 12.00
DCF	11.1	8.45 – 12.82
Domestic CAPM	12.5	10.75 – 14.45
Global CAPM	11.0	9.40 – 12.80

The ranges are merely suggestive—in this case they represent the judgmental estimates of SSI's financial managers. The summary of the most likely estimates suggests some congruence among the methods. However, in practice we expect more dispersion than shown above.

Retained Earnings versus Newly Issued Stock

One further complication regarding the cost of common equity is the effect of flotation costs when new stock is issued. A substantial underwriting cost is generally required to issue new common stock, and the announcement of plans to issue more stock has a psychological effect that increases the cost of new outside equity. However, most mature firms retain enough earnings each year to avoid the costs of issuing new common stock. Therefore, we shall omit a discussion of equity flotation costs and refer the interested reader to an advanced corporate finance text.[11]

---

[11]For example, see Eugene F. Brigham and Phillip R. Daves, *Intermediate Financial Management*, 8th edition (Mason, OH: South-Western Publishing, 2004), Chapters 9 and 14. If a firm has some wonderful new product that will increase earnings dramatically, but it needs capital to invest in the new product, then management would prefer to use debt rather than equity financing so all of the new earnings bonanza can be retained by current stockholders rather than shared with new stockholders. On the other hand, if the firm must make costly investments to upgrade plants or products to meet a competitive challenge, and those upgrades will just maintain revenues, not increase them, it would prefer to use stock financing so that new stockholders will absorb some of these "nonproductive" costs. Thus, managers have an incentive to issue stock when the future looks gloomy but not to issue stock if the future looks bright. As a result, stockholders might equate a new stock offering to a sign of bad times ahead, leading to a low issue price. This is a type of flotation cost, and it makes managers (1) retain more earnings during normal times than they otherwise would and (2) then use the *reserve borrowing capacity* supported by those extra retained earnings rather than issue new stock during hard times. In addition, the initial cost of going public now has a higher fixed cost component—the flotation costs are an additional incremental cost. For our purposes here, we can view the fixed cost as a sunk cost, though if the firm is not currently publicly traded this is not an issue.

APPLYING THE GLOBAL CAPM: NESTLÉ S.A.

Most valuation approaches used by U.S. companies were developed when the U.S. stock market accounted for most of the word's total capitalization and foreign investment was difficult. Today, the integration of international capital markets suggests that costs of capital should be calculated on a global basis. Mistakes due to using a local CAPM, rather than a global CAPM, can be substantial, especially for smaller firms. Professor René Stulz, of Ohio State University, identified the magnitude of this "mistake" to be

$$\text{Local CAPM error} = \beta_{iG} - \beta_{iH} \times \beta_{HG},$$

where β_{iG} is the beta of firm i using the global CAPM, β_{iH} is the beta of firm i using the local CAPM, and β_{HG} is the beta of the local index with respect to a global index.

Founded, headquartered, and traded in Switzerland, Nestlé S.A. markets its products throughout the world and provides an example of a multinational firm whose cost of equity estimate is challenging. The accompanying table summarizes Nestlé's beta with respect to two Swiss indices, two global indices, and two U.S. indices, as well as beta estimates of the two Swiss indices with respect to the remaining indices. As expected, Nestlé's beta with respect to the Swiss indices is closer to one than the other betas.

$$\text{Local CAPM error} = 0.585 - 0.885 \times 0.737$$
$$= 0.585 - 0.652 = -0.067.$$

This implies that using the local CAPM would cause Nestlé to overstate its beta by 0.067. Similarly, Stulz argues that the market risk premium is often overstated. He endorses a world risk premium that is roughly 0.74 times the U.S. risk premium.

Indices	$\beta_{\text{Nestlé}}$	$\beta_{\text{FTA Swiss}}$	$\beta_{\text{MSCI Swiss}}$
FTA Switzerland	0.885	—	—
MSCI Switzerland	0.838	—	—
FTA World	0.585	0.737	0.788
MSCI World	0.595	0.756	0.809
FTA US	0.712	0.842	0.897
MSCI US	0.709	0.838	0.893

To illustrate these CAPM errors, consider our example of Nestlé with a risk-free rate of 5 percent and market risk premium of 6 percent. Using the FTA Switzerland beta estimate for Nestlé, we find

$$r_s = 5\% + (6\%)(0.885) = 10.31\%.$$

However, if we use a global beta (FTA World estimate) and an adjusted world risk premium (0.74 times the local market risk premium), we find

$$r_s = 5\% + (0.74 \times 6\%)(0.585)$$
$$= 5\% + (4.44\%)(0.585) = 7.60\%.$$

In Nestlé's case, failure to apply the global CAPM results in overestimating the cost of common equity capital by 2.71 percent.

Source: René Stulz, "The Cost of Capital in Internationally Integrated Markets: The Case of Nestlé," *European Financial Management*, Vol. 1, no. 1, 1995, 11–22.

SELF-TEST QUESTIONS

Briefly explain what is meant by the term marginal investor. Why is this concept so important?

Why is the situation for determining the cost of common equity different from that for both debt and preferred stock?

Identify and briefly explain the four approaches used to estimate the cost of common equity capital.

When should you use the global CAPM to estimate a firm's cost of equity?

Why might the domestic CAPM overstate a firm's cost of equity?

Briefly explain the differences between the domestic and global versions of the CAPM.

THE WEIGHTED AVERAGE COST OF CAPITAL (WACC)

Now that we have component costs of the capital, we can calculate SSI's WACC. Because SSI has access to global markets, the firm correctly applies the global CAPM to calculate its cost of equity. The company's target capital structure calls for 30 percent debt, 10 percent preferred stock, and 60 percent common equity. We discuss setting the target capital structure in Chapter 13, but for now simply take it as given. SSI's WACC is calculated in the following table:

Capital Component	Target Weight	After-Tax Component Cost	After-Tax Weighted Cost
Debt	30%	8.0%(1 − 0.4)	1.44%
Preferred	10	7.2	0.72
Common	60	11.0	6.60
	100%		WACC = 8.76%

Of course, the actual WACC might be quite different from the calculated 8.76 percent. As we show in the model, the "reasonable range" is from 7 to 11 percent. We will consider the uncertainty about the WACC in Chapters 11 and 12, where WACC is an input in capital budgeting decisions.

A few additional points should be noted. First, the WACC is the weighted average cost of each new, or marginal, dollar of capital—it is not the average cost of all dollars raised in the past. Our primary interest is obtaining a cost of capital to use in discounting future cash flows, and for this purpose the cost of the new money to be invested is the relevant cost. On average, each new dollar will consist of some debt, some preferred, and some common equity.

Second, the percentages of each capital component, called weights, can be based on (1) accounting values shown on the balance sheet (book values), (2) current market values of the capital components, or (3) management's target capital structure. *The correct weights are based on the firm's target capital structure, since it is the best estimate of how the firm will, on average, raise money in the future.* Recent survey evidence indicates the majority of firms base their weights on target capital structures, and that target structures reflect market values.[12]

How is the weighted average cost of capital calculated? Write out the equation. On what should the weights be based?

How is the weighted average cost of capital affected by operating internationally?

DIFFERENT WACCs WITHIN A FIRM

The WACC calculated in the preceding section is an "overall corporate WACC" for all of SSI. Implicitly, that WACC reflects SSI's average cost of new debt, preferred stock, common equity, and the target capital structure. For capital budgeting purposes, the overall corporate WACC is appropriate for evaluating a project whose

---

[12]The appropriate capital structure for use in calculating a firm's WACC should focus on market weights rather than book weights. If a firm's market-to-book ratio is not equal to 1 (which is the typical situation), then book weights do not equal market weights and the resulting WACC calculation is different depending on which weights are used. We generally assume that market weights are accurate, so most firms base their target capital structure weights on market values. The *Excel* chapter model (refer to the Capital Structure tab) illustrates the "errors" that occur in a firm's WACC if book weights are used.

WACC ESTIMATES FOR SOME LARGE U.S. MULTINATIONAL CORPORATIONS

The accompanying table presents some recent WACC estimates as calculated by Stern Stewart & Company for a sample of U.S. multinational corporations, along with their debt ratios.

These estimates suggest that a typical company has a WACC somewhere in the 7 to 13 percent range and that WACCs vary considerably depending on (1) the company's risk and (2) the amount of debt it uses. Companies in riskier businesses, such as Intel, presumably have higher costs of common equity. Moreover, they tend not to use as much debt. These two factors, in combination, result in higher WACCs than those of companies that operate in more stable businesses, such as General Electric. We will discuss the effects of capital structure on WACC in more detail in Chapter 13.

Note that riskier companies may also have the potential for producing higher returns, and what really matters to shareholders is whether a company is able to generate returns in excess of its cost of capital.

Company[a]	WACC[b]	Book Value Debt Ratio[c]
Intel (INTC)	16.0%	2.6%
Motorola (MOT)	12.8	40.6
Wal-Mart (WMT)	8.8	33.3
Merck (MRK)	8.7	21.1
Walt Disney (DIS)	8.7	34.7
ToysR Us Inc. (TOY)	8.5	34.7
General Electric (GE)	8.1	68.8
ExxonMobil (XOM)	7.8	8.2
Coca-Cola (KO)	6.9	18.6
H.J. Heinz (HNZ)	6.5	73.0

Notes:
[a]Ticker symbols are shown in parentheses.
[b]Values are from *The 2002 Stern Stewart Performance 1000*, provided by Stern Stewart & Co.
[c]This is Long-term debt/(Long-term debt + Equity), obtained from **http://yahoo.marketguide.com**.

Sources: Various issues of *Fortune;* the General Electric Web site, **http://www.ge.com**; and the Stern Stewart & Co. Web site, **http://www.sternstewart.com**.

risk is about equal to the firm as a whole and assuming the project will be financed in accordance with the firm's target capital structure. However, different WACCs should be used for discounting cash flows of assets whose risk, financing, or other characteristics deviate from the average.

First, think of SSI as a composite of different "mini firms," with the mini firms being its different subsidiaries around the world, or its different operating divisions, or even different assets such as capital budgeting projects. The blended average of all the mini firms is reflected in SSI's risk, capital structure, and therefore its WACC. Now think about what would happen to SSI's overall risk if it acquired a company that was much riskier, say one with a beta of 2.0 versus SSI's current global beta of 1.2. The new and larger SSI would now have a higher beta, essentially a weighted average of 1.2 and 2.0, with the firm market values as weights. Obviously, such an acquisition affects the capital components' costs and the new corporate WACC. Similarly, if SSI decides to invest in a large, risky new capital budgeting project, this changes the company's overall risk and its WACC.

Now think of some factors that cause the WACCs of SSI's various mini firms to differ. Here is a partial list:

1. *Country risk.* Underlying risks vary across countries, and risk differentials affect WACCs.
2. *Exchange rate risk.* There are risks associated with exchange rates for operations outside the parent company's home country.
3. *Interest rates.* SSI has operations in many countries, and there are cross-country differences in interest rates. This situation could lead to different costs of debt, preferred, and common equity for each of its international subsidiaries.
4. *Tax rates and rules.* Tax rates and rules vary across countries and can affect the cost of debt, and possibly that of preferred and common equity.

5. *Capital structure.* The capital structure used to find the WACC in the preceding section was SSI's target for the total corporation. However, SSI might, for various reasons, choose to finance with other combinations of capital components in different countries. Companies sometimes finance different subsidiaries, even within a given country, with different debt/equity mixes. For example, McDonald's might have a separate subsidiary that owns and maintains its real estate and, as a result, uses more debt financing than its other operating subsidiaries. That would lead to different capital structure weights and different WACCs for different business units. However, the consolidated company's target capital structure would be reflected in the average WACC.

6. *Operating risk differences.* Different parts of a company, or different projects, have different operating risks. If SSI is considering two projects—one calling for the expansion of an established product line in the United States, where management is quite confident about revenue and cost projections, and another involving a new product to be produced in China for Chinese customers where results are highly uncertain—those projects will have different risks and different costs of capital.

It is apparent that different WACCs exist within a firm like SSI. Just as the beta of a portfolio is a weighted average of the individual stock betas, the firm's overall WACC is a weighted average of its individual units' WACCs. The overall WACC is appropriate for evaluating average-risk projects financed according to the firm's overall target capital structure, but wherever differences exist, they should explicitly be taken into account. Moreover, the surveys by Graham and Harvey and Bruner et al. indicate that firms, especially those with international operations, recognize and consider these differences.

Techniques for Measuring Project Risk

While corporate managers recognize the need to risk adjust the cost of capital for various projects, in practice it is hard to come up with reliable estimates of **risk-adjusted costs of capital**. Theoretically, we want to know each project's market risk (or beta). Unfortunately, it is difficult to directly estimate a project's market risk because projects, unlike common stocks, do not trade directly in the open market.

In some cases, managers use information from other publicly traded firms to estimate individual project or division betas. Using the **pure play method**, the company finds several single-product companies in the same line of business as the project it is evaluating and then averages these companies' betas to determine the project's cost of capital.[13] For example, several years ago when IBM considered going into personal computers, it was able to obtain data on Apple Computer and several other pure play personal computer companies. This is often the case when a firm considers a major investment outside its primary field. Generally, however, the pure play approach can be used only for major assets such as whole divisions, and even then it is difficult to implement because it is challenging to find pure play proxy firms.

An alternative (and more subjective) approach for risk adjusting the cost of capital is classifying the firm's projects according to their perceived stand-alone risk (which is generally measured by the standard deviation or variability of the project's returns). As we will see in Chapter 12, it is fairly easy to estimate a project's stand-alone risk. While market risk is theoretically a more appropriate risk measure, we take comfort in the fact that stand-alone risk and market risk are often highly cor-

Professor Campbell Harvey of Duke University has an interesting Web site that looks at country risk, emerging markets, and the global cost of capital. The site can be found at http://www.duke.edu/ ~charvey.

Risk-Adjusted Cost of Capital
The cost of capital appropriate for a particular project, given the riskiness of that project. The greater the risk, the higher the cost of capital.

Pure Play Method
An approach used for estimating the beta of a project in which a firm (1) identifies several companies whose only business is to produce the product in question, (2) calculates the beta for each firm, and then (3) averages the betas to find an approximation to the project's beta.

---

[13]Even when good pure play proxies can be found, different financing characteristics, like capital structure, can introduce new complications. We will deal with these issues in Chapter 13.

related.[14] Once project stand-alone risk is estimated, we classify projects into different subjective risk categories (e.g., above-average, average, and below-average risk). Then, starting with the firm's overall WACC, risk-adjusted costs of capital are developed for each category. For example, if the firm's overall WACC is 10 percent, its managers use 10 percent to evaluate average-risk projects, 12 percent for above-average risk projects, and 8 percent for below-average risk projects. While this approach is better than not making any risk adjustments, remember that these adjustments are subjective and somewhat arbitrary.

Effects of International Operations on WACC

As noted earlier, complications in determining the cost of capital for international operations include assessing variations in the level of international capital market integration across countries as well as differences in terms of country, political, and currency risks. Moreover, because international data on companies and industries are often difficult to obtain, especially in emerging markets, international cost of capital calculations are often done on a country-level basis. Rather than focusing on specific firms or industries in foreign markets, foreign cost of capital measures usually address overall risks in those markets. The cost of capital approaches for the domestic setting provide a useful framework for addressing international cost of capital issues. However, in an international setting, even greater challenges arise when calculating the cost of common equity.

Approaches for Determining the Cost of Equity for International Operations

Given the greater complications and lack of a consensus in calculating the international cost of capital, various approaches are used by academicians and industry practitioners. The various approaches are not only applicable to developed countries but also to emerging markets that are often segmented from developed capital markets and face even greater macroeconomic uncertainty. Although U.S. multinationals do not typically issue equity in emerging markets, they often acquire companies in these markets, and these approaches are useful when determining the values of those foreign companies. In addition, these approaches can be used by the domestic companies of such foreign countries. As discussed in Chapter 4, emerging markets are particularly interesting given their growing importance as receivers of capital flows through cross-border joint ventures and mergers and acquisitions.

Global CAPM with Partially Segmented Capital Markets A model that estimates the cost of equity in markets that are not perfectly integrated. The cost of equity is determined partly by an integrated market risk premium component and partly by a segmented market component.

The focus here is on appropriate cost of capital adjustments to address these additional risks. In Chapter 11, we discuss an alternative approach where cash flows are adjusted to account for various macroeconomic and other risk scenarios.

GLOBAL CAPM WITH PARTIALLY SEGMENTED CAPITAL MARKETS Earlier we discussed the use of the global CAPM when capital markets are perfectly integrated. However, for operations in markets that are not perfectly integrated, such as exist in many emerging markets, the cost of equity capital is equal to the risk-free rate, an integrated market risk premium component, and an additional segmented market component. The second factor is the risk premium associated with a country, or region, that is independent of the world risk premium. With this approach, the equation becomes

---

[14]The risk measure for market risk is beta. Mathematically, the beta for project i equals $\rho_{i,m}(\sigma_i/\sigma_m)$. Basing the risk adjustment only on σ_i, or project standard deviation, assumes implicitly that the correlation coefficient, $\rho_{i,m}$, is roughly the same for all projects. This often is a reasonable assumption, but you should also be aware of the potential for bias. The classification scheme presented in this section is probably sufficiently macro in scope to render such biases inconsequential.

$$r_s = r_{RF} + (RP_W)b_{i,W} + (SRP_j)b_{i,Seg}. \quad \textbf{(10-6)}$$

Here, r_{RF} is the risk-free rate, RP_W is the world risk premium, $b_{i,W}$ is the beta of firm i calculated with respect to the world risk premium, SRP_j is the risk premium associated with segmented country$_j$ (or region$_j$) risk, and $b_{i,Seg}$ is the beta of firm i with respect to the segmented country risk premium.[15]

Suppose that SSI has a Brazilian project and the SRP_j is 17 percent with a corresponding $b_{i,Seg}$ estimate of 0.7. The cost of equity estimate for a Brazilian project using the global CAPM and assuming partially segmented markets is calculated as 22.9 percent:

$$r_s = 5\% + (5\%)(1.2) + (17\%)(0.7)$$
$$= 22.9\%.$$

In this example, we see that the cost of equity more than doubled when we included the country-specific risk premium component. One benefit of this approach is that it allows for other country- or region-specific risk elements to be included in the cost of equity. Research shows that this approach works especially well for the Latin American region.[16]

COUNTRY-SPREAD APPROACH An additional problem arises when applying the global CAPM to emerging markets because the correlations of returns between emerging markets and developed markets are often low.[17] In this case, emerging-market betas calculated relative to the world portfolio are often indistinguishable from zero, or are even negative, implying that the emerging-market cost of equity is the risk-free rate or lower. While this could indicate significant diversification potential, it can partly be attributed to market segmentation, a potential risk. To address this problem, various consulting firms use a **country-spread model**, where the emerging-market cost of equity is determined by adding a country-credit spread to the U.S. risk-free rate along with an adjusted beta times the U.S. market risk premium.[18] In a sense, this approach is analogous to the bond-yield-plus-risk-premium approach described for estimating the domestic cost of equity.

The **country credit spread** is typically calculated as the spread between the 10-year yields on dollar-denominated foreign bonds (Yankee or Brady bonds) issued by foreign governments and U.S. Treasury bonds. It accounts for country-specific risk, including sovereign risk. This spread over U.S. government rates adds an additional foreign investment risk premium to the cost of equity, transforming an incorrectly low cost of equity estimate for emerging markets into a more reasonable estimate for evaluating investments. While the model anchors estimates to U.S. Treasury bonds and uses the U.S. market risk premium, the beta is calculated as the ratio of the country's market return variance divided by the U.S. market return variance. (Recall from the standard CAPM, beta is usually the covariance of an asset's return with the U.S. market return divided by the U.S. market return variance.) The beta

Country-Spread Model
This model estimates the emerging-market cost of equity by adding a country credit spread to the U.S. risk-free rate along with an adjusted beta times the U.S. market risk premium.

Country Credit Spread
Calculated as the difference between 10-year yields on dollar-denominated foreign bonds and U.S. Treasury bonds.

[15]SRP_j is the country (or region) risk premium that is statistically independent of the world risk premium. SRP_j is obtained by running a regression of the country returns against the world portfolio returns. The residuals from the regression are added to the model as the segmented country risk premium. The model parameters $b_{i,W}$ and $b_{i,Seg}$ are estimated by repeating the regression model shown in Equation 10-6.

[16]See Andrew Clare and Paul Kaplan, "A Globally Nested Capital Asset Pricing Model," *Ibbotson and Associates' Working Paper*, July 1998.

[17]We take the perspective of a U.S. multinational firm considering a project in an emerging market, though a similar problem exists when applying the global CAPM to individual stocks in emerging markets.

[18]See, for instance, Stephen Godfrey and Ramon Espinosa, "A Practical Approach to Calculating Costs of Equity for Investments in Emerging Markets," *Journal of Applied Corporate Finance*, Fall 1996, 80–89.

in this model is also scaled down by a constant factor of 0.6 to account for country credit spread representing some of the same risk factors as captured by the market risk premium.[19]

$$r_s = r_{RF} + (RP_M)[0.6(\sigma_j/\sigma_M)] + \text{Country credit spread.} \qquad (10\text{-}7)$$

Here, r_{RF} is the U.S. risk-free rate, RP_M is the U.S. market risk premium, and σ_j/σ_M is the ratio of the market return variance for country j to that of the United States.

For example, suppose the current U.S. risk-free rate is 5 percent, the United States market risk premium is 6 percent, the ratio of the market return variance for Brazil to that of the U.S. is 2.10, and the country credit spread is 13.5 percent. In this case, the cost of equity estimate for a Brazilian project using the country-spread approach is calculated as 26.06 percent:

$$r_s = 5\% + (6\%)(0.6)(2.10) + 13.5\%$$
$$= 26.06\%.$$

This cost of equity estimate is higher than our earlier estimate using the segmented CAPM approach (where we obtained an estimate of 22.9 percent) even after adjusting for the double counting problem. It is important to note that the country-spread approach provides an average estimate of the cost of equity in a particular country. This estimate is a measure of country risk, rather than project or firm risk. Therefore, to determine a specific project's discount rate, we must risk adjust the country's discount rate to reflect differences between the project's risk and that of an average investment in that country.[20]

COUNTRY-RISK-RATING APPROACH The **country-risk-rating approach** provides a good alternative to the country-spread approach when estimating country-level risk.[21] A key benefit of this approach is that it can be applied to well over 100 countries.[22] It uses the *Institutional Investor*'s country-risk ratings, which are based on weighted semiannual surveys of lenders from around the world.[23] The respondents rate each country on a scale from 0 to 100, with 100 representing the smallest default risk. Many political and economic risk factors influence a country's risk rating. If a country has higher credit risk (or a lower risk rating), then investors in that country will require a higher rate of return. The basic approach is to estimate a regression model of equity returns against corresponding country-risk ratings. The regression estimates allow inferences about expected returns in other developing markets. The corresponding regression model is

$$r_{sj}/2 = a + d_{cr}\ln(\text{Country-risk rating}_j). \qquad (10\text{-}8)$$

Here, $r_{sj}/2$ is the semiannual return in U.S. dollars for country j, a denotes the constant term of the regression equation, $\ln(\text{Country-risk rating}_j)$ is the natural logarithm of

Country-Risk-Rating Approach
It uses the *Institutional Investor*'s country-risk rating to estimate a regression model of equity returns against corresponding country-risk ratings.

---

[19]In another variation of this approach, the emerging-market beta is simply the U.S. beta.

[20]The country-spread approach has three major problems. First, it may result in a "double counting" and hence an overstatement in the international cost of equity. Second, there may be other equity risks not captured by the country credit spread, such as differences in liquidity. Finally, not all countries have appropriate country credit spread and equity market data, which are necessary inputs in the country-spread approach.

[21]See Claude B. Erb, Campbell R. Harvey, and Tadas E. Viskanta, "Country Risk and Global Equity Selection," *Journal of Portfolio Management*, Winter 1995, 74–83.

[22]The country-risk-rating approach also addresses some econometric deficiencies and measurement problems associated with the country-spread approach.

[23]*Institutional Investor* weights the responses by each bank's level of global prominence and credit analysis sophistication.

Institutional Investor's country-risk rating for country j at the end of March and September of each year, d_{cr} denotes the slope of the regression equation, and time is measured in half-years due to *Institutional Investor*'s semiannual data availability.

For example, suppose the estimated constant in the country-risk-rating model is 51.5 percent, the estimated slope is negative 10.5 percent, and the country-risk rating for Brazil is 45, then the cost of equity estimate for an average Brazilian project using the country-risk-rating approach is calculated as 23.06 percent:

$$
\begin{aligned}
r_{sj}/2 &= 51.5\% - 10.5\%[\ln(45)] \\
r_{sj} &= (11.53\%)(2) \\
&= 23.06\%.
\end{aligned}
$$

This approach provides an average country-level cost of equity estimate, which can be risk adjusted for different projects. However, unlike the country-spread approach, the country-risk-rating approach does not have a "double counting" problem, and the cost of equity estimate is generally lower.

INTERNATIONAL MULTI-BETA APPROACHES A final approach to calculating the international cost of equity incorporates macroeconomic and other asset pricing risk factors found in international capital markets. In addition to the world risk premium, factors may include GDP growth rates, current accounts, and exchange rates to explain the cost of equity for international capital markets.[24] Similarly, Fama and French find that their three-factor model also explains equity returns across countries.[25] While multi-beta extensions are intuitively appealing because they better estimate specific risk exposures across countries, their implementation is problematic for many countries due to varying levels of available data.

Summary: Estimating the Cost of Equity for International Operations

While calculating a firm's domestic cost of equity is difficult, estimating the international cost of equity requires an even greater dose of science and good judgment, especially in emerging markets. However, it is important that the cost of equity approach provides reasonable and consistent estimates for a wide range of countries.[26] Each international approach discussed has complications; however, the country-risk-rating approach provides reasonable and consistent estimates for the broadest set of countries. Therefore, the country-risk-rating approach should be given careful consideration when calculating the international cost of equity, particularly emerging-market operations. The following table shows the Brazilian cost of equity estimates using the different approaches discussed:

Approach	Cost of Equity Estimate
Two-component (segmented) CAPM	22.90%
Country-spread	26.06
Country-risk-rating	23.06

[24]See Andrew Clare and Paul Kaplan, "A Macroeconomic Model of the Equity Risk Premium," *Ibbotson and Associates' Working Paper*, November 1998.

[25]Professor John Griffin finds that country-level Fama-French three-factor models do a better job at explaining returns within each market than do international variations of the three-factor model. See John Griffin, "Are the Fama and French Factors Global or Country-Specific?" *University of Texas Working Paper*, 2003.

[26]See Campbell R. Harvey, "The International Cost of Capital and Risk Calculator (ICCRC)," *Duke Working Paper*, 2001; and Ibbotson Associates, *Stocks, Bonds, Bills, and Inflation: Valuation Edition, 2004 Yearbook* (Chicago: Ibbotson Associates, 2004), Chapter 9, "International Cost of Capital," 165–174.

As you can see, the estimates for an "average-risk" Brazilian project range from about 23 to 26 percent. Adjustments to these estimates would then be needed if the project were more or less risky than a "typical" Brazilian project.

What are some factors that contribute to making the international cost of equity hard to measure?

What is the global CAPM in partially segmented capital markets, and how is it implemented?

Compare the country-spread and country-risk-rating approaches. How do these estimates differ?

THE IMPACT OF GLOBALIZATION ON THE AMOUNT OF CAPITAL RAISED

Some research suggests that the WACCs of MNEs are actually higher than for equivalent domestic companies.[27] The extra premium is attributed to the existence of political and currency risk, higher agency costs from operating in a foreign marketplace, and asymmetric information because the company is not as knowledgeable as locals about how to operate effectively in the foreign marketplace. The magnitude of these extra risks, and the resulting upward pressure on the WACC, more than offsets any risk reduction from more effective diversification, leading to a higher WACC. Other research has concluded that just the opposite is true.[28] To look further into this controversy, we need to introduce two additional elements: the depth and liquidity of the domestic versus the global capital markets and the investment opportunity set confronting domestic versus global firms.

It is widely recognized that as a company attempts to raise additional capital, a point is reached where the marginal suppliers demand a higher rate of return before they will provide extra funds. Thus, the marginal cost of capital increases after a certain point. Because global firms can raise capital in multiple markets, it is reasonable to suppose that more capital can be raised at one time at a constant cost in the global marketplace than would be possible for a company restricted only to its domestic market.

Global companies also tend to have opportunities to invest significantly more money at higher rates of return than their domestic counterparts because of their expanded scope of operations. This means that they face a different investment opportunity schedule (IOS) than a purely domestic firm. If we plot availability of capital versus the cost of raising capital, and we place investment opportunity schedules on the same graph, we may be able to shed some light on this controversy. In Figure 10-2, the marginal WACC for the global firm, MCC_G, is lower than the WACC for the domestic firm, MCC_D, for the first increment of new capital raised. Because the local market is not as liquid or deep as global markets, though, the MCC_D curve rises more quickly than the MCC_G curve.

Superimposed on the MCC graphs are the investment opportunity schedules. IOS_D is plotted below and to the left of IOS_G to reflect the smaller number of good high-return investment projects available to the domestic company. The point of intersection between the MCC and IOS curves for a company defines both the return on the marginal project and the firm's marginal cost of capital. As shown in the figure, this intersection for the global firm occurs at a higher MCC than for the domestic firm, so its effective WACC is higher.

---

[27]See Reeb et al., "Systematic Risk of the Multinational Corporation," 263–279.

[28]See Stulz, "Globalization, Corporate Finance, and the Cost of Capital," 8–25.

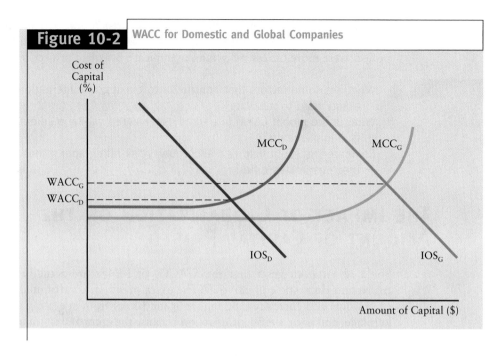

Figure 10-2 WACC for Domestic and Global Companies

Figure 10-2 illustrates that, depending on which WACC we focus on, the cost of the next unit of new capital raised or the effective cost of all capital raised at a point in time, it is possible to explain either side in the controversy. The salient point is that the MNE can invest more capital and earn a high rate of return because of its competitive advantages over a purely domestic firm.

What explanations are offered as to why the WACCs of MNEs might be higher than for equivalent domestic companies?

Some research has suggested that the WACCs of MNEs are higher than for equivalent domestic companies, while other research has reached the opposite conclusion. With a graph, explain both sides of this controversy.

SSI's PROCEDURES FOR CALCULATING DIFFERENT WACCS WITHIN THE FIRM

SSI is fairly typical of the firms surveyed by Graham and Harvey and Bruner et al. First, it raises capital throughout the world, obtaining it wherever costs at a given time are lowest after accounting for inflation and exchange rates. However, SSI (the parent company) generally guarantees its subsidiaries' debt in order to hold interest rates down. New equity in recent years has come only in the form of additions to retained earnings plus a relatively small amount of equity raised when employees exercise incentive stock options.[29] Operations are sometimes financed with different debt/equity combinations in different countries. When this occurs, the subsidiary generally finances with an above-target level of debt because debt happens to be relatively cheap in the given country and it is considered to be useful for ameliorating political risk. After an intense debate within the company, and over the objections of some of its executives, SSI decided to handle the WACC issue as follows:

---

[29]A relatively small amount of equity and debt has been raised from individuals in selected countries where SSI wants to have some local ownership for political reasons.

1. It uses the same target weights to calculate the WACC in all countries and for all divisions. Partly, this decision reflects the fact that the parent company guarantees most subsidiary debt, and this enables the subsidiaries to use above-average debt at a relatively low cost.

2. Similarly, the company builds an average cost of new debt and preferred into its WACC calculations, again on the grounds that cross-country cost differentials are affected by the parent company guarantees.

3. SSI uses different costs of equity in the calculation for its subsidiaries' WACCs. The equity costs are in part based on the betas of companies in similar industries whose stock trades in the country where the subsidiary operates. For example, the average beta of a group of Mexican technology companies is used as a proxy for SSI's Mexican subsidiary's beta.

As a result of these points, SSI now calculates different WACCs for its subsidiaries in different countries. Moreover, it classifies different projects in each country into one of three risk classes: high risk, average risk, and low risk. Each subsidiary's WACC is adjusted upward for high-risk projects, downward for low-risk projects, and left unchanged for those of average risk. These adjustments are often judgmental, and there have been some heated arguments within management over their proper level. We will discuss this issue in more detail in Chapter 12, where we take up risk analysis in capital budgeting.

SELF-TEST QUESTIONS   Is it reasonable for a company like SSI to calculate one WACC and then use that specific WACC, unadjusted, for decisions throughout the firm?

What are some factors that could lead to different WACCs for different parts of a firm?

SUMMARY

In this chapter, we discussed the basic concepts of the cost of capital for a purely domestic firm in an open, developed economy, and then we went on to show how international factors influenced a multinational firm's cost of capital. The basic concepts are the same for both multinationals and domestic firms; however, they are more complicated for multinationals, which have to deal with raising capital in different countries and in different currencies. The key concepts discussed in this chapter are listed below.

- The **cost of capital** used in capital budgeting is a **weighted average** of the types of capital the firm uses: typically debt, preferred stock, and common equity. The WACC is the weighted average cost of each new, or marginal, dollar of capital.

- The firm's **target capital structure** is the mix of debt, preferred stock, and common equity with which the firm plans to raise capital and which minimizes the firm's WACC. It is the best estimate of how the firm will, on average, raise money in the future.

- The **after-tax cost of debt** used to calculate the weighted average cost of capital (WACC) is found by multiplying the cost of new debt by $(1 - T)$, where T is the firm's marginal tax rate: $r_d(1 - T)$.

- The **cost of foreign-currency-denominated debt** should be calculated if a firm raises debt in another currency, and it is equal to: $r_d(1 - T)(1 + \Delta FX^e) + \Delta FX^e$, where ΔFX^e is the expected percentage change in foreign exchange rates between the domestic and foreign currency, stated in American terms.

- The **cost of preferred stock, r_{ps},** used to calculate a firm's WACC is calculated as the preferred dividend divided by the net issuing price after flotation costs are deducted: $r_{ps} = D_{ps}/P_n$. This calculation assumes the firm issues perpetual preferred. If preferred with a sinking fund is issued, then the equation would be similar to that used to estimate a bond's yield to maturity.
- The **marginal investor** is a representative investor whose actions reflect the beliefs of those people who are currently lending capital. It is the marginal investor who determines the cost of capital.
- The **cost of common equity, r_s,** is the required rate that investors require on a firm's common stock. It is not a contractually specified rate, and it is higher than both the costs of debt and preferred stock due to higher risk.
- For domestic operations, three approaches can be used to estimate the cost of common equity: **company-bond-yield-plus-risk-premium approach, discounted cash flow (DCF) approach**, and **capital asset pricing model (CAPM)**.
- The **company-bond-yield-plus-risk-premium approach** adds a subjectively determined risk premium to the firm's own bond yield.
- The **discounted cash flow (DCF) approach** evaluates stocks by forecasting a stream of dividends plus a future stock price and then discounting those cash flows at the required rate of return.
- A stock's **expected return must be equal to the stock's required return**, because, if it were not, buying or selling would occur to change the stock price and force equilibrium where the two returns were equal.
- The **CAPM approach** may be applied both domestically and internationally. The **domestic CAPM** uses the risk-free rate (r_{RF}), the firm's beta coefficient (b_i), and the market risk premium (RP_M) to estimate the firm's cost of equity as follows: $r_s = r_{RF} + (RP_M)b_i$. The **global CAPM** uses the risk-free rate (r_{RF}), the firm's global beta coefficient ($b_{i,W}$), and the world risk premium (RP_W) to estimate the firm's cost of equity as follows: $r_s = r_{RF} + (RP_W)b_{i,W}$.
- The **overall corporate WACC** is appropriate for use in evaluating a project whose risk is about equal to that of the firm as a whole, assuming the project will be financed in accordance with the firm's target capital structure. However, different WACCs should be used in situations where the WACC is used to evaluate assets whose risk, financing, or other characteristics are different from the firm's average. A firm's overall corporate WACC is an average of its individual divisions' WACCs.
- Various factors affect a firm's cost of capital. Some of these factors include **country risk, exchange rate risk, interest rates, tax rates and rules, capital structure**, and **operating risk differences**.
- The **risk-adjusted cost of capital** is the cost of capital appropriate for a particular project, given the project's riskiness.
- The **pure play method** is an approach used for estimating the beta of a project in which a firm (1) identifies several companies whose only business is to produce the product in question, (2) calculates the beta for each firm, and then (3) averages the betas to find an approximation to its own project's beta.
- Three main approaches can be used to estimate the cost of common equity for international operations particularly in emerging markets: **global CAPM with partially segmented markets, country-spread approach**, and **country-risk-rating approach**. In addition, various multi-beta approaches also exist.
- The **global CAPM with partially segmented capital markets** uses the risk-free rate (r_{RF}), the firm's global beta coefficient ($b_{i,W}$), the world risk premium (RP_W), the firm's segmented risk beta coefficient ($b_{i,Seg}$), and the risk premium (SRP_j) associated with segmented country j (or region j) risk to estimate the firm's cost of equity as follows: $r_s = r_{RF} + (RP_W)b_{i,W} + (SRP_j)b_{i,Seg}$.
- The **country-spread approach** adds the spread between the 10-year yields on dollar-denominated foreign bonds issued by foreign governments and U.S. Treasury securities to the U.S. risk-free rate and an adjusted beta times the U.S. market risk premium: $r_s = r_{RF} + (RP_M)[0.6(\sigma_j/\sigma_M)] +$ Country credit spread.

- The **country-risk-rating approach** uses a regression model of equity returns against country-risk ratings to calculate the semiannual cost of equity for an average country j project: $r_{sj}/2 = a + d_{cr} \ln(\text{Country-risk rating}_j)$.
- Depending on which WACC we focus on, the cost of the next unit of new capital raised or the effective cost of all capital raised at a point in time, it is possible to explain both a **higher or lower cost of equity** for MNEs than for equivalent domestic companies.
- MNEs can invest **more capital** and earn a high rate of return because of their **competitive advantages** over purely domestic firms.

The cost of capital as developed in this chapter is used in the following chapters to evaluate a firm's capital budgeting projects. In addition, we will extend the concepts developed here in Chapter 13, where we consider the effect of a firm's capital structure on its cost of capital.

QUESTIONS

(10-1) Is the following statement true or false: "Managers should calculate the cost of capital as a weighted average of the specific sources of financing employed in a particular year. Only if the WACC is calculated in this manner will the firm choose the value-maximizing set of projects over time." Explain your answer.

(10-2) Would logic suggest that the CAPM risk premium for an average company is larger or smaller than the risk premium on the company's stock over its bonds? Would your answer also hold for relatively risky and for relatively safe companies?

(10-3) In terms of the cost of capital equations, how does a firm's tax rate affect its cost of debt, preferred stock, and common stock, and thus its WACC?

(10-4) To be exactly precise, should flotation costs be considered when we estimate the cost of debt? Would it be more reasonable to ignore such costs if debt were being raised as bank loans or by issuing bonds to the public? How could flotation costs be worked into the estimate if the debt were a public bond issue? Say the bond flotation cost was 2 percent of the issue. Would flotation costs be more important if the bond had a 1-year maturity or a 50-year maturity?

(10-5) Holding everything else constant, how would a reduction in the corporate tax rate affect a company's WACC? After giving a rather mechanical answer to the first part of this question, go on to discuss other effects that a tax reduction might have, and the resulting effect on an average company's WACC. (Hint: Recognize that there is a definitive answer to the first part of the question but not to the second part.)

(10-6) The U.S. Commerce Department recently announced that wholesale price inflation in the latest reporting period was -1.5 percent, and core inflation was -0.9 percent. At the same time the Fed announced that it was concerned about deflation (as opposed to inflation) and was taking steps to prevent deflation. Would these events affect an average firm's cost of capital, and if so, how?

(10-7) In 2003, Congress passed a tax reform bill that reduced the tax on dividends. Before the law was enacted, dividends were taxed as ordinary income at an investor's marginal tax rate; however, now dividends are generally taxed at the same rate as capital gains (15 percent). Discuss how this action would affect corporate dividend payout ratios, the relative cost of debt versus common equity, corporations' capital structures, and, as a result of all these factors, firms' WACCs.

(10-8) Discuss the pros and cons of estimating a firm's cost of common equity by use of the domestic CAPM, global CAPM, the DCF, and the risk-premium-over-own-debt-cost method. Take both theoretical and data availability considerations into account, and think about the issue from the standpoint of both publicly traded and privately owned firms.

(10-9) If a multinational firm is operating in partially segmented international capital markets, discuss the approaches the firm could take in estimating the local subsidiary's cost of common equity. What relative strengths and weaknesses do the methods have?

(10-10) If a firm invests heavily in projects that are inherently more risky than its existing assets, but investors do not know that the newly acquired assets are more risky than the old assets, would the new investments raise the company's costs of debt, preferred, and common equity, and thus its WACC? If management recognizes the change in the company's risk profile, should it inform investors?

(10-11) Is the following statement true or false: "Just as the beta of a portfolio is a weighted average of the betas of the stocks in the portfolio, the firm's overall average WACC is an average of its individual units' WACCs." Explain your answer.

(10-12) Differentiate between the global CAPM and the global CAPM with partially segmented capital markets.

(10-13) What problem was encountered when the global CAPM was applied to emerging markets? Which approaches were developed in response to this problem?

(10-14) How is the country credit spread calculated? What risk is incorporated in this spread?

(10-15) Briefly explain why the cost of equity estimate obtained using the country-spread approach is higher than one obtained using the global CAPM with partially segmented capital markets.

(10-16) Briefly identify three major problems with the country-spread approach.

(10-17) Briefly explain whether the following statement is true or false: "The country-spread approach provides an average estimate of the cost of equity in a particular country, while the country-risk-rating approach provides an estimate of a specific project's discount rate. Thus, with the country-spread approach you would have to adjust the country's discount rate to reflect differences between the project's risk and that of an average investment in that country, while this adjustment would be unnecessary for the country-risk-rating approach."

(10-18) Why is time measured in half-years with the country-risk-rating approach?

(10-19) If a foreign project's risk were lower than that of an average investment in that foreign country, what adjustment would be needed to the cost of equity estimate obtained using the country-risk-rating approach?

(10-20) Which international cost of equity approach provides reasonable and relatively stable cost of equity estimates for the broadest set of countries?

SELF-TEST PROBLEMS   Solutions Appear in Appendix B

(ST-1) Define each of the following terms:
Key Terms
   a. Capital component; component cost
   b. Weighted average cost of capital (WACC); target capital structure
   c. New (marginal) debt; historical (embedded) rate
   d. After-tax cost of debt, $r_d(1 - T)$; cost of foreign-currency-denominated debt, $r_d(1 - T)(1 + \Delta FX^e) + \Delta FX^e$
   e. Cost of preferred stock, r_{ps}
   f. Marginal investor
   g. Cost of common equity, r_s
   h. Risk-adjusted cost of capital; pure play method
   i. Global CAPM; global CAPM with partially segmented capital markets
   j. Country-spread model; country credit spread
   k. Country-risk-rating approach

(ST-2) Lopez Inc., a U.S. multinational corporation with access to global capital markets
WACC and a producer of fine cigars, is developing next year's capital budget. To determine which projects should be included in the budget, the firm must estimate
its overall weighted average cost of capital (WACC), which will be applied to
average-risk projects. Lopez's financial staff has put together the following relevant information:

- Five years ago, the firm issued 20-year callable bonds with an 8 percent semiannual coupon and a face value of $1,000. The bonds currently trade for $920.
  The bonds originally had a call protection of 10 years, so the bonds can be
  called in 5 years at a call price of $1,080.
- The firm's treasurer has thoroughly reviewed the debt markets. He has narrowed the choice of bond issues between callable, U.S. dollar-denominated
  bonds and callable, Australian dollar-denominated bonds. The spot exchange
  rate is AUD 1.54 per U.S. dollar, and the 1-year forward exchange rate is AUD
  1.57 per U.S. dollar.
- Lopez's perpetual preferred stock currently trades for $105, and it pays a divi-
  dend of $5.80 per share. If the firm were to issue new perpetual preferred, it
  would incur a 2.5 percent flotation cost for underwriting fees.
- The current risk-free rate is 5.25 percent and the return on an average stock in
  the U.S. markets is 11 percent.
- The world risk premium is estimated to be 4.5 percent.
- Analysts estimate that the firm's beta calculated with respect to U.S. markets is
  equal to 0.85, while the firm's beta calculated with respect to the world markets is equal to 0.75.
- The firm has recently announced to investors that it would like to achieve a target capital structure of 5 percent preferred stock, 45 percent debt, and 50 percent common equity.
- The firm's marginal tax rate is 40 percent.
- Lopez is considering a project in Argentina, which will be 100 percent equity
  financed. The project is riskier than an average investment in Argentina. The
  segmented risk premium is 8 percent, and the beta calculated with respect to
  segmented markets is 0.8.
- The country credit spread for Argentina is 6 percent, and the ratio of the market return variance for Argentina to that of the United States is 1.4167. This
  ratio should be scaled down by 0.6 to reduce the possibility of overstatement in
  the estimate due to "double counting."
- A consultant recently hired by the firm has estimated that the following regression model can be used to estimate the expected cost of equity for an average
  investment in Argentina:

$$r_{sj}/2 = a + d_{cr} \ln(\text{Country-risk rating }_j)$$
$$= 25\% - 4.75\% \ln(40).$$

- For those models that calculate an average country-level cost of equity estimate,
  the firm risk adjusts by adding or subtracting 2 percent from the estimate for
  more- or less-risky projects.

a. What is the firm's component cost of debt used in calculating its WACC?
b. What is the firm's component cost of preferred stock used in calculating its
    WACC?
c. Assuming that global capital markets are perfectly integrated, what is the
    firm's cost of common equity used in calculating its WACC?
d. What is the firm's overall WACC, which should be applied to average-risk
    projects?
e. Assume that Argentinean capital markets are not perfectly integrated, and the
    firm uses the global CAPM with partially segmented capital markets. What
    should be the cost of equity estimate for the Argentinean project?
f. Using the country-spread approach, what should be the cost of equity estimate
    for the Argentinean project?

g. Using the country-risk-rating approach, what should be the cost of equity estimate for the Argentinean project?

h. If the Argentinean project's expected return is 20 percent, should the firm undertake the project? Explain your answer.

STARTER PROBLEMS

(10-1)
Cost of Debt
Podlecki Pottery Inc. (PPI) has bonds outstanding that currently sell at a discount and have a yield to maturity of 8 percent. Interest rates are expected to stay at current levels for the next year or so.

a. If the firm's marginal tax rate is 35 percent, what is the relevant cost of debt for use in calculating the firm's WACC for next year's capital budget?

b. Would the relevant cost of debt be different if the bonds were selling at a premium and were callable? Assume again that interest rates are expected to stay at this current level for the next year or so.

(10-2)
Cost of Preferred Stock
Juarez Cigar Co. (JCC) is planning a new perpetual preferred stock issue. Its preferred currently trades at $50 per share and has a dividend of $3.50 per share; however, the firm will incur an underwriting fee of approximately 2 percent on a new perpetual issue. What is JCC's cost of preferred?

(10-3)
CAPM: Cost of
Common Equity
Smythe-Davidson Inc. (SDI) is an international confectioner based in San Francisco. The firm estimates its cost of common equity by using the CAPM approach. Analysts estimate that the firm's beta is 0.75, the risk-free rate is 5.25 percent, and the return on an average stock in the market is 11 percent. The firm's marginal tax rate is 35 percent. What is the firm's cost of common equity?

(10-4)
Nonconstant DCF: Cost of
Common Equity
Keeley Software Products Co. (KSPC) estimates its cost of common equity using the nonconstant discounted cash flow approach. Its stock price is $22.50 per share, but it pays no dividends. However, analysts anticipate that the firm will begin paying a dividend of $1.50 per share 4 years from now and that dividend will grow at a constant 6.5 percent growth rate thereafter. What is the firm's cost of common equity? (Hint: You will need to use the chapter's *Excel* model to solve this problem.)

(10-5)
WACC
Shiels Inc., a trendy retail clothing store for women, is estimating its WACC for use in upcoming capital budgeting decisions. The firm's target capital structure is 5 percent preferred stock, 55 percent debt, and 40 percent common equity. The firm's currently outstanding noncallable long-term bonds (with a 20-year maturity) have a yield to maturity of 7.5 percent. The firm's perpetual preferred is trading for $52.00 per share, has a $3.60 dividend, and new perpetual preferred can be sold with a flotation cost of $2.00 per share. The risk-free rate is 5.2 percent, the market risk premium is 5.6 percent, the firm's beta is 0.95, and its tax rate is 40 percent. What is the WACC that Shiels should use for the firm's average-risk projects?

(10-6)
Cost of Foreign Debt
You are treasurer of International Foods Corporation (IFC). Your firm needs to raise capital and has decided to issue debt since it has reserve borrowing capacity. After a thorough review of global capital markets, you have narrowed the choice between issuing either yen-denominated debt or U.S. dollar-denominated debt. You have obtained the following information:

- Interest rate on similarly-rated U.S. dollar-denominated debt = 7%.
- IFC's marginal tax rate = 40%.
- Spot exchange rate = $0.0083 per yen.
- 1-year forward exchange rate = $0.0087 per yen.

a. What is IFC's after-tax cost of U.S. dollar-denominated debt?

b. What is IFC's after-tax cost of yen-denominated debt?

c. Given these two choices, where should the firm issue debt?

(10-7)
Global CAPM: Cost of
Common Equity

BWC Inc., a multinational firm with access to global capital markets, has a beta coefficient of 1.1 when calculated against the world index. Assume the risk-free rate is 5.5 percent and the world risk premium is 4.5 percent.
a. What is BWC's cost of equity using the global CAPM approach?
b. If you were told that BWC's treasurer had estimated the firm's cost of equity using the domestic CAPM, would you expect the estimate to be higher than, lower than, or equal to your estimate obtained in part a? Explain.

(10-8)
Cost of Equity for
Foreign Projects

La Tiempa Manufacturing Company has operations in Chile, whose capital markets are not perfectly integrated. The firm's treasurer is trying to estimate the cost of equity for one of its Chilean projects. She has obtained the following data:

$$
\begin{array}{ll}
r_{RF} = 5\% & SRP_j = 14\% \\
RP_W = 4.6\% & b_{i,Seg} = 0.9 \\
b_{i,W} = 1.4 & \sigma_j/\sigma_M = 2.5 \\
b_i = 1.5 & RP_M = 6\% \\
a = 40\% & \text{Country credit spread} = 12\% \\
d_{cr} = -8.5\% & \text{Country-risk rating} = 28
\end{array}
$$

a. Using the segmented CAPM, what should be her best estimate of the cost of equity for the Chilean project?
b. Estimate the cost of equity for the Chilean project using the country-spread approach. Assume that the project's risk is comparable to that of an average investment in Chile.
c. Estimate the cost of equity for the Chilean project using the country-risk-rating approach. Assume that the project's risk is comparable to that of an average investment in Chile.

EXAM-TYPE PROBLEMS

(10-9)
Cost of Domestic and
Foreign Debt

Five years ago, Glicken Pharmaceuticals issued 20-year callable bonds with a semiannual coupon of 8.5 percent and a face value of $1,000. The bonds currently trade for $1,145. The bonds originally had a call protection of 10 years, so the bonds can be called in 5 years at a call price of $1,085. The firm's marginal tax rate is 40 percent.
a. What is the firm's component cost of debt used to calculate its WACC? Explain.
b. Assume now that Glicken can issue callable, pound-denominated bonds in Great Britain. The spot exchange rate is $1.61 per pound, and the 1-year forward exchange rate is $1.58 per pound. Given that the yield calculated in part a is a good approximation of r_d and the tax rate remains at 40 percent, what is the after-tax cost of the pound-denominated debt?
c. Assuming that these are Glicken's only bond choices, which bond will the firm issue?

(10-10)
Cost of Domestic and
Foreign Debt

Last year, ABC Publishers issued 25-year callable bonds with a semiannual coupon of 7.2 percent and a face value of $1,000. The bonds currently trade for $990. The bonds originally had a call protection of 5 years, so the bonds can be called in 4 years at a call price of $1,072. The firm's marginal tax rate is 35 percent.
a. What is the firm's component cost of debt used to calculate its WACC? Explain.
b. Assume now that ABC can issue callable, Swiss-franc denominated bonds. The spot exchange rate is 1.37 Swiss francs per U.S. dollar, and the 1-year forward exchange rate is 1.35 Swiss francs per U.S. dollar. Given that the yield calculated in part a is a good approximation of r_d and the tax rate remains at 35 percent, what is the after-tax cost of the Swiss-franc denominated debt?

   c. Assuming that these are ABC's only bond choices, which bond will the firm issue?

(10-11)
Cost of Domestic and
Foreign Debt

Worldwide Manufacturing Company (WMC), a U.S. multinational, is considering raising debt capital in Finland, which is a member of the EMU, so the debt issued would be denominated in euros. WMC's treasurer has gathered the following information:

- Interest rate on similarly-rated U.S. dollar-denominated debt = 7.5%.
- WMC's tax rate = 35%.
- Spot exchange rate = 0.89 euro per U.S. dollar.
- 1-year forward exchange rate = 0.87 euro per U.S. dollar.

   a. Given this information, is the dollar expected to strengthen or weaken against the euro? Explain.
   b. Given this information and without doing any calculations, would you expect the cost of the euro-denominated debt to be lower than, higher than, or equal to the U.S. dollar-denominated debt?
   c. Given this information, what is the after-tax cost to WMC of the euro-denominated debt? Will the firm issue debt in the United States or Finland?
   d. Assume the same information given above, except now the 1-year forward exchange rate is 0.90 euro per U.S. dollar. What is the after-tax cost to WMC of the euro-denominated debt?
   e. If the assumptions in part d are correct, will WMC prefer to borrow in the United States or Finland? What is the after-tax cost of the least expensive source of debt?

(10-12)
Cost of Domestic and
Foreign Common Equity

Grunewald Manufacturing Company (GRMC), a well-known producer of electronics, is beginning to consider next year's capital budget. To determine which projects should be included in the budget, the firm must estimate its cost of common equity, which will be incorporated into its WACC calculation to determine its overall corporate WACC. The firm estimates its cost of common equity using the three different approaches discussed in the text. If a cost estimate is within 2 percentage points of the bond-yield-plus-risk-premium approach, which is used to arrive at a "ballpark" estimate, then the firm averages the three estimates to arrive at the cost of equity. However, if an estimate varies by more than 2 percentage points from the "ballpark" estimate, it is thrown out and only the average of the other approaches is used. The current risk-free rate is 5.5 percent, and the market risk premium is 5 percent. The yield to maturity on the firm's currently outstanding bonds is 6.5 percent, and the firm's subjective estimate of a risk premium that should be added to the firm's bond yield is 5 percent. GRMC does not currently pay dividends due to the high growth nature of its industry; however, analysts anticipate that in 3 years the firm will start paying an $0.80 dividend ($D_3 = 0.80$), and its dividend per share will grow 4.5 percent a year thereafter. These same analysts estimate the firm's beta is equal to 1.25. GRMC's current stock price is $10.
   a. What is GRMC's cost of common equity as estimated by the bond-yield-plus-risk-premium approach?
   b. What is GRMC's cost of common equity as estimated by the CAPM approach?
   c. What is GRMC's cost of common equity as estimated by the nonconstant discounted cash flow approach?
   d. What estimate will GRMC use as its cost of common equity in the WACC equation?

Assume now that GRMC has access to global capital markets. The firm's treasurer has obtained the following information:

$r_{RF} = 5.5\%$	$SRP_j = 6\%$
$RP_M = 5\%$	$\sigma_j/\sigma_M = 2.0833$
$b_i = 1.25$	$b_{i,Seg} = 0.9$
$RP_W = 4.35\%$	Country credit spread = 7%
$b_{i,W} = 1.15$	Country-risk rating = 37

e. Calculate the firm's cost of equity assuming that capital markets are perfectly integrated and the firm uses the global CAPM.

f. Assume that GRMC is considering operations in Peru and markets are not perfectly integrated there. Calculate the cost of equity estimate using the segmented CAPM for the Peruvian project.

g. Assume that GRMC is considering a risky project in Peru. In other words, the project is riskier than an average investment in Peru. Use the country-spread approach to estimate the cost of equity for this project. Assume that GRMC adjusts for project risk by adding plus or minus 3 percentage points to the estimate, depending on whether the project is more or less risky than a typical project.

h. Assume that GRMC is considering an average-risk project in Peru. The company uses the country-risk-rating approach to estimate the cost of equity. A consultant has estimated that the constant for use in this model is 28 percent and the estimated slope is negative 5.5 percent. What is the estimate of the cost of equity for this Peruvian project?

(10-13)
WACC: Access to Domestic and Global Markets

TMC Inc., an international conglomerate, is beginning its capital budgeting decision process for the upcoming year. In order for the company to select capital projects that will add shareholder value, it must first determine the appropriate WACC to use in its decision-making process. For this purpose, its financial staff has put together the following relevant information:

- Five years ago, the firm issued 30-year callable bonds with a 9 percent semiannual coupon and a face value of $1,000. The bonds currently trade for $1,200. The bonds originally had a call protection of 10 years, so the bonds can be called in 5 years at a call price of $1,090.
- TMC's perpetual preferred stock currently trades for $110, and it pays a dividend of $6.25 per share. If the firm were to issue new perpetual preferred, it would incur a 2 percent flotation cost for underwriting fees.
- The current risk-free rate is 5 percent, and the return on an average stock in the U.S. markets is 11.5 percent.
- The world risk premium is estimated to be 5.25 percent.
- To arrive at a "ballpark" estimate of the firm's cost of common equity, the firm adds a 7 percent subjective risk premium to the firm's own bond yield, estimated as either the YTM or YTC—whichever is more relevant.
- Analysts estimate that the firm's beta calculated with respect to U.S. markets is equal to 1.15, while the firm's beta calculated with respect to world markets is equal to 1.05.
- The firm is considered to be a mature firm in a very stable position, so the financial staff believes that the constant growth DCF model gives a good approximation of the firm's cost of common equity. The firm's expected dividend per share next year is $4.65 and dividends are anticipated to grow at approximately a 6 percent constant growth rate. The firm's common stock currently trades for $75 per share.
- TMC determines its cost of common equity by averaging the three approaches discussed in your text—unless an estimate deviates substantially from the "ballpark" estimate—in which case, the estimate is not used in the averaging process. (The firm defines a substantial deviation as 2 percentage points from the "ballpark" estimate.)
- TMC has recently announced to investors that it would like to achieve a target capital structure of 3 percent preferred stock, 52 percent debt, and 45 percent common equity.
- The firm's marginal tax rate is 35 percent.

For parts a through g, assume that the firm has access only to domestic U.S. capital markets.

a. What is the firm's component cost of debt used in calculating its WACC?

b. What is the firm's component cost of preferred stock?

c. What is the firm's "ballpark" estimate of its cost of common equity? (Hint: Be careful to use the yield that investors expect to earn in your calculation.)

    d. What is the firm's cost of common equity as estimated by the domestic CAPM approach?

    e. What is the firm's cost of common equity as estimated by the constant DCF approach?

    f. What is the firm's cost of common equity used in calculating its WACC?

    g. What is the firm's WACC?

For the remaining parts of this problem, assume that the firm has access to global markets.

    h. The firm's treasurer has thoroughly researched global capital markets. He has narrowed the choice of bond issues between callable, U.S. dollar-denominated bonds, the cost of which was calculated in part a, and callable, Canadian-dollar-denominated bonds. The spot exchange rate is CAD 1.40 per U.S. dollar, and the 1-year forward exchange rate is CAD 1.42 per U.S. dollar.

      (1) Assuming the firm's marginal tax rate remains constant at 35 percent, what is the after-tax cost of the Canadian-dollar-denominated bonds?

      (2) Assuming access to global capital markets, what is the firm's component cost of debt used in calculating its WACC?

    i. Assume that global capital markets are perfectly integrated. If the firm uses the global CAPM, what is the firm's cost of common equity used in determining its WACC?

    j. Assume that the firm's target capital structure is unaffected by its access to global markets. In addition, assume that the cost of the firm's preferred stock is unchanged from what you calculated in part b. What is the firm's WACC, assuming it has access to global markets?

(10-14)
WACC: Access to Global Markets
Global Communications Inc. (GCI), which consists of seven different subsidiaries around the world, is 100 percent equity financed and has an overall corporate beta calculated with respect to the world index of 1.3. GCI is in the middle of preparing its capital budget for next year. The company risk adjusts its divisional WACCs by ± 1.5 percentage points for project risk. One of its subsidiaries, a communications equipment manufacturer, is considering Project M, which will enhance manufacturing production in one of its plants. Project M's expected return is 8 percent. Analysts estimate that this subsidiary has a beta calculated with respect to the world index of 0.6, and Project M is considered to have lower risk than a typical project within this subsidiary. One of its other subsidiaries, which is responsible for research and development of new technology in the communications industry, has an estimated beta of 1.6 calculated with respect to the world index. The R&D subsidiary is considering Project T, which if successful will revolutionize the telecommunications industry. Project T is considered an average-risk project for this subsidiary, and its expected return is 14 percent. The current risk-free rate is 5.6 percent and the return on an average stock in the global markets is 11.5 percent. Assume that the firm has access to global capital markets, is not capital constrained, and these are independent projects.

    a. What is GCI's overall corporate WACC?

    b. What is the communications equipment subsidiary's WACC?

    c. What is the R&D subsidiary's WACC?

    d. Which project(s) should GCI include in its capital budget? Explain.

THOMSON ONE QUESTIONS

CALCULATING THE COST OF CAPITAL

Overview

In this chapter we described how to estimate a company's weighted average cost of capital (WACC). Simply put, a company's WACC is a weighted average of the firm's costs of debt, preferred stock, and common equity. Most of the data we need to estimate a company's WACC can be found in *Thomson One: Business School Edition*. Below, we walk through the steps to calculate a WACC estimate for entertainment conglomerate Vivendi Universal SA (EX-FR).

Discussion Questions

1. As a first step we need to estimate what percentage of Vivendi's capital comes from long-term debt, preferred stock, and common equity. If we click on "FINANCIALS," we can see immediately from the balance sheet Vivendi's long-term debt and common equity. (As of mid-2003, Vivendi had no preferred stock.) Alternatively, you can click on "FUNDAMENTAL RATIOS" in the next row of tabs below and then select Worldscope's "BALANCE SHEET RATIOS." Here, you will also find a recent measure of long-term debt as a percentage of total capital. Recall that the weights used in the WACC are based on the company's target capital structure. If we assume that the company wants to maintain the same mix of capital that it currently has on its balance sheet, what weights should you use to estimate the WACC for Vivendi? (Note that later in Chapter 13, we will see that we might end up with different estimates for these weights if we instead assume that Vivendi bases its target capital structure on the market values of debt and equity rather than the book values.)

2. Once again, we can use the CAPM to estimate Vivendi's cost of equity. *Thomson One: Business School Edition* provides various estimates of beta—select the measure that you think is best, and combine this with your estimates of the risk-free rate and the market risk premium to estimate Vivendi's cost of equity. (See the *Thomson One: Business School Edition* exercise for Chapter 5 for more details.) What is your estimate of Vivendi's cost of equity? Why might it not make much sense to use the DCF approach to estimate Vivendi's cost of equity?

3. Next, we need to calculate Vivendi's cost of debt. Unfortunately, *Thomson One: Business School Edition* doesn't provide us with a direct measure of the cost of debt. However, we can use a variety of approaches to estimate this cost. One approach is to take the company's long-term interest expense on the income statement and divide it by the amount of long-term debt on the balance sheet. Note, however, that this approach works only if the historical cost of debt equals the yield to maturity in today's market (i.e., if Vivendi's outstanding bonds are trading at close to their par value). Moreover, this approach may produce misleading estimates in years in which Vivendi issues a lot of new debt. For example, if a company issues a lot of debt at the end of the year, the full amount of debt will show up on the year-end balance sheet, yet we still may not see a sharp increase in interest expense on the annual income statement because the debt was outstanding for only a small portion of the entire year. When this situation occurs, the estimated cost of debt will likely understate the true cost of debt. Another approach would be to go to the company's annual report. (You can access this through the "FILINGS" section of *Thomson One: Business School Edition,* or click on the link to the company's home page, where you then look for the "INVESTOR RELATIONS" section.) Alternatively, you can go to other external sources to find estimates of the cost of debt. Once you find the cost of debt, remember that you need to multiply this by 1 minus Vivendi's tax rate (hard to determine, so just use a "guess" of 35 percent) to get the after-tax cost of debt. What do you estimate to be Vivendi's after-tax cost of debt?

4. Putting all this information together, what is your estimate for Vivendi's WACC? How confident are you in this estimate?

INTEGRATED CASE

Rick Schmidt, MRI's CFO, along with Mandy Wu, Schmidt's assistant, and John Costello, a consultant and college finance professor, comprise a team set up to teach the firm's directors and senior managers the basics of international financial management. The program includes 16 sessions, each lasting about 2 hours, and they are scheduled immediately before the monthly board meetings. Nine sessions have been completed, and the team is now preparing Session 10, which will deal with the cost of capital. Prior sessions have provided an overview of international finance, exchange rates, risk analysis, financial statements, bond valuation, stock valuation, and international security markets.

For the cost of capital session, the team will explain how the weighted average cost of capital is determined and then used in the capital budgeting process. They plan to go through the costs of the various types of capital, the process of calculating the weighted average cost, the appropriate set of weights to use for the calculation, and whether the corporate WACC should be used versus different WACCs for different purposes. Since MRI is a multinational firm that raises and invests capital around the world, international factors are especially important. For example, debt cost rates, tax rates, and capital structures vary for subsidiaries in different countries and even for different projects within a given country, and the team must address how those differences should be factored into the analysis.

Wu expressed concern about addressing controversial issues, where the proper analysis is in question. She recalled that in college some students simply "tuned out" when the instructor raised a question for which there was no definitive answer, and she was concerned that the directors might react similarly. Schmidt and Costello agree that this could be a problem, but they felt strongly that it would not be appropriate to "sweep problems under the carpet." So, they want to bring up relevant unresolved issues, discuss alternative ways of dealing with them, and point out the implications of different decisions. The directors are all intelligent, experienced in dealing with complex situations, and would rather know about potential problems than be kept in the dark.

With those thoughts in mind, the three compiled the following set of questions, which they plan to discuss during the session. As with the other sessions, they plan to use an *Excel* model to answer the quantitative questions. Assume that you are Mandy Wu and that you must prepare answers for use during the session.

QUESTIONS

a. MRI obtains some of its debt capital from sources in Europe and Japan, but it raises the bulk of its debt in the United States. Two dollar-denominated bonds are currently outstanding. Bond 1 has a 6 percent semiannual coupon, currently sells for 92.629 percent of par, has 20 years remaining to maturity, and can be called at a price of 107.50 percent of par in 4 years. Bond 2 has an 8.5 percent semiannual coupon, sells for 112.1 percent of par, has 20 years to maturity, and can also be called at a price of 107.50 in 4 years. MRI's federal-plus-state tax rate is 40 percent. Based on these data, what is a reasonable estimate of MRI's cost of debt for use in the WACC calculation?

b. MRI also raises capital with preferred stock. Its most recent issue was perpetual and noncallable, pays a $6 annual dividend, and currently sells for $94.20 per share. New shares could be sold with a flotation cost of 2 percent. What cost of preferred should be used in the WACC calculation? Is the relationship between the yields on debt and preferred consistent with their respective risks to investors?

c. Based on MRI's cost of debt plus a subjective risk premium (between 2 and 4 percent), what is the company's cost of common equity? What are the pros and cons of this estimation technique?

d. MRI's stock sells for $21 per share. The company currently does not pay a dividend, but a leading security analyst recently published a report that forecasted a dividend of $0.50 per share at the end of the 3rd year from today. The report also forecasted a growth rate of 20 percent in the 4th year, 15 percent in the 5th year, and 8 percent thereafter. Based on that information, what is MRI's DCF cost of equity? What are the pros and cons of the DCF method? (Hint: If you use the case model, you can get an exact solution for the DCF cost. Otherwise, just provide a "reasonable" approximation.)

e. MRI's beta coefficient calculated with respect to U.S. markets is 1.2. The risk-free rate is 4.75 percent, and the market risk premium (RP_M) with respect to U.S. markets is also estimated to be 6.0 percent. What is MRI's domestic CAPM cost of equity?

f. MRI's global beta coefficient is 1.1. The risk-free rate is 4.75 percent, and the world risk premium (RP_W) is estimated to be 5.0 percent. What is MRI's global CAPM cost of equity? When, and for which companies, should the global CAPM be given precedence over the domestic CAPM?

g. MRI expects to have enough retained earnings so that it will not have to issue any new common stock during the coming year. If it did plan to issue new stock, how would this affect its cost of common equity?

h. All things considered, what is a reasonable estimate of MRI's cost of common equity? Would it make a difference whether MRI had access to global capital markets?

i. MRI's capital structure, based on book and market values, is shown here:

	Book	Market
Debt	56.8%	25.0%
Preferred	6.5	4.5
Common	36.7	70.5
	100.0%	100.0%

These percentages are fairly close to the average of the group of companies against which MRI benchmarks. Rounding to whole percentage points, what capital structure should MRI use when calculating its WACC, assuming management's goal is to maximize the stock price? Justify your choice, and note that the company does not have to use either of the structures shown above.

j. Then, based on your capital structure, calculate MRI's WACC. Assume MRI has access to global capital markets. How different would the WACC be if you had chosen a different capital structure?

k. Now suppose MRI plans to use only retained earnings to finance its capital budgeting program during the coming year. In this case, should it use the calculated WACC to evaluate capital budgeting projects, or should it use just the cost of common equity?

l. Should the WACC that you calculated be used to evaluate all of MRI's proposed capital budgeting projects, regardless of the nature of the project or the country in which it would be located? Explain your answer. In particular, explain how the fact that MRI is a multinational company would affect the situation.

MRI is considering a project in Venezuela that would be financed with 10 percent debt and 90 percent equity due to its additional risk. Assume capital markets in Venezuela are not perfectly integrated. MRI's treasurer has obtained the following information:

- Spot exchange rate = VEB 1,598 per U.S. dollar.
- 1-year forward exchange rate = VEB 1,625 per U.S. dollar.
- r_{RF} = 4.75%.
- RP_M = 6%.
- b_i = 1.2.
- RP_W = 5%.
- $b_{i,W}$ = 1.1.
- SRP_i = 10%.
- $b_{i,Seg}$ = 0.7.
- σ_i = 0.38.
- σ_M = 0.19.
- Country credit spread = 6.5%.
- Country-risk-rating = 40.

m. MRI has decided that for this project it will issue debt denominated in bolivars, which is Venezuela's national currency. Assume that the yield calculated earlier in the case is a good approximation of the U.S. r_d and the tax rate remains at 40 percent. What is the after-tax cost of the bolivar-denominated debt?

n. Use the global CAPM with partially segmented markets to estimate the cost of equity for the Venezuelan project.

o. Use the country-spread approach to estimate the project's cost of equity. Assume that no additional risk adjustment is necessary since the company has adjusted the project's capital structure to reflect its risk.

p. Use the country-risk-rating approach to estimate the project's cost of equity. A consultant has estimated that the constant for use in this model is 31 percent and the estimated slope is negative 6 percent.

q. Using an average of your cost of equity calculations, what is the project's cost of equity?

r. Using your cost of equity estimate for the previous question, what is the Venezuelan project's weighted average cost of capital?

Capital Budgeting: The Basics

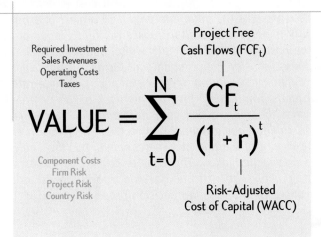

Required Investment
Sales Revenues
Operating Costs
Taxes

Project Free
Cash Flows (FCF$_t$)

$$\text{VALUE} = \sum_{t=0}^{N} \frac{\text{CF}_t}{(1+r)^t}$$

Component Costs
Firm Risk
Project Risk
Country Risk

Risk-Adjusted
Cost of Capital (WACC)

e-resource

The textbook's Web site, http://crum. swlearning.com, contains an Excel file that will guide you through the chapter's calculations. The file for this chapter is FIFC11-model.xls, and we encourage you to open the file and follow along as you read the chapter.

F irms generate cash flows by using assets—without assets, there would be no sales, profits, or cash flows. However, some potential asset acquisitions represent good investments while others are likely to be losers, and the most successful firms are those that make the best asset investment decisions. "Capital budgeting" is the name given to the asset investment decision process. Conceptually, capital budgeting decisions are no different than decisions relating to stocks and bonds. When evaluating securities, cash flows (coupon payments, dividends, etc.) are estimated and then discounted at an appropriate rate (the YTM or YTC for bonds and the required return for stocks) to find the present value of the cash flow stream. In capital budgeting, projects require an initial investment (perhaps spread over multiple years) and then they produce positive operating cash flows over some period. These cash flows are then discounted back to the present at a weighted average cost of capital (WACC) sufficient to compensate investors for bearing the risk inherent in the project.

The capital budgeting process requires coordination between several departments within the company. Most projects involve large initial investments and have an ongoing need for funding to cover operating costs throughout their lives. Managers must estimate the product demand and determine optimal prices and quantities so as to maximize profits. The evolving nature of global markets complicates these decisions. In the past, firms generally operated and sold only in their home countries, with markets in other countries served primarily through exports. Today, though, multinational firms operate in both industrial economies and emerging markets, and the complexities of producing and selling in many sovereign countries make the analyses of investment projects much more difficult.

Conceptually, capital budgeting is similar for both purely domestic and multinational companies, and in both cases we apply our basic valuation equation. We first estimate the project's investment requirements, both for acquiring productive assets and the related operating working capital, and this typically results in a negative cash flow at t = 0. For large projects that take several years to complete, there may be negative cash flows for several years, and in this instance the project's cost is calculated as the present value (PV) of those negative cash flows. Next, we estimate the FCFs for each year and find their present value. Finally, we estimate funds the firm can recover from selling the equipment and liquidating the working capital at the end of the project's operating life (the terminal value) and find their present value. The difference between the PV of the positive cash inflows and the PV of the project's investment cost is defined as the net present value, or NPV, and it represents the value the proposed project is expected to add to the firm. If a project's NPV is positive, then it increases the firm's value and should be accepted.

While the basic tenets of domestic capital budgeting still hold, international capital budgeting must consider some additional factors. In particular, multinationals must contend with different accounting and tax systems, exchange rate fluctuations, and the repatriation of funds from foreign investments back to the parent. A further complication arises because the analysis can be performed from either a local subsidiary's perspective or from the parent's home market perspective. The focus in either case should be on maximizing the wealth of the parent's shareholders, but the analysis itself is different depending on the perspective taken. This chapter covers the basics of capital budgeting in a global setting, while the next one goes on to bring in risk analysis and the role of real options in the capital budgeting decision process.

OVERVIEW OF CAPITAL BUDGETING

Capital Budgeting
The process of planning expenditures on assets whose cash flows are expected to extend beyond one year.

Capital budgeting is the decision process used to identify those investment projects that are likely to add value to the firm, and it is perhaps the most important task faced by financial managers and their staffs. First, a firm's capital budgeting decisions define its strategic direction because moves into new products, services, or markets must be preceded by capital expenditures. Second, the results of capital budgeting decisions continue for many years, thus reducing future flexibility. Third, poor capital budgeting can have serious financial consequences. If the firm invests too much, it will incur unnecessarily high depreciation and other expenses. On the other hand, if it does not invest enough, its equipment and computer software will become obsolete, and the firm will be unable to produce competitively. Also, if it has inadequate capacity, it may lose market share to rival firms, and regaining lost customers requires heavy selling expenses, price reductions, or product improvements, all of which are costly.

Security valuation concepts are also applied in capital budgeting. However, instead of investors selecting stocks and bonds from those available in the securities market, *capital budgeting projects are created by the firm.* For example, a sales representative may report that customers are asking for a product that the company does not currently produce. The sales manager then consults with the marketing research group to determine demand for the proposed product. If a significant market exists, cost accountants and engineers will estimate production costs. If management concludes that the product can generate sufficient profit, it will be formally proposed, and a project analysis will be conducted to verify that it will add value to the firm.

A firm's growth, and even its ability to hold its current position, depends on a constant flow of ideas for new projects, product improvements, and lower cost alternatives. Accordingly, a well-managed firm encourages good capital budgeting proposals from its employees. If a firm has capable and imaginative employees and executives, and if it has an efficient incentive system, capital investment ideas will flow freely. Some ideas will be good, but others will not, so companies must screen projects to ensure that they invest only in those likely to add value.

Why are capital budgeting decisions so important?
What are some ways firms obtain ideas for capital projects?

PROJECT CLASSIFICATIONS

Analyzing capital expenditure proposals is not a costless operation—benefits can be gained, but analysis has a cost. For certain projects, a detailed analysis may be warranted; for others, simpler procedures should be used. Accordingly, firms generally categorize projects and then analyze those in each category somewhat differently:

1. *Replacement: maintenance of business.* Replacement of worn-out or damaged equipment is necessary for the firm to remain competitive. The only issues here are (a) should this operation be continued and (b) should we continue to use the same production processes? If the answers are yes, maintenance decisions are normally made without an elaborate analysis.

2. *Replacement: cost reduction.* These projects lower the costs of labor, materials, and other inputs (such as electricity) by replacing serviceable but less efficient equipment. These decisions are often discretionary, and they generally require a somewhat more detailed analysis.

3. *Expansion of existing products or markets, including international markets.* These decisions may include new outlets, distribution facilities, or products and are more complex because they require an explicit forecast of demand, so a significantly more detailed analysis is required. Also, the final decisions are generally made at a high level within the firm.

4. *Expansion into new products or markets, including international markets.* These projects involve strategic decisions that could change the fundamental nature of the business, and they normally require the expenditure of large sums with delayed paybacks. Decisions are usually made at the very top—by the board of directors—as part of the firm's strategic plan.

5. *Downsizing and plant relocation decisions.* In recent years, many companies have found themselves with excess capacity, and studies have shown that closing some facilities and consolidating operations often increases profits. More and more, firms are concluding that closing domestic plants and moving production overseas will increase value.

Other types of projects include safety and/or environmental projects, research and development expenditures, or long-term contracts such as providing power to a military base where an initial investment is required to fulfill the contract.

In general, relatively simple calculations and only a few supporting documents are required for replacement decisions, especially maintenance-type investments in profitable plants. A more detailed analysis is required for cost-reduction replacements, for expansion of existing product lines, for investments in new products or areas, and for strategic relocation decisions. As we discussed in Chapter 4, international expansion can take several forms, including foreign direct investment (FDI), joint ventures/strategic alliances, and licensing and management contracts. Given the complexities that can arise with international expansions, these decisions require especially careful analyses.

Identify the major project classification categories, and explain how the decision process varies among these categories.

CAPITAL BUDGETING DECISION RULES

The three most commonly used methods for evaluating projects are (1) payback, (2) net present value (NPV), and (3) internal rate of return (IRR).[1] In the following sections we define each method, explain the calculations involved, and discuss how well each performs in terms of selecting the set of projects that will maximize the firm's value.

Payback Period

Payback Period
The length of time required for an investment's net revenues to cover its cost.

The **payback period**, defined as the number of years required to recover the investment in a project, was the first formal method used in capital budgeting. For example, if a project has a cost of $90,000 and expected cash inflows of $30,000 at the end of each of the next five years, then the payback would be three years because it would take three years to recover the $90,000 investment. If the project had cost $100,000, then its payback would have occurred some time between the third and fourth years, and we would calculate the exact payback period using this formula:[2]

$$\text{Payback period} = \text{Year before full recovery} + \frac{\text{Unrecovered cost at start of year}}{\text{Cash flow during year}}. \qquad \text{(11-1)}$$

Mutually Exclusive Projects
A set of projects where only one can be accepted.

In our example with a $100,000 project cost, the payback would be 3.33 years.

The shorter the payback, the better the project. Therefore, if we were comparing two projects, one with a payback of three years and the other five years, the three-year payback project would rank higher. If the projects were **mutually exclusive**, meaning that only one or the other could be accepted, the one with the shorter payback would be chosen.[3] If the projects were **independent**, then both could be chosen, but if the company had a rule that required projects to have a payback of four years or less, then the three-year payback project would be accepted and the five-year project rejected.

Independent Projects
Projects whose cash flows are not affected by the acceptance or nonacceptance of other projects.

Payback has three useful features: (1) It is simple to calculate; (2) it is easy to understand; and (3) it provides an indication of the "liquidity" of different projects by showing how long the firm's money will be tied up. However, it also has three

[1]Several additional methods are occasionally used in capital budgeting. Some of the less commonly used ones include discounted payback, accounting rate of return, profitability index, and modified IRR. See Eugene F. Brigham and Phillip R. Daves, *Intermediate Financial Management,* 8th edition (Mason, OH: South-Western Publishing, 2004), Chapter 11, for a discussion of these methods. For international projects, an adjusted present value approach is also sometimes considered. See Donald Lessard, "Evaluating International Projects: An Adjusted Present Value Approach," *International Financial Management: Theory and Application* (New York: John Wiley and Sons, Inc., 1985).

[2]When we use Equation 11-1, we are implicitly assuming that cash flows occur uniformly during the year at the rate of 1/365 per day. This is generally a reasonable assumption.

[3]An example of two mutually exclusive projects would be a conveyor belt system versus a fleet of forklifts for handling materials in a warehouse. Acceptance of one project would lower the cash flows from the other, so the projects' cash flows are dependent on one another, not independent.

serious flaws: (1) Since it gives equal weight to dollars received in different years, it does not consider the time value of money; (2) it does not take account of cash flows that occur after the payback year; and (3) it does not have a profitability-based benchmark to differentiate between acceptable and unacceptable projects.[4]

Firms calculate payback because it does provide some useful information, but because of its flaws, it is not a reliable guide for selecting the set of projects that will maximize the firm's value. Therefore, it is not given much weight in the final accept/reject decision in most regions of the world. Still, a majority of firms in India and Southeast Asia prefer the payback method to other more value-oriented measures because of its simplicity, low cost, and ease of explaining to upper management and also because firms in those regions often face severe liquidity constraints.

Net Present Value (NPV)

Net Present Value (NPV) Method
A method of ranking investment proposals using the NPV, which is equal to the present value of future net cash flows discounted at the cost of capital.

Once the flaws in the payback method were recognized, people began to search for better ways to evaluate projects. One obvious choice was the **net present value (NPV) method**, which utilizes the basic valuation equation. To implement this approach, we proceed as follows:

1. Find the present value of each cash flow, including both inflows and outflows, discounted at the project's risk-adjusted cost of capital (the project's WACC).
2. Sum these discounted cash flows to obtain the NPV.
3. If an independent project's NPV is positive, accept it because it adds value to the firm, but reject the project if the NPV is negative. If two projects are mutually exclusive, the one with the higher positive NPV should be chosen.

The equation for the NPV is as follows:

$$\text{Value added} = \text{NPV} = \frac{CF_0}{(1 + r)^0} + \frac{CF_1}{(1 + r)^1} + \frac{CF_2}{(1 + r)^2} + \cdots + \frac{CF_n}{(1 + r)^n}$$
$$= \sum_{t=0}^{n} \frac{CF_t}{(1 + \text{WACC})^t}. \tag{11-2}$$

Note that Equation 11-2 is a direct application of the basic valuation equation, where CF_t represents the expected cash flow at time t, WACC is the project's risk-adjusted cost of capital, and n is the project's life. Expenditures for assets such as buildings and equipment, along with the working capital required to operate new plants, are *negative* cash flows, and they generally occur before inflows begin. For most small projects, only CF_0 is negative, but for many large projects, such as an electric generating plant or a newly designed jet aircraft, outflows occur for several years before operations commence and cash inflows begin. For example, Boeing's new 7E7 aircraft is scheduled to fly in 2008, but the investment in that project began back in the 1990s.

To find a project's NPV, we estimate its CFs, its WACC, and n, after which we enter the data and solve the equation with a financial calculator or computer spreadsheet. An NPV of zero signifies that the project's cash flows are just sufficient to repay the invested capital and provide the required rate of return on that capital. If the NPV is positive, then the project is expected to generate more cash flow than

---

[4]A variant of the payback, the *discounted payback method,* has been used to help overcome the time value of money problem. See Brigham and Daves, *Intermediate Financial Management,* for a discussion. We do not cover discounted payback here, but some firms rely heavily on it, particularly as an indicator of project risk.

is needed to cover its cost of capital, and the excess cash accrues to the firm's stockholders and thus increases the firm's value. Therefore, if a firm undertakes a project with a positive NPV, stockholder wealth increases by the project's NPV. Viewed this way, it is easy to understand the logic of the NPV approach.[5]

Internal Rate of Return (IRR)

In Chapter 8 we found the yield to maturity on a bond as the discount rate that equates the present value of the expected future interest and principal payments to the bond's current market price. If the expected yield exceeds the required rate of return, then the bond is a good investment. This same concept applies to capital budgeting. Here, the project's cost corresponds to the bond price and the projected cash inflows correspond to the bond's interest and maturity payments. We are looking for projects whose expected rates of return (*IRRs*) are greater than their required rates of return, which are their risk-adjusted WACCs. To find the **internal rate of return, IRR**, we use the same basic formula as for the NPV, except here we solve the equation for the discount rate. When we found the NPV, we entered values for the expected cash flows and the WACC for r, and we then solved for NPV. When we find the IRR, we again enter the CFs, but now we enter 0 for NPV and then solve for r, the discount rate. The solution value of r—the value that forces NPV to 0—is defined as the IRR.

$$\text{Value added} = \text{NPV} = \frac{CF_0}{(1+r)^0} + \frac{CF_1}{(1+r)^1} + \frac{CF_2}{(1+r)^2} + \cdots + \frac{CF_n}{(1+r)^n}$$

$$0 = \sum_{t=0}^{n} \frac{CF_t}{(1+IRR)^t}. \tag{11-3}$$

The IRR is not easy to calculate numerically, but it can be found easily with a financial calculator or spreadsheet.[6]

If a project's IRR exceeds its cost of capital, then it will earn an extra return that accrues to stockholders, and this leads to a higher firm value. Therefore, under the **internal rate of return method**, all independent projects whose IRRs exceed their costs of capital should be accepted, and when choosing among mutually exclusive projects, the project with the highest IRR should be selected.

Comparison of the NPV and IRR Methods

The NPV and IRR criteria always lead to the same accept/reject decisions for independent projects.[7] In other words, if the NPV is positive, then the IRR must exceed the WACC. However, NPV and IRR can give conflicting rankings for mutually exclusive projects. Moreover, mutually exclusive projects are extremely common—

[5]A potential problem arises when using the NPV method to evaluate mutually exclusive projects that have different project lives. Methods such as the *replacement chain* or *equivalent annual annuity* must be employed. These methods are discussed in Brigham and Daves, *Intermediate Financial Management*.

[6]Most projects have negative cash flows (investment requirements) during the first year or perhaps the first few years, after which the sign of the cash flows changes from minus to plus. This is called a *normal* project. However, we occasionally encounter projects where the sign of the cash flows changes two or more times, as it might for a coal mining project where expenditures are required to open the mine, then cash inflows occur, and finally the company is required to spend money to clean up the mining site. This situation is defined as a *nonnormal* project. A complication can arise when we attempt to calculate the IRR for a nonnormal project—it may turn out that the project has two or more IRRs, or perhaps no IRR. The easiest way to deal with such a situation is to forget the IRR method and simply focus on the NPV. Alternatively, we can calculate the *modified IRR (MIRR)* or the *rate of return on capital (RORC)*. For a discussion of multiple IRRs, see Brigham and Daves, *Intermediate Financial Management*.

[7]This assumes that the IRR exists and is unique. This may not always be the case, as explained in Footnote 6.

Net Present Value Profile
A graph showing the relationship between a project's NPV and different values for the firm's cost of capital.

there is almost always more than one way to do something, and when there is, we have mutually exclusive projects.

Consider Figure 11-1. Here we examine two projects, S and L. Focus first on Project S, and look at the graph in Panel A of the figure. That graph is called a **net present value profile**, and it shows the project's NPV at different costs of capital. Notice that NPV declines as the discount rate increases, and the rate where NPV = 0 is the IRR, which is 18.46 percent for Project S. Notice also that at any cost of capital (WACC) less than the IRR of 18.46 percent, NPV_S is greater than zero, so if WACC is less than 18.46 percent, then NPV_S and IRR_S both indicate that S should be accepted. Conversely, if the WACC is greater than 18.46 percent, then the NPV and IRR methods both indicate rejection. Therefore, in a situation where we are dealing with only one project, the NPV and IRR methods can never conflict—if one method indicates acceptance, then so will the other method.[8]

Now assume that Projects S and L are mutually exclusive. They both have a cost of $1,000, and both produce cash flows for four years. However, S's inflows come primarily in the early years, giving it a relatively short payback, while L's inflows come later, giving it a longer payback. The two projects are equally risky, and a WACC of 10 percent is assigned to them. At the 10 percent WACC, NPV_L = $144.12 and NPV_S = $118.64, so based on the NPV criterion, L should be selected. However, as we can see from the data and from Panel B, S has the higher IRR, 18.46 percent versus 14.84 percent for Project L. Therefore, a conflict exists between the two methods: The NPV method says choose L, while the IRR method says choose S. Notice also in Panel B that there would be no conflict between the methods if the WACC were greater than the **crossover rate** of 11.56 percent, because at that WACC, Project S would dominate in the sense that NPV_S would be greater than NPV_L and IRR_S would exceed IRR_L.[9]

Crossover Rate
The cost of capital at which the NPV profiles of two projects cross, and thus at which the projects' NPVs are equal.

We see from Panel B of Figure 11-1 that the NPVs of both projects decline as the cost of capital increases. At low costs of capital, Project L has the higher NPV, but its NPV profile line declines more rapidly than that of S, and at a WACC of 11.56 percent the NPV profiles cross. Project L's NPV declines more rapidly as the WACC increases because most of its cash flows occur late in its life, and those distant cash flows are exponentially affected by a higher cost of capital. Most of S's cash flows come in early, so its cash flows are not hurt as badly by high WACCs. The situation here is like that with bonds, where we saw long-term bonds' prices decline more than those of short-term bonds when interest rates rise. The NPV profile lines are analogous to the bond interest rate sensitivity curves we discussed in Chapter 8.

Logic suggests that NPV is a better decision criterion than IRR because NPV selects the project that adds the most to shareholder wealth. Therefore, this method should generally be given the most weight in capital budgeting decisions. However, the IRR is still useful because decision makers like to know what rate of return they can expect on different investments.[10]

[8]This statement is always true for normal projects. Nonnormal projects, with more than one change in the sign of the cash flows, can have more than one IRR and thus can have conflicts between NPV and IRR.

[9]The crossover rate, where two NPV profiles intersect, is calculated in the *Excel* chapter model, and it is discussed more fully in Brigham and Daves, *Intermediate Financial Management*.

[10]We do sometimes find situations where one project's NPV is larger than that of another, but the project with the smaller NPV has an IRR that is so much higher that it is reasonable to accept the one with the higher IRR. IRR advocates illustrate this point with an extreme situation: "Suppose one project has a cost of $100,000, a 50 percent IRR, and an NPV of $1 million, while another has a cost of $10 million, an IRR of 15 percent, and an NPV of $1.01 million. Which is the better project?" Most people would choose the small project in spite of its slightly lower NPV because so much less money is being put at risk. To deal with such situations, a method called the "profitability index," which gives return per dollar invested, may be advocated.

| **Figure 11-1** | NPV Profile Analysis: Projects S and L |

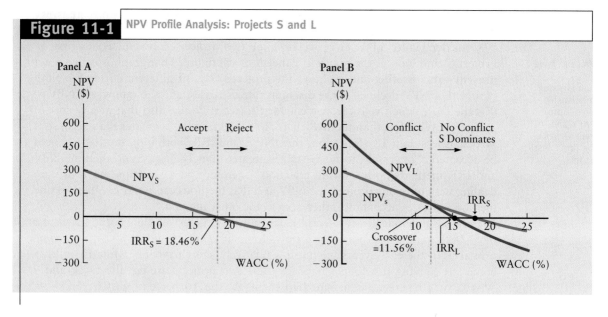

NET CASH FLOWS					WACC = 10.00%		
Year	Project S	Project L				Project S	Project L
0	−1,000	−1,000		NPV =		$118.64	$144.12
1	800	100		IRR =		18.46%	14.84%
2	300	200		Crossover =		11.56%	
3	100	500					
4	100	750					

Notes:
1. In Panel A, we see that if WACC < IRR, then NPV > 0, and vice versa.
2. Thus, for "normal and independent" projects, there can be no conflict between NPV and IRR rankings.
3. However, if we have mutually exclusive projects, conflicts can occur. In Panel B, we see that IRR_S is always greater than IRR_L, but if WACC < 11.56%, then NPV_L > NPV_S, in which case a conflict occurs.
4. Summary: (a) For normal, independent projects, conflicts can never occur, so either method can be used. (b) For mutually exclusive projects, if WACC > Crossover, there is no conflict, but if WACC < Crossover, then there will be a conflict between NPV and IRR.

Conclusions on Capital Budgeting Methods

We have discussed the three most frequently used capital budgeting decision methods and highlighted their relative strengths and weaknesses. In making accept/reject decisions, sophisticated firms calculate and consider all available measures because each provides a different piece of relevant information.

Payback provides an indication of a project's liquidity and risk—a long payback means (1) that the investment dollars will be locked up for many years, hence the project is relatively illiquid, and (2) that the project's cash flows must be forecasted far out into the future, hence the project is probably risky. NPV is important because it gives a direct estimate of the project's profitability by showing how much it is expected to add to shareholder wealth. IRR also measures profitability, but it is expressed as a percentage rate of return, which many decision makers prefer. If conflicts exist between the NPV and IRR methods, then more weight should be given to NPV because it shows how much wealth a project adds, and that is the ultimate test of a project's value.

Each method provides a different piece of information to decision makers. Because it is easy to calculate all of them, they should all be considered in the decision process.

We recommend that the most weight should be given to NPV, but it would be foolish to ignore the information the other methods provide. It should also be noted that sophisticated managers do not make important decisions based solely on the results of quantitative measures such as NPV. Qualitative factors such as the chances of a tax increase, a military conflict, or a major product liability suit should also be considered. In summary, informed capital budgeting decisions should be the product of sound managerial judgment that reflects such quantitative measures as NPV and IRR, along with judgmental, qualitative factors that simply cannot be quantified.

SELF-TEST QUESTIONS
Define the three capital budgeting decision methods discussed in this section, and explain the rationale for each.

What information does the payback provide that is not provided by NPV and IRR? What information is provided by NPV? IRR?

Describe how NPV profiles are constructed. What information do they provide?

In general, should more weight be given to the NPV or to the IRR if those two methods produce conflicting results? Explain.

Should capital budgeting decisions be based solely on whether or not the NPV is positive and/or the IRR exceeds the WACC? Explain.

ESTIMATING CASH FLOWS

The most important, and also the most difficult, step in capital budgeting is estimating the cash flows—the investment outlays and the annual cash inflows after a project goes into operation. Many variables are involved, and many individuals and departments participate in the process. For example, the forecasts of unit sales and sales prices are normally made by the marketing group, based on their knowledge of basic product demand, price elasticity, advertising effects, the state of the economy, competitors' reactions, and consumer trends. Similarly, the capital outlays associated with a new product are generally obtained from engineering and product development experts, personnel specialists, purchasing agents, and so forth.

It is difficult to forecast the costs and revenues associated with a large, complex project, so forecast errors can be quite large. For example, when several major oil companies decided to build the Alaska Pipeline, the original cost estimates were in the neighborhood of $700 million, but the actual cost was closer to $7 billion. Similar (or even worse) miscalculations are common in forecasts of product design costs, such as the costs to develop a new aircraft such as Boeing's 7E7. Further, as difficult as plant and equipment costs are to estimate, sales revenues and operating costs over the project's life are even more uncertain. Just ask Polaroid, which recently filed for bankruptcy, or stockholders of now-defunct dot-com companies.

International projects are even more difficult to analyze than domestic ones for at least three different reasons:

1. The quality of data available in many countries is poor, and forecasts are subject to significant errors.
2. Exchange rates are often hard to forecast, and they rely on questionable assumptions such as purchasing power and interest rate parity that we discussed in Chapter 3.
3. Many of the costs associated with foreign projects are subject to political negotiations with host governments instead of being determined in the marketplace, and government officials can change their minds.

Such complexities often introduce a great deal of uncertainty into the forecasting process, and some of the required inputs may be little more than educated guesses.

A good forecast includes these steps: (1) Obtaining information from various departments such as engineering and marketing, (2) ensuring that everyone involved with the forecast uses a consistent set of economic and political assumptions, and (3) ensuring that no biases exist in the forecast. This last point is extremely important, because some managers become emotionally involved with pet projects or else seek to build empires. Both problems lead to cash flow forecasting biases that make bad projects look good, but only on paper.

It is almost impossible to overstate the problems one can encounter in cash flow forecasts. It is also difficult to overstate the importance of these forecasts. Still, observing the principles discussed in the next several sections will help minimize forecasting errors.

What is the most important step in a capital budgeting analysis?

What departments are involved in estimating a project's cash flows?

Why are international projects more difficult to analyze than domestic projects?

What steps does a proper forecast analysis include?

IDENTIFYING THE RELEVANT CASH FLOWS

Relevant Cash Flows
The specific cash flows that should be considered in a capital budgeting decision.

The first step in estimating cash flows for use in a capital budgeting analysis is to identify the **relevant cash flows**, defined as the specific set of cash flows that should be considered in the current decision. Analysts often misestimate cash flows, but two cardinal rules can help you minimize mistakes: (1) Capital budgeting decisions must be based on *cash flows*, not accounting income. (2) Only *incremental cash flows*, caused by accepting the project, are relevant.

Remember from Chapter 6 that *free cash flow* is the cash flow available for distribution to investors. In a nutshell, the relevant cash flow for a project is the *additional* free cash flow that the company expects to realize if it accepts a project. It is the cash flow above and beyond what the company could expect if it does not implement the project. The following sections discuss the relevant cash flows in more detail.

Project Cash Flow versus Accounting Income

Recall from Chapter 6 that free cash flow is calculated as follows:

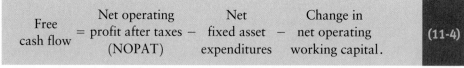

$$\text{Free cash flow} = \text{Net operating profit after taxes (NOPAT)} - \text{Net fixed asset expenditures} - \text{Change in net operating working capital.} \quad (11\text{-}4)$$

Just as a firm's value depends on its free cash flows, so does the value of its proposed projects. We illustrate cash flow estimation later in the chapter with a comprehensive example, but it is important to understand how project cash flow differs from accounting income.

CASH FLOWS ASSOCIATED WITH FIXED ASSETS Most projects require an investment in assets, and asset purchases require cash. Note too that substantial shipping and installation costs are often required, and those costs must be included along with the purchase price of the assets themselves. Finally, the fixed assets associated with a project can often be sold for cash at the conclusion of the project's life, and the cash invested in the project's working capital can also be recovered. We must consider these factors when we calculate projects' net cash flows.

NONCASH CHARGES Accountants do not subtract the cash purchase price of fixed assets when calculating accounting income, but they do subtract a noncash charge each year for depreciation.[11] We handle things differently in capital budgeting—we show the project's cost as an outflow in the year or years when those costs are incurred, and we add the annual depreciation charge back to net income when calculating annual cash flows. Since accountants take depreciation out when they calculate net income, we must add it back in when we find the annual cash inflows (i.e., Cash flow = Net income + Annual depreciation).[12]

CHANGE IN NET OPERATING WORKING CAPITAL The net operating working capital associated with a new project is calculated as follows:[13]

$$\begin{pmatrix} \text{Required change} \\ \text{in net operating} \\ \text{working capital} \end{pmatrix} = \begin{pmatrix} \text{Required} \\ \text{additions to} \\ \text{inventory} \end{pmatrix} + \begin{pmatrix} \text{Increase} \\ \text{in accounts} \\ \text{receivable} \end{pmatrix} - \begin{pmatrix} \text{Increase in} \\ \text{accounts payable} \\ \text{and accruals} \end{pmatrix}. \quad (11\text{-}5)$$

The investment in net new operating working capital requires capital, and like the investment in fixed assets, it represents a negative cash outlay. Note that projects that simply reduce costs, like replacing inefficient machinery with newer and more efficient machines, generally do not require additional working capital and may in fact even reduce it. However, expansion projects generally require additional working capital. Investors must provide this capital, and they expect to earn a return on it. Note too that during the project's later years, or at the end of its life, annual sales will decline, and when that occurs, inventories will be sold off and receivables will be collected. Thus, the funds initially invested in net operating working capital will eventually be recovered, and that amounts to a cash inflow in the recovery year.[14]

INTEREST EXPENSES ARE NOT INCLUDED IN PROJECT'S CASH FLOWS Recall that we discount a project's free cash flows by its cost of capital, and the cost of capital is a risk-adjusted weighted average, the WACC, which is the rate of return necessary to satisfy all the firm's investors. A bad mistake is to subtract interest payments when estimating a project's cash flows. Because the cost of debt is included in the WACC, which is then used to discount the cash flows, subtracting interest payments from the project's cash flows would result in double counting interest expenses.[15]

Note that our treatment of interest differs from the procedures used to calculate accounting income. Accountants measure the profits available for *stockholders*, and for that purpose interest expenses must be subtracted. However, in capital budgeting we are interested in the cash flows available to all investors, creditors as well as shareholders, so interest expenses are not subtracted. This is analogous to the procedures used in the corporate valuation model discussed in Chapter 9, where the company's free cash flows were discounted at the WACC. *Therefore, you must not subtract interest expenses when finding a project's cash flows.*

---

[11]Depreciation does shelter income from taxation, and that increases cash flow, but depreciation itself is not a cash flow.

[12]If any other noncash charges had been deducted when determining the expected net income, we would also have to add them back, but generally depreciation is the only noncash charge of concern.

[13]If additional cash or any other type of current asset was required as a result of the investment, it too would be shown as part of the investment in net operating working capital.

[14]The return of the investment in working capital is not generally subject to taxes.

[15]If someone subtracted interest (or interest plus principal payments) from the project's cash flows, then they would be calculating the cash flows available to the equity holders, and these cash flows should be discounted at the cost of equity. This technique can give the correct answer, but in order for it to work you must be very careful to adjust the amount of debt outstanding each year to keep the riskiness of the equity cash flows constant. This process is very complicated, and we do not recommend it.

Incremental Cash Flows

Incremental Cash Flows
The cash flows representing the change in the firm's total cash flows that occurs as a direct result of accepting the project.

In a project analysis, we focus on those cash flows that occur if and only if we accept the project. These cash flows, called **incremental cash flows**, represent the change in the firm's total cash flows that occurs as a direct result of accepting the project. Three special issues in finding incremental cash flows are discussed next.

Sunk Cost
A cash outlay that has already been incurred and that cannot be recovered regardless of whether the project is accepted or rejected.

SUNK COSTS   A **sunk cost** is an outlay that has already occurred and hence is not affected by the decision under consideration. Since sunk costs are not incremental costs, they should not be included in the analysis. To illustrate, in 2005, Northeast BankCorp was considering whether to establish a branch office in a newly developed section of Boston. To help with its evaluation, Northeast had, back in 2004, hired a consulting firm to perform a site analysis; the cost was $100,000, and this amount was expensed for tax purposes in 2004. Is this 2004 expenditure a relevant cost with respect to the 2005 capital budgeting decision? The answer is no—the $100,000 is a *sunk cost*, and it will not affect Northeast's future cash flows regardless of whether or not the new branch is built. It often turns out that a particular project has a negative NPV if all the associated costs, including sunk costs, are considered. However, on an incremental basis, the project may be a good one because the *future incremental cash flows* are large enough to produce a positive NPV on the *incremental investment*. That is, they more than cover their future cost and generate at least some revenue to help cover the sunk costs.[16]

Opportunity Cost
The return on the best alternative use of an asset, or the highest return that will not be earned if funds are invested in a particular project.

OPPORTUNITY COSTS   A second potential problem relates to **opportunity costs**, which are cash flows that could be generated from an asset the firm already owns if it is not used for the project in question. To illustrate, Northeast BankCorp already owns a piece of land that is suitable for a branch location. When evaluating the prospective branch, should the cost of the land be disregarded because no additional cash outlay would be required? The answer is no, because there is an *opportunity cost* inherent in the use of the property. For example, suppose the land could be sold for $150,000 after taxes. Use of the site for the branch would require forgoing this inflow, so the $150,000 must be charged as an opportunity cost against the project. Note that the proper land cost in the example is the $150,000 market-determined value, regardless of whether Northeast originally paid $50,000 or $500,000 for the property. (What Northeast paid would, of course, have an effect on taxes, hence on the after-tax opportunity cost.)

Externalities
Effects of a project on cash flows in other parts of the firm.

EFFECTS ON OTHER PARTS OF THE FIRM: EXTERNALITIES   The third potential problem involves the effects of a project on other parts of the firm, which economists call **externalities**. For example, some of Northeast's customers who would use the new branch are already banking with Northeast's downtown office. The loans and deposits, hence profits, generated by these customers would not be new to the bank; rather, they would simply be transferring from the main office to the branch. Thus, the net income produced by these customers should not be treated as incremental income in the capital budgeting decision. On the other hand, having a suburban branch would help the bank attract new business to its downtown office because some people would like to be able to bank both close to home and close to work. In this case, the additional income that would actually flow to the downtown office should be attributed to the branch. Although they are often difficult to quantify, *externalities* (either positive or negative) should be considered.

---

[16]A caveat about sunk costs is appropriate. Managers who want to bias the analysis in favor of some pet project have been known to make significant expenditures that will benefit the project prior to conducting the formal analysis. These costs, then, are sunk, so there is an upward bias in the analysis—the "true" NPV is negative, but the NPV of the incremental cash flows is positive. Managers who deliberately bias projects ought to be fired!

When a new project takes sales from an existing product, this is an externality
called **cannibalization**. Cannibalization occurs when a firm builds a plant abroad
and substitutes foreign production for parent company exports. To the extent that
the new project takes sales from existing corporate units, the new project's estimated
profits should be reduced by the earnings lost on existing sales. Naturally, firms do
not like to cannibalize existing products, but it often turns out that if they do not,
someone else will. To illustrate, IBM for years refused to provide full support for its
PC division because it did not want to steal sales from its highly profitable mainframe business. That turned out to be a huge strategic error, because it allowed Intel,
Microsoft, Dell, and others to become dominant forces in the computer industry.
Therefore, when contemplating externalities, the long-run implications of the proposed new project should be included in the analysis.

Timing of Cash Flows

We must account properly for the timing of cash flows. Accounting income statements are for periods such as years or months, so they do not reflect exactly when
during the period cash revenues or expenses actually occur. Because of the time value
of money, capital budgeting cash flows should, in theory, be analyzed exactly as they
occur. Of course, there must be a compromise between accuracy and feasibility. A
time line with daily cash flows would in theory be most accurate, but daily cash flow
estimates would be costly to construct, unwieldy to use, and probably no more accurate than annual cash flow estimates because we simply cannot forecast well enough
to warrant this degree of detail. Therefore, in most cases, we simply use three rules
of thumb when assigning cash flows to time periods: (1) We assume that capital
expenditures occur at the beginning of periods; (2) we assume that capital inflows
(return of capital) occur at the end of periods; and (3) we assume that operating cash
flows, both revenues and expenses, are netted out and reported at the end of the
period in which they were generated. These are very conservative assumptions, so
projects that pass the NPV hurdle with them in place are almost certain to pass under
more favorable assumptions. However, for projects with highly predictable cash
flows, it might be best to assume that cash flows occur at mid-year, or even quarterly
or monthly, to avoid imparting a downward bias to the NPV.

Why should companies use project cash flows rather than accounting income
when calculating a project's NPV?

What is the most common noncash charge that must be added back when
finding project cash flows? Why is it added back?

What is net operating working capital, and how does it affect a project's cash
flows?

Explain the following terms: relevant cash flow, incremental cash flow, sunk
cost, opportunity cost, externalities, and cannibalization.

Explain why in most capital budgeting analyses we simply assume that all
cash flows occur at the end of every year.

ADJUSTING FOR INFLATION

Inflation is a fact of life all over the world, so it must be considered in any sound
capital budgeting analysis; failure to do so can corrupt the analysis.[17] Accounting

---

[17]For some articles on this subject, see Phillip L. Cooley, Rodney L. Roenfeldt, and It-Keong Chew, "Capital Budgeting Procedures under Inflation," *Financial Management*, Winter 1975, 18–27; and "Cooley, Roenfeldt, and Chew vs.
Findlay and Frankle," *Financial Management*, Autumn 1976, 83–90.

for differences in inflation rates across countries is also important because it can change a firm's competitive position, especially when exchange rate changes are slow to adjust to differences in inflation rates.

In capital budgeting analysis, some analysts mistakenly use base-year, or constant (unadjusted), dollars throughout the analysis—say, 2005 dollars if the analysis is done in 2005—along with a cost of capital as determined in the marketplace as we described in Chapter 10. This is wrong: *If the component costs of capital include an inflation premium, as they typically do, but the cash flows are all stated in constant purchasing power (unadjusted) dollars, then the calculated NPV will be lower than the true NPV.* The denominator will be high because it reflects inflation, but the numerator will not have an upward adjustment, and this will produce a downward-biased NPV.

The most common method for inflation adjustment involves leaving the cost of capital in its nominal form and then adjusting the individual cash flows, both revenues and expenses, to reflect expected inflation. For example, we might assume that sales prices and variable costs will increase by 2 percent per year, that fixed costs will increase by 1 percent per year, and that depreciation charges (since they are based on historical costs) will be unaffected by inflation. In general, we should always build inflation into the cash flow analysis, with the specific adjustments reflecting as accurately as possible the most likely set of circumstances. With a spreadsheet, it is easy to make these adjustments. For companies that operate in high inflation environments or in circumstances where inflation is highly variable, it is often useful to analyze projects in both nominal and real (constant currency) terms.[18]

SELF-TEST QUESTIONS
Explain why inflation should be considered in a capital budgeting analysis.
What is the most common way of handling inflation, and how does this procedure eliminate a potential bias?

EVALUATING FOREIGN PROJECTS

Multinational enterprises with projects in foreign countries can use the analytical methods described above in the same way as purely domestic companies. However, they face challenges that are not usually encountered in a single-country analysis that significantly affect cash flows and discount rates. First, cash flows are often generated in foreign currencies, and they are subject to different accounting and tax treatments than in the home country. Because exchange rates often fluctuate over time, the dollar-equivalent amounts are even less certain than the original foreign currency cash flows. Second, some countries either place restrictions on the amount of money that can be repatriated from the local subsidiary to the parent or impose taxes on funds sent abroad. In the extreme, countries may prohibit the repatriation of capital or earnings to the parent until the subsidiary is liquidated or sold to local investors. Third, MNEs face unique risks when they operate abroad. For instance, the host government may change the conditions for repatriating funds, or adopt confiscatory tax policies, or even expropriate local operations.

---

[18]Although the nominal and real approaches should yield roughly similar answers if done properly, consulting firms such as McKinsey and Company argue that the two approaches provide some additional insights and also reveal potential shortcomings in the analysis. See, for instance, Tom Copeland, Tim Koller, and Jack Murrin, *Valuation: Measuring and Managing the Value of Companies* (New York: John Wiley and Sons Inc., 2000).

Adjust for Risk in the Discount Rate or the Cash Flows?

The additional risks of foreign investments need to be incorporated into the valuation equation, and the adjustment can be made to either the cash flows in the numerator or the discount rate in the denominator. Traditionally, risk is incorporated into the analysis by increasing the risk premium embedded in the discount rate. However, a second alternative, which is conceptually superior if it can be implemented, is to make the risk adjustment by lowering the cash flows and then discounting at the domestic cost of capital. For instance, future cash flows in foreign currency can be estimated using forward rates that eliminate unexpected changes in exchange rates.[19] Risks associated with nonconvertibility and expropriation, as well as political violence to business income and assets in place, can be eliminated through insurance issued by organizations such as the Overseas Private Investment Corporation (OPIC). If insurance is used, the premium is subtracted from the cash flows themselves, and the remaining cash flows are discounted at the domestic cost of capital. Note, though, that insurance is not feasible for all foreign investments, and other adjustments to the cash flows are often nothing more than informed guesses.

Compartmentalizing Risks Using Alternative Perspectives

A second procedure that companies use to deal with risk is to compartmentalize risks by using three separate types of analysis. First, the firm conducts a financial analysis of the project in the traditional manner, but strictly from the perspective of the local subsidiary. This analysis is exactly like one that would be done for the project by a local company in the host country, and it is called a **project perspective** analysis. If the project does not have a positive NPV in this evaluation, this probably means that our company does not have a competitive advantage over local companies in this line of business. Projects should generally have a positive NPV to warrant further consideration.

Assuming that the project passes the first screen, many companies then recalculate the NPV—focusing not on the operating cash flows of the project itself but on the capital transfers from the parent to the subsidiary and the cash flows from the project that can be repatriated back to the parent. These cash flows are very different from the ones developed for the project perspective, and they usually include both operating and financial components. Thus this analysis, called the **parent perspective** analysis, mixes the investment and financing decisions, which is usually a questionable procedure. Still, the parent perspective is important for investments in some countries where there is a high likelihood that cash flows will be blocked from redistribution elsewhere in the MNE, including the servicing of debt and payment of dividends. In this case, the traditional NPV overstates the value of the project to the parent firm. Daewoo learned this lesson the hard way when it encountered severe financial difficulties but was unable to use the cash flows from its subsidiary in Uzbekistan to help relieve its problems.

A third screen, called the **country perspective** analysis, is beginning to be used by MNEs to gauge the long-run potential of the project. This evaluation, which often employs subjective factors that are hard to quantify, looks at the project's contribution to the host nation and the local stakeholders who will be most affected. The underlying rationale here is that if the project does not make a positive contribution

Project Perspective
Evaluation of a capital budgeting project from the perspective of a local company undertaking a project.

Parent Perspective
Evaluation of a capital budgeting project from the perspective of the parent company; it is mainly concerned with the cash flows to be realized by the parent.

Country Perspective
Evaluation of a capital budgeting project that looks at the project's contribution to the host nation and local stakeholders who will be most affected.

---

[19]As we saw in Chapter 3, forward swap rates go out at least to five years and can be used for this purpose.

to the country and local stakeholders, there may well be tension between the company and the government, possibly leading to harassment and even confiscation. Governments do change, and harsh measures might well be imposed if a new nationalist government replaced the officials now in power. So, projects are less risky if the host country as well as the company itself benefits.

Identify three major challenges companies face when implementing foreign projects.

What are the three perspectives from which projects may be evaluated?

EVALUATING CAPITAL BUDGETING PROJECTS: AN EXAMPLE

We illustrate capital budgeting analysis by examining an investment being considered by Sound Systems International (SSI), a California-based multinational manufacturer of sound systems. The company currently has subsidiaries in Mexico, Argentina, and Germany, but sales in Asia are forecasted to expand rapidly. The Asian market is now being served by SSI Germany, but, because of high transportation costs, the profit margin is only 5 percent. Several of the company's directors have been pushing the creation of a subsidiary in Shanghai to serve the growing Asian market. This group points out that Chinese labor costs are low, transportation systems are well developed, and thus that it would be comparatively inexpensive to serve SSI's Asian markets from Shanghai. The Business Development Team (BDT) from SSI's headquarters in California has been negotiating with Chinese officials for almost two years to find mutually acceptable requirements for establishing a subsidiary in the Pu Dong Special Economic Area of Shanghai, and the two sides are now close to agreement. The BDT has negotiated the terms under which the investment would be made, and SSI must now undertake a formal analysis of the project to decide if it would be profitable.

The Chinese Investment Project

We first evaluate the Shanghai operation from a project perspective. If it passes that hurdle, then it is examined from the perspective of SSI-USA, the parent, to see if the cash flows that can be returned are sufficient to cover the original investment. Finally, we consider the country perspective to see how China would benefit from the project.

We use an *Excel* model to analyze the project, finding its cash flows and then the NPV, IRR, and payback. Selected portions of the model are printed out and shown as tables throughout this section.

REQUIRED INVESTMENT SSI has located a building with a secure storage area in the Pu Dong industrial zone. The site has the utilities required for production, and it has easy access to transportation connections that serve both the domestic market, by rail and by barge up the Yangtze River, and export sales through the port of Shanghai. The building's cost is $7.5 million, payable in dollars but recorded on the books of the subsidiary as CNY 62.1 million at the spot exchange rate of CNY 8.28/$. The money to purchase the building will come from SSI-USA as a $10 million equity infusion. An additional equity contribution from SSI will come from both standard and specialized production equipment developed and patented by SSI worth $5 million or CNY 41.4 million. Thus, the equity contribution will be $15 million: $10 million in cash and $5 million in assets. Chinese import regulations require that equipment acquired from other countries must use the latest technology before an import license will be granted, and misrepresentations of the technology subject the company to a hefty penalty, but SSI has obtained approval for the equipment it intends to send. The remainder of the cash supplied by SSI will be used to acquire additional standard production equipment in China for a total cost of CNY 20.7 million, or $2.50 million. This acquisition brings the total investment in equipment to CNY 62.1 million.

China requires companies to use straight-line depreciation unless special permission is given to use accelerated methods. SSI has not been able to secure such permission, so all fixed assets will be depreciated using straight-line depreciation, but for differing periods. Chinese tax regulations classify buildings as 20-year assets, mechanical production equipment as 10-year assets, and specialized electronics production equipment as 5-year assets. Thus, the cost, depreciable life, and annual depreciation will be as follows:

Asset	Cost	Depreciable Life	Annual Depreciation Expense
Building	CNY 62.10 million	20	CNY 3.105 million
Mechanical equipment	CNY 31.05 million	10	CNY 3.105 million
Electronic equipment	CNY 31.05 million	5	CNY 6.210 million

Working capital will also be needed by the operation. The best estimate of required net operating working capital is CNY 41.4 million. As production and sales increase, net operating working capital is expected to increase by CNY 2 million per year. The initial working capital will be obtained by a yuan-denominated loan of CNY 41.4 million for five years at a borrowing rate of 6 percent.

STUDY PERIOD The subsidiary is expected to operate indefinitely. SSI has a policy of investing in a country for the long run and will not make the first investment if it does not believe that the long-run potential is positive. However, for project analysis, the company always uses a five-year study period. When the project's economic life is longer than five years, as it is in this investment, the company estimates the project's salvage value as of the end of Year 5 and adds it to the cash flows.

PROJECTED SALVAGE VALUES SSI uses two methods for estimating salvage values at the end of the study period. First, it estimates the market value of the fixed assets, adjusted for taxes, and adds the value of recovered net operating working capital.[20] This is a *liquidating value concept*. Table 11-1 shows the after-tax salvage values (according to the liquidating-value concept) for the project's building and equipment at the end of the study period.

The second method for estimating a salvage value takes the net operating cash flow in Year 5, $NOCF_5$, estimates the growth rate in NOCF for the future, and uses the terminal value formula,

$$SV_5 = NOCF_5(1 + g)/(WACC - g),$$

[20]Note that if an asset is sold for exactly its book value, there will be no gain or loss, hence no tax liability or credit. However, if an asset is sold for other than its book value, a gain or loss will be created. For example, SSI's building will have a book value of CNY 46,575,000, but the company expects to realize CNY 58,218,750 when it is sold. This would result in a gain of CNY 11,643,750. This indicates that the building should have been depreciated at a higher rate—if depreciation had been CNY 11,643,750 more, the book and market values would have been equal. So, the U.S. Tax Code stipulates that gains on the sale of operating assets indicate that the depreciation rates were too low, so the gain is called "depreciation recapture" by the U.S. Internal Revenue Service and is taxed as ordinary income. On the other hand, if an asset is sold for less than its book value, then the difference can be used to reduce ordinary income, just as depreciation reduces income. The tax rules are essentially the same in other countries.

TABLE 11-1 | **Annual Depreciation and Salvage Value for SSI's Shanghai Project (Currency in Thousands of Chinese Yuan)**

	A	B	C	D	E	F
34	ANNUAL DEPRECIATION					
35	Building				3,105	
36	Mechanical equipment				3,105	
37	Electronic equipment				6,210	
38	Total depreciation				12,420	
39						
40	CALCULATING SALVAGE VALUE			Building	Mftg. Equip.	Elec. Equip.
41	Purchase price			62,100	31,050	31,050
42	Less: Accumulated depr.			15,525	15,525	31,050
43	Book value			46,575	15,525	0
44	Market value (BV x 1.25)			58,219	19,406	0
45	Excess depreciation taken			11,644	3,881	0
46	Tax on excess depreciation			4,658	1,553	0
47	After-tax salvage value			53,561	17,854	0

to estimate the Year 5 value of the future cash flow. This procedure is a *going concern concept* and is appropriate if the project will continue beyond the study period. Note that if the project is treated as a "going concern," the salvage value is not actually recovered in Year 5. It is added to the Year 5 total cash flows to represent the value of the continuing operations as of that point in time. Generally SSI computes the salvage value using both methods and uses the lower estimate in its project analysis as a conservative estimate. If the going concern value is significantly greater than the liquidating value, though, this fact is included as part of the decision information.

EXCHANGE RATES   The exchange rate for the Chinese yuan has been stable at CNY 8.28 per dollar since 1998, and the government has announced that it foresees no change in the rate for at least the next five years. In 2003, the IMF reported that it did not believe the yuan to be undervalued, but private economists assert that it is undervalued by some 10 to 15 percent. Even so, forward quotations going out as far as five years indicate that the market expects the rate to be steady at CNY 8.28 to the dollar. Note that the actual rate is not determined in the market but is set by the government based on mainly political considerations, although not entirely divorced from the underlying economics. In this analysis, to serve as the base case, we will assume that the exchange rate will be constant at CNY 8.28/$ for the next five years. In Chapter 12, we explore the implications for the project of a revaluation of the yuan.

CASH FLOWS TO THE PARENT   China has a reputation as a country from which it is sometimes challenging to repatriate funds or to acquire foreign inputs to the production process because of rather stringent foreign exchange and capital controls. In general, capital must remain in China as long as the company continues operations, and companies can acquire foreign exchange to use in repatriating operating funds or paying for imports only up to the amount of foreign exchange the company earns on its export sales. SSI believes that the level of exports will be more than enough to satisfy this requirement, but they are worried about other restrictions the government might decide to place on repatriating funds. Thus, they would like to have the flexibility to move funds back to California as quickly and in as large an amount as possible. The Chinese government has agreed to allow three sources of cash flow to be sent to the parent annually:

1. License fees—equal to 2 percent of gross sales.
2. Management fees—equal to a fixed CNY 1.656 million plus 0.5 percent of gross sales.
3. Dividends after required reinvestment.

None of these transfers are subject to withholding taxes, but, as pointed out earlier, SSI must generate sufficient foreign exchange from export sales to cover the payments. If they do not do so, the payments are blocked. Also, it is conceivable that in the future China might impose withholding taxes on the company, but the team considers it unlikely in the next 5 years because of the agreement with the government.

GENERAL COMPANY DATA The marginal tax rate in China is 40 percent, comprised of a 30 percent national rate plus a 10 percent local rate. However, new investments receive concessionary treatment so that in the first year profits are earned, the tax rate is zero. Then, in Years 2 and 3, the tax rate is one-half of the normal rate, or 20 percent. Thereafter the full 40 percent rate applies. In the United States, a federal-plus-state tax rate of 40 percent applies for all years.

FIRST-YEAR PROJECTIONS The marketing department has made a series of forecasts of expected unit sales, sales growth, and sales price. While local and export unit sales are expected to grow, the sales prices are expected to be stable. The domestic price in China, though, will have to be lower because of the lower purchasing power in the country. This lower price is justified in terms of cheaper transportation and distribution costs. The department has also put together cost and inflation estimates for the project's expenses. All of these estimates can be seen in Table 11-2.

CANNIBALISM The export sales in China will come at the expense of German sales to those export markets. The local sales in China are new sales, as Germany currently sells almost nothing in China. The computation of the erosion is as follows:

$$\frac{\text{Erosion}}{\text{opportunity cost}} = \frac{\text{Export}}{\text{sales revenue}} \times \frac{\text{Profit margin}}{\text{in Germany}}.$$

There is a controversy, though, about whether the erosion figures should be included in the analysis. Some of the analysts point out that the German capacity will not remain idle but will be used to penetrate other markets in Europe and the former Soviet Union that are not being served to the fullest extent. These analysts suggest that the only reason the capacity to serve these new markets exists is because of the Chinese expansion, so the extra sales should also be attributed to China. Alternatively, the erosion calculations could be eliminated from the evaluation of the Shanghai facility. However, at least in the initial stage of the analysis, SSI will take a conservative approach and consider the lost German sales as an externality, while ignoring possible new German sales.

Project Perspective Analysis

The project perspective looks at the economic feasibility of investing in the Shanghai production unit from the point of view of a local Chinese company considering the investment. When evaluating a potential project from this perspective, the starting

TABLE 11-2 | Input Data for SSI's Shanghai Project (Currency in Thousands)

	A	B	C	D	E	F	G	H	I
5	INPUT DATA (all yuan and dollars in thousands)								
6	INVESTMENT & FINANCING					1ST YEAR PROJECTIONS & GROWTH RATES			
7	Parent investment					Local sales			
8	Cash			USD 10,000		Unit sales			20,000
9	Manufacturing equipment			USD 5,000		Expected growth			5%
10	Subsidiary investment					Sales price (per unit)			CNY 10
11	Locally borrowed funds (NOWC)			CNY 41,400		Export sales			
12	Local borrowing rate			6%		Unit sales			30,000
13	REQUIRED ASSET INVESTMENT					Expected growth			8%
14	Building cost			CNY 62,100		Sales price (per unit)			USD 2
15	Mechanical equipment			CNY 31,050		Direct Materials (per unit)			CNY 5
16	Electronic equipment			CNY 31,050		Expected growth			1.0%
17	Annual increase in NOWC			CNY 2,000		Direct Labor (per unit)			CNY 4
18	PROJECT & ASSET DEPRECIABLE LIVES					Expected growth			2.0%
19	Project life			5		General and adminstrative expenses			CNY 122,500
20	Building depr. life			20		Expected growth			1.5%
21	Mechanical equip. depr. life			10		Insurance			CNY 1,750
22	Electronic equip. depr. life			5		Expected growth			1.5%
23	GENERAL COMPANY DATA					CASH FLOWS TO THE PARENT			
24	Chinese marginal tax rate					License fees (% of sales)			2.00%
25	Tax rate on Year 1 profits			0.00%		Management fees (fixed)			USD 200
26	Tax rate on Year 2 and 3 profits			20.00%		Management fees (% of sales)			0.50%
27	Tax rate, thereafter			40.00%		Profit Margin in Germany			5.00%
28	US marginal tax rate			40.00%		Market Value Excess			25%
29	Domestic WACC			8.76%					
30	Risk-adjusted foreign WACC			11.75%					
31	Exchange rate (CNY/USD)			8.28					

point is to estimate the expected cash flows, which typically include the following items:

1. *Required investment.* This includes the cost of the fixed assets associated with the project plus any investment in net operating working capital (NOWC), such as raw materials, accounts receivable, or cash. Many projects have levels of NOWC that change during the project's life. For example, if sales increase, more NOWC will be required, and if sales fall, less NOWC will be needed.

2. *Annual project operating cash flow.* The operating cash flow is the net operating profit after taxes (NOPAT) plus depreciation. Recall (a) that depreciation is added back because it is a noncash expense and (b) that financing costs (including interest expenses) are not subtracted out because they are incorporated in the firm's cost of capital used to discount the project's cash flows.

3. *Terminal year cash flow.* At the end of the project's life, or at the end of the study period if the project is to continue, some extra capital cash flow is usually generated from the salvage value of the fixed assets, adjusted for taxes if the assets are not sold at their book value. Any return of net operating working capital not already included in the annual cash flow must also be added to the terminal year capital cash flow.

The classification of cash flows is not always as distinct as we have indicated here. For example, in some projects the acquisition of fixed assets is phased in throughout the project's life, and for other projects, some fixed assets are sold off at times other than the project's terminal year. The important point to remember is to include all required investment cash flows in your analysis using the rules mentioned earlier to get the timing right, no matter how you classify them or when they occur.

For each year of the project's life, the *free cash flow* is the sum of the required investment and operating cash flows. These annual free cash flows are then placed on a time line and used to calculate the project's NPV and IRR.

Multinational firms analyzing projects in foreign countries must consider the additional issue of fluctuating exchange rates when conducting the analysis from the project perspective. Consequently, in this situation, modifications to the domestic NPV analysis must be made. There are two main approaches for handling projects with cash flows that are denominated in foreign currencies:

1. Estimate the project's cash flows in the foreign currency (e.g., Chinese yuan) and discount them at the appropriate Chinese-based discount rate to find the yuan-denominated NPV. Then, use the spot exchange rate (e.g., CNY/$ rate) to convert the yuan-denominated NPV to a dollar-denominated equivalent NPV. This is the methodology we will follow in our Shanghai project example.

2. Estimate the project's cash flows in the foreign currency and use forward exchange rates, interest rate parity, purchasing power parity, or an alternative foreign exchange rate forecasting model to determine expected CNY/$ exchange rates that correspond to the time period for each of the cash flow estimates. After converting annual yuan cash flows to annual dollar cash flows, calculate the project's expected dollar-denominated NPV using an appropriate U.S.-based discount rate. Because the Chinese government mandates a pegged value of the yuan versus the dollar, we will defer this analysis to the next chapter when we talk about the possibility of the exchange rate changing.

Surveys of discounted cash flow practices in an international setting indicate that financial practitioners and consultants use each of these approaches about equally.[21] These two approaches will yield the same answer if the foreign exchange parity conditions covered in Chapter 3 hold perfectly. However, in practice, deviations from the parity conditions do occur.

CALCULATING THE REQUIRED INVESTMENT, OPERATING, AND TOTAL CASH FLOWS We begin the project perspective analysis by developing the investment cash flows as shown on the top five rows of Table 11-3. The data are given in a time-line format corresponding to the five-year study period. Row 53 shows the purchase price of the building at time zero and the after-tax salvage value at Year 5. Rows 54 and 55 record similar entries for the two classes of machinery, while Row 56 shows the required net operating working capital. Notice that the initial working capital must be supplemented over time as production and sales increase. Then, in Year 5, the investment in working capital is recovered. Row 57 sums these data and thus shows the total required investment cash flows required for the Chinese project.

Note that all entries in Table 11-3 are denominated in yuan even though the building and much of the machinery were actually paid for with dollars. This is consistent with the philosophy of the project perspective in that we look at the investment from the point of view of local management in Shanghai and ask, "Would this investment add value if it were made by a local Chinese company that had the same opportunities as our subsidiary?" Also note that we assumed that the entire CNY 49.4 million investment in working capital would be recovered. If bad debts or inventory shrinkages occur, the recoverable working capital would be substituted in Year 5.

---

[21]See, for instance, Tom Keck, Eric Levengood, and Al Longfield, "Using Discounted Cash Flow Analysis in an International Setting: A Survey of Issues in Modeling the Cost of Capital," *Journal of Applied Corporate Finance*, Fall 1998, 82–99.

TABLE 11-3 | SSI's Shanghai Project, Cash Flow Analysis (Currency in Thousands of Chinese Yuan)

	A / B	C	D	E	F	G	H
50		Time period					
51		0	1	2	3	4	5
52	**1. Req. investment CFs**						
53	Building	-62,100					53,561
54	Mechanical Machinery	-31,050					17,854
55	Electrical Machinery	-31,050					0
56	NOWC	-41,400	-2,000	-2,000	-2,000	-2,000	49,400
57	Req. investment CFs	-165,600	-2,000	-2,000	-2,000	-2,000	120,815
58							
59	**2. Operating cash flows**						
60	Local unit sales		20,000	21,000	22,050	23,153	24,310
61	Export unit sales		30,000	32,400	34,992	37,791	40,815
62	Local revenues		200,000	210,000	220,500	231,525	243,101
63	Export revenues		422,280	456,062	492,547	531,951	574,507
64	Total revenues		622,280	666,062	713,047	763,476	817,609
65	Direct Materials		-225,000	-242,703	-261,848	-282,557	-304,961
66	Direct Labor		-200,000	-217,872	-237,386	-258,696	-281,973
67	G&A		-122,500	-124,338	-126,203	-128,096	-130,017
68	Insurance		-1,750	-1,776	-1,803	-1,830	-1,857
69	License Fees		-12,446	-13,321	-14,261	-15,270	-16,352
70	Management Fees		-4,767	-4,986	-5,221	-5,473	-5,744
71	Depreciation		-12,420	-12,420	-12,420	-12,420	-12,420
72	Total expenses		-578,883	-617,416	-659,142	-704,342	-753,324
73	BT operating income		43,397	48,646	53,905	59,134	64,284
74	Less: Taxes		0	9,729	10,781	23,654	25,714
75	NOPAT		43,397	38,917	43,124	35,480	38,570
76	Add back: Depreciation		12,420	12,420	12,420	12,420	12,420
77	Net After-Tax Cash Flow		55,817	51,337	55,544	47,900	50,990
78	Less: Cannibalism		-21,114	-22,803	-24,627	-26,598	-28,725
79	Operating CFs		34,703	28,534	30,917	21,303	22,265
80	**3. TOTAL CFs**	-165,600	32,703	26,534	28,917	19,303	143,080
81							
82	**4. Financial results:**						
83	NPV	CNY 110	USD 13				
84	IRR	11.77%					
85	Payback	4.41					

Now consider the project's operating cash flows. Rows 60 and 61 represent annual local and export sales in units, and Rows 62 and 63 show units multiplied by the price per unit, or sales revenues. Annual expenses, based on the assumptions set earlier, come next, and total revenues minus total expenses yields before-tax operating income. Note that we did not include interest as an expense in the operating cash flows.

The tax calculation is in accordance with the Chinese investment incentives, where tax rates are reduced for the first three years of profitable operations. We then show net operating profit after taxes (NOPAT), and then we add back depreciation (because it is a noncash expense) to find the net after-tax cash flow. Row 77 represents a cash flow time line, and these are the numbers that would generally enter our analysis. Some members of the evaluation team believe these are the numbers that should be used to calculate the NPV, but the majority view is that the reduction in German export sales is an externality (cannibalization) that should be charged to this project. Therefore, we subtract the cannibalized costs on Row 78 to find the effective operating cash flows on Row 79.

The final step is to sum the required investment and operating cash flows to obtain the project's total annual cash flows on Row 80. When these cash flows are discounted at the 11.75 percent WACC, an NPV of CNY 110,000, or approximately $13,000 (at the current spot rate of CNY 8.28/$) is obtained. We also calculate an IRR, which turns out to be 11.77 percent, barely greater than the 11.75 percent WACC. Note also that the payback is nearly as long as the five-year projected operating life, and the only reason the project pays back at all is due to the projected salvage value. However, note that if we omitted the cannibalization deduction as advocated by some SSI staff members, the NPV would increase to CNY 88.4 million or $10.7 million, more than enough to make the project pay back from the operations.

Note too that we have assumed that the project will be liquidated after Year 5, even though sales, profits, and cash flows are all projected to be growing nicely. Therefore, a good case could be made for using the going concern concept for estimating the project's value at Year 5. From Table 11-3, the growth rate in the operating cash flow between Years 4 and 5 (when the full impact of the 40 percent tax rate is felt) is 4.52 percent.[22] If we assume that the cash flow will grow indefinitely at this rate, we can use the formula developed in Chapter 9 to estimate the Year 5 value of the continuing stream of cash flows as follows:[23]

$$SV_5 = NOCF_5(1 + g)/(WACC - g)$$
$$= CNY\ 22.265\ million(1.0452)/(0.1175 - 0.0452)$$
$$= CNY\ 321.9\ million,\ or\ \$38.9\ million.$$

This is considerably higher than the CNY 120.8 million liquidating value used for the salvage value in the base case, and it would make the project look much better at an NPV of CNY 115.3 million ($14.0 million). If we also ignored the cannibalization issue in calculating the going concern value, it would be even higher.

Our conclusions from the project perspective analysis are that the project is marginally acceptable, but it is quite risky—all of the cash flows are uncertain, and the factor that makes the NPV turn positive, the salvage value, is extremely difficult to estimate. We take some consolation from the fact that we used a very conservative liquidating value assumption in estimating the salvage value, but it is still worrisome.

Parent Perspective Analysis

The second analysis conducted by most MNEs recognizes that foreign investments that look good on a project-perspective basis may not really be worthwhile if their cash flows cannot be integrated into the corporate network. Thus, SSI wants to know whether cash generated by the Shanghai project can be reallocated to other operating units of the company or used to service debt or pay dividends. If the funds are blocked and cannot be removed from the host country, the investment will not be attractive in the short run, and perhaps not even in the long run. This analysis looks at the investment project from the parent's perspective, focusing on the cash flows moving between the foreign subsidiary and the parent.

Table 11-4 illustrates the types of cash flows analysts use to calculate the NPV from the parent perspective. Notice that many of the intracorporate cash flows represent financial transactions. In our discussion of the project perspective, we emphasized that interest should not be included in the cash flows because we were concerned

[22]The continuing growth rate is assumed to be the growth rate in net operating cash flows between Years 4 and 5. Thus, g = (NOCF_5 − NOCF_4)/NOCF_4 = (22,265,000 − 21,303,000)/21,303,000 = 0.0452, or 4.52 percent.

[23]Note that this formula assumes that the cash flows continue to grow forever. This is unrealistic, but if a shorter period such as 25 years is used, this does not change the result materially because the PV of the distant cash flows rapidly approach zero unless the growth rate is high relative to the WACC used as the discount rate.

TABLE 11-4 | Parent/Subsidiary Cash Flows

	Parent to Subsidiary	Subsidiary to Parent
Financial Cash Flows:	Contributions of equity capital	Cash dividends
	Loans to the subsidiary (not used in the SSI case)	Return of capital
		Interest payments
		Principal repayment
Operating Cash Flows:	Providing machinery parts	License fees
	Providing inventory items	Management fees
		Royalties
		Payment for parts and inventory items

only with *operating* cash flows, with financial effects being reflected in the WACC. However, in the parent perspective analysis, this separation principle must be violated. Nevertheless, the ability to transfer funds among all of its operating units is a critical source of competitive advantage for an MNE. Therefore, the implications of blockages should be assessed before a foreign investment is made, and a strategy must be developed to deal with blockages if they occur. The parent perspective analysis focuses on the implications of the project for transferring funds and allows us to develop proper strategies for dealing with this issue *prior to making the commitment and implementing the project.*

China has a reputation for closely regulating funds flowing across its borders. Regulations are becoming more flexible as China continues to embrace capitalism and especially since it entered the WTO, but restrictions still exist. If SSI is to invest $15 million in China, it wants to be sure that it can get its money back on a reasonable timetable. The Business Development Team (BDT) was able to negotiate unrestricted remittance of cash dividends up to NOPAT less the required increase in net working capital, provided the company generates sufficient foreign exchange to offset the payment. (Yuan must be converted to dollars to make the dividend payment.) No withholding taxes are required for these payments. Contributed capital, though, must remain in China until the company decides to shut down the operation and leave the country or else sell it to Chinese nationals. This is the assumption made in the analysis at the end of the study period, when the terminal value of the required investment is assumed to be returned to SSI-USA. The BDT decided not to recommend a parent-to-subsidiary loan because money at a reasonable interest rate can be obtained from a local bank in Shanghai, given that the parent company will provide adequate equity capital. On the operating side, the BDT negotiated license fees to be used to pay for the advanced technology transferred to the Shanghai operation, plus a management fee to cover the Shanghai operation's share of the entire corporation's overhead. Many countries are sensitive about management fees, so such fees should be explicitly covered in negotiations with the host government. SSI decided to source all production inputs in China, as this will increase the project's value to the Chinese and also avoid import licenses and transfer pricing issues, both of which are closely regulated by the government.

In the project perspective analysis, license fees and management fees were included in operating cash flows as expenses, hence they reduced the taxes paid in China. However, when the parent receives these fees, they represent taxable income and are taxed at the parent's tax rate. Cash dividends sent to the parent from China were calculated as NOPAT minus the increase in required net operating working capital.[24] Taxes will already have been paid in China on these earnings, but when they are sent back to the United States, they will again be subject to taxation. In general, if the tax paid in the host country is less than what would have been paid on the same before-tax earnings in the United States, the IRS charges additional taxes when the dividends are repatriated to the parent. The calculation of this tax obligation is shown in Table 11-5.

On Row 90 of Table 11-5, the dividend repatriated to SSI-USA is NOPAT minus the investment in working capital. The figure needed to determine the U.S. tax liability is the before-tax equivalent of the dividend actually sent. This is shown on Row 92. To calculate the deemed-paid tax on Row 91, the dividend received is divided by NOPAT and then multiplied by the tax actually paid in the host country. For example, the Year 4 NOPAT is projected to be CNY 35.48 million, dividends received are CNY 33.48 million (calculated as NOPAT less the increase in required NOWC), and the taxes paid in China are CNY 23.654 million. Thus, the deemed-paid tax for Year 4 is 22.32 million yuan:

$$\begin{aligned} \text{Deemed-paid tax} &= (\text{Dividends received/NOPAT}) \times \text{Taxes paid} \\ &= (\text{CNY 33.48 million/CNY 35.48 million}) \times \text{CNY 23.654 million} \\ &= 0.943630 \times \text{CNY 23.654 million} = \text{CNY 22.32 million.} \end{aligned}$$

If we add this deemed-paid tax to the amount of the dividend, we obtain the grossed-up dividend shown on Row 92. The applicable U.S. federal-plus-state tax rate is assumed to be 40 percent, and Row 93 shows the tentative amount of tax due to the IRS. However, the company receives a foreign tax credit equal to the deemed-paid tax, which is reported on Row 94. Subtracting Row 94 from Row 93 gives the U.S. tax due on the foreign dividend shown on Row 95. Subtracting this from Row 90 gives the after-U.S.-tax dividend to the parent denominated in yuan on Row 96, and it is translated into dollars on Row 97. Note that no U.S. taxes are due in Years 4 and 5 because in those years the Chinese tax rate is the same as the U.S. rate. However, for Years 1, 2, and 3, U.S. taxes would be due when the dividends are repatriated to SSI-USA. Even though the subsidiary gets a "tax break" during the first three years of profitable operations, sending the money back to the United States wipes out the benefits to the company. This is why companies often

TABLE 11-5 | Calculation of the After-Tax Dividend (Currency in Thousands)

	A	B	C	D	E	F	G	H
88					Time period			
89	Currency in yuan:		0	1	2	3	4	5
90	Dividend Sent		0	41,397	36,917	41,124	33,480	38,570
91	Deemed-Paid Tax			0	9,229	10,281	22,320	25,714
92	Grossed-Up Dividend			41,397	46,146	51,405	55,801	64,284
93	U.S. Tax			16,559	18,458	20,562	22,320	25,714
94	Less: Foreign Tax Credit			0	9,229	10,281	22,320	25,714
95	U.S. Tax Due			16,559	9,229	10,281	0	0
96	A-T Dividend in Yuan			24,838	27,688	30,843	33,480	38,570
97	A-T Dividend in USD		USD 0	USD 3,000	USD 3,344	USD 3,725	USD 4,044	USD 4,658

[24]Some analysts believe that the correct figure to use in calculating the dividend is net income from the income statement instead of using NOPAT from the operating cash flow statement.

do not repatriate dividends from subsidiaries in countries whose tax rates are less than the U.S. rate.[25]

Table 11-6 gives the cash flows required to analyze the Chinese project from the parent's perspective. Rows 102 and 103 represent the cash flows going from the parent to the subsidiary in the form of cash and machinery. License and management fees are taken from Table 11-3 and converted into dollars at the spot rate. The total fees sent to the parent are fully taxable at the U.S. tax rate of 40 percent, so the net fees after paying U.S. taxes are reported on Row 109. We add to this the after-tax dividend from Table 11-5 to obtain the total cash flow on Row 111.

Two adjustments must be made to the numbers on Row 111 to arrive at the parent cash flows. First, the cannibalism of after-tax profits from Germany also affects the parent, so we subtract these flows on Row 112. Also, the after-tax salvage values of the building, equipment, and working capital contributed above the initial allotment (remember the initial NOWC was financed with a local loan) are added back even though the company has no intention of abandoning the Shanghai operation. Their inclusion reflects the assumed Year 5 market value of the assets in place that are "owned" by the parent that could be realized by selling the operations to a Chinese company. Row 114 shows the parent cash flows. Discounting the parent's cash flows at its foreign-risk-adjusted cost of capital, 11.75 percent, gives an NPV of approximately −$1.8 million, an IRR of 8.14 percent, and a payback of 4.56 years. Because the NPV is negative, the project appears to be unprofitable from the parent perspective. Also, the same two caveats apply here that we mentioned in the project perspective analysis. First, the only reason the project "pays back" is because of the salvage value recovery. This is worrisome because the salvage value is especially uncertain. Second, if it is determined that subtracting the cannibalism value is

TABLE 11-6 | Cash Flows from Parent Perspective (Currency in Thousands of Dollars)

	A	B	C	D	E	F	G	H
100					Time period			
101			0	1	2	3	4	5
102	Equity Investment		-10,000					
103	Equipment		-5,000					
104								
105	License Fee			1,503	1,609	1,722	1,844	1,975
106	Management Fee			576	602	631	661	694
107	Total Fees			2,079	2,211	2,353	2,505	2,669
108	U.S. Tax			-832	-884	-941	-1,002	-1,067
109	Net Fees (after-tax)			1,247	1,327	1,412	1,503	1,601
110	Dividend (after-tax)			3,000	3,344	3,725	4,044	4,658
111	Total CFs			4,247	4,671	5,137	5,547	6,259
112	Less: Cannibalism			-2,550	-2,754	-2,974	-3,212	-3,469
113	Plus: SV							9,591
114	Parent CFs		-15,000	1,697	1,917	2,162	2,334	12,381
115								
116	Financial results:							
117	NPV	-USD 1,796						
118	IRR	8.14%						
119	Payback	4.56						

[25]This is a political issue as we write this text in 2004. Estimates indicate that hundreds of billions of U.S. taxes have been avoided by multinational U.S. firms that leave their profits overseas. Some see the existing tax regime as being necessary to compete in global markets, while others see it as providing a bonanza to multinational corporations.

not appropriate because Germany is able to use the freed-up production capacity to expand in other markets, the NPV will increase by $10.7 million, rising to $8.9 million. Note that cannibalization had a similar impact in the project perspective analysis, and this effect passes through directly to the parent as well. Also, if the going concern salvage value (adjusted for the yuan loan) is used instead of the liquidating value, the NPV will increase by nearly $14 million, more than enough to make the NPV positive.

The other procedure for adjusting for foreign risk is to build it into the cash flows. This can be done by adding (1) the cost of *forward cover* (i.e., purchasing forward contracts and thereby eliminating unexpected changes in the exchange rates) and (2) purchasing OPIC insurance and including the premium as a cost. The Overseas Private Investment Corporation is a development agency of the U.S. government that was established in 1971. According to its Web site, "OPIC helps U.S. businesses invest overseas, fosters economic development in new and emerging markets, complements the private sector in managing the risks associated with foreign direct investment, and supports U.S. foreign policy." It does this by offering insurance coverage for most types of projects in almost all countries for three types of foreign risks: currency inconvertibility, expropriation, and political violence. Premiums for the various types of coverage generally fall in the range of $0.20 to $0.85 per $100 of coverage, depending on the nature of the industry and the country in question. It also offers enhanced inconvertibility coverage for an additional premium in some areas.

For this project, using the average premium charged for the three types of coverage offered for China, the unique foreign risk can be eliminated by a before-tax charge of $370,000 per year or $222,000 after taxes. We assume that OPIC insurance must be acquired at the beginning of the year, and the adjusted cash flows are shown in Table 11-7. At the domestic WACC of 8.76 percent, the present value increases to approximately −$1.3 million even though the IRR decreases to 6.4 percent. This analysis suggests that SSI's foreign direct investment risk premium, approximately 3 percent, might be a bit too high. It is still a marginal project from the parent perspective unless SSI changes its mind about the cannibalism issue or uses the "going concern" salvage value.

Country Perspective Analysis

The analyses shown in Tables 11-1 through 11-7 appear quite precise and provide consistent NPV results that signal the project's marginal acceptability. While it is theoretically possible to quantify the project's value to the country, we will not go

TABLE 11-7 | Parent Perspective Analysis with Risk Adjustment to Cash Flows (Currency in Thousands of Dollars)

	A	B	C	D	E	F	G	H
124			Time period					
125			0	1	2	3	4	5
126	Parent CFs		-$15,000	$1,697	$1,917	$2,162	$2,334	$12,381
127	A-T OPIC insurance		-222	-222	-222	-222	-222	
128	Risk-adjusted CFs		-$15,222	$1,475	$1,695	$1,940	$2,112	$12,381
129								
130	Financial results:							
131	NPV	-USD 1,279						
132	IRR	6.40%						

into detail on this topic.[26] Instead, we list in Table 11-8 the information that SSI's Business Development Team used to negotiate with Chinese government authorities. Note that the project would bring no disadvantages to China, but if there had been disadvantages, they would also be shown in Table 11-8.

SSI's team made the points listed in Table 11-8 in its negotiations with the Chinese authorities. Even though such a listing may seem overly simplistic, it has three important uses: (1) It allows SSI-USA's management to assess whether the project adds value to the host country. If it does not, then the project will probably not be allowed, or if it is permitted, then it may experience problems down the road. (2) Because the host country is vitally concerned with its balance of payments position and its trade position, this list reassures the government that the project will help them manage the economy.[27] Most emerging markets, but also advanced industrial countries, are keenly interested in this impact of FDI. (3) The project makes a contribution to politically important areas such as job creation, training, social services, and technology access. Governments are comprised of politicians, and projects that contribute positively to their political agenda tend to be looked upon favorably.

In the initial negotiations between SSI and local Shanghai officials, the Chinese took a hard-line stance about license fees, withholding taxes on remittances abroad, and transfer prices for imported components. At first, management fees were not

TABLE 11-8 | Project's Contribution to China

- The project will create approximately 75 jobs in the first year, mainly semiskilled, and provide training and social services for these workers. Additional hiring is expected in later years as production expands. The new workers will be trained to do their jobs, so they will not be hired away from local companies.

Export sales in hard currency	$299,196,000
Less: dollar remittances to the parent	34,944,000
Net inflow of hard currency	$264,252,000

- This net inflow of hard currency will be a net credit balance in China's current account and serves to increase the huge trade surplus China is running with the United States. Because China is running a large budget deficit, the extra hard currency represents an additional buffer to ensure that the country can continue its rapid rate of growth.
- The initial investment inflow of $15,000,000 will be reported as a credit balance in the capital account of China's balance of payments.
- Chinese tax authorities will collect taxes in the amount of CNY 69,878,000 or $8,439,372.
- There will be a transfer to China of proprietary process technology embodied in specialized equipment, and local workers will be trained to use the technology.
- The project will develop industrial capacity in a product line that has no competitors in China, so it will enable China to expand its export reach.
- All inputs will be sourced in China, thus increasing the profits of local companies and perhaps creating some new suppliers to meet the needs of the company.
- The project is relatively "clean"—it will not add to China's environmental problems. SSI will use state-of-the-art containment technology to ensure that no pollutants are released into the atmosphere or water.

---

[26]The World Bank has developed a methodology using economic shadow prices that it calls *economic analysis* to perform such calculations. It is left to interested readers to delve into this methodology on their own.

[27]China is running a huge trade surplus with the U.S. and it has huge holdings of U.S. Treasury securities. Thus China, unlike many developing nations, has no problem with obtaining hard currencies to use to purchase import goods. However, China does want to keep foreign investors in the country, hence it restricts repatriating funds. Also, the yuan is by most accounts undervalued, which the Chinese like because it stimulates exports and thus economic growth. If companies like SSI could freely buy dollars with yuan for repatriation purposes, this would strengthen the yuan, and this is another reason for restricting the repatriation rules.

permitted. However, as negotiations progressed and government officials recognized the potential contributions of the investment, they relaxed their initial positions, leading to increased profitability for SSI. Thus, developing a country analysis as a negotiating tool clarified the project's impact on things that were important to the local officials, and the BDT found it useful for this purpose.[28] At this point the company managers are disappointed that the project is not as profitable for SSI as they expected it to be. They are inclined to think that using the going concern salvage value is justifiable, because SSI is not likely to pull out in five years if it invests. However, opinions on cannibalization are mixed. What is abundantly clear, though, is that more information is needed before the BDT should recommend the project to the board of directors. Thus, they need to perform a full risk analysis to put the project's uncertainties into better perspective. This analysis will be taken up in Chapter 12.

SELF-TEST QUESTIONS

What are the two different treatments for estimating salvage values?

Identify and explain the three different classifications of cash flow.

What are the two main approaches for handling projects with cash flows that are denominated in foreign currencies?

What are the differences among the project perspective, the parent perspective, and the country perspective analyses?

---

[28]For an example of how such information can lead to a redesign of the project in a manner that increases the NPV to the company, as well as the benefits to the country, see Lee A. Tavis and Roy L. Crum, "Performance-Based Strategies for MNC Portfolio Balancing," *The Columbia Journal of World Business*, Summer 1984, 85–94.

SUMMARY

In this chapter, we discuss the basic concepts of capital budgeting and then illustrate how international factors affect the capital budgeting process. We discuss how payback, net present value, and internal rate of return are used to evaluate capital budgeting decisions. Each method provides different information, so managers look at all of them when evaluating projects. However, NPV is the best single measure, and almost all firms now use NPV. Although purely domestic and multinational companies use the same conceptual framework, capital budgeting is more complicated for multinationals because they must decide where to locate operations, worry about fluctuations in exchange rates, and consider their ability to repatriate cash flows from foreign operations to the parent. This chapter illustrates the evaluation of a foreign project from a project perspective, a parent perspective, and a country perspective. The differences among these three types of analyses are highlighted. The key concepts discussed in this chapter are listed below.

- **Capital budgeting** is the decision process that managers use to identify those projects that add to the firm's value. The same general concepts that are used in security valuation are also involved in capital budgeting. Whereas a set of stocks and bonds exists in the securities market, capital budgeting projects are created by the firm.
- Firms generally categorize projects into five main classifications: **replacement for maintenance of business, replacement for cost reduction, expansion of existing products or markets (including international markets), expansion into new products or markets**, and **downsizing and plant relocation decisions**.
- The **payback period** is the length of time required for an investment's net revenues to cover its cost. The shorter the payback period, the better the project is.
- Payback has three **advantages:** (1) It is simple to calculate; (2) it is easy to understand; and (3) it provides an indication of both the **risk** and **liquidity** of different projects by showing how long the firm's money will be tied up (indicating relative

liquidity) and that the project's cash flows must be forecasted way out into the future (indicating relative risk).

- Payback has three very serious **flaws**: (1) It **ignores the time value of money** because it gives equal weight to dollars received in different years; (2) it **does not consider cash flows that occur after the payback year**; and (3) **it does not have a natural (market-determined) benchmark to differentiate between acceptable and unacceptable projects.**

- **Mutually exclusive projects** are a set of projects in which only one project can be accepted.

- **Independent projects** are those whose cash flows are not affected by the acceptance or nonacceptance of other projects.

- The **net present value (NPV) method** is a method of ranking investment proposals using the NPV, which is equal to the present value of future net cash flows discounted at the cost of capital. It gives a direct measure of the project's dollar benefit to shareholders. A project should be accepted if the NPV is positive.

- The **internal rate of return (IRR)** is the discount rate that forces the present value of a project's inflows to equal the present value of its costs. If a project's IRR exceeds its cost of capital, then it will earn an extra return that will go to stockholders, and that leads to a higher firm value. IRR measures profitability, but it is expressed in terms of percentage rate of return.

- The **internal rate of return method** is a method of ranking investment proposals using the rate of return on an investment, calculated by finding the discount rate that equates the present value of future cash inflows to the project's cost. The project should be accepted if the IRR is greater than the cost of capital.

- The NPV and IRR criteria always lead to the **same accept/reject decisions for independent projects**. If the NPV is positive, then the IRR must exceed the WACC. However, NPV and IRR **can give conflicting rankings for mutually exclusive projects**. Logic suggests that NPV is a better decision criterion than IRR because NPV selects the project that adds the most to shareholder wealth.

- A **net present value profile** is a graph showing the relationship between a project's NPV and the different values for firm's cost of capital.

- The **crossover rate** is the cost of capital at which the NPV profiles of two projects cross and, thus, at which the projects' NPVs are equal.

- In the real world, a quantitative analysis using NPV, IRR, and payback is not the **sole determinant** in important capital budgeting decisions. Qualitative factors should also be considered. **Informed capital budgeting decisions** should be the product of **sound managerial judgment** that reflects qualitative factors as well as quantitative measures.

- The most important, but also the most difficult, step in capital budgeting is **estimating projects' cash flows.**

- International projects are even more difficult to analyze than domestic ones because of at least three different factors: (1) The **quality of data available** in many countries is very poor and forecasting is subject to significant errors; (2) **exchange rates are often hard to forecast**, and they rely on assumptions such as purchasing power parity or interest rate parity; and (3) many of the **costs associated with foreign projects** are subject to political negotiations with host governments instead of being determined in the marketplace.

- A proper analysis of forecasts includes (1) **obtaining information** from various departments, (2) ensuring that everyone involved with the forecast uses a **consistent set of economic assumptions**, and (3) ensuring that **no biases exist** in the forecasts.

- **Relevant cash flows** are defined as the specific cash flows that should be considered in a capital budgeting decision. Only **incremental cash flows**, those cash flows representing the change in the firm's total cash flow that occurs as a direct result of accepting a project, are relevant.

- **Free cash flow** is the cash flow available for distribution to all investors. A project's relevant cash flow is the additional free cash flow that the company expects from the project.

- **Project cash flow** is different from accounting income. Project cash flow reflects (1) **cash outlays for fixed assets**, (2) the **tax shield provided by depreciation**, and (3) cash flows due to **changes in net operating working capital**. Project cash flow does not include **interest payments**.
- In determining incremental cash flows, **opportunity costs** (the cash flows forgone by using an asset) must be included, but **sunk costs** (cash outlays that have been made and that cannot be recouped) are not included. Any **externalities** (effects of a project on other parts of the firm) should also be reflected in the analysis.
- **Cannibalization** occurs when a new project leads to a reduction in sales of an existing product. To the extent that a new project takes sales from existing corporate sales, the new project's estimated profits should be reduced by earnings lost on existing sales.
- **Inflation effects** must be considered in project analysis. If the component costs of capital include an inflation premium, as they typically do, but the cash flows are all stated in constant purchasing power dollars, then the calculated NPV will be lower than the true NPV. The **most common inflation adjustment procedure is to build expected inflation into the cash flow estimates.** For companies that operate in high inflation environments, it is often useful to do the analysis in both nominal and real (constant currency) terms.
- The incremental cash flows from a typical project can be classified into three categories: (1) **required investment**, (2) **annual operating cash flows over the project's life**, and (3) **terminal year cash flow.**
- Firms must consider additional issues when undertaking international capital budgeting projects, such as **exchange rates, political risk**, and **repatriation of funds.** All will influence a foreign project's capital budgeting analysis.
- Additional foreign risks need to be incorporated into the formal project analysis, and there are two very different approaches: (1) Traditionally, risk is incorporated in the analysis by increasing the risk premium in the discount rate to account for the added uncertainties. (2) The other alternative is to make the adjustment to the cash flows and then to discount at a domestic rate that does not adjust for the unique foreign risks.
- The **project perspective** is the evaluation of a capital budgeting project from the perspective of a local company undertaking a project.
- The **parent perspective** is the evaluation of a capital budgeting project from the perspective of the parent company, which is mainly concerned with the cash flows to be realized by the parent.
- The **country perspective** is the evaluation of a capital budgeting project from the perspective of the host country and the benefits to be realized.
- There are two methods for estimating salvage values. (1) The **liquidating value concept** estimates the market value of the fixed assets, adjusted for taxes, and adds the value of recovered NOWC. (2) The **going concern concept** estimates the salvage value by taking the final year of the study period's NOCF, increasing it by 1 + growth rate in NOCF and dividing it by the difference between WACC and g. This, of course, is the formula for calculating the present value of a constantly growing perpetuity.
- There are essentially **two main approaches** for handling projects whose **cash flows are denominated in foreign currencies:** (1) Estimate the project cash flows in the foreign currency, discount them at the appropriate foreign-based discount rate, and then convert the foreign-denominated NPV at the spot exchange rate to a dollar-denominated NPV. (2) Estimate project cash flows in the foreign currency, use forward exchange rates or an alternative foreign exchange rate forecasting model to convert foreign cash flows to dollars, and then calculate the dollar-denominated NPV using an appropriate U.S.-based discount rate.
- These two approaches for evaluating international projects will yield the same answer if **foreign exchange parity conditions** hold perfectly. However, in practice, deviations from parity conditions occur, so both approaches are used.

QUESTIONS

(11-1) Briefly explain how the valuation equation relates to capital budgeting.

(11-2) Why are capital budgeting decisions considered one of the most important tasks faced by financial managers and their staffs?

(11-3) Briefly explain whether the following statement is true or false: "The same general concepts that are used in security valuation are also involved in capital budgeting."

(11-4) Identify the five general capital budgeting classifications, and differentiate how a capital budgeting decision would be made in each classification.

(11-5) Identify the advantages and disadvantages of payback.

(11-6) What is the decision rule for payback? In other words, when would a project be accepted under this decision method?

(11-7) What steps are involved when analyzing a project using the NPV method?

(11-8) How does the NPV equation relate to the general valuation equation given at the introduction to the chapter?

(11-9) What is the decision rule for NPV?

(11-10) When a firm is considering a foreign project, what two approaches using the NPV methodology can be used?

(11-11) Differentiate between the equation used to solve for NPV and the one used to solve for IRR.

(11-12) What is the decision rule for IRR?

(11-13) Do the NPV and IRR decision methods always lead to the same capital budgeting decisions? Explain.

(11-14) What information is provided by each of the following decision methods: (1) payback, (2) NPV, and (3) IRR?

(11-15) Briefly explain whether the following statement is true or false: "Financial managers base their capital budgeting decisions solely on quantitative analyses."

(11-16) Why is it so difficult to estimate a project's cash flows?

(11-17) What are the relevant cash flows for an international investment—the cash flows produced by the subsidiary in the country where it operates or the cash flows in the home currency that it sends to its parent company?

(11-18) What two cardinal rules can help you minimize mistakes when estimating cash flows?

(11-19) Why must depreciation be added back to NOPAT when estimating a project's cash flow?

(11-20) Why is interest expense not included in a project's cash flows?

(11-21) Briefly explain how sunk costs, opportunity costs, externalities, and cannibalization affect a project's cash flows.

(11-22) Why will ignoring inflation "corrupt" a capital budgeting analysis, and how should you incorporate inflation into the analysis?

(11-23) Briefly explain the three categories into which a project's incremental cash flows can be classified.

(11-24) If you were responsible for analyzing a capital project, what information would you need to begin your analysis, and what steps would you use to proceed with your analysis?

(11-25) What additional complications arise when one is considering an international capital budgeting project?

(11-26) Why do U.S. corporations build manufacturing plants abroad when they could build them at home?

SELF-TEST PROBLEMS   Solutions Appear in Appendix B

(ST-1) Define each of the following terms:
Key Terms a. Capital budgeting
    b. Payback period; net present value (NPV); net present value method; internal rate of return (IRR); internal rate of return method
    c. Mutually exclusive projects; independent projects
    d. Net present value profile; crossover rate
    e. Relevant cash flows; incremental cash flows
    f. Sunk cost; opportunity cost; externalities; cannibalization
    g. Project perspective; parent perspective; country perspective

(ST-2) Global Publishing, a U.S. multinational, is considering entering a new line of busi-
Project NPV ness in Great Britain. In analyzing the potential business, their financial staff has accumulated the following information:

- The new business will require a capital expenditure of £5 million at t = 0. This expenditure will be used to purchase new equipment.
- This equipment will be depreciated at rates of 33 percent, 45 percent, 15 percent, and 7 percent, respectively.
- The equipment will have no salvage value after 4 years.
- If Global goes ahead with the new business, inventories will rise by £500,000 at t = 0, and its accounts payable will rise by £200,000 at t = 0. This increase in net operating working capital will be recovered at t = 4.
- The new business is expected to have an economic life of 4 years. The business is expected to generate sales of £3 million at t = 1, £4 million at t = 2, £5 million at t = 3, and £2 million at t = 4. Each year, operating costs excluding depreciation are expected to be 75 percent of sales.
- The company's tax rate is 40 percent.
- The company is very profitable, so any accounting losses on this project can be used to reduce the company's overall tax burden.
- The project's cost of capital, which includes a foreign exchange risk premium, is 10 percent.
- The spot exchange rate is $1.65 per pound.

    a. Use the NPV method to estimate the project's cash flows in pounds, and then use the spot exchange rate to convert the pound-denominated NPV to a dollar-denominated NPV. What is the project's NPV (stated in U.S. dollars)?
    b. Assume now that the pound is expected to depreciate by 2 percent per year during the project's life. In addition, the project's cost of capital, excluding the foreign exchange risk premium, is 9.6 percent. Estimate the project's cash flows in pounds, and then use the expected exchange rates to convert to dollar-denominated cash flows. What is the project's NPV (stated in U.S. dollars)? (Hint: Because the cash flows have been adjusted for foreign exchange risk, no such adjustment is needed for the WACC.)

STARTER PROBLEMS

(11-1) a. Project X requires an initial investment of $60,000, its annual after-tax cash
Payback Period flows (including depreciation) are expected to be $14,000 for 7 years, and its cost of capital is 9 percent. What is the project's payback period?

b. Assume now that Project X is one of many projects of a U.S. firm; however, it is located in Argentina. If the Argentinean peso were expected to depreciate relative to the U.S. dollar, would you expect the project's payback period to be shorter, longer, or the same as the one calculated in part a? Assume that differences in the project's cash flows are strictly related to differences in exchange rates.

(11-2) a. Project Y requires an initial investment of $100,000 and produces annual
NPV   after-tax cash flows (including depreciation) of $30,000 in Years 1 through 3 and $20,000 in Years 4 and 5. If the project's cost of capital is 10 percent, what is Project Y's NPV?

b. Assume now that Project Y is one of many projects of a British company, Heath & Smythe (H&S). The spot exchange rate is $1.5776 per pound. Calculate the project's pound-denominated NPV by using the spot exchange rate to convert the dollar-denominated NPV to a pound-denominated NPV. Assume that 10 percent is the appropriate WACC. Should H&S undertake this project?

c. Again, assume that Project Y is one of many projects of Heath & Smythe. Assume that the dollar is expected to depreciate against the pound by 1 percent per year during this project's life. Estimate the project's cash flows in dollars, and then use the expected rates to convert to pound-denominated cash flows. Assume that a 9.7 percent WACC appropriately excludes the foreign exchange rate risk premium. Should H&S undertake this project?

(11-3) a. Project Z is expected to produce annual after-tax cash flows of $15,000,
IRR $20,000, $20,000, and $25,000 over the next 4 years. To initiate Project Z, a $55,000 investment must be made today. What is Project Z's IRR?

b. Assume that Project Z is one of many projects of a Canadian firm, British Columbia Enterprises. The spot exchange rate is CAD 1.3958 per U.S. dollar. From the Canadian firm's perspective, once cash flows are converted to Canadian dollars, what is the project's IRR?

(11-4) LLT International is considering expanding its technological development facilities
Relevant Cash Flows in New Zealand. The spot exchange rate is NZD 1.7544 per U.S. dollar; however, the New Zealand dollar is expected to depreciate in value relative to the U.S. dollar by 2 percent next year. LLT's financial staff has made the following estimates (stated in New Zealand dollars) of incremental changes for the next year due to the expansion project:

Increased sales revenue	NZD 15 million
Operating costs (excluding depreciation)	NZD 9 million
Depreciation expense	NZD 4 million
Interest expense	NZD 3 million

The firm is subject to a 40 percent tax rate. What is the project's estimated U.S. dollar-denominated operating cash flow for the first year of operations (t = 1)?

(11-5) Walton International Communications is evaluating a new project, which will be
Initial Investment Outlay located in Hong Kong, and it will require the purchase of an HKD 12 million facility. Walton also will have to spend HKD 5 million to purchase new equipment necessary for the project. To help finance the project, Walton must increase its net operating working capital by HKD 2 million. The spot exchange rate is HKD 7.7992 per U.S. dollar. If the company's tax rate is 40 percent, what is the project's initial investment outlay stated in terms of U.S. dollars?

(11-6) Three years ago, Garvin purchased $13 million of equipment. Garvin depreciated
After-Tax Salvage Value the equipment using the 3-year MACRS accelerated depreciation method. The appropriate 3-year MACRS depreciation rates are 33 percent, 45 percent, 15 percent, and 7 percent. Garvin expects to sell the used equipment today for $1 million. If the company's tax rate is 40 percent, what is the equipment's after-tax net salvage value?

EXAM-TYPE PROBLEMS

(11-7)
Payback, NPV, and IRR

Kaufman Enterprises, a U.S. multinational, is evaluating two independent projects (Projects A and Z) of its British subsidiary for inclusion in this year's capital budget. The projects are of equal risk and should be evaluated at a risk-adjusted 11 percent cost of capital, which includes the foreign exchange risk premium. The projects' after-tax cash flows (stated in pounds), including depreciation, are as follows:

Year	Project A	Project Z
0	(£120,000)	(£75,000)
1	20,000	30,000
2	20,000	30,000
3	50,000	30,000
4	50,000	10,000
5	50,000	10,000

The spot exchange rate is $1.45 per pound. Calculate payback, NPV, and IRR for each project. Indicate the correct accept/reject decision for each criterion. For purposes of answering this question, assume Kaufman requires a payback of 3 years or less.

(11-8)
Missing Cash Flow, IRR, and NPV

Rao Technologies is considering a project that is expected to generate annual after-tax cash flows of $2,200 for each of the next 20 years. The project's cost of capital is 8.5 percent, and it has an IRR of 9.058 percent. What is this project's NPV?

(11-9)
NPV and IRR

a. Project Alpha is expected to produce annual after-tax cash flows (including depreciation) of $20,000 for the next 7 years. It requires an initial investment of $75,000 and an additional investment of $25,000 at the end of the 4th year. The project's cost of capital is 10 percent. What are Project Alpha's NPV and IRR?

b. Assume that Project Alpha is one of many projects of a Japanese firm, Tokyo Manufacturing Company (TMC). The spot exchange rate is ¥117.425 per U.S. dollar. Assume that 10 percent is the appropriate WACC. From the Japanese firm's perspective, once cash flows are converted to yen, what are Project Alpha's NPV and IRR? Should TMC undertake the project?

c. Assume again that Project Alpha is one of many projects of Tokyo Manufacturing Company (TMC). Assume now that the yen is expected to depreciate in value relative to the U.S. dollar by 0.5 percent per year during the life of this project. Assume that a 9.2 percent WACC appropriately excludes the foreign exchange rate risk premium. From the Japanese firm's perspective, once cash flows are converted to yen, what are Project Alpha's NPV and IRR? Should TMC undertake this project?

(11-10)
IRR and NPV Profiles

Murphy Chemicals is considering two mutually exclusive investments with the following after-tax cash flows (including deprecation):

Year	Project X	Project Y
0	($3,000)	($6,000)
1	500	1,000
2	500	1,000
3	500	1,000
4	1,750	3,000
5	1,750	3,000

a. What is each project's IRR?

b. Construct NPV profiles for Projects X and Y.
c. For what range of WACCs would Murphy Chemicals choose to accept Project X?

(11-11) Bruner Fashions, a U.S. multinational, has a subsidiary located in Australia.
Mutually Exclusive Projects Average-risk projects in this subsidiary have a weighted average cost of capital of 10.5 percent, which includes a foreign exchange risk premium. Bruner is considering two mutually exclusive, average-risk projects for its new Australian facility. Each requires an initial investment of AUD 4 million. The projects are expected to produce the following after-tax cash flows, including depreciation (stated in Australian dollars):

Year	Project A	Project B
1	AUD 1,500,000	AUD 2,500,000
2	1,500,000	1,500,000
3	1,500,000	1,000,000
4	1,500,000	500,000

The spot exchange rate is AUD 1.5623 per U.S. dollar. There is no limitation on the repatriation of funds, so all project cash flows will be available to Bruner.
a. What are the projects' U.S. dollar-denominated net present values, and which project should be selected by Bruner? To answer this question, estimate the projects' cash flows in Australian dollars, and then use the spot exchange rate to convert the Australian-dollar-denominated NPVs to U.S.-dollar-denominated NPVs.
b. Assume that the Australian dollar is expected to appreciate in value relative to the U.S. dollar by 2.5 percent per year over the project's life. In addition, assume that the appropriate WACC excluding the foreign exchange risk premium is 10.2 percent. What are the projects' U.S.-dollar-denominated net present values, and which project should be selected by Bruner? To answer this question, estimate the projects' cash flows in Australian dollars and then use the expected exchange rates to convert to U.S.-dollar-denominated cash flows. (Hint: Because the cash flows have been adjusted for foreign exchange risk, no such adjustment is needed for the WACC.)

(11-12) Holmes Waste Disposal is legally required to clean up a former dumping site to
PVs of Cash Outflows minimize the ecological damage done to the area. Two alternatives have been suggested: a quick cleanup plan (with larger costs early in the plan) and a slow cleanup plan (with smaller costs spread out over a longer time period). Holmes is only required to complete the cleanup in 6 years, although the quicker the cleanup effort moves, the better off the area's ecosystem will be. The after-tax costs of the two plans are as follows:

Year	Quick Plan	Slow Plan
0	($800,000)	($300,000)
1	(500,000)	(300,000)
2	(500,000)	(300,000)
3	(50,000)	(300,000)
4	(50,000)	(300,000)
5	(50,000)	(300,000)
6	(50,000)	(300,000)

Holmes has assigned a 10 percent cost of capital to each project. From a financial perspective, which plan should be adopted? From a societal benefit perspective, which plan should be adopted?

(11-13) McCormick Solutions, a U.S. multinational, is considering instituting a new inven-
Payback, NPV, and IRR   tory identification system to improve its efficiency in its Swiss plants. Although the
system costs SwF 5 million, it is expected to reduce operating costs associated
with inventory management by SwF 800,000 per year in after-tax cash flows for
the next 10 years. The spot exchange rate is SwF 1.4114 per U.S. dollar. After 10
years, the system is expected to be obsolete and retired with no salvage value. The
firm's cost of capital is 9.6 percent, including a foreign exchange risk premium.
What are the project's payback, NPV, and IRR?

(11-14) Yerkes International, a U.S. multinational, uses the NPV method to decide
Mutually Exclusive   between mutually exclusive projects. Yerkes is currently evaluating two product
Projects, NPV, and IRR   delivery systems for its operations in Germany. Both projects require a €200,000
initial investment and have a 9.8 percent cost of capital, which excludes a foreign
exchange risk premium. The two systems have the following after-tax cash flows,
including depreciation (stated in euros):

Year	Project C	Project D
1	€20,000	€110,000
2	40,000	90,000
3	50,000	20,000
4	80,000	20,000
5	120,000	20,000

The spot exchange rate is €0.9173 per U.S. dollar; however, the euro is expected
to depreciate by 1.5 percent per year over the next 5 years. What is the IRR of the
better project's dollar-denominated cash flows, if cash flows are adjusted for
expected exchange rates?

(11-15) Bailey Communications, a U.S. multinational, is evaluating the proposed acquisi-
NPV Analysis: Project and   tion of a new satellite system in Italy that will boost its transmission area in
Parent Perspectives   Europe. The satellite system will cost €25 million and will require an increase in
net operating working capital of €1.5 million. The analysis will focus upon the
next 4 years, in which the new satellite system is expected to provide additional
revenues of €13.25 million per year and incur operating costs of €2 million per
year. The system will be depreciated at rates of 33 percent, 45 percent, 15 percent,
and 7 percent, respectively. After 4 years, the satellite system is expected to have
no salvage value, but the increase in net operating working capital will be fully
recovered.
    The spot exchange rate is €0.95 per U.S. dollar. The project's cost of capital,
which includes a foreign exchange risk premium, is 10 percent, and the firm's tax
rate is 30 percent. The company is extremely profitable; and the satellite represents just one project for the firm, so losses in any one year on this project can be
used to partially offset taxes paid on the company's other projects.
a. What is the project's dollar-denominated NPV? To answer this question, esti-
    mate the project's cash flow in euros, and then use the spot exchange rate to
    convert the euro-denominated NPV to a dollar-denominated NPV.
b. In part a, Bailey Communications performed an NPV analysis from the project
    perspective. Now, the firm is interested in analyzing the project from a parent
    perspective. Assume that the $2 million in operating costs includes €750,000
    of annual license and management fees, the U.S. tax rate is 40 percent, and the
    spot exchange rate between euros and dollars is a good indicator of what
    exchange rates will be during the next 4 years. What are the after-tax divi-
    dends (stated both in euros and dollars) repatriated to the firm during the
    project's life? What is the project's dollar-denominated NPV from the parent
    perspective?

INTEGRATED CASE

Rick Schmidt, MRI's CFO, along with Mandy Wu, Schmidt's assistant, and John Costello, a consultant and college finance professor, comprise a team set up to teach MRI's directors and senior managers the basics of international financial management. The program includes 16 sessions, each lasting about 2 hours, which are held immediately before the monthly board meetings. Ten sessions have been held, and they have included studies of exchange rates, risk analysis, financial statements, bond valuation, stock valuation, and the cost of capital. The team is now preparing Session 11, which will deal with the basics of capital budgeting. The next session will extend the discussion of capital budgeting to formal procedures dealing with risk.

The introductory capital budgeting session will focus on two main points: (1) The different criteria that are used to evaluate proposed capital expenditures and (2) identifying the cash flows that are relevant in capital budgeting decisions. The team decided that the session would be most productive if they analyze an actual decision that MRI now faces: whether or not to produce a new heat-sensing device that would be used by airlines to determine if passengers are too sick to be allowed on flights. After the SARS epidemic in 2003, airlines are very much interested in such capabilities in order to protect other passengers and thus to convince the flying public that airline travel is safe. The project has been dubbed HSD, for heat-sensing device, in internal discussions, and Schmidt is quite sure the directors will be interested in analyzing it in detail.

The devices will be sold to airlines all over the world, and they are small enough to be transported economically by airfreight. Therefore, they can be manufactured anywhere, in the United States or overseas. Other things held constant, MRI favors basing its operations in the United States, but if a project would be more profitable based elsewhere, then management will not hesitate to locate a facility overseas. For the HSD project, the most promising overseas location is northern Italy. MRI has several facilities in the Milan area, and the labor force in northern Italy is highly skilled, which is important for a high-tech product such as HSD. Italy also has the advantages of a relatively stable government, operating in the euro zone, and no significant repatriation problems. Therefore, Schmidt wants to evaluate the project in Italy. He has stressed to his global management team to look at issues from all angles and, therefore, wants the project analyzed from the project perspective, parent perspective, and the country perspective. Schmidt has instructed MRI's staff to use a risk adjustment of 1.5 percent above its WACC, since the project is being carried out in Italy. That assessment may change later.

MRI has a capital budgeting model that is used to analyze all proposed projects, with modifications made to accommodate specific situations. The model is used to obtain the most-likely estimates of NPV, IRR, and payback for each location, and then it is run under alternative sets of assumptions to get an idea of the project's riskiness. Schmidt, Wu, and Costello plan to restrict their analysis in the upcoming session to the most-likely results and then, in the next session, go on to include risk analysis.

Table IC11-1 shows the basic assumptions regarding the HSD project in Italy. There are several important things to note about the input data. Some of the directors have criticized the choice of Italy for this project. They cite labor costs that are similar to U.S. labor costs and far exceed labor costs if taken to the Far East or Latin America. Schmidt has maintained that alternate locations, while cheaper, will not provide MRI the skilled labor it requires for this project. In addition, he has noted that he has negotiated higher license and management fees with the Italian government than has been possible with any other nation. Also, required NOWC will be funded by a loan borrowed by the subsidiary from a local lender. Fixed assets will be depreciated using the straight-line method and are expected to be worth 15 percent above book value at the end of the project. And the project is expected to take away from a less-sophisticated security device MRI is currently selling. That product is produced at a plant in the southeastern United States and the unit responsible has a profit margin of 6 percent.

In addition, Table IC11-2 was created to list the advantages as well as disadvantages this project brings to Italy. MRI's Business Development Team used these points listed in Table IC11-2 to negotiate with Italian government authorities. Note that this project would bring no disadvantages to Italy.

Wu stated that she thought it would be best to lead off with an explanation of the three capital budgeting criteria, using a simplified set of data. Schmidt and Costello agreed, so they decided to use the following data for illustrative purposes:

Year (t)	0	1	2	3	4
Project S	($10,000)	$8,000	$3,000	$1,000	$1,000
Project L	(10,000)	1,000	2,000	5,000	7,500

Also for illustrative purposes, they plan to assume a 10 percent cost of capital.

TABLE IC11-1 | Input Data for HSD's Project in Italy
(All Euros and Dollars in Thousands)

Investment and Financing		First-Year Projections and Growth Rates	
Parent investment		Local sales	
Cash	USD 12,000	Unit sales	15,000
Manufacturing equipment	USD 6,500	Expected growth	5%
Subsidiary investment		Sales price (per unit)	EUR 10.50
Locally borrowed funds (NOWC)	EUR 4,900	Export sales	
Local borrowing rate	6%	Unit sales	6,000
Required Asset Investment		Expected growth	7%
Building cost	EUR 7,700	Sales price (per unit)	USD 13.0
Mechanical equipment	EUR 3,800	Direct materials (per unit)	EUR 2.15
Electronic equipment	EUR 3,250	Expected growth	1.5%
Annual increase in NOWC	EUR 750	Direct labor (per unit)	EUR 4.75
Project and Asset Depreciable Lives		Expected growth	3.0%
Project life	5	General and administrative expenses	EUR 55,500
Building depreciable life	20	Expected growth	1.5%
Mechanical equipment depreciable life	10	Insurance	EUR 600
Electronic equipment depreciable life	5	Expected growth	1.5%
General Company Data		Cash Flows to the Parent	
Italian marginal tax rate	30.00%	License fees (% of sales)	2.50%
U.S. marginal tax rate	40.00%	Management fees (fixed)	USD 15
Domestic WACC	8.50%	Management fees (% of sales)	0.75%
Risk-adjusted foreign WACC	10.00%	Profit margin in southeastern United States	6.00%
Exchange rate (EUR/USD)	0.7973	Market value excess	15%

TABLE IC11-2 | Project's Contribution to Italy

- The project will create approximately 300 jobs in the first year, about half skilled and the rest semi-skilled, and provide training for these workers. Additional hiring is expected in later years as production expands.

- The export sales will be a net credit balance in Italy's current account, so it will not put downward pressure on the country's ability to support the euro.

- Italian tax authorities will collect taxes in the amount of €11,212,043.

- There will be a transfer to Italy of proprietary process technology embodied in specialized equipment, and local workers will be trained to use the technology.

- All inputs will be sourced in Italy, thus increasing the profits of local companies and perhaps creating some new suppliers to meet the needs of the company.

- The project, as proposed, is relatively "clean"—it will not add to Italy's environmental problems. MRI will use state-of-the-art containment technology to ensure that no pollutants are released into the atmosphere or water.

Wu, Schmidt, and Costello then compiled the following set of questions, which they plan to discuss during the session. As with the other sessions, they plan to use an *Excel* model to answer the quantitative questions. Assume that you are Mandy Wu and that you must prepare answers for use during the session.

QUESTIONS

a. What are the three most commonly used capital budgeting decision rules? What are the primary advantages and disadvantages of each? Is one of them better than the others, and if so, why should the team explain more than the best method?

b. Now, for the illustrative data, calculate the values for each of the three decision criteria. If the two projects are independent, should they be accepted?

c. Now suppose Projects S and L are mutually exclusive. Which one, if either, should be accepted? Some of the directors are likely to ask for an explanation, so be prepared to explain why any conflicts arise and why you might choose one project over the other. Graph the projects' NPV profiles and use this graph in your explanation.

d. In general terms, what would be included in a project's required investment? Its terminal year cash flows? What is the required investment and terminal year cash flow for the HSD project, and what cash flows are included in each? Discuss the use of different terminal cash flow calculations and determine which makes the most sense in this case.

e. Given the data in Table IC11-1, find HSD's annual euro free cash flows, and then calculate its NPV, IRR, and payback. On the basis of your project analysis, should the project be accepted if it is to be produced in Italy?

f. Suppose that a year ago MRI performed a feasibility study for the HSD project. The cost of this study was $100,000, and it was expensed for tax purposes last year. Describe in words how this would be incorporated in your capital budgeting analysis.

g. Suppose instead of having to build an entire new plant MRI could renovate an existing plant that currently lies idle. The cost of the renovation would be $20,000,000. Describe in words how this would be incorporated in your capital budgeting analysis.

h. A serious problem of locating production in other countries is the inability to repatriate funds back to the parent. In the current situation, MRI is considering production in Italy so this is not a problem; however, suppose that MRI was considering production in a country where repatriation of funds is limited. Explain in words how you would incorporate this in your capital budgeting analysis. (No numbers are needed here.)

i. In the Italian capital budgeting analysis, it was assumed that the exchange rate stayed constant throughout the project's life. Obviously, this is an unrealistic assumption. Describe in words how you would incorporate a fluctuating exchange rate in your capital budgeting analysis.

j. Analyze the project from the parent perspective. What kind of dividend can the Italian subsidiary send back to MRI? What are the total free cash flows the parent expects, and what are the NPV, IRR, and payback of the project from the parent's perspective? If MRI can purchase OPIC insurance, what effect does that have on project NPV and IRR?

k. Discuss the country perspective analysis developed in Table IC11-2. What are three important uses for this type of analysis?

CHAPTER 12

Capital Budgeting: Risk Analysis and Real Options

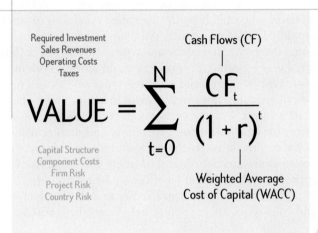

$$VALUE = \sum_{t=0}^{N} \frac{CF_t}{(1+r)^t}$$

Required Investment
Sales Revenues
Operating Costs
Taxes

Cash Flows (CF)

Capital Structure
Component Costs
Firm Risk
Project Risk
Country Risk

Weighted Average
Cost of Capital (WACC)

e-resource

The textbook's Web site, *http://crum. swlearning.com,* contains an Excel file that will guide you through the chapter's calculations. The file for this chapter is *FIFC12-model.xls,* and we encourage you to open the file and follow along as you read the chapter.

I n the last two chapters we explained how the WACC is calculated, how cash flows are estimated, and how the WACC and project cash flows are combined to produce project NPVs. In this chapter we look at cash flows again, but we now focus on their risk and how that risk affects the required WACC and the NPV. We must estimate each project's risk and then incorporate it into the capital budgeting decision. Note that the analysis can be applied to either domestic or foreign projects, but because foreign projects typically have more risk, risk analysis is especially important for multinational firms.

The chapter also discusses a related topic—real options. An option is the right to take some specified action, and in finance we distinguish between two types of options: financial and real. A call option on a stock, which gives the option holder the right to buy the stock at a specified price within a specified time period, is one type of financial option, as is an option to buy a foreign currency at some future date. Financial options are important for managing currency and other risks, and we cover them in detail in Chapter 15. A real option is an action a manager can take to alter the cash flow stream after a project has been accepted. For example, suppose a relatively small project can be expanded if demand for the product turns out to exceed expectations. The option to expand is a type of real option, and it can increase actual cash flows above what was originally projected and thus raise the project's true NPV. Real options are especially important for multinational firms because these firms almost always have more flexibility than purely domestic firms.

PROJECT RISK ANALYSIS

Stand-Alone Risk
The risk an asset would have if it were a firm's only asset and if investors owned only one stock. It is measured by the standard deviation or coefficient of variation of the project's expected NPV.

Corporate (Within-Firm) Risk
Risk not considering the effects of stockholders' diversification; it is measured by a project's effect on uncertainty about the firm's future earnings.

Market Risk
The part of a project's risk that cannot be eliminated by diversification; it is measured by the project's beta coefficient.

In Chapter 11 we explained how a potential investment's cash flows are estimated and then evaluated to see if it should be accepted. However, different projects' cash flows have different degrees of risk, so estimating project risk is an important aspect of capital budgeting.[1] To begin, note that risk can be categorized in three ways: (1) **Stand-alone risk** is the risk the project would have if it were the firm's only project and if investors owned only the one firm's stock. Thus, stand-alone risk does not reflect diversification by either the firm or its stockholders. It is measured by the standard deviation or coefficient of variation of the project's expected NPV. (2) **Corporate**, or **within-firm**, **risk**, is a project's risk when it is considered as one asset in the firm's portfolio of assets. Because it is just one of the firm's assets, some of a project's stand-alone risk can be diversified away. (3) **Market risk** is a project's risk to investors who hold broadly diversified portfolios of stocks. In theory, security prices should be based on market risk, so market risk should be our primary consideration. However, stand-alone and corporate risk are both important for these reasons: It is easier to estimate a project's stand-alone risk than its corporate or market risk. Moreover, in most cases all three types of risk are highly correlated. Thus, if the overall economy does well, so will the firm, and if the firm does well, so will most of its projects. Because of this high correlation, stand-alone risk is generally a good proxy for hard-to-measure corporate and market risk.[2]

Even though we focus on stand-alone risk, it should be noted that not all investors are diversified, and for them corporate risk is also important. In addition, corporate risk can have an effect on a firm's ability to obtain debt capital, the cost of that capital, and the firm's ability to deal effectively with its customers, suppliers, and employees. So, corporate risk cannot be ignored.

SELF-TEST QUESTIONS

Identify and briefly explain the three categories of risk.

Why are stand-alone and corporate risk important, even if market risk should be our primary consideration?

STAND-ALONE RISK

A project's stand-alone risk is determined largely by the degree of uncertainty inherent in its cash flows. To illustrate what is involved in analyzing stand-alone risk, consider again Sound Systems International's (SSI) project in China. Many of the key inputs shown in Tables 11-2 and 11-3 are subject to uncertainty. For example, local sales in China were projected at 20,000 units to be sold at a net price of CNY 10,000 each. However, actual unit sales will almost certainly be higher or lower than 20,000 units, and the sales price will probably turn out to be different from the projected CNY 10,000 per unit. *In effect, the sales quantity and price estimates are really expected values based on probability distributions, as are many of the other values in Tables 11-2 and 11-3.* The distributions could be relatively "tight," reflecting small standard deviations and low risk, or they could be "wide," denoting a

---

[1]Recall that in Chapter 11 we considered foreign projects from three different perspectives: the project itself, the parent company, and the host country. In this chapter we consider all three perspectives, but our primary focus is from the project perspective. Note that the techniques used here can also be performed from the perspectives of the parent and the host country.

[2]Note that any Project J's beta coefficient is the product of the project's standard deviation of returns times the correlation coefficient between the project and the market divided by the standard deviation of the market's returns, $b_j = \sigma_j(\rho_{jM}/\sigma_M)$. Therefore, the higher its standard deviation and greater the correlation with the market, the higher the project's beta. Because stand-alone risk is measured by the standard deviation, and because most projects are correlated with both the firm's other projects and the market, the higher its standard deviation, the higher its market risk. This makes stand-alone risk as reflected by the project's σ quite important.

great deal of uncertainty as to what the actual value of the variable will be. If most of the input variables are subject to a lot of risk, then the project will probably have a high degree of stand-alone risk.

While uncertainty about input variables is the major determinant of a project's stand-alone risk, correlations between the inputs also have a bearing—the more highly the inputs are correlated with one another, the greater the project's risk. In the following sections, we explore these ideas and discuss three techniques for assessing stand-alone risk: (1) *sensitivity analysis*, (2) *scenario analysis*, and (3) *Monte Carlo simulation*.

<table>
<tr><td>SELF-TEST QUESTIONS</td><td>Briefly explain whether the following statement is true or false: "Input values for sales quantity and price are point estimates determined from the firm's marketing department."

What determines a large part of a project's stand-alone risk? Does anything else impact it?</td></tr>
</table>

SENSITIVITY ANALYSIS

Sensitivity Analysis
A risk analysis technique in which key variables are changed one at a time and the resulting changes in the NPV are observed.

Base-Case NPV
The NPV when sales and other input variables are set equal to their most likely (or base-case) values.

Intuitively, we know that many of the variables that determine a project's cash flows could turn out to be different from the values used in the base-case analysis. We also know that a change in an input such as local units sold will cause the NPV to change. **Sensitivity analysis** is a technique that indicates how much NPV will change in response to a given change in an input variable, other things held constant.

Sensitivity analysis begins with a *base case*, which is developed using the *expected* values for each input. To illustrate, consider the data given back in Tables 11-2 and 11-3, where projected cash flows for SSI's Shanghai project were shown. The values of inputs used to develop the tables are all base-case (i.e., most likely) values, and the resulting NPV of approximately CNY 110,000 shown in Table 11-3 is called the **base-case NPV**. Now we ask a series of "what if" questions:

- What would happen to the NPV if the yuan appreciated or depreciated against the dollar instead of remaining pegged at CNY 8.28/$ as we expect?
- What if unit export sales fall below the most likely level?
- What if the local sales price per unit falls?
- What if general and administrative (G&A) expenses are higher than CNY 122,500,000?

Sensitivity analysis provides decision makers with answers to questions such as these.

In a sensitivity analysis, input variables are increased or decreased from their expected values while holding all other variables constant. Then a new NPV is calculated using each revised input value. Finally, the set of NPVs is plotted on a graph to show how sensitive NPV is to changes in each variable. Figure 12-1 shows the speaker project's sensitivity graphs for the five most important variables, while the table below the graph shows the NPV sensitivities to all eight of the key inputs, ranked by sensitivity. The data and the graph were developed in the chapter's *Excel* model. The slopes of the lines show how sensitive NPV is to changes in each of the inputs: *The steeper the slope, the more sensitive the NPV is to a change in the variable.*

SSI focuses primarily on the operating variables because they are the factors it can control, but the company must also consider the effects of possible changes in the exchange rate. SSI has no influence over this variable, which has been pegged at 8.28 yuan per dollar for the last few years. The Chinese government has not indicated any intention to "re-peg" the yuan-to-dollar exchange rate, but it is vital that SSI plan for that possibility.

Figure 12-1 | Evaluating SSI's Shanghai Project's Risk: Sensitivity Analysis (Dollars in Thousands)

Summary Data Used to Make the Graph: NPV Sensitivity
to the Different Variables Ranked by Sensitivity

(%) Deviation	Export Price	Exchange Rate	Direct Materials	Direct Labor	Local Price	Export Units	G&A Expenses	Local Units
−30	−$44,647	−$63,539	$26,123	$23,609	−$21,630	−$14,266	$12,900	−$2,307
−20	−29,761	−37,059	17,420	15,744	−14,416	−9,506	8,604	−1,533
−10	−14,874	−16,463	8,717	7,878	−7,201	−4,746	4,309	−760
0	13	13	13	13	13	13	13	13
10	14,900	13,494	−8,690	−7,852	7,228	4,773	−4,282	787
20	29,787	24,728	−17,393	−15,717	14,442	9,533	−8,578	1,560
30	44,674	34,234	−26,096	−23,582	21,657	14,292	−12,873	2,333
Sensitivity index	11228%	11073%	−6564%	−5932%	5441%	3590%	−3240%	583%
Rank	1	2	3	4	5	6	7	8

The graph and accompanying data show that NPV is extremely sensitive to variations in the export sales prices, exchange rate, materials, labor, and the local sales price. NPV is less sensitive to units sold and G&A (general and administrative) expenses. The steeper the sensitivity lines, the riskier the project, because if NPV is very sensitive to a variable, then even a small change in the variable would result in a large change in NPV. Thus, sensitivity analysis provides useful insights into project risk.[3]

---

[3]Note that the sensitivities in the table below Figure 12-1 are elasticities, and the index is the percentage change in the NPV that would result from a 1% change in the variable. A positive sign indicates that NPV would increase if the variable increased, and vice versa for negative signs. The sensitivities for the project are quite large because the expected NPV is relatively small. They would be different if the NPV were different, but their relative sizes would in all likelihood remain the same. Note too that except for exchange rates, the sensitivities indicate the slopes of the lines in the graph—the larger the sensitivity, the steeper the sensitivity line. The exchange rate has a non-linear relationship because it affects both sales prices and cost rates.

The idea behind sensitivity analysis is that the greater the sensitivity of NPV to changes in an input variable, the greater the risk. While this conclusion is intuitive, it is not always correct. We must also consider the likelihood that the input variable will deviate substantially from its expected value and our ability to forecast its value accurately. For the Shanghai project, the second most sensitive variable is the exchange rate. However, if management were confident that the exchange rate would not be changed, then this variable would not be an important risk factor in spite of its high sensitivity index. For each variable, the company can assess subjectively the likelihood that the variable will deviate substantially from its forecasted level. This is done for the Shanghai project and is shown in Table 12-1.

We now have two important pieces of information about the input variables for use in deciding which should be of the most concern. We portray each variable in a 3 × 3 matrix in Table 12-2. The variables that need to be looked at most carefully are those that are high in importance and hard to forecast. In other words, variables shown in the top row and left column are the ones of greatest concern. Fortunately, for the Shanghai project none of the variables plots in the upper left cell, but several are shown in adjacent cells.

Most multinational companies have developed procedures for dealing with the variables shown in each cell, as shown in Table 12-3. If one or more variables appear in the upper left corner, management will often defer making a decision on the project. Probably, they will ask that the project be modified to make the NPV less sensitive to the variable or ask the sponsors to find ways to forecast it more accurately. For example, maybe an alternative production process with less operating leverage would make the project less sensitive to the uncertain variables, or perhaps hedges could be put in place to improve results under bad conditions.

For variables that appear in cells adjacent to the upper left one, the company has a formal tracking system. This system identifies who will track the actual value for

TABLE 12-1 | Importance and Forecast Ability for Input Variables

	Sensitivity	Forecast Ability
Export selling price	High	Average
Spot exchange rate	High	Good
Direct materials cost	Moderate	Average
Direct labor cost	Moderate	Average
Local selling price	Moderate	Poor
Export unit sales	Moderate	Good
G&A expense	Moderate	Average
German profit rate	Low	Average
Local unit sales	Low	Poor
Discount rate	Low	Average
Growth in export unit sales	Low	Good
Growth in direct labor cost	Low	Poor
Growth in direct materials cost	Low	Poor
Growth in G&A expense	Low	Average
Salvage premium over book	Low	Poor
Insurance cost	Low	Average
Growth in local unit sales	Low	Poor
Growth in insurance cost	Low	Average

TABLE 12-2 | Input Variable Importance Matrix for Shanghai Project

Forecast Ability	IMPORTANCE INDICATOR		
	High	Moderate	Low
Poor		Local selling price	Salvage premium Local unit sales Growth in direct labor Growth in direct materials Growth in local unit sales
Average	Export selling price	Direct materials cost Direct labor cost G&A expense	Discount rate Insurance cost Growth in G&A Growth in insurance German profit rate
Good	Spot exchange rate	Export unit sales	Growth in export sales

the variable, specifies what the acceptable upper and lower limits are for the variable before corrective actions are needed, and establishes regular reporting procedures under which the responsible person must file a report on the variable. For other variables that are farther away from the critical cell, the monitoring is not as frequent because it is not as critical, and reports are filed only if the variable goes out of established bounds. Finally, variables appearing in the bottom-right cell are checked once a year, during the annual review. These rules allow SSI to focus its resources on those inputs that matter the most, and the tracking system gives management an early warning when some of the input assumptions start to deviate from their expected values. Having such information on a timely basis allows the company to react early to changes in the environment, enabling it to take advantage of unexpected opportunities or to head off unexpected losses.

Before moving on, we should note that spreadsheet computer programs such as *Microsoft Excel* are ideally suited for sensitivity analysis. We used *Excel*'s "Data Table" feature in the chapter model to generate the sensitivity analysis. To conduct such an analysis by hand would be quite time consuming.

TABLE 12-3 | Managerial Actions to Track Input Variables

Forecast Ability	IMPORTANCE INDICATOR		
	High	Moderate	Low
Poor	Evaluate further. Re-engineer the project to reduce importance.	Try to obtain better forecasting information. Track closely and report regularly.	Monitor frequently. Report exceptions.
Average	See if the project can be modified to reduce sensitivity. Track closely and report regularly.	Track closely and report regularly.	Monitor and report exceptions.
Good	Track closely and report regularly.	Monitor, then report only exceptions.	Review periodically.

What is sensitivity analysis?
What is the idea behind sensitivity analysis? Is this conclusion always correct? Explain.
Explain the purpose behind Tables 12-2 and 12-3.

SCENARIO ANALYSIS

Scenario Analysis
A risk analysis technique in which "bad" and "good" sets of financial circumstances are compared with a most likely, or base-case situation.

Base Case
An analysis in which all of the input variables are set at their most likely values.

Worst-Case Scenario
An analysis in which all of the input variables are set at their worst reasonably forecasted values.

Best-Case Scenario
An analysis in which all of the input variables are set at their best reasonably forecasted values.

Although sensitivity analysis is the most widely used risk analysis technique, it does have limitations. Perhaps most serious is the fact that only one variable is tested for sensitivity at a time; all others are held constant at their expected (or base-case) values. This is generally unreasonable, because, for example, when demand for a product changes, there is generally a change in the product's price. Similarly, if input prices rise, the output price may also increase. Other variable interactions exist, but they are ignored in sensitivity analysis.

For low-risk projects that do not have high funding requirements, sensitivity analysis is generally sufficient for getting a handle on the project's risk. However, for projects that require significant investment or are strategically important, extending the sensitivity analysis to show the combined effects of simultaneous variable changes is generally necessary. **Scenario analysis** provides this extension. Here the analyst begins with the **base case**, or most likely set of values for the input variables. This is usually the same as the base case used in sensitivity analysis because it represents the analyst's "best guess" about the future. Then, he or she asks the marketing, engineering, and other operating managers to specify a **worst-case scenario** (low unit sales, low sales price, high variable costs, and so on) and a **best-case scenario** (high unit sales, high sales price, low variable costs, and so on). These scenarios should reflect pessimistic and optimistic business cases that could realistically be experienced rather than "gloom and doom" or "pie in the sky" fantasies. The managers who develop the scenarios are not usually asked to provide probability estimates for them (although this information might be important for the evaluation of an embedded real option as discussed later in the chapter), but often the scenarios are interpreted as the three points of a triangular distribution, or the mean and plus or minus two standard deviations of a normal distribution. Obviously, conditions could actually take a variety of other values, but framing the questions in terms such as these are useful to focus on the central issues in risk analysis.

Each member of SSI's Shanghai project team was asked to give his or her assessments for the optimistic and pessimistic scenarios, and the consensus forecasts are given in Table 12-4. Three points should be noted about these forecasts. First, they represent assessments from people who are knowledgeable about the project itself, conditions in China, and export markets in general. Therefore, it is realistic to assume that these combinations of input values could actually occur. Second, the forecasts are not for "gloom and doom" or "pie in the sky" scenarios. Finally, the forecasters who developed the scenarios were not asked to assess the probability of the three scenarios occurring, but they understood that the expected values should lie in the middle of the range and that values above the optimistic and/or below the pessimistic values should have about a 25 percent probability of occurrence.

The NPVs of the three scenarios indicate that SSI would lose heavily if things go badly or do exceptionally well if things go well. As we have seen with previous analyses, the expected scenario is profitable, but not by very much. We conclude from these three scenarios that the Shanghai project has substantial stand-alone risk and that the concerns raised by the sensitivity analysis are valid. One question that needs to be answered, though, is this: How accurate are these scenario numbers? If people who really understand the business environment developed the scenarios,

TABLE 12-4 Scenarios: Input Values and Outcomes

	Pessimistic Value	Expected Value	Optimistic Value
Export selling price	$1.65	$1.70	$1.85
Spot exchange rate	CNY 8.00/$	CNY 8.28/$	CNY 8.30/$
Direct materials cost	CNY 4.75	CNY 4.50	CNY 4.25
Direct labor cost	CNY 4.25	CNY 4.00	CNY 3.90
Local selling price	CNY 9.50	CNY 10.00	CNY 10.50
Export unit sales	29,000	30,000	32,000
G&A expense	CNY 124,000	CNY 122,500	CNY 121,000
German profit rate	6.00%	5.00%	4.00%
Local unit sales	18,000	20,000	22,000
Discount rate	12.5%	11.75%	11.00%
Growth in export unit sales	6.00%	8.00%	10.00%
Growth in direct labor cost	2.25%	2.00%	1.75%
Growth in direct materials cost	1.25%	1.00%	0.75%
Growth in G&A expense	1.60%	1.50%	1.40%
Salvage premium over book	0.00%	25.00%	40.00%
Insurance cost	CNY 1,800	CNY 1,750	CNY 1,700
Growth in local unit sales	4.00%	5.00%	7.00%
Growth in insurance cost	1.60%	1.50%	1.40%
NPV (CNY)	CNY −234,107,800	CNY 109,800	CNY 312,251,000
NPV ($)	−$29,263,500	$13,300	$37,620,600
IRR	undefined	11.77%	66.09%
Payback	0.00 years	4.41 years	1.45 years

there is evidence that they offer approximations of the extreme end points of the NPV distribution. However, we only have a single point estimate of expected value, and scenario analysis has not proved in practice to be very good at identifying the true midpoint of the NPV distribution. This situation leads us to Monte Carlo simulation, our next topic.

SELF-TEST QUESTIONS Does sensitivity analysis have any limitations? Explain.

What is scenario analysis?

In what situations is scenario analysis generally sufficient, and when is it not sufficient?

MONTE CARLO SIMULATION

Monte Carlo Simulation
A risk analysis technique in which probable future events are simulated on a computer, generating estimated rates of return and risk indices.

Scenario analysis provides useful information about a project's stand-alone risk. If it is done correctly, the analyst should get a sense of the extreme tails of the NPV distribution. However, as we pointed out earlier, it is not particularly useful for identifying the shape of the NPV distribution because it considers only three discrete outcomes (NPVs), two of which are at the tails. We know that in reality, there are an infinite number of possibilities, and we really need additional data points to give us a more accurate description of the whole distribution.

Monte Carlo simulation ties together scenarios and probability distributions. It grew out of work in the Manhattan Project to build the first atomic bomb, and its

FOLLOW THE SIGNPOSTS

For many companies, scenario planning is a passive exercise. Planning teams scramble to make predictions about a volatile future, but no action is taken to guard against or take advantage of these scenarios. Scenario planning should be used to help companies become more aware of possible outcomes, and as a springboard for action. Even the brightest of future scenarios is useless if companies do not act on them.

A recent study by the Corporate Strategy Board reports that one-third of major American companies use scenario planning, but it estimates that only one-third of them do it right (testing the robustness of strategies and updating scenarios as conditions shift).

According to Rick Eno, vice-president at Arthur D. Little in Cambridge, the key is to identify "signposts" that signal when a scenario is unfolding, such as a changing rate of new technology adoption or a wave of debt defaults in a particular industry.

One of the first major corporations to establish an effective scenario planning protocol was Royal Dutch/Shell. The Shell method, as it is called, helped make the company an oil giant. Today, Shell has forecasts of energy markets out to 2050 and a series of 20-year scenario plans (updated every three years) to help manage Shell's strategic planning. A long process (up to nine months) is used to identify the *problematique*, the issue on which the company wants to focus. A team of economists, sociologists, and energy experts analyzes the issue and determines what is important and what challenges exist. After the analysis stage, the scope of the *problematique* is determined and the research phase proceeds (with board approval). The research phase goes into great detail (lasting as much as a year) generating scenarios. Once plans have been approved, the team tests the company's strategies against these scenarios (called "wind tunneling").

According to Peter Schwartz (former head of scenario planning at Royal Dutch/Shell), scenarios can be as narrowly or broadly focused as the company wishes but are best suited for capital intensive firms with long product life cycles and high inventory levels. He continues, "They're not good for fashion-focused or short-cycle companies, where there are infinite possible scenarios. In those cases, the risks are not analyzable."

Tragic events such as September 11 have made the range of possible scenarios even wider. However, Ged Davis, vice-president of global business environment at Shell International, says that the basics of scenario planning have not changed. According to Davis, "We view these events as a wild-card concept. They don't happen very often. To spend significant resources to deal with them is to move into a state of paranoia."

Source: Kris Frieswick, "Follow the Signposts," *CFO Magazine,* February 2002, 65–66.

name came about because it utilized the mathematics of casino gambling. While Monte Carlo simulation is considerably more complex than scenario analysis, simulation software packages make this process manageable. Some of these packages can be run as add-ons to spreadsheet programs such as *Excel.*

In a simulation analysis, the managers are asked to provide information about each of the important input variables. Usually variables that do not have a strong effect on NPV are set at their expected values and the analysis focuses on the more critical inputs, such as the highly and moderately sensitive variables identified in the sensitivity analysis. Often, the managers are asked to give the best-case, worst-case, and most-likely value for each input, just as for the scenario analysis. If multiple managers are asked to provide estimates, Delphi techniques are sometimes used to refine the consensus forecasts. Also, if historical price and volume information is available, it should be used. The data for the input variables are then entered into the computer using an assumed probability distribution (such as normal or triangular distributions). Once the data are entered into the model, the computer begins by picking from the input probability distributions a random value for each variable—export unit sales, export sales price, direct materials cost per unit, and so on. Then those values are inserted into the spreadsheet model, which then calculates a value for the NPV and stores the value in the computer's memory. Then, a second set of input values is selected at random, and a second NPV is calculated.[4] This process is repeated perhaps 2,000 times, generating 2,000 NPVs. The mean and standard deviation of the set of NPVs are determined, and the mean value is used as a measure of the project's expected NPV, and the standard deviation (or coefficient of variation) is used as a measure of risk.

Monte Carlo simulation is, in essence, a highly refined and mechanized scenario analysis, with a very large number of scenarios generated in a manner that conforms to input probability distributions. The end result is a table like Table 12-4, but with many possible outcomes rather than just three, along with descriptive statistics for the NPV distribution. We conducted a Monte Carlo simulation of the Shanghai project using the add-on risk analysis program called *Crystal Ball*.[5] The three estimates for each of the input variables rated high or moderate importance were assumed to be the end points and middle of triangular distributions, and these data were entered into *Crystal Ball*. Because we did not have any reasonable information about correlations between variables, we assumed that they were uncorrelated, although *Crystal Ball* permits the analyst to specify correlations.[6] A simulation of the project with 2,500 iterations was conducted and the output report shown in Table 12-5 was generated by the computer.

The report shows that the mean NPV of the project is CNY 1,490,000, which is more than 10 times higher than the CNY 110,000 estimated in the scenario analysis. However, the median NPV is a *negative* CNY 413,000, so the NPV distribution is skewed to the left (downward).[7] The standard deviation is also very large—CNY 38,751,000—indicating substantial risk. The other interesting parameters are the range minimum of *negative* CNY 126,151,000 and range maximum of positive CNY 130,449,000. This suggests that the optimistic and pessimistic values in the scenario analysis are perhaps too far into the tails of the distribution—they could occur, but the probabilities are much less than supposed.

If we have reliable estimates of the input variables' probability distributions, along with the correlations between the inputs, then simulation analysis can be extremely useful. It is the only one of the three methodologies that can give reasonable estimates of the entire NPV distribution. Unfortunately, objective (historical) data, or even reliable subjective estimates of the probabilities and correlations, are rarely available for new projects, so Monte Carlo simulations are used sparingly in capital budgeting analyses. However, they are used often for oil exploration projects, where good statistical data are available, and also for projects requiring a huge investment, when the consequences of making a wrong decision are significant for the company's future. With the availability of relatively inexpensive and easy-to-use spreadsheet add-on packages such as *Crystal Ball*, it is being tried more and more frequently on smaller projects like SSI's Shanghai investment. Notice from Table 12-5 that a desktop computer (Pentium IV, 2 gigahertz) ran the 2,500 iteration simulation in only 10 seconds.

---

[4]Values for the input variables are selected at random, but the random selection is based on the variable's probability distribution. Values close to the center of the distribution have a higher probability of being selected than values out toward the tails. Thus, in the various runs during the simulation, the most likely input value will be used far more often than the least likely high and low values.

[5]*Crystal Ball* is a registered trademark of Decisioneering, Inc.

[6]There is no rigorous technique available for assessing correlations other than with historical data. If historical data are available, these can be used to estimate correlations, but for this project, historical data are unavailable. We could, however, make subjective estimates of "reasonable" correlations and run the simulations with a series of such estimates, in effect, doing a sensitivity analysis of a simulation analysis. This could yield insights into the risk inherent in the project, but it would not yield reliable statistical confidence data.

[7]The primary reason the mean is so much larger than the median is the fact that when a high price is combined with a high unit volume the result is a very high NPV, which results in a relatively high mean NPV. This can be misleading, and it is one reason analysts must be careful when interpreting Monte Carlo simulation results.

TABLE 12-5 | Report of the Monte Carlo Simulation for the Shanghai Investment Project

Crystal Ball Report

Simulation started on 3/20/04 at 12:08:19

Simulation stopped on 3/20/04 at 12:08:29

Forecast: NPV(Y)

Summary

Display range is from (Y97,009) to Y98,468

Entire range is from (Y126,151) to Y130,449

After 2,500 trials, the standard error of the mean is Y775

Statistics	*Value*
Trials	2500
Mean	Y1,490
Median	(Y413)
Mode	—
Standard deviation	Y38,751
Variance	Y1,501,620,041
Skewness	0.15
Kurtosis	2.85
Coefficient of variability	26
Range minimum	(Y126,151)
Range maximum	Y130,449
Range width	Y256,600
Mean standard error	Y775.01

Probability (2,500 Trials) / Frequency (2,472 Displayed)

Forecast: NPV(Y) Frequency Chart

Probability	Frequency
.025	62
.019	46.5
.012	31
.006	15.5
.000	0

−$97,009   −$48,140 $729 $49,599 $98,468

The big hurdle today is not the cost and computational difficulty of doing a Monte Carlo simulation—it is the availability of reasonable input data and the difficulty of validating outputs obtained from subjectively estimated inputs.[8]

SELF-TEST QUESTIONS

What is Monte Carlo simulation? Why is it not used more often?

What are the hurdles today with respect to Monte Carlo simulation?

---

[8]See Eugene F. Brigham and Phillip R. Daves, *Intermediate Financial Management*, 8th edition (Mason, OH: South-Western Publishing, 2004), Chapter 12, for a further discussion of simulation analysis.

REAL OPTIONS AND DECISION TREES

Overview

Option
The right, but not the obligation, to take some action in the future. In finance, we deal with financial and real options.

Call Option
An option to buy, or "call," a share of stock at a certain price within a specified period.

Real Option
Involves real, rather than financial, assets. Real options exist when managers can influence the size and riskiness of a project's cash flows by taking different actions during or at the end of a project's life.

Decision Tree
A diagram that shows all possible outcomes that might result from a decision. Each possible outcome is shown as a "branch" on the tree. Decision trees are especially useful for analyzing the effects of real options.

For those students interested in learning more about real options, here are two web sites that provide more information: http://www. real-options.de/ index.html and http://sphere.rdc. puc-rio.br/marco. ind. The second Web site highlights the discussion of real options in the petroleum industry.

To have an **option** means to have a choice. If someone has joint majors in finance and foreign languages, then he or she is more likely to have the option of working for an international financial institution than someone with a finance degree but no foreign language skills. Because few people have this highly desirable combination, a person with both majors stands out in the job market and has a better chance of finding just the right employment opportunity. Thus, possessing such an option expands a person's opportunity set and reduces the risk of not experiencing a good outcome. There are also options in financial markets. A **call option** on a stock gives the holder the right to buy a share of the stock at a specified price within a specified period of time. Importantly, though, the holder of the call option has the choice of whether to buy the share or not. In other words, the option may be exercised, in which case the share is purchased, or it may be allowed to expire unexercised. Other financial options give the holder the right, but not the obligation, to sell stock at specific prices, to buy real estate, and so on. In capital budgeting, if a manager has the flexibility to take some type of strategic action that will alter the cash flow stream after a project has been initiated, then the project is said to have an "embedded **real option**." For example, if SSI could expand its Shanghai plant in the event that things work out particularly well, or abandon it if things go badly, then these opportunities constitute real options. The first is called an expansion option, the second an abandonment option. As we shall see, real options are sometimes automatically embedded in projects, but in other situations managers must take actions to create them. In either case, their existence can greatly increase a project's expected return while simultaneously decreasing its risk.

Analyzing Real Options for SSI's China Project

The tree diagram in Panel A at the top of Table 12-6 shows the cash flows under each of three scenarios. (The "expected" base-case scenario was presented earlier in Table 11-3.) To illustrate the use of **decision trees** in evaluating real options, we assume that the managers who developed the scenarios also estimated the probability of occurrence for each outcome. We then found the expected NPV and risk measures as shown. This format is especially useful for analyzing real options, where some action can be taken after the project has been implemented that would alter the initially estimated cash flows. To deal with such situations, we add a new decision point after 2004 and then set up a new branch that shows the cash flows that would occur if that action were taken. Panel B of Table 12-6 illustrates such a real option—the option to produce speakers and other products in Beijing for the North China market.

Note that there are two decision points in Panel B. The first is at the end of 2004, when the initial decision must be made and CNY 165.6 million must be spent. The second is at the end of 2006, when SSI has the (real) option to expand production in China if things go well during 2005 and 2006. This option more than doubles the expected NPV, from CNY 19.6 million to CNY 52.8 million, and it also lowers risk as measured by the CV. In many cases, real options can turn a negative NPV into a positive one. Clearly, a failure to recognize such real options could lead to turning down valuable projects, which would mean a failure to maximize the firm's value.

The option illustrated here is an *expansion option* because it would expand Chinese operations. If having existing operations in Shanghai allows the company to build another factory in Beijing to serve more effectively the northern China market

TABLE 12-6 | Decision Tree Incorporating Beijing Expansion and Abandonment (Yuan in Thousands)

Panel A: Base-Case Scenarios
China: Base-Case Scenarios: Free Cash Flows, NPVs, and Risk Measures

		2004	2005	2006	2007	2008	2009	NPV	WACC
Optimistic	25%		118,187	104,692	117,490	94,414	233,053	312,251	11.00%
Expected	50%	−165,600	32,703	26,534	28,917	19,303	143,080	110	11.75%
Pessimistic	25%		−35,413	−34,423	−38,549	−36,692	72,351	−234,108	12.50%

Expected NPV: 19,591
SD: 194,147
CV: 9.91

Panel B: Expansion to Beijing

		2004	2005	2006	2007	2008	2009	NPV	WACC
				−82,800	45,510	63,694	210,505		
Optimistic			118,187	104,692	117,490	94,414	233,053		
	25%		118,187	21,892	163,000	158,108	443,558	445,207	11.00%
Expected	50%	−165,600	32,703	26,534	28,917	19,303	143,080	110	11.75%
Pessimistic	25%		−35,413	−34,423	−38,549	−36,692	72,351	−234,108	12.50%

Expected NPV: 52,830
SD: 245,892
CV: 4.65

Panel C: Abandonment after One Year

		2004	2005	2006	2007	2008	2009	NPV	WACC
				−82,800	45,510	63,694	210,505		
			118,187	104,692	117,490	94,414	233,053		
Optimistic	25%		118,187	21,892	163,000	158,108	443,558	445,207	11.00%
Expected	50%	−165,600	32,703	26,534	28,917	19,303	143,080	110	11.75%
Pessimistic 1	0%		−35,413	−34,423	−38,549	−36,692	72,351		
			41,400	0	0	0	0		
Pessimistic 2	25%		5,987	0	0	0	0	−160,278	12.50%

Expected NPV: 71,287
SD: 225,594
CV: 3.16

and without having to go through the arduous and expensive negotiating process with the government, it is valuable for two reasons. First, the cost of setting up another production site in China is lower than it would be if SSI were trying to enter the market for the first time. McDonald's often makes initial investments in foreign countries and then expands operations to other cities or countries in the region if the initial investment works out well. In addition to lowering costs, success in the first stage generally means less risk for the second stage, as by then the company has a much better idea of cost and demand conditions in the new market.[9]

---

[9]Options to expand are the essence of test markets and pilot production experiments that are used extensively in marketing and production. Entering one narrowly defined market that is representative of the broader marketplace—or producing on a small scale using a new process—allows the company to gain information about the acceptance of the product by consumers, the cost of producing and distributing it, and other important but currently unknown inputs to the capital budgeting analysis. Having this information, then, lowers the risk of the full-scale roll-out.

Abandonment Option
The option of discontinuing a project if operating cash flows turn out to be lower than expected. This option can both raise expected profitability and lower project risk.

Investment Timing Option
An option as to when to begin a project. Often, if a firm can delay a decision, it can increase a project's expected NPV.

Other common real options include **abandonment** and **investment timing options.** If abandonment is possible, then the "Pessimistic" branch as shown in Panels A and B would be modified as shown in Panel C. Here we assume that the project could be abandoned at the end of 2005 if cash flows were poor and that CNY 41.4 million could be recovered as a salvage value. The originally projected negative cash flows for 2005 through 2008 would not occur. Thus, under the pessimistic scenario with abandonment, the relevant cash flows are those shown on the bottom row of Panel C, and the NPV of that row declines from CNY −234,108,000 to CNY −160,278,000. As a result, the expected NPV increases from CNY 52.8 million to CNY 71.3 million and the CV falls from 4.65 to 3.16.

Up to this point we have assumed that SSI must decide now whether to undertake the Shanghai project. However, suppose the company has the option to invest in market research to get a better idea of what the domestic Chinese market for speakers is likely to be and also to build a small pilot plant in Shanghai to better judge the costs of producing those speakers. The marketing study and pilot plant will have a total cost of $2 million or CNY 16.56 million, and those costs will be incurred at the end of 2004. If things work out well, then the original CNY 165.6 million will be spent one year later, at the end of 2005, and the project will go forward beginning in 2006 rather than 2005. Table 12-7 shows a decision tree that incorporates the timing option. Note that the abandonment option is no longer relevant because the project will be stopped after the pilot phase if bad conditions are experienced.

Notice that all the cash flows beyond 2004 will be delayed under the timing option, hence they must be discounted back for an extra year. This, along with the CNY 16.56 million cost of the option, causes the NPVs of the best- and base-case scenarios to be smaller than if this real option were not considered. However, the timing option provides information that would enable SSI to avoid building the plant under bad conditions, and that lowers the loss that would be incurred from CNY −160.3 million to CNY −16.56 million. As a result, the NPV with the timing option rises to CNY 83.76 million. SSI's management decided to accept the Shanghai project with the timing option, which meant investing CNY 16.56 million in 2004 and then waiting to see how things turn out before committing the additional CNY 165.6 million.

It would be possible to consider other real options and to make additional adjustments to the analysis. Here is a listing of some possible refinements:

1. The company might design the Shanghai plant so that it could produce other products in case the demand for the speakers falls below expectations. Simi-

TABLE 12-7 | Decision Tree with Both Expansion and Timing Options (Yuan in Thousands)

	2004		2005	2006	2007	2008	2009	2010	NPV	WACC
					−82,800	45,510	63,694	210,505		
Optimistic				118,187	104,692	117,490	94,414	233,053		
		25%		118,187	21,892	163,000	158,108	443,558	384,528	11.00%
Expected	−16,560	50%	−165,600 → 32,703		26,534	28,917	19,303	143,080	−16,462	11.75%
Pessimistic		25%	Stop	0	0	0	0	0	−16,560	12.50%
								Expected NPV:	83,761	
								SD:	173,648	
								CV:	2.07	

larly, it might build a plant that allows it to substitute one input for another in case the original inputs turn out to cost more than was expected or are not available. These are examples of **flexibility options**, which can be very important.

Flexibility Option
The option to modify operations depending on how conditions develop during a project's life, especially the type of output produced or the inputs used.

2. Our original analysis assumed that all input variables would grow at a constant rate. That assumption could be changed, which would mean adding more branches to the decision tree.

3. We used the same WACCs throughout the analyses. Analysts often alter the WACCs after introducing real options because, as in our example, those options can dramatically lower a project's risk. This is especially true when abandonment and timing options are added.

The Value of a Real Option: SSI's China Project

Real options are often "free" in the sense that they are a part of the project. However, they may have a cost, as was true for our timing option. Also, it often costs something to design flexibility into a plant. When options have a cost, it is useful to find the value of the option, compare that value to the related cost, and then decide whether or not to create the option depending on whether the benefits exceed the cost.

Option Value
Value that is not accounted for in a conventional NPV analysis. Positive option value expands the firm's opportunities.

Various methods of differing complexity are used to estimate the value of real options. We can simply recognize them subjectively and then bump up a project's NPV by some arbitrary amount if the options would probably be valuable. A method that is more rigorous is demonstrated in Table 12-8. Here, using DCF analysis, we simply find the expected NPV of the project with no options considered, then find its value recognizing the real option or options, and then calculate the difference in the expected NPVs as the **option value**. Table 12-8 calculates the values of our Shanghai project's growth, abandonment, and timing options. Other more complex methods, based on option-pricing procedures such as the *Black-Scholes model*, can be used, but the use of such techniques is limited by the difficulty of obtaining the required inputs.

If SSI had to incur costs to obtain the three options, it would pay the company to spend up to CNY 33.2 million to have the option to expand production in China; it would be worth an additional CNY 18.5 million to be able to abandon the project under poor conditions; and it would be worth an additional CNY 30.9 million to delay the project one year to do the marketing study and build the pilot plant.

TABLE 12-8 | **Shanghai Project: Value of Various Real Options (Yuan in Thousands)**

NPV recognizing the growth option	CNY 52,830
NPV not recognizing the growth option	19,591
Value of the growth option	CNY 33,239
NPV recognizing the abandonment option	CNY 71,287
NPV not recognizing the abandonment option	52,830
Value of the abandonment option	CNY 18,457
NPV recognizing the timing option	CNY 83,761
NPV not recognizing the timing option	52,830
Value of the timing option	CNY 30,931

Real option analysis can be applied to entire companies as well as to projects.[10] Traditional DCF analysis, when applied to companies such as those engaged in biotech research, typically results in very low valuations because these firms have never produced much in the way of cash flows that can be projected and then discounted. However, the research done by such firms can be considered as producing real growth options, and the values of those options are what give the firms their values. The same general situation also exists for other firms, in varying degrees. Some companies have primarily assets-in-place—factories, stores, and so forth—that produce their cash flows. Those firms can be valued by traditional DCF procedures. However, other firms have less of their values based on assets-in-place and more based on potential future growth resulting from research and development efforts. For such firms, analysts need to think in terms of real options. If the probability is high that good results will be obtained and that cash flows will follow, then the stock might be valuable in spite of its not having any current earnings. There is obviously a lot of uncertainty in such an approach, but it is the best way to approach corporate valuation for firms whose primary assets are growth options.

SELF-TEST QUESTIONS

What are real options? How might they be used by a multinational corporation?

Briefly explain whether the following statement is true or false: "The existence of real options has no effect on either a project's risk or its expected return."

When might a decision tree be used?

Differentiate among the following real options: growth, abandonment, investment timing, and flexibility options.

How might the failure to recognize a growth option lead to the underestimation of a project's NPV?

How might an abandonment option increase a project's NPV? Lower its risk?

Briefly explain how to estimate the value of a project's real options.

Briefly explain what is meant by the following statement: "Real options are often free . . . However, they may have a cost . . ."

Briefly explain whether the following statement is true or false: "While real option analysis has been applied to a firm's individual projects, it cannot be applied to the firm as a whole."

CONCLUSIONS ON RISK ANALYSIS AND REAL OPTIONS

Risk Analysis
An assessment of the uncertainty inherent in projects' cash flows, which should then be reflected in the WACCs used to evaluate the projects.

Risk analysis is an essential component of capital budgeting. The uncertainty inherent in projects' cash flows should be assessed, and that assessment should be reflected in the WACCs used to estimate the projects' NPVs. It would be best if we could determine how the returns on individual projects are correlated with returns on the stock market, making it possible to calculate project betas and use them as risk measures. However, that is generally not possible. Still, it is usually reasonable to assume that a project's returns are positively correlated with the economy and thus with stock returns, and also with returns on other projects in the firm's portfolio of assets. If a positive correlation does exist, then a project's stand-alone risk, as measured by the standard deviation or coefficient of variation of its NPV, can be used to judge its market risk for capital budgeting purposes. Sensitivity analysis, sce-

---

[10]For a summary of this work, see the panel discussion entitled "Real Options and Corporate Practice," *Journal of Applied Corporate Finance,* Winter 2003, 8–23. See also Thomas Arnold and Richard L. Shockley, Jr., "Real Options, Corporate Finance, and the Foundations of Value Maximization," *Journal of Applied Corporate Finance,* Winter 2003, 82–88.

HAS THE REAL OPTIONS APPROACH LOST ITS LUSTER?

Despite the fact that option pricing models have been around for 30 years, the real options approach has yet to catch on at most companies. In fact, recent surveys suggest that it has actually lost ground. A 2002 survey of *Fortune* 1000 CFOs found that the real options approach finished last in a field of 13 supplementary capital budgeting tools. Only 11.4 percent of CFOs responding to the survey used the real options approach, whereas 85.1 percent used sensitivity analysis and 66.8 percent used scenario analysis. Of course, the NPV method, with 96 percent usage, was the most used capital budgeting tool.

Do these results mean that real option valuation is disappearing? No. Academics point out that it took decades for NPV to become a widely accepted practice. Because the real options approach is a more sophisticated tool, it will take it at least as long to become integrated in corporations. Most companies, particularly in industries such as oil and gas, mining, pharmaceuticals, high tech, and biotechnology, have only been using it since the mid-1990s.

Real options are widely discussed in finance textbooks, academic literature, and business classes. Proponents of real options analysis point out that NPV assumes passive asset management, while real options valuation recognizes that managers often obtain valuable information after projects have been undertaken and take actions on the basis of new information to alter projects' values. More and more managers are considering project contingencies and their reactions to them. This is particularly true in industries that require large capital investments with a lot of uncertainty and flexibility. However, managers in these industries tend to be more engineering-oriented, hence not averse to using complex mathematical tools like the real options approach. Managers are also discovering that real options analysis can be used in more situations, such as supply-chain management and information technology (IT).

Opponents of real options analysis assert that there are four problems with the approach:

1. It is a black box.
2. It is a new economy tool.
3. It works only for tradable assets.
4. It discounts management realities.

It is clear that real options analysis uses sophisticated mathematics and is not as transparent as other tools such as NPV. However, more and more software applications are being developed for modeling real options.

The association of real options with Enron has given them a bad name. However, while Enron was an innovative user of real options, this tool had little to do with its financial difficulties. Note too that growth option analysis may have fueled the high valuations of Internet companies before their bubble burst, but again, these high valuations were more a result of garbage-in-garbage-out analysis than a poor technique. A more meticulous application of the data used in a real options analysis would have shown that many of these companies were overvalued.

Another assertion about the approach is that it does not work if the assets are not traded. However, the data can be created for real assets by identifying the assumptions underlying a project's value, the risks associated with these assumptions, and its statistical returns distribution using Monte Carlo simulation.

Finally, opponents point out that real options do not expire like financial options, so managers may be reluctant to abandon a project. However, real options analysis often helps managers make such decisions. Indeed, this approach may actually promote greater project management discipline, though this will happen only in companies that promote change and that have established appropriate incentive-based compensation systems.

What are the prospects for real options analysis? There has been substantial progress in getting managers to think about real options; however, companies have been slow to adopt real option tools for evaluating projects. The final step of an "integrated value-based management system that analyzes a company's portfolio of real options" is still a long way off.

Source: Edward Teach, "Will Real Options Take Root?," *CFO Magazine*, July 1, 2003, **http://www.cfo.com**.

nario analysis, and Monte Carlo simulation are all available to help us assess project risk.

Real options are actions that management can take to alter the cash flow stream after an initial investment has been made. Real options can result in new revenue streams, cost reductions, increased profits if the market does better than expected, and smaller losses in the event that things work out poorly. Thus, recognizing their existence typically increases a project's expected NPV and lowers its risk. A decision tree can be used to evaluate the value and effects of a real option. More sophisticated (but complicated) approaches can be taken, but these approaches can generally be applied only in specialized situations where statistical data on inputs and outputs are available. Note, though, that more and more data are becoming available every day, so more and more sophisticated real option analysis can be expected in the future.

Our example of SSI's Chinese speaker project showed strong sensitivity to variations in exchange rates. That situation is generally true when products are made and sold in world markets at costs and prices that are affected by exchange rates, such as French wine, Florida orange juice, or Japanese automobiles. Exchange rate risk is a significant factor in capital budgeting decisions for firms that deal with such projects, and the effects of changes in exchange rates on NPVs must be considered.

SELF-TEST QUESTIONS

Why is risk analysis an essential component of capital budgeting?

What tools can be used to assess a project's risk?

How do real options affect the capital budgeting analysis?

What tools can be used to evaluate the value and effects of real options?

Briefly explain whether the following statement is true or false: "Exchange rate risk is not a significant factor in capital budgeting decisions for firms whose products are sold in international markets."

SUMMARY

The last three chapters have focused on capital budgeting. In Chapter 10 we showed how companies estimate the cost of capital and how international factors influence a multinational firm's cost of capital. In Chapter 11, given an estimated cost of capital, we described several approaches for evaluating projects, how to estimate a project's cash flows, and how international factors impact the capital budgeting process. In this chapter, we discussed several techniques for evaluating a project's risk and introduced real option analysis—both of which are important considerations for firms with international operations. The key concepts discussed in this chapter are listed below.

- Cash flows are subject to varying degrees of **risk**, so risk should be considered in capital budgeting decisions. There are three different types of risk: stand-alone risk, corporate (or within-firm) risk, and market risk.
- **Stand-alone risk** is the risk a project would have if it were the firm's only project and if investors owned only the stock of the firm. It is measured by the standard deviation of the project's expected NPV.
- **Corporate** (or **within-firm**) **risk** is a project's risk when it is considered as one asset in the firm's portfolio of assets, in which case some of its individual risk is diversified away.
- **Market risk** is a project's risk given that it is part of the firm's asset portfolio and also given that investors hold a broadly diversified portfolio of stocks.
- In theory, market risk should be our primary consideration, and stand-alone risk should be relatively unimportant. However, stand-alone risk is actually of great importance because (1) it is **easier to measure** than both corporate or market risk and (2) in the vast majority of cases, **all three types of risk are highly correlated**. Because of this high correlation, stand-alone risk is generally a **good proxy** for both corporate and market risk.
- **Sensitivity analysis** is a risk analysis technique that shows how much a project's NPV will change in response to a given change in an input variable such

as sales, other things held constant. NPV is then plotted on a graph to show how sensitive NPV is to changes in each variable. The steeper the slope, the more sensitive the NPV is to a change in the variable.

- **Scenario analysis** is a risk analysis technique in which the **best-** and **worst-case NPVs** are compared with the project's **expected NPV.** It extends the information provided by sensitivity analysis by incorporating the probability distributions of inputs and combining the effects of changes in variables.
- **Monte Carlo simulation** is a risk analysis technique that uses a computer to simulate future events and to estimate the profitability and riskiness of a project.
- **Decision tree analysis** shows how different decisions in a project's life affect its value.
- A **decision tree** is a diagram that shows all possible outcomes that result from a decision. Each possible outcome is shown as a "branch" on the tree. Decision trees are especially useful in analyzing the effects of real options in investment decisions.
- Investing in a new project often brings with it a potential increase in the firm's future opportunities. Opportunities are, in effect, **options**—the right but not the obligation to take some future action.
- A **real option** involves real, rather than financial, assets. They exist when managers can influence the size and riskiness of a project's cash flows by taking different actions during or at the end of a project's life.
- If an investment creates the opportunity to make other potentially profitable investments that would not otherwise be possible, then the investment is said to contain a **growth (expansion) option.**
- An **abandonment option** is the ability to stop a project if the operating cash flows turn out to be lower than expected. This option can both reduce the riskiness of a project and increase its value.
- An **investment timing option** involves not only the decision of *whether* to proceed with a project but also the decision of *when* to proceed with it. This opportunity to affect a project's timing can dramatically change its estimated value.
- A **flexibility option** is the option to modify operations depending on how conditions develop during a project's life, especially the type of output produced or the inputs used.
- A project may have an **option value** that is not accounted for in a conventional NPV analysis. Any project that expands the firm's set of opportunities has positive option value. Using DCF analysis, find the expected NPV of the project, then find its value recognizing the real option, and then calculate the difference in the expected NPVs as the option value.
- **Risk analysis** is an essential component of capital budgeting. It involves an assessment of the uncertainty in projects' cash flows, which should then be reflected in the WACCs used to evaluate the projects.

QUESTIONS

(12-1) Briefly explain whether you agree or disagree with the following statement: "In theory, market risk should be our primary consideration, and it is significantly more important than stand-alone risk."

(12-2) Why can corporate risk not be ignored?

(12-3) Why is risk analysis so essential to capital budgeting decisions?

(12-4) Differentiate among sensitivity analysis, scenario analysis, and simulation analysis. If General Motors were considering two investments, one calling for the expenditure of $500 million to develop a state-of-the-art assembly plant in Mexico and the other involving the expenditure of $15,000 for computer software, for which one would the company be more likely to use simulation analysis?

(12-5) In a sensitivity graph, what information does the steepness of the slope tell us about changes in an input variable? About the project's risk?

(12-6) Briefly explain how you might set up base-case, worst-case, and best-case scenarios for analyzing a particular project.

(12-7) What is the difference between financial and real options? What are some specific types of real options, and are they "created" or do they just occur?

(12-8) What is a decision tree, and when might you use it?

(12-9) What factors should a company consider when it decides whether to invest in a project today or to wait until more information becomes available?

(12-10) In general, do timing options make it more or less likely that a project will be accepted today?

(12-11) If a company has an option to abandon a project, would this tend to make the company more or less likely to accept the project today?

(12-12) Why might a different WACC be used in evaluating a project after real options were considered? For which type of real options might this be true?

(12-13) Identify several methods that could be used to estimate the value of a real option. How would you use this information when making decisions about an option?

(12-14) Suppose a company does not explicitly consider real options in its capital budgeting decisions, and it uses the corporate WACC to calculate the NPV of a specific project. Now suppose the company decides to consider several real options embedded in the project, such as a timing option, a flexibility option, and an abandonment option. Should it continue to use the corporate WACC in the analysis once options are considered? Explain your answer.

(12-15) Good managers not only identify and evaluate real options in projects—they also structure projects so as to produce real options. If a multinational company is considering a project to build a manufacturing plant abroad, name some real options that might be built into the project, explain how they could be evaluated, and discuss their effects on the project's NPV.

SELF-TEST PROBLEMS   Solutions Appear in Appendix B

(ST-1) Define each of the following terms:
Key Terms a. Risk; stand-alone risk; corporate (within-firm) risk; market risk
b. Sensitivity analysis; scenario analysis; Monte Carlo simulation; risk analysis
c. Base-case NPV; base case; worst-case scenario; best-case scenario
d. Option; call option; real option; decision tree; option value
e. Growth (expansion) option; abandonment option; investment timing option; flexibility option

(ST-2) Schneider Inc., a U.S. multinational, is considering a project in France that has an
Investment Timing Option up-front cost of 4.5 million euros and produces an expected cash flow of 750,000 euros at the end of each of the next 5 years. The spot exchange rate is €0.89/$, and the euro is expected to depreciate against the dollar by 1 percent a year during the project's life. The project's cost of capital, excluding the foreign exchange rate risk premium, is 9 percent.
a. What is the project's net present value (NPV) stated in dollars?
b. If Schneider goes ahead with this project today, the project will create additional opportunities five years from now (t = 5). The company can decide at t = 5 whether it wants to pursue these additional opportunities. On the basis

of the best information that is available today, the company estimates that there is a 40 percent chance that its technology will be successful, in which case the future investment opportunities will have a net present value of 8.5 million euros at t = 5. There is a 60 percent chance that its technology will not succeed, in which case the future investment opportunities will have a net present value of −8.5 million euros at t = 5. Schneider does not have to decide today whether it wants to pursue these additional opportunities. Instead, it can wait until after it finds out if its technology is successful. However, Schneider cannot pursue these additional opportunities in the future unless it makes the initial investment today. What is the estimated net present value of the project today stated in dollars, after taking into account the future opportunities? Assume that the NPV estimates of the future investment opportunities have properly adjusted the cash flows for changes in future exchange rates.

STARTER PROBLEMS

(12-1)
Investment Timing Option

Beckham Manufacturing Company (BMC), a U.S. multinational, is considering an investment in a proposed project in Australia. Rather than making the investment today, the company wants to wait a year to collect additional information about the project. If BMC waits a year, it will not have to invest any cash flows unless it decides to make the investment. If it waits, there is a 20 percent chance the project's expected NPV 1 year from today will be AUD 12.4 million, a 60 percent chance that the project's expected NPV 1 year from now will be AUD 5 million, and a 20 percent chance that the project's expected NPV 1 year from now will be AUD −12.4 million. The spot exchange rate is AUD 1.50/$; however, next year the Australian dollar is expected to appreciate by 1 percent against the U.S. dollar. All expected cash flows are discounted at a 9 percent cost of capital, which excludes the foreign exchange rate risk premium. What is the expected NPV today (stated in U.S. dollars) if the company chooses to wait a year before deciding whether to make the investment? Assume that the NPV estimates of the future investment opportunities have properly adjusted the cash flows for changes in future exchange rates.

(12-2)
Abandonment Option

Sorrento Supplies Inc., a U.S. multinational, recently purchased a new forklift for one of its Canadian subsidiaries. Because of high transportation costs, it was cheaper for the firm to purchase the forklift in Canada rather than in the United States. The forklift cost CAD 35,000 and is expected to generate net after-tax operating cash flows, including depreciation, of CAD 8,900 at the end of each year. The forklift has a 5-year expected life. The expected abandonment values at different points in time are given below. (Note that these abandonment value estimates assume that the forklift is sold after receiving the project's cash flow for the year.)

Year	Abandonment Value
1	CAD 27,000
2	22,500
3	14,000
4	8,450
5	0

The spot exchange rate is CAD 1.36/$, and the Canadian dollar is expected to appreciate by 1 percent a year against the U.S. dollar during the forklift's life. The firm's cost of capital is 8 percent and excludes the foreign exchange rate risk premium. At what point in time would the company choose to sell (abandon) the forklift in order to maximize its NPV stated in U.S. dollars? What is the forklift's NPV (stated in U.S. dollars) at that point in time?

EXAM-TYPE PROBLEMS

(12-3)

Investment Timing Option

Worldwide Satellites Inc. (WSI), a U.S. multinational, is considering a proposed project in Switzerland. The firm estimates that if it invests in the project today, the project's estimated NPV is SwF 16.25 million, but there remains a lot of uncertainty about the project's profitability.

As an alternative to making the investment today, the company is considering waiting a year. In particular, it is considering spending some money today to collect additional information, which would enable the firm to make a better assessment of the project's value 1 year from now. WSI believes that if it waits a year, there is a 60 percent chance the information collected will be positive and the project's expected NPV 1 year from now (not including the cost of obtaining the information) will be SwF 32 million. There is also a 40 percent chance the information collected will be negative and the project's expected NPV 1 year from now (not including the cost of obtaining the information) will be SwF −20 million.

If WSI chooses to collect additional information, the cost of collecting this information will be incurred today. Moreover, if the firm chooses to wait a year, it has the option to invest or not invest in the project after receiving information about the project's prospects. The spot exchange rate is SwF 1.39/$, and the Swiss franc is expected to depreciate against the dollar by 2 percent next year. Assume that all cash flows are discounted at 10 percent, which excludes the foreign exchange rate risk premium. What is the maximum amount of money (stated in U.S. dollars) that the company would be willing to spend to collect this information? Assume that the NPV estimates of the future investment opportunities have properly adjusted the cash flows for changes in future exchange rates.

(12-4)

Abandonment Option

Global Technology Inc. (GTI), a U.S. multinational, is considering a project in England that has an up-front cost of £375,000. The project's subsequent cash flows critically depend on whether its products become the industry standard. There is a 45 percent chance that the products will become the industry standard, in which case the project's expected cash flows will be £150,000 at the end of each of the next 5 years. There is a 55 percent chance that the products will not become the industry standard, in which case the project's expected cash flows will be £50,000 at the end of each of the next 5 years. The spot exchange rate is $1.59 per pound, and the British pound is expected to depreciate by 1 percent per year relative to the dollar during the project's life. Assume that the cost of capital is 10 percent, which excludes the foreign exchange rate risk premium.

a. What is the project's expected net present value (NPV) stated in U.S. dollars?

b. Now assume that 1 year from now GTI will know if the products will have become the industry standard. Also assume that after receiving the cash flows at t = 1, the company has the option to abandon the project. If it abandons the project it will receive an additional £215,000 at t = 1, but will no longer receive any cash flows after t = 1. Assume that the abandonment option does not affect the cost of capital. What is the estimated value of the abandonment option stated in U.S. dollars?

INTEGRATED CASE

Rick Schmidt, MRI's CFO, his assistant, Mandy Wu, and John Costello, a consultant and college finance professor, have the task of teaching MRI's directors and senior managers the basics of international financial management. Their program consists of 16 sessions, each lasting about 2 hours, and the sessions are held immediately before the monthly board meetings. Eleven sessions have been held thus far, and they have covered exchange rates, risk and return, financial statements, bond and stock valuation, cost of capital, and the basics of capital budgeting. The team is now preparing Session 12, which will deal with methods of risk analysis and the role of real options in capital budgeting.

The introductory capital budgeting session focused on identifying a project's relevant cash flows and then evaluating the project using the NPV, IRR, and payback criteria. The procedures were illustrated with an actual decision that MRI now faces, a major project to produce a heat-sensing device for use by airlines to determine if passengers are too sick to be allowed on flights. After the SARS epidemic in 2003, airlines became interested in this issue because they wanted to protect other passengers and thus to convince the flying public that airline travel is safe. The venture was dubbed Project HSD, for heat-sensing device, and because this is a very large project, the directors were quite interested in the capital budgeting analysis as presented in the last session.

The HSD devices will be sold to airlines all over the world, and they are small enough to be transported economically by air freight. Therefore, they can be manufactured anywhere, in the United States or overseas. For the HSD project, the most promising overseas location is northern Italy. MRI has several facilities in the Milan area, and the labor force in northern Italy is highly skilled, which is important for a high-tech product like HSD. Italy also has a relatively stable government, it is in the euro zone, and it does not have a repatriation problem.

The initial analysis was based on the assumption that Project HSD is about as risky as an average project. That initial assessment is one of the focal points of the current session, and it may be changed as a result of the risk analysis to be discussed in this session. MRI has a three-stage capital budgeting model. Stage 1 is used to obtain the most-likely estimates of NPV, IRR, and payback for each location, and that model was run for the analysis presented in Session 11. The project's NPV was projected to be negative from the project perspective, but, because of first-rate negotiations with the Italian government, the project provides positive value to the parent firm. However, in this analysis, exchange rates were assumed to remain constant, which is highly unlikely. In Stage 2, management will study the project's risk using sensitivity and scenario analyses, and in Stage 3 real options and their effects on risk and expected returns will be considered. It is possible that the Italian project is not as risky as it was thought to be so that a lower WACC may be justified. In addition, it is possible that additional opportunities made available by the investment have not been considered. The directors expressed great interest in the results of Stages 2 and 3 because they have seen quite a few projects projected to have positive NPVs that turned out to be losers. Therefore, they left the last session looking forward to this one.

Table IC12-1 shows management's assessment of its ability to forecast key input variables for this project. Table IC12-2 shows the key variables MRI wants to analyze. The variables not focused on in this analysis are mostly the up-front costs of the project, tax rates, and depreciation, which are known with a high degree of certainty. This is why Session 12 focuses on the variables in Table IC12-2. The first column shows expected input values for the project, while the next two columns show the pessimistic and optimistic projections of these variables. MRI is using a naïve approach to generating most of these values (except for the discount rate) by assuming that the optimistic values are 20 percent more favorable than the expected case, and the pessimistic values are 20 percent less favorable.

MRI's managers put a lot of stock in simple sensitivity analysis and want to analyze certain inputs. They have identified a series of variables for which they want to see a sensitivity analysis, including local

TABLE IC12-1 | Forecast Ability of Key Input Variables

Forecast Ability	Variables
Poor	Local selling price, local unit sales, growth in local unit sales, salvage premium, growth in direct labor, growth in direct materials
Average	Exchange rate, export selling price, discount rate, U.S. profit margin, direct materials cost, direct labor cost, G&A expense, insurance cost, growth in G&A, growth in insurance cost
Good	Export unit sales, growth in export unit sales

TABLE IC12-2 | Expected, Pessimistic, and Optimistic Input Values

	Expected Value	Pessimistic Value	Optimistic Value
Local unit sales	15,000	12,000	18,000
Growth in local unit sales	5.00%	4.00%	6.00%
Local selling price	€10.50	€8.40	€12.60
Export unit sales	6,000	4,800	7,200
Growth in export unit sales	7.00%	5.60%	8.40%
Export selling price	$13.00	$10.40	$15.60
Direct materials cost	€2.15	€2.58	€1.72
Growth in direct materials cost	1.50%	1.80%	1.20%
Direct labor cost	€4.75	€5.70	€3.80
Growth in direct labor cost	3.00%	3.60%	2.40%
G&A expense	€55,500	€66,600	€44,400
Growth in G&A expense	1.50%	1.80%	1.20%
Insurance cost	€600	€720	€480
Growth in insurance cost	1.50%	1.80%	1.20%
Spot exchange rate ($/€)	0.7973	0.63784	0.95676
U.S. profit margin	6.00%	7.20%	4.80%
Discount rate	10.00%	10.50%	9.50%
Salvage premium over book	15.00%	12.00%	18.00%

unit sales, local sales price, export unit sales, export sales price, exchange rate, G&A expenses, direct labor costs, and direct materials costs. This subset was chosen because using sensitivity analysis on every variable can be tedious, and MRI's managers have considerable experience in similar projects and have a reasonable idea about which variables are the most important. The remaining variables in MRI's Forecast Ability Chart (Table IC12-1) are considered to be of low importance.

First, in Stage 2 of MRI's model, a sensitivity analysis is completed, where the input variables are changed systematically to see just how sensitive NPV is to changes in each input. The greater the sensitivity, the riskier the project, other things held constant, because if the NPV is highly sensitive to a variable such as unit sales or sales price, then NPV could be wildly different if the estimates for the inputs turn out to be incorrect. After the sensitivity analysis, a scenario analysis is implemented, where each key input variable is set at "expected," "optimistic," and "pessimistic" levels, and three scenarios are run—a base case, a best case, and a worst case. Operating managers are responsible for setting the input values, and they are set such that the best-case scenario has a 25 percent probability of occurrence, the base-case scenario has a 50 percent probability, and the worst-case scenario has a 25 percent probability of happening. The scenario inputs are entered in the model as percentage deviations from their expected values. For example, if local demand is expected to result in sales of 15,000 units, but the marketing manager thinks that under bad conditions they could actually turn out to be 20 percent lower while under good conditions they could be 20 percent higher, then those percentages are entered in the model and used to find the worst- and best-case scenarios' unit sales. The model then calculates the NPV under each of the three scenarios, the expected NPV, and two risk measures (the standard deviation and the coefficient of variation).

Some of the directors have been asking about simulation analysis and would like to know how it can be used at MRI. Until now, MRI has not done Monte Carlo simulation analysis, but some of its competitors have. Wu thinks that for this project, where variables are moderately predictable (because they are in a developed market), Monte Carlo simulation would provide results consistent with the scenario analysis. By assuming the pessimistic and optimistic values are 20 percent below and above the expected value, Wu is assuming that the variables are normally distributed. This might make sense in a developed country, but as the analysis moves to developing markets this assumption is poor and simulation analysis becomes more valuable.

MRI also requires operating executives to identify any real options that exist or can be created for each proposed project. The model then, in Stage 3, calculates the option-adjusted expected NPV and risk measures, and it finds the value of each option. Specifically, operating executives are expected to explore future growth opportunities, benefits of delaying production, and any options to abandon the project. Sometimes there are costs to obtaining the real options, so their values need to be compared with the relevant costs. The following three embedded options for this project have been identified:

- In the event of the best-case scenario, operating executives have determined that 2 years later (at the end of 2006), an additional €8 million investment can be made in a different, though related, project that is expected to produce cash flows of €1.5 million in perpetuity.

- If the worst-case scenario occurs, operating executives estimate that at the end of the second year (2006), the project may be abandoned. The abandonment will generate an after-tax cash flow of €3.5 million at the end of 2006, which will include any operating or terminal cash flows.

- If MRI is willing to invest €4 million in a test site, executives can wait a year to see whether market conditions will be favorable for the project. Therefore, MRI can postpone the required investment for a year to determine whether either the best-case scenario or base-case scenario is likely to occur, or MRI can even cancel the project altogether if it looks as if the worst-case scenario is more likely to happen.

Depending on the results of the risk analysis, the WACC used in the analysis may be raised or lowered, and a modified NPV and risk measures may be calculated. For example, if the risk analysis indicates that a project is much more risky than average, then the WACC would be raised and a new NPV and coefficient of variation (CV) would be calculated. On the other hand, if the project appears to have relatively little risk, then the WACC would be lowered. Just how much to adjust the WACC under various conditions is a contentious issue, and MRI does not have a specific formula for these adjustments. Schmidt wants adjustments to be made, because in his words, "It's better to be approximately correct than exactly wrong." Others dislike making adjustments when they have little or no idea about how large they should be. In practice, the analyst in charge of a given project analysis generally does a final sensitivity analysis, where the NPVs at different WACCs are calculated. If the NPV is positive even at a very high WACC, then the analyst reports that fact, and the project will probably be accepted. On the other hand, if the NPV would be negative at a WACC only slightly higher than the company's unadjusted average WACC, then the project will be deemed questionable, and it might well be rejected even if the NPV is positive.

After much discussion, Schmidt, Wu, and Costello compiled the following set of questions for use during the session. As with the other sessions, they will use the *Excel* model to develop answers for the quantitative questions. Assume that you are Mandy Wu and must now prepare answers for use during the session. Most of the quantitative information is calculated in the case model, but if you use it, be prepared to answer questions about the model. The directors don't like analysts who use models as black boxes and can't explain how they actually work.

QUESTIONS

a. Define and differentiate among stand-alone risk, within-firm risk, and market risk. Which ones should be used to assess the riskiness of a capital budgeting project? If one of them is theoretically better, but a firm actually focuses on another type of risk, could this be justified?

b. What is sensitivity analysis, and how is it used in capital budgeting? Which type of risk does sensitivity analysis typically measure?

c. Now perform a sensitivity analysis for Project HSD and discuss the results. Which variables should concern management the most? Calculate sensitivity indices based on an input change of 1 percent, and construct an importance matrix for the project similar to the one in this chapter.

d. What is scenario analysis, and how does it differ from sensitivity analysis? Which type of risk does scenario analysis typically reflect? Can you think of any way that scenario analysis could be used to help assess the project's other types of risk?

e. Now perform a scenario analysis (using Table IC12-2) for Project HSD, and calculate the expected NPV and the CV. If the CV of an average MRI project is 1.0, how might that fact affect the evaluation of Project HSD?

f. What are decision trees, and how are they used in capital budgeting?

g. What is a real option, and how does the existence of real options affect a scenario analysis? What real options are considered in the HSD analysis? How do the real options affect HSD's estimated NPV and CV? If MRI must spend money up front for a particular option, how much should it be willing to spend to obtain each of the options discussed in the case?

h. What do you regard as the weakest aspects of scenario analysis after real options have been included in the analysis? What are its principal advantages versus other procedures?

i. How is Monte Carlo simulation used in capital budgeting, and how does it differ from scenario analysis? Which type of risk does simulation typically reflect? Can you think of a way that simulation analysis could be used to help assess the project's other types of risk? What are the major pros and cons of simulation for capital budgeting analysis?

j. On the basis of the data given in the case and your analysis, what action should MRI take with regard to Project HSD? Explain.

CHAPTER 13

Capital Structure and Distribution Policy

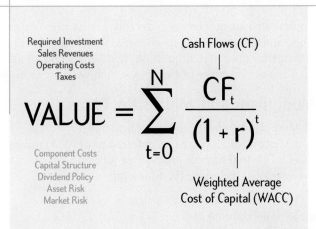

e-resource

The textbook's Web site, **http://crum. swlearning.com,** contains an Excel file that will guide you through the chapter's calculations. The file for this chapter is **FIFC13-model.xls,** and we encourage you to open the file and follow along as you read the chapter.

I n previous chapters we noted that free cash flow is the primary determinant of firm value, and our focus thus far has been on assets. In this chapter, though, we focus on two other issues: (1) How should the firm finance its assets—that is, what mix of debt and equity should it use? (2) How much of its cash flow should it distribute to stockholders, either as cash dividends or by repurchasing stock?

Capital structure has several important effects on the denominator of the valuation equation, r, which is the firm's WACC. First, it determines the weights used to calculate the WACC. Second, it affects the riskiness and thus the cost of the firm's debt and equity capital. Third, because interest is tax deductible, the more debt the firm uses, the lower its tax bill and thus the more of its operating income is available to its investors (bondholders and stockholders). Fourth, the higher the debt ratio, the greater the probability of bankruptcy, and if this threat becomes excessive, it will lower the cash flows in the numerator. Our first task in this chapter is to try to determine the optimal capital structure—the one that strikes a balance between the risk and return attributes of debt so as to maximize the firm's value. Capital structure is important for all firms but especially for multinational corporations, which deal in global capital markets and must take account of local issues when they finance foreign investments. Our capital structure discussion concludes with guidelines that can help a company estimate its optimal capital structure range.

Regarding cash distribution policy, note first that bondholders receive specified returns in the form of interest, whereas stockholders are paid for the use of their money in the form of expected (but not guaranteed) dividends and/or capital gains. Interest payments are contractual obligations, so firms have little flexibility *with regard to interest payments. However, management can choose to retain and reinvest after-interest cash flow or to distribute it to stockholders in the form of dividends or as payments for repurchased stock. The distribution decision can affect both the numerator and the denominator of the valuation equation, and thus the value of the firm. Therefore, the chapter's second task is to explore distribution policy. Again, this is especially important for multinational firms because of their ability to defer taxes on income earned in countries whose tax rates are lower than U.S. rates.*

CAPITAL STRUCTURE THEORY

Two video clips of Steve Walsh, Assistant Treasurer at JC Penney, talking about capital structure are available at http://fisher.osu.edu/fin/clips.htm. The first clip on capital structure discusses the cost of capital and debt, while the second clip discusses optimal capital structure at JC Penney relative to the capital structure theory of Modigliani/Miller.

Capital structures vary considerably across firms in given industries, across industries, and from country to country. What factors explain these differences? In an attempt to answer this question, academics and practitioners have developed and then tested a number of theories, which we discuss in this section.

Modigliani and Miller: No Taxes

Modern capital structure theory began in 1958, when Professors Franco Modigliani and Merton Miller (hereafter referred to as MM) published what has been called the most influential finance article ever written.[1] MM's study was based on some strong assumptions, including the following:

1. There are no brokerage costs.
2. There are no taxes.
3. There are no bankruptcy costs.
4. Investors can borrow at the same rate as corporations.
5. All investors have the same information as management about the firm's future investment opportunities.
6. EBIT is not affected by the use of debt.

MM proved that if these assumptions hold true then a firm's value will be unaffected by its capital structure, hence the following situation must exist:

$$V_L = V_U = S_L + D. \tag{13-1}$$

Here V_L is the value of a levered firm, which is equal to V_U, the value of an identical but unlevered firm; S_L is the value of the levered firm's equity, and D is the value of its debt.

Recall that the WACC combines the costs of debt and equity. Debt costs less than equity, so as leverage increases, more weight is given to low-cost debt, which tends to lower the WACC. However, increasing leverage makes the equity become riskier, which increases its cost, r_s.[2] Under MM's assumptions, r_s increases by exactly enough to keep the WACC constant. Therefore, if MM's assumptions were correct, it would not matter how a firm finances its operations, so its capital structure decisions would be irrelevant.

Despite some of their unrealistic assumptions, MM's irrelevance result is extremely important. By indicating the conditions under which capital structure would be irrelevant, MM also provides us with clues about what is required to make capital struc-

---

[1]Franco Modigliani and Merton H. Miller, "The Cost of Capital, Corporation Finance, and the Theory of Investment," *American Economic Review*, June 1958. Modigliani and Miller both won Nobel Prizes for their work.

[2]The cost of debt also rises with leverage, but in their initial article MM ignore this point. It is, however, dealt with in subsequent research.

ture relevant and thus to affect a firm's value. MM's work marked the beginning of modern capital structure research, and subsequent research has focused on relaxing the MM assumptions to develop more realistic capital structure theories.

Modigliani and Miller: The Effect of Corporate Taxes

MM published a follow-up paper in 1963 that relaxed the assumption of no corporate taxes.[3] The U.S. Tax Code (and that of most other nations as well) allows corporations to deduct interest payments as an expense, which reduces taxable income, but stockholders' dividend payments are not deductible. Accordingly, if a firm uses debt, more of its operating cash flow is available to investors. This differential tax treatment encourages corporations to use more debt in their capital structures than they otherwise would.

As in their earlier paper, MM introduced a second important way of looking at capital structure: The value of a levered firm is the value of an otherwise identical unlevered firm *plus the value of any "side effects."* While others expanded this idea, the only "side effect" MM considered was the present value of the interest tax shield. Here is their expanded equation:

$$V_L = V_U + \text{Value of side effects} = V_U + \text{PV of interest tax shield.} \qquad \text{(13-2)}$$

Under their assumptions, they showed that the present value of the interest tax shield is equal to the corporate tax rate, T, multiplied by the amount of debt, D:

$$V_L = V_U + TD. \qquad \text{(13-3)}$$

With a federal-plus-state tax rate of 40 percent, every dollar of debt adds about 40 cents of value to the firm, and this implies that the optimal capital structure is virtually 100 percent debt.[4] MM also demonstrated that the cost of equity, r_s, increases as leverage increases, but that it does not increase quite as fast as it would if there were no taxes. As a result, under MM with corporate taxes, the WACC falls as debt is added.

Miller: The Effect of Corporate and Personal Taxes

In 1977 Merton Miller (this time without Modigliani) took up the effects of personal taxes.[5] He noted that most of the income that bonds provide is interest, which is taxed in the United States (and most other countries) as personal income at rates (T_d) going up to 35 percent, while stock income comes from dividends and long-term capital gains taxed at a maximum rate of 15 percent. Further, long-term capital gains are deferred until the stock is sold and the gain realized. As a result, returns on stock are taxed at T_s, which is lower than the rate on debt.

Because of the tax situation, Miller argued that investors are willing to accept relatively low before-tax stock returns relative to before-tax bond returns. Thus, Miller concluded that (1) the *deductibility of interest* favors the use of debt financing, but (2) the *favorable tax treatment of stock income* lowers the required rate of return and thus favors equity financing. The reduction of tax rates on dividend income and capital gains in 2003 only accentuates Miller's earlier findings.

---

[3]Franco Modigliani and Merton H. Miller, "Corporate Income Taxes and the Cost of Capital: A Correction," *American Economic Review,* Vol. 53, June 1963, 433–443.

[4]Firms must have some equity or else the debt would de facto be equity. Pure-form MM would lead firms to get as close to 100 percent debt as they can.

[5]Merton H. Miller, "Debt and Taxes," *Journal of Finance,* Vol. 32, May 1977, 261–275. Miller was president of the American Finance Association, and he delivered the paper as his presidential address.

Miller showed that the net effect of taxes on value, when both corporate and personal taxes are considered, is as follows:

$$V_L = V_U + \left[1 - \frac{(1 - T_c)(1 - T_s)}{(1 - T_d)} \right] D. \qquad (13\text{-}4)$$

Here T_c is the corporate tax rate, T_s is the personal tax rate on income from stocks, and T_d is the tax rate on income from debt. Miller argued that the marginal tax rates on stock and debt balance in such a way that the bracketed term in Equation 13-4 is zero, so $V_L = V_U$. However, most researchers who followed Miller have concluded that there is still a tax advantage to debt. For example, with a 40 percent marginal corporate tax rate, a 30 percent marginal rate on debt, and a 12 percent marginal rate on stock, the advantage of debt financing is

$$V_L = V_U + \left[1 - \frac{(1 - 0.4)(1 - 0.12)}{(1 - 0.30)} \right] D$$

$$= V_U + 0.2457D.$$

Thus, it appears that the presence of personal taxes reduces, but does not completely eliminate, the advantage of debt financing.

Trade-off Theory

Both MM and Miller did not consider the possibility that firms may go bankrupt, hence they do not bring in potential bankruptcy costs. However, bankruptcy can be quite costly, as firms in bankruptcy have very high legal and accounting expenses plus a hard time retaining customers, suppliers, and employees. Moreover, bankruptcy often forces firms to liquidate or sell assets for less than they would be worth if the firms continued operations.

Note, too, that the *threat of bankruptcy*, not just bankruptcy per se, produces these problems. Key employees jump ship, suppliers refuse to grant credit, customers seek more stable suppliers, and lenders demand higher interest rates to compensate them for the additional risk and impose more restrictive loan covenants if potential bankruptcy looms.[6]

Trade-Off Theory
States that firms trade off the benefits of debt financing against higher interest rates and bankruptcy costs. A levered firm's value is equal to the value of an unlevered firm plus the value of any side effects, including the benefits of the interest tax shield minus the costs associated with potential financial distress.

These factors led to the development of "the **trade-off theory** of leverage," in which firms trade off the benefits of debt financing (favorable corporate tax treatment) against higher interest rates and bankruptcy-related costs. In essence, the trade-off theory says that the value of a levered firm is equal to the value of an unlevered firm plus the value of any side effects, which include the interest tax shield less the costs associated with potential financial distress. Figure 13-1 gives a graphic summary of the trade-off theory. Here are some observations:

1. Under the assumptions of Modigliani-Miller with corporate taxes, a firm's value will be maximized if it uses virtually 100 percent debt, and the line labeled "MM Result Incorporating the Effects of Corporate Taxation" in Figure 13-1 illustrates the relationship between value and debt under their assumptions.

---

[6]An interesting effect of bankruptcy on customers occurred in the airline industry a few years ago. Laker Airlines declared bankruptcy when one of its planes, full of passengers, was en route from London to New York. The pilot was ordered to return to London so Laker's creditors could seize the plane. That incident hurt weaker airlines worldwide, as passengers turned toward stronger companies. Those declining sales led to further bankruptcies. Similar situations have occurred with regard to suppliers. Boeing Aircraft once had hundreds of millions of dollars' worth of partially completed planes hung up because one of its suppliers went bankrupt and was unable to provide an essential part. Thereafter, Boeing checked suppliers carefully before contracting with them to provide essential components. So, financial strength can definitely affect operating income.

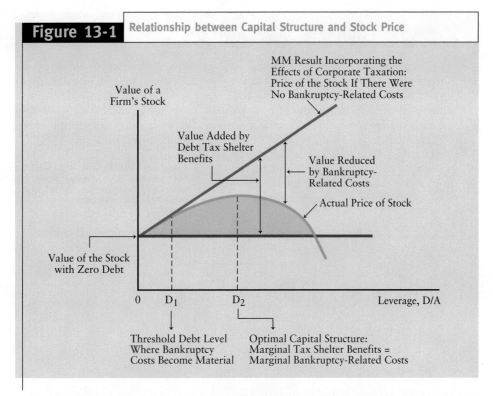

Figure 13-1 Relationship between Capital Structure and Stock Price

MM Result Incorporating the
Effects of Corporate Taxation:
Price of the Stock If There Were
No Bankruptcy-Related Costs

Value of a
Firm's Stock

Value Added by
Debt Tax Shelter
Benefits

Value Reduced
by Bankruptcy-
Related Costs

Actual Price of Stock

Value of the Stock
with Zero Debt

0   D_1 D_2 Leverage, D/A

Threshold Debt Level
Where Bankruptcy
Costs Become Material

Optimal Capital Structure:
Marginal Tax Shelter Benefits =
Marginal Bankruptcy-Related Costs

2. There is some threshold level of debt, labeled D_1 in Figure 13-1, below which the probability of bankruptcy is so low as to be immaterial. Beyond D_1, however, bankruptcy-related costs become increasingly important, and they reduce the tax benefits of debt at an increasing rate. In the range from D_1 to D_2, bankruptcy-related costs reduce but do not completely offset the tax benefits of debt, so the stock price rises (but at a decreasing rate) as the debt ratio increases. However, beyond D_2, bankruptcy-related costs exceed the tax benefits, so from this point on increasing the debt ratio lowers firm value. Therefore, D_2 is the optimal capital structure. Of course, D_1 and D_2 vary from firm to firm and over time, depending on firms' business risks and bankruptcy costs.

3. While theoretical and empirical work support the general shape of the curve in Figure 13-1, this graph must be taken as an approximation, not as an exact curve.

Asymmetric Information
The situation in which managers have different (better) information about firms' prospects than do investors.

Pecking Order
The idea that firms have a preference order for raising capital, first using retained earnings, then debt, and new stock only as a last resort.

While there are other extensions of these basic ideas, such as the **asymmetric information** and **pecking order** theories, this discussion gives a theoretical outline of capital structure theory.[7] If you find this discussion of capital structure theory imprecise, you are not alone. In truth, no one knows how to precisely identify a firm's optimal capital structure or how to measure capital structure's effects on stock prices and the cost of capital. In practice, capital structure decisions are made using a combination of judgment and numerical analysis.

SELF-TEST QUESTIONS

What were the original assumptions of MM's paper? Are they realistic? How are they important?

Why does the MM theory with corporate taxes lead to an optimal capital structure of 100 percent debt?

What is the trade-off theory?

[7]For a more thorough discussion of capital structure theory see Eugene F. Brigham and Phillip R. Daves, *Intermediate Financial Management*, 8th edition (Mason, OH: South-Western Publishing, 2004), Chapters 14 and 15.

TAKING A LOOK AT GLOBAL CAPITAL STRUCTURES

To what extent does capital structure vary across different countries? The following table, which is taken from a study by Raghuram Rajan and Luigi Zingales, both of the University of Chicago, shows the median debt ratios of firms in the largest industrial countries.

Rajan and Zingales also show that there is considerable variation in capital structures among firms within each of the seven countries. However, they also show that capital structures for the firms in each country are generally determined by a similar set of factors: firm size, profitability, market-to-book ratio, and the ratio of fixed assets to total assets. All in all, the Rajan-Zingales study suggests that the points developed in this chapter apply to firms around the globe.

Source: Raghuram G. Rajan and Luigi Zingales, "What Do We Know about Capital Structure? Some Evidence from International Data," *Journal of Finance,* Vol. 50, no. 5, December 1995, 1421–1460. Used with permission.

Median Percentage of Debt to Total Assets in Different Countries

COUNTRY	BOOK VALUE DEBT RATIO
Canada	32%
France	18
Germany	11
Italy	21
Japan	21
United Kingdom	10
United States	25

GLOBAL COMPANIES AND CAPITAL STRUCTURE

The capital structure theories just outlined were developed in the United States, and they are intended to describe the optimal capital structure for companies whose shares are traded in a mature, liquid, and highly efficient capital market like in North America. Are they equally applicable in countries that do not have such efficient and liquid capital markets? If a multinational company operates in many different countries, should it try to find the optimal capital structure for each subsidiary, or should it only be concerned with the capital structure of the consolidated company? In the following sections we attempt to answer these questions.

Optimum Capital Structures in Different Countries

If we look at capital structures in firms around the world, greater differences are observed from country to country than among industries within a given country. This is due to country-specific factors that make the use of debt more or less useful in different countries. Some of these environmental factors include the following:

1. *Cultural characteristics (particularly toward risk aversion).* Investors in different countries differ significantly in their willingness to assume risk, and this translates into more or less aggressive capital structures.[8] In segmented capital markets, these culturally defined dissimilarities result in different market risk premiums in different countries.

---

[8]See Geerte Hofstede, *Culture's Consequences: International Differences in Work-Related Values* (Beverly Hills: Sage Publications, 1980), for a description of these ideas.

2. *Corporate governance and agency costs.* Earlier in the book, we described two types of corporate governance—shareholder based and bank based. Information asymmetries, and thus agency costs, are thought to be higher in shareholder-based governance systems (like those in the United States and United Kingdom) than in bank-based systems (like those in Germany and Japan), so different capital structures would be expected.

3. *The breadth and depth of local equity markets.* In many countries, stock markets are not very efficient, making it challenging to raise capital through new stock issues. Capital structures in these countries tend to be skewed toward higher debt ratios.

4. *Tax policy.* According to the MM theories, higher tax rates make debt more valuable to a company because of the interest tax shelter. While the trade-off theory suggests that other side effects offset this advantage for higher debt levels, the curve in Figure 13-1 reaches a maximum (the optimal capital structure) at a larger debt ratio when tax rates are higher.

5. *Government policies and regulation.* Some countries are more concerned about employment and social stability than economic efficiency, and their policies favor continuity and discourage bankruptcy except in extreme circumstances. (See the box titled, "The French Help Again.") For instance, South Korea is infamous for propping up ailing chaebols rather than letting market forces determine which survive and which go bankrupt. When the government intervenes in this way, the usual restraints on excessive debt do not operate as they would in open markets.

Depending on the mix of environmental factors, managerial risk aversion, and industry practices within its home country, a particular company might have a relatively high or low consolidated debt ratio. Therefore, when an MNE operates in a foreign market, its local competitors may have very different attitudes toward risk and thus capital structures, and far more or less debt than the parent wants to use. This raises the issue of using local capital structures for different operating units versus financing all subsidiaries with the same debt/equity mix.

Local versus Global Capital Structure

If each country has distinct capital structure tendencies, and if these tendencies vary across countries, should an MNE try to conform to local norms for its various subsidiaries? The answer varies by situation, depends on several economic and political factors, and may not always provide clear-cut policy guidance. However, because our goal is to maximize firm value, the best capital structure is the one that maximizes the value of the entire MNE in its home market. Investors typically focus on the consolidated capital structure, translated into market values, so the consolidated structure should be of primary concern.[9] Factors supporting this conclusion include the following:

1. Creditors generally expect the parent to guarantee debt issued by subsidiaries in other countries. This is often formalized in the bond indenture, so subsidiary borrowings are really the obligations of the parent. Even if there is no legal responsibility to guarantee the subsidiary's debt, most companies feel compelled to do so because of the negative signals sent to capital markets if

---

[9]Recall that accountants use historical costs, not market values, when they develop the balance sheet. However, unless a firm is in imminent danger of bankruptcy, the market value of its debt is normally close to its book value, and for publicly traded companies it is easy to multiply shares outstanding times the stock price to find the value of the equity. Therefore, sophisticated investors, who really determine stock prices, can easily translate a book value capital structure into the more relevant market value structure.

THE FRENCH HELP AGAIN

The European Union Commission recently launched an investigation into the French government's cancellation of debt owed by Bull S.A., one of the world's 10 largest suppliers of information systems. In 2002, France loaned Bull €450 million. The EUC approved this controversial emergency loan, provided that the company repaid it no later than June 2003. The loan was never repaid, despite the EUC's stern requests that France recover the money, so in November 2003 France decided to forgive 90 percent of the loan.

This is not the first time the French have come to the computer company's rescue. In 1993, France spent €1.3 billion ($1.61 billion) to bail out Bull, and over the prior decade it loaned the firm an additional $2.5 billion. Nor is Bull the only company the government has bailed out. Recently, France bailed out France Telecom, Air France, and Alstom (an engineering firm). Thus, France has a history of propping up weak companies rather than letting market forces determine survival.

Now the French government again hopes to keep Bull alive with a proposed aid package worth €520 million (roughly $631 million), which would begin in January 2005. Under the terms of the deal, French Telecom and Japanese computer company NEC (each owns 16.9 percent of Bull's shares) will contribute €7.5 million ($9.3 million), a German insurer (a Bull client) will provide €3 million ($3.7 million), French insurer AXA will invest €9 million ($11.1 million), and 350 employees will raise €6 million ($7.4 million). Bull would

use part of this aid to repay the unforgiven 10 percent of the 2002 government loan. Under European Union aid rules, governments can only grant subsidies to businesses that have not received state aid during the last 10 years. Because Bull's bailout will not start until January 2005, the plan would meet this criterion.

The generous terms of the deal have continued to strain the already rocky relationship between the EUC and France, and days after France's loan restructuring announcement, the Commission began proceedings to sue the French government for failure to recover the loan. Unfortunately, France is notorious for stretching, or even breaking, European rules governing state subsidies to financially struggling companies, so the EUC also plans to look into France's bailouts of other companies.

Students may believe that only developing countries implement fiscal policies that interfere with market forces due to concerns over their own economy. However, this story demonstrates that at certain times even a developed country will interfere with market forces in the name of its own economic stability. Obviously, this government help hurts IBM, Dell, and computer companies in other nations, including those in Europe.

Sources: "EU Opens Investigation into French Govt Aid to Bull," *Dow Jones Newswires*, March 16, 2004, **http://online.wsj.com**; and "French Government Looks to Push through Bull Rescue Plan," *Computer Business Review Online*, March 8, 2004, **http://www.cbronline.com**.

the subsidiary defaults. Raising capital with future debt issues by any subsidiary would be difficult if it defaults.

2. If the MNE decided to optimize each subsidiary's local capital structure, then subsidiaries from countries with a high tolerance for debt would not necessarily be offset by other more conservatively financed units. This method could conflict with the "whole firm" approach, which could increase the cost of capital and reduce the firm's value.

3. Competitive advantage theories suggest that MNEs receive benefits from their global network that domestic companies cannot duplicate. Why should the MNE surrender its global financing advantage just because local subsidiaries use different leverage than local companies?

4. Local governments often see MNEs as their connection to international capital markets, supplying outside capital to subsidize perhaps meager domestic resources. Companies that finance subsidiaries mainly with local debt do not provide this benefit, and such **shell corporations** may be perceived by the local government as lacking a strong commitment to the country. This may lead the local government to penalize the company in various ways.

Shell Corporation
The situation in which a foreign company raises most of its subsidiary's capital in the local market.

Point 4 is probably more valid than the others because the first three are based on questionable assumptions. Others have suggested that conforming to local capital structure norms helps top management compare managerial performance in each subsidiary with that of its local peers. This might be true to some extent, but the proper metrics for such comparisons should be based on operating assets and operating income, and financing should be taken out of the equation. For example, the Economic Value Added (EVA) approach should use a global cost of capital (which we discussed in Chapter 10) instead of a local one, again suggesting the local capital structure is irrelevant.

However, in some countries, capital is scarce and more expensive than risk considerations warrant. In such cases, conforming to local norms would lead to the rejection of positive NPV projects based on global capital costs. If an MNE has a competitive financing advantage, it might invest in projects that return less than the local required return, as long as they add value to the company. You should carefully evaluate arguments justifying a local optimal capital structure because they might imply not taking advantage of a competitive advantage.

SELF-TEST QUESTIONS

Identify some of the factors attributable to varying capital structures across countries.
What is an MNE's best capital structure? What factors support your answer?

THE TARGET CAPITAL STRUCTURE

Target Capital Structure
The mix of debt, preferred stock, and common equity with which the firm plans to raise capital.

From the preceding discussion, we conclude that there is an optimal, but hard to quantify, combination of debt and equity financing. This optimum might be defined as a precise, specific debt ratio or as a range where the "best" capital structure is thought to be somewhere within the range. Debt and equity should be measured in market value, not book value, terms. Consistent with this optimum, whether global or local, the firm should set a **target capital structure** for the consolidated company. This target can change over time as conditions change, but at any given moment, management should have a specific target in mind. If the actual debt ratio is below the target level, or outside the optimal range, new capital should be raised as debt, whereas if the actual debt ratio is above the target, equity should be used.

Optimal Capital Structure
The mix of debt, preferred stock, and common equity that strikes a balance between risk and return so as to maximize the firm's stock price.

Capital structure policy involves a trade-off between risk and return. Using more debt increases the risk borne by shareholders, but more debt generally leads to a higher expected return on equity. Higher risk exerts a downward pressure on a stock's price, but a higher expected rate of return pushes it up. *Therefore, the optimal capital structure is the one that strikes a balance between risk and return so as to maximize the stock price.*

Five primary factors influence capital structure decisions:

1. *Business risk.* This is the risk inherent in the firm's operations if it used no debt. In general, the greater the firm's business risk, the lower its optimal debt ratio. For a global company, business risk in different countries varies, but since these risks are not perfectly correlated, diversification tends to lower business risk vis-à-vis the risks of subsidiaries operating independently. This is another factor that provides competitive advantage to multinational corporations.
2. *The firm's tax position.* A major reason for using debt is that interest is tax deductible, which lowers the effective cost of debt. However, if most of a firm's income is already sheltered from taxes by depreciation tax shields, by interest on currently outstanding debt, or by tax loss carry-forwards, its tax rate will be low already, so additional debt will not be as advantageous as it

would be to a firm with a higher effective tax rate. We also saw in Chapter 11 that concessionary, or low, tax rates in other countries may not translate into tax advantages in the United States. If income is repatriated to the United States, the IRS requires the company to pay taxes up to the appropriate U.S. rate. Only if the company keeps earnings offshore does the firm benefit from concessionary tax rates.

3. *Financial flexibility.* The ability to raise capital on reasonable terms under adverse conditions is important. Corporate treasurers know that a steady supply of capital is necessary for stable operations, which is vital for long-term success. They also know that when money is tight, or when a firm is experiencing operating problems, banks and other suppliers of capital favor companies with strong balance sheets. Therefore, both the potential need for funds and the consequences of a funds shortage influence the target capital structure—the greater the probable need for capital and the worse the consequences of a capital shortage, the stronger the balance sheet should be. Companies with access to international capital markets have a competitive advantage over purely domestic companies because their potential supply of capital is greater. Even if one unit of an MNE experiences financial stress, other units of the company may still be able to acquire capital easily. Hence, MNEs generally have more financial flexibility than purely domestic firms.

4. *Managerial conservatism or aggressiveness.* Some managers are more aggressive than others, hence some firms are more inclined to use leverage in an effort to boost profits. While managerial risk aversion varies from firm to firm within given countries, it may be exaggerated by MNEs that employ managers from host countries or employ third-country nationals. This factor does not affect the true optimal, or value-maximizing, capital structure, but it could influence the manager-determined target capital structure.

5. *Investor risk aversion.* The costs of both debt and equity are determined in the marketplace by investors, and, like managers, investors in different countries exhibit different degrees of risk aversion. However, as capital markets become more integrated, and shares of a company's stock are traded on multiple national exchanges, investors' risk aversion in different countries may converge, leading to similar views regarding the required returns on different types of securities and the collective view of an appropriate capital structure.

These five factors help determine the target capital structure, but operating conditions can cause the actual capital structure to vary from the target. For example, a company may have a target debt ratio of 50 percent, but unforeseen circumstances may force it to write down its common equity, which raises its debt ratio well above the target level. Presumably, the company will in the future return its capital structure to the target level.

SELF-TEST QUESTIONS
What is meant by the term "target capital structure"? Is it a constant for a particular firm? Explain.

Should the target be based on book value or market value data?

What are five factors that influence capital structure decisions?

In what sense does capital structure policy involve a trade-off between risk and return?

BUSINESS AND FINANCIAL RISK

In Chapter 5, we examined risk from the viewpoint of a stock investor, and we distinguished between *market risk*, which is measured by the firm's beta coefficient, and *stand-alone risk*, which includes both market and diversifiable risk. Now we introduce two new dimensions of risk: (1) *business risk*, or the riskiness of the stock if the firm uses no debt, and (2) *financial risk*, which is the additional risk borne by common shareholders if the firm does use debt.[10]

Conceptually, each company has some risk inherent in its operations—this is its business risk. If it uses any debt, then it partitions its investors into two groups and concentrates its business risk on one class—the common stockholders. The *additional* risk the stockholders face is the firm's financial risk. Naturally, a leveraged firm's shareholders will demand more compensation for bearing the additional (financial) risk, so the required rate of return on common equity increases with the use of debt.

Business Risk

Business Risk
The riskiness inherent in the firm's operations if it uses no debt.

As noted earlier, **business risk** is the risk common shareholders would face if the firm had no debt. Business risk arises from uncertainty in the firm's operating cash flows, which means uncertainty about operating profit and capital investment requirements. In other words, we do not know how large consolidated operating profits will be, nor do we know how much we will have to invest to develop new products, build new plants, and so forth. The return on invested capital (ROIC) combines these two sources of uncertainty, and its variability (σ_{ROIC}) can be used to measure business risk on a stand-alone basis:

$$
\begin{aligned}
\text{ROIC} &= \frac{\text{NOPAT}}{\text{Invested capital}} = \frac{\text{EBIT}(1 - T)}{\text{Invested capital}} \\[2ex]
&= \frac{\substack{\text{Net income to} \\ \text{common stockholders}} + \substack{\text{After-tax} \\ \text{interest payments}}}{\text{Invested capital}}.
\end{aligned}
\tag{13-5}
$$

Here NOPAT is net operating profit after taxes, and invested capital is the required amount of operating capital, which is numerically equivalent to the sum of the consolidated firm's interest-bearing debt plus common equity. If the firm's capital requirements are stable, we can use σ_{EBIT} as an alternative measure of stand-alone business risk.

Business risk depends on a number of factors, which we describe here:

1. *Demand variability.* The more stable the demand for a firm's products, the lower its business risk. Companies operating in many countries can often offset weak sales in one country with strong sales in another, assuming there is no worldwide recession, so global diversification decreases demand variability.
2. *Sales price variability.* Firms whose products are sold in highly volatile markets are exposed to more business risk than similar firms whose output prices are more stable. Sales price variability is often associated with intense competition in a mature or declining market. Global firms that operate in markets where products are still in the high-growth phase of the business cycle are partly protected from the full effects of competitive price pressures.
3. *Input cost variability.* Firms whose input costs are relatively uncertain are exposed to a relatively high degree of business risk. Flexibility options (which we discussed in Chapter 12) add value by allowing the firm to shift to alternative inputs. Global companies that can shift sourcing, or entire production

---

[10]Preferred stock also adds to financial risk. To simplify matters, we concentrate on debt and common equity in this chapter.

processes, to other locations have a competitive advantage in stabilizing input costs when input price increases are localized.

4. *Ability to adjust output prices for changes in input costs.* Some firms are able to raise their own output prices when input costs rise. The greater the ability to adjust output prices to reflect cost conditions, the lower the business risk. MNEs do not necessarily have an advantage in the price elasticity of demand for its products. However, if the elasticity in foreign markets differs from that in domestic markets, it is possible that an advantage could exist.

5. *Ability to develop new products in a timely, cost-effective manner.* Firms in high-tech industries such as pharmaceuticals and computers depend on a constant stream of new products. The faster its products become obsolete, the greater a firm's business risk, because failure to innovate leads to declining market shares. For global companies, new-product innovation in one market translates to innovation throughout the MNE.

6. *Foreign risk exposure.* Firms that generate significant earnings overseas are subject to earnings volatility due to exchange rate fluctuations. Also, if a firm operates in a politically unstable area, it may be subject to specific political risks that negatively affect the subsidiary and the consolidated firm.

7. *The extent to which costs are fixed: operating leverage.* If a high percentage of its costs are fixed (high **operating leverage**), hence do not decline when demand falls, then the firm is exposed to higher business risk. This is true for domestic companies as well as MNEs.

Operating Leverage
The extent to which fixed costs are used in a firm's operations.

Most of these factors are partly determined by the firm's industry characteristics, but they are all somewhat subject to managerial controls. For example, most firms can stabilize both unit sales and sales prices through their marketing policies. However, this stabilization may require larger advertising expenditures and/or price concessions to obtain future commitments from customers to purchase fixed quantities at fixed prices. Similarly, firms can reduce future input cost variability by negotiating long-term labor and materials supply contracts, but they may have to pay above market prices to obtain these contracts. Many firms also use hedging techniques to reduce exchange rate risk.

Financial Risk

Financial Risk
An increase in stockholders' risk, over and above the firm's basic business risk, resulting from the use of financial leverage.

Financial Leverage
The extent to which fixed-income securities (debt and pre-ferred stock) are used in a firm's capital structure.

Financial risk is the additional risk common shareholders bear as a result of debt financing. If a firm uses debt (**financial leverage**), this concentrates its business risk on the common stockholders. The concentration of business risk occurs because creditors, who receive fixed interest payments independent of operating earnings, bear very little of the business risk.[11]

To illustrate the concentration of business risk, we can use the following example. Assume that to date a company with $200,000 of capital has never used debt, but its treasurer is now considering a change in the capital structure. In addition, assume that only two financing choices are being considered—remaining at zero debt or shifting to $100,000 debt and $100,000 book equity.

First, focus on Section I of Table 13-1, which assumes that there are only five possible states of demand for the product and that the company uses no debt. Because there is no debt, interest is also zero, hence pre-tax income is equal to EBIT. Taxes are deducted to obtain net income, which is then divided by the $200,000 of book equity to calculate ROE. Note that the company receives a tax credit if the demand is either terrible or poor (the two scenarios where net income is negative). We assume

---

[11]Holders of corporate debt generally bear some business risk, because they generally lose some of their investment if the firm goes bankrupt.

that the company's losses can be carried back to offset income earned in prior years. ROE ranges from −18 percent under terrible conditions to 42 percent if times are wonderful. We then multiply the ROE at each sales level by its probability to calculate the expected ROE, which is 12 percent.

Section II shows the same demand states as in Section I; that is, Columns 1, 2, and 3 are unchanged, but now $100,000 of 10 percent debt is used. Because neither demand nor operating costs are affected by this financing decision, the EBIT values shown in Column 3 are identical in the two cases. However, the $100,000 of debt results in an interest expense of $10,000, which we show in Column 4. This interest must be paid regardless of the economy—otherwise, the company will be forced into bankruptcy and the stockholders will be wiped out. Column 5 shows pre-tax income, Column 6 the applicable taxes, and Column 7 gives the resulting net income. When net income is divided by book equity—which now will be only $100,000 because

TABLE 13-1 Effects of Financial Leverage: Firm Financed with Zero Debt or with $100,000 of Debt

Section I. Zero Debt

Debt $0
Book equity $200,000

Demand for Product (1)	Probability (2)	EBIT (3)	Interest (4)	Pre-Tax Income (5)	Taxes (40%) (6)	Net Income (7)	ROE (8)
Terrible	0.05	($60,000)	$0	($60,000)	($24,000)	($36,000)	−18.0%
Poor	0.20	(20,000)	0	(20,000)	(8,000)	(12,000)	−6.0
Normal	0.50	40,000	0	40,000	16,000	24,000	12.0
Good	0.20	100,000	0	100,000	40,000	60,000	30.0
Wonderful	0.05	140,000	0	140,000	56,000	84,000	42.0
Expected value		$ 40,000	$0	$ 40,000	$16,000	$24,000	12.0%
Standard deviation							14.8%
Coefficient of variation							1.23

Section II. $100,000 of Debt

Debt $100,000
Book equity $100,000
Interest rate   10%

Demand for Product (1)	Probability (2)	EBIT (3)	Interest (4)	Pre-Tax Income (5)	Taxes (40%) (6)	Net Income (7)	ROE (8)
Terrible	0.05	($60,000)	$10,000	($70,000)	($28,000)	($42,000)	−42.0%
Poor	0.20	(20,000)	10,000	(30,000)	(12,000)	(18,000)	−18.0
Normal	0.50	40,000	10,000	30,000	12,000	18,000	18.0
Good	0.20	100,000	10,000	90,000	36,000	54,000	54.0
Wonderful	0.05	140,000	10,000	130,000	52,000	78,000	78.0
Expected value		$ 40,000	$10,000	$ 30,000	$ 12,000	$18,000	18.0%
Standard deviation							29.6%
Coefficient of variation							1.65

Assumptions:
1. Sales and operating costs, hence EBIT, are not affected by the financing decision. Therefore, EBIT under both financing plans is identical.
2. All losses can be carried back to offset income in the prior year.

$100,000 of the $200,000 total capital requirement was obtained as debt—we find the ROEs under each demand state. They range from −42 percent to 78 percent, with an expected ROE of 18 percent.

Typically, debt increases the common stockholders' expected return, but it also increases their risk. This situation holds with our example—financial leverage raises the expected ROE from 12 to 18 percent, but it also increases risk, as measured by the standard deviation, which increases from 14.8 to 29.6 percent, and the coefficient of variation, which increases from 1.23 to 1.65.[12]

We see, then, that using financial leverage has both good and bad effects: Higher leverage increases the expected ROE, but it also increases risk.

SELF-TEST QUESTIONS

What is business risk, and how is it measured?

What are some determinants of business risk?

What is financial risk, and how does it arise?

Explain this statement: "Using financial leverage has both good and bad effects."

CHECKLIST FOR CAPITAL STRUCTURE DECISIONS

Firms generally consider the following factors when making capital structure decisions:

1. *Business risk.* A firm with relatively little business risk can safely take on more debt and incur higher fixed charges than a company with more volatile operating income. Many food companies, because of stable demand and low operating leverage, have historically been able to use more financial leverage than heavy equipment companies. Similarly, global companies that operate in countries whose business cycles are not perfectly correlated tend to have more stable sales than their purely domestic counterparts, so they can safely employ more leverage.

2. *Asset structure.* Firms whose assets are suitable as security for loans tend to use debt rather heavily. General-purpose assets that can be used by many businesses make good collateral, whereas special-purpose assets do not. Thus, real estate companies are usually highly leveraged, while technology companies are not. Global companies in extractive industries with large reserves of untapped resources—such as oil, mining, and agricultural firms—can afford to use more debt than manufacturing companies.

3. *Growth rate.* Other things the same, faster-growing firms must rely more heavily on external capital. Further, the flotation costs involved in selling common stock exceed those incurred when selling debt, which encourages rapidly growing firms to rely more heavily on debt. At the same time, however, these firms often face greater uncertainty, which tends to reduce their willingness to use debt. Global companies in this position tend to concentrate funds in strategic locations from which they can be deployed quickly and with minimum transaction and exchange rate costs.

4. *Profitability.* It is often observed that firms with very high rates of return on investment use relatively little debt. Although there is no theoretical rationale for this empirical fact, one practical explanation is that very profitable

---

[12]See Chapter 5 for a review of the standard deviation and coefficient of variation calculations. Recall that the advantage of the coefficient of variation is that it permits better comparisons when the expected values vary, as they do here for the two capital structures.

firms such as Intel, Microsoft, and Coca-Cola simply do not need much debt financing. Their high rates of return enable them to finance mostly with internally generated funds and still maintain a healthy growth rate.

5. *Taxes.* Interest is a tax deductible expense in most countries, and deductions are most valuable to firms with high tax rates. Therefore, the higher a firm's tax rate, the greater the advantage of using debt.

6. *Control.* The effect of debt versus stock on a management's control position can influence capital structure. If management currently has voting control (more than 50 percent of the shares) but is not in a position to purchase any more stock, then it may choose debt for new financings. However, if too little debt is used, management runs the risk of a takeover. On the other hand, management may decide to use equity if the firm's financial situation is so weak that the use of debt might subject it to serious risk of default, because if the firm goes into default, the managers will almost surely lose their jobs. Thus, control considerations could lead to the use of either debt or equity because the type of capital that best protects management will vary from situation to situation. In any event, if management is at all insecure, it will consider the control issue.

7. *Management attitudes.* Because no one can prove that one capital structure will lead to higher stock prices than another, management can exercise its own judgment about the firm's proper capital structure. Some managements tend to be more conservative than others, and thus use less debt than the average firm in their industry, whereas aggressive managements use more debt in their quest for higher profits.

8. *Lender and rating agency attitudes.* Regardless of managers' own analyses of the proper leverage factors for their firms, lenders' and rating agencies' attitudes frequently influence capital structure decisions. In the majority of cases, the corporation discusses its capital structure with lenders and rating agencies and gives much weight to their advice. Bond ratings play less of a role in eurobond markets, but recently more issues are being rated than ever before. Some analysts are predicting that this trend will accelerate causing euromarkets to look more like the United States and United Kingdom markets in the future.

9. *Market conditions.* Stock and bond market conditions undergo both long- and short-run changes that can have an important bearing on a firm's optimal capital structure. For example, during a recent credit crunch, the junk bond market dried up, and there was simply no market at a "reasonable" interest rate for new, long-term, non-investment-grade bonds. Therefore, low-rated companies in need of capital were forced to go to the stock market or to the short-term debt market, regardless of their target capital structures. When conditions eased, however, these companies sold bonds to get their capital structures back on target. Global firms have an advantage over domestic companies in this regard because they can raise debt in many national markets as well as in the euromarkets. These markets are not perfectly correlated, so when conditions in the United States limit the ability of companies to finance with long-term debt, MNEs may be able to obtain financing in the eurodollar bond market.

10. *The firm's internal condition.* A firm's own internal condition can also have a bearing on its target capital structure. For example, suppose a firm has just successfully completed an R&D program, and it forecasts higher earnings in the immediate future. However, the new earnings are not yet anticipated by investors, hence are not reflected in its stock price. This company would not want to issue stock—it would prefer to finance with debt until the higher

earnings materialize and are reflected in its stock price. Then it could sell common stock, retire the debt, and return to its target capital structure.

11. *Financial flexibility.* Firms with profitable investment opportunities need to be able to fund them. An astute corporate treasurer made this statement to the authors:

> Our company can earn a lot more money from good capital budgeting and operating decisions than from good financing decisions. Indeed, we are not sure exactly how financing decisions affect our stock price, but we know for sure that having to turn down a promising venture because funds are not available will reduce our long-run profitability. For this reason, my primary goal as treasurer is to always be in a position to raise the capital needed to support operations.
>
> We also know that when times are good, we can raise capital with either stocks or bonds, but when times are bad, suppliers of capital are much more willing to make funds available if we give them a secured position, and this means debt. Further, when we issue new stock, this sends a negative "signal" to investors, so stock sales by a mature company such as ours are not desirable.

12. *Market values.* Our focus throughout this chapter has been on *market values,* not book values. Managers should maximize market values, not book values, so capital structure theory is developed only in a market value context. In Chapter 10, we stated that the weights used to find the WACC should be based on the target capital structure, which is a market value concept, and not on accounting values. The reason for that choice was based on the thought process set forth in this chapter—the *optimal capital structure* is the one that maximizes the firm's *market value,* that structure should be estimated and then used as the *target capital structure,* and the target structure should be used to set the *weights for the* WACC. Before MM's work in the 1950s and 1960s, people generally focused on accounting book values and found the WACC using book values. That was wrong, and it led to seriously incorrect WACC estimates and to incorrect capital budgeting decisions. This is yet another example of how advances in finance theory have led to better financial decisions.

Reserve Borrowing Capacity
The ability to borrow money at a reasonable cost when good investment opportunities arise. Firms often use less debt than specified by the MM optimal capital structure in "normal" times to ensure that they can obtain debt capital later if necessary.

Putting all these thoughts together gives rise to the goal of *maintaining financial flexibility,* which, from an operational viewpoint, means *maintaining adequate reserve borrowing capacity.* Determining an "adequate" **reserve borrowing capacity** is judgmental, but it clearly depends on the factors discussed in this chapter, including the firm's forecasted need for funds, predicted capital market conditions around the world, management's confidence in its forecasts, and the consequences of a capital shortage.

How does sales stability affect a firm's target capital structure?

How do the types of assets used affect a firm's capital structure?

How do taxes affect a firm's target capital structure?

How do lender and rating agency attitudes affect a firm's capital structure?

How does the firm's internal condition affect its target capital structure?

What is "financial flexibility," and how is it affected by a high debt ratio?

DIVIDEND DISTRIBUTIONS IN THE GLOBAL FIRM

In a global environment, dividend policy has two distinct aspects: internal payout policy within the corporate network, which merely transfers funds from subsidiaries to the parent to make them available for reallocation to other units or other purposes, and external payout policy, from the firm to its shareholders. In domestic

An excellent source of recent dividend news releases for major corporations is available at the Web site of Corporate Financials Online at http:// www.cfonews.com/. By clicking the down arrow of the "News Category" box to the left of the screen, students may select "Dividends" to obtain a list of companies with dividend news. Click on any company listed and you will see its latest dividend news.

finance, internal payout policy is not much of an issue because payment blockages, capital and foreign exchange controls, and political risk are not encountered. However, in global finance, these issues are critical. Once the internal policies have been established, based mainly on the strategic and operating realities of doing business in many different countries, the parent company can turn its attention to the distribution of cash to its shareholders.

Internal Corporate Dividend Policy

Within the global corporate network there is an inherent conflict between preserving corporate flexibility and maintaining the value of monetary assets versus financing growth in ongoing operations. Monetary assets held in countries whose currencies are expected to devalue will lose value unless they can be changed into hard currencies. Thus, it is a good idea to remove monetary assets from such countries. Moreover, if there is a chance that funds may be blocked in the future, this too calls for moving monetary assets to other countries where blockage is not likely. These factors create a preference for a high internal dividend payout from subsidiaries in at least some countries.[13] Of course, host governments may not care for such policies and may institute constraints on payouts, thereby giving rise to even greater apprehension about blockages. There are also tax implications for the payout decision. If the foreign tax rate is lower than the U.S. rate, additional taxes will be due when dividends are repatriated to a U.S. parent. Also, many countries impose withholding taxes on repatriated dividends, lowering their value even more. Even if foreign tax rates are higher than in the United States, leading to a foreign tax credit in excess of the U.S. tax obligation for those cash flows, the company may not be able to use the entire credit and may be forced to carry it forward to a future tax year when it is less valuable.

A further complication arises if the foreign subsidiary is not wholly owned by the MNE, a fairly common situation. Local minority interests and joint venture partners may want to receive steady and predictable dividends. Thus, the MNE's interest in shifting monetary assets to other countries to maximize its own position must be weighed against the legitimate desires of these other owners to receive cash dividends.

MNEs also need to finance their local subsidiaries' growth, and there are usually good reasons to use internally generated equity and local debt financing. Internal equity can come from the local operation itself or from earnings generated by units in other countries where the need for funds is not as great. Of course, this means that dividend policies for all countries must be considered as an integrated group when setting the internal dividend policy. Taxes, including withholding taxes and foreign tax credits, blockages, expected future exchange rate movements, and local capital requirements constrain actions to preserve value and finance global operations at the lowest possible cost. We will consider the effects of tax issues in greater detail in Chapter 16.

Parent Dividend Policy

The parent company's policy with regard to paying dividends to its stockholders must be established simultaneously with the internal policies regarding funds transfers within the overall corporation. The central issue here is this: Do shareholders prefer dividends or reinvestment, or perhaps a combination of the two? This question has interested finance professionals for years, and the following sections summarize research on the subject.

---

[13]Also, other devices to remove funds such as license and management fees will be used in addition to dividends.

IS IT TIME TO START PAYING A DIVIDEND?

By July 2003, many European telecommunications companies had rebounded from the slump that had been plaguing the global telecommunications industry, and they were expected to generate tens of billions of dollars worth of cash in the very near future. What should these again cash-rich firms do with their funds? Good question. Managers might be tempted to use the influx of cash to finance acquisitions and other investments, but shareholders still felt the sting of the market collapse only a couple of years earlier and wanted dividends.

Several companies, having controlled their debt through the crisis, had giant war chests of cash, and their CEOs were ready to fund a new wave of acquisitions. However, many investors were still recovering from the overly ambitious expansions of the 1990s that left them drowning in losses. These investors want the firms to distribute their excess funds, either as dividends or through stock repurchases. Inefficient uses of funds in the past had conditioned investors not to give free rein to companies that wanted to use cash to fund acquisitions.

In the United States, Microsoft has initiated a dividend, and Citigroup increased its dividend payout by 75 percent. In Europe, telecommunications companies are expected to generate a net inflow of $47 billion in cash, but it remains to be seen what they will do with the money. Spanish Telefonica SA expects to bring in more than €6 billion in cash (before dividends); Orange SA expects to generate €14 billion in cash (before interest, taxes, and license payments); and even Deutsche Telekom AG and France Telecom, once in financial dire straits, can now see the light at the end of the tunnel. Still, Orange SA is showing interest in expanding on three continents, and Vodaphone Group PLC continues to funnel money into risky, unproven wireless technology.

In the late 1990s, many European companies had generated even larger debts than their U.S. counterparts but have been able to recover more quickly (mostly due to lighter competition in Europe). In 2000, the European telecommunications industry suffered from a $71 billion cash outflow, but by 2003 that had turned around to a $47 billion cash inflow. During the 1990s, the European telecom giants had gobbled up cell-phone companies at sky-high prices and invested in new technology and equipment. A vivid example of this excess was the Deutsche Telekom acquisition of Voicestream Wireless Corp (then the sixth-leading U.S. mobile phone service provider) for a whopping €39 billion.

As the market unraveled in 2001, many telecom executives were replaced with cost-cutting specialists, whose sole mission was to revive the companies' finances. A few years later, with the cost-cutting measures in full swing, the European companies find themselves with traditional fixed-line phone businesses that are spinning off lots of cash, and they must decide what to do with this newfound cash. Many investors are calling for a return to the 1980s, when telephone companies such as AT&T were boring but paid out great dividends. Still smarting from the last several years, investors doubt the telecom industry's ability to recognize successful new-growth opportunities. Approximately 80 percent of the European population already uses cell phones, and British regulators are calling for a 15 percent annual cut in charges for mobile handsets. All this, coupled with plummeting land-line telephone rates, suggests that cash flows might be losing some steam.

Most European telecommunications companies have never paid a dividend, but the time to do so may be approaching. Vodafone officers have been asking investors what they want done with the cash, and in meetings with T. Rowe Price executives the Vodafone heads asked whether they preferred dividends or a share buyback. T. Rowe Price telecom analyst Dale West responded, "Our answer to them was the form is not important, but the timing and the amount are important. Basically . . . we'd like to get the money sooner rather than later." A Vodafone spokeswoman stated that some investors still want the cash spent on expansion, but for many, dividends are a higher priority. Even so, some of the new telecom executives still plan further expansion.

Source: "Europe's Telecoms Bring in Cash, and Investors Want a Share," *The Wall Street Journal,* July 21, 2003, **http://www.wsj.com.**

Target Payout Ratio
The percentage of net income paid out as cash distributions (dividends and/or stock repurchases) as desired by the firm.

Dividends versus Capital Gains: What Do Investors Prefer?

When deciding how much of its cash to distribute, financial managers must keep in mind that the firm's objective is to maximize shareholder value. Consequently, the **target payout ratio**—defined as the percentage of net income to be paid out as cash distributions—should be based on investors' preferences for dividends versus capi-

observed that an increase in the dividend is often accompanied by an increase in the stock price, while a dividend cut generally leads to a stock price decline. Before MM, it was argued that this indicated that investors prefer dividends to capital gains. However, MM argued differently. They noted that corporations are reluctant to cut dividends, hence they do not raise dividends unless they anticipate the higher future earnings necessary to support the higher dividends. Thus, MM argued that a higher-than-expected dividend increase is a **signal** to investors that the firm's management forecasts good future earnings. Conversely, a dividend reduction, or a smaller-than-expected increase, is a signal that management forecasts poor earnings in the future. Thus, MM argued that investors' reactions to changes in dividend policy do not show that investors prefer dividends to retained earnings. Rather, they argued that price changes following dividend actions simply indicate that dividend announcements have **information**, or **signaling**, **content**.

Like most other aspects of dividend policy, empirical studies of signaling have had mixed results. There is clearly some information content in dividend announcements. However, it is difficult to tell whether stock price changes that follow increases or decreases in dividends reflect only signaling effects or both signaling and dividend preference. Still, signaling effects should definitely be considered when a firm is contemplating a change in its dividend policy.

Clientele Effect

As we indicated earlier, different groups, or **clienteles**, of stockholders prefer different dividend payout policies. For example, retired individuals, pension funds, and university endowment funds generally prefer cash income, so they often want the firm to pay out a high percentage of its earnings. Such investors are frequently in low or even zero tax brackets, so taxes are of little concern. On the other hand, stockholders in their peak-earning years might prefer reinvestment, because they have less need for current investment income and would simply reinvest dividends received, incurring both income taxes and brokerage costs.

If a firm retains and reinvests income rather than paying dividends, those stockholders who need current income would be disadvantaged. The value of their stock might increase, but they would be forced to go to the trouble and expense of selling off some of their shares to obtain cash. Also, some institutional investors (or trustees for individuals) would be legally precluded from selling stock and then "spending capital." On the other hand, stockholders who are saving rather than spending dividends would favor the low dividend policy: the less the firm pays out in dividends, the less these stockholders will have to pay in current taxes, and the less trouble and expense they will have to go through to reinvest their after-tax dividends.[17] Therefore, investors who want current investment income should own shares in high-dividend payout firms, while investors with no need for current investment income should own shares in low-dividend payout firms. For example, investors seeking high cash income might invest in electric utilities, which had an average payout of 63 percent in 2003, while those favoring growth could invest in the software industry, which paid out only 4 percent that same year.

All this suggests that dividend policy is affected by a **clientele effect**, which means that firms cater to specific clienteles, and if a firm's dividend policy changes this could upset its clientele and have a negative impact on its stock price.[18] MM and others have argued that one clientele is as good as another, so the existence of a

Signal
An action taken by a firm's management that provides clues to investors about how management views the firm's prospects.

Information Content (Signaling) Hypothesis
The theory that investors regard dividend changes as signals of management's earnings forecasts.

Clienteles
Different groups of stockholders that prefer different dividend payout policies.

Clientele Effect
The tendency of a firm to attract a set of investors who like its dividend policy.

---

[17]The 2003 tax law changes will certainly have an effect on this argument, but it is too soon to judge the strength of its impact.

[18]For example, see R. Richardson Pettit, "Taxes, Transactions Costs and the Clientele Effect of Dividends," *Journal of Financial Economics*, December 1977, 419–436.

clientele effect does not necessarily imply that one dividend policy is better than any other. MM may be wrong, though, and neither they nor anyone else can prove that the aggregate makeup of investors permits firms to disregard clientele effects. This issue, like most others in the dividend arena, is still up in the air.

Define (1) information content and (2) the clientele effect, and explain how they may affect dividend policy.

ESTABLISHING THE DIVIDEND POLICY IN PRACTICE

Investors may or may not prefer dividends to capital gains; however, they almost certainly prefer *predictable* dividends. Given this situation, how should firms set their basic dividend policies? In particular, how should a company establish the specific percentage of earnings it will distribute, the form of this distribution, and the stability of its distributions over time? In this section, we describe how most firms answer this question.

Setting the Target Payout Ratio: The Residual Dividend Model[19]

When deciding how much cash to distribute to stockholders, two points should be kept in mind: (1) The overriding objective is to maximize shareholder value, and (2) the firm's cash flows really belong to its shareholders, so management should refrain from retaining income unless they can reinvest it at higher rates of return than shareholders could earn themselves. On the other hand, recall from Chapter 10 that internal equity (retained earnings) is cheaper than external equity (new common stock). This encourages firms to retain earnings to avoid issuing new stock.

When establishing a dividend policy, one size does not fit all. Some firms produce a lot of cash but have limited investment opportunities—this is true for firms in profitable but mature industries where few growth opportunities exist. Such firms typically distribute a large percentage of their cash to shareholders, thereby attracting investor clienteles who prefer high dividends. Other firms generate little or no excess cash but have many good investment opportunities. Such firms generally distribute little or no cash but enjoy rising earnings and stock prices, thereby attracting investors who prefer capital gains.

As Table 13-2 suggests, dividend payouts and dividend yields for large corporations vary considerably. Generally, firms in stable, cash-producing industries such as utilities, food, and tobacco pay relatively high dividends, whereas companies in rapidly growing industries such as computer software and biotechnology tend to pay lower dividends. Average dividends also differ significantly across countries. Higher payout ratios in some countries can be partially explained by lower tax rates on earnings distributed as cash dividends relative to applicable rates on reinvested income. This biases the dividend policy toward higher payouts.

For a given firm, the optimal payout ratio is a function of four factors: (1) investors' preferences for dividends versus capital gains, (2) the firm's investment opportunities, (3) its target capital structure, and (4) the availability and cost of external cap-

---

[19]The term "payout ratio" can be interpreted in two ways: (1) the conventional way, where the payout ratio means the percentage of net income paid out as cash dividends, or (2) the percentage of net income distributed to stockholders through both dividends and share repurchases. In this section, we assume that no repurchases occur. Increasingly, though, firms are using the residual model to determine "distributions to shareholders" and then making a separate decision as to the form of those distributions. Further, an increasing percentage of the distribution is in the form of share repurchases. For a discussion on repurchases refer to Brigham and Daves, *Intermediate Financial Management*, Chapter 16.

TABLE 13-2 | Dividend Payouts (March 2004)

Company	Industry/ Country Headquarters	Dividend Payout	Dividend Yield
I. Some Companies That Pay High Dividends			
Rayonier Inc.	Forestry & Wood Products/United States	87.93%	5.17%
Great Northern Iron Ore Properties	Metal Mining/United States	85.09	7.62
United Utilities PLC	Electric Utilities/United Kingdom	83.84	7.91
Flanigan's Enterprises Inc.	Restaurants/United States	81.33	4.70
Gallaher Group PLC	Tobacco/United Kingdom	77.90	4.30
Tate & Lyle PLC	Food Processing/United Kingdom	73.31	5.23
II. Some Companies That Pay Little or No Dividends			
Serona SA	Biotechnology & Drugs/Switzerland	22.04%	0.69%
Wal-Mart Stores	Retail/United States	17.71	0.89
Marriott International	Hotels & Motels/United States	14.43	0.72
Apple Computer	Computer Hardware/United States	0	0
British Airways	Airline/United Kingdom	0	0
Info Vista SA	Software & Programming/France	0	0

Source: **http://www.marketguide.com**, March 2004.

Residual Dividend Model
The dividend paid is set equal to net income minus the amount of retained earnings necessary to finance the firm's optimal capital budget.

ital. The last three elements are combined in what we call the **residual dividend model**. Under this model, we assume that investors in the aggregate are indifferent between dividends and capital gains and that firms follow these three steps when establishing their target payout ratios: (1) Each firm determines its optimal capital budget. (2) The firm then determines the amount of equity needed to finance that budget, given its target capital structure. (3) It then uses retained earnings to meet equity requirements to the extent possible, and thus pays dividends only if more earnings are available than are necessary to support the capital budget. The word *residual* implies "left over," and the residual policy implies that dividends are paid from "leftover" earnings.

If a firm rigidly follows the residual dividend policy, then dividends paid in any given year can be expressed as follows:

$$\text{Dividends} = \text{Net income} - \text{Retained earnings needed to finance new investments}$$
$$= \text{Net income} - [\text{Target equity ratio} \times \text{Total capital budget}]. \quad (13\text{-}6)$$

For example, suppose the target equity ratio is 60 percent and the firm plans to spend $50 million on capital projects. In that case, it would need $50(0.6) = $30 million of common equity (along with $20 million of new debt). Then, if its net income were $100 million, its dividends would be $100 − $30 = $70 million, producing a payout ratio of $70/$100 = 70%. The $30 million of the retained earnings plus the $50 − $30 = $20 million of new debt would keep the capital structure on target. Note that the amount of equity needed to finance new investments might exceed the firm's net income; in our example, this would happen if the capital budget were $200 million. In that case, no dividends would be paid, and the

DIVIDEND YIELDS AROUND THE WORLD

Dividend yields vary considerably in different stock markets throughout the world. In 1999 in the United States, dividend yields averaged 1.6 percent for the large blue-chip stocks in the Dow Jones Industrials, 1.2 percent for a broader sample of stocks in the S&P 500, and 0.3 percent for stocks in the high-tech-dominated Nasdaq. Outside the United States, average dividend yields ranged from 5.7 percent in New Zealand to 0.7 percent in Taiwan. The accompanying table summarizes the dividend picture in 1999.

World Stock Market (Index)	Dividend Yield	World Stock Market (Index)	Dividend Yield
New Zealand	5.7%	United States (Dow Jones Industrials)	1.6%
Australia	3.1	Canada (TSE 300)	1.5
Britain FTSE 100	2.4	United States (S&P 500)	1.2
Hong Kong	2.4	Mexico	1.1
France	2.1	Japan Nikkei	0.7
Germany	2.1	Taiwan	0.7
Belgium	2.0	United States (Nasdaq)	0.3
Singapore	1.7		

Source: From Alexandra Eadie, "On the Grid Looking for Dividend Yield Around the World," *The Globe and Mail,* June 23, 1999, B16. Eadie's source was Bloomberg Financial Services. Reprinted with permission from *The Globe and Mail.*

company would have to issue new common stock to maintain its target capital structure.[20]

Because both investment opportunities and earnings will surely vary from year to year, strict adherence to the residual dividend policy would result in unstable dividends. One year the firm would pay zero dividends because it needed the money to finance good investment opportunities, but the next year it might need to pay a large dividend because investment opportunities were poor and it did not need to retain as much. Similarly, fluctuating earnings would also lead to variable dividends, even if investment opportunities were stable. Therefore, following the residual dividend policy rigidly would lead to fluctuating, unstable dividends. Since investors desire stable, dependable dividends, r_s would be high, and the stock price low, if the firm followed the residual model in a strict sense. Therefore, firms tend to

1. Estimate earnings and investment opportunities over some time horizon (next five or so years).
2. Use this forecasted information to find the average residual model payout ratio and dollars of dividends during the planning period.
3. Then set a *target payout ratio* based on the average projected data.

Thus, it makes sense for firms to use the residual policy to help set their long-run target payout ratios, but not as a guide to the payout in any one year.

---

[20]Most firms have a target capital structure that calls for at least some debt, so new financing is generally done partly with debt and partly with equity. As long as the firm finances with the optimal mix of debt and equity and only uses internally generated equity (retained earnings), the marginal cost of each new dollar of capital will be minimized. Thus, internally generated equity is available for financing a certain amount of new investment, but beyond that amount, the firm must turn to more expensive new common stock. At the level of investment where new stock must be sold, the cost of equity, and consequently the marginal cost of capital, increases. If we drew a graph with the WACC on the vertical axis and the amount of capital raised and invested on the horizontal axis, the WACC would be constant until the investment level where new stock was needed, at which point it would rise.

Companies use the residual dividend model as discussed to help understand the determinants of an optimal dividend policy, along with computerized financial forecasting models. Most larger corporations forecast their financial statements for the next 5 to 10 years. Projected capital expenditures and working capital requirements are entered into the model, along with sales forecasts, profit margins, depreciation, and other data required to forecast cash flows. The target capital structure is also specified, and the model shows the amounts of debt and equity needed to meet the capital budgeting requirements while maintaining the target capital structure. Then, dividend payments are introduced. Naturally, the higher the payout ratio, the greater the required external equity. Most companies use the model to find a dividend pattern over the forecast period (generally five years) that provides enough equity to support the capital budget, but neither requires a new common stock issue nor a departure of the capital structure from its optimal range.

Companies whose earnings and funds requirements are especially unstable can set a very low "regular" dividend and then supplement it with an "extra" dividend when cash flow exceeds internal requirements. General Motors, Ford, and other auto companies have followed the **low-regular-dividend-plus-extras policy** in the past. The companies announced a low regular dividend that could be easily maintained and thus that stockholders could expect under virtually all conditions. Then, when profits and cash flows were high, the companies paid out a specially designated extra dividend. Investors recognize that the extra would not necessarily be maintained in the future, so they did not interpret it as a signal that earnings were permanently increasing, nor did they take the elimination of the extra as a negative signal.

At times, however, companies must make substantial cuts in dividends in order to conserve cash. In October 2000, facing increasing competition, technology changes, a decline in its bond rating, and a cutoff from the commercial paper market, Xerox Corporation rolled back its quarterly dividend from $0.20 per share to $0.05 per share. This was a dividend not seen by Xerox shareholders since 1966. In the week prior to the dividend cut, the share price had declined significantly in response to an announcement that there would be a loss for the quarter rather than a modest profit and a warning that a dividend cut was likely. Xerox took a substantial stock price hit when it conceded that cash flows would be insufficient to cover the old dividend—indeed, the price declined from $15 to $8. However, most analysts thought the dividend cut was exactly the right action—it would preserve cash, maintain Xerox's ability to service its debt, and lay the groundwork for further growth in the future; without the cut Xerox's stock price would have ended up even lower. Note too that in 2004 Xerox's share price was back at the 2000 level, which is better than the performance of most other stocks during that time period.

Low-Regular-Dividend-plus-Extras Policy
The policy of announcing a low, regular dividend that can be maintained no matter what and then, when times are good, paying a designated "extra" dividend.

SELF-TEST QUESTIONS

Explain the logic of the residual dividend model, the steps a firm takes when implementing it, and why it is more likely to be used in establishing a long-run payout target than an actual year-by-year payout ratio.

How do firms use planning models to help set dividend policy?

SUMMARY OF FACTORS INFLUENCING DIVIDEND POLICY

In earlier sections, we described the major theories regarding the effects of dividend policy on firm value. We also discussed the residual dividend model for setting a firm's long-run target payout ratio. In this section, we discuss several other factors that affect the dividend decision. These factors may be grouped into four broad categories: (1) constraints on dividend payments, (2) investment opportunities, (3) availability and cost of alternative sources of capital, and (4) effects of dividend policy on r_s. Each of these categories has several subparts, which we discuss below.

Constraints

1. *Bond indentures.* Debt contracts often limit dividend payments to earnings generated after the loan was granted. Also, debt contracts often stipulate that no dividends can be paid unless the current ratio, times-interest-earned ratio, and other safety ratios exceed stated minimums.
2. *Preferred stock restrictions.* Typically, common dividends cannot be paid if the company has omitted its preferred dividend, and preferred arrearages must be paid off before common dividends can be resumed.
3. *Impairment of capital rule.* Dividend payments cannot exceed the balance sheet item "retained earnings." This legal restriction, known as the *impairment of capital rule*, is designed to protect creditors. Without this rule, a company that is having financial problems might distribute most of its assets to stockholders, leaving debtholders high and dry. (*Liquidating dividends* can be paid out of capital, but they must be indicated as such, and they must not reduce capital below the levels required by debt contracts.)
4. *Availability of cash.* Cash dividends can be paid only with cash, so a shortage of cash can restrict dividend payments. However, the ability to borrow can offset this factor.
5. *Penalty tax on improperly accumulated earnings.* To prevent wealthy individuals from using corporations to avoid personal taxes, the U.S. Tax Code has a special surtax on improperly accumulated income. Thus, if the IRS can demonstrate that a firm's dividend payout ratio is being deliberately held down to help stockholders avoid personal taxes, the firm is subject to heavy penalties. This rule has, to our knowledge, never been invoked against a publicly owned firm, so it is really relevant only to privately owned firms.

Investment Opportunities

1. *Number of profitable investment opportunities.* If a firm expects many profitable investment opportunities, its target payout ratio will probably be low, but the payout will be high if there are few profitable opportunities. Global firms generally have a large number of investment alternatives all around the world, so these firms are expected to have lower target payout ratios.
2. *Accelerating or delaying projects.* The ability to accelerate or postpone projects permits firms to adhere more closely to a stable dividend policy.

Alternative Sources of Capital

1. *Cost of selling new stock.* If a firm needs to finance a given capital budget, it can obtain equity by retaining earnings or by issuing new common stock. If flotation costs (including any negative signaling effects of a stock offering) are high, the cost of external equity will be significantly higher than the cost of retained earnings, and this will favor a low payout ratio and thus the use of retained earnings rather than new common stock. On the other hand, a higher dividend payout ratio is more feasible for a firm whose flotation costs are low. Flotation costs differ across firms, and they are generally higher for small firms, so they tend to set low payout ratios.
2. *Ability to substitute debt for equity.* A firm can finance investments with either debt or equity. As noted earlier, low stock flotation costs permit a more

flexible dividend policy because equity can be raised by retaining earnings or by selling new stock. A similar situation holds for capital structure: If the firm can adjust its debt ratio without raising capital costs sharply, it can pay its expected dividend even if its earnings fluctuate by increasing its debt ratio.

3. *Control.* If management is concerned about maintaining control, it may be reluctant to sell new stock, hence the firm may retain more earnings than it otherwise would. However, if stockholders want higher dividends and threaten a proxy fight, then the dividend will probably be increased.[21]

Effects of Dividend Policy on r_s

The effects of dividend policy on r_s may be considered in terms of four factors:

1. Stockholders' desire for current versus future income.
2. Perceived riskiness of dividends versus capital gains.
3. The tax advantage of capital gains over dividends.
4. The information content of dividends (signaling).

We discussed each of these factors in detail earlier, so we need only note here that the importance of each factor varies from firm to firm depending on the makeup of its current and possible future stockholders.

It should be apparent that dividend policy decisions are truly exercises in informed judgment—they are not decisions that can be quantified precisely. Even so, to make rational dividend decisions, financial managers must address all the issues discussed in this chapter.

SELF-TEST QUESTIONS

Identify four broad groups of factors that affect dividend policy.

What are some factors that constrain dividend policy?

How do investment opportunities affect dividend policy?

How does the availability and cost of outside capital affect dividend policy?

---

[21]Generally, most proxy-fight-induced dividend increases result because stockholders believe that managers have been making investments that do not add value, and stockholders want the free cash flow returned to them so they can deploy it, presumably at higher returns than the firm can earn on its investments.

SUMMARY

In Chapter 10, we took the firm's financing choice as given and then calculated the cost of capital based on that capital structure. Then, in Chapters 11 and 12, we described capital budgeting techniques, which use the firm's cost of capital as an input. Capital budgeting decisions determine the types of projects that the firm accepts and where it locates facilities across the globe, and these decisions affect the nature of the firm's assets and its business risk. In this chapter we reversed the process, taking the firm's assets and business risk as given and then seeking to determine the best way to finance those assets.

More specifically, this chapter focused on a firm's capital structure and dividend policy decisions and their effect on its stock price. In this chapter we presented the relevant capital structure and dividend theories, and then we discussed the specific factors that affect a multinational's capital structure and dividend policy decisions. The key concepts discussed in this chapter are listed below.

• In 1958, **Franco Modigliani** and **Merton Miller (MM)** proved, under a restrictive set of assumptions including zero taxes, that capital structure is irrelevant; that is, according to the original MM article, a firm's value is not affected by its financing mix. Despite some of the unrealistic assumptions, MM's irrelevance result is extremely important. By indicating the conditions under which capital structure is irrelevant, MM also provides clues about what is required for capital structure to be relevant and affect a firm's value.

- MM later added **corporate taxes** to their model and reached the conclusion that capital structure does matter. Indeed, their model led to the conclusion that debt financing creates value-adding tax shelters.

- MM's model with corporate taxes demonstrated that the primary benefit of debt stems from the **tax deductibility of interest payments**.

- Later, Miller extended the theory to include **personal taxes**. The introduction of personal taxes reduces, but does not eliminate, the benefits of debt financing.

- The **trade-off theory of leverage** showed that debt is useful because interest is **tax deductible**, but also that debt brings with it costs associated with actual or potential bankruptcy. The **optimal capital structure** strikes a balance between the tax benefits of debt and the costs associated with bankruptcy.

- **Asymmetric information** is the situation in which managers have different (better) information about firms' prospects than do investors.

- **Pecking order** is the idea that firms have a preference order for raising capital, first using retained earnings, then debt, and new stock only as a last resort.

- If we looked at capital structures across countries, greater differences would be observed among countries than among industries within a given country. This is attributable to various country-specific factors that make the use of debt more or less risky to local companies. Some environmental factors include **cultural characteristics, corporate governance and agency costs**, the **breadth and depth of local equity markets, tax policy**, and **government policies and regulation.**

- The best capital structure is the one that **maximizes the value of the entire MNE in its home market.** Factors that support this conclusion include the following: (1) Creditors generally expect the parent to guarantee a foreign subsidiary's debt. (2) If the MNE were to optimize each subsidiary's local capital structure, then subsidiaries from countries with a high debt tolerance might not be offset by more conservatively financed units. (3) MNEs receive benefits from their global network that domestic companies cannot duplicate. (4) Local governments often see MNEs as their connection to international capital markets.

- In defining the optimal capital structure (whether global or local), firms should set a **target capital structure**—the mix of debt, preferred stock, and common equity with which the firm plans to raise capital—for the consolidated company. This target can change over time as conditions change, but at any given moment, management should have a specific capital structure in mind.

- **Capital structure policy** involves a trade-off between risk and return. Using more debt increases the risk borne by shareholders; however, using more debt generally leads to a higher expected rate of return on equity.

- Five primary factors that influence capital structures are **business risk**, the firm's **tax position, financial flexibility, managerial conservatism and aggressiveness**, and **investor risk aversion.** While these factors help determine the target capital structure, **operating conditions** can cause the actual capital structure to vary from the target.

- **Business risk** is the riskiness inherent in the firm's operations if it uses no debt. Business risk arises from uncertainty in the firm's operating cash flows, which means uncertainty about operating profit and capital investment requirements.

- Business risk depends on the following factors: **demand variability, sales price variability; input cost variability; ability to adjust output prices for changes in input costs; ability to develop new products in a timely, cost-effective manner; foreign risk exposure;** and **operating leverage.**

- **Financial leverage** is the extent to which fixed-income securities (debt and preferred stock) are used in a firm's capital structure. **Financial risk** is the added risk borne by stockholders as a result of financial leverage.
- The firm should maintain **financial flexibility**, which, from an operational viewpoint, means maintaining adequate reserve borrowing capacity. **Reserve borrowing capacity** is the ability to borrow money at a reasonable cost when good investment opportunities arise. Firms often use less debt than specified by the MM optimal capital structure in "normal" times to ensure that they can obtain debt capital later if necessary.
- Determining an adequate reserve borrowing capacity is judgmental, but it clearly depends on the firm's **forecasted need for funds**, predicted global **capital market conditions, management's confidence in its forecasts**, and the **consequences of a capital shortage**.
- In a global environment, dividend policy has two distinct aspects: **internal payout policy** within the corporate network and **external payout policy** from the firm to its shareholders. In global finance, payment blockages, capital and foreign exchange controls, and political risk are critical issues that are not factors in domestic finance.
- **Dividend policies** for all countries must be considered as an **integrated group** in setting the internal dividend policy. **Taxes, including withholding taxes and foreign tax credits; blockages; expected future exchange rates for each of the currencies; and local capital requirements** serve as **constraints** to preserving as much value as possible while financing global operations at the lowest feasible cost.
- The parent company's dividend policy is decided **simultaneously** with each subsidiary's internal dividend policy.
- The **target payout ratio** is the percentage of net income paid out as cash distributions (dividends and/or stock repurchases) as desired by the firm.
- The **optimal dividend policy** is one that strikes a balance between current dividends and future growth and maximizes the firm's stock price.
- The **dividend irrelevance theory** is the theory proposed by Merton Miller and Franco Modigliani that states a firm's dividend policy has no effect on either its value or its cost of capital.
- The **bird-in-the-hand theory** is MM's name for the theory proposed by Myron Gordon and John Lintner suggesting that a firm's value will be maximized by setting a high dividend payout ratio.
- The **tax preference theory** suggests there are tax-related reasons for investors preferring a low dividend payout to a high payout.
- The **information content (signaling) hypothesis** suggests that investors regard dividend changes as signals of management's earnings forecasts.
- The **clientele effect** is the tendency of a firm to attract a set of investors who like its dividend policy.
- The **residual dividend model** is a model in which the dividend paid is set equal to net income less the amount of retained earnings necessary to finance the firm's optimal capital budget.
- The **low-regular-dividend-plus-extras policy** is one in which a firm announces a low, regular dividend that can be maintained no matter what and then, when times are good, pays a designated "extra" dividend.
- There are four broad categories of additional factors that affect the firm's dividend decision: (1) **constraints** on dividend payments, (2) **investment opportunities**, (3) **availability and alternative sources of capital**, and (4) **effects of dividend policy on the cost of equity**.

QUESTIONS

(13-1) Explain why the following statement is true: "Other things the same, firms with relatively stable sales are able to carry relatively high debt ratios."

(13-2) If a firm went from zero debt to successively higher debt levels, why would you expect its stock price to first rise, then hit a peak, and then begin to decline?

(13-3) If Congress considers a change in the Tax Code that will increase personal tax rates but reduce corporate tax rates, what effect would this Tax Code change have on the average company's capital structure decision?

(13-4) How does a firm's capital structure decision affect the valuation equation?

(13-5) How would each of the following changes tend to affect aggregate (i.e., average for all corporations) payout ratios, other things held constant? Explain your answers.
   a. An increase in the personal income tax rate.
   b. A liberalization of depreciation for federal income tax purposes—that is, faster tax write-offs.
   c. An increase in interest rates.
   d. An increase in corporate profits.
   e. A decline in investment opportunities.
   f. Permission for corporations to deduct dividends for tax purposes as they now do interest charges.

(13-6) Discuss the following statement: "The cost of retained earnings is less than the cost of new outside equity capital. Consequently, it is totally irrational for a firm to sell a new issue of stock and to pay dividends during the same year."

(13-7) Would it ever be rational for a firm to borrow money to pay dividends? Explain.

(13-8) "Executive salaries have been shown to be more closely correlated to firm size than to its profitability. If a firm's board of directors is controlled by management instead of by outside directors, this might result in the firm's retaining more earnings than can be justified from the stockholders' point of view." Discuss the statement, being sure (a) to discuss the interrelationships among cost of capital, investment opportunities, and new investment and (b) to explain the implied relationship between dividend policy and stock prices.

(13-9) One position expressed in the financial literature is that firms set their dividends as a residual after using income to support new investment.
   a. Explain the residual dividend policy and what it implies.
   b. Consider the relationship between capital structure and cost of capital. If the WACC-versus-debt-ratio plot were shaped like a sharp V, would this have a different implication for the importance of setting dividends according to the residual policy than if the plot were shaped like a shallow bowl (or a flattened U)?

(13-10) Indicate whether the following statements are true or false. If the statement is false, explain why.
   a. The Tax Code encourages companies to pay a large percentage of their net income in the form of dividends.
   b. If your company has established a clientele of investors who prefer large dividends, the company is unlikely to adopt a residual dividend policy.
   c. If a firm follows a residual dividend policy, holding all else constant, its dividend payout will tend to rise whenever the firm's investment opportunities improve.

(13-11) Explain the conclusions reached and their implications under (1) MM's capital structure theory with no taxes, (2) MM's theory with corporate taxes, and (3) Miller's theory with the addition of personal taxes.

(13-12) How did the trade-off theory develop, and what are its implications for capital structure? What is meant by the terms "asymmetric information" and "pecking order"?

(13-13) How does a global company's capital structure decision differ from that of a purely domestic firm?

(13-14) Briefly identify and explain the "checklist" of factors relevant to any firm's capital structure decision.

(13-15) How does a global company's dividend policy decision differ from that of a purely domestic firm?

(13-16) Using the information learned in this chapter, does a firm's dividend policy matter? Explain.

(13-17) How should a firm go about setting its dividend payout in practice?

SELF-TEST PROBLEMS   Solutions Appear in Appendix B

(ST-1)
Key Terms

Define each of the following terms:
a. Trade-off theory; asymmetric information; pecking order
b. Shell corporation
c. Target capital structure; optimal capital structure
d. Business risk; operating leverage
e. Financial risk; financial leverage
f. Reserve borrowing capacity
g. Target payout ratio; optimal dividend policy
h. Dividend irrelevance theory; bird-in-the-hand theory; tax preference theory
i. Signal; information content (signaling) hypothesis
j. Clienteles; clientele effect
k. Residual dividend model; low-regular-dividend-plus-extras policy

(ST-2)
Capital Structure Theory

Heuser Manufacturing Inc. (HMI) is a global furniture manufacturer with production facilities located across the globe. The firm's value with no debt is $10 billion. Heuser uses $2 billion of debt financing, and its corporate tax rate is 35 percent. The personal tax rates of Heuser's investors are 33 percent on interest income and 15 percent on stock income.
a. What is the firm's value according to the original MM paper written in 1958 with its restrictive set of assumptions?
b. What is the firm's value according to MM with corporate taxes?
c. What is the firm's value according to the Miller model with the inclusion of personal taxes?

(ST-3)
Residual Dividend Model

Global Publications Inc. expects to have net income of $7 billion this year. The company has an estimated capital budget of $6 billion, and its capital structure consists of 45 percent common equity and 55 percent debt. If the company follows a strict residual dividend policy, what is the company's expected dividend payout ratio?

STARTER PROBLEMS

(13-1)
Capital Structure Theory

Worldwide Foods Inc. (WFI) is an international food processor of grains with processing facilities located in North and South America. The firm's value with no debt is $800 million. WFI uses $320 million of debt financing, and its corporate tax rate is 38 percent. The personal tax rates of WFI's investors are 28 percent on interest income and 15 percent on stock income.
a. What is the firm's value according to the original MM paper written in 1958 with its restrictive set of assumptions?

b. What is the firm's value according to MM with corporate taxes?

c. What is the firm's value according to the Miller model with the inclusion of personal taxes?

(13-2) HendersonCutterSmythe Pharmaceuticals (HCSP) is an international pharmaceuti-
Residual Dividend Model cals company with production plants located in Canada, Central America, Asia, and Europe. The firm uses the residual dividend model to determine its common dividend payout. This year HCSP expects its net income to be $2.5 billion, and it expects to have a 15 percent dividend payout ratio. The company's target common equity ratio is 70 percent, and the firm is financed with only common equity and debt. What is HCSP's forecasted total capital budget for the year?

(13-3) Kricos Apparel Company (KAC), a global manufacturer of women's clothing and
Residual Dividend Model shoes, has manufacturing plants located in Central and South America, Europe, and Asia. The firm expects to have net income of $950 million during the next year. KAC's target capital structure is 40 percent debt and 60 percent common equity. The company's capital budgeting director has determined that the optimal capital budget for the upcoming year is $1.25 billion. If KAC follows a residual dividend policy to determine next year's dividend, what is the firm's payout ratio?

EXAM-TYPE PROBLEMS

(13-4) You are an analyst for TRD Incorporated and have the following data:
Capital Structure Theory

$$V_U = \$775,000$$
$$V_L = \$803,427$$
$$T_d = 25\%$$
$$T_c = 39\%$$
$$T_s = 12\%$$

According to the Miller model, what is the market value of TRD's debt?

(13-5) You are an analyst for TransWorld Financial Company and have the following
Capital Structure Theory data:

$$V_U = \$9,691,666$$
$$V_L = \$10,000,000$$
$$T_d = 28\%$$
$$T_s = 12\%$$
$$D = \$1,500,000$$

According to the Miller model, what is TransWorld's corporate tax rate, T_c?

(13-6) Global Biotechnology Services (GBS) is an international company responsible for
Capital Structure Theory designing and manufacturing artificial knee and hip joints used by surgeons per-forming artificial knee and hip replacements. The firm's value with no debt is $500 million. GBS uses $100 million of debt financing and its corporate tax rate is 40 percent. The personal tax rate of GBS investors (on average) is 35 percent on interest income and 15 percent on stock income.

a. What is the firm's value according to the original MM paper written in 1958 with its restrictive set of assumptions?

b. What is the firm's value according to MM with corporate taxes?

c. What is the firm's value according to the Miller model with the inclusion of personal taxes?

    d. According to the Miller model, what happens to a firm's value when
       (1) Corporate tax rates increase?
       (2) Tax rates on stock income decrease?
       (3) Personal tax rates on interest income decline?

(13-7)
Residual Dividend Model International Beverage Company (IBC) has production plants worldwide that produce and distribute alcoholic beverages. The firm uses the residual dividend model to determine its common dividend payout. This year IBC expects its net income to be $4.5 billion, and it expects to have a 35 percent dividend payout ratio. The company's target common equity ratio is 45 percent, and the firm is financed with only common equity and debt. What is IBC's forecasted total capital budget for the year?

EXPLORING THE CAPITAL STRUCTURES FOR FOUR OF THE WORLD'S LEADING AUTO COMPANIES

Overview

This chapter provides an overview of the effects of leverage and describes the process that firms use to determine their optimal capital structure. The chapter also indicates that capital structures tend to vary across industries and across countries. If you are interested in exploring these differences in more detail, *Thomson One: Business School Edition* provides information about the capital structures of each of the companies it follows.

The following discussion questions demonstrate how we can use this information to evaluate the capital structures for four of the world's leading automobile companies: General Motors (GM), Ford (F), BMW (BMW), and Toyota (J:TYMO). As you gather information on these companies, be mindful of the currencies in which these companies' financial data are reported.

Discussion Questions

1. To get an overall picture of each company's capital structure, it is helpful to see a chart that summarizes the company's capital structure over the past decade. To obtain this chart, choose a company to start with and select FINANCIALS. Next, select MORE>THOMSON REPORTS & CHARTS> CAPITAL STRUCTURE. This should generate a chart that plots the companies' long-term debt, common equity, and total current liabilities over the past decade. What, if any, are the major trends that emerge from looking at these charts? Do these companies tend to have relatively high or relatively low levels of debt? Do these companies have significant levels of current liabilities? Have their capital structures changed over time? (Note an alternative chart can be found by selecting FINANCIALS>FUNDAMENTAL RATIOS>WORLDSCOPE RATIOS>DEBT TO ASSETS & EQUITY RATIOS.)

2. To get more details about the companies' capital structures over the past 5 years, select FINANCIALS>FUNDAMENTAL RATIOS>THOMSON RATIOS. From here you can select ANNUAL RATIOS and/or 5 YEAR AVERAGE RATIOS REPORT. In each case, you can scroll down and look for LEVERAGE RATIOS. Here you will find a variety of leverage ratios for the past 5 years. (Notice that these two pages offer different information. The ANNUAL RATIOS page offers year-end leverage ratios, while the 5 YEAR AVERAGE RATIOS REPORT offers the average ratio over the previous 5 years for each calendar date. In other words, the 5 YEAR AVERAGE RATIOS REPORT smoothes the changes in capital structure over the

reporting periods.) Do these ratios suggest that the company has significantly changed its capital structure over the past 5 years? If so, what factors could possibly explain this shift? (Financial statements might be useful to detect any shifts that may have led to the company's changing capital structure. You may also consult the company's annual report to see if there is any discussion and/or explanation for these changes. Both the historical financial statements and annual report information can be found via *Thomson One: Business School Edition*.)

3. Repeat this procedure for the other three auto companies. Do you find similar capital structures for each of the four companies? Do you find that the capital structures have moved in the same direction over the past 5 years, or have the different companies changed their capital structures in different ways over the past 5 years?

4. The financial ratios investigated thus far are based on book values of debt and equity. Determine whether using the market value of equity (current market capitalization is found on the OVERVIEW page) makes a significant difference in the most recent year's LT DEBT PCT COMMON EQUITY and TOTAL DEBT PCT TOTAL ASSETS, which are book value ratios as shown. (Note: LT DEBT is defined by *Thomson One: Business School Edition* as LONG TERM DEBT listed on the balance sheet, while TOTAL DEBT is defined as LONG TERM DEBT plus ST DEBT & CURRENT PORTION DUE LT DEBT.) Are there big differences between the capital structures measured on a book (as shown) or market basis (as you've calculated)?

5. To obtain information about dividend policy, select OVERVIEW>FULL REPORTS>THOMSON FULL REPORTS>FULL COMPANY REPORT. Go to the STOCK & EARNINGS DATA section and look for the subheading ANNUAL HISTORICAL DATA. What has happened to these companies' dividends per share, dividend yields, and dividend payouts over the past 5 years? Do you have any explanations?

6. We are using a set of peers in our analysis, but to get another peer set from *Thomson One: Business School Edition*, have a company selected and select PEERS>OVERVIEWS>PER SHARE DATA to see their peers' last annual dividends. Accessing PEER>OVERVIEWS>VALUATION COMPARISON shows their peers dividend yields. Have the companies selected behaved differently from the *Thomson One: Business School Edition* peers or have there been industrywide shifts?

7. Refer back to the FULL COMPANY REPORT used in question 1. Manually, plot earnings and dividends over time for two of our companies. In the text we point out that dividends are often much more stable than earnings. Do you see a similar pattern for your companies?

8. Now, select INTERIM FINANCIAL DATA from the THOMSON FULL COMPANY REPORT page. Identify the dividend declared date, ex date, and pay date for the two companies. Explain the significance of these dates. Go back to OVERVIEW, and access the INTERACTIVE PRICE CHART from the COMPANY OVERVIEW page. Can you observe price shifts around these dates?

9. Investors are more concerned with future dividends than historical dividends, so click on ESTIMATES and scroll down to the CONSENSUS ESTIMATES section. Click on the AVAILABLE MEASURES menu to toggle between earnings per share and dividends per share. How do analysts expect your two companies' payout policies to behave in the future?

10. Refer back to the FULL COMPANY REPORT and click on 5 YR ANNUAL BALANCE SHEET section. Does it appear that either of your companies has repurchased any stock recently or have they been issuing new stock?

INTEGRATED CASE

Rick Schmidt, MRI's CFO, along with Mandy Wu, Schmidt's assistant, and John Costello, a consultant and college finance professor, comprise a team set up to teach the firm's directors and senior managers the basics of international financial management. The program includes 16 sessions, each lasting about 2 hours, and they are scheduled immediately before the monthly board meetings. Twelve sessions have been completed, and the team is now preparing Session 13, which will deal with capital structure and distribution policy. Prior sessions have provided an overview of international finance, exchange rates, risk analysis, financial statements, bond and stock valuation, international security markets, the cost of capital, and capital budgeting.

For the capital structure and distribution session, the team will explain the implications of using different capital structures and how firms make their decisions. They will also discuss the methods firms use to distribute funds to investors, while focusing on cash dividends and stock repurchases. Because MRI is a multinational firm that raises and invests capital around the world, the capital structure decision is a multifaceted one. The types and sources of capital employed for operations in different parts of the globe can be quite different. MRI must consider this when setting its strategic capital structure policy. Stakeholders around the world have widely different perceptions, so MRI must also consider how its distribution policy affects the entire firm and how it will be perceived abroad.

For illustrative purposes, Wu has drawn up a sample corporation that has $2 million in assets, funded entirely by equity. This firm is considering a shift in capital structure that would call for $1 million to be raised as debt to replace $1 million in equity. The firm would now have 50 percent equity and 50 percent debt. This firm's tax rate is 40 percent, and the interest rate on new debt is expected to be 10 percent. Next year's probability distribution of operating income is shown in Table IC13-1.

Wu expressed concern about addressing controversial issues, where the proper analysis is in question. She recalled that in college some students simply "tuned out" when the instructor raised a question for which there was no definitive answer, and she was concerned that the directors might react similarly. Schmidt and Costello agree that this could be a problem, but they felt strongly that it would not be appropriate to "sweep problems under the carpet." So, they want to bring up relevant unresolved issues, discuss alternative ways of dealing with them, and point out the implications of different decisions. The directors are all intelligent, experienced in dealing with complex situations, and would rather know about potential problems than be kept in the dark.

With those thoughts in mind, the three compiled the following set of questions, which they plan to discuss during the session. As with the other sessions, they plan to use an *Excel* model to answer the quantitative questions. Assume that you are Mandy Wu and that you must prepare answers for use during the session.

QUESTIONS

a. Before MRI has a serious discussion about capital structure, Schmidt wants everyone to have a firm grasp on the theoretical underpinnings of capital structure. Discuss the following theories: Modigliani and Miller (especially how corporate and personal taxes affect capital structure), trade-off, asymmetric information, and pecking order.

b. How can the idea of an optimal capital structure change when looking at a multinational entity with a number of subsidiaries across the globe? What factors drive this result? Compare local versus global capital structure decisions.

c. What is the optimal capital structure? What major factors affect the optimal capital structure?

d. Define the terms (1) business risk and (2) financial risk. Identify some factors that affect each of them, and indicate how they combine to affect the firm's investment risk.

TABLE IC13-1 | Probability Distribution of Operating Income

Probability	Operating Income
0.05	($700,000)
0.20	(300,000)
0.50	500,000
0.20	1,100,000
0.05	1,500,000

e. On the basis of Table IC13-1 and the data given earlier for the illustrative company, what is the expected return on equity (ROE) under each of the financing plans? Standard deviation? Coefficient of variation?

f. Which financing plan appears to be more risky? Explain your answer.

g. Is the ROE or the return on invested capital (ROIC) affected by the amount of financial leverage used? Why does this result occur? Should the company choose the capital structure that maximizes its expected ROE? Explain.

h. Is the capital structure that maximizes the value of a firm consistent with the capital structure that minimizes the firm's WACC? Explain.

i. Describe the difference between internal and external payout policies.

j. What is the target payout ratio? What is the optimal dividend policy? Do investors prefer dividends or capital gains? Discuss any relevant theories.

k. Describe the signaling hypothesis and the clientele effect.

l. What is the residual dividend model? How does it help firms establish their dividend policies? Are there any shortcomings to this model? How should MRI use this model to examine its own dividend policy?

m. To illustrate the calculations for the residual dividend model the following data for an illustrative firm were given:

Net income = $5 billion.
Dividend payout = 30%.
Capital structure = 55% common equity and 45% debt.

Given these data, what is the firm's forecasted capital budget for the year?

CHAPTER 14

Working Capital Management and Global Cash Flow Integration

Required Investment
Sales Revenues
Operating Costs
Taxes

Cash Flows (CF)

$$VALUE = \sum_{t=0}^{N} \frac{CF_t}{(1+r)^t}$$

Capital Structure
Component Costs
Asset Risk
Market Risk

Weighted Average
Cost of Capital (WACC)

e-resource

The textbook's Web site, http://crum. swlearning.com, contains an Excel file that will guide you through the chapter's calculations. The file for this chapter is FIFC14-model.xls, and we encourage you to open the file and follow along as you read the chapter.

A**t the most fundamental level, working capital management answers two primary questions: (1) What is the appropriate investment in each current asset account, and in total, and (2) how should current assets be financed? To answer the first question, we must look beyond the traditional boundaries of finance to explore issues usually dealt with in marketing (the relationship between credit policy and sales), production (raw materials needed each day to support production), logistics (receiving inputs from suppliers once orders are placed), and information technology (streamlining the supply chain to eliminate inefficiencies). The finance staff must evaluate the profitability of alternative working capital proposals, including the optimal way to obtain the cash needed to support continuing operations.*

For a multinational enterprise, these questions must be answered for each foreign subsidiary as well as for the entire MNE. In previous chapters, we identified the MNE's ability to move resources around the world as an important competitive advantage. This flexibility allows the MNE to support subsidiaries from an internal pool of resources or from external sources, whichever yields the greatest value. Of course, such flexibility involves complex decisions by the MNE, and significant attention must be paid to mechanisms used to convert one currency to another and to move cash from one country to another.

Working capital decisions affect both the numerator and denominator of the valuation equation. Current assets investments affect free cash flows directly, for if management can reduce required investments without decreasing inflows or increasing risk, free cash flows will increase, thus increasing the value of the firm. Working capital decisions also affect the WACC, because short-term interest rates are normally lower than long-term rates, and supplier credit usually has no explicit interest cost.

OVERVIEW OF WORKING CAPITAL MANAGEMENT

Working Capital
A firm's investment in short-term assets—cash, marketable securities, inventory, and accounts receivable.

Before beginning our discussion of working capital, we review some basic definitions and concepts that are used throughout the chapter:

1. **Working capital**, sometimes called *gross working capital*, simply refers to current assets used in operations. They can be divided into two classes: (a) **permanent working capital**, which are those current assets required to support operations at the minimum anticipated level of demand, and (b) **temporary working capital**, which are current assets above permanent working capital required to support operations during peak periods.

Permanent Working Capital
Current assets that a firm must carry even at the trough of its cycles.

2. **Net working capital** is current assets minus current liabilities, or the amount of current assets that are financed with long-term capital.

3. **Net operating working capital (NOWC)** is operating current assets minus operating current liabilities. Generally, NOWC is equal to cash and near-cash required to support operations, accounts receivable, and inventories minus accounts payable, customer deposits, and accrued liabilities.

Temporary Working Capital
Current assets that fluctuate with seasonal or cyclical variations in sales.

With these definitions in mind, we review the basic structure of the company's working capital management in a single country, and then explain how the various subsidiaries' operations are linked together to make operations more efficient.

Differentiate between working capital and net working capital.
Differentiate between permanent and temporary working capital.
What is net operating working capital, and how does it differ from net working capital?

THE CASH CONVERSION CYCLE

Net Working Capital
Current assets minus current liabilities.

Focusing first on the assets side of the balance sheet, let us look at the production and sales functions. The working capital management process begins when the company places an order for raw materials. Materials are received sometime after the order was placed (depending on delivery lead times); then they are stored and are recorded in raw materials inventory at their invoice prices. Raw materials are drawn from inventory for production, converted into finished goods, and carried as finished goods inventory until they are sold. As shown in Figure 14-1, which illustrates the **cash conversion cycle**, the average time required to convert raw materials into finished goods and to sell those goods is called the **inventory conversion period**. The period extending from the time the sale is recorded and a receivable is created until the cash is collected is called the **receivables collection period**. The top half of Figure 14-1 shows the time that passes between when raw materials are received and cash is collected from sales. During this period, inventory and accounts receivable must be financed.

Net Operating Working Capital (NOWC)
Operating current assets minus operating current liabilities.

Cash Conversion Cycle
Focuses on the length of time a dollar is tied up in current assets other than cash.

When raw materials are recorded as an asset on the inventory records, the purchase invoice is recorded as a liability, an account payable. As shown in the bottom part of Figure 14-1, the time between recording the invoice and paying the bill is

Inventory Conversion Period
The average time required to convert raw materials into finished goods and then to sell those goods.

Receivables Collection Period
The average length of time required to convert the firm's receivables into cash, that is, to collect cash following a sale.

Payables Deferral Period
The average length of time between the purchase of materials and labor and the payment of cash for them.

Cash Conversion Period
Equal to the sum of the inventory conversion period and the receivables collection period minus the payables deferral period.

called the **payables deferral period.**[1] During this period the supplier is providing credit that usually has no explicit cost.[2] The sum of the inventory conversion period and the receivables collection period, minus the payables deferral period, is defined as the **cash conversion period.** When the cash conversion period is positive, as it is in Figure 14-1, the company must pay for the raw materials and their processing before it collects the money from sales, so financing is required to "bridge the gap" between when payments are made and when cash is received. The cash conversion period can be negative, but that means that cash is received prior to when payment must be made. In this situation, no "bridge" financing is needed.[3] In fact, the company can pay down loans or make short-term investments and earn a positive return with the excess funds.

If we look at the financial statements for SSI-USA given in Table 14-1, we see that the inventory conversion period (also called days inventory held or DIH) is 86.42 days. We note that this is less than the 97.05 days (calculated earlier in Chapter 6) for the consolidated company, but it still seems long. This conclusion is reinforced when we note that the production period for all series of speakers is less than 3 days and the average inventory conversion period for the industry is 65.84 days. Also, the receivables collection period (also called days sales outstanding or DSO) is 81.89 days, only slightly less than the 83.51 days (calculated earlier in Chapter 6) for the consolidated company, but longer than the 44-day industry average. Because the payment terms for almost all of the speaker lines are net 45 days, we need to look more carefully at DSO to determine why it is so long. However, the payables deferral period (also called days payables outstanding or DPO) of 43.20 days (44.70 days, calculated earlier in Chapter 6 for the consolidated company) is better than the 30.25-day industry average, *assuming* that the company has negotiated better terms than other companies and is not simply delaying payment past the due date (which would be a bad policy). As a result, the cash conversion period is a very long 125.11 days for the U.S. subsidiary (135.86 days for the consolidated company), substantially above the 79.59-day industry average.

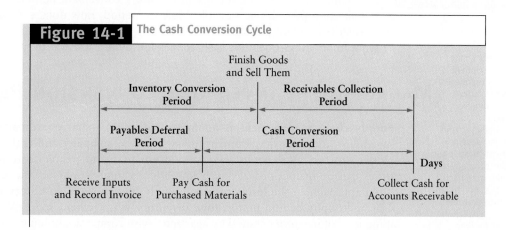

Figure 14-1   The Cash Conversion Cycle

---

[1]Paying the bill is not when the check is written. It is when the money is actually withdrawn from the account and is no longer available for other uses. There can be a delay between writing the check and the actual withdrawal of funds.

[2]If the supplier offers a cash discount or other inducements to pay early, or if there is a penalty for late payment, then the credit is not costless and the cost must be factored into the analysis. We explain this later in more detail, but for a more comprehensive discussion of these issues see Eugene F. Brigham and Phillip R. Daves, *Intermediate Financial Management*, 8th ed. (Mason, OH: South-Western Publishing, 2004), Chapter 20.

[3]Firms in which customers order goods over the Internet using a credit card often have negative cash conversion periods.

TABLE 14-1 | The Cash Conversion Period Calculations for SSI-USA, December 31, 2003

INPUT DATA

Income Statement Data (in millions):

Sales	$4,367.9
Cost of goods sold	$2,972.1

Balance Sheet Data (in millions):

Accounts receivable (total)	$980.0
Inventories	$703.7
Accounts payable (total)	$351.8

FORMULAS

$$\text{Days inventory held (DIH)} = \frac{\text{Inventories}}{\text{Cost of goods sold}/365} = \frac{\$703.7}{\$2,972.1/365} = 86.42 \text{ days.}$$

$$\text{Days sales outstanding (DSO)} = \frac{\text{Accounts receivable}}{\text{Sales}/365} = \frac{\$980.0}{\$4,367.9/365} = 81.89 \text{ days.}$$

$$\text{Days payables outstanding (DPO)} = \frac{\text{Accounts payable}}{\text{Cost of goods sold}/365} = \frac{\$351.8}{\$2,972.1/365} = 43.20 \text{ days.}$$

Cash conversion period = DIH + DSO − DPO = 86.42 + 81.89 − 43.20 = 125.11 days.

Note: SSI-USA's financial statement data are taken from Table 7-6.

SSI is not managing its working capital very well, either from a subsidiary perspective or as an integrated MNE. What can be done to improve its performance? There are many options. In the next section, we look at ways to manage inventories, accounts receivable, and accounts payable more effectively.

SELF-TEST QUESTIONS

Differentiate between the following: inventory conversion period, receivables collection period, and payables deferral period. How does each affect the cash conversion period?

What information does the cash conversion period provide to management?

Supply Chain Management
An integrated process that coordinates production scheduling and sales development throughout the company and with manufacturers' suppliers and retail customers.

MANAGING THE INVENTORY CONVERSION PERIOD

Supply chain management is an integrated process that coordinates production scheduling and sales development throughout the company and with suppliers and retail customers. With better and faster information, and greater coordination, inventories can be maintained at much lower levels than would otherwise be possible, often approaching the levels associated with "just-in-time" inventory management. The philosophy behind **just-in-time inventory management** suggests that the optimum level of inventory should be near zero, with companies holding just enough raw materials to avoid production interruptions. Also, producing to order, or convincing others in the supply chain to carry the finished goods, lowers inventory holdings and thus inventory carrying costs. Holding inventory at a reduced level minimizes storage and handling costs, insurance, property taxes, spoilage or obsolescence, and the cost of capital needed to finance inventory. However, ordering costs might be higher because more orders must be placed, although coordination and information sharing could offset some of these costs. Allowances need to be made throughout the supply chain for shipment delays, defective inputs and outputs, unexpected demand, and the like. Therefore, most companies hold *precautionary balances* to cover these contin-

Just-In-Time Inventory Management
Suggests that the optimum level of inventory is near zero, with companies holding the minimum levels of raw materials required to avoid production interruption.

gencies. Determining the appropriate precautionary balances is important but difficult because of the many uncertainties.

Economic Order Quantity (EOQ) Model
A technique for finding the optimal inventory balance.

Some finance textbooks discuss the **economic order quantity (EOQ) model** as a technique for finding the optimal inventory balance. Since the EOQ model ignores the time value of money, it often leads to a suboptimal long-run inventory strategy.[4] Many of the newer inventory solutions recognize the complex issues that could not be handled in the EOQ framework, and they explicitly incorporate the time value of money.

In emerging markets, companies often carry larger inventory stocks than would otherwise seem optimal because of high inflation. When inflation is high, the local currency ceases to serve as a storehouse of value, so individuals do not want to hold money. They prefer to hold real assets such as gold, gemstones, or foreign currencies that are expected to maintain or increase their values. Companies react in the same way, but instead of buying gold or diamonds, they often hold large amounts of commodities such as steel, wood, microchips, and other raw materials needed in the production processes. Due to purchasing power parity, discussed in Chapter 3, these real assets generally hold their value better than many local currencies. Thus, the inventory levels in Argentina for 2003 could be expected to be relatively high because of its 42 percent inflation rate. However, inflation was not a problem for the other countries in which SSI operates, so inventories elsewhere should be maintained at lower levels.

SELF-TEST QUESTIONS

What are supply chain management and just-in-time inventory management?
What are precautionary inventory balances, and what purpose do they serve?
What is the economic order quantity (EOQ) model?

MANAGING THE RECEIVABLES COLLECTION PERIOD

Accounts receivable exist because companies believe their sales will increase if they offer credit to prospective customers.[5] Empirically this situation holds, so companies need to determine the credit structure that maximizes sales and profitability. This is termed the **credit policy**. Four variables are associated with credit policy:

Credit Policy
A set of decisions that include a firm's credit period, credit standards, collection procedures, and discounts offered.

1. The *credit period* is the length of time buyers have to pay for their purchases. In some industries and countries, there is a traditional credit period, or "standard practice," followed by most firms, but in other industries and countries such standards may not exist. In either case, the company should evaluate the costs and benefits of alternative credit periods.

   The company should be aware of its customers' cash flow situation when it establishes its credit terms. For example, if most customers will not have the money to pay SSI until they sell the speakers to final consumers and collect the cash 40 days later, then setting a 30-day credit period is not logical, since customers will tend to pay late by about 10 days. Terms of 40 or 45 days make better sense in this case because then the credit period is consistent with the customers' underlying credit needs.

---

[4]A good presentation of inventory practices and other working capital topics can be found in Terry S. Maness and John T. Zietlow, *Short-Term Financial Management*, 2nd ed. (Mason, OH: South-Western Publishing, 2002).

[5]We assume here that the receivables arise from supplier credit to other companies rather than consumer credit. The evaluation of both types of credit is similar, but SSI deals mainly with distributors, so supplier credit is a reasonable assumption. Also, in this section we ignore the fact that some of the receivables may be in currencies other than the home currency. We will consider this issue later in the chapter.

Of course, if customers have adequate capital, then they can finance the gap between required payments and collections. However, if they do not, then credit granted by SSI is vitally important. This situation is likely to exist in emerging markets where banking systems are not highly developed. Many western suppliers found a ready market in Russia after the fall of the Soviet Union because they offered good credit terms when there were virtually no other working capital financing alternatives available.

2. A *discount* may be offered for early payment to reward customers who have the ability and desire to make early payments. For example, SSI might use a credit period of 30 days but offer a discount of 2 percent if a customer pays within 10 days of the invoice date. Customers who pay within 10 days would then have to pay only 98 percent of the invoice price, while those who delay payment until the 30th day would have to pay the full invoice price. If possible, the invoice price should reflect the cost of the merchandise plus the cost of capital tied up in receivables for the net period, $30 - 10 = 20$ days in our example. Because SSI incurs a real economic cost for capital tied up in accounts receivable, it is also important to specify an additional financing charge if the customer pays late, that is, after 30 days in our example, providing such charges are allowed by the host country. When customers have no other reasonable source of credit, they should be willing to pay for the credit granted by SSI in this way.

3. *Credit standards* refer to the credit quality, or required financial strength, of acceptable credit customers. If SSI insisted on extremely high credit standards for its customers, then it would likely experience no bad debt losses. However, it would lose sales and profits from groups of companies with lesser financial strength but most of whom would be able to honor their obligations. A highly restrictive credit policy would seriously hurt SSI's sales, so such a policy would really not be feasible. Of course, with less restrictive credit standards, some customers will default, so SSI will experience bad debt losses. Therefore, SSI must assess the creditworthiness of each customer and set its credit standards such that the costs of lost sales and bad debts offset one another.

   In foreign markets, and particularly emerging markets, there are a number of serious challenges when setting credit standards. First, reliable data may not be available to assess the creditworthiness of customers. In such situations companies must look at general payment histories and underlying cultural characteristics to gain insights into potential default risks in each specific country.[6] They might also want to place extra restrictions on accounts, such as ensuring that previous invoices have been paid before granting additional credit, setting specific credit limits, retaining a security interest in the merchandise until the account is paid, or having the customer provide formal acknowledgment of the debt. In the latter case, the credit would not be on open account (recorded by SSI as an account receivable) but rather as a note receivable secured by a promissory note, often with a specified interest charge. Notes are always used for some types of products (such as diamonds or furs), and in some countries promissory notes are the rule rather than the exception.

4. *Collection policy*, or the steps taken to collect overdue accounts, is a particularly sensitive issue in many countries. A company doesn't want to alienate

---

[6]It is known, for instance, that defaults of sovereign debt are very rare in Asia but very common in Latin America. While not wanting to stereotype individual customers, and though private companies are not the same as sovereign governments, information of this type can be used to temper judgment in assessing whether and how to extend credit.

good customers experiencing temporary problems, but strong steps should be taken if customers have no intention of paying or are flagrantly abusing the credit policy. If SSI were very passive and did not act against slow-paying customers, then there would be no penalty for delaying payments, and the costs of carrying the credit would be very high.[7] Note, though, that as the collection policy becomes more aggressive, the probability of collection increases, but so do the chances of alienating customers. Thus, a balance must be struck, and it is essential to be aware of how people in different countries react to collection efforts.

MNEs can often use credit policies to gain a competitive advantage over local companies because, as we saw in Chapter 10, they tend to have access to capital at a lower cost than most purely domestic firms. Thus, they can extend trade credit more aggressively than local competitors and still make an adequate profit. However, they may not have good cultural insights into local business practices, and that can lead to errors in judgment when establishing and implementing credit policy.

SELF-TEST QUESTIONS   What is credit policy?

Identify and briefly explain the four variables associated with credit policy.

MANAGING THE PAYABLES DEFERRAL PERIOD

Accounts payable represent supplier trade credit, not investor-supplied capital.[8] Often, there is no explicit interest charge for trade credit, but as we discussed in the previous section, some companies include an implicit interest cost in the invoice price. If there is no cash price and no discount offered for early payment, the buyer would like to negotiate the longest payment period possible with its suppliers and pay on the last possible day. If the company has bargaining power over its suppliers, it may be able to negotiate terms long enough to cause the cash conversion period to be negative. In any case, the company will try to minimize the cash conversion period because investor-supplied financing at a positive interest rate is required to bridge the gap.[9]

If there is a cash price for immediate payment, or if there is no cash price but there is a discount for early payment, the buying firm must calculate the implicit interest rate associated with forgoing the discount and compare this rate with its external borrowing rate to determine whether or not to take the discount. There are two ways to calculate the implicit interest rate: (1) annualize the nominal discount percent and (2) calculate the effective annual rate. The formula for the annualized discount is

$$\text{Nominal annual cost} = \frac{\text{Discount percent}}{100 - \text{Discount percent}} \times \frac{365 \text{ days}}{\text{Days credit is outstanding} - \text{Discount period}}. \tag{14-1}$$

---

[7]One of the authors is familiar with a situation in Poland where a company never asked a customer with an overdue account to pay its bills, explaining that they were "sure" the company would pay when they had the money. On the other hand, the same company had a policy (very common at the time in Poland) of never paying a bill until they received the third overdue notice from their suppliers with a threat to cut them off from future credit. They were proud that they were able to make sales in a tough environment but wondered why their accounts receivable balance continued to rise sharply.

[8]Accrued liabilities—accrued taxes, wages, and interest—are also liabilities that do not come from investors and are subtracted in the calculation of NOWC. Companies should employ these to the extent they can, but they tend to be outside of the managerial control we are concerned with in this section. Thus, we will not cover them here.

[9]We will consider a possible exception later in the chapter when we introduce expected exchange rate losses.

If the credit terms offered to the company are 3/15, net 45, then the nominal annual cost would be

$$\begin{array}{l} \text{Nominal} \\ \text{annual} \\ \text{cost} \end{array} = \frac{3}{97} \times \frac{365}{45 - 15}$$

$$= 0.030928 \times 12.166667$$

$$= 0.376289 \text{ or } 37.63\%.$$

The first term of the equation, $3/97 = 3.0928\%$, is the cost per dollar of credit divided by the funds made available by not taking the discount, or the cost per period for the trade credit. The second term is the number of times per year this cost must be incurred, 12.17 times. If the company buys from the supplier regularly and does not take the discount, it is paying a nominal annual rate of 37.63 percent for the supplier-provided trade credit.

This 37.63 percent is a high cost for credit, but the effective cost is even higher! Equation 14-1 does not consider compounding, and when compounding is taken into account, the effective annual rate comes to 44.86 percent:

$$\text{Effective annual rate} = [(1.030928)^{12.166667} - 1] \times 100 = 44.86\%.$$

Costly Trade Credit
Credit taken in excess of free trade credit, whose cost is equal to the discount lost.

These calculations clearly demonstrate that forgoing cash terms or discounts results in extremely expensive credit. Most companies have alternative sources of less expensive financing, so companies would generally try to find financing elsewhere. On the other hand, if alternatives are not available, the **costly trade credit** may be the only means the customer has to finance inventories. This was the situation for many companies in Russia during the mid-1990s, and it is true for smaller companies in many emerging-market countries. Companies that find themselves in this situation should ignore the discounts and pay the net amount so long as the operation remains profitable after paying the high effective rate. Many companies, including some in industrialized countries, find themselves in this situation, and the costly trade credit allows them to stay in business. Note that suppliers should understand this fact as well, and many progressive MNEs pass on interest savings to their customers in the form of lower net prices. This creates goodwill and strengthens the relationship between supplier and customer.

Note also that the effective annual rate can be reduced if the company pays late and the seller imposes no extra interest penalties. However, this practice is not recommended because it destroys goodwill and brands the company as a slow payer. In the future, suppliers might not be as willing to extend additional credit to a slow payer as it would to a customer that can be counted upon to pay on time.

SELF-TEST QUESTIONS

Briefly explain whether the following statement is true or false: "Accounts payable represent investor-supplied capital."

Explain the difference between the two ways to calculate the implicit interest rate of trade credit.

GLOBAL CASH MANAGEMENT

The last major net operating working capital components are cash and near-cash (marketable securities). Cash, which consists of demand deposits and currency, earns no interest in the United States and very little, if any, elsewhere. Excess cash not needed in the short run is usually invested in short-term, highly liquid marketable securities that provide at least a small return, and for most purposes these investments are treated as cash.

Motives for Holding Cash

Because cash is a nonearning (or minimal earning) asset, most companies minimize the amount held. At the same time, cash is needed to take trade discounts, to pay bills as they come due; to pay salaries, taxes, and interest; and to meet unexpected funding needs. Thus, cash cannot be eliminated entirely. Over the years, several motives have been suggested to explain why firms hold cash balances:

1. *Transactions motive.* Companies must pay their bills as they come due. In the United States, such payments tend to be made using checks, but in other countries payments are usually made through manual or electronic debit systems. Likewise, receipts, whether in the form of cash, checks, or credit entries, are deposited and recorded in the company's demand deposit account. Positive balances are created by deposits and then used to pay bills as they come due. Thus, **transactions balances** are held to make payments on accounts payable by the due date; to take discounts when available; and to pay salaries, taxes, interest, dividends, and all other payments usually required of a company.

2. *Precautionary motive.* Cash inflows and outflows are unpredictable, so most firms tend to hold extra cash balances "in reserve," just in case unforeseen needs arise. These "safety stocks" of cash are called **precautionary balances**, and the more unpredictable the cash flows are, the higher these balances should be.

3. *Compensating balances motive.* Banks make money by providing services that customers need and by lending out deposited money at a higher rate than they pay on deposits, that is, to earn a credit spread. Companies that use banking services can pay for them in two different ways. First, they can pay directly a small service charge each month to compensate the bank for the services provided. Second, the company can leave a minimum sum of money on deposit at all times that earns zero or very little interest. The bank can then lend out this money and earn a return on it. For each dollar left on deposit the bank applies an *earnings credit rate* (or ECR) and uses the resulting credit to offset the cost of providing services. It is easy to calculate how many dollars of deposits are needed to generate sufficient earnings credit to offset the entire service charge. This minimum deposit amount is called a **compensating balance**. If a company chooses to use compensating balances to pay for bank services, it will maintain higher cash balances than an otherwise similar firm that prefers to pay service charges directly. Historically, most companies used compensating balances to pay for bank service charges. However, in the age of electronic commerce, when companies can shift funds globally quickly and at low cost, the majority are now switching to direct payments for banking services.

Transactions Balances
Cash balances associated with payments and collections; the balance necessary for day-to-day operations.

Precautionary Balances
Cash balances held in reserve for random, unforeseen fluctuations in cash inflows and outflows.

Compensating Balances
Bank balances that firms must maintain to compensate the bank for services rendered.

Cash balances serve as a buffer when the timing of inflows and outflows is uncertain. If the cash conversion period is positive, then its cash balance allows a company to pay bills when they come due and to replenish the balance when receivables are collected. If the company does not have enough cash on hand, then marketable securities can be liquidated, or the firm can use short-term bank loans until it receives additional cash inflows. If a company has more cash than it needs for transactions purposes, it can pay it out to investors, pay down debt, or "park" it temporarily in marketable securities until the money is needed to pay bills. Knowing when the company will need to borrow or when it will have the cash to pay off loans or to invest is vital information for a good cash management system. The device that is used by most companies to forecast cash needs and availability is

Cash Budget
The device used by most companies to forecast cash needs and availability.

called the **cash budget**.[10] For multinational companies, the cash budget is prepared by each subsidiary and, depending on how the company is structured, either actions are taken locally to acquire or invest cash or the information is sent to a central coordinating location and the necessary actions are taken there.

Centralization of Cash Management

One of the most important working capital decisions for an MNE is whether to centralize or decentralize the cash management function.[11] In previous chapters, we suggested that MNEs have a competitive advantage over purely domestic companies in raising capital globally. The same is true on the investing side—an MNE can search globally for the instrument that gives the highest available yield, while domestic firms are largely constrained to invest only in local securities. To capitalize on this advantage, many MNEs centralize the cash management function rather than have subsidiaries manage this function individually.

There are at least three areas of competitive advantage for MNEs that favor centralization of cash management:

1. *Scale advantages.* When a company centralizes its cash management operations, individual subsidiaries remit excess cash to the central pool on a daily basis, or, if they have a shortage, it is replenished daily from the central pool. Thus, the money in the system is concentrated rather than being dispersed, and there are economies of scale present in dealing with larger cash flows.

   An important scale effect relates to information availability at the centralized treasury department. Because of the large amount of business given to a single global bank (or a small group of banks), to brokers, and to other institutions, a great deal of information can be obtained from these institutions' research departments about risks in various currencies and countries, the institutions may offer more competitive rates, and it is likely that the company's transactions will receive higher priority in execution. This is particularly true if the company locates the central depository in one of the world's money centers, where the financial institutions are larger, have greater scope, are more efficient, and have greater focused expertise.

   A second scale effect is the ability to develop a highly competent financial staff at a single location. It is generally not cost efficient to maintain a high level of expertise at each separate subsidiary, but it makes sense to do so in one centralized location.

2. *Diversification advantages.* If there are 10 subsidiaries and each subsidiary holds a precautionary balance of $2 million, the decentralized precautionary balance would total $20 million. It is unlikely, though, that unfavorable circumstances would simultaneously strike all 10 subsidiaries so that they each need the full amount. Through diversification, a central pool can reduce the precautionary balance from $20 million to a smaller amount, say $12 million, without increasing the risk of a cash shortage. If a subsidiary has an urgent need for cash, the central pool can wire transfer the funds. Thus, the precautionary cash needs at the consolidated level will decline, thereby increasing the firm's profitability.

[10]For a detailed description of cash budgets and how they are prepared and used see Brigham and Daves, *Intermediate Financial Management*, Chapter 20.

[11]This is also an important decision for domestic companies. With the rise of nationwide branching in the United States and the availability of low-cost electronic funds transfer systems, corporate treasurers have far more latitude than ever before to exercise centralized control over cash payments and receipts. The same is true of international companies who use multinational banks to perform the same services globally. For a good discussion of these issues that goes beyond what we can cover here, see Maness and Zietlow, *Short-Term Financial Management*.

Another diversification advantage results from the ability to use internal matching, along with global capital markets to acquire funds and or invest surplus cash. If cash management is decentralized, a subsidiary that needs cash may be forced to borrow at high rates while another subsidiary with excess cash must invest at low rates. A centralized pool allows excess cash from one subsidiary to flow to other subsidiaries, thus improving results for the consolidated company.

3. *Tax advantages.* Locating the centralized depository in a "tax haven" country such as Lichtenstein or the Cayman Islands has several advantages. These countries specialize in global financial operations and have sophisticated infrastructures designed to serve the needs of MNEs. They do not restrict the movement of cash into or out of the country, and they are called **tax havens** because they impose very low or no taxes on most transactions, along with favorable income taxes. They also have strict secrecy regulations, so MNEs do not have to disclose information they consider to be trade secrets. Finally, as we will see shortly, locating the central depository in a tax haven country can reduce a consolidated firm's tax liability.

Tax Havens
Locations with low or no taxes on most transactions and no restrictions on the movement of cash into or out of these locations.

SELF-TEST QUESTIONS

Identify and briefly explain the three motives generally given as reasons firms hold cash balances.

What are the three areas of competitive advantage enjoyed by MNEs that favor the centralization of the cash management function? Briefly explain each one.

WORKING CAPITAL INTEGRATION OVERVIEW

Many companies also centralize intracompany receivables, payables management, and working capital financing. Integrating global working capital management is an exceptionally complex activity because so many factors must be considered, including highly variable laws, regulations, and business practices in different countries. Also, working capital issues must be integrated with other dimensions of global operations, including exchange-rate risk management, tax planning, research and development, and providing centralized services to the internal market. To facilitate our discussion, we focus on 10 different decision areas that companies must consider when integrating global working capital and cash flow management activities. These include the following:

1. Mechanisms for global repositioning of funds.
2. Transactions costs incurred when repositioning funds.
3. Tax treatment of different repositioning channels.
4. Blockages that prevent the use of certain repositioning channels.
5. Minority interests of local shareholders or joint venture partners.
6. Exchange-rate expectations for all the currencies used by the company.
7. Liquidity needs and compensating balances for each subsidiary and for the combined MNE.
8. Borrowing and investing opportunities.
9. The availability of and need for funds in each subsidiary.
10. The company's willingness to assume risk.

SELF-TEST QUESTIONS

Identify some of the factors that must be considered when integrating global working capital management.

With what areas of global operations must working capital be integrated?

MECHANISMS FOR GLOBAL REPOSITIONING OF FUNDS

The decision to centralize working capital functions implies that the MNE can reposition funds globally whenever and wherever it desires and that this can be done quickly and at a low cost. In developed industrial countries this is a reasonable assumption, but in many emerging markets it may not be correct. We alluded to this in Chapter 11 when we discussed project cash flows from the parent perspective. Now we must look more closely at global funds repositioning when assessing opportunities for centralized working capital management.

As shown in Table 14-2, we can divide the mechanisms for moving funds into or out of a country into two groups: capital-related flows and operations-related flows. The left column lists flows related to investor-supplied equity and debt, both from internal sources (such as the contribution of parent equity or debt investment) and from external sources (minority interest equity or a bond issue in the euromarkets), to the affiliate's country. Most countries encourage such inflows, but getting money back out is sometimes a problem. Generally, repatriating earnings as dividends is easier than repatriating equity capital, and interest and principal repayments to external lenders are less problematic than those to related affiliates. At times, countries have claimed a "loan" from the parent to the local subsidiary is really "disguised equity," and thus subjected it to strict regulations. However, if an intrafirm loan carries a market-derived interest rate and contractual payments similar to external loans, it is more likely that interest and principal payments can be made.

Royalties, license fees, management fees, and administrative overhead allocations as discussed in SSI's Shanghai investment are examples of operations-related flows, and we also discussed intrafirm accounts receivable and payable when we translated and consolidated SSI's financial statements in Chapter 7. Note too that MNEs with similar operations in several different countries have the flexibility to serve global markets from different production sites. Suppose a company has determined that a particular production plan results in the lowest total cost and the maximum consolidated free cash flow. Markets are dynamic, though, with costs and revenues changing at different rates in different countries. As these costs and revenues change, shifting production between countries and serving markets from different facilities could lead to greater consolidated free cash flow for the MNE. A purely domestic company would have less flexibility to change its operating environment, so the MNE's ability to adapt in response to changing conditions provides an advantage over domestic competitors.

TABLE 14-2 | Mechanisms for Moving Funds Into and Out of a Country

Capital-Related Flows	Operations-Related Flows
Parent equity investment	Payments for purchases of goods and services (intracompany)
Other party equity investment	Payments for purchases of goods and services (external)
Intracompany loan	Receipts for sales (intracompany)
External loan	Receipts for sales (external)
Payment of dividends	Royalties paid/received
Repatriation of invested equity	License fees paid/received
Payment of interest	Management fees paid/received
Repayment of principal	Administrative overhead allocations paid/received

Ramping production up or down at different locations, or serving markets from alternative production locations, requires that the company be able to reallocate resources quickly and at a low cost. This resource reallocation is difficult if the MNE is decentralized and each subsidiary has significant autonomy. However, if operations are centralized, the MNE can use its internal market to react quickly and reconfigure operations to take advantage of changing conditions.[12] This is why we placed so much emphasis on the repatriation of funds in our Chapter 11 discussion and why the Chapter 4 country attractiveness scorecard emphasized this factor.

What are the two categories of mechanisms for moving funds into or out of a country?

Identify examples of capital-related flows.

Identify examples of operations-related flows.

TRANSACTIONS COSTS WHEN REPOSITIONING FUNDS

Moving funds between two affiliated units through the MNE's internal market is not costless, but for some transactions, costs are significantly lower than if the external market were used. For instance, an MNE with operating affiliates that trade with each other can use the internal market to reduce transactions costs and increase the efficiency of receivables and payables management. Table 14-3 lists the accounts receivable and payable for an illustrative MNE's affiliates. Looking at Panel A, the columns represent each subsidiary's accounts receivable from affiliates, while the rows show the subsidiaries' accounts payable to affiliates. Thus, total intrafirm accounts receivable for the Argentine affiliate is $500, shown at the bottom of its column, and it consists of $300 due from Germany and $100 each from Japan and the U.S.[13]

Netting
A technique for minimizing transactions costs by simply "canceling" the obligation of one affiliate with obligations of another.

The Argentine subsidiary's accounts payable to affiliates, shown in row one in the far right column, total to $800, with $400 payable to Germany and $200 to both Japan and the United States. Notice that each pair of affiliates, say, Argentina and Germany, have receivables and payables to each other: Argentina owes $400 to Germany, and Germany owes $300 to Argentina. It would be possible for each subsidiary to acquire foreign exchange and physically remit payments to one another, thereby incurring transactions costs. Over time these costs would accumulate to a significant amount, so it is useful to find a mechanism to help minimize these costs.

Bilateral Netting
A technique in which receivables and payables entries are "netted out" between pairs of affiliates, and then the sum of the remaining nonzero entries represents the total accounts payable and accounts receivable in the internal market. Payments are now made in only one direction.

Netting

One technique for minimizing transactions costs among affilitates is called **netting**. Because the affiliates are part of the internal market, some of their obligations can be "canceled out," as we saw in Chapter 7. **Bilateral netting** is shown in Panel B of Table 14-3. For Germany and Argentina, we note that Argentina owes $400 to Germany while Germany owes only only $300 to Argentina. After netting, Argentina would still owe $100 to Germany. On the other hand, the payables and receivables between Germany and Japan are equal, so they can be netted out completely. Once

---

[12]Of course, there are human resources issues that have to be considered during such reallocations that may be challenging. In general, managers should be compensated on the basis of their contribution to consolidated value creation instead of looking only at the local affiliate.

[13]For ease of effecting the netting transactions, all intrafirm accounts for all affiliates are translated into the reporting currency, in this case the U.S. dollar.

TABLE 14-3 | Netting of an Illustrative MNE's Affiliates' Intrafirm Accounts

Panel A: Total Firm Example

| | Accounts Receivable from Affiliates | | | | |
	Argentina	Germany	Japan	United States	Total Accounts Payable
Argentina	—	$400	$200	$200	$ 800
Germany	$300	—	200	400	900
Japan	100	200	—	300	600
United States	100	200	200	—	500
Total accounts receivable	$500	$800	$600	$900	$2,800

(left margin label: Accounts Payable)

Panel B: Bilateral Netting Example

| | Accounts Receivable from Affiliates | | | | |
	Argentina	Germany	Japan	United States	Total Accounts Payable
Argentina	—	$100 / 400	$100 / 200	$100 / 200	$300
Germany	$ 0 / 300	—	0 / 200	200 / 400	200
Japan	0 / 100	0 / 200	—	100 / 300	100
United States	0 / 100	0 / 200	0 / 200	—	0
Total accounts receivable	$ 0	$100	$100	$400	$600

(left margin label: Accounts Payable)

Panel C: Multilateral Netting Example

| | Accounts Receivable | | | | |
	Argentina	Germany	Japan	United States	Total Accounts Payable
Argentina	—	$ 0 / 100	$ 0 / 100	$300 / 100	$300
Germany	$ 0	—	0	100 / 200	100
Japan	0	0	—	0 / 100	0
United States	0	0	0	—	0
Total accounts receivable	$ 0	$ 0	$ 0	$400	$400

(left margin label: Accounts Payable)

we net out the entries for each pair of affiliates, we can sum the remaining nonzero entries to obtain the total accounts payable and accounts receivable in the internal market. The value of total transactions has been reduced from $2,800 in Panel A to $600 in Panel B, and now payments are made only in one direction. This reduces transactions costs because there are fewer and smaller transactions.

**Multilateral
Netting**
Where affiliates
make payments
for other affiliates
to reduce transac-
tions costs even
further.

Multilateral netting can reduce transactions costs even more. Panel C starts with the positive numbers from Panel B. Thus, Argentina owes Germany, Japan, and the United States $100 each, Germany owes the United States $200, and Japan owes the United States $100. Through accounting entries, Argentina will pay an additional $100 to the United States versus the Panel B figure (increasing its total payment to the United States from $100 to $200), and the payment from Germany to the United States will be reduced from $200 to $100. Likewise, Argentina owes Japan $100 and Japan owes the United States $100, so again we can net out the $100 payment by Argentina to Japan and increase the payment from Argentina to the United States by another $100 (for a new total of $300). Japan's obligations net out to zero. So, we are left with just two payments, $300 by Argentina and $100 by Germany, both to the United States.

Without netting, the company had to engage in 12 separate transactions to balance out its accounts. This number was cut to 5 transactions through bilateral netting and down to 2 with multilateral netting. These reductions save money and thus are a source of competitive advantage for the MNE.

However, there is one problem with netting—not all countries permit it. Countries with strong foreign exchange and capital restrictions often prohibit netting because they want all receivables to flow into the country while they can restrict which payables can be sent out.

Reinvoicing Centers

Reinvoicing Center
A separate affili-
ate, often located
in a tax haven
country, through
which intracom-
pany transactions
pass.

A **reinvoicing center** is a separate affiliate, often located in a tax haven country, through which intracompany transactions pass. Reinvoicing centers often have an in-house bank, along with centralized foreign currency and interest-rate risk management operations. Physical transfers of goods, though, pass directly from one operating affiliate to another—only payables and receivables are handled by the reinvoicing center.

All intracompany sales are transactions between an affiliate and the reinvoicing center, and they are denominated in the currency of the local operating affiliate. Thus, an account receivable of the operating subsidiary becomes a liability of the reinvoicing center, and because all sales to operating affiliates are made by the reinvoicing center, the subsidiaries' accounts payable are assets of the reinvoicing center. Again, all of these transactions are denominated in the currency of the operating affiliate.

Continuing our example from Table 14-3, assume that the company opens a reinvoicing center in the Cayman Islands. The appropriate cash flows are given in Table 14-4. Panel A shows the situation after intracompany receivables and payables have been transferred to the reinvoicing center (RC). Panel B shows the situation after RC has netted these items out. The totals at the bottom of the columns show that Argentina, Germany, and Japan have no net receivables after their payables have been deducted, while the United States has $400 of net receivables. The last column shows that Argentina has $300 of net payables, Germany owes a net of $100, and Japan and the United States have zero net payables. All of the accounts are based on local currencies, translated into dollars. From the subsidiaries' standpoint, the results are the same as in Panel C of Table 14-3, except now funds are due from or owed to the RC rather than other operating subsidiaries. Two important points should be made about Table 14-4:

1. All currency risk is centralized with the reinvoicing center because all transactions are recorded in the operating affiliates' local currencies. This facilitates risk management by concentrating all internal foreign currency transactions at a single location where specialized expertise can be developed.

TABLE 14-4 | Netting for an Illustrative MNE with a Reinvoicing Center

Panel A: Situation with Receivables and Payables held by Reinvoicing Center

			Accounts Receivable			
Accounts Payable		Argentina	Germany	Japan	United States	Reinvoicing Center	Total
	Argentina	—	$ 0	$ 0	$ 0	$800	$ 800
	Germany	$ 0	—	0	0	900	900
	Japan	0	0	—	0	600	600
	United States	0	0	0	—	500	500
	Reinvoicing Center	500	800	600	900	—	
	Total	$500	$800	$600	$900		$2,800

Panel B: Subsidiaries Net Receivables or Payables

			Accounts Receivable			
Accounts Payable		Argentina	Germany	Japan	United States	Reinvoicing Center	Total
	Argentina	—	$ 0	$ 0	$ 0	$300 / 800	$300
						100	100
	Germany	$ 0	—	0	0	900	
	Japan	0	0	—	0	0 / 600	0
	United States	0	0	0	—	0 / 500	0
	Reinvoicing Center	500	800	600	400 / 900	—	$400
	Total	$ 0	$ 0	$ 0	$400		$400

2. The RC participates in all intracompany transactions, which facilitates the netting process. Panel B of Table 14-4 produces results similar to those in Panel C of Table 14-3, but with simple bilateral netting rather than having to use the more complex multilateral netting.

Thus, we see that a reinvoicing center facilitates the management of intrafirm trade credit.

SELF-TEST QUESTIONS

What is netting?

What is a reinvoicing center?

TAX TREATMENT OF DIFFERENT REPOSITIONING CHANNELS

Tax rules and regulations differ across countries and affect the choice of repositioning channels. In terms of affiliate earnings, some countries provide tax incentives via a low rate on earnings. If these earnings are repatriated to the United States (or to

TABLE 14-5 | Differing Tax Treatment of Illustrative MNE Subsidiary

Panel A: Repatriate Dividends to Receive Funds		Panel B: Use License Fees to Receive Funds	
Sales	$2,500	Sales	$2,500
Operating costs	(1,500)	Operating costs	(1,500)
License fee	(0)	License fee	(1,000)
Taxable income	$1,000	Taxable income	$ 0
Taxes (35%)	(350)	Taxes (40%)	0
Net income	$ 650	Net income	$ 0
Withholding (10%)	(65)		
After-tax dividend	$ 585	No dividend is paid BUT	
Taxable income per IRS	$1,000	License fee	$1,000
U.S. taxes (40%)	400	U.S. taxes (40%)	(400)
Foreign Tax Credit (FTC) = $350 + $65 =	415	After-tax license fee	$ 600
Net tax due (all foreign)	$ 415		
After-tax dividend = $1,000 − $350 − $65 =	$ 585		
Have $15 of excess FTC which could be used later.			

most other industrial nations), a foreign tax credit is given for foreign taxes paid, but additional taxes are due in the home country to bring the effective rate up to that of the parent. This process was illustrated in Chapter 11 when we discussed the parent perspective analysis. If the affiliate's host country also imposes a withholding tax (as do many emerging-market countries) on the repatriated dividends to the parent (there was none in our Shanghai example), the total of the local tax rate plus the withholding rate may be higher than the home country's tax rate, so an excess foreign tax credit will exist. The company may or may not be able to use the full tax credit, but the supposedly lower taxes in the foreign host country will be illusory. Of course, the primary purpose of withholding taxes is to pressure MNEs to reinvest their earnings locally.[14]

License Fees

Faced with these tax issues regarding repatriating earnings, MNEs might choose to use fees or assessments to get money home. In Panel A of Table 14-5, we assume that the local tax rate on earnings is 35 percent versus the U.S. federal-plus-state tax rate of 40 percent. However, suppose that if the subsidiary pays a dividend to the parent, the dividend is subject to a 10 percent withholding tax, causing the total effective tax rate to be 41.5 percent ([$350 + $65]/$1,000), which exceeds the U.S. rate. No tax will be due on the repatriated dividend in the United States, but local taxes will be $415, thus providing an excess foreign tax credit (FTC) of $15. This credit can be applied against other foreign income, if any, but it cannot be applied against this subsidiary's dividend.

Panel B of Table 14-5 illustrates the use of license fees as an alternative for getting money home. License fees are a deductible expense in the host country, but they are subject to the full 40 percent U.S. tax rate. The after-tax license fee received is $600, which is $15 more than if the subsidiary repatriated the money as a dividend.

---

[14]Another mechanism for achieving this result is to constrain the maximum dividend to a fixed percentage of invested equity capital.

Notice that even if the company can use the excess FTC elsewhere, the maximum that can be realized through dividends is $585 + $15 = $600, but such income is subject to more uncertainty than license fees. Of course, if the company wants to remove as much value from the subsidiary as quickly as it can, all channels may be used simultaneously. We will consider this possibility in a later section when we discuss exchange-rate expectations.

Transfer Prices

Transfer Price
The price charged for a transaction between affiliates.

Transfer pricing is another device affecting intrafirm payables and receivables that can be used to shift funds from one operating unit to another. If one affiliate sells to another subsidiary through the internal market, what price should it charge for the transaction? Economic theory suggests setting the **transfer price** equal to the marginal cost of the item, but that answer ignores many practical issues. High transfer prices increase the profitability of the selling affiliate but depress the profitability of the buying affiliate, and vice versa. Managerial performance evaluation and compensation systems are often tied directly to their units' profitability, so selling at marginal costs would penalize the selling group's managers. A more significant complication arises due to taxes. The tax authorities in each country want their "fair share" of taxes, and setting the transfer price (sales price) equal to the marginal cost would eliminate taxes in the selling country. Countries have sovereignty, so they have the power to "impute" a higher transfer price that will result in profits and thus taxes.

To the extent that companies have flexibility to vary transfer prices, taxes usually dominate the decision process.[15] The MNE would prefer to realize the profit in the country with the lowest tax rates in order to minimize the firm's global tax burden. Table 14-6 illustrates how the tax burden can be shifted from a high-tax country to one with lower tax rates. Assume that the tax rate in Country A is 40 percent and the tax rate in Country B is 30 percent. Also assume that the MNE's affiliate in Country A sells to the affiliate in Country B. The simplified income statements shown in Table 14-6 assume that the sales of A translate into cost of goods sold for B. In Case 1, the selling price is set at $10 per unit. At this price, net income is $120 and taxes paid to Country A are $80. In Country B, net income is $140 and taxes paid are $60. Consolidating these two income statements yields $140 of total taxes and $260 of net income.

In Case 2, the transfer price is lowered to $9 per unit. This lowers taxes and net income in Country A by half, to $40 and $60, respectively. However, taxes in Country B are increased by 50 percent, to $90, and net income rises to $210. From the consolidated MNE's perspective, the total tax burden has been reduced from $140 to $130, and the extra $10 has flowed directly to net income, which rises from $260 to $270. At the limit, if the transfer price were set at $8 per unit (the fully allocated cost), no taxes would be paid in Country A, and the consolidated tax burden would be lowered even more.

The minister of finance in Country B would probably like these last two scenarios, but the minister from Country A would be unhappy. If the ministry concluded that the low transfer price was a tax avoidance scheme that did not reflect true underlying market values, a higher transfer price would be imputed, and the tax owed by the company would be based on that price.[16]

---

[15]In addition to income tax rates, tariff and quota issues need to be factored into the analysis. We will abstract from these complications as we provide an overview of transfer pricing.

[16]Transfer pricing is also an issue for domestic companies operating in multiple states. In July 1983, Florida passed a law creating a "unitary tax" environment for companies in which the percentage of total tax paid by the company in Florida could be no less than the percentage of total assets located in the state. The intent was to increase tax collections to a "fair" level, but in the face of threats by companies to pull out of Florida entirely if the tax were not repealed, the legislature backed down and repealed the law in 1984. Transfer pricing, though, is still a sensitive issue.

TABLE 14-6 | Transfer Pricing and Taxation Effects for an Illustrative MNE's Affiliates

Case 1: Transfer Price = $10 per Unit

Affiliate A (High Taxes)		Affiliate B (Low Taxes)	
Sales (100 units @ $10)	$1,000	Sales	$1,600
Cost of goods sold	(600)	Cost of goods sold	(1,000)
Other costs	(200)	Other costs	(400)
Taxable income	$ 200	Taxable income	$ 200
Taxes (40%)	(80)	Taxes (30%)	(60)
Net income	$ 120	Net income	$ 140

Total consolidated taxes paid = $80 + $60 = $140
Total consolidated net income = $120 + $140 = $260

Case 2: Transfer Price = $9 per Unit

Affiliate A (High Taxes)		Affiliate B (Low Taxes)	
Sales (100 units @ $9)	$900	Sales	$1,600
Cost of goods sold	(600)	Cost of goods sold	(900)
Other costs	(200)	Other costs	(400)
Taxable income	$100	Taxable income	$ 300
Taxes (40%)	(40)	Taxes (30%)	(90)
Net income	$ 60	Net income	$ 210

Total consolidated taxes paid = $40 + $90 = $130
Total consolidated net income = $60 + $210 = $270

"Arms-Length" Price
The theoretically correct transfer price; the amount an unrelated customer would have to pay in a free market for the product.

Countries are keenly interested in transfer prices, so companies do not have as much flexibility today as they enjoyed in the past (although there is still some latitude in instances when the country might prefer to give a break to the company using this "invisible" mechanism rather than one that is more visible for all to see and oppose). Theoretically, the "correct" transfer price from a country's perspective that should satisfy the ministers of finance of both countries is the amount an unrelated customer would have to pay in a free market, or an **"arms-length" price.** If the MNE sells the same products in the external market, or if the item is a widely traded generic commodity, this price is easier to obtain. However, because of factors such as quantity discounts, variations in quality, or product branding effects through proprietary trademarks, it is often difficult to establish such prices. Also, many items may be intermediate goods for which there is no external market. When we cannot directly observe an arms-length or uncontrolled price for comparable items, two other methods for setting transfer prices are suggested by the Organization for Economic Cooperation and Development (OECD) Committee on Fiscal Affairs:

1. *Resale price method.* The sales price to the ultimate external consumer is determined and then reduced by an "appropriate" distributor markup to arrive at a fair price to the distributor. Determining the appropriate markup is difficult, and various factors such as the value added by the distributor can complicate the computation. Also, if the item is only one component of the final product, this method is almost impossible to use.
2. *Cost-plus method.* The full cost of the item, including both direct costs and overhead allocations, is the starting point in the cost-plus method. Then an

Advance Pricing Agreement (APA) An approach to determining the appropriate cost-plus transfer price through negotiation with tax authorities of both governments of the affiliates involved in the transaction.

"appropriate" markup is applied to arrive at the transfer price. Of course, there are issues of what the direct cost really is (e.g., do you use FIFO or LIFO?), and the overhead allocation is always somewhat subjective. Determination of the appropriate margin is also subjective. One approach to finding the appropriate cost-plus transfer price is through negotiation of an **advance pricing agreement (APA)** with the tax authorities of both governments of the affiliates involved in the transaction. While these agreements take time and money to negotiate, they reduce the risk that one or both governments may challenge the transfer price.

SELF-TEST QUESTIONS

What is a foreign tax credit?

What is a transfer price?

BLOCKAGES THAT PREVENT THE USE OF CERTAIN REPOSITIONING CHANNELS

Blockage Government regulations or laws restricting an MNE's ability to transfer funds into or out of an affiliate country.

The term **blockage** refers to government regulations or laws that restrict an MNE's ability to transfer funds into or out of a country in which the company has an affiliate. In previous sections, we noted that some countries do not permit foreign companies to repatriate equity investments until the subsidiary is sold to others and limits can be placed on dividends. Sometimes, there is a numerical limit on dividends, such as paying no more than a specified percentage (15 percent is common) of invested capital. Or, as described in our Chinese project in Chapter 11, the government may insist that the company generate sufficient foreign exchange earnings to cover dividends and other foreign transfers. Also in Chapter 11, we discussed the difficulties associated with paying fees or assessments to the parent.

Basically, there are two dimensions to dealing with blockages: (1) figuring out ways to get money out of a subsidiary in a country where a blockage exists and (2) financing local operations without having to send more money to a host country where it might be blocked. To develop effective strategies for managing blockages, we need to appreciate why countries impose such restrictions in the first place.

Why Countries Block Funds

At least four reasons for countries to block international funds flows have been suggested in the academic literature:

1. *To manage the country's foreign exchange reserves and currency's value.* In Chapter 2, we discussed various exchange-rate management strategies used by governments. We also suggested that emerging-market nations might benefit from one of the fixed-exchange-rate regimes. This requires the country to maintain a strong reserve position to counter pressures on the exchange rate in the short run, so the government must actively manage the supply and demand for the local currency. Usually this translates into capital and/or foreign exchange controls. Thus, certain types of transactions will be blocked while others will be permitted—but only to a limited extent and subject to explicit government permission. China's policy of keeping the yuan at a fixed parity rate against the dollar is a good example of a government that follows such a policy.

2. *To stimulate local investment and increase capital availability.* Countries that do not have deep local capital markets and have only limited access to international sources of capital often see the MNE as their link to external invest-

ment capital. By allowing MNEs to enter the country, external capital that benefits the local economy is attracted. To ensure that the company maintains its stake in the country and continues to expand the capital base, the government may constrain the company's ability to repatriate capital and earnings.[17]

3. *To encourage exports.* Many countries establish free trade zones to attract investments that produce goods only for export. Companies recover their investment by "repatriating" profits through exporting products and selling them in another market, bringing back to the host country only part of the revenues. Countries often constrain the company's ability to use many of the global repositioning channels given in Table 14-2, but license fees and transfer pricing are often allowed to remove funds.

4. *To increase MNEs' commitment to the local economy.* If a country is to obtain the maximum benefits from an MNE's investment, then a network of local suppliers and workers, and the social and economic infrastructure to support them, must be developed. In negotiations with the host government, MNEs are often required to invest in worker training, housing, medical facilities, schools, roads, and similar infrastructure. If the company is required to invest depreciation cash flows along with earnings back into the community, either in the form of a plant expansion or more supporting infrastructure, the country benefits. Likewise, if an MNE can be encouraged to shift other parts of its global operations to the host country to use blocked funds, then the country benefits.

These four motives for blocking funds are not mutually exclusive. In fact, they are all used as parts of an integrated development strategy of some countries. Faced with such blockages, what strategies can MNEs employ to minimize disruptions to their internal markets, and how can they circumvent blockages? We now explore these questions.

Strategies for Dealing with Blockages

Blockages are a fact of life for MNEs, and it is usually not possible to avoid them entirely. However, it is important for an MNE to develop a strategy to minimize the disruption caused by blockages. Four dimensions of strategies need to be considered to deal effectively with blockages:

1. *Negotiations prior to investment.* The time to think about how blockages will affect the firm is before the investment is made. Often, the bargaining power of the company vis-à-vis the host government will be the strongest at this time. We described briefly in Chapter 11 the negotiations between SSI and the Chinese government that established the ground rules for the Shanghai investment. License and management fees, repatriation restrictions on earnings, and taxation—all of which are relevant aspects of global repositioning and blockages—were explicitly included in the discussions and both sides compromised about the terms of participation.

   Recall from Chapter 4 that companies sometimes define minimum acceptable terms for such things as earnings repatriation, technology licensing, integrated working capital management flexibility, and other items that are vital

---

[17]There are examples of companies whose invested equity consisted mainly of overvalued used machinery that had been largely depreciated. They structured the investment to pull out of the country as much cash flow as possible in just a few years, making the project "payback" very short. After the payback point, the company could afford, literally, to walk away from the investment. A company in such a situation is in an extremely strong bargaining position. However, governments do not like to be put in this position, so they attempt to prevent "thin capitalization" from occurring in the first place.

Strike-Out Rules
Designations
given to critical
conditions in the
country evaluation
process that mean
if it is not possi-
ble to negotiate
acceptable terms,
the company will
not make the
investment.

for maintaining flexibility and managing the internal market. Often these critical conditions are included in the country evaluation process as **strike-out rules** instead of trade-off variables. This designation means that if it is not possible to negotiate acceptable terms, the company will not make the investment. Thus, the negotiation process can be a critical aspect of FDI.

2. *Operating strategies to increase the ability to reposition funds globally.* Once the structure has been defined through negotiations, management knows how much flexibility it has in using the internal market to respond to changing conditions. Sometimes this means moving money out of weak currency areas to stronger ones or sourcing inputs from different locations and selling in new markets. At other times it may mean building up stocks of raw materials as a hedge against inflation in a particular country, or using local-currency debt financing instead of retained earnings. These operating strategies go beyond traditional working capital management, but at the same time they are implemented through actions that affect working capital. Thus, once the investment has been made, the emphasis of working capital management activities is on operating efficiency broadly defined for the entire MNE. In this context, there may be legitimate reasons for sacrificing working capital objectives such as minimizing the cash conversion period.

3. *Alternatives to direct capital contributions in financing foreign affiliates.* If a country places significant restrictions on the MNE's ability to move funds into or out of the country, but the company decides to make the investment anyway, then a strategy for managing local working capital must be developed.[18] This situation is most common in countries with depreciating currencies, unstable prices, and poor access to international capital markets. Perhaps the subsidiary will be financed with a minimal equity contribution (and this may be in the form of used machinery or raw materials that are not available locally) plus, if possible, local borrowing or equity contributed by local investors if control is not an issue. Reinvested earnings and depreciation cash flows will be used to finance growth, and the techniques mentioned later in this section to circumvent blockages will be employed to the fullest.

4. *Exit strategy.* Companies often expend significant amounts of resources to evaluate whether to invest in a country and to find the best entrance strategy. Although it is also important, companies often do not pay much attention to potential exit strategies in the event things do not go as planned. It is important to think about this issue during negotiations with the government to minimize such things as redundancy payments to discharged workers, steep withholding taxes on repatriated capital if the operation is sold to a local owner, and similar impediments to an orderly withdrawal. Companies facing such possibilities will want to structure their operations to maximize value repatriation in the early years, particularly from sources that are not tied directly to profitability. This shortens the payback and therefore reduces risk.

Devices for Lessening the Effects of Blockages

Even when governments block repatriation of cash flows and cannot be persuaded to relax restrictions, there may still be legal ways to remove value from the country. Assuming that the country does not require reinvestment of operating earnings and depreciation cash flows in low-yielding government bonds (which does happen

---

[18]While this situation does not sound particularly attractive, we assume that the investment has a positive NPV when evaluated from the parent perspective (otherwise the investment should not be made). We point out that investments in these countries likely have real option value because they would be quite valuable if things turn out well, and this may explain the positive NPV.

sometimes), there are at least three devices that can be used to mitigate the effects of blockages:

1. *Unrelated exports.* Countries encourage the export of most products because foreign exchange is generated and the balance of payments is affected in a positive manner. Blocked funds can be employed to purchase some local commodity, which can then be exported. With the concurrence of the host government, the money generated from selling the products abroad is placed in the central depository for use by the MNE. Pepsico used this type of arrangement when it first entered the U.S.S.R. market. It used rubles earned in Russia to buy vodka, which it then exported to the United States and was paid with dollars. McDonnell Douglas also used a similar technique when it built a factory to produce airplanes near Shanghai. Part of the production was flown out of China and sold for dollars. For both Pepsico and McDonnell, the dollars received constituted repatriated subsidiary "profits." Less common, but still a viable alternative, is to use spare production capacity to produce other products for export.

2. *Outsourcing.* If funds are blocked and must be spent locally, the company may find that it is not feasible or desirable to engage in unrelated export activities. Instead, it might use the blocked money to purchase from local providers services needed by other affiliates. Advances in computers, communications, and information technology have, in many cases, made it just as easy to provide needed services from emerging-market countries as in another floor of the parent company's home office building. These expenditures, then, become substitutes for equivalent payments that would have to be made anyway to support the MNE and its global operations. Here are some examples of services that might be purchased with blocked funds depending on the characteristics of the host country and its capabilities:

   - *Back-office operations, information processing (including data entry), report preparation, account processing, and similar services.* These activities must be done somewhere, and if blocked funds can be used to purchase them, money elsewhere is freed up and made available for other purposes.

   - *Customer service call centers and product support services.* As long as customer service representatives who are fluent in the appropriate language and who have the requisite technical training are available, it doesn't matter where the centers are located.

   - *Software development.* Some types of software development and maintenance are becoming routine. For activities that fall into this category, people with the required educational background are available in developing countries such as India. Using blocked funds locally to develop software releases funding elsewhere.

   - *Product testing and research.* Two types of product testing can be done just as easily in other countries as at home. First, reliability assessment is normally done in a laboratory and is valid if done under proper conditions in any country. Second, testing involving animals or human subjects can sometimes be done more inexpensively in other countries that do not have such elaborate protocols as Europe and the United States. This is not to suggest that people should be placed at risk or that safety controls should be less strenuously enforced, but at least in early trials it may be easier and less expensive to conduct such tests abroad.

   - *Conferences and employee vacations.* Some countries that block funds may qualify as attractive tourist destinations. If this is the case, the company can hold conferences and company meetings in that country, using the blocked funds for payment. Similarly, they can sponsor holiday packages for tourists, paying the local charges with the blocked funds and retaining the convertible currency received from the tourists.

These examples are but a few of the possibilities for using the blocked funds and, in effect, converting them into hard currencies for use elsewhere.

3. *Fronting loans.* If a company has operations in a country that blocks funds to manage its global economic relationships, it is understandable that the company might want to minimize capital contributed through the internal market. Equity capital invested in the affiliate is likely to be blocked until the company sells the facility and departs the country. Direct loans made to the subsidiary by other affiliates tend to be blocked less often, but there is always the chance that the host government will declare the direct loan as "disguised equity" and treat it according to the usually stricter rules governing equity. Loans from nonaffiliated banks, though, tend to be treated as bona fide loans, and the affiliate is not likely to be restricted from servicing such loans to outsiders. This type of lending arrangement is often structured as a **fronting loan.**

Fronting Loan
A type of lending arrangement structured as an indirect loan from a nonaffiliated bank. It is denominated in local currency to prevent blockage from the local host government.

One alternative for funding a foreign subsidiary is for the parent to make a direct loan as shown in the top section of Figure 14-2. The dollars would be converted into local currency and then recorded on the balance sheets of both units in the local currency. Upon the loan's maturity, the subsidiary would have to convert local currency into dollars to repay the principal plus interest to the parent, assuming that the local government would permit the repatriation. Thus, this transaction is subject to both repatriation risk and exchange rate risk.

An alternative to a direct loan is shown in the bottom half of Figure 14-2. In the indirect loan approach, the U.S. parent places dollars in a time deposit (certificate of deposit or CD) at Citibank New York to earn a modest interest rate for a fixed maturity (flow 1). This time deposit serves as collateral for a local-currency-equivalent loan to the foreign subsidiary by Citibank's host country branch at a local market-determined interest rate (flow 2). Over the life of the loan, as exchange rates change, Citibank might have the right to ask the company to deposit additional collateral in New York, or the time deposit may be reduced, so that the dollar amount of collateral maintains the same real value as the local-currency loan principal. At maturity, the foreign subsidiary repays the local-currency loan with interest (flow 3), and the par-

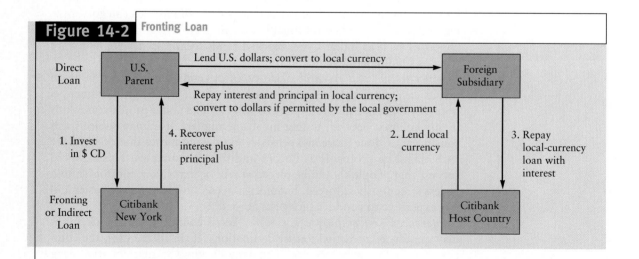

Figure 14-2 Fronting Loan

ent recovers the time deposit funds with interest (flow 4). Notice that there is no exchange rate risk on the principal in this indirect, or fronting loan, and that the effective interest rate on the total transaction is the differential interest rate (adjusted for the tax consequences in both countries). Because it is a local loan denominated in local currency, there is no worry about a blockage. If the collateral is provided by the central depository and it is located in a tax haven country, it may be possible to lower the effective cost of the loan because the foreign subsidiary will receive a tax deduction on the interest paid, but there may be no tax due on the interest received.[19]

In spite of efforts such as those just described, it may turn out that some funds are completely blocked and cannot be made available for use throughout the MNE's operation. This might happen, for instance, if depreciation funds must be reinvested in plant and equipment or else in government bonds, and a further investment in physical assets is not warranted. If this possibility poses a danger, it should be addressed before the investment is made.

SELF-TEST QUESTIONS

What are blockages?
What are strike-out rules?
Why do countries encourage exports?
What is outsourcing? Provide some examples.
What is a fronting loan?

MINORITY INTEREST OF LOCAL SHAREHOLDERS OR JOINT VENTURE PARTNERS

If a foreign affiliate is 100 percent owned and controlled by an MNE, it is free, within local government constraints, to alter prices, change expenses, set dividend repatriation policies, and engage in other actions that will maximize the MNE's value. However, if the subsidiary has local shareholders or is part of a joint venture, this flexibility is constrained. Actions benefiting the MNE might not be in the best interests of the other stakeholders, so they would prefer some other course of action. For instance, local shareholders might prefer high cash dividends at a time when the MNE wants to use earnings to finance expansion. Also, because of high local tax rates, the MNE might prefer low internal transfer prices to minimize the consolidated tax bill, but this would lower local earnings and potential dividends.

In Chapter 4, we also noted that the interests of joint venture partners might diverge over time, leading to tensions among the partners. Indeed, it is often difficult to simultaneously satisfy the value-maximizing desires of diverse partners. Each would benefit the most from a particular combination of policies and actions, but the combination is different for each. This reality is why we suggested that detailed agreements should be negotiated at the onset regarding the responsibilities and rights of each party. Also, an MNE's participation in the joint venture needs to be reevaluated periodically to ensure that it remains in the best interests of the company to continue its involvement.

The potential conflicts between the MNE and minority shareholders or joint venture partners explain why many companies insist on 100 percent ownership and

---

[19]One other situation for a fronting loan would be to engage in this transaction with the host government rather than a commercial bank. The parent could deposit dollars in the host government's account with the Federal Reserve Bank of New York (FRBNY), and, in turn, the government would make the loan to the local subsidiary. The company probably would not earn any interest on the FRBNY deposit, though.

shun joint ventures. Only when local regulations prohibit 100 percent ownership but the company believes a presence in the country is of great strategic importance does it relent and take on local shareholders or do a joint venture with a local company. Many companies, though, are unwilling to take this step and include 100 percent ownership as a strike-out rule in the country attractiveness scorecard.

Why may it be difficult to simultaneously satisfy the value-maximizing desires of diverse partners?

Why do many companies insist on 100 percent ownership and actually shun joint ventures?

EXCHANGE RATE EXPECTATIONS FOR CURRENCIES IN WHICH THE MNE DOES BUSINESS

As we saw in Chapter 3, forward exchange rates are predictors of future spot rates. Thus, forward contracts lock in expected changes in the exchange rate and thus protect against unexpected changes. But what happens if a company expects a particular currency to depreciate (or appreciate) against the home currency, and management wants to benefit from this change? Forward contracts or other hedging techniques (which we will cover in Chapter 15) cannot be used, so another strategy must be developed.[20] Basically, management should use the mechanisms described earlier in this chapter to remove as much value as possible from subsidiaries with depreciating currencies and relocate that value to other affiliates whose currencies are appreciating. For intrafirm trade, a technique called "leading and lagging" can be used to assist with this strategy, as we explain in the next section.

Leading and Lagging

In most cases, intrafirm trade involves two currencies, so there is a chance that exchange rates will change and cause gains or losses. We look closely at this discrete exchange rate risk in Chapter 15, but in this section we consider an operational arrangement that enables the company to minimize expected losses. Assume that the Argentine subsidiary has an account payable of $1,000 to its U.S. parent due in 30 days, and the exchange rate on the date the payable was booked was A$1.00 = $1.00. Our foreign exchange forecasting service predicts that the Argentine peso is likely to be devalued soon to a level of A$1.45/$. If we hedge this exposure in the forward market, we will lock in the expected depreciation (the unbiased predictor parity condition from Chapter 3). If the exchange rate does not change, we would need A$1,000 to pay the $1,000 account payable. However, if the rate changes as predicted, we would need $1,000 × A$1.4500/$ = A$1,450, or 45 percent more. Note, though, that if the Argentine subsidiary paid cash for the materials instead of taking the trade credit, it could avoid the expected foreign exchange loss. However, the payables deferral period would be eliminated, so its cash conversion period would lengthen.

Leading Strategy The company alters the timing of intrafirm payments in order to preserve wealth by getting it out of weak currencies and into strong currencies as quickly as possible.

If the exchange rate is depreciating in a predictable manner, the company might even want to prepay for materials. This strategy is called *leading* the account payable, and the idea is to move wealth out of the weak currency and into the strong currency as quickly as possible. Of course, the expected wealth savings must be compared with the increased cost of financing working capital due to the longer cash conversion period, but often the **leading strategy** will allow the company to preserve value.

---

[20]Option contracts might be used here but at a positive cost.

If we change the scenario so that the U.S. parent has an account payable of A$1,450 to the Argentine subsidiary due in 30 days, the situation is reversed. If the exchange rate does not change, we would need to convert $1,450 into pesos at A$1.00/$ to pay the obligation. However, if the exchange rate changes as predicted, we would need only A$1,450/A$1.45 = $1,000 to cover the payable. Here, we want to preserve our wealth in the stronger currency (the U.S. dollar) for as long as possible, so we would want to stretch out the payment to the maximum and perhaps even pay late, for the longer we delay, the fewer the required U.S. dollars. This is called a **lagging strategy**.

Lagging Strategy
The company alters the timing of intrafirm payments in order to preserve wealth by keeping it in strong currencies for as long as possible.

Leading and lagging strategies allow the company to alter the timing of intrafirm payments in order to maximize wealth by keeping funds in strong currencies to the greatest extent possible. Many countries place limits on the maximum prepayment or postponement period, so the company does not have unconstrained flexibility to engage in these strategies. However, to the extent that they can be used, they represent working capital management policies that can help manage currency risk. Leading and lagging strategies can also be used for payables to outside vendors when exchange rates are expected to change. In this case, companies need to trade off the exchange-rate gains against the effective interest cost to assess the best payment policy.

SELF-TEST QUESTION   What are leading and lagging strategies? What is their primary purpose?

LIQUIDITY NEEDS AND COMPENSATING BALANCES FOR EACH SUBSIDIARY AND THE COMBINED MNE

In the preceding sections we discussed numerous reasons an MNE might want to reposition a particular subsidiary's cash to another location. We also identified several techniques that can be used to accomplish this objective. However, as we indicated earlier in the chapter, each affiliate has requirements for local currency to use for transactions purposes, to cover compensating balance requirements, and as a precautionary reserve. Thus, management must balance the desire to create or preserve value by drawing funds out of the subsidiary to a central depository versus the need for liquidity that cannot be met through transfers from the central depository.

SELF-TEST QUESTION   What are the trade-offs that management must consider regarding liquidity needs?

THE AVAILABILITY OF AND NEED FOR FUNDS IN EACH SUBSIDIARY

When we talked about strategies for repositioning funds within the MNE, we assumed that the parent company had information about the magnitude and timing of cash receipts and required cash payments for each of the operating affiliates. Thus, daily cash budgets that must be prepared by the subsidiaries and forwarded electronically to headquarters are the basic documents on which global integrated working capital and cash flow management are based. It is beyond the scope of this chapter to discuss how the cash budgets are combined and translated into a global plan for reallocating cash flows, but such plans give directions for each of the subsidiaries to remit excess funds to a particular centralized account or to plan for a specific amount to be deposited in its local account at a particular time.[21] In the most advanced cash flow management systems, these instructions are transmitted at a fixed time each day to cover actions expected in the following 24-hour period.

What are the basic documents used for global integrated working capital and cash flow management?

BORROWING AND INVESTING OPPORTUNITIES

It would be a rare event if the operating affiliates all had excess cash or all required infusions of cash at the same time. Instead, because business cycles are not synchronized around the world, some contribute cash to the central pool while others draw cash from it. However, at times it is likely that the central pool will have cash surpluses or deficits. To deal with these imbalances effectively at the aggregate level, the centralized cash flow management system must supplement internal market information from the subsidiaries' cash budgets with external market data. Specifically, to determine the least expensive borrowing possibilities and the highest return, short-term investment alternatives, system managers need daily information about exchange rates, borrowing rates, and investment rates on financial instruments in both the various domestic money markets and the international markets. They also know from which sources, in what currencies, how much, and the maturities of all the loans and investments currently outstanding. As shown in Figure 14-3, all of this information flows into the centralized cash flow management system where decisions are made and then transmitted to the central depository and each subsidiary.

In Figure 14-3, the cash cycles for two subsidiaries are depicted in the diagrams. Each subsidiary is connected to the central depository with one arrow indicating transfer of excess cash to the central pool and another arrow showing infusions of cash from the pool. Because the central depository is the primary location for maintaining precautionary balances and engaging in transactions with the external market, it is connected to the rectangles representing these markets by solid arrows. Notice that the individual subsidiaries are also connected to external loan and investment markets, but with dashed lines. These are secondary linkages that can be used to acquire funds or to park excess cash without involving the central depository. They would be used whenever a subsidiary has access to external sources or uses of funds at subsidized rates that are not available to the central depository. This could happen, for instance, if the host government grants concessionary terms to locally chartered companies or there are favorable tax effects such as no tax on interest received by local companies from certain securities. Even though these alternatives are available only to the local subsidiary, the MNE as a whole can benefit by using them to the fullest extent through the subsidiary, thereby substituting for external transactions that would otherwise need to be made elsewhere. While they are not shown in Figure 14-3, lines connecting subsidiaries with the central depository representing the various mechanisms for moving funds into and out of a country shown in Table 14-2 could also be included in the centralized global cash flow management system.

---

[21]Each subsidiary is likely to have several bank accounts for receiving deposits and making payments, but the process through which these accounts are integrated into a locally centralized account network is beyond the scope of this chapter. We simply assume that there is such a centralized local account that is linked to the MNE's central depository through the internal market.

| Figure 14-3 | The Global Cash Flow Management System |

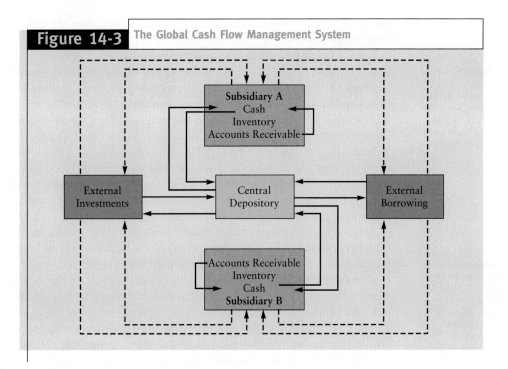

What information is needed by managers to determine the least expensive borrowing possibilities and the highest return, short-term investment alternatives? When might a subsidiary have access to external sources or uses of funds at subsidized rates that are not available to the central depository?

COMPANY ATTITUDES TOWARD RISK

The preceding decision areas for globally integrating working capital and cash flow management describe different sources and uses of cash flows, mechanisms for moving cash flows among subsidiaries, procedures for selecting channels, and timing cash flow movements to create maximum values. Before we can implement the integrated management system, though, we need to consider how net operating working capital (NOWC) will be financed. This decision will be determined largely by the company's attitude toward risk. Because long-term interest rates are usually higher than short-term rates, interest charges could generally be minimized if the firm financed NOWC mainly by borrowing in the short-term market. However, this strategy might be risky, because short-term loans must be renewed or rolled over frequently and interest rates can rise sharply and quickly. Thus, interest charges under a short-term loan strategy are likely to be less stable and possibly higher than if the company had locked in rates with long-term loans.

How does a company decide on an appropriate financing mix? Traditional financial theory suggests that companies should try to match the maturity of the financing instrument with the useful life of the asset to be financed. Because NOWC is short term, this rule of thumb implies that short-term loans are the most appropriate instruments for use in financing NOWC. However, this interpretation ignores the permanent NOWC that always exists on the balance sheet to support continuing operations. Permanent NOWC has characteristics more like fixed assets, so our rule of thumb suggests that it should be financed with long-term funds. Temporary increases in NOWC that support cyclical increases in production and sales, though, are short term in nature, and our rule suggests that they should be financed from short-term sources.[22]

Moderate Financing Strategy
A financing policy that matches asset and liability maturities. This is a moderate policy.

If a company follows exactly the traditional view of working capital financing, it will use the strategy shown in the top graph of Figure 14-4, a **moderate financing strategy**. Over time, the level of permanent NOWC will increase as production and sales expand. Because of flotation costs associated with long-term financing, the line representing long-term financing in the graph will not be as smooth as shown, but the company will try to increase long-term financing approximately in line with increases in permanent NOWC. This capital could come from additions to retained earnings, new common stock issues, or long-term bonds, but what is important here is the pattern.[23] Temporary NOWC, then, is financed with short-term loans that are obtained as needed from global sources, mainly through the centralized cash flow and working capital management system.

Conservative Financing Strategy
With this financing policy, part of temporary NOWC is financed from long-term sources and, when it is not needed to support operations, it is parked temporarily in short-term investments.

Some companies are uncomfortable with the level of risk implied in the traditional rule of thumb—they prefer to maintain higher levels of liquidity and also to lock in long-term interest rates. These companies tend to follow a more **conservative financing strategy**, portrayed in the middle graph of Figure 14-4. In this case, part of the temporary NOWC is financed from long-term sources and, when it is not needed to support operations, it is "parked" temporarily in short-term investments. Occasionally, short-term loans might be required to support particularly high NOWC needs, but only for short periods.[24] On average, the cost of capital with this strategy will be higher than with the moderate strategy, and the borrowing rate is almost always higher than the investment rate, so the company is paying a real economic price for the extra liquidity.

Aggressive Financing Strategy
With this financing policy, not only is temporary NOWC financed with short-term debt, part of permanent NOWC is also financed with short-term funds.

The bottom graph of Figure 14-4 portrays an **aggressive financing strategy**. Not only is temporary NOWC financed with short-term debt, part of the permanent NOWC is likewise financed with short-term funds. In this case, the interest charges are likely to be less than in the other two cases, but there is much more "rollover risk."

An integrated MNE that centralizes its working capital and cash flow management activities might well use different working capital financing strategies in each of its operating affiliates. For countries in which blockages are a significant problem, the aggressive strategy may be called for, with the central pool providing short-term financing as needed. In this way, the equity investment can be minimized, with mainly local sources of long-term debt supplementing it. On the other hand, if the host-country government offers subsidized long-term loans at particularly good rates, then a conservative strategy might be used.[25] In this case, any excess cash would be moved to the central pool and reallocated wherever it is needed. In this manner, the subsidized financing replaces other loans and produces benefits beyond the borders of the country of origin. Thus, even though each subsidiary is a separate legal entity and is physically separated from the others, the integrated management system treats the whole of the internal market as a single entity. It is the consolidated position that is important to the stock market when it values the MNE's shares.

---

[22]We assume here that accounts payable and accrued liabilities are used to the maximum extent possible after considering the cost and exchange rate risk factors discussed earlier in the chapter. Thus, this discussion focuses on net operating working capital (NOWC) that must be financed with investor-supplied capital.

[23]These capital structure issues are discussed in detail in Chapter 13.

[24]In the extreme, some companies might want to acquire long-term financing for both permanent and temporary NOWC, place any excess cash in short-term securities, and draw it down as needed. When it appears that additional capital will be needed, another bond issue is used and the process repeats itself.

[25]Such loans are often available from various national development organizations to companies willing to locate in depressed areas of the country with high unemployment rates. This was why John DeLorean decided to build his sports car in Belfast, Northern Ireland—the British government provided heavily subsidized loans to go there.

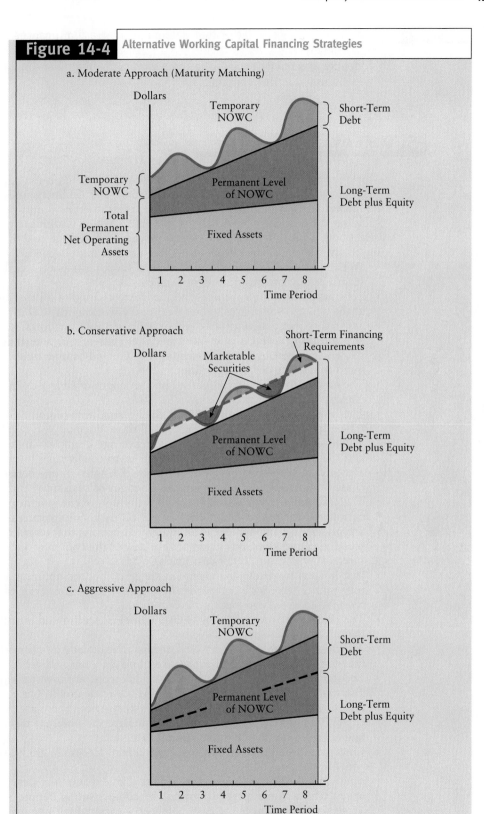

Figure 14-4 Alternative Working Capital Financing Strategies

a. Moderate Approach (Maturity Matching)

b. Conservative Approach

c. Aggressive Approach

What is the biggest factor that determines how a firm finances its working capital?

Identify and briefly explain the three working capital financing strategies discussed in this chapter.

SUMMARY

Working capital answers two primary questions: (1) What is the appropriate investment in each current asset account, and in total, and (2) how should current assets be financed? For a multinational enterprise, these questions must be answered for each foreign subsidiary as well as for the entire MNE. Working capital decisions affect both a firm's free cash flows and its weighted average cost of capital, affecting the firm's value. The key concepts discussed in this chapter are listed below.

- **Working capital** is a firm's investment in short-term assets—cash, marketable securities, inventory, and accounts receivable.
- **Permanent working capital** is those current assets that a firm must carry even at the trough of its cycles, while **temporary working capital** is those current assets that fluctuate with seasonal or cyclical variations in sales.
- **Net working capital** is calculated as current assets minus current liabilities, while **net operating working capital** is calculated as operating current assets minus operating current liabilities.
- The **cash conversion cycle** focuses on the length of time a dollar is tied up in current assets other than cash.
- The **inventory conversion period** is the average time required to convert materials into finished goods and then to sell those goods.
- The **receivables collection period** is the average length of time required to convert the firm's receivables into cash, that is, to collect cash following a sale.
- The **payables deferral period** is the average length of time between the purchase of materials and labor and the payment of cash for them.
- The **cash conversion period** is equal to the sum of the inventory conversion period and the receivables collection period minus the payables deferral period.
- **Supply chain management** is an integrated process that coordinates production scheduling and sales development throughout the company and with manufacturers' suppliers and retail customers.
- **Just-in-time inventory management** suggests that the optimum level of inventory is near zero, with companies holding the minimum levels of raw materials required to avoid production interruption.
- The **economic order quantity (EOQ) model** is a technique for finding the optimal inventory balance.
- A firm's **credit policy** is a set of decisions that include a firm's credit period, credit standards, collection procedures, and discounts offered.
- **Accounts payable** represent supplier trade credit, not investor-supplied capital. Often, there is no explicit interest charge for trade credit, but some companies include an implicit interest cost in the invoice price. There are two ways to calculate the **implicit interest rate**: (1) **annualize the nominal discount percent** and (2) calculate the **effective annual rate**.
- **Costly trade credit** is credit taken in excess of free trade credit, whose cost is equal to the discount lost.
- There have been several motives suggested to explain why firms hold cash balances: **transactions**, **precautionary**, and **compensating balances**.
- **Transactions balances** are cash balances associated with payments and collections or the balance necessary for day-to-day operations.
- **Precautionary balances** are cash balances held in reserve for random, unforeseen fluctuations in cash inflows and outflows.

- **Compensating balances** are bank balances that firms must maintain to compensate the bank for services rendered.
- The **cash budget** is used by most companies to forecast cash needs and availability.
- There are three areas of competitive advantage for MNEs that favor centralization of cash management: **scale, diversification**, and **taxes.**
- **Tax havens** are locations with low or no taxes on most transactions and no restrictions on the movement of cash into or out of these locations.
- The mechanisms for moving funds into or out of a country can be divided into two groups: **capital-related flows** and **operations-related flows.** Capital-related flows include investor-supplied equity and debt (both from internal and external sources) to an affiliate's country. Royalties, license fees, and administrative overhead allocations are examples of operations-related flows.
- **Netting** is a technique that minimizes transactions costs by simply canceling the obligation of one affiliate with obligations of another.
- **Bilateral netting** is a technique in which receivables and payables entries are "netted out" between pairs of affiliates and then the sum of the remaining nonzero entries represents the total accounts payable and accounts receivable in the internal market.
- **Multilateral netting** is a technique in which affiliates make payments for other affiliates to reduce transactions costs even further from that achieved with bilateral netting.
- A **reinvoicing center** is a separate affiliate, often located in a tax haven country, through which intracompany transactions pass.
- A **transfer price** is the price charged for a transaction between affiliates. An **arms-length price** is the amount an unrelated customer would have to pay in a free market for the product. It is the theoretically correct transfer price from a country's perspective.
- Besides an arms-length price, there are two other methods for setting transfer prices suggested by the Organization for Economic Cooperation and Development (OECD) Committee on Fiscal Affairs: (1) resale price method and (2) cost-plus method. With the **resale price method**, the sales price to the ultimate external consumer is determined and then reduced by an "appropriate" distributor markup to arrive at a fair price to the distributor. With the **cost-plus method**, an appropriate markup is applied to the full cost of the item, including both direct costs and overhead allocations.
- An **advance pricing agreement (APA)** is an approach used to determine the appropriate cost-plus transfer price through negotiation with tax authorities of both governments of the affiliates involved in the transaction.
- A **blockage** occurs when government regulations or laws restrict an MNE's ability to transfer funds into or out of an affiliate country.
- Four reasons have been suggested to explain why countries block international funds flows: (1) to **manage** the **country's foreign exchange reserves and currency's value,** (2) to **stimulate local investment and increase capital availability,** (3) to **encourage exports,** and (4) to **increase MNEs' commitment to the local economy.**
- Four types of strategies need to be considered for dealing effectively with blockages: (1) **Negotiations** prior to investment, (2) **operating strategies** to increase the ability to **reposition funds globally,** (3) **alternatives to direct capital contributions in financing foreign affiliates,** and (4) an **exit strategy.**
- **Strike-out rules** are designations given to critical conditions in the country evaluation process that mean, if it is not possible to negotiate acceptable terms, the company will not make the investment.
- There are at least three devices that an MNE can use to mitigate the effects of blockages: (1) **unrelated exports,** (2) **outsourcing,** and (3) **fronting loans.**
- A **fronting loan** is a type of lending arrangement structured as an indirect loan from a nonaffiliated bank. It is denominated in local currency to prevent blockage from the local host government.

- With a **leading strategy**, the company alters the timing of intrafirm payments to preserve wealth by getting it out of weak currencies and into strong currencies as quickly as possible.
- With a **lagging strategy**, the company alters the timing of intrafirm payments to preserve wealth by keeping it in strong currencies for as long as possible.
- There are three different types of working capital financing policies that a firm can use. A **moderate financing strategy** is a financing policy that matches asset and liability maturities. A **conservative financing strategy** is a financing policy in which part of temporary NOWC is financed from long-term sources and, when it is not needed to support operations, it is parked temporarily in short-term investments. An **aggressive financing strategy** is a financing policy in which not only temporary NOWC is financed with short-term debt, but part of permanent NOWC is also financed with short-term funds.

QUESTIONS

(14-1) Why might an MNE prefer license fees to dividend repatriation?

(14-2) Why might a foreign government impose a withholding tax?

(14-3) Briefly explain what the theoretically correct transfer price is from an economic perspective. What is it from a country's perspective? Are your answers different? Explain.

(14-4) Identify and briefly explain two methods suggested by the OECD for setting transfer prices when arms-length prices cannot be directly observed.

(14-5) What is an advance pricing agreement (APA), and what is its primary purpose?

(14-6) What are two dimensions for managing blockages in which the MNE is interested?

(14-7) Why do countries block funds?

(14-8) What are some strategies that MNEs can use in dealing with blockages?

(14-9) Within an MNE, could there ever be legitimate reasons for sacrificing working capital objectives (such as minimizing the cash conversion period) in order to achieve a broader objective? Explain.

(14-10) Even when governments block repatriation of cash flows, and cannot be persuaded to relax restrictions, are there still legal ways to remove value from the country that the host government would welcome? Explain.

(14-11) What is a fronting loan? How does it work? What is its purpose?

(14-12) Should NOWC be financed mainly by borrowing in the short-term market? Explain your answer.

(14-13) How does a company decide on an appropriate financing mix for its NOWC?

(14-14) Identify three different working capital financing strategies mentioned in this chapter. How do they differ from one another? Which one is riskier? Explain. Which one will provide the highest expected return? Explain.

(14-15) In what situations might an MNE use each of the three different working capital financing strategies? Explain.

SELF-TEST PROBLEMS   Solutions Appear in Appendix B

(ST-1) Define each of the following terms:
Key Terms   a. Working capital; permanent working capital; temporary working capital
b. Net working capital; net operating working capital (NOWC)

c. Cash conversion cycle; inventory conversion period; receivables collection period; payables deferral period; cash conversion period
d. Supply chain management; just-in-time inventory management; economic order quantity (EOQ) model
e. Credit policy; costly trade credit
f. Transactions balances; precautionary balances; compensating balances
g. Cash budget; tax havens
h. Netting; bilateral netting; multilateral netting; reinvoicing center
i. Transfer price; arms-length price; advance pricing agreement (APA)
j. Blockage; strike-out rule; fronting loan
k. Leading strategy; lagging strategy
l. Moderate financing strategy; conservative financing strategy; aggressive financing strategy

(ST-2)
Cash Conversion Period
HMC Inc., a U.S. multinational conglomerate, has $25 million in inventory and $20 million in accounts receivable. Annual sales are $365 million, and the firm's annual cost of goods sold represents 45 percent of annual sales. The firm's payables deferral period is 35 days.
a. What is HMC's inventory conversion period?
b. What is HMC's receivables collection period?
c. What is HMC's cash conversion period?

(ST-3)
Trade Credit
SRT Enterprises, a U.S. multinational, is offered trade credit terms of 2/10, net 35. SRT does not take the discount, but pays its account after 35 days.
a. What is the nominal cost of the firm's trade credit?
b. What is the effective annual cost of the firm's trade credit?

STARTER PROBLEMS

(14-1)
Cash Conversion Period
LSI Corporation, a U.S. multinational, has an average accounts receivable balance of $12.5 million, an average inventory balance of $18.5 million, and an average accounts payable balance of $8 million. Its annual sales are $150 million, and its cost of goods sold represents 75 percent of annual sales.
a. What is LSI's inventory conversion period?
b. What is LSI's receivables collection period?
c. What is LSI's payables deferral period?
d. What is LSI's cash conversion period?

(14-2)
Trade Credit
Jericho Imports, a U.S. multinational, buys on terms of 4/20, net 40. Jericho does not take discounts, but pays its account after 40 days.
a. What is the nominal cost of the firm's trade credit?
b. What is the effective annual cost of the firm's trade credit?

(14-3)
Working Capital Financing
RSO International Manufacturing Company and KTS Manufacturing Company, both U.S. multinational furniture manufacturers, had the following balance sheets as of December 31, 2004 (thousands of dollars):

	RSO	KTS
Current assets	$ 500,000	$ 400,000
Fixed assets (net)	500,000	600,000
Total assets	$1,000,000	$1,000,000
Current liabilities	$ 100,000	$ 400,000
Long-term debt	400,000	100,000
Common stock	250,000	250,000
Retained earnings	250,000	250,000
Total liabilities and equity	$1,000,000	$1,000,000

Earnings before interest and taxes for both firms are $150 million, and the effective federal-plus-state tax rate is 40 percent.

a. What is the return on equity for each firm if the interest rate on current liabilities is 7 percent and the rate on long-term debt is 10 percent?

b. Assume that the short-term rate rises to 14 percent. While the rate on new long-term debt rises to 12 percent, the rate on existing long-term debt remains unchanged. What would be the return on equity for RSO and KTS under these conditions?

c. Which company is in a riskier position? Why?

EXAM-TYPE PROBLEMS

(14-4)
Cash Conversion Period

Hiers International has annual sales of $126,837,500 and maintains an average inventory level of $30,024,000. The firm's annual cost of goods sold represents 70 percent of its annual sales, and its average accounts receivable balance outstanding is $22,518,000. The company makes all purchases on credit and always pays on the 30th day.

a. What is the firm's average accounts payable balance?

b. What is the firm's inventory conversion period?

c. What is the firm's receivables collection period?

d. What is the firm's cash conversion period?

e. Assume that the company is now going to take full advantage of trade credit and pay its suppliers on the 40th day. Assume that sales and cost of goods sold remain at existing levels, but inventory and receivable balances can each be lowered by $4,865,000. What will be the net change in the firm's cash conversion period?

(14-5)
Trade Credit

Espinoza Food Corporation's business is booming, and it needs to raise more capital. The company purchases supplies on terms of 1/10, net 20, and it currently takes the discount. One way of receiving the needed funds would be to forgo the discount. The firm's management believes that it could delay payment for 20 additional days from the existing credit terms (in other words, the firm would pay on Day 40) without adverse effects.

a. What is the nominal annual cost of stretching accounts payable?

b. What is the effective annual cost of stretching accounts payable?

(14-6)
Netting

You are a financial analyst for Jamison Computers and have been given the following data regarding the firm's international subsidiaries' intrafirm accounts.

		ACCOUNTS RECEIVABLE FROM AFFILIATES				
		Brazil	Italy	Malaysia	USA	Total Accounts Payable
Accounts Payable	Brazil	—	$ 560	$ 350	$ 350	$1,260
	Italy	$420	—	350	560	1,330
	Malaysia	150	350	—	420	920
	United States	150	350	350	—	850
	Total accounts receivable	$720	$1,260	$1,050	$1,330	$4,360

a. From the data given, use bilateral netting to reduce the intrafirm account balances. What is the new balance of intrafirm accounts?

b. Now, from part a, use multilateral netting to reduce the intrafirm account balances even further. What is the new balance of intrafirm accounts?

INTEGRATED CASE

Rick Schmidt, MRI's CFO, along with Mandy Wu, Schmidt's assistant, and John Costello, a consultant and college finance professor, comprise a team set up to teach the firm's directors and senior managers the basics of international financial management. The program includes 16 sessions, each lasting about 2 hours, and they are scheduled immediately before the monthly board meetings. Thirteen sessions have been completed, and the team is now preparing Session 14, which will deal with working capital management and global cash flow integration. Prior sessions have provided an overview of international finance, exchange rates, risk analysis, financial statements, international markets and security valuation, the cost of capital, capital budgeting, and capital structure and cash distribution policy.

For this session, the team will explain how multinational entities manage their current assets and liabilities and use these strategies to maximize shareholder wealth. More than one story has graced the headlines in which a company with a successful business model has crashed and burned because they lacked sound working capital strategies. The team has prepared Table IC14-1, which gives key financial data for various MRI subsidiaries around the world. They plan to go through basic working capital issues and spend a lot of time discussing how MNEs position funds globally and how MNEs manage working capital across different subsidiaries. In the earlier days of MRI's global expansion, MRI was slow to react to cultural differences in their subsidiaries and tried to enforce its domestic attitudes about asset management in each of its subsidiaries.

Wu expressed concern about addressing controversial issues, where the proper analysis is in question. She recalled that in college some students simply "tuned out" when the instructor raised a question for which there was no definitive answer, and she was concerned that the directors might react similarly. Schmidt and Costello agree that this could be a problem, but they felt strongly that it would not be appropriate to "sweep problems under the carpet." So, they want to bring up relevant unresolved issues, discuss alternative ways of dealing with them, and point out the implications of different decisions. The directors are all intelligent, experienced in dealing with complex situations, and would rather know about potential problems than be kept in the dark.

With those thoughts in mind, the three compiled the following set of questions, which they plan to discuss during the session. As with the other sessions, they plan to use an *Excel* model to answer the quantitative questions. Assume that you are Mandy Wu, and that you must prepare answers for use during the session.

QUESTIONS

a. Differentiate between permanent and temporary working capital. How can more or less aggressive working capital strategies be used to satisfy permanent and temporary working capital requirements?

b. What is the cash conversion period? What are its components and how is each component interpreted? Use Table IC14-1 to calculate MRI's and its subsidiaries' cash conversion periods. How do the working capital positions of the various subsidiaries compare with each other and with the total firm?

c. Discuss ways in which MNEs actively manage their inventory conversion, receivables collection, and payables deferral periods. MRI conducts credit sales on the terms of 3/20, net 45. What is the cost of trade credit MRI extends to its customers?

TABLE IC14-1 2004 MRI Key Financial Data[a]

	United States	Japan	Italy	Indonesia	Consolidated
Sales	$475,970.0	$196,659.0	$238,127.0	$92,381.0	$1,003,137.0
Cost of goods sold	299,907.0	137,299.0	171,506.0	51,969.0	660,681.0
Accounts receivable[b]	47,461.0	38,202.4	37,330.4	40,703.6	122,255.2
Inventories	47,097.0	37,147.9	66,705.9	28,180.2	179,131.0
Accounts payable[b]	46,554.0	38,141.0	36,775.8	13,334.7	93,363.1

Notes:
[a]Data taken from MRI's 2004 consolidated income statement and balance sheet.
[b]Subsidiary numbers reflect intrafirm sales.

d. Identify the reasons MNEs keep cash on hand. How do firms forecast cash requirements, and why might cash management operations be centralized?

e. Describe the types of mechanisms used to reposition funds within an MNE.

f. Discuss how transactions costs can play a role in global working capital management. What steps can firms take to minimize these costs in intrafirm transactions? What are bilateral and multilateral netting? How are reinvoicing centers used by MNEs?

g. How can different tax systems affect an MNE's ability to reposition funds? What is transfer pricing? Describe the methods suggested by the OECD for setting transfer prices.

h. Explain what a funds blockage is and why countries might choose to block funds. How can an MNE minimize the disruption caused by blockages?

i. Exchange-rate fluctuations often cause headaches for firms with global operations, and MRI is no different. What are some strategies the firm can employ to minimize the damage caused by fluctuating exchange rates?

j. Building on your answer to part a, demonstrate how a firm's risk aversion can play a role in its decision to manage working capital conservatively or aggressively.

International Corporate Strategy

Part Four

Derivatives and Risk Management

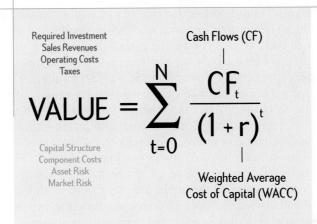

The essence of business is risk taking. If one is not prepared to take risks, one should not run a company. These statements imply that management should not attempt to eliminate all risks, or even to minimize them, because that would also reduce the potential for high returns. Instead, the firm's objective should be to manage its risks in a prudent manner and to strike a balance between risk and return that maximizes the firm's value. Risks that do not contribute sufficiently to the company's success should be eliminated. Moreover, managers should monitor events closely to ensure that risky conditions are identified early, allowing the company to react quickly. All of this was discussed in Chapter 12, when we considered SSI's Shanghai project. Now, we need to look more closely at how SSI and other multinational companies assess and manage their risks.

All firms face risks, but several types of risk are more important for MNEs than for most purely domestic firms. Moreover, some of those risks can be managed, using derivatives or other techniques, and those are the risks that we focus on in this chapter. First, MNEs' cash flows are earned in various currencies, and they must be translated into each parent's reporting currency. Therefore, cash flows are subject to exchange rate risk. Second, MNEs often use commodities extensively in their operations, and if commodity prices rise or fall sharply, this could have a significant effect on free cash flows. However, as we shall see, there are ways to minimize the effects of commodity price variability. Third, MNEs raise capital all across the globe, and they are affected in important ways by interest rate shifts. Again, though, techniques we discuss in this chapter can reduce the risks of changing interest rates.

The firm's stock price will be maximized if management manages the risks associated with exchange rate volatility, interest rates, and commodity prices in an optimal manner. Proper risk management can maximize the cash flows in the numerator of the valuation equation and also minimize the WACC in the denominator. Thus, risk management, using the techniques discussed in this chapter, is quite important for multinational corporations.

Forward Contract
A contract in which one party agrees to buy or sell an asset or commodity at a specific price on a specific future date from another party, and physical delivery occurs.

Futures Contract
A standardized agreement similar to a forward contract that is traded on exchanges, but no physical delivery occurs.

OVERVIEW OF DERIVATIVES[1]

Financial managers use derivatives to transfer several different risks, for a price, to others.[2] There are thousands of different derivatives, but they can be categorized as three basic types: (1) *forward contracts,* (2) *futures contracts,* and (3) *option contracts.* Under the **forward contract**, one party agrees to buy or sell something at a specific price on a specific future date from another party, and physical delivery occurs. **Futures contracts** are similar to forwards, but no physical delivery occurs. One party simply pays the other an amount that reflects the change in the price of the underlying asset. Both forwards and futures allow parties to "lock in" interest rates, commodity prices, and exchange rates, and thus remove the effects of variability in those items. **Options** give the holder the right, but not the obligation, to buy or sell an asset at a set price (the "strike" price) within a specific time period. A **call option** gives the holder the right to buy, while a **put option** gives the holder the right to sell the asset. Risk managers use these three types of derivatives to manage risks related to unexpected market fluctuations.

SELF-TEST QUESTIONS

What are the three basic types of derivatives?
Differentiate between forward and futures contracts.
What is an option?
Differentiate between call and put options.

SOURCES OF RISK

Option
A contract that gives the buyer the right, but not the obligation, to buy or sell an asset at a set price (the "strike" price) on or before a specific date.

Call Option
Gives the holder the right to buy an asset.

Put Option
Gives the holder the right to sell an asset.

Multinationals have advantages over purely domestic firms in terms of diversifying operations and using their internal markets to react quickly to global disequilibria, but they still face many risks. In fact, MNEs have to contend with the same risks as domestic firms, plus an additional layer related to their global operations. In previous chapters, we have already discussed business risk, financial risk, market risk, political risk, forecasting uncertainties, and the risk of cash flow blockages. Now we focus on strategies for dealing with three risks that, while not unique to MNEs, are especially important for firms competing in the global business environment: exchange rate risk, interest rate risk, and commodity price risk.

Before discussing these specific risks, we need to clarify exactly what we mean by *risk* as we use the term in this chapter. Expected changes in exchange rates, interest rates, or commodity prices are built into forward or futures prices, exchange rates, and interest rates. Therefore, firms can only hedge against expected changes using

---

[1]Derivative securities are covered in detail in most advanced finance sources. For further discussion, see Eugene F. Brigham and Phillip R. Daves, *Intermediate Financial Management,* 8th ed. (Mason, OH: South-Western Publishing, 2004), Chapter 23.

[2]The first derivative was the "forward contract," under which farmers would contract in the spring to sell wheat at a specified price to millers in the fall. The forward contract protected the farmers from a low price later and millers from a high price. Now many different types of derivatives are used, and they are applied to commodities such as wheat and copper as well as to currencies and interest rates.

various operating techniques, as we discussed in Chapter 14. However, the expected changes may not be realized, so there are risks associated with *unexpected* changes. The key focus of risk management in this chapter involves managing the uncertainty that results from such unexpected changes. Some techniques allow the company to shift this risk to others by fixing rates or prices at a constant level. Other instruments allow the company to protect itself from downside risk while retaining upside potential. Typically, companies need to use several different devices simultaneously to manage risk most efficiently. In the sections that follow, we describe in detail the various types of risks and procedures used to manage them.

Exchange Rate Risk

In Chapter 2, we identified two broad strategies that countries use to manage the value of their currencies: fixed- and floating-rate regimes. Under fixed-exchange-rate systems, companies, in theory, do not have to worry about exchange rate risk because rates should be stable. Indeed, under the Bretton Woods Agreement, which lasted from 1944 to 1971, exchange rates were fixed throughout the developed world, so most of the instruments used to manage exchange rate risk today were unnecessary.[3] However, that agreement was eventually abandoned, and today, even if rates are fixed, it is recognized that it is always possible for a country to succumb to pressures on its reserves or internal politics and devalue or revalue its currency. Forecasting the timing of such events is difficult, because while they are influenced by economic trends, they are really political decisions. The current situation in China falls into this category. As we discussed in Chapter 11, the yuan exchange rate has been pegged at CNY8.28/$ since 1998. If market forces were allowed to operate, the yuan's rate would rise, but the rate is fixed and the Chinese government has been unwilling to adjust it. However, many private forecasters are suggesting that potential inflation, along with pressure from trading partners such as the United States, will eventually cause the Chinese government to revalue the yuan upward by some 10 to 15 percent, to somewhere in the CNY7.53/$ to CNY7.20/$ range, in the future. The risk, then, is related to if and when such a change might occur. This was one of the considerations that went into the evaluation of SSI's Shanghai project as discussed in Chapter 12.

When the Bretton Woods system collapsed in 1971, most exchange rates were allowed to float. Exchange rates were then determined in the market, so they became subject to fluctuations, which led to the **exchange rate risk** that companies seek to manage. The strategies for managing this risk are discussed later in the chapter, and they are quite important to multinational corporations.

Risks Related to Changing Interest Rates

When we discussed debt securities in Chapter 8 we focused on risk as seen by the debtholders, not the firms that issued them. There, we defined interest rate risk as "the risk of a decline in bond values due to rising interest rates." Now, however, we look at the effects of changes in interest rates on the issuers of debt, *so here interest rate risk refers to issuer risk*. Multinational enterprises, as borrowers, are subject to three types of risk from changing interest rates. The first relates to changes in their **credit risk**, or the possibility that they will default on their debt. The interest rate on debt is determined by lenders' assessments of borrowers' creditworthiness.[4]

Exchange Rate Risk The risk that relates to what the foreign currency cash flows will be worth in the parent company's home currency.

Credit Risk The risk that relates to the possibility that a borrower will default on its debt.

[3]The Bretton Woods Agreement established the international monetary system that was used from 1944 to 1971. It called for fixed exchange rates, but in 1971 market forces caused it to be abandoned and replaced with a floating-exchange rate system.

[4]For fixed-rate debt, the creditworthiness results in the risk premium added to the risk-free rate. For floating-rate debt, the risk premium is added to LIBOR or some other reference rate.

Repricing (Rollover) Risk
The risk that relates to the possibility (1) that a company will have to pay a higher interest rate when renewing maturing credit, or (2) that it will receive a lower interest rate on securities it holds due to changing market rates.

Corporations often renew maturing debt, and when debt matures, the lender will reappraise the situation. If the borrower's creditworthiness has declined, then the risk premium will be increased, the credit line reduced, or possibly the lender will refuse to renew the loan. The risk due to a change in credit risk is greater the shorter the debt maturity, because if such changes occur further in the future, it will give firms time to recover from temporary setbacks. Thus, this aspect of credit risk tends to make companies look favorably at longer-term bond issues.

Even if creditworthiness is unchanged, if market interest rates have risen above the level when the debt was issued, companies will have to pay higher rates when they renew, or roll over, their debt. This type of risk is known as **repricing**, or **rollover**, **risk**. If the company lends rather than borrows, repricing risk means that the company will receive a lower interest stream if market rates have fallen.

Counterparty Risk
The risk that the other party to a contractual arrangement will not be able to carry out its obligations as specified in the contract.

Counterparty risk is the risk that the other party to a contractual arrangement will not be able to carry out its obligations as specified in the contract. It is not unique to debt contracts, but it is particularly important with some kinds of interest-rate-risk management strategies as discussed later in the chapter.

Commodity Price Risk

Commodity Price Risk
The risk that the prices of a company's generic production inputs or outputs (commodities) may change.

Many MNEs participate in commodity markets, either as buyers (such as cocoa for Nestlé or Hershey, and wheat and corn for General Mills) or as sellers (such as oil and gas for ExxonMobil or agricultural products for Archer Daniels Midland). All manufacturing companies require raw materials for their production processes, and these raw materials can change in price. What distinguishes the goods mentioned in this section from other types of production inputs is that they are standardized, generic products and that contracts for their future delivery are traded on financial markets such as the Chicago Board of Trade or the Coffee, Sugar & Cocoa Exchange in New York. Thus, it is possible to use forward or futures contracts to manage **commodity price risk**, which is the risk that the prices of a company's generic production inputs or outputs (commodities) may change.

SELF-TEST QUESTIONS

What are the three types of risk that are critical for firms competing in the global business environment?

What are the three types of interest rate risk?

What is a commodity?

RISKS THAT CAN BE MANAGED

MNEs face many different types of risk. Some of them can be managed in the sense that they can be transferred to other parties, while some cannot be readily transferred. For example, risks associated with exchange rate changes can be managed, but the risk that our products will be rendered obsolete by a competitor cannot be managed in the sense that we use the term "manage" in this chapter. We discuss some major types of manageable risks in this section, after which we discuss the tools and techniques used to manage them. It is useful to divide manageable risks into two broad categories: discrete risks and continuing risks.

Discrete Risks

Discrete Risks
Related to specific transactions that lead to economic gains or losses as underlying variables change.

Discrete risks are related to specific transactions, such as placing an order for a specific amount of some commodity or arranging to borrow a given amount of money. **Continuing risks** are ones that are ongoing rather than related to specific transac-

Continuing Risks
Risks that are ongoing and not related to specific transactions.

tions, with one example being the periodic translation of foreign operating results that can lead to changes in reported income due to changes in exchange rates.

Discrete risks are often referred to as **transaction exposure**, because accrual accounting rules require transactions to be recorded on the books at the spot exchange rate, interest rate, or commodity price when the relevant contract was signed. However, if a transaction will not be completed until a later date, the final rate or price might end up with a different value. Depending on how the variables change, a gain or loss may result when the transaction is closed out on the company's books. Credit sales that result in accounts receivable and purchases that lead to accounts payable are examples of such transactions.

Another type of discrete risk arises when the company knows that a specific transaction will probably have to be made in the future, but the exact exchange rate, price, or interest rate for the deal is unknown at the present. Because such a transaction has not yet been made, it is not recorded by the company, so the situation is different from the one just described. There will not be an accounting gain or loss if the underlying variables change between today and when the transaction is made because the spot rate when the transaction occurs will be recorded once the deal is done. However, the ultimate price or rate could differ from what we expect today, yielding a real economic loss or gain in an opportunity cost sense.

FOREIGN-DENOMINATED ACCOUNTS PAYABLE AND RECEIVABLE Accounts payable and receivable are recorded on the date the relevant transaction occurs. If the payable or receivable is denominated in a foreign currency, then because these are monetary liabilities or assets, the spot exchange rate on the transaction date is used to translate it into the reporting currency, and that amount is recorded in the accounting records. Later, when the payment is actually made, a change in the spot rate will cause either more or less local currency units to be required to complete the transaction. For example, assume that an American company purchases goods on open account from a German supplier for €1,250,000, payable in euros, but with credit terms of net 30 days. Assume that today's spot exchange rate is $1.270400/€, so the American firm records the transaction at €1,250,000 × $1.270400/€ = $1,588,000. In 30 days, the accounts payable department notices that the dollar has weakened, and the spot rate is now $1.2721/€, so it will take €1,250,000 × $1.2721/€ = $1,590,125 to pay the bill, or $2,125 more than the recorded value. This extra $2,125 will flow through the income statement, reducing both reported income and the tax liability. If the dollar had strengthened, it would have taken fewer dollars to pay the bill, so the American company would have enjoyed a gain. There would have been no impact on the German company in either case because the transaction is in the local currency.

If the American firm had sold to the German firm rather than purchased from it, an accounts receivable would have been created, and in that case the weaker dollar would have led to a gain. In general, as the dollar weakens, monetary assets denominated in a foreign currency will increase in value because the dollar-equivalent amount will rise, and vice versa if the dollar strengthens.

Monetary liabilities denominated in a foreign currency also change in value when exchange rates change. A weakening of the dollar will increase the firm's liability and result in a loss, while a stronger dollar will lower the dollar value of the liability and lead to a gain. Therefore, if a company has both monetary assets and liabilities denominated in the same foreign currency, they will tend to offset each other and thus mitigate the effects of exchange rate changes. Indeed, if the beginning book values of the two are equal, gains and losses will exactly offset one another, thus eliminating this aspect of exchange rate risk. This property will be used later in the chapter when we discuss risk management strategies for dealing with payables and receivables denominated in foreign currencies.

Transaction Exposure
The risk that arises because accrual accounting rules require that transactions be recorded at a spot rate or price even though the transaction will not be completed until a later date.

LENDING AND BORROWING IN A FOREIGN CURRENCY If a company, whose reporting currency is the dollar, invests some excess cash in a euro-denominated certificate of deposit, or decides to borrow euros, then monetary assets or liabilities denominated in foreign currencies will be shown on the balance sheet. These have exactly the same impact as accounts payable and receivable. For example, assume that the company invests $1,588,000 in a euro-denominated CD for 30 days at a 30-day interest rate of 0.10 percent. The spot exchange rate when the marketable security investment is recorded is $1.2704/€, so the amount invested in euros is $1,588,000/$1.2704/€ = €1,250,000. The company expects to receive €1,250,000 × 1.001 = €1,251,250 in 30 days, which at today's spot rate is equivalent to $1,589,588. If in 30 days, when the CD matures, the spot exchange rate is $1.2721/€, then €1,251,250 × $1.2721/€ = $1,591,715 will be received, so the effective gain is $1,591,715 − $1,588,000 = $3,715. This amount is $1,591,715 − $1,589,588 = $2,127 more than what would have been earned had the dollar not weakened. The increase in value of $3,715 is fully taxable. Two things should be noted about this transaction:

1. The dollar return on the investment is $3,715/$1,588,000 = 0.002339 = 0.2339%. This would be the 30-day U.S. periodic interest rate if the rates conform to interest rate parity.
2. The dollar-equivalent principal amount at the end of the 30 days is €1,250,000 × $1.2721/€ = $1,590,125. Thus, the "gain" of principal is $1,590,125 − $1,588,000 = $2,125. This is the same increase in value we obtained in the previous account receivable example, so it shows that monetary assets offset monetary liabilities as long as the recorded amounts are the same. The fact that one pays or charges interest and the other does not is irrelevant.

Of course, if the company had borrowed euros, the situation would have been reversed.

SERVICING FLOATING-RATE DEBT Even if a company decides to borrow in its home currency rather than in a foreign currency subject to exchange rate risk, there may still be risk that must be managed. For example, assume that a company needs $10 million for one year. It has three choices, listed in order of increasing risk:

1. Borrow $10 million at a fixed rate for one year. There is no credit-related rollover risk and no repricing risk because the interest rate is fixed for the duration of the loan. However, the company will suffer an opportunity loss if interest rates fall.
2. Borrow $10 million at a floating rate of LIBOR + 1% with quarterly resets. In this case there is no credit rollover risk because the loan's maturity matches the time the funds will be needed, but there is repricing risk due to possible LIBOR increases. Of course, the company will benefit if LIBOR declines.
3. Borrow $10 million at a fixed rate for three months, planning for three quarterly renewals at the then-prevailing rates. This loan is subject to both credit-related rollover risk and repricing risk.

Alternative 3 gives the company flexibility on both the upside and the downside, and if the yield curve is upward sloping, it will probably have the lowest *expected* interest cost. However, Alternative 3 also has the most risk, particularly for firms with less-than-stellar financial strength. Very strong "blue chip" companies do not have to worry as much as weaker firms about credit-related rollover risk, but their repricing risk is generally just as significant. Alternative 2 might be preferred over Alternative 3 by weaker companies worried about credit risk, but it is likely to be slightly more expensive. Alternative 1 is the least risky, but with a normal (upward-sloping) yield curve, it is likely to be the most expensive.[5]

---

[5]These choices are also available for foreign-currency-denominated debt, thus compounding the risks faced by the company on top of those discussed previously.

PLANNING FOR KNOWN FUTURE BORROWING As an outgrowth of the capital and cash budgeting processes, it is common for companies to anticipate future borrowing requirements. One source of uncertainty in planning for future borrowing is that the interest rate will be not be set until the loan agreement is signed. Of course, the company can estimate the future rate using the expectations theory of the term structure of interest rates, but this is an expected rate that may be different from the actual rate. Another possibility is to borrow now, locking in the interest rate and eliminating this source of uncertainty. But if the company doesn't need the money now, paying interest until the funds are needed is an expensive way to eliminate the risk of changing interest rates.

SUPPLY CHAIN COORDINATION Manufacturing firms must plan for the timely acquisition of raw materials, and two discrete risks might be relevant. First, input prices might fluctuate, leading to swings in profitability. Also, if inputs are priced in a foreign currency, the company may be faced with foreign exchange risk on transactions that are known today but which will be finalized in the future. If production for a given order will not start immediately, or if inputs are not needed until a later stage in the production process, both commodity prices and exchange rates could affect the profitability of orders.

Continuing Risks

Continuing risks arise in connection with aggregated items in the company's financial statements whose values are affected by changing exchange rates, interest rates, or commodity prices. Instead of focusing on individual transactions, as we did in the discrete category, here we focus on broad macroeconomic forces relating to two risk exposures: *accounting exposures* and *economic exposures*.

Accounting Exposure
The effect on the firm of the different currency translation methods and resulting translation gains and losses.

ACCOUNTING EXPOSURES **Accounting exposures** are related to the effect of the different currency translation methods. In Chapter 7, we discussed the translation and consolidation of subsidiary financial statements for an MNE. We noted that if exchange rates change between two balance sheet dates, the translated statements may not balance after translation; that is, translated assets may not equal translated liabilities and capital. This can give rise to translation (noneconomic) gains and losses that are used to balance the statement. Depending on the translation methodology (current rate or temporal method), firms can have a net asset or liability exposure; that is, it can have either more exposed assets or more exposed liabilities that are affected by exchange rate changes.[6]

Monetary Balance
Implies that gains/ losses on the assets side of the balance sheet will exactly offset losses/gains on the capital side, so the company is completely insulated against translation gains or losses.

If the temporal method is required and the company has a zero net exposure position for all subsidiaries and currencies, then monetary assets equal monetary liabilities in the same currency, and we have **monetary balance**. Monetary balance implies that gains/losses on the assets side of the balance sheet will exactly offset losses/gains on the capital side, so the company is completely insulated against *translation* gains or losses.[7] As we stated in Chapter 7, these translation gains and losses are phantom adjustments that have little if any economic consequences. We concluded that if it makes good economic or business sense to match currencies to

---

[6]Recall that, with the current rate method, assets and liabilities are translated at the spot exchange rate on the day the financial statements are prepared, while equity accounts are translated at historical exchange rates in effect on the dates the items were recorded. On the other hand, with the temporal method all monetary assets and all liabilities are translated at the spot exchange rate on the day financial statements are prepared. However, nonmonetary items must be translated or remeasured at the historical exchange rates in effect on the dates the items were first recorded.

[7]One might think that monetary balance also leads to no *transaction* exposure for the discrete risks. This is not necessarily the case because individual transactions can cause gains or losses if the timing and maturity of assets and liabilities are not exactly matched. In other words, if the asset is used before the offsetting liability matures, then the exchange rate might change again during the timing gap, thus yielding a different gain or loss. Later in the chapter, when we discuss managing the transaction exposure, we will be careful to ensure that the amount and the timing of asset and liability transactions are the same.

achieve monetary balance, then there is no reason not to do it. However, if the company must incur real economic gains and losses to achieve monetary balance, then this is not a value-maximizing strategy.[8]

ECONOMIC EXPOSURES Throughout the book we have assumed that management's primary objective should be to maximize shareholder value created by the company.[9] **Economic exposure**, often called **operating exposure** or **strategic exposure**, is defined as the effect of changing economic variables (such as exchange rates, interest rates, and commodity prices) on firm value and the reaction of competitors to these variables.[10]

Some managers view economic exposure management as occurring over three time horizons, or tiers. In the short run (the first tier), the company should be concerned about the kinds of discrete risks and transaction exposures discussed above. These transactions are generally contractual and cannot be changed in the near-term.

The second tier (from one to five years) often corresponds with five-year operating plans that are rolled forward each year. The company may be able to use the parity conditions discussed in Chapter 3 to forecast equilibrium prices and costs and thus make free cash flow predictions more accurate.

The third tier is the long run, extending out more than five years. Strategic decisions regarding where and what to produce and sell, where to obtain key inputs, and what pricing strategies to use are obviously important. The firm must also anticipate actions by competitors. These third-tier actions are outside the main scope of finance, but financial managers are necessarily involved in the strategic planning process. SSI's decision to invest in Shanghai to serve the Asian market instead of supplying it from Germany is an example of such a strategy, and making the right decisions is critical for maximizing the value of the firm.

Economic (Operating or Strategic) Exposure
The impact of changing economic variables on firm value and the reaction of competitors to these variables.

SELF-TEST QUESTIONS

What are the two broad groups of manageable risks?
What are discrete risks?
What are continuing risks?
What are the two types of broad exposures to macroeconomic forces?

MANAGING RISKS

In Chapter 14, we discussed procedures for mitigating the problem of currency blockages, ways to reposition funds globally to get assets out of depreciating currencies and into stable ones, ways to use the firm's internal market to gain competitive advantage, and ways the MNE's global knowledge can help it obtain low-cost loans and high-return short-term investments. These are all important components of a comprehensive risk management program, but when we use the term **risk management**, we are generally referring to various strategies used to manage discrete foreign exchange, interest rate, and commodity price risks. Risk management in this sense is discussed in the following sections.

Risk Management
Refers to various strategies used to manage discrete foreign exchange, interest rate, and commodity price risk.

---

[8]Note that if the company is required to use the current rate method for translation, it is very difficult to obtain a zero net exposure because all assets are exposed but all equity accounts are, by definition, not exposed. While it is possible to obtain a zero net exposure, doing so almost always distorts the balance sheet and leads to suboptimal asset allocations and financing arrangements among the firm's operating units. We do not advocate trying to do this—instead, we focus on maximizing value and let the translation exposure be whatever it is.

[9]Recall that this view is common in the Anglo-American world but less prevalent elsewhere where the stakeholder concept holds sway. In either case, maximizing value is appropriate, and only the allocation of benefits is subject to controversy.

[10]Some writers suggest that economic exposure is concerned only with changes in exchange rates. We call this concept *currency exposure* and note that properly understood, economic exposure is the impact of all changes in the macroeconomic environment.

Managing Currency Risk

Hedging
Refers to creating offsetting assets and liabilities so that gains in one offset losses in the other. It locks in expected losses or gains and protects against unexpected changes.

The most common technique for managing currency risk involves **hedging**. Fundamentally, hedging refers to creating offsetting assets and liabilities so that gains in one offset losses in the other. If the hedge is "perfect," then the assets and liabilities are matched exactly, and all uncertainty caused by exchange rate fluctuations is eliminated. Sometimes hedges are not perfect, but they still reduce risk. It is important to recognize that hedging does not protect the firm from all currency changes. Most hedging techniques are based on parity relationships, and as such they lock in *expected* currency changes (losses or gains) but protect against loss from *unexpected* changes.

In terms of the probability distribution of free cash flows, hedging generally decreases expected free cash flows because it has an economic cost, but the risk of the cash flows, as measured by the standard deviation, is decreased. Managers must determine the proper level of hedging, defined as the amount and type that strikes the optimal balance between risk and return.

To Hedge or Not to Hedge

There is a debate among international financial scholars about the usefulness of hedging techniques. The major arguments of both sides are given in Table 15-1. Neither side dominates, but a consensus appears to be developing that the correct answer is somewhere in the middle.

1. There is no single right answer to the question of whether a firm should hedge or not. The extreme positions, that firms should hedge all risks or should do no hedging, are not likely to lead to value maximization.
2. Selective hedging of specific transactions appears to be useful when managers believe that the parity conditions do not hold and that they can accurately forecast currency fluctuations for the relevant period.
3. Currency risk management makes more sense for a consolidated firm than for each subsidiary because some currency positions will offset one another and more expertise can be used to address the problem.

TABLE 15-1 | Pros and Cons of Hedging

Arguments *for* Currency Hedging	Arguments *against* Currency Hedging
1. Management understands the currency risk situation better than shareholders, and this creates an information asymmetry.	1. Shareholders are better able to diversify currency risks and match their own risk tolerances and currency preferences.
2. All markets are usually not in equilibrium and parity conditions do not always hold for all countries, so the NPV of hedging could easily be positive.	2. Many managers engage in currency hedging because they are more risk averse than investors and fear that they will be criticized for currency losses but not rewarded for currency gains.
3. The greater the volatility of free cash flows, the greater the chance that the firm might violate bond provisions related to its operations. Hedging reduces the probability of this occurrence, thus lowering risk.	3. Managerial compensation programs are often tied to accounting results, and managers do not want to incur currency losses that would reduce their total compensation.
4. Planning capability is enhanced by greater stability and predictability of free cash flows.	4. When the parity conditions hold, the NPV of hedging is zero; managers cannot consistently beat the market.
	5. If the market is efficient, currency risk is already factored into the company's stock price.

| SELF-TEST QUESTIONS |

What is risk management?

What is hedging? What is a perfect hedge?

Is there a consensus regarding the proper amount of hedging?

TECHNIQUES FOR HEDGING CURRENCY RISK

Natural (Operating) Hedges
Arise from the firm's operating cash flows. Occur when monetary assets denominated in a particular foreign currency on the balance sheet offset liabilities in the same currency and same maturity. There are no transaction or translation gains or losses.

Contractual Hedges
Exist when a formal contractual relationship is established to lock in the exact terms of a future transaction.

Forward Market Hedge
Involves a contract to exchange specific amounts of two currencies at an exact time in the future and a source of funds to fulfill the contract.

If a company decides to hedge a specific transaction, a number of techniques can be used. We can divide these techniques into two major groups: *natural hedges,* also called *operating hedges,* and *contractual hedges.* **Natural** (or **operating**) **hedges** arise from the firm's operating cash flows. A natural hedge mentioned earlier is to have monetary assets denominated in a particular foreign currency on the balance sheet offset liabilities in the same currency and same maturity. In this case, losses on one side are offset by gains on the other. If the hedge is perfect, then there is an exact matching, and there are no transaction (or translation) gains or losses whatever. **Contractual hedges** are created when a formal contractual relationship is established to lock in the exact terms of a future transaction. There are three kinds of contractual hedges for managing discrete currency risk—forward market, money market, and OTC option hedges. There is also one type of hedge for managing continuous risk—exchange-traded currency derivatives. These terms are explained next, and the data for the numerical examples are given in Table 15-2.

Forward Market Hedge

A **forward market hedge** involves two elements: (1) a contract to exchange specific amounts of two currencies at an exact time in the future and (2) a source of funds to fulfill the contract.[11] The basic structure of a forward market hedge is shown in Figure 15-1. Here the company has an account payable for €1,250,000 due in 30 days, and the company expects to have dollars, but not euros, to make the payment (Case 1). To hedge this account payable in the forward market, the company executes a forward contract to buy euros forward 30 days for dollars. If the forward rate is $1.2721/€, the dollar equivalent to the euro payment is €1,250,000 × $1.2721/€ = $1,590,125. This means that the company agrees to pay $1,590,125 in 30 days to fulfill its obligation under the forward contract and in return will receive €1,250,000. It then takes the euros and makes the payment on the account payable. Note three things about this transaction:

TABLE 15-2 | Data for Hedging Examples

Amount of the account payable/receivable = €1,250,000.

Days before payment must be made/received = 30 days.

Spot exchange rate = $1.2704/€.

30-day forward exchange rate = $1.2721/€.

U.S. 30-day periodic interest rate = 0.2339%.

Euro 30-day periodic interest rate = 0.10%.

An OTC call option for €1,250,000 is available at a strike price of $1.2720/€ at a premium, or cost, of 0.50% or €6,250 ($7,940). An OTC put option with the same terms and cost is also available.

---

[11]If only the first part of the requirement, the contract itself, is present, then the contract is "open" or "naked," and this is called *speculation* rather than a risk-reducing hedge.

| Figure 15-1 | Structure of Forward Market Hedging for Payables and Receivables |

Today	30 Days from Now
Case 1:	
2. Execute forward contract to pay dollars and receive euros in 30 days.	1. Cash payment due in euros.
	3. Pay dollars to fulfill the forward contract, receive euros in return. Use euros to pay payable.
Case 2:	
2. Execute forward contract to pay euros and receive dollars in 30 days.	1. Cash receipt expected in euros.
	3. Receive euros from the receivable. Use euros to fulfill forward contract. Receive dollars in return.

1. The exchange rate is set when the forward contract is signed, but the exchange will not take place for 30 days.
2. Before the forward contract, the company had a liability of €1,250,000 and no corresponding euro-denominated asset. After the forward contract is signed, the company still has a liability to pay €1,250,000, but it also has a call (an asset) on €1,250,000 to meet the liability. It also has a liability to pay $1,590,125 in 30 days to purchase the euros. The net result is that the foreign-currency-denominated liability has been converted into a U.S.-currency-denominated liability.
3. The only risk in this transaction is counterparty risk, but that is minimal and is usually ignored if the counterparty is a reputable bank or dealer.

If the firm is to collect on an account receivable rather than pay off an account payable, the situation is just the opposite (Case 2). Now the company has an account receivable of €1,250,000 due in 30 days. Its primary currency is the dollar, so it wants to know exactly how many dollars it will receive. It can execute a forward contract to sell €1,250,000 at a rate of $1.2721/€ and receive the dollar equivalent or €1,250,000 × $1.2721/€ = $1,590,125 in 30 days. The transaction is a mirror image of the hedge for the account payable.

Money Market Hedge

Money Market Hedge
Similar to forward market hedge, but it involves an investment or loan contract.

Like the forward market hedge, the **money market hedge** also involves a contract, but in this case it is an investment or loan contract. The basic structure of the hedge is shown in Figure 15-2. Assume the company has a euro-denominated account payable due in 30 days, but no euros (Case 1). To hedge, the company converts dollars into euros at the spot rate, invests the euros for 30 days, and thus lines up the necessary euros to pay the account payable. How many dollars must the company invest for this hedge? If the account payable is for €1,250,000 and the 30-day euro investment rate is 0.10 percent, the principal to be invested today is €1,250,000/1.001 = €1,248,751.25. How many dollars are needed to obtain €1,248,751.25? The dollars required are €1,248,751.25 × $1.27040/€ = $1,586,413.59. Thus, the entire transaction consists of taking $1,586,413.59, converting it into €1,248,751.25 at the current spot rate of $1.27040/€, and investing €1,248,751.25 at 0.10 percent for 30 days, ending up with the €1,250,000 required for the account payable.

There are three significant differences between a money market hedge and a forward market hedge:

1. With a forward market hedge, the company does not have to come up with the dollars for the transaction until the end of the period. With the money market hedge, the funds must be available at the beginning of the period. The money market hedge requires fewer dollars because the investment is made in advance and thus earns interest. If we adjust for the time value of money based on the U.S. rate, the same amount of funds is required: $1,590,125 for the forward hedge and $1,586,413.59 × 1.002339 = $1,590,125 for the money market transaction.

2. In both the forward market and money market hedges, the goal is to create a foreign-currency offset to the payable or receivable so that the dollar cost or benefit can be locked in. The two hedging techniques use different mechanisms, but they are equally effective.

3. Because the money market hedge requires the company to borrow or invest, an additional issue is whether or not the company is a net borrower or a net investor. If the company has excess cash, then the $1,590,125 − $1,586,413.59 = $3,711.41 represents the opportunity cost of using money for hedging instead of investing it at the U.S. equilibrium rate of 0.2339 percent for 30 days. If the company is a net borrower, then this is a real interest cost instead of an opportunity cost.[12] In either situation, the cost is included when comparing the money market and forward market hedges.

In Case 2 of Figure 15-2, the company has a foreign-currency account receivable instead of a payable. To use a money market hedge in this instance, the company needs to borrow euros today, convert at the spot rate to dollars, and then use the euros received from the account receivable to repay the euro loan. If the 30-day account receivable is for €1,250,000 and the periodic interest rate on the euro loan is 0.10 percent, the company needs to borrow €1,250,000/1.001 = €1,248,751.25.

Figure 15-2 Structure of Money Market Hedging for Payables and Receivables

Today	30 Days from Now
Case 1:	1. Cash payment due in euros.
2. Take dollars, convert at the spot rate of $1.27040/€ into euros.	
3. Invest the euros for 30 days at a rate of 0.10%.	
	4. Receive principal plus interest from the euro investment. Use the euros to pay payable.
Case 2:	1. Cash receipt expected in euros.
2. Borrow euros at 0.10% for 30 days.	
3. Convert the euros into dollars at the spot rate of $1.27040/€.	
	4. Receive euros from the receivable. Use the euros to repay the loan with interest.

[12]In the real world, the borrowing rate will be greater than the lending rate. This would tend to bias the choice toward the money market hedge even if the rates were at parity.

In other words, the company borrows €1,248,751.25 today and must repay the principal plus interest (€1,250,000) in 30 days. To repay the loan, the company has a source of euros that can meet the account receivable. The €1,248,751.25 received by the company today will be converted into dollars at the spot rate of $1.27040/€, yielding $1,586,413.59. Compounding this to the end of the 30-day period at the dollar rate of 0.2339 percent gives $1,586,413.59 × 1.002339 = $1,590,125. This is exactly the same dollar cost as in the previous example.

OTC Option Hedge

OTC Option Hedge
Foreign currency exposure is hedged using an option contract. Currency options are priced relative to the forward rate, but the price of the option is paid immediately.

Forward-at-the-Money
Near the forward rate.

The company could also hedge the euro exposure using an option contract, which is called an **OTC option hedge.** OTC (over-the-counter) option contracts are written by many large multinational banks for their clients. Currency options are priced relative to the forward rate, but payment of the premium on (or price of) the option is made when it is acquired. To hedge the €1,250,000 account payable, the firm can purchase a 30-day call option on €1,250,000. A quote is available at a strike price of $1.2720/€, which is very near the forward rate of $1.2721/€, so it is approximately a **forward-at-the-money** transaction, which means it is near the forward rate. This quote has a premium of 0.50 percent, so the cost of the call is €1,250,000 × 0.0050 × $1.27040/€ = $7,940 payable immediately. However, we need to evaluate everything at the end of the period, so we compound this price forward 30 days at the 30-day U.S. interest rate of 0.2339 percent: $7,940 × 1.002339 = $7,958.57. The company has the right, but not the obligation, to exercise the option. At the end of 30 days, when the account payable must be paid, the decision to exercise the option or to let it expire will be made. Of course, the company prefers to use the fewest dollars to acquire the €1,250,000, so if the spot rate in 30 days is less than the strike price of $1.2720/€, the call will be allowed to expire, and the euros will be acquired in the spot market. If the spot exchange rate in 30 days is greater than the strike price ($1.2720/€), the option will be exercised, and the total cost will be €1,250,000 × $1.2720/€ + $7,958.57 = $1,597,958.57, no matter how high the actual spot rate turns out to be. The option thus protects the firm from the downside risk (high exchange rate) but allows it to take advantage of the upside potential (low exchange rate). However, in making our decision to use options we must factor in the cost of the option, which exceeds the cost of the forward contract.

Figure 15-3 shows the relationship of the future spot exchange rate to the dollar cost of acquiring €1,250,000 in 30 days under each of the three scenarios. At exchange rates lower than the strike price ($1.2720/€), the option will not be exercised, so the total cost is the dollars required to obtain spot euros plus the cost of the option (€1,250,000 × Spot rate + $7,958.57). The other sloping line in the figure is the cost of acquiring euros to pay the account payable if the company remains unhedged. Note that for exchange rates less than the strike price, the unhedged line is less than the option line by the cost of the option. Considering the cost of the option, the exchange rate at which the cost of hedging is the same as remaining unhedged can be calculated as

$$\text{Break-even rate} = \$1,597,958.57/€1,250,000 = \$1.2784/€.$$

If the company expects the future exchange rate to be greater than this "break-even" rate, then the option hedge is superior to remaining unhedged. Otherwise, the cost will be less if the company remains unhedged. Of course, no one knows what the rate will be in 30 days, so this course of action is risky.

The horizontal line at a cost of $1,590,125 represents the cost of the transaction using either the forward contract or the money market hedge. The two lines are the

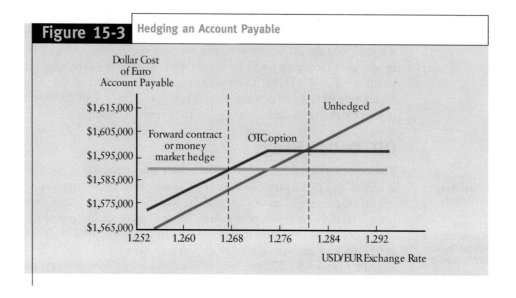

Figure 15-3 Hedging an Account Payable

same because interest rate parity holds, but they would be different if a disequilibrium existed. We can compute the break-even rate between these alternatives and the call option as we did for the unhedged position:

$$\text{Break-even rate} = \frac{(\text{Spot dollar-equivalent of obligation} - \text{Cost of option})}{\text{Foreign currency obligation}}$$

$$= (\$1,590,125 - \$7,958.57)/\text{€}1,250,000$$

$$= \$1.2657/\text{€}.$$

If the company expects the future spot rate to exceed $1.2657/€, then the forward contract or money market hedge is superior to the call option hedge. Otherwise, the call is preferred.

To hedge the account receivable of €1,250,000, the firm would need to exchange foreign currency for dollars, so it needs to purchase a put option on €1,250,000. Assume the same approximately forward-at-the-money strike price of $1.2720/€. This quote has the same premium of 0.50 percent as in the previous example, so the cost of the put is €1,250,000 × 0.0050 × $1.2704/€ = $7,940 payable immediately. The value of this cost at the end of the period is still $7,940 × 1.002339 = $7,958.57. The company has the right, but not the obligation, to exercise the option. At the end of 30 days when the receivable is collected, the decision to exercise the option or to let it expire will be a function of the current spot rate at that time. The company prefers to gain the most dollars from the €1,250,000, so if the spot rate in 30 days is greater than the strike price of $1.2720/€, the put will be allowed to expire, and the euros will be exchanged in the spot market. If the spot exchange rate in 30 days is less than the strike price ($1.2720/€), the option will be exercised, and the total receipt will be €1,250,000 × $1.2720/€ − $7,958.57 = $1,582,041.43, no matter how low the actual spot rate turns out to be.

Figure 15-4 shows the relationship of the future spot exchange rate to the dollar receipts from €1,250,000 worth of accounts receivable in 30 days. At the strike price of $1.2720/€, the option will be exercised, so the minimum dollar receipt from the account receivable is $1,582,041.43. At exchange rates higher than the strike price, the option will not be exercised, so the total receipt is calculated as the dollars received in the spot market less the cost of the option. The other sloping line in

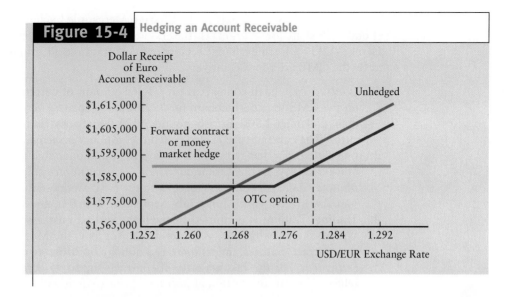

Figure 15-4 Hedging an Account Receivable

the figure is the dollars received by exchanging the euro account receivable funds if the company remains unhedged. Note that for exchange rates greater than the strike price, the option line is lower than the unhedged line by the cost of the option. Considering the cost of the option, the exchange rate at which the cost of hedging is the same as remaining unhedged can be calculated as

$$\text{Break-even rate} = \$1,582,041.43/€1,250,000 = \$1.2656/€.$$

If the company expects the exchange rate to be less than this break-even rate, then the option hedge is superior to remaining unhedged because it places a floor on the dollar-equivalent receipts.

The horizontal line at a cost of $1,590,125 represents the proceeds of the transaction using either the forward or money market hedge. We can compute the break-even rate between these alternatives and the put option:

$$\text{Break-even rate} = (\$1,590,125 + \$7,958.57)/€1,250,000$$
$$= \$1.2785/€.$$

If the company expects the future spot rate to be less than $1.2785/€, then the forward or money market hedges are superior to the put option hedge. Otherwise, the put is the preferred hedging technique.

Exchange-Traded Currency Derivatives

Exchange-traded currency futures and options exist for most major currencies. However, they are distinct from the forwards and OTC options discussed earlier. Most importantly, exchange-traded derivatives are standardized, "prepackaged" instruments, while forwards and OTC options are custom tailored to meet the needs of the firm seeking a hedge. For this reason, **exchange-traded currency derivatives** tend to be used extensively for speculation, although some companies use them to hedge continuing exposures that cannot be neutralized with natural hedges.

A **currency futures contract** calls for delivery (1) at a preset location, (2) of a standardized amount of a particular currency, (3) at a specific time in the future, and (4) at a specified price. Currency futures can be obtained in most world money centers. In the United States, most currency futures are traded on the International

Exchange-Traded Currency Derivatives
They are standardized, prepackaged instruments used more for speculation than for hedging, although some companies use them to hedge continuing exposures that cannot be neutralized with natural hedges.

Currency Futures Contract
Calls for delivery, at a preset location, of a standardized amount of a particular currency, at a specific time in the future, and at a fixed price.

Monetary Market (IMM), a part of the Chicago Mercantile Exchange (CME), while in London the major market is the London International Financial Futures Exchange (LIFFE). Each exchange sets its own contract specifications, but the ones used by the CME are representative:

1. *Contract size.* Each contract is for a fixed amount of currency. For instance, on the CME the contracts are for 12,500,000 Japanese yen, 100,000 Canadian dollars, 62,500 British pounds, 125,000 Swiss francs, and 125,000 euros. The contract size is also called the *notional principal.*

2. *Quotations.* Exchange rates are always the U.S. dollar cost of one unit of the other currency, so the quotations are in "American terms."

3. *Maturity date.* All contracts mature on the third Wednesday of eight months: January, March, April, June, July, September, October, and December.

4. *Trading.* Trading is permitted through the second business day prior to the Wednesday on which the contract matures; this is the Monday of the week the contract matures, unless there is a holiday on Monday or Tuesday.

5. *Settlement.* For the vast majority of contracts (up to 95 percent), buyers and sellers close out their original positions prior to delivery by buying an opposite contract. The total transaction—taking an original position and then an opposite one to cancel it out—is called a *round turn.*

6. *Counterparty.* All contracts are between a buyer and the exchange clearinghouse. Because the clearinghouse is owned by the members of the exchange who guarantee the contracts, counterparty risk is not an issue.

7. *Collateral.* The buyer must deposit a fixed sum as an initial margin or collateral. This requirement can be met by a letter of credit, Treasury bills, or cash.

8. *Maintenance margins.* The value of the contract is "marked to market" daily; that is, it is revalued daily using the closing price for the day. All changes in value must be paid in cash daily, and the amount to be paid is called the *variation margin.*

Table 15-3 illustrates CME quotations and gives the information for euro futures on the CME as of Wednesday, April 28, 2004. Looking at the various columns, "Open" means the price at which the future opened that day. "High" and "Low" are the high and low prices for the day. "Settle" is the closing price for the day. Thus, the June contract closed lower than it opened, as shown in the "Chg" column. Over the lifetime of the June contract it has traded at a lifetime high and low of 1.2875

TABLE 15-3 | Euro Futures Quotations for April 28, 2004

Euro/US Dollar (CME)-€125,000; $ per €

	Open	High	Low	Settle	Chg	LIFETIME High	Low	Open Int
June	1.1909	1.1939	1.1805	1.1825	−.0094	1.2875	1.0570	118,216
Sept	1.1895	1.1901	1.1785	1.1802	−.0094	1.2800	1.0500	937
Dec	1.1860	1.1860	1.1780	1.1788	−.0094	1.2781	1.0735	403

Est vol 25,633; vol Tue 69,254; open int 119,710, +1,706.

Source: Data excerpted from *The Wall Street Journal,* April 29, 2004, C12.

and 1.0570, respectively. The final column, "Open Int," is the number of contracts outstanding.

Businesses find futures contracts to be inefficient and hard to use for transaction hedging in comparison to forwards. The "mark-to-market" feature must be monitored constantly, even if the company doesn't have to pay or receive cash daily, and the futures contract can result in frequent margin calls. Forwards are much easier to work with because they can be negotiated for exact maturity dates and amounts of money, and they do not require frequent monitoring. However, they may have more counterparty risk unless the counterparty is a strong bank or dealer.

Traded Option Contract
Similar to OTC options, but like traded futures contracts, they are standardized.

A **traded option contract** is similar to the OTC options we discussed. However, like the traded futures contracts, traded options are standardized. Technically, there are two different kinds of options. An *American option* gives the buyer the right, but not the obligation, to exercise the option at any time between the dates at which it is written and on which it expires. A *European option* cannot be exercised until the date on which it expires. The difference in valuation between them is small because American options are rarely exercised before they expire—instead, they are sold to someone else at a premium because they still have time remaining before they expire.

Option contracts are traded on several U.S. and foreign exchanges. In the United States, the Philadelphia Stock Exchange and the Chicago Mercantile Exchange are the two most widely used, and we can find option market quotations from the CME in *The Wall Street Journal,* as shown in Table 15-4. The options on the euro (both calls and puts) are for a fixed amount of €125,000, and, like traded futures, they are quoted in American terms. The "Price" column refers to the strike price (11750 is equivalent to $1.1750), or the price that must be paid for one euro if the option is exercised. The entries in the other columns are the premium or price of the option expiring in that month (calls in the first three columns and puts in the last three columns). In other words, a June call with a strike price of $1.1800 has a cost of 2.03 U.S. cents per euro, or $0.0203/€. Because each contract involves €125,000, the total cost of a June call with a strike price of $1.1800 is €125,000 × $0.0203/€ = $2,537.50. If there is no numerical entry in a particular column, it means that no

TABLE 15-4 | Euro Options Quotations for April 28, 2004

Euro Fx (CME)
125,000 euros; cents per euro

Strike Price	CALLS—SETTLE			PUTS—SETTLE		
	May	June	July	May	June	July
11750	. . .	1.65	. . .	0.40	. . .	. . .
11800	. . .	2.03	2.73	0.28	0.98	1.51
11850	1.31	2.10	. . .	0.56	1.35	. . .
11900	1.01	1.83	. . .	0.76	1.58	2.33
11950	0.76	. . .	. . .	1.01	. . .	. . .
12000	0.56	1.36	1.90	1.31	2.11	2.88

Est vol 4,400 Tu 2,689 calls 1,524 puts

Op int Tues 32,381 calls 29,290 puts

Source: Data excerpted from *The Wall Street Journal,* April 29, 2004, C12.

trading occurred for that contract on that day. At the bottom of the table, we see the estimated volume for Wednesday, April 28, 2004, and the actual volume for Tuesday, April 27, 2004. Also, open interest (Op int) is the number of call and put contracts outstanding for euros. The actual spot rate for the euro on April 28, 2004, which isn't included in the table, can be compared with the strike price. This information is given elsewhere on the same page of the *Journal* as $1.1834/€.

Companies may use traded options to hedge continuing or aggregate balance sheet exposures in the same way they might consider traded currency futures. There is little or no counterparty risk with traded options because all contracts have the exchange as the counterparty. However, most traded options are used by speculators or people who want to hedge but do not have easy access to the OTC market makers.

SELF-TEST QUESTIONS

What are the two major groups of hedging techniques designed for specific transactions?

What are the three types of contractual hedges for managing discrete currency risk?

What type of contractual hedge is used for managing continuous risk?

What does forward-at-the-money mean?

How do you calculate the break-even exchange rate between hedging and remaining unhedged?

What are the two different types of options?

HEDGING OTHER EXPOSURES

We focused the preceding discussion of hedging on a foreign-currency-denominated account payable where no offsetting source of the foreign currency was on the firm's books. Borrowing or lending in a foreign currency gives rise to the same types of exposures as with payables and receivables, and the same techniques and instruments can be used for hedging them. Remember, the essence of currency risk is a future receipt or payment in a foreign currency for which there is no offsetting liability or asset. These risks can be hedged, provided the amount, timing, and currency are known. If debt contracts are involved and the risk issue is managing the currency risk associated with servicing them, some other specialized risk management techniques are available to complement procedures already described.

Managing Interest Rate Risk

For a multinational enterprise operating in many countries, interest-rate-risk management is especially complex. Even if the finance function is centralized, managers must recognize that some countries have segmented capital markets, use their own national currencies, have different yield curves, and often have dissimilar attitudes regarding capital structure. As Table 15-5 illustrates, interest payments are also calculated differently in different countries.

Environmental diversity can convey advantages to MNEs that know how to manage currencies effectively, yielding better returns without appreciably higher risk. In the sections that follow, we demonstrate how MNEs manage risks associated with (1) servicing foreign-currency-denominated debt, (2) servicing floating-rate debt, and (3) planning for future borrowings.

Assume that SSI has just borrowed on a one-year floating-rate loan of $10 million for LIBOR + 1%, with quarterly resets. Details on the loan are shown in Table 15-6. The three-month LIBOR rate is currently 1.12 percent, and that rate was set

TABLE 15-5 | Interest Calculation Conventions

Convention	Number of Days in a Period	Number of Days in a Year
British	Actual number of days	365
International	Actual number of days	360
Swiss (eurobond)	Assume 30 days/month	360

TABLE 15-6 | Cash Flows from Servicing SSI's $10 Million Floating-Rate Loan

	Origination	1st Quarter	2nd Quarter	3rd Quarter	4th Quarter
1. Loan Interest					
LIBOR		1.12%	1.12%	1.12%	1.12%
Fixed premium		1.00	1.00	1.00	1.00
Total interest rate		2.12%	2.12%	2.12%	2.12%
Total interest dollars		($212,000)	($212,000)	($212,000)	($212,000)
2. Principal					
Receipt/repayment	$9,800,000[a]				($10,000,000)
3. Total Loan CFs	$9,800,000	($212,000)	($212,000)	($212,000)	($10,212,000)
Effective rate, or all-in-cost (AIC) 2.653604%					

Note:
[a]A 2 percent loan origination fee reduces the proceeds from $10 million to $9.8 million.

in the loan. This is the rate per quarter, not per year. The interest rate paid by SSI, then, is 1.12% + 1% = 2.12% for the first quarter. SSI also had to pay a 2 percent origination fee at the time the loan contract was signed (today). The expected cash flows associated with this loan, assuming that LIBOR remains at 1.12 percent, are given in the table. Of course, LIBOR could rise or fall, causing the dollar interest paid to increase or decrease, so the effective rate of the loan (IRR), also called the *all-in cost,* can rise or fall. SSI's treasurer really wanted to borrow at a fixed rate, but the quotes were too high, so the firm decided to use the floating-rate loan instead. The treasurer is reasonably comfortable with the terms of this contract right now, but rising rates could pose a problem. Thus, it is useful to consider mechanisms that could eliminate the risk associated with changes in LIBOR, and three procedures can be used for this purpose: (1) *interest rate futures,* (2) *forward rate agreements,* and (3) *interest rate swaps.*

Interest Rate Futures
Standardized contracts traded on exchanges around the world whose underlying security is a debt obligation.

INTEREST RATE FUTURES As we noted earlier, **interest rate futures** are standardized contracts traded on exchanges around the world, including the Chicago Mercantile Exchange (CME) in the United States. They are highly liquid and easy to use, and corporate managers find them valuable for hedging interest rate exposures. Table 15-7 shows *The Wall Street Journal* quotes for a three-month eurodollar futures contract. The September 2004 contract opened at 98.53 and closed at 98.52. The yield at the close was 100.00 − 98.52 = 1.48 percent per quarter. SSI's treasurer is interested in using interest rate futures to hedge the company's interest rate risk for its floating-rate interest payment due in September 2004.

TABLE 15-7 | Eurodollar Futures Quotations for April 28, 2004

Eurodollar (CME)-$1,000,000; pts of 100%

	Open	High	Low	Settle	Chg	Yield	Chg	Open Int
Mar04	98.78	98.78	98.77	98.77	−.01	1.23	.01	89,323
June	98.67	98.68	98.67	98.67	−.01	1.33	.01	838,970
Sept	98.53	98.53	98.52	98.52	−.02	1.48	.02	38,789
Dec	98.39	98.39	98.39	98.39	. . .	1.61	. . .	350
Mar05	98.32	98.32	98.26	98.27	−.04	1.73	.04	881,763
June	97.88	97.88	97.80	97.81	−.06	2.19	.06	761,202

Source: Data excerpted from *The Wall Street Journal*, April 29, 2004, C12.

It is important to differentiate between when the company is hedging a future interest payment (this situation) or interest to be received on a floating-rate investment. If it must *pay* interest in the future, it needs to *sell* a futures contract, while if it will *receive* future interest, it needs to *buy* a futures contract:

1. *The firm must pay interest: hedging a debt obligation.* If you sell a futures contract, you are selling something you do not now own—in effect, you borrow the item, sell it now, and then buy it back later at the then-prevailing price. This is called taking a *short position.* As we saw in Chapter 8, if interest rates rise, the price of debt instruments will fall (in this case, the futures contract on some amount of debt). Thus, if rates rise, the seller of the futures contract could purchase the debt at a lower price in the future and earn a profit on the transaction. Accordingly, falling interest rates cause debt futures to rise in value, and rising rates cause futures prices to decline. If the company has taken out a loan, then if LIBOR increases it will have to pay more interest than it expected. Therefore, if the company sells 10 futures contracts (for a total notional principal of $10 million), then the gain on the short position would approximately offset the extra interest on the loan. Of course, if interest rates fall, the price of the futures contract will increase, leading to a loss on the transaction because the company earlier sold it at a lower price and must replace it at the higher price. However, the interest payments will be lower because LIBOR has fallen, so the firm again has offsetting gains and losses. *So, to hedge a debt obligation with a futures contract, the firm must sell the futures contract short.*

2. *The firm will receive interest: hedging a floating-rate investment.* If a person buys a futures contract, he or she owns it. This is called a *long position.* If interest rates fall, the price of the futures contract will increase and the owner will earn a profit, and the futures owner will suffer a loss if rates rise. The interest earned on a floating-rate investment will decline if rates fall and rise if rates rise. Thus, the lower interest earned on the investment if rates fall is offset by the profit on the futures contract, and vice versa if rates rise. Thus, a long position in interest rate futures can be used to hedge floating-rate investments.

We see, then, that interest rate futures can be used to hedge floating-rate obligations on both the liabilities and assets sides of the balance sheet. Historically, treasurers have been more concerned with their floating-rate debt, but companies are now making use of futures for both purposes.

Forward Rate Agreements (FRAs) **Forward rate agreements**, or **FRAs**, are contracts restricted mainly to major markets and currencies that can be tailored to fit specific company situations, much like forward contracts. FRAs are an important hedging tool because they allow firms to lock in future interest rates. Suppose SSI is concerned that LIBOR will increase and in the second quarter the interest rate will be higher than 2.12 percent. The treasurer can purchase an FRA on $10 million to lock in the payment at 2.12 percent. If LIBOR moves above 1.12 percent, SSI would receive a cash payment from the FRA seller to offset the increase.[13] However, if LIBOR falls below 1.12 percent, SSI would have to pay cash to the seller to bring the total up to the agreed 1.12 percent. In this way, SSI can lock in the 1.12 percent LIBOR and eliminate all variability.

Interest Rate, or Coupon, Swaps Assume that SSI now has $10 million of floating-rate debt tied to LIBOR. However, assume that the treasurer believes that dollar interest rates will rise over the next year. Thus, the effective cost of the loan is expected to be greater than the 2.653604 percent calculated in Table 15-6. We have already discussed how the company can use interest rate futures and FRAs to eliminate the interest rate volatility, but a third technique is also available. **Interest rate**, or **coupon**, **swaps** allow a company that has floating-rate debt to switch debt servicing to a fixed-rate basis or a firm with fixed-rate debt to switch to floating-rate debt service. There are many reasons for preferring one type of debt servicing over the other, including matching asset and liability exposures and the relative costs of both types of borrowing, but we will focus on SSI's belief that rates will rise over the next year, which would increase its interest expense. Remember from an earlier discussion, the company really wanted fixed-rate debt when it borrowed the $10 million on a floating basis, but it couldn't raise the funds at an acceptable fixed rate. Now, though, a swap may allow it to effectively convert the debt to a fixed-rate basis.

At the most basic level, a **swap** is simply a contractual agreement to exchange a series of cash flows. SSI wants to replace the cash flows associated with servicing its floating-rate debt with fixed interest payments on the same notional principal ($10 million). It would, of course, like the fixed interest rate to be lower than it could have obtained had it borrowed at a fixed rate in the first place. Is this a realistic expectation? Frequently, the answer is yes, and the reason is *comparative advantage* as discussed back in Chapter 4.

Table 15-8 shows the rates available to two companies, SSI and G&T Industries, for both fixed- and floating-rate debt. To use the terminology of Adam Smith and David Ricardo, we see that G&T has an absolute advantage in both fixed- and floating-rate borrowing—it can borrow at a lower cost on either type instrument. However, G&T's advantage is 0.27 percent for fixed-rate borrowing but only 0.10 percent for floating-rate debt, so SSI has the least absolute disadvantage on floating-rate debt. As long as these two numbers are not the same, both companies can gain from "specialization and trade"—or in this case, swapping interest payment streams. SSI prefers to borrow fixed, but it would have to pay 3.27 percent. G&T prefers to have floating-rate debt to match against its floating-rate assets, but in a swap transaction it might be able to pay less than LIBOR + 0.90%.

Forward Rate Agreements (FRAs) Contracts restricted mainly to major markets and currencies that can be tailored to fit specific company situations, much like forward contracts. They allow firms to lock in future interest rates.

Interest Rate (Coupon) Swaps Allow a company that has floating-rate debt to switch debt servicing to a fixed-rate basis, or vice versa.

Swap A contractual agreement to exchange a series of cash flows.

---

[13]Remember, only part of the interest rate is floating LIBOR. The rest is the 1 percent fixed premium.

TABLE 15-8 | Anatomy of an Interest Rate Swap on $10 Million Notional Principal

SSI	G&T Industries	Differences
Fixed: 3.27%	Fixed: 3.00%	$\Delta = 0.27\%$
Floating: LIBOR + 1%	Floating: LIBOR + 0.90%	$\underline{\Delta = 0.10}$
Prefers fixed	Prefers floating	$\Delta = 0.17\%$
Borrow floating at LIBOR + 1%	Borrow fixed at 3.00%	
Swap the debt service streams:		
Pay fixed: 3.20%	Pay floating: LIBOR + 0.83%	
	Inflows: LIBOR + 0.83% + 3.20% = LIBOR + 4.03%	
	Outflows: LIBOR + 1% + 3.00% = LIBOR + 4.00%	
	Net + 0.03%	

A broker then puts the two companies together and arranges a swap. SSI borrows $10 million of floating-rate debt at an interest rate of LIBOR + 1%, while G&T borrows $10 million of fixed-rate debt at 3.00%. The two contracts have the same notional principal, so the companies can swap their debt service streams. Assume that the broker has arranged for SSI to pay a fixed rate of 3.20 percent, which is less than it would have had to pay if it had borrowed directly at a fixed rate. Also, G&T must pay LIBOR + 0.83%, also less than it would have had to pay if it had borrowed directly at a floating rate. Thus, both companies are able to obtain debt of the type they prefer at a lower cost than they could achieve without the swap.

What is the broker's profit for arranging this deal? SSI pays a fixed rate of 3.20 percent, and G&T pays LIBOR + 0.83%. Total inflows equal LIBOR + 0.83% + 3.20% = LIBOR + 4.03%. Outflows to service the actual borrowings are LIBOR + 1% + 3.00% = LIBOR + 4.00%. Netting out the inflows and outflows, a positive remainder of 0.03% exists, or $3,000 on a notional principal of $10 million, which represents the broker's profit.

What would happen if one of the companies failed to live up to its end of the deal? This is what is meant by *counterparty risk*. If this happens, then the debt service immediately reverts to the original unswapped stream—liability for payment of the floating-rate debt service remains with SSI even if it swaps with G&T. The risk is that SSI expects to have a fixed-rate debt service at 3.20 percent, and after default by G&T, it would again have to pay a variable rate, LIBOR + 1%.

Interest rate swaps of this kind are sometimes called *plain vanilla swaps*. The market for plain vanilla swaps is the single largest financial derivative market in the world. In reality, though, most swaps are transactions between a company and a swap dealer, not directly between companies. SSI could swap debt service for the entire $10 million, or for any part of it. Having a dealer means that a company does not have to search for a partner to take the other side of the transaction—the dealer "makes the market." If markets were complete and efficient, the comparative advantages would disappear and no company could be made "better off" by engaging in swap transactions. However, markets are neither complete nor completely efficient, and there may be other reasons for swapping. Therefore, the swap market serves an important function in making the market more efficient.

It is also possible to swap the currency in which payments are made. That is, the company can swap debt service in dollars for debt service in euros for the same notional principal. This is called a **currency swap**. Currency swaps can be combined with interest rate swaps, making it possible to swap, for example, floating-rate dol-

Currency Swap
A contractual agreement to exchange the currency of the debt service for the same notional principal.

lar payments for fixed-rate Swiss franc payments. Table 15-9 shows interest rate swaps for five currencies as reported in the *Financial Times* on April 28, 2004. Three features of the quotations in Table 15-9 are highlighted:

1. All of the rates in the table are derived from the yield curves for government securities in the respective countries, plus a credit risk premium appropriate for investment-grade corporate borrowers in the respective national markets.
2. Swap rates do not vary with the credit rating of the borrower. As we saw in the plain vanilla swap example, the credit risk premium is the fixed component added to LIBOR or embedded in the fixed rate, and the variable component, LIBOR, is what is being swapped.
3. The note at the bottom of Table 15-9 specifies that the U.S. dollar quotes are in percent per year and use the international convention from Table 15-5. The yen and pound are quoted as semiannual rates using the British convention, and the euro and Swiss franc quotes are percent per year and employ the Swiss or eurobond convention.

Within a particular row of the table (corresponding to the maturity of the contract), all of the ask rates are interchangeable. In other words, if SSI had five-year yen-denominated debt at an interest rate of 0.76 percent per annum, it could swap the debt service stream for another one: 3.96 percent in dollars, 2.24 percent in Swiss francs, 5.27 percent in pounds sterling, or 3.57 percent in euros. These rates are all at interest rate parity, so moving from one to the other does not change the

TABLE 15-9 | Bid/Ask Data for Interest Rate Swaps on April 28, 2004

Apr 28	EURO Bid	Ask	£ STERLING Bid	Ask	SW FRANC Bid	Ask	US$ Bid	Ask	YEN Bid	Ask
1-year	2.25	2.28	4.83	4.85	0.74	0.80	1.74	1.77	0.07	0.10
2-year	2.65	2.68	5.01	5.05	1.28	1.36	2.54	2.57	0.20	0.22
3-year	3.00	3.03	5.12	5.16	1.64	1.72	3.15	3.18	0.36	0.38
4-year	3.30	3.33	5.18	5.23	1.92	2.00	3.59	3.62	0.54	0.56
5-year	3.54	3.57	5.22	5.27	2.16	2.24	3.93	3.96	0.73	0.76
6-year	3.75	3.78	5.25	5.29	2.36	2.44	4.20	4.23	0.93	0.96
7-year	3.93	3.96	5.26	5.31	2.54	2.62	4.41	4.44	1.12	1.15
8-year	4.08	4.12	5.27	5.32	2.68	2.76	4.58	4.61	1.28	1.31
9-year	4.21	4.24	5.28	5.33	2.80	2.88	4.73	4.76	1.41	1.44
10-year	4.32	4.35	5.28	5.33	2.90	2.98	4.85	4.88	1.53	1.56
12-year	4.48	4.51	5.27	5.34	3.06	3.15	5.05	5.08	1.72	1.75
15-year	4.66	4.69	5.23	5.32	3.25	3.35	5.28	5.31	1.92	1.95
20-year	4.85	4.88	5.16	5.29	3.45	3.55	5.47	5.50	2.14	2.17
25-year	4.94	4.97	5.09	5.22	3.55	3.65	5.52	5.55	2.27	2.30
30-year	4.97	5.00	5.04	5.17	3.60	3.70	5.54	5.57	2.33	2.36

Notes:
Bid and ask rates are as of close of London business. U.S. dollars are quoted on an annual money actual/360 basis against three-month LIBOR. Pounds and yen are quoted on a semiannual actual/365 basis against six-month LIBOR. Euros and Swiss francs are quoted on an annual bond 30/360 basis against six-month Euribor/LIBOR with the exception of the one-year rate, which is quoted against three-month Euribor/LIBOR.

Source: Data excerpted from *Financial Times*, April 29, 2004, 29.

home-currency-equivalent value of the interest stream when the contract is signed. It could also move from fixed to floating (or vice versa), as we discussed previously.

Option-Based Instruments

Just as there are options designed to manage currency risks, several option products can be used for interest-rate-risk management. A thorough discussion of these derivative products is beyond the scope of this book, but we discuss below several standard over-the-counter (interbank) options that companies with significant expertise sometimes obtain from their banks. Currency options include both puts and calls. Interest rate options, though, are of three types—*caps, floors,* and *collars.* Assume that a company has $10 million of three-year floating-rate debt (maturities can be up to about 10 years) tied to a reference rate such as three-month LIBOR. This means that the interest rate will be reset every three months, or 11 times over the life of the loan (no reset exists for the first three-month period because it is set when the contract is signed). Assume also that the company is willing to accept some variability in LIBOR, but it wants to constrain the maximum value of LIBOR over the life of the loan. The instrument designed to achieve this constraint is basically a call option called an **interest rate cap**. The value of LIBOR at the fixed upper bound is called the *strike rate,* the three-month reset period is called the *tenor* of the cap, and the buyer pays an upfront premium as with other options. If LIBOR is above the strike rate on the exact date the rate will be reset, the buyer of the cap will receive a cash payment from the seller that is equal to the difference between the actual LIBOR rate and the strike rate times the notional principal. For instance, if the cap is set at 1.25 percent and LIBOR goes to 1.28 percent, for a notional principal of $10,000,000, the seller would have to pay the buyer $10,000,000 $\times$ (1.0128 − 1.0125) = $3,000.

Just as an interest rate cap is essentially a call option, an *interest rate floor* is a put option. **Interest rate floors** are options that set a minimum effective interest rate to be received on an invested notional principal. They are used when the company is willing to assume some interest rate risk on a security investment, but it wants to constrain the minimum earnings rate to a particular level. Assume that a company will receive operating cash flows in the future and wants to set a lower bound on the effective rate it will receive when investing these flows. The instrument designed to offer this kind of protection is the interest rate floor. Like the cap (but in the opposite direction), if the market rate goes below the strike rate, the buyer of the floor will receive a cash payment from the writer of the instrument equal to the difference in rates times the notional principal.

If a company believes that the reference rate (such as dollar LIBOR) is more likely to increase than to decrease, or vice versa, purchasing a cap (floor) and selling a floor (cap) might be worth considering. The premium earned on the cap or floor can cover part or even the entire premium paid on the other side of the deal.[14] This simultaneous buying and selling of caps and floors is called an **interest rate collar**. The difference between the cap rate and the floor rate is called the width of the collar, and a zero-width collar is effectively a forward rate agreement. Collars allow the company to benefit from constraints on the upside or downside, whichever it is concerned with, while having a reduced premium cost. Later, the cost may be nonzero if the company has to pay the buyer of the position because the reference rate penetrated the strike rate.

Interest Rate Cap
A type of call option that constrains the maximum interest rate value over the life of the loan.

Interest Rate Floor
A type of put option that sets a minimum effective interest rate to be received on an invested notional principal.

Interest Rate Collar
The simultaneous buying and selling of caps and floors. It allows the company to benefit from constraints on the upside or downside, whichever it is concerned with, while having a reduced premium cost.

---

[14]If the premium earned is equal to the premium paid on the other side of the deal, the position is called a *zero-premium collar.*

Swaption
Shorthand for swap option. Gives the firm the right, if it chooses, to enter into a swap on some notional principal at a fixed date and at a designated strike rate.

A final type of option is called a **swaption**, which is shorthand for *swap option*. Basically, a swaption gives the firm the right, if it chooses, to enter into a swap on some notional principal at a fixed date and at a designated strike rate. There are two different types of swaptions, one that conveys the right to pay a fixed rate and receive a floating rate (a *payer's swaption*) and the other the right to receive a fixed rate and pay a floating rate (a *receiver's swaption*). MNEs generally purchase *payer's swaptions,* and banks generally purchase *receiver's swaptions.*

Managing Commodity Price Risk

While commodity price risk is not unique to MNEs, the internal market gives the MNE several competitive advantages over purely domestic companies. These advantages occur because MNEs have access to commodities and materials from many different sources plus flexibility in how they deploy these resources. Depending on the production processes and industry, commodity price changes can affect input costs, output prices, or both. We can divide commodities into two broad groups—those that can be "packaged" in a standardized manner and traded in an organized financial futures market (e.g., wheat) and those whose characteristics do not lend themselves to such generic standardization.

Commodity Futures

Commodities that are traded in futures markets are usually grouped into three categories: (1) agricultural products, (2) metals, and (3) energy. Agricultural products can be further divided into grains and oil seeds (such as corn, oats, soybeans, rough rice, and wheat), livestock (cattle, hogs, and pork bellies), and food and fiber (lumber, milk, cocoa, coffee, sugar, cotton, and orange juice). Metals usually include copper, gold, platinum, and silver, and energy includes crude oil, heating oil, gasoline, and natural gas. Commodity futures contracts are traded mainly in the United States, on the Chicago Board of Trade; Kansas City Board of Trade; Minneapolis Grain Exchange; Chicago Mercantile Exchange; Coffee, Sugar & Cocoa Exchange of New York; New York Cotton Exchange; COMEX; New York Mercantile Exchange; and the International Petroleum Exchange (London also trades commodities). Table 15-10 gives the quotations for cocoa on the Coffee, Sugar & Cocoa Exchange of New York as they appeared in *The Wall Street Journal* for trading activity on Wednesday, April 28, 2004. There are two points we should make. First, the format for Table 15-10 is exactly the same as we described for Table 15-3, Euro

TABLE 15-10 | Cocoa Futures Prices on April 28, 2004

Cocoa (CSCE)-10 metric tons; $ per ton.

	Open	High	Low	Settle	Chg	LIFETIME High	LIFETIME Low	Open Int
May	1,390	1,397	1,390	1,400	22	2,265	1,310	491
July	1,383	1,408	1,381	1,405	27	2,307	1,325	46,423
Sep	1,387	1,410	1,387	1,409	25	2,402	1,345	14,069
Dec	1,398	1,421	1,398	1,421	26	2,065	1,360	11,180

Est vol 4,917; vol Tue 3,090; open int 105,091, -212.

Source: Data excerpted from *The Wall Street Journal,* April 29, 2004, C12.

Futures Quotations. This reinforces the idea that currencies are nothing more than a different type of commodity. Second, the lifetime high price for all contracts is significantly higher than the closing price on April 28, 2004, and the range between the lifetime highs and lows is huge, indicating huge price fluctuations. Companies such as Hershey or Nestlé cope with such price risks by locking in input prices with futures contracts or forward purchases. They may not be able to prevent the price swings, but they can eliminate the effects of unexpected swings through hedging. Their basic businesses are quite stable and thus produce stable, predictable earnings, which investors like. However, commodity price swings would, in the absence of hedging, lead to volatile, unpredictable earnings, and this would have a negative impact on their stock prices. So, hedging helps maximize the prices of these and other companies that would otherwise be subject to volatile earnings due to changes in commodity prices, interest rates, or exchange rates.

Another mechanism for managing commodity price risk that companies use is to develop output products whose demand is driven by the same factors as commodity prices. For instance, during periods of rapid economic growth, demand for energy-intensive products may grow strongly, matching the growth in demand for related input commodities such as electricity or natural gas. When economic growth slows, the demand for both outputs and inputs declines, so that revenue variability tracks expense variability quite closely. This strategy doesn't necessarily reduce input price variability, but it tries to ensure that when input prices are high, the company will have high revenues as well. Of course, the success of this strategy depends on the ability of the firm to scale production up and down as demand varies and to recognize when such demand shifts are occurring.

On the producer side, the futures markets also permit greater price predictability. For many agricultural commodities, though, various government organizations run price stabilization programs to assist farmers by setting minimum prices to be paid for covered products. Floor prices of this kind are touted as ensuring the health of the agricultural sector, but many large producers also utilize the futures markets to eliminate price variability above the government's floor price.

SUPPLY CONTRACTS For input materials not traded on organized exchanges, the primary means for ensuring price predictability is to develop long-term contracts with suppliers for regular delivery. Sometimes these are arms-length discrete contracts with other companies, but at other times more formal, long-term linkages are developed to ensure smooth functioning of the supply chain. In Chapter 4, we discussed strategic alliances as mechanisms for tying together two or more companies into a coherent group that for some purposes can operate as an integrated whole. One of the biggest motivators for these types of relationships is supply chain management. Producers at both ends of the supply chain benefit because they have a more predictable supply of inputs and demand for their output products. Any time the ultimate demand for the final product changes, the entire strategic alliance coordinates its response instead of having individual firms dealing with the issue independently.

As an alternative to strategic alliances, companies can acquire their suppliers (and perhaps customers as well) through the process of vertical integration. MNEs in extractive industries often use this strategy to exert complete control over the supply chain, and they use their internal markets to absorb price variability in whatever manner makes the most economic sense.

Managing Economic Exposure

Total economic exposure, which is exposure to all changes in long-term macroeconomic variables, is of paramount concern to management. Transaction exposures to exchange rates, interest rates, and commodity prices over the short to medium run are an integral part of economic exposure, but managing the strategic implications of all changing macroeconomic variables cannot be accomplished using only the financial markets. Instead, effective economic exposure management must be based on strategic operating decisions made mainly by marketing and production managers in response to expected changes in input and output prices, and the impact of changing demand for the company's products. We have discussed most of these issues elsewhere in the book, but this section reviews some of the more important issues and ties them together in an integrated decision framework.

MARKETING DECISIONS THAT INFLUENCE ECONOMIC EXPOSURE   MNEs generate revenues by selling products demanded by customers, in markets where the customers are located, with the quality they expect, and at prices customers find attractive. These, then, are the areas of operations upon which we need to focus.

1. *What products?* Not all products are appropriate for all countries. In deciding which products to make available in different countries we must consider income effects, cultural effects, national security effects, and country of origin effects, among others. Also, products that are not appropriate now may gain acceptance later when the environment changes.
2. *What markets?* In Chapter 4, we discussed the country selection process. Generally, the larger the market the more likely it is to be profitable, but the company also needs to make sure that the effects relating to the product decision are valid for the particular market. Over time, marginal markets may develop and become good candidates for the firm while currently good markets may wane in profitability.
3. *What quality?* Somewhere in the world there is a market for junk. Maybe not in Japan or Germany, but maybe elsewhere. Companies need to assess the quality requirements of the markets it intends to serve and adjust the product accordingly. In newly emerging markets, price is probably more important than quality, but this can change quickly depending on how the economy develops.
4. *What price?* The price charged for the product must be competitive in the marketplace and be perceived as giving good value for the money.

Once the decision is made to sell a particular product in a specific market at an expected price, the company needs to question the effects of macroeconomic variables on profitability. These "what if" questions need to be answered: What will be the effect if inflation increases and the local currency is devalued? What if it is revalued upward? Depending on the price elasticity of demand, the ability of our company to maintain real local currency prices and absorb reductions in margin, and reactions of competitors to these same forces, inflation could cause the revenue stream to increase, decrease, or remain stable. If the product is targeted toward affluent consumers, perhaps the price elasticity will be less than for mass market items, so the effect of inflation will not be too great. However, if price elasticity is high, should the local price be maintained at the same real level so as to stabilize demand, or should the company increase the real price, thereby lowering demand, and if so, can it still make an adequate profit? Can the company use various promotional strategies to entice customers to continue buying the product? If the margin increases, should the company just keep the extra profits, or should it lower the real price to gain market share? If the country starts to experience balance of payments problems, might the government institute foreign exchange or capital controls? All of these different scenarios should be evaluated for each product in each country, and the evaluations should be done within a comprehensive company model designed to maximize value.

PRODUCTION DECISIONS THAT INFLUENCE ECONOMIC EXPOSURE In Chapter 4, we discussed the major issues associated with the location of production facilities and the sourcing of production inputs. As real input prices change, optimal sourcing strategies will also change. This is one reason given by U.S. companies that have moved factories to Asia or Latin America and for outsourcing computer-related jobs to India, Russia, and elsewhere. Similarly, exchange rate and import controls may make it more efficient to serve particular markets from new locations. Japanese auto companies moved production of cars to the United States for sales in the American market for just these reasons.

In managing total economic exposure, changes in exchange rates, interest rates, labor rates, tariffs, and price controls must be continually monitored to ensure that current production allocation decisions are still optimal. Of course, this is an enormously complex decision process. Fortunately, technology allows companies to link together the operations of subsidiaries all over the world into a single integrated model of company cash flows. Such integrated models are essential for effective management of global corporations.

SELF-TEST QUESTIONS

What is the essence of currency risk?

Why is interest-rate-risk management more complex for an MNE operating in many countries than for a domestic company operating in a single country?

What are three procedures used for coping with the uncertainty in future LIBOR?

What is meant by a plain vanilla swap?

What are the three types of interest rate options?

What are the two broad groups of commodities?

What are the four fundamental questions regarding operations that MNEs need to address?

SUMMARY

The firm's objective should be to manage its risks in a prudent manner and to strike a balance between risk and return that maximizes its value. Risks that do not contribute sufficiently to the company's success should be eliminated. Managers should monitor events closely to ensure that risky conditions are identified early, allowing the company to react quickly. The key concepts discussed in this chapter are listed below.

- A **forward contract** is a contract in which one party agrees to buy or sell an asset or commodity at a specific price on a specific future date from another party, and physical delivery occurs.
- A **futures contract** is a standardized agreement similar to a forward contract that is traded on exchanges, but no physical delivery occurs.
- An **option** is a contract that gives the buyer the right, but not the obligation, to buy or sell an asset at a set price (the "strike" price) on or before a specific date.
- A **call option** gives the holder the right to buy an asset, while a **put option** gives the holder the right to sell an asset.
- The key focus of **risk management** involves managing the uncertainty that results from unexpected changes.

- **Exchange rate risk** is the risk that relates to what foreign currency cash flows will be worth in the parent company's home currency.
- **Credit risk** is the risk that relates to the possibility that a borrower will default on its debt.
- **Repricing (rollover) risk** is the risk that relates to the possibility (1) that a company will have to pay a higher interest rate when renewing maturing credit or (2) that it will receive a lower interest rate on securities it holds due to changing market rates.
- **Counterparty risk** is the risk that the other party to a contractual arrangement will not be able to carry out its obligations as specified in the contract.
- **Commodity price risk** is the risk that the prices of a company's generic production inputs or outputs (commodities) may change.
- **Manageable risks** are those that can be transferred to other parties, and they can be classified as discrete risks or continuing risks.
- **Discrete risks** are related to specific transactions that lead to economic gains or losses as underlying variables change.
- **Continuing risks** are risks that are ongoing and not related to specific transactions.
- **Transaction exposure** is the risk that arises because accrual accounting rules require that transactions be recorded at a spot rate or price even though the transaction will not be completed until a later date.
- If a company has both **monetary assets and liabilities denominated in the same foreign currency**, they will tend to offset each other and thus **mitigate the effects of exchange rate changes**.
- With continuing risks, we focus on broad macroeconomic forces relating to two risk exposures: **accounting exposures** and **economic exposures**.
- **Accounting exposure** is the effect on the firm of the different currency translation methods and resulting translation gains and losses.
- **Monetary balance** implies that gains/losses on the assets side of the balance sheet will exactly offset losses/gains on the capital side, so the company is completely insulated against translation gains or losses.
- **Economic (operating or strategic) exposure** is the impact of changing economic variables on firm value and the reaction of competitors to these variables.
- **Risk management** refers to various strategies used to manage discrete foreign exchange, interest rate, and commodity price risks.
- **Hedging** refers to creating offsetting assets and liabilities so that gains in one offset losses in the other. It locks in expected losses or gains and protects against unexpected changes.
- **Natural (operating) hedges** arise from the firm's operating cash flows, such as when a firm has monetary assets denominated in a foreign currency that are offset by liabilities with the same currency and same maturity.
- **Contractual hedges** are created when a formal contractual relationship is established to lock in the exact terms of a future transaction.
- A **forward market hedge** involves two elements: (1) a contract to exchange specific amounts of two currencies at an exact time in the future and (2) a source of funds to fulfill the contract.
- A **money market hedge** involves a contract, like the forward market hedge, but in this case it is an investment or loan contract.
- An **OTC (over-the-counter) option hedge** uses customized contracts written by banks for their clients.
- A **forward-at-the-money** option is an option where the strike price is very near the forward rate.
- **Exchange-traded currency derivatives** tend to be used extensively for speculation, although some companies use them to hedge continuing exposures that cannot be neutralized with natural hedges.
- A **currency futures contract** calls for delivery (1) at a preset location, (2) of a standardized amount of a particular currency, (3) at a specific time in the future, and (4) at a specified price.

- A **traded option contract** is similar to an OTC option, but the contract is standardized. *American options* give the buyer the right, but not the obligation, to exercise the option at any time until the expiration of the option. *European options* can only be exercised at maturity.
- **Interest rate futures** are highly liquid, standardized contracts that allow companies to hedge interest rate exposures.
- **Forward rate agreements**, or **FRAs**, are contracts that can be tailored to fit specific company situations, because they allow firms to lock in future interest rates.
- **Interest rate**, or **coupon**, **swaps** allow a company that has floating-rate debt to switch debt servicing to a fixed-rate basis, or a firm with fixed-rate debt to switch to floating-rate debt service.
- A **currency swap** allows firms to swap the currency in which payments are made. That is, the company can swap debt service in dollars for debt service in a foreign currency for the same notional principal. Currency swaps can be combined with interest rate swaps, making it possible to swap, for example, floating-rate dollar payments for fixed-rate Swiss franc payments.
- An **interest rate cap** is similar to a call option that constrains the maximum value of LIBOR over the life of the loan, while allowing the company to accept some variability in LIBOR.
- **Interest rate floors** are options that set a minimum effective interest rate to be received on an invested notional principal.
- An **interest rate collar** is the simultaneous buying and selling of interest rate caps and floors, where the premium earned on the cap or floor can cover part or even the entire premium paid on the other side of the deal. The difference between the cap rate and the floor rate is called the width of the collar.
- A **swaption** gives the firm the right, if it chooses, to enter into a swap on some notional principal at a fixed date and at a designated strike rate. A *payer's swaption* (usually purchased by MNEs) conveys the right to pay a fixed rate and receive a floating rate, while a *receiver's swaption* (usually purchased by banks) gives the right to receive a fixed rate and pay a floating rate.

QUESTIONS

(15-1) Explain whether the following statement is true or false: "Because MNEs can more easily diversify operations than domestic firms and have an internal market to react quickly to global disequilibria, they are devoid of risk."

(15-2) Identify and briefly describe some basic derivative instruments.

(15-3) Compare forward and futures contracts. Describe how both can be used to hedge similar risks and identify when one method should be used over another.

(15-4) What risks are multinational enterprises chiefly concerned about guarding against?

(15-5) Describe how interest rate, credit, and repricing risks are viewed differently from the perspective of issuers as compared with investors.

(15-6) Compare discrete and continuing risks, and describe how each is managed.

(15-7) Explain how risk management plays a role in supply chain management.

(15-8) Describe economic exposure management. Is it a short- or long-term process?

(15-9) Briefly explain the following statement from the CFO of a medium-sized manufacturing firm, "We pay a lot of attention to risk management and our best hedging strategy is not to hedge."

(15-10) Compare and contrast forward market, money market, and OTC options as hedging techniques. When does each make sense? Does it ever make sense to remain unhedged?

(15-11) Why might businesses find futures contracts inefficient (compared with forwards) when hedging?

(15-12) A firm has debt obligations on which it must pay interest and it is interested in using futures contracts to hedge itself. Does the firm need to buy or sell a futures contract? Describe this hedging process.

(15-13) What is a plain vanilla swap?

(15-14) Describe how firms can use an interest rate collar to benefit from constraints on LIBOR.

(15-15) How can marketing decisions affect economic exposure management?

SELF-TEST PROBLEMS   Solutions Appear in Appendix B

(ST-1) Define each of the following terms:
Key Terms
  a. Forward contract; futures contract; option; call option; put option
  b. Risk management; counterparty risk; commodity risk
  c. Exchange rate risk; credit risk; repricing risk
  d. Discrete risk; continuing risks
  e. Transaction exposure; accounting exposure; economic exposure
  f. Hedging; natural hedges; contractual hedges
  g. Forward market hedge; money market hedge; OTC option hedge
  h. Interest rate futures; FRAs; interest rate swaps; currency swaps
  i. Interest rate cap; interest rate floor; interest rate collar; swaptions

(ST-2) Bishop International recently purchased ¥5.5 million worth of materials on credit,
Forward Market, due in 30 days. The spot exchange rate is currently ¥113.25/$, the 30-day periodic
Money Market, and rate on Japanese securities is 0.12 percent, and the 30-day U.S. rate is 0.7875
OTC Option Hedges percent. The 30-day forward exchange rate is ¥112.5/$. A call option can be purchased at a premium of 1.20 percent at a strike price of ¥112/$. Outline the appropriate transactions using forward market, money market, and OTC option hedges. Draw a graph showing the expenditures for each case, and determine the corresponding break-even points.

STARTER PROBLEMS

(15-1) An investor bought a European put option on XYZ Inc.'s stock at a cost of $2.50.
Options The current price of the stock is $52.25, and the strike price of the option is $50.00. If the stock price is $48.80 when the option expires, what will be the profit (per share of stock) from the transaction?

(15-2) A firm just received payment on an account receivable denominated in euros. The
Transaction Exposure account was created 30 days ago when an €800,000 sale was made to a German customer. At the time of the sale, the spot rate was $1.2575/€, and now the spot rate is $1.2650/€. The firm did not engage in any hedging practice. What is the gain/loss due to exchange rates on this transaction?

(15-3) DigiCom has $600,000 in excess cash it wants to invest in a euro-denominated
Transaction Exposure CD. The 30-day periodic rate on the CD is 0.11 percent. The spot exchange rate is $1.2750/€. If the spot exchange rate is $1.2685/€ in 30 days, what will be the return on the investment? Was there a gain or loss from exchange rate fluctuations?

(15-4) An investor purchased an interest rate cap on LIBOR set at 2.55 percent. If actual
Interest Rate Cap LIBOR is 2.61 percent on the day the rate is being reset and the notional principal is $3 million, how much must the seller pay the buyer?

EXAM-TYPE PROBLEMS

(15-5)
Forward Market,
Money Market, and
OTC Option Hedges

Rowe Tech just made a £1.75 million credit sale to one of its British customers, and the balance is due in 30 days. The spot exchange rate is currently $1.7525/£, the 30-day periodic rate on British securities is 0.13 percent, and the 30-day rate on U.S. securities is 0.9870 percent. The 30-day forward exchange rate is $1.7675/£. A call option can be purchased at a premium of 0.60 percent at a strike price of $1.7750/£. Outline the appropriate transactions using forward market, money market, and OTC option hedges. Draw a graph showing the expenditures for each case, and determine the corresponding break-even points.

(15-6)
Options

A Japanese investor bought a European call option on Dynamo Tech's stock at a cost of $4.25. The current price of the stock is $71.125, and the strike price of the option is $70.00. The option gives the investor the right to buy 100 shares of Dynamo Tech's stock at the strike price.
a. If the stock price is $69.25 when the option expires, what will be the net profit/loss from the transaction?
b. If the stock price is $76.375 when the option expires, what will be the net profit/loss from the transaction?
c. If the exchange rate when the option was purchased was ¥109/$ and it is ¥107.5/$ when the option matures, what is the yen-denominated return to the Japanese investor if the stock price is $76.375 at expiration?

(15-7)
Forward Contract Hedging

Mirzadeh Corp. is headquartered in Florida but has a large operation in France. This morning, Mirzadeh purchased some goods from a French supplier for €600,000 and also sold equipment to a different French company for €400,000. Both transactions were made on credit due in 30 days, so the appropriate accounts payable and receivable have been created. The current exchange rate is $1.220/€, and the 30-day forward rate is $1.235/€. Mirzadeh wants to hedge itself from currency exposure on these transactions. Construct a strategy that hedges Mirzadeh from currency exposure on these transactions using a forward contract.

(15-8)
Floating-Rate Loan

Three years ago, Dolberg Industries took out a 3-year loan on $10 million, with an initiation fee of 1.5 percent. The terms of the loan were for quarterly interest payments of LIBOR + 1%, resetting annually (so there are two resets). When the loan was initiated LIBOR was 1.56 percent. The next year, LIBOR was 1.76 percent and was 1.83 percent the following year. What was the effective quarterly rate of the loan?

INTEGRATED CASE

Rick Schmidt, MRI's CFO, along with Mandy Wu, Schmidt's assistant, and John Costello, a consultant and college finance professor, comprise a team set up to teach the firm's directors and senior managers the basics of international financial management. The program includes 16 sessions, each lasting about 2 hours, and they are scheduled immediately before the monthly board meetings. Fourteen sessions have been completed, and the team is now preparing Session 15, which will deal with derivative securities and global risk management. Prior sessions have provided an overview of international finance, exchange rates, risk analysis, financial statements, international markets and security valuation, the cost of capital, capital budgeting, capital structure, cash distribution policy, and global working capital management.

For the risk management session, the team will explain how firms manage the risks created by operating globally. MRI's directors recognize that risk is a part of doing business, and its role has grown as MRI has increased its international presence. Previous sessions have focused on business risk, financial risk, market risk, political risk, forecasting uncertainties, and cash flow blockages. This session will deal with managing exchange rate, interest rate, and commodity price risks. Schmidt has stressed to Wu that he wants MRI's directors to understand that risk management does not eliminate risk, but rather, it reduces risk by minimizing losses due to unexpected changes in market conditions.

Risk management involves the reduction of variability. Some of the mechanisms introduced in this session are designed to shift the risk to other parties by locking in prices, while others are designed to guard against downside risk and protect upside potential. Effective risk management requires the coordination of many different devices simultaneously to manage risks.

Wu expressed concern about addressing controversial issues, where the proper analysis is in question. She recalled that in college some students simply "tuned out" when the instructor raised a question for which there was no definitive answer, and she was concerned that the directors might react similarly. Schmidt and Costello agree that this could be a problem, but they felt strongly that it would not be appropriate to "sweep problems under the carpet." So, they want to bring up relevant unresolved issues, discuss alternative ways of dealing with them, and point out the implications of different decisions. The directors are all intelligent, experienced in dealing with complex situations, and would rather know about potential problems than be kept in the dark.

With those thoughts in mind, the three compiled the following set of questions, which they plan to discuss during the session. As with the other sessions, they plan to use an *Excel* model to answer the quantitative questions. Assume that you are Mandy Wu and that you must prepare answers for use during the session.

QUESTIONS

a. Identify and describe the three major sources of risk.

b. Most risk factors that MNEs face can be collected into two broad groups: discrete and continuing risks. Identify some of the different discrete and continuing risks.

c. Last month, MRI made a large purchase (¥110 million) from a Japanese supplier on account, due in 30 days. At the time, the spot exchange rate was $0.008846/¥, but the spot rate has since changed to $0.008925/¥. Describe how this transaction is originally recorded in MRI's financial statements, how the transaction is closed out, and what effect this has on MRI's financial statements. Are there any tax consequences?

d. Last month, MRI also invested (¥140 million) in a yen-denominated CD for 30 days at a periodic rate of 0.20 percent. The exchange rates in the previous question are applicable here. What are the tax implications of this transaction? If interest rate parity holds, what can we say about the expected 30-day U.S. periodic interest rate?

e. Define hedging. Should managers hedge all risks? Explain your answer. What are natural and contractual hedges?

f. Describe forward market and money market hedges and over-the-counter options. Show how each can be used to manage the accounts payable discussed in part c. The periodic rate on a yen-denominated CD is 0.20 percent.

g. How do traded futures and options differ from forward and OTC option contracts?

h. What are interest rate futures? Describe how a firm would hedge using interest rate futures.

i. What is an interest rate swap? Use the data in Table IC15-1 to construct an agreement between MRI and SJY Electronics in which both would gain from an interest rate swap. MRI prefers to borrow on fixed terms but could not get an acceptable fixed rate. Hence, MRI borrowed floating-rate debt. SJY, meanwhile, prefers floating-rate debt, but the most attractive offer they received was for fixed-rate debt. The notional principal being swapped in this agreement is $3 million.

j. What are interest rate caps, interest rate floors, interest rate collars, and swaptions?

k. How do marketing decisions affect a firm's economic exposure?

TABLE IC15-1 | Interest Rate Swap Data on $3 Million Notional Principal

MRI	SJY Electronics
Fixed: 4.20%	Fixed: 3.95%
Floating: LIBOR + 1.25%	Floating: LIBOR + 1.10%
Prefers fixed	Prefers floating
Borrow floating at LIBOR + 1.25%	Borrow fixed at 3.95%

CHAPTER 16

International Tax Planning

$$\text{VALUE} = \sum_{t=0}^{N} \frac{CF_t}{(1+r)^t}$$

Required Investment
Sales Revenues
Operating Costs
Taxes

Cash Flows (CF)

Capital Structure
Component Costs
Asset Risk
Market Risk

Weighted Average
Cost of Capital (WACC)

e-resource

*The textbook's Web site, **http://crum. swlearning.com,** contains an Excel file that will guide you through the chapter's calculations. The file for this chapter is **FIFC16-model.xls,** and we encourage you to open the file and follow along as you read the chapter.*

For every nation, the tax laws pertaining to international transactions have two central goals: to provide tax revenues while promoting the global competitiveness of its own domestic firms. However, these two objectives are sometimes in conflict, and it is also difficult to craft simple rules that fit all situations. Companies find creative mechanisms for circumventing regulations, leading countries to replace them with laws that are harder to get around but more complex. Moreover, tax laws do not always achieve their intended goals. Other countries may also object to complex regulations that they perceive as granting unfair subsidies to local businesses or penalizing foreign companies. Attempts to resolve such conflicts often lead to even more complexity in international tax regulations and also to escalating tax competition among countries.

Of course, global companies legitimately desire to reduce their worldwide tax liability, and this means trying to structure the corporation and its diverse operations so as to achieve the lowest legally possible overall tax rate. This is particularly important for U.S. companies today, because the United States has one of the highest combined federal and state corporate tax rates among major industrial nations—only Belgium, Italy, and Japan are higher. Many economists suggest that the high U.S. tax rate discourages MNEs from locating their headquarters in America, and it also encourages firms headquartered in the United States to move elsewhere. Indeed, we have recently seen several U.S. companies change their headquarters to countries with lower tax rates, such as Bermuda. Relatively high U.S. tax rates also put American companies at a disadvantage as they compete with MNEs from lower-tax countries, because taxes are a cost of doing business. Thus, firms must be creative in designing tax strategies that *allow them to remain competitive and retain the flexibility to reposition funds within their internal markets.*

In previous chapters, we have suggested numerous strategies that companies can use to increase their global flexibility and minimize taxes. While we do not want to duplicate those discussions, it is useful to consider the various tax strategies already mentioned, and several more that have not been covered, in an overall tax planning context. Seeing the "big picture" will help you understand why tax issues often dominate, or are at least very important, in defining global corporate strategy.

Taxes obviously have a strong impact on stock prices. They affect both the cash flows in the numerator and the discount rate in the denominator of the valuation equation. We have the curious situation in which a reduction in the tax rate (generally considered to be a positive development) causes the effective cost of debt to increase (a negative development). Usually, though, the positive effects of lower taxes on the cash flows far more than offset any increase in the discount rate.

INTRODUCTORY CONCEPTS AND DEFINITIONS

International taxation is a complex subject because of the interplay of different national legal systems, economic objectives, and accounting philosophies. Before we delve into these issues, though, it will be useful to illustrate how tax rates vary across countries and to define certain terms. Only then can we place the various topics into their proper place as we discuss corporate tax plans.

National Tax Rates

Effective tax rates vary greatly around the world and they even fluctuate over time in many countries. Table 16-1 shows effective tax rates (national plus state or provincial rates) for 30 OECD countries. You should notice two things about this table. First, the effective tax rate in the United States, 40 percent, is near the top—indeed, U.S. firms are at an 8.6 percentage point (or 27.3 percent) tax disadvantage on average when they go head-to-head with foreign competitors. Second, two-thirds of the countries cut their maximum rates from 1996 to 2002, but the United States kept its rate high. Thus, the disadvantage has increased in recent years.

Different Types of Taxes

There are many types of taxes. First, there are *direct taxes,* the name given to taxes that are based on income, and *indirect taxes,* which are all types of taxes based on something other than income. Indirect taxes include sales taxes, ad valorem taxes on the year-end value of inventory (a sort of property tax), value-added taxes (VAT), and taxes imposed when financial assets are transferred. We discuss the more important types of taxes in the following sections.

INCOME TAXES The tax rates given in Table 16-1 are applied to corporate income generated in the various countries.[1] Some countries impose different tax rates on different activities, such as one rate for reinvested profits and another rate for earnings paid out as cash dividends. The usual reason income is taxed is to raise revenue for government programs. However, many economists, going all the way back to Adam

---

[1]Most countries also impose personal income taxes on their citizens. While we limit our discussion to corporate taxes, it should be noted that personal taxes can have an effect on where global corporations locate their executive offices, because the executives who make these location decisions are interested in their own personal taxation. Of course, individual stockholders can reside in locations different from the locations where corporations operate.

TABLE 16-1 | Combined National and State Corporate Income Tax Rates, 1996–2002

Country	1996	1997	1998	1999	2000	2001	2002	1996–2002 Change
Australia	36.0	36.0	36.0	36.0	36.0	34.0	30.0	−6
Austria	34.0	34.0	34.0	34.0	34.0	34.0	34.0	0
Belgium	40.2	40.2	40.2	40.2	40.2	40.2	40.2	0
Canada	44.6	44.6	44.6	44.6	44.6	42.1	38.6	−6
Czech Republic	39.0	39.0	35.0	35.0	31.0	31.0	31.0	−8
Denmark	34.0	34.0	34.0	32.0	32.0	30.0	30.0	−4
Finland	28.0	28.0	28.0	28.0	29.0	29.0	29.0	+1
France	36.7	36.7	41.7	40.0	36.7	35.3	34.3	−2
Germany	57.4	57.4	56.7	52.3	51.6	38.4	38.4	−19
Greece	40.0	40.0	40.0	40.0	40.0	37.5	35.0	−5
Hungary	33.3	18.0	18.0	18.0	18.0	18.0	18.0	−15
Iceland	33.0	33.0	30.0	30.0	30.0	30.0	18.0	−15
Ireland	38.0	36.0	32.0	28.0	24.0	20.0	16.0	−22
Italy	53.2	53.2	41.3	41.3	41.3	40.3	40.3	−13
Japan	51.6	51.6	51.6	48.0	42.0	42.0	42.0	−10
Korea	33.0	30.8	30.8	30.8	30.8	30.8	29.7	−3
Luxembourg	40.3	39.3	37.5	37.5	37.5	37.5	30.4	−10
Mexico	34.0	34.0	34.0	35.0	35.0	35.0	35.0	+1
Netherlands	35.0	35.0	35.0	35.0	35.0	35.0	34.5	−1
New Zealand	33.0	33.0	33.0	33.0	33.0	33.0	33.0	0
Norway	28.0	28.0	28.0	28.0	28.0	28.0	29.0	0
Poland	40.0	38.0	36.0	34.0	30.0	28.0	28.0	−12
Portugal	39.6	39.6	37.4	37.4	35.2	35.2	33.0	−7
Slovak Republic	n/a	n/a	n/a	n/a	n/a	29.0	25.0	n/a
Spain	35.0	35.0	35.0	35.0	35.0	35.0	35.0	0
Sweden	28.0	28.0	28.0	28.0	28.0	28.0	28.0	0
Switzerland	28.5	28.5	27.8	25.1	25.1	24.7	24.5	−4
Turkey	44.0	44.0	44.0	33.0	33.0	33.0	33.0	−11
United Kingdom	33.0	31.0	31.0	31.0	30.0	30.0	30.0	−3
United States	40.0	40.0	40.0	40.0	40.0	40.0	40.0	0
Average for 30 OECD countries	37.6	36.8	35.9	34.8	34.0	32.8	31.4	−6

Source: Data excerpted from Chris Edwards and Veronique de Rugy, "International Tax Competition: A 21st-Century Restraint on Government," *Tax Notes International,* July 1, 2002, 63–110.

Smith, have argued that using corporate taxes to raise revenues in open economies is inefficient. Economic theory suggests that high taxation on capital—including business income, dividends, capital gains, and interest—creates an increasing brake on overall growth as capital mobility increases. In other words, excessive taxation of capital causes capital flight, thus reducing domestic productivity and income, and, if capital is internationally mobile (which it certainly is today), it also transfers the tax burden to immobile factors such as labor. Adam Smith recognized this phenomenon when he wrote in 1776:

> . . . land, is a subject which cannot be removed, whereas stock easily may. The proprietor of land is necessarily a citizen of a particular country in which his estate lies. The proprietor of

stock is properly a citizen of the world, and is not necessarily attached to any particular country. He would be apt to abandon the country in which he was exposed to a vexatious inquisition, in order to be assessed to a burdensome tax, and would remove his stock to some other country where he could either carry on his business, or enjoy his fortune more at his ease. By removing his stock he would put an end to all the industry which it had maintained in the country which he left. Stock cultivates land; stock employs labour. A tax which tended to drive away stock from any particular country, which would so far tend to dry up every source of revenue, both to the sovereign and to the society. Not only the profits of stock, but the rent of land and the wages of labour, would necessarily be more or less diminished by its removal.[2]

Nevertheless, income taxes are likely to remain a part of the business landscape for the foreseeable future, and MNEs need to learn how to cope with them and to minimize their global tax liability.

WITHHOLDING TAXES Income earned by the residents of one country from passive investments made in other countries, such as interest, dividends, rents, and royalties on foreign securities and intangible assets, is generally subject to tax. However, most foreigners will not file tax returns in every country in which they have passive income, so governments have to resort to other means for collecting the taxes. The device they use is to have the payor, either a bank, a company, or some other organization, hold back some of the payment (usually from 0 to 30 percent) and instead send it to the government. This is called *withholding*. Thus, taxes will be withheld from dividends paid by the Dutch insurance company Aegon to its U.S. stockholders. Those stockholders can then receive a credit for the taxes withheld when they file their U.S. tax returns.

SALES TAXES In some countries (or regions of countries), a tax will be levied on purchases of goods and services at the point of sale. This is a **consumption-based tax** and is borne only by those who consume specific products or services.[3] The sales tax is an important device used by U.S. cities and states to raise revenues.

VALUE-ADDED TAXES As an alternative to a consumption-based sales tax, some countries (including the European Union) levy a **value-added tax (VAT)** at each stage of the production process as a primary device for raising revenues. As the name indicates, at various production stages the firm involved in a particular production stage pays a tax on the value it adds to the product. The VAT is called a consumption-based tax because final consumers end up paying it, but it is really a **production-based tax** that is paid on units produced rather than units consumed, so even if no one ends up buying and consuming the product, the tax will still have been paid. Depending on the nature of the product, the value-added tax may be charged at different rates at different stages of the production process. For example, farmers might be charged one rate, distributors a second rate, and food retailers a third rate. Today, the rates in the EU range from a low of 2.1 percent to a high of 25 percent depending on the product and the country.

OTHER NATIONAL TAXES Many other taxes, including ad valorem taxes on real estate and intangible assets such as stocks and bonds, taxes on undistributed profits, and transfer taxes on securities and other assets, are also important. Such taxes vary from country to country, and they are generally intended to raise revenues and/or to achieve social goals, including wealth redistribution.

In this chapter, we are primarily interested in income and withholding taxes. Other types of taxes are often important, but income and withholding taxes gener-

Consumption-Based Tax A tax borne only by those who wish to consume specific products or services. This is a primary device for raising revenues by U.S. cities and states.

Value-Added Tax (VAT) The tax paid by an entity on the value added to the product by that particular stage of production.

Production-Based Tax A tax paid on units produced rather than units consumed.

[2]Adam Smith, *An Inquiry into the Nature and Causes of the Wealth of Nations* (1776; Chicago: University of Chicago Press, 1990), 293.

[3]Many times certain types of products, such as food, medicine, and other necessities, will be exempted from sales taxes, while "luxury" products such as furs and jewelry may be charged an extra tax.

ally have the greatest impact on MNEs' international tax planning, hence they deserve special consideration.

Tax Havens

In Chapter 14, we suggested that one strategy for maximizing the benefits of a firm's internal market is to establish a reinvoicing center in a low-tax, or "tax haven," country. This center can also centralize risk management activities and possibly financing activities as well. We will have more to say about such operations later in this chapter, but first we need to clarify what a tax haven is and what it is not. Basically, there are four major characteristics to look for when setting up a subsidiary in a tax haven:

1. A stable government that encourages foreign-owned service facilities within its borders and establishes a predictable environment in which the firm can operate.
2. A stable financial system and currency that permits resident companies to engage in transactions and maintain accounts in many different currencies and to move from one currency to another one easily, inexpensively, and quickly.
3. An infrastructure that supports sophisticated financial services, including advanced telecommunications and computer capabilities, highly trained professional office workers, and financial institutions of unquestioned strength and integrity.
4. Low tax rates on income from foreign investments earned by resident corporations and a low withholding rate on dividend transfers to foreign owners.

Many MNEs use the tax haven financial subsidiary as the nexus, or connecting point, for ownership of the foreign operating subsidiaries. Typically, the financial subsidiary is 100 percent owned and controlled by the parent, and then the financial subsidiary owns the operating subsidiaries. Then, through the devices to be discussed in the following sections, the existence of the financial subsidiary allows the parent corporation to reduce its overall tax rate below what it would otherwise be.

SELF-TEST QUESTIONS   Differentiate between direct and indirect taxes.
Differentiate between a consumption-based tax and a production-based tax.
Why are we primarily interested in income and withholding taxes as opposed to the other types of taxes?

THEORIES OF INTERNATIONAL TAXATION

While every country designs its own unique system for taxing both domestic and foreign income, there are some general principles that tend to be used when deciding how to accomplish the country's objectives. In the domestic setting, most economists believe that taxation should be neutral in the sense of causing capital to flow to uses that create the highest value for society. Thus, tax regulations should not favor one industry or type of investment over another, nor should it encourage consumption over saving or vice versa. Obviously, politicians do not always agree with economists, nor do all economists agree with one another. Thus, while countries whose leaders believe in government-directed industrial policies deviate from this notion of neutrality, most countries acknowledge the importance of the concept. In an international context, though, things are not so clear-cut, even when the country truly believes in the value of tax neutrality, because tax neutrality itself can take on different meanings.

Capital Export Neutrality (CEN) Suggests that investors should have to pay exactly the same total amount of taxes on income from foreign investments as they do on domestic investments.

Capital export neutrality (CEN), sometimes called *domestic neutrality*, suggests that investors should pay exactly the same total amount of taxes on income from foreign investments as they do on income from domestic investments. To achieve capital export neutrality, investors should be taxed in their home country on a *worldwide basis*, but with a credit given for foreign taxes paid in order to prevent double taxation. Table 16-2 illustrates CEN taxation from the perspective of Country A. The MNE based in Country A portrayed in the table has $1,000 of domestic income taxed at 40 percent and $500 of foreign income taxed at 30 percent in Country B. If the $350 of net income from Country B is sent to Country A as a dividend, then additional taxes will be owed—total taxes on $500 of income in Country A would have been $500 × 0.4 = $200, which is $50 greater than the taxes actually paid in Country B. By allowing the foreign tax credit (FTC) of $150 for taxes paid in Country B, the net taxes owed in Country A for the dividend is the extra $50. Thus, total taxes paid by the consolidated company will equal $600, which represents an effective tax rate of 40 percent on worldwide income.[4] Of course, if the foreign tax rate is greater than the domestic tax rate, more taxes will be paid in the host country than would have to be paid on equivalent income at home. However, the FTC is limited to the home tax owed, so there will be an excess FTC that the company may or may not be able to use elsewhere. Notice that if no FTC had been allowed, total taxes paid would have been ($400 + $150 + $200)/$1,500 = 50%. Advocates of CEN suggest that this concept of tax neutrality promotes economic efficiencies by removing tax considerations from global location decisions so that decisions can be made on the basis of their underlying economic profitability. This is, in theory, the guiding principle followed by the United States in designing its international tax regulations, but there are many exceptions to CEN built into the U.S. Tax Code.

Capital Import Neutrality (CIN) Suggests that investments in any country should all be taxed at the same rate no matter where the investor resides.

An alternative philosophy of international tax neutrality is called **capital import neutrality (CIN)**, or *foreign neutrality*. This perspective suggests that investments in any country should all be taxed at the same rate no matter where the investor resides. In other words, investors from all countries would face exactly the same total tax rate on their investments in a particular country. This means that countries would not place any local tax on foreign-source income received by residents of the

TABLE 16-2 | Capital Export Neutrality: Taxation of Foreign-Source Income

Country A (Tax rate = 40%)		Country B (Tax rate = 30%)	
Domestic income	$1,000	Foreign income	$500
Taxes (40%)	(400)	Taxes (30%)	(150)
Net income	$ 600	Net income	$350

Dividend received from B	$350
A's tax due on dividend = $500 × 0.4	$200
Less FTC	(150)
Tax still owed to A on dividend	$ 50
Net dividend received = $350 − $50	$300

Total after-tax income = $600 + $300 = $900.
Effective tax rate = ($400 + $150 + $50)/$1,500 = 40%.

[4]In Chapter 11, the computation of taxes due on the repatriated dividend in the parent perspective analysis used this procedure.

country, no matter where that income was generated or how much tax was paid. Extending the example in Table 16-2, under a CIN regime, sometimes called a *territorial system* of business taxation, total income in Country A would be $600 + $350 = $950 because no additional local tax would be imposed. The effective tax rate would be $550/$1,500 = 36.67%. Supporters of CIN argue that if investors from Country A have to pay more tax on an investment in Country B than do the residents of Country B (or residents of other countries that use a territorial tax regime), then they are at a competitive disadvantage in the global marketplace. About half of OECD member countries, including France, Germany, and the Netherlands, use a territorial tax regime for foreign-source income and do not impose extra taxes when the foreign tax rate is less than the local rate. The implication of this statistic is that MNEs from the other half of OECD countries that use a CEN system, including the United States, face higher costs when doing business in many foreign countries than MNEs from CIN countries and are thereby placed at a competitive disadvantage in the global marketplace.

SELF-TEST QUESTIONS   What is capital export neutrality (CEN)?
How is CEN achieved?
What is capital import neutrality (CIN)?

INTERNATIONAL TAX PLANNING

As the world moves closer to a true global marketplace, an MNE's ability to manage its tax expenses becomes increasingly important. In a purely domestic situation, all companies face the same tax rates and rules, so no one has a tax advantage over the others. This is not true in the global environment. As we saw in Table 16-1, Irish companies face a combined tax rate of only 16 percent, while U.S. companies are taxed at 40 percent. This is a tremendous difference, and it causes significant disadvantages to U.S.-based MNEs in today's competitive marketplace. This suggests that three major areas must be taken into consideration as part of an MNE's international tax planning.

Nature of Business Activities: Passive versus Active

Passive Investment Income
Consists of such things as dividends, interest, royalty income from securities investments, and the licensing of intangible assets to foreigners. Foreign countries typically apply a withholding tax rate to the gross amount of the transfer of passive investment income.

Most of the international cash flows identified in Chapters 11 and 14 are from either (1) passive investments or (2) active business operations. **Passive investment income** consists of such things as dividends, interest, royalty income from securities investments, and the licensing of intangible assets to foreigners. Generally, foreign countries may apply a withholding tax rate to the gross amount of transferred passive investment income. Usually these cash flows are also taxable when they are received in the home country. The license fees paid to SSI-USA by the Shanghai subsidiary fall into this category, although no withholding tax was charged because it was waived during negotiations. However, when an MNE conducts **active business operations** in a host country, that country will typically tax the net income of the activity rather than the gross income. That is, deductions will be allowed for operating expenses to reduce taxable income to the net amount, but the applicable tax rate applied to the net is often higher than the withholding rate on passive income.

Active Business Operations
Operations in which the net income of the activity rather than the gross income is taxed by the host country.

Type of Organization

Generally, foreign affiliates are organized either as independent companies chartered in the host country but owned largely or wholly by the parent company or as foreign extensions of the parent in the host country. The first form of organization is called a *subsidiary*, and it is legally separate from the parent/owner. Foreign-source income earned by subsidiaries, except as discussed later in the chapter, is not subject to any additional tax by the parent until it is repatriated.[5] When the affiliate is simply an extension of the parent, it is called a *branch*, and the income generated in the host country is consolidated with the parent income for tax purposes. In this chapter, we usually assume that the foreign affiliate is a subsidiary, but in several instances we indicate where organizing foreign operations as a branch (or designating them as a branch for U.S. tax purposes even though they are a subsidiary for foreign tax purposes) might be beneficial.

Tax Treaties

Tax treaties between countries provide MNEs with at least three forms of tax assistance. First, for passive income, treaties may eliminate or reduce the tax rate applicable to the gross income subject to withholding tax. Second, for active business income, treaties provide protection against host-country taxation of what are called "transient" operations. That is, treaties almost always restrict taxes imposed by the host-country taxation to situations where the foreign corporation is engaging in a trade or business in the host country through a **permanent establishment** located in that country. The term "permanent establishment" means that the activities of the company in the host country rise beyond some minimal level. Activities that create a permanent establishment include opening a local office, building a factory and starting manufacturing operations, or establishing some other fixed place of business. Treaties also specify activities that do not lead to a permanent establishment, including such things as maintaining inventories in a distributor's warehouse or engaging in a temporary construction project. Treaty provisions generally take precedence over local tax codes and regulations.

The United States has entered into bilateral tax treaties with more than 50 countries, but there are many other countries in which MNEs might have a presence that are not covered by such treaties. In this situation, the permanent establishment determination is replaced by a more subjective test of whether or not the company is "engaged in a trade or business" within the host country. Also, the MNE might find itself in a situation in which it wants to engage in a specific internal market transaction with an affiliate in a non-tax-treaty country, but finds that the absence of a tax treaty means that there will be a substantial withholding tax. Assume for this example that the company also has a subsidiary in another country with which the United States has negotiated a tax treaty, and the withholding rate in this case would be zero. All else equal, engaging in the internal market transaction with the second subsidiary instead of the first will reduce the taxes paid, thus increasing the return to the MNE system. If this alternative is not feasible and the first subsidiary must be involved in the transaction, the MNE may try to get around the tax payment through what is called *treaty shopping*, if the two countries in which the subsidiaries are located have a tax treaty between them that allows a zero withholding rate.

As an example of treaty shopping, assume that a U.S.-based MNE needs to borrow money from its Peruvian subsidiary but finds that the United States does not have a tax treaty with Peru. Thus, there will be a 30 percent withholding tax on the interest paid by the U.S. parent to the Peruvian subsidiary. The company also has a subsidiary in Venezuela, and there is a tax treaty in place that calls for a zero withholding tax on interest transfers. Unfortunately, though, the Venezuelan subsidiary is not in a position to make the loan to the parent at this time, so this is not really

Permanent Establishment Activities of the company in the host country rise beyond a minimal level. These activities include opening a local office, building a factory and starting manufacturing operations, or establishing some other fixed place of business.

---

[5]Of course, the tax treatment will depend on the tax neutrality philosophy used by the parent or home country. If the country uses a territorial system (CIN), no tax would be due upon repatriation, but if home country taxes are viewed on a worldwide basis (CEN), then there is a tax issue.

an option. However, the company notes that Peru and Venezuela have signed a tax treaty with each other that calls for a zero withholding rate. If the company can structure the loans as legitimate business transactions, the Peruvian subsidiary can lend the money to the Venezuelan affiliate, and there will be a zero withholding rate on the interest paid by Venezuela to Peru. Then the Venezuelan affiliate can lend money to the U.S. parent, and interest payments on this loan will have a zero percent withholding rate as well. Unfortunately, if it discovers that the goal of the transactions is to avoid taxes, the United States is likely to take an anti-treaty-shopping position on the combined transaction and charge a 30 percent withholding tax anyway. However, sometimes legitimate business reasons allow the company to direct cash flows among subsidiaries in a way that minimizes withholding taxes because of tax treaty provisions. The various funds repositioning techniques discussed in Chapter 14 need to be evaluated in terms of the tax implications of the various transfers given the tax treaties in place between pairs of countries.

Another important component of tax treaties is the inclusion of "competent authorities," which refer to administrative methods covered in tax treaties that can benefit the MNE. Competent authorities allow for the resolution of double taxation problems encountered with international transactions that arise by virtue of the two countries viewing the same transaction differently. Transfer pricing is an example of this situation when an advance pricing agreement has not been negotiated. In this situation, the administrative methods can lead to resolution of the issues quickly, although perhaps not entirely to the liking of the company.

What are the three areas that must be taken into consideration as part of international tax planning?

Differentiate between the tax treatment applied to passive investment operations as opposed to active business operations.

Differentiate between a subsidiary and branch.

What are the three forms of tax assistance provided to MNEs by tax treaties?

Possessions Credit
A credit that reduces the effective tax rate meant to encourage U.S. companies to aid in the economic development of U.S. possessions. Domestic corporations can claim a credit for income derived from sources within one of these possessions even when little or no foreign taxes are actually paid on it.

Extra-Territorial Income (ETI)
Allows U.S. exporters to exclude from U.S. tax a portion of export profits from goods produced domestically in the United States.

HOW TO PLAN WITH RESPECT TO THE U.S. TAX SYSTEM

U.S. resident business entities are subject to U.S. tax on their worldwide income. In other words, their foreign-source income is taxed in the same manner as domestic-source income. However, foreign-source income may be able to benefit from special provisions in the Tax Code either to reduce U.S. taxes below the normal U.S. rate or to defer U.S. tax payments to a later date. Good tax advice is critical, though, because if one is not careful, these special provisions can lead to circumstances in which the effective U.S. tax rate is considerably higher than the normal U.S. rate.

Permanent Deferral or Reduction of U.S. Tax

Currently there are two provisions in the Tax Code for permanent deferral or reduction of U.S. taxes, but these will probably soon be eliminated or radically changed. The first provision is called **possessions credit**. To encourage U.S. companies to aid in the economic development of U.S. possessions such as Guam and Puerto Rico, domestic corporations can claim a credit for income derived from sources within one of these possessions even when little or no foreign taxes were actually paid on it. This credit can be used to reduce the effective rate, but the credit expires after 2005.

The other provision for reduction of U.S. tax is on what is called **extra-territorial income**, or **ETI**. The ETI regime allows U.S. exporters to exclude from U.S. taxes a portion of export profits on goods produced domestically in the United States. The original idea behind the ETI was to "level the playing field" with regions of the world such as the European Union, where companies receive a rebate of value-added taxes paid for exports. However, other countries see the issues differently, and the United States has lost its battle with the EU and the World Trade Organization over ETI. As of March 2004, the United States became subject to increasing trade sanctions if the ETI rules are not repealed or modified to address WTO concerns. It is likely that Congress will repeal the ETI Act and replace it with another vehicle in an effort to grant tax relief to domestic exporters, but it remains to be seen if the new innovation will pass muster at the WTO or not.[6]

Temporary Deferral of U.S. Tax

U.S. taxes payable on foreign-source income may be deferred to a later date in some circumstances through the use of a foreign subsidiary. Subsidiaries, rather than branches, are independently chartered foreign corporations owned partly or wholly by the MNE. Because foreign corporations are generally subject to U.S. tax only on their U.S.-source income, the earnings of foreign subsidiaries of U.S. companies are not subjected to U.S. taxes until those earnings are distributed to the U.S. parent as a dividend.[7] This provision is very useful to companies because, when the tax rate in the foreign country is lower than the U.S. rate, it permits deferral of the additional taxes that would be due in the United States (for an effective rate up to the U.S. tax rate) until the earnings are repatriated. If the foreign tax rate is higher than the U.S. rate, no U.S. taxes will be due on repatriated earnings, and there will be an excess foreign tax credit (FTC) created.

The deferral of U.S. taxes on foreign subsidiaries' earnings often encourages U.S. MNEs to use foreign corporations. The various devices for repositioning funds globally through the internal market (discussed in Chapter 14) can be used to ensure that these earnings are profitably employed overseas. This deferral provision is particularly valuable when the foreign subsidiary is located in a country that imposes little or no income tax.

Antideferral Provisions of U.S. Tax Law

Deferral provisions obviously reduce taxes collected by the U.S. government, hence Congress has passed legislation over the years limiting deferrals for three types of foreign entities: a foreign personal holding company (FPHC), a passive foreign investment company (PFIC), and a controlled foreign corporation (CFC).

The Foreign Personal Holding Company Act of 1937 prevents U.S. citizens from deferring U.S. tax on investment income by transferring their investment assets to a corporation chartered in a low-tax foreign country. The earnings of an FPHC are taxed in the United States whether or not they are actually distributed.

The Passive Foreign Investment Companies Act was passed as part of the Tax Reform Act of 1986 to prevent the use of foreign-controlled offshore mutual funds by U.S. investors to shield income from taxation until it is remitted to investors. As

---

[6]Actually the ETI is the third successor device that has been declared an illegal trade subsidy. First was the Domestic International Sales Corporation (DISC), which was found to be an illegal subsidy under the General Agreement on Tariffs and Trade (GATT). To get around the problems with DISC, Congress passed the Foreign Sales Corporation Act. However, in 2000 the WTO ruled that this act suffered the same problems as the DISC and was thus an illegal subsidy. Congress then passed the FSC Repeal and Extra-Territorial Income Exclusion Act of 2000 (the ETI Act), but this was declared to be illegal by the WTO in 2002. As of mid-May 2004, the U.S. Congress had neither repealed nor modified the ETI Act, so sanctions granted to the EU by the WTO in August 2002 took effect in March 2004, with increasingly punitive rates each month until the act is repealed or the maximum level is reached.

[7]If the foreign earnings are never expected to be repatriated, the tax deferral does not have to be reported on the balance sheet. However, if repatriation is expected at some foreseeable future date, the deferred taxes are included as a liability on the balance sheet.

a result of this act, the proportional share of such income is taxable to the U.S. shareholder in the current period whether remitted or not, and a penalty tax plus an interest charge is levied on any excess distribution of PFIC income or gain on the disposition of PFIC stock.

Of more relevance for corporations, prior to 1963, foreign subsidiary income that was not repatriated to the United States enjoyed complete deferral of U.S. tax. In this environment, organizing a subsidiary in a low-tax environment had great tax advantages. After 1962 this ability was severely restricted for companies with foreign subsidiaries that qualified as controlled foreign corporations (CFCs) and had what is called "Subpart F" income for the taxable year, whether or not it was distributed.[8] Subpart F income is income that is easily shifted from one foreign location to another or has little or no economic connection with the CFC's country of incorporation. Some examples of Subpart F income include (1) passive income, such as interest or dividends earned by owning financial securities, and rents or royalties from intangible property; (2) sales income where neither production of the goods nor the final customers to whom they are sold are located in the CFC's host country, and either the supplier of the goods or the customer is related to the CFC (such as through the internal market); and (3) service income when the CFC is providing services outside its host country on behalf of the U.S. parent. However, if the CFC has other income that does not qualify as Subpart F income, U.S. taxes can be deferred on it until the time it is repatriated to the U.S. parent.

As an example of how Subpart F income is taxed, assume that SSI-USA exports $1 million of speakers to customers in Ireland. If the cost of goods sold on these exports is $600,000 and the U.S. combined tax rate is 40 percent, SSI reports the taxes and income from the transaction as follows:

Sales	$1,000,000
Cost of goods sold	600,000
Taxable income	$ 400,000
Taxes (40%)	160,000
Net income	$ 240,000

Now assume that SSI decides to create a wholly-owned foreign subsidiary in the Cayman Islands (where no income taxes are imposed on corporate income). Now SSI-USA sells the speakers to SSI-Cayman for a transfer price of $750,000, and SSI-Cayman turns around and resells them to the customers in Ireland for the full $1 million. As we have structured the transaction, SSI-Cayman does not add value to the speakers in any way, merely passing them on to the final customers. Thus, the subsidiary is only involved in a paper transaction. With this structure, if there were no tax law restrictions, the taxes and income from the transactions would be as follows:

	SSI-USA	SSI-Cayman
Sales	$750,000	$1,000,000
Cost of goods sold	600,000	750,000
Taxable income	$150,000	$ 250,000
Taxes (40%)	60,000	0
Net income	$ 90,000	$ 250,000

[8]Basically, a CFC is a foreign corporation in which more than 50 percent of the aggregate voting power from all classes of voting stock is owned by U.S. shareholders, or the total voting stock of the foreign company is owned by a U.S. shareholder on any day during the taxable year of the foreign company. By this definition, virtually all subsidiaries of MNEs are CFCs with very few exceptions.

In this circumstance, there is a tax savings of $100,000. However, the U.S. taxing authorities would likely challenge the strategy from two directions. First, they would say that SSI-Cayman does not contribute any value to the speakers, so the appropriate transfer price is $1,000,000, not $750,000. At this transfer price, the U.S. taxes would be the same $160,000 as in the previous case, so there would be no tax savings. The second challenge would be that this transaction and the ensuing income fall under Subpart F of the Tax Code. In this situation, the U.S. tax would again be $160,000 and there would be no tax benefits from using the Cayman subsidiary.

If we change the scenario and incorporate the sales subsidiary in Ireland, where the corporate tax rate is only 16 percent, then have the Irish sales subsidiary sell the speakers in the local market, the income from the transaction does not qualify as Subpart F income, and tax savings can be realized. However, if SSI-Ireland sells the speakers in the United Kingdom, a foreign country, income generated by those sales would be considered Subpart F income under the scenario we described. On the other hand, if SSI-Ireland does some assembly work, purchasing the incomplete units from SSI-USA and adding some value to them, and then sells them in the United Kingdom, the income from the sales would not be Subpart F income because there would be economic substance to the Irish subsidiary that earns the income. The fact that the 16 percent tax rate is much lower than the 40 percent in the United States is irrelevant for determining the tax status of the transaction. With this scenario, the company saves taxes as long as it keeps the income offshore and does not repatriate it to the United States.

In Chapter 14, we suggested that there might be cost advantages if a company establishes a reinvoicing center in a low-tax country such as the Cayman Islands. Having all internal sales transactions channeled through the reinvoicing center helps centralize risk management operations and facilitates netting of intrafirm accounts, thereby lowering costs. The downside of this suggestion is that the centralized financial subsidiary will almost certainly run afoul of the Subpart F taxation rules, hence income generated from the sales will be taxed immediately at the U.S. tax rate. Also, the transfer prices used for these transactions must be set carefully, perhaps using advance pricing agreements that allow the reinvoicing center to earn just enough revenues to cover centralized risk management costs but leave most of the operating profits in the manufacturing subsidiaries. Particularly if the operating subsidiaries are in countries whose tax rates are less than that in the United States, this will allow the company to defer the U.S. tax if it so chooses because the income in the operating subsidiaries will not be Subpart F income.

Prevention of Excessive U.S. Tax

While it is becoming increasingly difficult to reduce or defer U.S. taxes on foreign-source income, MNEs should ensure that they do not pay excessive taxes in the United States or anywhere else. There are at least eight sections of the U.S. Internal Revenue Code that pertain to taxation of foreign income that companies should factor into business decisions. We have already talked about a few of these issues, but now we reiterate them in greater detail.

FOREIGN TAX CREDITS As we discussed earlier, U.S. taxation of international income is based largely on the capital export neutrality, or CEN, philosophy, under which the government retains the right to tax residents on their worldwide taxable income. In our example of CEN taxation, we demonstrated that in the absence of a foreign tax credit (FTC), double taxation of foreign-source income would result in a higher rate than on domestic income, which would violate the basic idea behind

CEN neutrality. The FTC provides a dollar-for-dollar reduction of U.S. taxes owed on foreign-source income.[9]

The organizational form of the foreign operation is also an issue when applying the FTC. If the operation is a branch of the parent, then a direct credit can be taken against taxes on the branch's earnings. However, if the foreign operation is incorporated as a subsidiary, then the foreign taxes were paid not by the parent but by a separate foreign entity. In this case, the direct credit for foreign taxes paid is not available, but an indirect credit, called a **deemed-paid credit**, is available if the parent receives actual or constructive dividends from the subsidiary. It is called a deemed-paid credit because the foreign taxes are deemed paid by the parent shareholder in the same proportion as the dividends actually or constructively received to the subsidiary's total undistributed income. To take the FTC, the parent must "gross-up" or add to its taxable income both the dividend itself and the deemed-paid credit. This was the procedure used in Chapter 11, when we forecasted the after-tax dividend to be received by SSI-USA from the Shanghai subsidiary.

There are limits on the amount of foreign taxes that can be used as credits. First, only foreign *income* taxes are creditable, so other types of foreign taxes paid are excluded. Second, in any tax year, the allowed FTC is restricted to the amount of U.S. tax imposed on the foreign-source income that is included on the U.S. tax return. This gives rise to a limit calculated as follows:

$$\text{FTC} = \frac{\text{Foreign-source taxable income}}{\text{Worldwide taxable income}} \times \text{U.S tax liability before FTC.}$$

Any FTC that is disallowed because of this limit may be carried back two years or forward five years, subject to the same limit in those years.

To illustrate this limit, assume that a U.S. company, the XYZ Corporation, invests in the bonds of Nestlé, a Swiss corporation. Assume that XYZ's worldwide taxable income for the tax year is $6 million, consisting of $5 million of profits from U.S. sales and $1 million of interest income from the Nestlé (foreign-source) bonds. Foreign taxes were withheld by Switzerland on the interest income in the amount of $450,000. XYZ's total U.S. tax on the $6 million worldwide income before any FTC is $6,000,000(0.4) = $2,400,000 at an effective tax rate of 40 percent. Its FTC is limited to ($1,000,000/$6,000,000) × $2,400,000 = $400,000. The difference between the foreign taxes paid and the maximum FTC, or $450,000 − $400,000 = $50,000, can be carried back and, if not exhausted, then forward.

Notice that the reason the FTC was limited to only $400,000 is because the withholding tax rate in Switzerland (45 percent) was greater than the U.S. tax rate (40 percent). In the past, if the company could mix its foreign-source income from both high- and low-tax-rate countries so that the combined foreign rate were no higher than the U.S. tax rate, then the entire credit could be taken. For example, suppose XYZ's foreign-source income consisted of $500,000 in interest from Switzerland with foreign taxes of $225,000 paid, and $500,000 of interest from Ireland, taxed at 30 percent, or $150,000. In this scenario, the FTC limit would still be $400,000, but total foreign taxes paid would be only $375,000; hence all of the foreign taxes could be offset by the credit.

However, the U.S. Congress understands this mixing process and has taken steps to reduce companies' ability to increase the usable FTC by mixing foreign-source income from high- and low-tax countries. This was done by creating nine separate foreign tax credit limitation categories, or baskets. The nine income categories are

---

Deemed-Paid Credit
An indirect credit available if the parent received actual or constructive dividends from the subsidiary. Foreign taxes are deemed paid by the parent shareholder in the same proportion as the dividends actually or constructively received to the total undistributed income of the subsidiary.

---

[9]The FTC cannot be used to reduce taxes on domestic sources of income. Also, MNEs can take a deduction for foreign taxes paid rather than a credit, but in most cases the credit is more valuable.

passive, high withholding tax interest, financial services, shipping, noncontrolled foreign corporations, dividends from DISC, foreign trade income, FSC distributions, and general (all other income sources). Today, the credit is defined as the lesser of taxes paid or the FTC limit *within each separate basket.* This device essentially segregates income subject to high foreign tax from that subject to lower tax rates. DISCs and FSCs are no longer valid, but the other seven categories remain.

To see how these categories affect the foreign tax credit, assume that XYZ has foreign-source income in three of the baskets plus domestic U.S. earnings. Table 16-3 gives the relevant information. The three foreign-income sources and the domestic source are identified in Column 1, and the net taxable amount in each category is given in Column 2. Multiplying Column 2 by the relevant tax rate in Column 3 gives the foreign taxes actually paid. Column 5 is the U.S. tax that would be due at a tax rate of 40 percent on the income in Column 2. If there were only one category, the total FTC would be the lesser of the foreign taxes paid in Column 4, $1,215,000, or the formula amount:

$$\text{FTC limit} = [\$3,000,000/\$8,000,000 \times \$3,200,000] = \$1,200,000.$$

This same amount is shown in the total foreign row in Column 5. In this case, because the actual taxes paid exceed the limit, an excess FTC of $1,215,000 − $1,200,000 = $15,000 would be carried back or carried forward. However, because we have to make the computations category by category, the maximum FTC allowed is given in Column 6 as only $1,150,000. Now the firm would have to actually pay an additional $50,000 of taxes in the current year and then carry back or forward $65,000. Because of the basket approach, the firm could not mix the low-tax-rate passive income with the high-tax-rate manufacturing and financial services income to average out the rate. Because of these different categories of foreign-source income, tax planning is much harder today, but it is even more important than before to ensure that the company does not get into a situation where it has to pay too much tax because the system was improperly structured.

SECTION 482 ALLOCATIONS In the United States, the IRS has the authority to adjust the income of a U.S. party to a transaction with a controlled entity (a subsidiary in most cases) in order to accurately reflect "true income." This could prove beneficial to the company, particularly when there is a tax treaty between the host country and the United States. However, without a tax treaty, it is not usually possible to obtain a corresponding adjustment from the foreign tax authorities.

SECTION 367 If, in the organization, reorganization, or liquidation of a foreign subsidiary, a transaction involves the transfer of appreciated property to a foreign

TABLE 16-3 Calculation of Foreign Tax Credit with Different Categories of Income

(1) Foreign Income Category	(2) Net Taxable Income	(3) Tax Rate	(4) Foreign Taxes Paid	(5) U.S. Tax Before FTC	(6) FTC Allowed with Separate Limits
Manufacturing	$2,000,000	42%	$ 840,000	$ 800,000	$ 800,000
Financial services	500,000	45%	225,000	200,000	200,000
Passive	500,000	30%	150,000	200,000	150,000
Total foreign	$3,000,000		$1,215,000	$1,200,000	$1,150,000
U.S. income	5,000,000	40%		2,000,000	
Total income	$8,000,000			$3,200,000	

corporation, then the company may have to pay a "toll charge" in the form of gains recognition on the transfer.

DEDUCTIBILITY OF FOREIGN OPERATING LOSSES A U.S. parent cannot deduct losses incurred by a foreign corporation, so if the foreign operation is expected to have losses during the early years of operation, perhaps it should be organized as a branch. However, if the branch is reorganized into a corporation (subsidiary) after it becomes profitable, the tax benefits of writing off the branch losses will have to be recaptured. The recapture will occur in the future, though, so this strategy may still be advisable.

USING FLOW-THROUGH ENTITIES Special hybrid entities have been developed that are classified as a corporation for foreign tax purposes but as a partnership or unincorporated branch for U.S. tax purposes. These can be advantageous for flowing foreign operating losses through to the parent.

CHECK-THE-BOX REGULATIONS Some foreign business entities with a single U.S. owner can elect to be treated as either a corporation or an unincorporated branch for tax purposes.[10] This regulation, passed in 1997, excludes 80 types of foreign business entities, including the German AG, French SA, Dutch NV, and UK plc, but where it can be used it represents a significant tax advantage to MNEs. It is called a "check-the-box regulation" because to choose these options the company must put a checkmark in the appropriate box on the tax form. As an example of how this choice can benefit the MNE, assume that XYZ Corporation creates a controlled foreign corporation (CFC) holding company in a low-tax area such as the Cayman Islands to serve as the "owner" of two other operating subsidiaries. The holding company lends money to the operating subsidiaries, both of which are located in countries with high tax rates. The interest paid by the subsidiaries to the holding company is deductible locally for tax purposes (and is valuable because of the high tax rates), and the Cayman Islands does not charge tax on the interest income. The only problem with this arrangement is that the interest payments to the holding company may be construed as Subpart F income and trigger a constructive dividend back to the U.S. parent. If this happens, the tax savings may be largely offset by the U.S. taxes on the Subpart F income. However, under the check-the-box regulations, the two operating subsidiaries can be treated as unincorporated branches of the holding company for U.S. tax purposes. In this case, there are no loans and no interest payments because all three entities (the two operating subsidiaries and the holding company) are treated as a single entity for purposes of U.S. taxes. Without interest income, there is no Subpart F income, and no U.S. taxes are due. The foreign tax savings still exist, though, because the subsidiaries are still foreign corporations for purposes of local taxes in the host countries. This structure might allow the company to circumvent some of the problems with reinvoicing centers mentioned earlier in the chapter.

EARNINGS AND PROFITS To calculate the indirect FTC on dividends received by a U.S. company from its foreign subsidiary (as discussed in Chapter 11 and earlier in this chapter), it is necessary to apply U.S. Generally Accepted Accounting Principles (GAAP) to the foreign information. Because U.S.-GAAP sometimes differs significantly from foreign accounting principles, it is often possible to accelerate indirect FTCs and thereby defer more U.S. tax.

LIQUIDATION OF AN UNSUCCESSFUL SUBSIDIARY Generally, losses by a foreign corporation are not deductible for U.S. companies. However, if the MNE is careful

---

[10]If they have more than one owner, they can elect to be treated as a corporation or as a partnership for tax purposes.

to build the subsidiary's capital structure using the proper securities, then at least part of the losses may be recoverable. No loss is recognized for equity investments on complete liquidation of subsidiaries. This suggests that if the company is worried about the success of the venture, it should minimize contributed equity until later when the uncertainties are resolved and the subsidiary has proven its viability. However, if part of the foreign subsidiary's capital structure is noncommon equity—meaning mainly parent-supplied debt—it is possible to obtain an ordinary loss deduction for worthless securities in an affiliated corporation. Of course, the parent company must actually charge off the debt on the books within the tax year in order to claim this deduction.

SELF-TEST QUESTIONS

What are the only two provisions in the U.S. Tax Code for permanent deferral or reduction of U.S. taxes?

How can a foreign subsidiary be used to temporarily defer U.S. taxes?

What is Subpart F income? Give some examples.

What is a deemed-paid credit?

How do you calculate the limit on the allowed FTC that is restricted to the amount of U.S. tax imposed on the foreign-source income that is included on the U.S. tax return?

What has Congress done to reduce the ability of companies to increase the usable FTC by mixing foreign-source income from high- and low-tax countries?

SUMMARY

The tax laws of any particular country pertaining to international transactions have two central goals: to promote the global competitiveness of local industry and to protect the country's tax revenue base. On the other hand, global companies legitimately desire to reduce their worldwide tax liability by structuring the company and its global operations to achieve the lowest possible effective tax rate. The key concepts discussed in this chapter are listed below.

- **Effective tax rates** vary greatly around the world and they even fluctuate over time in many countries. The U.S. effective tax rate is near the top, which puts U.S. firms at a distinct disadvantage when they go head-to-head with foreign competitors. Two-thirds of the countries have cut their maximum tax rates over the 1996–2002 period, but the United States has kept its rate stable.
- Taxes are generally classified into two broad categories: direct and indirect. **Direct taxes** are based on income, while **indirect taxes** are based on some other measurable attribute, such as ad valorem taxes on year-end inventory value.
- Most countries impose both **corporate income taxes** and **personal income taxes** on their citizens. Some countries have different income tax rates for different activities, such as one rate for reinvested profits and another rate for earnings paid out as cash dividends.
- **Withholding tax** is the device that the payor—a bank, a company, or some other organization—uses to hold back some of the payment (usually from 0 to 30 percent) and send it to the government.
- A **consumption-based tax** is borne only by those who wish to consume specific products or services. This is a primary device for raising revenues by U.S. cities and states.
- A **value-added tax (VAT)** is a tax levied on the entity involved in each production stage of the production process for goods, and it is based on the value added to the product by that particular production stage.
- A **production-based tax** is a tax paid on units produced rather than units consumed.

- Income taxes and withholding taxes are the two major taxes that directly affect **international tax planning** for the MNE.
- There are four major characteristics that are desired when a firm discusses setting up a subsidiary in a **tax haven**: (1) A **stable government**, (2) a **stable financial system and currency**, (3) the necessary **infrastructure** to support sophisticated financial services and institutions, and (4) **low tax rates** on foreign investment or sales income and a low withholding tax rate on dividend transfers.
- **Capital export neutrality (CEN)**, sometimes called *domestic neutrality,* is an international tax theory that suggests that investors should pay exactly the same total amount of taxes on income from foreign investments as they do on income from domestic investments.
- **Capital import neutrality (CIN),** or *foreign neutrality,* suggests that investments in any country should all be taxed at the same rate no matter where the investor resides.
- The three major issues that must be considered when developing an MNE's tax plan are the **nature of business activities**, the **type of organization**, and **tax treaties.**
- **Passive investment income** consists of such things as dividends, interest, royalty income from securities investments, and the licensing of intangible assets to foreigners.
- **Active business operations** are operations in which the net income of the activity rather than the gross income is taxed by the host country.
- **Permanent establishment** means that the activities in the host country rise beyond some minimal level. Activities that create a permanent establishment include opening a local office, building a factory and starting manufacturing operations, or establishing some other fixed place of business.
- Currently, there are two provisions in the Tax Code for permanent deferral or reduction of U.S. taxes: (1) The **possessions credit** encourages U.S. companies to aid in the economic development of U.S. possessions by allowing domestic corporations to claim a credit for income derived from sources within these possessions, even when little or no foreign taxes were actually paid on it, and (2) the **extra-territorial income**, or **ETI**, regime allows U.S. exporters to exclude from U.S. taxes a portion of export profits on goods produced domestically in the United States.
- Foreign tax credits provide a dollar-for-dollar reduction in U.S. taxes owed on foreign-source income. If the operation is a branch of the parent, then a direct credit can be taken against taxes on the branch's earnings. However, if the foreign operation is incorporated as a subsidiary, then the foreign taxes were paid not by the parent but by a separate foreign entity. In this case, the direct credit for foreign taxes paid is not available, but there is an indirect credit, called a **deemed-paid credit.**
- The U.S. Congress created nine separate foreign tax credit limitation categories, or baskets, to prevent the mixing of foreign-source income from high- and low-tax countries. The nine income categories are: **passive, high withholding tax interest, financial services, shipping, noncontrolled foreign corporations, dividends from DISC, foreign trade income, FSC distributions**, and **general**. DISCs and FSCs are no longer valid but the other seven categories remain.
- The U.S. Tax Code must be factored into an MNE's business decisions. MNEs should consider **Section 482 allocations**, **Section 367**, using **flow-through entities**, and **check-the-box regulations.**

QUESTIONS

(16-1) What are the two central goals of tax laws pertaining to international transactions?

(16-2) How do taxes affect the valuation equation?

(16-3) Why is international taxation so complex?

(16-4) What reasons have economists given in their arguments that corporate taxes to raise revenues in open economies are inefficient?

(16-5) Why do governments withhold taxes on passive income?

(16-6) What is a value-added tax (VAT)? Is it a consumption-based or production-based tax? Explain your answer.

(16-7) What is a tax haven? What are the four major characteristics a firm looks for when setting up a subsidiary in a tax haven?

(16-8) Differentiate between capital export neutrality and capital import neutrality. Give the supporting arguments for each system.

(16-9) Differentiate between the typical international tax treatment applied to passive investment income versus active business operations.

(16-10) Differentiate between the typical international tax treatment applied to foreign subsidiaries versus foreign branches.

(16-11) What are the three forms of tax assistance provided to MNEs by tax treaties?

(16-12) What is the importance of the inclusion of "competent authorities" in a tax treaty?

(16-13) Identify and explain special provisions in the Tax Code that reduce U.S. taxes on foreign-source income below the normal U.S. rate or defer U.S. tax payments to a later date.

(16-14) What legislation has Congress passed limiting deferrals of U.S. taxes on foreign-source income?

(16-15) Briefly identify and explain the eight sections of the U.S. Internal Revenue Code highlighted in this chapter pertaining to taxation of foreign income that companies should factor into business decisions.

SELF-TEST PROBLEMS   Solutions Appear in Appendix B

(ST-1) Define each of the following terms:
Key Terms
a. Consumption-based tax; value-added tax; production-based tax
b. Capital export neutrality (CEN); capital import neutrality (CIN)
c. Passive investment income; active business operations
d. Permanent establishment
e. Possessions credit; extra-territorial income (ETI)
f. Deemed-paid credit

(ST-2) Global Electronics Incorporated (GEI) has subsidiaries that operate in Country X
Taxation on Foreign- and in Country Y, and its home country is X. Country X's income tax rate is 40
Source Income percent, while Country Y's tax rate is 20 percent. Assume that GEI's domestic income earned in Country X is $25 million, while the income earned in Country Y is $10 million. GEI repatriates all income after taxes from Country Y to Country X. Assume that Country X operates under a capital export neutrality regime.
a. What is the dividend received from Country Y?
b. What is Country X's tax due on Country Y's dividend?
c. What is the foreign tax credit?
d. What is the actual net dividend received after all taxes have been considered?
e. What is GEI's total after-tax income?
f. What is GEI's effective tax rate?

STARTER PROBLEMS

(16-1) Refer back to problem ST-2. Assume that Country X operates under a capital import neutrality regime.

Taxation on Foreign-Source Income

a. What is GEI's total after-tax income?
b. What is GEI's effective tax rate?

(16-2) Assume that Lopez Cigar Manufacturers (LCM) is a U.S. company that has invested in bonds of a Japanese corporation. LCM's worldwide taxable income for the year is $25 million, consisting of $20 million of profits from U.S. sales and $5 million of interest income from the Japanese corporation. Foreign taxes withheld by the Japanese corporation total $2,250,000, representing 45 percent of the interest earned. Assume a U.S. tax rate of 40 percent.

Foreign Tax Credit

a. What is the U.S. tax liability before the foreign tax credit (FTC)?
b. What is the allowed FTC?
c. What is the difference between the foreign taxes paid and the maximum FTC that can be carried back and, if not exhausted, carried forward?

EXAM-TYPE PROBLEMS

(16-3) Heuser Imports (HI) has subsidiaries that operate in Country M and in Country N, and its home country is M. Country M's income tax rate is 35 percent, while Country N's tax rate is 15 percent. Assume that HI's domestic income earned in Country M is $10 million, while the income earned in Country N is $2 million. HI repatriates all income after taxes from Country N to Country M. Assume that Country M operates under a capital export neutrality regime.

Taxation on Foreign-Source Income

a. What is the dividend received from Country N?
b. What is Country M's tax due on Country N's dividend?
c. What is the foreign tax credit?
d. What is the actual net dividend received after all taxes have been considered?
e. What is HI's total after-tax income?
f. What is HI's effective tax rate?

(16-4) Refer back to problem 16-3. Assume that Country M operates under a capital import neutrality regime.

Taxation on Foreign-Source Income

a. What is HI's total after-tax income?
b. What is HI's effective tax rate?

(16-5) Assume that International Designs Incorporated (IDI) is a U.S. company that has invested in bonds of a French corporation. IDI's worldwide taxable income for the year is $125 million, consisting of $87.5 million of profits from U.S. sales and $37.5 million of interest income from the French corporation. Foreign taxes withheld by the French corporation total $15,000,000, representing 40 percent of the interest earned. Assume a U.S. tax rate of 35 percent.

Foreign Tax Credit

a. What is the U.S. tax liability before the foreign tax credit (FTC)?
b. What is the allowed FTC?
c. What is the difference between the foreign taxes paid and the maximum FTC that can be carried back and, if not exhausted, carried forward?

INTEGRATED CASE

Rick Schmidt, MRI's CFO, along with Mandy Wu, Schmidt's assistant, and John Costello, a consultant and college finance professor, comprise a team set up to teach the firm's directors and senior managers the basics of international financial management. The program includes 16 sessions, each lasting about 2 hours, and they are scheduled immediately before the monthly board meetings. Fifteen sessions have been completed, and the team is now preparing Session 16, which will deal with international tax systems, tax planning, and strategy. Prior sessions have provided an overview of international and corporate financial topics, and this final session is intended to integrate a lot of those concepts and show how MNEs develop global tax strategies.

For the international tax planning session, the team will explain how tax systems and rates vary across the world, how competing theories on the role of taxation guide policy, and how government regulation affects tax strategy. MRI is a multinational firm that operates worldwide. Some operations are quite large with factories and distribution centers, while others are restricted to just exports. Schmidt thinks it is very important to make sure that all of MRI's directors understand how their activities fit in the overall corporate tax scheme.

Wu expressed concern about addressing controversial issues, where the proper analysis is in question. She recalled that in college some students simply "tuned out" when the instructor raised a question for which there was no definitive answer, and she was concerned that the directors might react similarly. Schmidt and Costello agree that this could be a problem, but they felt strongly that it would not be appropriate to "sweep problems under the carpet." So, they want to bring up relevant unresolved issues, discuss alternative ways of dealing with them, and point out the implications of different decisions. The directors are all intelligent, experienced in dealing with complex situations, and would rather know about potential problems than be kept in the dark.

With those thoughts in mind, the three compiled the following set of questions, which they plan to discuss during the session. Assume that you are Mandy Wu and that you must prepare answers for use during the session.

QUESTIONS

a. Describe the kinds of taxes MNEs and individuals face around the world.

b. What major characteristics do firms look for when setting up a subsidiary in a tax haven?

c. Explain what is meant by tax neutrality, and describe the two competing neutrality theories.

d. Tax rates and systems vary greatly across the world, and MNEs must develop a cohesive strategy for international tax planning. Describe the three major issues that must be addressed.

e. How is foreign-source income taxed for U.S. business entities? What provisions exist to help defer or reduce the U.S. tax liability? What antideferral provisions of U.S. taxes exist?

f. Describe how some sections of the U.S. IRS Tax Code must be factored into business decisions.

Currencies of the World

Country	Currency	Symbol	Subdivision	ISO-4217 Code	Regime
Afghanistan	afghani	Af	100 puls	AFA 004	float
Albania	lek	L	100 qindarka (qintars)	ALL 008	float
Algeria	dinar	DA	100 centimes	DZD 012	composite
American Samoa	(see United States of America)				
Andorra	Andorran Peseta (1/1 to Spanish peseta) and Andorran franc (1/1 to French franc)				
Angola	kwanza	Kz	100 lwei	AOK —	(replaced)
Angola	kwanza (kwanza reajustado, -2000)	Kz	100 lwei	AON 024	m.float
Angola	kwanza (new kwanza, 2001-)	Kz	100 lwei	AOA 024	m.float
Anguilla	dollar	EC$	100 cents	XCD 951	US$ (2.7)
Antarctica	(each Antarctic base uses the currency of its home country)				
Antigua and Barbuda	dollar	EC$	100 cents	XCD 951	US$ (2.7)
Argentina	austral (-1991)	double dashed A	100 centavos	ARA —	(replaced)
Argentina	peso (1991-)	$	100 centavos	ARS 032	float
Armenia	dram		100 luma	AMD 051	
Aruba	guilder (a.k.a. florin or gulden)	Af.	100 cents	AWG 533	US$ (1.79)
Australia	dollar	A$	100 cents	AUD 036	float
Austria (-1998)	schilling	S	100 groschen	ATS 040	euro-13.7603
Austria (1999-)	(see European Union)				
Azerbaijan	manat		100 gopik	AZM 031	
Bahamas	dollar	B$	100 cents	BSD 044	US$ (1.0)
Bahrain	dinar	BD	1,000 fils	BHD 048	US$ (lim.flex.)
Bangladesh	taka	Tk	100 paisa (poisha)	BDT 050	composite
Barbados	dollar	Bds$	100 cents	BBD 052	US$ (2.0)

Country	Currency	Symbol	Subdivision	ISO-4217 Code	Regime
Belarus (-1999)	ruble	BR		BYB 112	replaced, 1000 BYB = 1 BYR
Belarus (2000-)	ruble	BR		BYR 112	m.float
Belgium (-1998)	franc	BF	100 centimes	BEF 056	euro-40.3399
Belgium (1999-)	(see European Union)				
Belize	dollar	BZ$	100 cents	BZD 084	US$ (2.0)
Belorussia	(old name of Belarus)				
Benin	franc	CFAF	100 centimes	XOF 952	French franc (100.0)
Bermuda	dollar	Bd$	100 cents	BMD 060	US$ (1.0)
Bhutan	ngultrum	Nu	100 chetrum	BTN 064	Indian rupee (1.0)
Bolivia	boliviano	Bs	100 centavos	BOB 068	float
Bosnia-Herzegovina (-1999)	B.H. dinar		100 para	BAD 070	
Bosnia-Herzegovina (1999+)	convertible mark	KM	100 fennig	BAM 977	DM (1.0)
Botswana	pula	P	100 thebe	BWP 072	composite
Bouvet Island	(see Norway)				
Brazil	cruzeiro (-1993)		100 centavos	BRE 076	(replaced)
Brazil	cruzeiro (1993-94)		100 centavos	BRR 076	(replaced)
Brazil	real (1994-)	R$	100 centavos	BRL 986	float
British Indian Ocean Territory	(legal currency is GBP, but mostly USD is used)				
British Virgin Islands	(see United States)				
Brunei	ringgit (a.k.a. Bruneian dollar)	B$	100 sen (a.k.a. 100 cents)	BND 096	S$ (1.0)
Bulgaria	leva	Lv	100 stotinki	BGL 100	German mark (1.0)
Burkina Faso	franc	CFAF	100 centimes	XOF 952	French franc (100.0)
Burma	(now Myanmar)				
Burundi	franc	FBu	100 centimes	BIF 108	composite
Cambodia	new riel	CR	100 sen	KHR 116	m.float
Cameroon	franc	CFAF	100 centimes	XAF 950	French franc (100.0)
Canada	dollar	Can$	100 cents	CAD 124	float
Canton and Enderbury Islands	(see Kiribati)				
Cape Verde Island	escudo	C.V.Esc.	100 centavos	CVE 132	composite
Cayman Islands	dollar	CI$	100 cents	KYD 136	US$ (0.85)
Central African Republic	franc	CFAF	100 centimes	XAF 950	French franc (100.0)

Country	Currency	Symbol	Subdivision	ISO-4217 Code	Regime
Chad	franc	CFAF	100 centimes	XAF 950	French franc (100.0)
Chile	peso	Ch$	100 centavos	CLP 152	indicators
China	yuan renminbi	Y	10 jiao = 100 fen	CNY 156	m.float
Christmas Island	(see Australia)				
Cocos (Keeling) Islands	(see Australia)				
Colombia	peso	Col$	100 centavos	COP 170	m.float
Comoros	franc	CF	–	KMF 174	French franc (75.0)
Congo	franc	CFAF	100 centimes	XAF 950	French franc (100.0)
Congo, Dem. Rep. (former Zaire)	franc		100 centimes	CDF 180	US$ (2.50)
Congo, Dem. Rep. (2001-)	franc		100 centimes	CDF 976	float
Cook Islands	(see New Zealand)				
Costa Rica	colon	¢	100 centimos	CRC 188	float
Côte d'Ivoire	franc	CFAF	100 centimes	XOF 952	French franc (100.0)
Croatia	kuna	HRK	100 lipas	HRK 191	float
Cuba	peso	Cu$	100 centavos	CUP 192	US$ (1.0)
Cyprus	pound	£C	100 cents	CYP 196	1.7086 EUR/CYP +/−2.25%
Cyprus (Northern)	(see Turkey)				
Czechoslovakia	(split into Czech Republic and Slovak Republic on January 1, 1993)				
Czech Republic	koruna	Kc (with hacek on c)	100 haleru	CZK 203	float
Denmark	krone (pl. kroner)	Dkr	100 øre	DKK 208	EMS-II
Djibouti	franc	DF	100 centimes	DJF 262	US$ (177.72)
Dominica	dollar	EC$	100 cents	XCD 951	US$ (2.7)
Dominican Rep.	peso	RD$	100 centavos	DOP 214	m.float
Dronning Maud Land	(see Norway)				
East Timor	(see Indonesia)				
Ecuador	sucre	S/	100 centavos	ECS 218	m.float
Ecuador (15-Sep-2000-)	(country has adopted the US dollar)				
Egypt	pound	£E	100 piasters or 1,000 milliemes	EGP 818	m.float
El Salvador	colon	¢	100 centavos	SVC 222	float
Equatorial Guinea	franc	CFAF	100 centimos	GQE 226	French franc (100.0)
Eritrea	nakfa	Nfa	100 cents	ERN 232	
Estonia	kroon (pl. krooni)	KR	100 senti	EEK 233	German mark (8.0)

Country	Currency	Symbol	Subdivision	ISO-4217 Code	Regime
Ethiopia	birr	Br	100 cents	ETB 230	float
European Union (-1998)	European Currency Unit	ecu		XEU 954	
European Union (1999-)	Euro	€	100 euro-cents	EUR 978	
Faeroe Islands (Føroyar)	(see Denmark)				
Falkland Islands	pound	£F	100 pence	FKP 238	British pound (1.0)
Fiji	dollar	F$	100 cents	FJD 242	composite
Finland (-1998)	markka (pl. markkaa)	mk	100 penniä (sg. penni)	FIM 246	euro-5.94573
Finland (1999-)	(see European Union)				
France (-1998)	franc	F	100 centimes	FRF 250	euro-6.55957
France (1999-)	(see European Union)				
French Guiana	(see France)				
French Polynesia	franc	CFPF	100 centimes	XPF 953	French franc (18.18)
Gabon	franc	CFAF	100 centimes	XAF 950	French franc (100.0)
Gambia	dalasi	D	100 butut	GMD 270	float
Gaza	(see Israel and Jordan)				
Georgia	lari		100 tetri	GEL 981	float
Germany (-1998)	deutsche mark	DM	100 pfennig	DEM 276	euro-1.95583
Germany (1999-)	(see European Union)				
Ghana	new cedi	¢	100 psewas	GHC 288	float
Gibraltar	pound	£G	100 pence	GIP 292	British pound (1.0)
Great Britain	(see United Kingdom)				
Greece (-2000)	drachma	Dr	100 lepta (sg. lepton)	GRD 300	euro-340.750
Greece (2001-)	(see European Union)				
Greenland	(see Denmark)				
Grenada	dollar	EC$	100 cents	XCD 951	US$ (2.7)
Guadeloupe	(see France)				
Guam	(see United States)				
Guatemala	quetzal	Q	100 centavos	GTQ 320	float
Guernsey	(see United Kingdom)				
Guinea-Bissau (-Apr 1997)	peso	PG	100 centavos	GWP 624	m.float
Guinea-Bissau (May 1997-)	franc	CFAF	100 centimes	XOF 952	French franc (100.0)
Guinea	syli	FG	10 francs, 1 franc = 100 centimes	GNS 324	m.float
Guinea	franc			GNF 324	

Country	Currency	Symbol	Subdivision	ISO-4217 Code	Regime
Guyana	dollar	G$	100 cents	GYD 328	float
Haiti	gourde	G	100 centimes	HTG 332	float
Heard and McDonald Islands	(see Australia)				
Honduras	lempira	L	100 centavos	HNL 340	m.float
Hong Kong	dollar	HK$	100 cents	HKD 344	US$ (7.73 central parity)
Hungary	forint	Ft	none	HUF 348	composite
Iceland	krona	IKr	100 aurar (sg. aur)	ISK 352	composite
India	rupee	Rs	100 paise	INR 356	float
Indonesia	rupiah	Rp	100 sen (no longer used)	IDR 360	m.float
International Monetary Fund	Special Drawing Right	SDR		XDR 960	
Iran	rial	Rls	10 rials = 1 toman	IRR 364	US$ (4750)
Iraq	dinar	ID	1,000 fils	IQD 368	US$ (0.3109)
Ireland (-1998)	punt or pound	IR£	100 pingin or pence	IEP 372	euro-0.787564
Ireland (1999-)	(see European Union)				
Isle of Man	(see United Kingdom)				
Israel	new shekel	NIS	100 new agorot	ILS 376	m.float
Italy (-1998)	lira (pl. lire)	Lit	no subdivision in use	ITL 380	euro-1936.27
Italy (1999-)	(see European Union)				
Ivory Coast	(see Côte d'Ivoire)				
Jamaica	dollar	J$	100 cents	JMD 388	float
Japan	yen	¥	100 sen (not used)	JPY 392	float
Jersey	(see United Kingdom)				
Johnston Island	(see United States)				
Jordan	dinar	JD	1,000 fils	JOD 400	composite
Kampuchea	(see Cambodia)				
Kazakhstan	tenge		100 tiyn	KZT 398	float
Kenya	shilling	K Sh	100 cents	KES 404	float
Kiribati	(see Australia)				
Korea, North	won	Wn	100 chon	KPW 408	
Korea, South	won	W	100 chon	KRW 410	float
Kuwait	dinar	KD	1,000 fils	KWD 414	composite
Kyrgyzstan	som		100 tyyn	KGS 417	float
Laos	new kip	KN	100 at	LAK 418	m.float
Latvia	lat	Ls	100 santims	LVL 428	SDR
Lebanon	pound (livre)	L.L.	100 piastres	LBP 422	float
Lesotho	loti, pl. maloti	L, pl. M	100 lisente	LSL 426	South African rand (1.0)

Country	Currency	Symbol	Subdivision	ISO-4217 Code	Regime
Liberia	dollar	$	100 cents	LRD 430	US$ (1.0)
Libya	dinar	LD	1,000 dirhams	LYD 434	SDR (8.5085)
Liechtenstein	(see Switzerland)				
Lithuania	litas, pl. litai		100 centu	LTL 440	euro (3.4528)
Luxembourg (-1998)	franc	LuxF	100 centimes	LUF 442	euro-40.3399
Luxembourg (1999-)	(see European Union)				
Macao (Macau)	pataca	P	100 avos	MOP 446	HK$ (1.03)
Macedonia (Former Yug. Rep.)	denar	MKD	100 deni	MKD 807	composite
Madagascar	ariayry = 5 francs	FMG	1 franc = 100 centimes	MGF 450	float
Malawi	kwacha	MK	100 tambala	MWK 454	float
Malaysia	ringgit	RM	100 sen	MYR 458	m.float
Maldives	rufiyaa	Rf	100 lari	MVR 462	m.float
Mali	franc	CFAF	100 centimes	XOF 952	French franc (100.0)
Malta	lira, pl. liri	Lm	100 cents	MTL 470	composite
Martinique	(see France)				
Mauritania	ouguiya	UM	5 khoums	MRO 478	composite
Mauritius	rupee	Mau Rs	100 cents	MUR 480	composite
Micronesia	(see United States)				
Midway Islands	(see United States)				
Mexico	peso	Mex$	100 centavos	MXN 484	float
Moldova	leu, pl. lei			MDL 498	float
Monaco	(see France)				
Mongolia	tugrik (tughrik?)	Tug	100 mongos	MNT 496	float
Montserrat	dollar	EC$	100 cents	XCD 951	US$ (2.7)
Morocco	dirham	DH	100 centimes	MAD 504	composite
Mozambique	metical	Mt	100 centavos	MZM 508	float
Myanmar	kyat	K	100 pyas	MMK 104	US$ (5.86of, 200-300bm)
Nauru	(see Australia)				
Namibia	dollar	N$	100 cents	NAD 516	South African rand (1.0)
Nepal	rupee	NRs	100 paise	NPR 524	composite
Netherlands Antilles	guilder (a.k.a. florin or gulden)	Ant.f. or NAf.	100 cents	ANG 532	US$ (1.79)
Netherlands (-1998)	guilder (a.k.a. florin or gulden)	f.	100 cents	NLG 528	euro-2.20371
Netherlands (1999-)	(see European Union)				
New Caledonia	franc	CFPF	100 centimes	XPF 953	FFr (18.18)

Country	Currency	Symbol	Subdivision	ISO-4217 Code	Regime
New Zealand	dollar	NZ$	100 cents	NZD 554	float
Nicaragua	gold cordoba	C$	100 centavos	NIO 558	indicators
Niger	franc	CFAF	100 centimes	XOF 952	French franc (100.0)
Nigeria	naira	double-dashed N	100 kobo	NGN 566	US$ (82.0)
Niue	(see New Zealand)				
Norfolk Island	(see Australia)				
Norway	krone (pl. kroner)	NKr	100 øre	NOK 578	float
Oman	rial	RO	1,000 baizas	OMR 512	US$ (1/2.6)
Pakistan	rupee	Rs	100 paisa	PKR 586	m.float
Palau	(see United States)				
Panama	balboa	B	100 centesimos	PAB 590	US$ (1.0)
Panama Canal Zone	(see United States)				
Papua New Guinea	kina	K	100 toeas	PGK 598	composite
Paraguay	guarani	slashed G	100 centimos	PYG 600	float
Peru	inti		100 centimos	PEI —	(replaced)
Peru	new sol	S/.	100 centimos	PEN 604	float
Philippines	peso	dashed P	100 centavos	PHP 608	float
Pitcairn Island	(see New Zealand)				
Poland	zloty	z dashed l	100 groszy	PLN 985	m.float
Portugal (-1998)	escudo	Esc	100 centavos	PTE 620	euro-200.482
Portugal (1999-)	(see European Union)				
Puerto Rico	(see United States)				
Qatar	riyal	QR	100 dirhams	QAR 634	US$ (lim.flex.)
Reunion	(see France)				
Romania	leu (pl. lei)	L	100 bani	ROL 642	float
Russia (-1997)	ruble	R	100 kopecks	RUR 810	(replaced, 1000/1)
Russia (1998-)	ruble	R	100 kopecks	RUB 810	float
Rwanda	franc	RF	100 centimes	RWF 646	SDR (201.8)
Samoa (Western)	(see Western Samoa)				
Samoa (American)	(see United States)				
San Marino	(see Italy)				
Sao Tome & Principe	dobra	Db	100 centimos	STD 678	m.float
Saudi Arabia	riyal	SRls	100 halalat	SAR 682	US$ (lim.flex.)
Senegal	franc	CFAF	100 centimes	XOF 952	French franc (100.0)
Serbia	(see Yugoslavia)				
Seychelles	rupee	SR	100 cents	SCR 690	SDR (7.2345)
Sierra Leone	leone	Le	100 cents	SLL 694	float

Country	Currency	Symbol	Subdivision	ISO-4217 Code	Regime
Singapore	dollar	S$	100 cents	SGD 702	m.float
Slovakia	koruna	Sk	100 halierov	SKK 703	float
Slovenia	tolar	SIT	100 stotinov (stotins)	SIT 705	m.float
Solomon Island	dollar	SI$	100 cents	SBD 090	composite
Somalia	shilling	So. Sh.	100 centesimi	SOS 706	float
South Africa	rand	R	100 cents	ZAR 710	float
Spain (-1998)	peseta	Ptas	100 centimos	ESP 724	euro-166.386
Spain (1999-)	(see European Union)				
Sri Lanka	rupee	SLRs	100 cents	LKR 144	m.float
St. Helena	pound	£S	100 new pence	SHP 654	GBP (1.0)
St. Kitts and Nevis	dollar	EC$	100 cents	XCD 951	US$ (2.7)
St. Lucia	dollar	EC$	100 cents	XCD 951	US$ (2.7)
St. Vincent and the Grenadines	dollar	EC$	100 cents	XCD 951	US$ (2.7)
Sudan (-1992)	pound		100 piastres	SDP 736	m.float
Sudan (1992-)	dinar		100 piastres	SDP 736	m.float
Suriname	guilder (a.k.a. florin or gulden)	Sur.f. or Sf.	100 cents	SRG 740	m.float
Svalbard and Jan Mayen Islands	(see Norway)				
Swaziland	lilangeni, pl. emalangeni	L, pl., E	100 cents	SZL 748	South African rand (1.0)
Sweden	krona (pl. kronor)	Sk	100 öre	SEK 752	m.float
Switzerland	franc	SwF	100 rappen/ centimes	CHF 756	float
Syria	pound	£S	100 piasters	SYP 760	US$ (11.225)
Tahiti	(see French Polynesia)				
Taiwan	new dollar	NT$	100 cents	TWD 901	
Tajikistan (-5-Nov-2000)	ruble			TJR 762	replaced, 1000 TJR = 1 TJS
Tajikistan (6-Nov-2000-)	somoni		100 dirams	TJS 762	
Tanzania	shilling	TSh	100 cents	TZS 834	float
Thailand	baht	Bht or Bt	100 stang	THB 764	float
Togo	franc	CFAF	100 centimes	XOF 952	French franc (100.0)
Tokelau	(see New Zealand)				
Tonga	pa'anga	PT or T$	100 seniti	TOP 776	composite
Trinidad and Tobago	dollar	TT$	100 cents	TTD 780	float
Tunisia	dinar	TD	1,000 millimes	TND 788	m.float (1.0)
Turkey	lira	TL	100 kurus	TRL 792	m.float

Country	Currency	Symbol	Subdivision	ISO-4217 Code	Regime
Turkmenistan	manat		100 tenga	TMM 795	US$ (10.0; 230.0)
Turks and Caicos Islands	(see United States)				
Tuvalu	(see Australia)				
Uganda	shilling	USh	100 cents	UGS —	(replaced)
Uganda	shilling	USh	100 cents	UGX 800	float
Ukraine	Hryvnia		100 kopiykas	UAH 980	float
United Arab Emirates	dirham	Dh	100 fils	AED 784	US$ (lim.flex.)
United Kingdom	pound	£	100 pence	GBP 826	float
United States of America	dollar	$	100 cents	USD 840	float
Upper Volta	(now Burkina Faso)				
Uruguay (-1975)	peso	Ur$	100 centésimos	UYP —	(replaced)
Uruguay (1975-93)	new peso	NUr$	100 centésimos	UYN —	(replaced)
Uruguay (1993-)	peso uruguayo	$U	100 centésimos	UYU 858	m.float
Uzbekistan	som		100 tiyin	UZS 860	
Vanuatu	vatu	VT	100 centimes	VUV 548	composite
Vatican	(see Italy)				
Venezuela	bolivar	Bs	100 centimos	VEB 862	float
Vietnam	(new) dong	dashed d, or D	10 hao or 100 xu	VND 704	m.float
Virgin Islands	(see United States)				
Wake Island	(see United States)				
Wallis and Futuna Islands	franc	CFPF	100 centimes	XPF 953	French franc (18.18)
Western Sahara	(see Spain, Mauritania, and Morocco)				
Western Samoa	tala	WS$	100 sene	WST 882	composite
Yemen	rial	YRls	100 fils	YER 886	float
Yugoslavia	dinar	Din	100 paras	YUM 891	
Zaïre (-Nov 1994)	zaire	Z	100 makuta		(replaced)
Zaïre (-1997)	new zaire	NZ	100 new makuta	ZRN 180	float
Zaïre	(country renamed in 1997 to Democratic Republic of Congo)				
Zambia	kwacha	ZK	100 ngwee	ZMK 894	float
Zimbabwe	dollar	Z$	100 cents	ZWD 716	float

Source: The University of British Columbia Sauder School of Business Pacific Exchange Rate Service, "Currencies of the World,"
http://fx.sauder.ubc.ca/currency_table.html.

Solutions to Self-Test Problems

Note: Except for Chapter 1, we do not show an answer for ST-1 problems because they are verbal rather than quantitative in nature.

Chapter 1

ST-1   Refer to the marginal glossary definitions or relevant chapter sections to check your responses.

Chapter 2

ST-2   a. I = Change in price/Initial price
$$= (\$2,600 - \$2,500)/\$2,500$$
$$= 0.04 = 4\%.$$

   b.
$$r_{RF} = r^* + I + r^*I$$
$$0.0764 = r^* + 0.04 + 0.04r^*$$
$$0.0764 - 0.04 = 1.04r^*$$
$$0.035 = r^*.$$

   c. IP = I + r*I
$$= 0.04 + 0.035(0.04)$$
$$= 0.04 + 0.0014$$
$$= 0.0414.$$

   Or,
$$r_{RF} - r^* = IP$$
$$0.0764 - 0.035 = 0.0414.$$

ST-3   IP = I + r*I
$$= 0.03 + (0.025)(0.03)$$
$$= 0.03075 = 3.075\%.$$

ST-4   r = r* + IP + DRP + LP + MRP + CRP + ERP
$$= 2.5\% + 3.2\% + 0.4\% + 0.5\% + 1.2\% + 0.1\% + 0.2\%$$
$$= 8.1\%.$$

ST-5   Suppose you have $1,000 to invest today. (You can start with any amount and you will arrive at the same answer.)

	Today		1 Year Later
		Invest at (1.032)(1.04) − 1 = 7.328%	
United States:	$1,000	──────────────────────────────────►	$1,073.28
	LC 2/$	Invest at (1.032)(1.10) − 1 = 13.52%	
Country X:	LC 2,000	──────────────────────────────────►	LC 2,270.40

$$LC\ 2,270.40/x = \$1,073.28$$
$$x = LC\ 2.115385/\$.$$

Next year's exchange rate would be LC 2.115385/$.

Chapter 3

ST-2   By convention, the spot rate for the British pound will be quoted in American terms, while the Chinese yuan spot rate will be given in European terms. To calculate the cross rates, the spot rate for the British pound must first be converted to European terms by finding the reciprocal of the quotation given.

Pound: $1.8271/£   or   1/$1.8271/£ = £0.547315/$

Yuan: CNY 8.2781/$

Now, the cross rates can be calculated.

a. Yuan/pound exchange rate $= \dfrac{\text{Yuan/\$}}{\text{Pound/\$}}$

$$= \frac{\text{CNY } 8.2781}{£0.547315} = \text{CNY } 15.1249/£.$$

b. Pound/yuan exchange rate $= \dfrac{\text{Pound/\$}}{\text{Yuan/\$}}$

$$= \frac{£0.547315}{\text{CNY } 8.2781} = £0.0661/\text{CNY}.$$

Alternatively, you should realize that this cross rate is just the reciprocal of the answer given in part a.

Pound/yuan exchange rate = 1/CNY 15.1249/£ = £0.0661/CNY.

ST-3   a.

	1/22/04	1/22/05
$/€	$1.270400	$1.260013

Because the euro quotations are given in American terms, they are direct quotations. Therefore, the direct quotation formula must be used to determine the percentage change in the euro relative to the dollar for the year.

$\%\Delta FX$ = [(Ending rate − Beginning rate)/Beginning rate] × 100
         = [(1.260013 − 1.270400)/1.270400] × 100
         = −0.010387/1.270400 × 100
         = −0.8176% ≈ −0.82%.

This indicates that during the year, the euro depreciated slightly against the dollar by 0.82 percent.

b. Table 3-4 gives the following information:

	British Pound	Canadian Dollar
Outright spot	1.841600	1.297800
3-month forward (points)	−132.90	44.53
3-month forward (outright)	1.828310	1.302253

c. Because the British pound quotation is given in American terms (direct quotation), then the direct formula would be used. Because the Canadian dollar is given in European terms (indirect quotation), then the indirect formula would be used.

British pound:

Forward premium or discount % = [(Forward rate − Spot rate)/Spot rate] × 360/n × 100
         = [(1.828310 − 1.841600)/1.841600] × 360/90 × 100
         = (−0.007217) × 4 × 100
         = −2.8866% discount to the dollar.

Canadian dollar:

Forward premium or discount % = [(Spot rate − Forward rate)/Forward rate] × 360/n × 100
= [(1.297800 − 1.302253)/1.302253] × 360/90 × 100
= (−0.003419) × 4 × 100
= −1.3678% discount to the dollar.

d. Table 3-4 provides the following information:

	Midrate	Bid	Offer
Spot rate	1.841600		
1-month forward	1.837200	−44.10	−43.90

		Bid	Offer
Outright spot		1.841600	1.841600
1-month forward (points)		−44.10	−43.90
1-month forward (outright)		1.837190	1.837210

The dealer would sell pounds:	£100,000,000 × $1.837210/£ =	$183,721,000
The dealer would purchase pounds:	£100,000,000 × $1.837190/£ =	$183,719,000
Difference = Spread = Dealer profit		$ 2,000

ST-4 You are given the following data:

Price of television in United States	$425.00
Spot rates	¥106.63/$
	€0.00785/¥

The price of the same television in Italy according to PPP:

$425 × ¥106.63/$ × €0.00785/¥ = €355.74.

ST-5 You are given the following data:

Spot rate	$1.8192/£
1-year forward rate	$1.7606/£
1-year U.S. Treasury yield	1.35%

According to interest rate parity, the yield on 1-year risk-free British securities is calculated as follows:

$(1 + r_\$) = S_{£/\$} \times (1 + r_£) \times 1/F_{£/\$}.$

However, the exchange rates for the pound are given in American terms, so the reciprocals must be calculated in order to use the formula above.

Spot rate	$1/\$1.8192/£ = £0.549692/\$$
1-year forward rate	$1/\$1.7606/£ = £0.567988/\$$

Now, the yield on 1-year risk-free British securities can be calculated as follows:

$1.0135 = 0.549692 \times (1 + r_£) \times 1/0.567988$
$1.0135 = 0.967788(1 + r_£)$
$0.045712 = 0.967788 r_£$
$0.0472 = r_£$
$4.72\% = r_£.$

Chapter 4

ST-2 a. Yes, Country G is more efficient and can produce more barrels of tea and bushels of corn per unit of input than Country F. Thus, Country G has an absolute advantage in the production of both tea and corn.

b. While Country G has an absolute advantage in the production of both products, its relative advantage is not the same for the two products. Country G's advantage over F in tea production is 15-to-7.5, or $15/7.5 = 2.00$, while its advantage in corn is only 10-to-7.5, or $10/7.5 = 1.33$. Thus, G has a larger absolute advantage in the production of tea, which means that it has a comparative advantage in the production of tea. Country F has the least absolute disadvantage in harvesting corn.

c. From the answer given in part b, G should specialize in tea, F should specialize in corn, and the two countries should trade with each other to obtain the proper mix of products.

d. Using barrels of tea as a medium of exchange, a bushel of corn in Country G is worth 1.5 barrels of tea.

e. Country F will produce only corn and Country G will produce only tea.

Trade at G's Domestic Price (1 bushel of corn = 1.5 barrels of tea)

	Tea (Barrels)			Corn (Bushels)	
Country F					
Produces	0	Given	Produces	18,750	2,500 × 7.5
Imports	13,125	Same as G's exports	Exports	8,750	Same as G's imports
Consumes	13,125		Consumes	10,000	
Advantage over No Trade:	937.5	= 13,125 − 12,187.5		3,437.5	= 10,000 − 6,562.5
Country G					
Produces	37,500	2,500 × 15	Produces	0	Given
Exports	13,125	37,500 − 24,375	Imports	8,750	8,750 − 0
Consumes	24,375	Given	Consumes	8,750	Given
Advantage over No Trade:	0	Country G consumes exactly as what it did in no-trade case		0	

From this table you can see that Country F is better off than in the "no-trade" situation. F now consumes 937.5 more barrels of tea and 3,437.5 more bushels of corn. Country G is exactly the same as it was in the "no-trade" situation. In the "no-trade" situation, GWP was 36,562.5 barrels of tea and 15,312.5 bushels of corn. By having F specialize in corn and G specialize in tea, GWP has increased. There are now 37,500 barrels of tea produced and 18,750 bushels of corn produced, an increase of 937.5 barrels of tea and 3,437.5 bushels of corn.

f. Using barrels of tea as a medium of exchange, a bushel of corn in Country F is worth 1 barrel of tea.

g. Again, Country F will produce only corn and Country G will produce only tea.

Trade at F's Domestic Price (1 bushel corn = 1 barrel of tea)

	Tea (Barrels)			Corn (Bushels)	
Country F					
Produces	0	Given	Produces	18,750	2,500 × 7.5
Imports	12,187.5	12,187.5 − 0	Exports	12,187.5	18,750 − 6,562.5
Consumes	12,187.5	Given	Consumes	6,562.5	
Advantage over No Trade:	0	Country F consumes exactly as what it did in no-trade case		0	
Country G					
Produces	37,500	2,500 × 15	Produces	0	Given
Exports	12,187.5	Same as F's imports	Imports	12,187.5	Same as F's exports
Consumes	25,312.5		Consumes	12,187.5	
Advantage over No Trade:	937.5	= 25,312.5 − 24,375		3,437.5	= 12,187.5 − 8,750

From this table you can see that Country G is better off than in the "no-trade" situation. G now consumes 937.5 more barrels of tea and 3,437.5 more bushels of corn. Country F is exactly the same as it was in the "no-trade" situation. In the "no-trade" situation, GWP was 36,562.5 barrels of tea and 15,312.5 bushels of corn. By having F specialize in corn and G specialize in tea, GWP has increased. There are now 37,500 barrels of tea produced and 18,750 bushels of corn produced, an increase of 937.5 barrels of tea and 3,437.5 bushels of corn.

h. Again, Country F will produce only corn and Country G will produce only tea.

Trade at Market-Determined Price (Assume 1 bushel of corn = 1.43 barrels of tea)

	Tea (Barrels)			Corn (Bushels)		
Country F						
Produces	0	Given	Produces	18,750	$2,500 \times 7.5$	
Imports	12,512.5	Same as G's exports	Exports	8,750	Same as G's imports	
Consumes	12,512.5		Consumes	10,000		
Advantage over No Trade:	325	$= 12,512.5 - 12,187.5$		3,437.5	$= 10,000 - 6,562.5$	
Country G						
Produces	37,500	$2,500 \times 15$	Produces	0	Given	
Exports	12,512.5	$8,750 \times 1.43$	Imports	8,750	$8,750 - 0$	
Consumes	24,987.5		Consumes	8,750	Given	
Advantage over No Trade:	612.5	$24,987.5 - 24,375$		0		

From this table you can see that both countries are better off than in the "no-trade" situation. Country F now consumes 325 more barrels of tea and 3,437.5 more bushels of corn, while Country G consumes 612.5 more barrels of tea. (G consumes exactly the same amount of corn as in the "no-trade" case.) Consequently, GWP has improved by 937.5 barrels of tea and 3,437.5 bushels of corn.

Chapter 5

ST-2 a. Expected return, $\hat{r} = 0.05(-20\%) + 0.25(-5\%) + 0.4(10\%) + 0.25(25\%) + 0.05(40\%)$
$= -1\% + -1.25\% + 4.00\% + 6.25\% + 2.00\%$
$= 10.00\%$.

b. Standard deviation $= [0.05(-20\% - 10\%)^2 + 0.25(-5\% - 10\%)^2 + 0.4(10\% - 10\%)^2$
$+ 0.25(25\% - 10\%)^2 + 0.05(40\% - 10\%)^2]^{1/2}$
$= [0.0045 + 0.005625 + 0 + 0.005625 + 0.0045]^{1/2}$
$= [0.02025]^{1/2} = 0.142302495 \approx 14.23\%$.

c. CV = Standard deviation/Expected return.
$= 14.23\%/10\% = 1.423$.

ST-3 a. IP = I + r*I
$= 0.0425 + (0.025)(0.0425)$
$= 0.0435625$
$= 4.35625\% \approx 4.36\%$.

b. $r_{RF} = r^* + IP$
$= 2.50\% + 4.36\%$
$= 6.86\%$.

c. $RP_M = r_M - r_{RF}$
$0.0575 = r_M - 0.0686$
$0.1261 = r_M$
$12.61\% = r_M$.

d. $r = r_{RF} + (r_M - r_{RF})b_V$
   $\quad = r_{RF} + (RP_M)b_V$
   $\quad = 6.86\% + (5.75\%)(1.50)$
   $\quad = 6.86\% + 8.625\%$
   $\quad = 15.485\% \approx 15.5\%.$

e. The investor's expected return, r̂, of 16 percent is greater than the stock's required return, r, of 15.5 percent. Therefore, the investor would purchase the Valdez stock.

ST-4 $1.1 = 1/20(0.6) + (19/20)b.$
   b is the average beta for the other 19 stocks.
   $1.07 = (19/20)b.$
   New beta $= 1.07 + 1/20(1.5) = 1.145.$

Chapter 6

ST-2   a. Looking back at the income statement, we realize that the depreciation and amortization expense can be found as the difference between EBITDA and EBIT. Therefore, we need to break down NOPAT to determine EBIT:

$$NOPAT = EBIT(1 - T)$$
$$\$14,000,000 = EBIT(1 - 0.4)$$
$$\$14,000,000 = EBIT(0.6)$$
$$\$23,333,333 = EBIT.$$

Now that we have EBIT, we can find the depreciation and amortization expense by subtracting EBIT from EBITDA, which is given in the problem.

EBITDA	$30,000,000
Depreciation and amortization	− ? ? ? ? ? ? ?
EBIT	$23,333,333

Therefore, depreciation and amortization expense is equal to $6,666,667.

b. To get the firm's interest expense, we must use the income statement to determine earnings before taxes (EBT). Then, we can subtract EBT from EBIT to find the interest expense.

EBIT	$23,333,333
Int	− ? ? ? ? ? ? ?
EBT	
Taxes	
NI	$ 8,500,000

$$NI = EBT(1 - T)$$
$$\$8,500,000 = EBT(0.6)$$
$$\$14,166,667 = EBT.$$

Interest expense is simply the difference between EBIT and EBT.

$$EBIT - Int = EBT$$
$$\$23,333,333 - Int = \$14,166,667$$
$$\$9,166,666 = Int.$$

c. Remember, free cash flow (FCF) can be calculated as after-tax operating income less net capital expenditures. Therefore,

$$FCF = EBIT(1 - T) - \text{Net capital expenditures}$$
$$= \$23,333,333(1 - 0.4) - \$10,000,000$$
$$= \$14,000,000 - \$10,000,000$$
$$= \$4,000,000.$$

d. Recall, EVA is after-tax operating income less the after-tax capital costs.

$$EVA = EBIT(1 - T) - \text{AT capital costs}$$
$$= \$14,000,000 - \$11,500,000$$
$$= \$2,500,000.$$

ST-3   Write down equations with given data, then find the unknowns:

$$\text{Profit margin} = \frac{\text{NI}}{\text{S}} = 0.08.$$

$$\text{Debt ratio} = \frac{\text{D}}{\text{A}} = \frac{\text{D}}{\$250,000,000} = 0.45; \text{D} = \$112,500,000.$$

$$\text{TA turnover} = \frac{\text{S}}{\text{A}} = 3.6 = \frac{\text{S}}{\$250,000,000} = 3.6; \text{S} = \$900,000,000.$$

Now plug sales into profit margin ratio to find NI:

$$\frac{\text{NI}}{\$900,000,000} = 0.08; \text{NI} = \$72,000,000.$$

Now set up an income statement:

Sales	$900,000,000	
Cost of goods sold		
EBIT	$128,437,500	(EBIT = EBT + Interest)
Interest	8,437,500	($112,500,000 × 0.075 = $8,437,500)
EBT	$120,000,000	(EBT = $72,000,000/(1 − T) = $120,000,000)
Taxes (40%)	48,000,000	
NI	$ 72,000,000	

Chapter 7

ST-2   Translation of Balance Sheet for Foreign Subsidiary
(Remeasured from local currency to dollars using the temporal method)

	Foreign	$/LC	$ Equivalent
Cash	LC 42.5	0.009500	$ 0.4
Accounts receivable	50.4	0.009500	0.5
Accounts receivable from intrafirm	884.9	0.009500	8.4
Inventories	2,613.8	0.008000	20.9
Prepaid expenses	—		—
Current assets	LC 3,591.6		$30.2
Net plant and equipment	4,467.5	0.008500	38.0
Total assets	LC 8,059.1		$68.2
Accounts payable	LC 896.9	0.009500	$ 8.5
Accounts payable to intrafirm	1,258.4	0.009500	12.0
Notes payable	366.7	0.009500	3.5
Current maturities LTD	94.4	0.009500	0.9
Accrued liabilities	944.4	0.009500	9.0
Current liabilities	LC 3,560.8		$33.9
Long-term debt	1,295.5	0.009500	12.3
Total liabilities	LC 4,856.3		$46.2
Preferred stock	—		—
Common stock	1,280.0	0.007500	9.6
Retained earnings	1,922.8		12.4
Total equity	LC 3,202.8		$22.0
Cumulative translation adjustment	—		—
Total capital	LC 8,059.1		$68.2

MST International December 31, 2004, Financial Statements

Income Statements (USD)

	USA	Foreign	Consolidated
Sales	$5,678.3	$517.3	$6,195.6
Cost of goods sold	3,974.8	362.1	4,336.9
General and administrative	903.4	35.8	939.2
EBITDA	$ 800.1	$119.4	$ 919.5
Depreciation and amortization	361.0	55.6	416.6
EBIT	$ 439.1	$ 63.8	$ 502.9
Interest	77.4	12.4	89.8
EBT	$ 361.7	$ 51.4	$ 413.1
Taxes	144.7	20.6	165.3
NI before preferred	$ 217.0	$ 30.8	$ 247.8
Preferred stock dividends	45.5	—	45.5
Net income to common stockholders	$ 171.5	$ 30.8	$ 202.3

Balance Sheets (USD)

	USA	Foreign	Consolidated
Cash	$ 695.0	$ 0.4	$ 695.4
Accounts receivable	1,132.1	0.5	1,132.6
Accounts receivable from intrafirm	12.0	8.4	—
Inventories	914.8	20.9	935.7
Prepaid expenses	—	—	—
Current assets	$2,753.9	$30.2	$2,763.7
Net plant and equipment	3,403.6	38.0	3,441.6
Investment in foreign subsidiary	22.0	—	—
Total assets	$6,179.5	$68.2	$6,205.3
Accounts payable	$ 225.3	$ 8.5	$ 233.8
Accounts payable to intrafirm	8.4	12.0	—
Notes payable	284.2	3.5	287.7
Current maturities LTD	219.4	0.9	220.3
Accrued liabilities	335.6	9.0	344.6
Current liabilities	$1,072.9	$33.9	$1,086.4
Long-term debt	1,455.2	12.3	1,467.5
Total liabilities	$2,528.1	$46.2	$2,553.9
Preferred stock	600.0	—	600.0
Common stock	2,050.0	9.6	2,050.0
Retained earnings	1,001.4	12.4	1,001.4
Total equity	$3,051.4	$22.0	$3,051.4
Total capital	$6,179.5	$68.2	$6,205.3

ST-3   Translation of Balance Sheet for Foreign Subsidiary
        (Restated from local currency to dollars using the current rate method)

	Foreign	$/LC	$ Equivalent
Cash	LC 498.2	1.025	$ 510.7
Accounts receivable	2,038.1	1.025	2,089.0
Accounts receivable from intrafirm	125.0	1.025	128.1
Inventories	803.4	1.025	823.5
Prepaid expenses	—	1.025	—
Current assets	LC 3,464.7		$3,551.3
Net plant and equipment	4,440.5	1.025	4,551.5
Total assets	LC 7,905.2		$8,102.8
Accounts payable	LC 305.6	1.025	$ 313.3
Accounts payable to intrafirm	85.0	1.025	87.1
Notes payable	576.1	1.025	590.5
Current maturities LTD	57.0	1.025	58.4
Accrued liabilities	923.5	1.025	946.6
Current liabilities	LC 1,947.2		$1,995.9
Long-term debt	2,257.2	1.025	2,313.6
Total liabilities	LC 4,204.4		$4,309.5
Preferred stock	—		—
Common stock	2,205.0	0.620	1,367.1
Retained earnings	1,495.8		435.3
Total equity	LC 3,700.8		$1,802.4
Cumulative translation adjustment			1,990.9
Total capital	LC 7,905.2		$8,102.8

Hubbard International December 31, 2004, Financial Statements

	USA	Foreign	Consolidated
Income Statements (USD)			
Sales	$13,977.3	$8,537.6	$22,514.9
Cost of goods sold	9,510.7	6,103.0	15,613.7
General and administrative	2,223.7	1,339.6	3,563.3
EBITDA	$ 2,242.9	$1,095.0	$ 3,337.9
Depreciation and amortization	888.7	479.7	1,368.4
EBIT	$ 1,354.2	$ 615.3	$ 1,969.5
Interest	190.4	89.0	279.4
EBT	$ 1,163.8	$ 526.3	$ 1,690.1
Taxes	465.5	210.5	676.0
NI before preferred	$ 698.3	$ 315.8	$ 1,014.1
Preferred stock dividends	112.0	—	112.0
Net income to common stockholders	$ 586.3	$ 315.8	$ 902.1
Balance Sheets (USD)			
Cash	$ 1,710.9	$ 510.7	$ 2,221.6
Accounts receivable	2,786.8	2,089.0	4,875.8
Accounts receivable from intrafirm	87.1	128.1	—
Inventories	2,251.9	823.5	3,075.4
Prepaid expenses	—	—	—

	USA	Foreign	Consolidated
Current assets	$ 6,836.7	$3,551.3	$10,172.8
Net plant and equipment	8,378.0	4,551.5	12,929.5
Investment in foreign subsidiary	1,802.4	—	—
Total assets	$17,017.1	$8,102.8	$23,102.3
Accounts payable	$ 600.3	$ 313.3	$ 913.6
Accounts payable to intrafirm	128.1	87.1	—
Notes payable	522.8	590.5	1,113.3
Current maturities LTD	540.2	58.4	598.6
Accrued liabilities	1,200.7	946.6	2,147.3
Current liabilities	$ 2,992.1	$1,995.9	$ 4,772.8
Long-term debt	3,567.7	2,313.6	5,881.3
Total liabilities	$ 6,559.8	$4,309.5	$10,654.1
Preferred stock	500.0	—	500.0
Common stock	5,000.0	1,367.1	5,000.0
Retained earnings	4,957.3	435.3	4,957.3
Total equity	$ 9,957.3	$1,802.4	$ 9,957.3
Cumulative translation adjustment		1,990.9	1,990.9
Total capital	$17,017.1	$8,102.8	$23,102.3

Chapter 8

ST-2

N = 30; I = 5; PMT = 30; FV = 1000. Solve for PV = $692.55.
Number of bonds: $5,000,000/$692.55 ≈ 7,220 bonds.*

*Rounded up to next whole bond.

ST-3

Step 1: Enter zeros for each unknown PMT as follows and solve for the NPV of the cash flow stream:
$CF_0 = -1000$; $CF_{1-2} = 50$; $CF_3 = 0$; $CF_4 = 1000$; I = 4.52. Solve for NPV = $68.4736.

Step 2: Calculate the FV of the PV determined in Step 1:
N = 2; I = 4.52; PV = -68.4736; PMT = 0. Solve for FV = $74.80351.

Step 3: Determine the semiannual coupon payment in Year 2:
N = 2; I = 4.52; PV = -74.80351; FV = 0. Solve for PMT = $39.96 ≈ $40.

Chapter 9

ST-2   a. Here are the relevant data to solve this part of the problem:

$D_0 = \$2.05$; $g_1 = 25\%$; $g_2 = 15\%$; $g_3 = 10\%$; $g_n = 6\%$; and $r_s = 12\%$.

Step 1: Calculate dividends during the nonconstant growth period:
$D_1 = D_0 \times (1 + g_1) = \$2.05 \times 1.25 = \$2.5625$.
$D_2 = D_1 \times (1 + g_2) = \$2.5625 \times 1.15 = \$2.946875$.
$D_3 = D_2 \times (1 + g_3) = \$2.946875 \times 1.10 = \$3.2415625$.

Step 2: Calculate the stock price at t = 3 when dividend growth becomes constant:

$$\hat{P}_3 = \frac{D_4}{(r_s - g)} = \frac{D_3(1 + g_n)}{(r_s - g)} = \frac{\$3.2415625(1.06)}{0.12 - 0.06} = \$57.2676042.$$

Step 3: Now we can enter the relevant data on a time line.

```
0    12%    1         2          3             4
|           |         |          |             |
         2.5625   2.946875   3.2415625
                            57.2676042
                            60.5091667
```

Using your financial calculator, solve for the firm's stock price. Enter the following data:

$CF_0 = 0$; $CF_1 = 2.5625$; $CF_2 = 2.946875$; $CF_3 = 60.5091667$; I = 12. Then, solve for NPV = P_0 = $47.71.

b. Step 1: Calculate the free cash flow amount (in millions of dollars):

$$FCF_1 = EBIT(1 - T) + \text{Depreciation} - \frac{\text{Capital}}{\text{expenditures}} \pm \Delta\left(\begin{array}{c}\text{Net operating}\\\text{working capital}\end{array}\right)$$

$$= \$650 + \$75 - \$240 - \$30$$

$$= \$455.$$

Step 2: Calculate the firm value today (in millions of dollars) using the constant growth corporate value model:

$$\text{Firm value} = \frac{FCF_1}{WACC - g}$$

$$= \frac{\$455}{0.09 - 0.04}$$

$$= \frac{\$455}{0.05}$$

$$= \$9,100.$$

This is the total firm value today.

Step 3: Determine the market value of the equity (in millions of dollars) and price per share:

$$MV_{Total} = MV_{Equity} + MV_{Debt}$$
$$\$9,100 = MV_{Equity} + \$1,750$$
$$MV_{Equity} = \$7,350.$$

This is today's market value of the firm's equity. Divide by the number of shares to find the current price per share: $7,350/150 = $49.00.

Chapter 10

ST-2 a. Cost of U.S. dollar-denominated bonds:

N = 15 × 2 = 30; PV = −920; PMT = 0.08/2 × 1,000 = 40; FV = 1,000; i = r_d/2 = 4.49%; r_d = 8.98%.

$r_d(1 - T)$ = 8.98%(0.6) = 5.39%. Since the bonds are selling at a discount, use YTM as r_d.

Need to determine the cost of the foreign-denominated debt to see which bonds should be issued.

Need to convert the exchange rates so they're stated as $/foreign currency.

Spot exchange rate: $1/AUD 1.54 = $0.6494 per Australian dollar.
Forward exchange rate: $1/AUD 1.57 = $0.6369 per Australian dollar.

U.S. dollar has appreciated relative to the Australian dollar.

$$\Delta FX^e = (0.6369 - 0.6494)/0.6494$$
$$= -0.0191.$$

Cost of foreign-denominated debt $= r_d(1 - T)(1 + \Delta FX^e) + \Delta FX^e$
$$= (0.0539)(1 - 0.0191) - 0.0191$$
$$= 0.033771 = 3.3771\%.$$

Because the cost of the Australian debt is lower, the firm will issue Australian dollar-denominated bonds.

b. $r_{ps} = \$5.80/[(\$105)(1 - 0.025)] = 0.056654 = 5.6654\%.$

c. Global CAPM:

$$r_s = r_{RF} + (RP_W)(b_{i, W})$$
$$= 5.25\% + (4.5\%)(0.75)$$
$$= 5.25\% + 3.375\%$$
$$= 8.625\%.$$

d. WACC $= (w_d)[r_d(1 - T)(1 + \Delta FX^e) + \Delta FX^e] + w_{ps}r_{ps} + w_c r_s$
$$= (0.45)(0.033771) + (0.05)(0.056654) + (0.50)(0.08625)$$
$$= 0.061155 \approx 6.12\%.$$

e. Global CAPM with partially segmented capital markets:

$$r_s = r_{RF} + (RP_W)(b_{i, W}) + (SRP_j)(b_{i, Seg})$$
$$= 5.25\% + (4.5\%)(0.75) + (8\%)(0.8)$$
$$= 5.25\% + 3.375\% + 6.4\%$$
$$= 15.025\%.$$

f. Country-spread approach:

$$r_s = r_{RF} + (RP_M)[0.6(\sigma_j/\sigma_M)] + \text{Country credit spread}$$
$$= 5.25\% + (11\% - 5.25\%)[0.6(1.4167)] + 6\%$$
$$= 5.25\% + 4.8876\% + 6\%$$
$$= 16.1376\%.$$

However, this is the cost of equity for an average investment in Argentina. Since this is a risky project, 2 percent is added to the estimate: $16.1376\% + 2\% = 18.1376\%.$

g. Country-risk-rating approach:

$$r_{sj}/2 = a + d_{cr}\ln(\text{Country-risk rating}_j)$$
$$r_{sj} = [0.25 - 0.0475(\ln 40)] \times 2$$
$$= [0.25 - 0.0475(3.688879)] \times 2$$
$$= (0.074778)(2)$$
$$= 0.149556 = 14.9556\%.$$

Again, 2 percent must be added to the estimate since this is a riskier project than the average investment in Argentina: $14.9556\% + 2\% = 16.9556\%.$

h. Accept the project, since the 20 percent expected return is greater than the required return estimated in all three approaches.

Chapter 11

ST-2 a. Depreciation cash flows:

Year	Depreciation Rates	Depreciable Basis	Annual Depreciation
1	0.33	£5,000,000	£1,650,000
2	0.45	5,000,000	2,250,000
3	0.15	5,000,000	750,000
4	0.07	5,000,000	350,000
			£5,000,000

Analysis in pounds:

Year	0	1	2	3	4
Project cost	(5,000,000)				
NOWC*	(300,000)				
Sales		3,000,000	4,000,000	5,000,000	2,000,000
Operating costs (75%)		2,250,000	3,000,000	3,750,000	1,500,000
Depreciation		1,650,000	2,250,000	750,000	350,000
Operating income before taxes		(900,000)	(1,250,000)	500,000	150,000
Taxes (40%)		(360,000)	(500,000)	200,000	60,000
Operating income after taxes		(540,000)	(750,000)	300,000	90,000
Plus: Depreciation		1,650,000	2,250,000	750,000	350,000
Operating cash flow		1,110,000	1,500,000	1,050,000	440,000
Recovery of NOWC					300,000
Net cash flows (stated in pounds)	(5,300,000)	1,110,000	1,500,000	1,050,000	740,000

*An increase in inventories is a use of funds for the company, and an increase in accounts payable is a source of funds for the company. Thus, the change in net operating working capital will be £200,000 − £500,000 = −£300,000 at time 0.

Using your financial calculator, enter the pound cash flows as follows: $CF_0 = -5300000$; $CF_1 = 1110000$; $CF_2 = 1500000$; $CF_3 = 1050000$; $CF_4 = 740000$; $I = 10$; and then solve for $NPV = -£1,756,929$. The NPV stated in dollars is $-1,756,929 \times 1.65 = -\$2,898,933$. Therefore, because $NPV < 0$, the firm would not enter the new line of business.

b. Begin with the net cash flows stated in pounds that were found in part a:

	0	1	2	3	4
Cash flows (in pounds)	(5,300,000)	1,110,000	1,500,000	1,050,000	740,000
Exchange rate*					
$/£	$1.65	$1.6176	$1.5859	$1.5548	$1.5243
U.S. cash flows	(8,745,000)	1,795,588	2,378,893	1,632,573	1,128,015

*Since the pound depreciates relative to the U.S. dollar by 2 percent per year during the project's life, fewer dollars will be required in each year to purchase one pound. The expected exchange rate in Year 1 is calculated as $1.65 ÷ 1.02 = $1.6176.

The project's NPV is calculated by entering the cash flows as follows: $CF_0 = -8745000$; $CF_1 = 1795588$; $CF_2 = 2378893$; $CF_3 = 1632573$; $CF_4 = 1128015$; $I = 9.6$; and then solve for $NPV = -\$3,104,472$. Because $NPV < 0$, the firm will not enter the line of business.

Chapter 12

ST-2 a.

	0	1	2	3	4	5
Euro cash flows	(4,500,000)	750,000	750,000	750,000	750,000	750,000
Exchange rate*						
€/$	€0.89	€0.8989	€0.9079	€0.9170	€0.9261	€0.9354
U.S. cash flows	(5,056,180)	834,353	826,092	817,913	809,815	801,797

*Since the euro depreciates relative to the U.S. dollar by 1 percent per year during the project's life, more euros will be required in each year to purchase one dollar. The expected exchange rate in Year 1 is calculated as €0.89 × 1.01 = €0.8989.

Using a financial calculator, enter the dollar cash flows as follows: $CF_0 = -5056180$; $CF_1 = 834353$; $CF_2 = 826092$; $CF_3 = 817913$; $CF_4 = 809815$; $CF_5 = 801797$; $I = 9$; and then solve for $NPV = -\$1,869,028$.

b. At t = 5, the additional expected euro cash flow is calculated as follows:

$(0.4)(€8,500,000) + (0.6)(€0) = €3,400,000.$

Note that at t = 5 you will not do the additional part of the project if its NPV is negative, so that's why we use zero in the calculation to determine the expected additional cash flow in Year 5.

This cash flow can be translated into U.S. dollars as follows: 3,400,000/0.9354 = $3,634,813.

The present value of this cash flow is calculated as $3,634,813/(1.09)^5 = $2,362,379.

Therefore, this project will turn out to have a positive cash flow after considering the embedded real option: $-$1,869,028 + $2,362,379 = $493,351.$

Chapter 13

ST-2   a. In the 1958 MM paper under the original restrictive assumptions, the firm's value with debt is equal to its value without debt of $10 billion.

b. The firm's value according to MM with corporate taxes is given by the following formula:

$$
\begin{aligned}
V_L &= V_U + TD \\
&= \$10,000,000,000 + (0.35)(\$2,000,000,000) \\
&= \$10,000,000,000 + \$700,000,000 \\
&= \$10,700,000,000.
\end{aligned}
$$

c. The firm's value according to the Miller model with personal taxes included is given by the following formula:

$$
V_L = V_U + \left[1 - \frac{(1 - T_c)(1 - T_s)}{(1 - T_d)}\right]D
$$

$$
= \$10,000,000,000 + \left[1 - \frac{(1 - 0.35)(1 - 0.15)}{(1 - 0.33)}\right]\$2,000,000,000
$$

$$
= \$10,000,000,000 + \left[1 - \frac{(0.65)(0.85)}{(0.67)}\right]\$2,000,000,000
$$

$$
= \$10,000,000,000 + (0.175373)(\$2,000,000,000)
$$

$$
= \$10,000,000,000 + \$350,746,269
$$

$$
= \$10,350,746,269.
$$

ST-3   The capital budget is $6 billion. Of that budget, 45 percent will be paid for with common equity to keep the capital structure the same. The equity will come from additions to retained earnings or net income.

$0.45 \times $6 billion capital budget = $2.7 billion.

This leaves $7 - $2.7 = $4.3 billion of net income to pay as dividends.

Payout ratio = $4.3 billion/$7.0 billion = 61.43%.

Chapter 14

ST-2   a. Inventory conversion period = DIH = $\dfrac{\text{Inventories}}{\text{Cost of goods sold}/365}$

$$
= \frac{\$25,000,000}{(0.45 \times \$365,000,000)/365}
$$

$$
= 55.56 \text{ days.}
$$

b. Receivables collection period = DSO = $\dfrac{\text{Accounts receivable}}{\text{Sales}/365}$

$$
= \frac{\$20,000,000}{\$365,000,000/365}
$$

$$
= 20 \text{ days.}
$$

c. Cash conversion period = DIH + DSO − DPO
$$= 55.56 + 20 - 35$$
$$= 40.56 \text{ days.}$$

ST-3 a. $\dfrac{\text{Nominal}}{\text{Annual}}_{\text{Cost}} = \dfrac{\text{Discount percent}}{100 - \text{Discount percent}} \times \dfrac{365 \text{ days}}{\underset{\text{is outstanding}}{\text{Days credit}} - \underset{\text{period}}{\text{Discount}}}$

$$= \frac{2}{98} \times \frac{365}{35 - 10}$$

$$= 0.020408 \times 14.6$$

$$= 0.2980 = 29.80\%.$$

b. Effective annual cost = $[(1.020408)^{14.6} - 1] = 1.3431 - 1 = 0.3431 = 34.31\%.$

Chapter 15

ST-2   Structure of Forward Market Hedge for Payable

Today	30 Days from Now
	1. Cash payment of ¥5.5 million due.
2. Execute forward contract to pay ¥5.5 million/ ¥112.5/$ = $48,888.89 and receive ¥5.5 million in 30 days.	
	3. Pay $48,888.89 to fulfill the forward contract and receive ¥5.5 million in return to pay payable.

Structure of Money Market Hedge for Payable

Today	30 Days from Now
	1. Cash payment of ¥5.5 million due.
2. Take dollars, convert at the spot rate of 1/¥113.25/$ into yen.	
3. Invest the yen for 30 days at a rate of 0.12 percent. Dollars needed are calculated as ¥5,500,000/1.0012 × 1/¥113.25 = $48,506.91.	
	4. Receive principal plus interest from yen investment. Pay ¥5.5 million payable.

Structure of OTC Option Hedge for Payable

Today	30 Days from Now
1. Purchase a 30-day call option on ¥5,500,000. So, ¥5,500,000 × 0.012 × 1/¥113.25/$ = $582.78 payable immediately. The cost of the option compounded forward 30 days is $582.78(1.007875) = $587.37.	2a. Company will let option expire and purchase yen in the spot market, if the dollar has strengthened over the 30-day period. The dollar cost of the payable is ¥5,500,000 × Spot rate + $587.37.

OR

Today	30 Days from Now
	2b. Company exercises the option and purchases yen at ¥112/$, if the dollar weakens. The dollar cost of the payable is ¥5,500,000 × (1/¥112/$) + $587.37 = $49,694.51.

Break-even point between OTC and forward or money market hedge $= \dfrac{\$48,888.89 - \$587.37}{¥5,500,000} = \$0.008782/¥.$

Break-even point between OTC option and unhedged position $= \dfrac{\$49,694.51}{¥5,500,000} = \$0.009035/¥.$

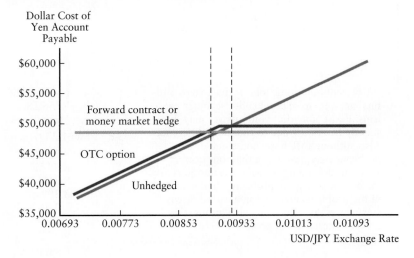

Chapter 16

ST-2 Capital Export Neutrality: Taxation of Foreign-Source Income

Country X (Tax rate = 40%)		Country Y (Tax rate = 20%)	
Domestic income	$25,000,000	Foreign income	$10,000,000
Taxes (40%)	10,000,000	Taxes (20%)	2,000,000
Net income	$15,000,000	Net income	$ 8,000,000
Dividend received from Y	$ 8,000,000		
X's tax due on dividend	$ 4,000,000	($10,000,000 × 0.4)	
Less FTC	−2,000,000		
Tax still owed to X on dividend	$ 2,000,000		
Net dividend received	$ 6,000,000	($8,000,000 − $2,000,000)	

a. Dividend received from Country Y is $8,000,000.

b. Country X's tax due on Y's dividend is $10,000,000 × 0.4 = $4,000,000.

c. FTC = $10,000,000 × 0.2 = $2,000,000.

d. Net dividend received = $8,000,000 − $2,000,000 = $6,000,000.

e. Total after-tax income = $15,000,000 + $6,000,000 = $21,000,000.

f. Effective tax rate = ($10,000,000 + $2,000,000 + $2,000,000)/$35,000,000 = 40%.

APPENDIX C

Answers to End-of-Chapter Problems

We present here some intermediate steps and final answers to selected end-of-chapter problems. Please note that your answer may differ slightly from ours due to rounding differences. Also, although we hope not, some of the problems may have more than one correct solution, depending on what assumptions are made in working the problem. Finally, many of the problems involve some verbal discussion as well as numerical calculations; this verbal material is not presented here.

2-1 a. I = 3.6675%.
b. r_{RF} = 6%.

2-2 a. r_{RF} = 5.7%.
b. RP = 2.8%.

2-3 ERP = 0.3%.

2-4 a. LC4.115854/$.

2-5 a. CRP + ERP = 0.4%.
b. r_{BBB} = 8.5%.

2-6 a. LC2.66/$.

2-7 r_{RF} = 5.2672%.

2-8 a. IP = 3.2672%.
b. r_{RF} = 5.3672%.

2-9 a. IP = 2.5%.
b. r_{RF} = 5.25%.
c. r = 9.00%.

3-1 $0.1605/Dkr.

3-2 a. kr5.9049/SwF.
b. SwF0.1694/kr.

3-3 a. JD0.7093/$.
b. $1.4098/JD.

3-4 $r_\$$ = 2.5%.

3-5 a. R21.6145/A$.
b. A$0.0463/R.

3-6 a. %ΔFX = −2.92%.
b. 1.264490; 105.711495.
c. −0.93%; +1.17%.
d. $2,186.40.

3-7 a. NZ$129.99.
b. R556.28.
c. Mex$956.45.

3-8 SwF1.2997/$.

3-9 a. +3.30%.
b. 6.0875%.
c. 9.71%.
d. 3.30%.
e. −3.30%.
f. −3.30%.

4-1 b. Country C; return ranking = 22.
c. Country B; risk ranking = 10.
d. Overall country ranking: B, C, D, and A.
e. Overall country ranking: C, D, and A.

4-2 a. Yes, Country X.
b. Country Y.
c. Country Y: wheat; Country X: widgets.
d. P_{Wheat} = 1.5 crates of widgets.
e. Country Y; +1,200 bushels of wheat and +34,600 crates of widgets; ΔGWP = +1,200 bushels of wheat and +34,600 crates of widgets.
f. P_{Wheat} = 0.72 crate of widgets.
g. Country X; +1,200 bushels of wheat and +34,600 crates of widgets; ΔGWP = +1,200 bushels of wheat and +34,600 crates of widgets.
h. Both; Country X: +900 bushels of wheat and +24,225 crates of widgets; Country Y: +300 bushels of wheat and +10,375 crates of widgets; ΔGWP = +1,200 bushels of wheat and +34,600 crates of widgets.

4-3 b. Country P; return ranking = 16.
c. Country M; risk ranking = 7.
d. Overall country ranking: N, M, P, and O.

e. Overall country ranking: M, P, and O.

4-4   a. Yes, Country N.
 b. Country M.
 c. Country M: coffee; Country N: corn.
 d. P_{Coffee} = 1.33 bushels of corn.
 e. Country M; +1,500 bushels of corn and +2,250 bags of coffee; ΔGWP = +1,500 bushels of corn and +2,250 bags of coffee.
 f. P_{Coffee} = 1.11 bushels of corn.
 g. Country N; +1,500 bushels of corn and +2,250 bags of coffee; ΔGWP = +1,500 bushels of corn and +2,250 bags of coffee.
 h. Both; Country M: +300 bushels of corn and +1,250 bags of coffee; Country N: +1,200 bushels of corn and +1,000 bags of coffee; ΔGWP = +1,500 bushels of corn and +2,250 bags of coffee.

5-1   a. RP_M = 0.0575.
 b. b_{P1} = 0.9; b_{P2} = 1.0.
 c. r_{P1} = 10.425%; r_{P2} = 11.00%.
5-2 r_p = 13%; b_p = 1.25.
5-3   a. $\hat{r}$ = 11.95%.
 b. σ = 23.6421%.
 c. CV = 1.9784.
5-4   a. IP = 3.06%.
 b. r_{RF} = 5.06%.
 c. RP_M = 10.46%.
 d. r = 9.65%.
5-5 r_p = 10.24%.
5-6   a. b_p = 0.95.
 b. r_{RF} = 4.8%.
 c. r_D = 13.8%.
5-7 b_X = 2.175.
5-8 r_p = 14.20%; b = 1.4833.

6-1 $8,480,769.
6-2   EVA = $3,412,500.
6-3 P_0 = $50.00.
6-4 ΔROE = 2.15%.
6-5   New PM = 15.74%.
6-6   a. $NOPAT_{04}$ = $731,250,000.
 b. $NOWC_{04}$ = $1,440,000,000.
 c. TOC_{04} = $3,690,000,000.
 d. FCF_{04} = $449,050,000.
6-7   New ROE = 19.9%.
6-8   TIE = 4.66$\times$.
6-9   New CR = 1.91$\times$.
6-10 ΔStock price = $6.41.

7-1   a. Temporal method.
 c. ($ in thousands) Total assets = $156,519.0; A/P = $14,229.2; R/E = $68,380.5.

7-2   a. Current rate method.
 c. ($ in thousands) Net plant and equipment = $749.3; C/S = $204.0; CTA = ($10.80).
7-3   a. Temporal method.
 c. ($ in thousands) A/R = $12.16; Total assets = $26.46; C/S = $4.13.
7-4   HK: ($ in thousands) Net plant and equipment = $3,016.5; Total assets = $4,792.9; R/E = $1,823.0; GB: ($ in thousands) Cash = $1,485.2; N/P = $1,061.8; CTA = ($1,472.8); Consolidated: ($ in thousands) A/R = $5,930.7; Total assets = $32,164.7; Total liabilities = $17,379.4.
7-5   Mex: Inventories = $233.2; Total assets = $699.7; N/P = $29.3; R/E = $239.4; Ger: Cash = $222.6; Total assets = $3,184.3; Total liabilities = $1,771.0; R/E = $913.3; Arg: Net plant and equipment = $110.4; Accrued liabilities = $21.6; Total liabilities = $61.8; Total capital = $202.5; Consolidated: A/R = $1,581.5; Net plant and equipment = $4,724.5; Total assets = $8,105.0; Total liabilities = $3,717.6; Total common equity = $3,887.4.

8-1   YTM = 5.35%; YTC = 5.21%.
8-2   a. CY = 10.21%.
 b. Capital gains yield = 1.79%.
8-3 V_B = $810.92.
8-4   a. CY = 10.59%.
 b. YTM = 11.57%.
 c. V_B = $878.95.
8-5   Total value of debt = $18,768,895.
8-6 V_B = $1,326.72.
8-7   Open market purchase = $43,117.58.
8-8   PMT = $54.11.

9-1 $\hat{P}_3$ = $47.64.
9-2 P_0 = $60.67.
9-3 $\hat{P}_0$ = $32.00.
9-4 P_0 = $91.78.
9-5 P_0 = $36.48.
9-6 $\hat{P}_0$ = $30.17.
9-7 P_0 = $25.00.
9-8   a. P_0 = $14.28.
 b. P_5 = $21.19.
9-9   a. FCF_1 = $325,000,000.
 b. P_0 = $56.00.

10-1   a. $r_d(1 - T)$ = 5.2%.
10-2 r_{ps} = 7.14%.
10-3 r_s = 9.56%.
10-4 r_s = 11.33%.

10-5 $r_d(1 - T) = 4.5\%$; $r_{ps} = 7.2\%$;
        $r_s = 10.52\%$; WACC = 7.043%.

10-6   a. U.S. $r_d(1 - T) = 4.2\%$.
        b. $\Delta FX^e = 0.048193$; Yen $r_d(1 - T) = 9.22\%$.

10-7   a. $r_s = 10.45\%$.

10-8   a. $r_s = 24.04\%$.
        b. $r_s = 26.00\%$.
        c. $r_s = 23.35\%$.

10-9   a. $r_d(1 - T) = 3.91\%$.
        b. $\Delta FX^e = -0.018634$; Pound $r_d(1 - T) = 1.98\%$.
        c. Issue pound-denominated debt.

10-10   a. $r_d(1 - T) = 4.74\%$.
        b. $\Delta FX^e = 0.014815$; SwF $r_d(1 - T) = 6.29\%$.
        c. Issue U.S.-dollar-denominated debt.

10-11   a. Weaken.
        b. Higher.
        c. $\Delta FX^e = 0.022989$; Euro $r_d(1 - T) = 7.29\%$; United States.
        d. $\Delta FX^e = -0.01111$; Euro $r_d(1 - T) = 3.71\%$.
        e. Finland; 3.71%.

10-12   a. $r_s = 11.5\%$.
        b. $r_s = 11.75\%$.
        c. $r_s = 10.99\%$.
        d. $r_s = 11.41\%$.
        e. $r_s = 10.50\%$.
        f. $r_s = 15.90\%$.
        g. $r_s = 21.75\%$.
        h. $r_s = 16.28\%$.

10-13   a. $r_d(1 - T) = 3.83\%$.
        b. $r_{ps} = 5.80\%$.
        c. $r_s = 12.90\%$.
        d. $r_s = 12.475\%$.
        e. $r_s = 12.2\%$.
        f. $r_s = 12.525\%$.
        g. WACC = 7.80%.
        h. (1). $\Delta FX^e = -0.014085$;
                  CAD $r_d(1 - T) = 2.37\%$.
            (2). 2.37%.
        i. $r_s = 10.51\%$.
        j. WACC = 6.1%.

10-14   a. WACC = 13.27%.
        b. $WACC_{Communications} = 9.14\%$.
        c. $WACC_{R\&D} = 15.04\%$.
        d. Accept only Project M.

11-1   a. 4.29 years.
        b. Longer.

11-2   a. $684.26.
        b. NPV = £433.7348; accept project.
        c. NPV = −£748.04; reject project.

11-3   a. IRR = 15.51%.
        b. IRR = 15.51%.

11-4 $2,905,859.11.

11-5 $2,436,147.30.

11-6 $964,000.

11-7

Criterion	Project A	Project Z
Payback	3.6 yrs.; no	2.5 yrs.; yes
NPV	$19,813.03; yes	$15,708.23; yes
IRR	14.65%; yes	17.83%; yes

11-8   NPV = $819.27.

11-9   a. NPV = $5,293.04; IRR = 12.17%.
        b. NPV = ¥621,535.22; IRR = 12.17%.
        c. NPV = ¥1,044,490.97; IRR = 12.73%.

11-10   a. $IRR_X = 15.13\%$; $IRR_Y = 12.06\%$.
        c. WACC < 8.61%, choose Project Y and 8.61% < WACC < 15.13%, choose Project X.

11-11   a. $NPV_A = \$450,481.67$; $NPV_B = \$363,213.84$; accept Project A.
        b. $NPV_A = \$654,558.24$; $NPV_B = \$513,306.78$; accept Project A.

11-12   Financial perspective, choose Slow Plan; PV of costs = −$1,606,578.21.

11-13   Payback = 6.25 years; NPV = $900.01; IRR = 9.61%.

11-14 $IRR_D = 12.76\%$.

11-15   a. NPV = $6,031,871.56.
        b. Year 4 AT $Div_€$ = €5,700,000; Year 3 AT $Div_\$$ = $4,736,842.11; NPV = −$15,935,350.98.

12-1 $3,385,199.

12-2   Year 4; NPV = $1,219.

12-3   Maximum cost = $620,360.

12-4   a. NPV = −$39,386.
        b. $47,392.

13-1   a. $V_U = V_L = \$800$ million.
        b. $V_L = \$921,600,000$.
        c. $V_L = \$885,777,778$.

13-2 $3,035,714,286.

13-3   Payout ratio = 21.05%.

13-4   D = $100,000.

13-5 $T_C = 35\%$.

13-6   a. $V_U = V_L = \$500$ million.
        b. $V_L = \$540,000,000$.
        c. $V_L = \$521,538,462$.

13-7 $6,500,000,000.

14-1   a. DIH = 60.02 days.
        b. DSO = 30.42 days.
        c. DPO = 25.96 days.
        d. CCP = 64.48 days.

14-2   a. 76.04%.
        b. 110.64%.

14-3 a. RSO: ROE = 12.36%;
         KTS: ROE = 13.44%.
     b. RSO: ROE = 11.52%;
         KTS: ROE = 10.08%.
     c. KTS.

14-4 a. A/P = $7,297,500.
     b. DIH = 123.43 days.
     c. DSO = 64.80 days.
     d. CCP = 158.23 days.
     e. ΔCCP = −44 days.

14-5 a. 12.29%.
     b. 13.01%.

14-6 a. $820.
     b. $610.

15-1 $2.50.

15-2 0.5964%.

15-3 −0.4004%; −0.51%.

15-4 $1,800.

15-6 a. $425.
     b. $212.15.
     c. 47.94%.

15-8 2.856%.

16-1 a. $23,000,000.
     b. 34.29%.

16-2 a. $10,000,000.
     b. $2,000,000.
     c. $250,000.

16-3 a. $1,700,000.
     b. $700,000.
     c. $300,000.
     d. $1,300,000.
     e. $7,800,000.
     f. 35%.

16-4 a. $8,200,000.
     b. 31.67%.

16-5 a. $43,750,000.
     b. $13,125,000.
     c. $1,875,000.

Selected Equations and Data

Chapter 1

$$\text{Value} = \text{NPV} = \frac{CF_0}{(1+r)^0} + \frac{CF_1}{(1+r)^1} + \frac{CF_2}{(1+r)^2} + \cdots + \frac{CF_n}{(1+r)^n}$$

$$= \sum_{t=0}^{n} \frac{CF_t}{(1+\text{WACC})^t}.$$

Chapter 2

$r_{RF} = r^* + I + r^*I.$

$IP = I + r^*I.$

$r = r^* + IP + RP = r_{RF} + RP.$

$r = r^* + IP + RP = r_{RF} + DRP + LP + MRP + CRP + ERP.$

Chapter 3

$\%\Delta FX_{Direct} = [(\text{Ending rate} - \text{Beginning rate})/\text{Beginning rate}] \times 100.$

$\%\Delta FX_{Indirect} = [(\text{Beginning rate} - \text{Ending rate})/\text{Ending rate}] \times 100.$

$$\begin{array}{l}\text{Forward premium} \\ \text{or discount }\%_{Direct}\end{array} = \left[\left(\begin{array}{c}\text{Forward} \\ \text{rate}\end{array} - \begin{array}{c}\text{Spot} \\ \text{rate}\end{array}\right)\Big/\begin{array}{c}\text{Spot} \\ \text{rate}\end{array}\right] \times 360/n \times 100.$$

$$\begin{array}{l}\text{Forward premium} \\ \text{or discount }\%_{Indirect}\end{array} = \left[\left(\begin{array}{c}\text{Spot} \\ \text{rate}\end{array} - \begin{array}{c}\text{Forward} \\ \text{rate}\end{array}\right)\Big/\begin{array}{c}\text{Forward} \\ \text{rate}\end{array}\right] \times 360/n \times 100.$$

Absolute PPP: Spot rate$_{\$/€}$ = $PI_\$/PI_€$.

Interest Rate Parity: $S_{P/\$}/F_{P/\$} = (1 + r_\$)/(1 + r_P)$
$F_{P/\$} = S_{P/\$} \times [(1 + r_P)/(1 + r_\$)].$

International Fisher Effect: $[S_{P/\$} - EFS_{P/\$}]/EFS_{P/\$} = -[(1 + r_P) - (1 + r_\$)]/(1 + r_P)$
$= -[r_P - r_\$]/(1 + r_P)$
$= [r_\$ - r_P]/(1 + r_P).$

Chapter 5

$$\text{Holding period rate of return} = \frac{\text{Total proceeds} - \text{Amount invested}}{\text{Amount invested}}.$$

Expected rate of return $= \hat{r} = P_1 r_1 + P_2 r_2 + \cdots + P_n r_n$

$$= \sum_{i=1}^{n} P_i r_i.$$

Variance $= \sigma^2 = \sum_{i=1}^{n} (r_i - \hat{r})^2 P_i.$

Standard deviation $= \sigma = \sqrt{\sum_{i=1}^{n} (r_i - \hat{r})^2 P_i}.$

Estimated $\sigma = S = \sqrt{\dfrac{\sum_{t=1}^{n} (\bar{r}_t - \bar{r}_{\text{Avg}})^2}{n - 1}}.$

Coefficient of variation $= CV = \dfrac{\sigma}{\hat{r}}.$

$\hat{r}_p = w_1 \hat{r}_1 + w_2 \hat{r}_2 + \cdots + w_n \hat{r}_n$

$\quad = \sum_{i=1}^{n} w_i \hat{r}_i.$

$b_i = \left(\dfrac{\sigma_i}{\sigma_M} \right) \rho_{iM}.$

$b_p = w_1 b_1 + w_2 b_2 + \cdots + w_n b_n$

$\quad = \sum_{i=1}^{n} w_i b_i.$

$RP_M = r_M - r_{RF}.$

SML equation: $\dfrac{\text{Required return}}{\text{on Stock i}} = \dfrac{\text{Risk-free}}{\text{rate}} + \left(\begin{array}{c} \text{Market risk} \\ \text{premium} \end{array} \right) \left(\begin{array}{c} \text{Stock i's} \\ \text{beta} \end{array} \right)$

$$r_i = r_{RF} + (r_M - r_{RF}) b_i$$

$$= r_{RF} + (RP_M) b_i.$$

Chapter 6

$\dfrac{\text{Net operating}}{\text{working capital}} = \dfrac{\text{Operating current}}{\text{assets}} - \dfrac{\text{Operating current}}{\text{liabilities}}.$

$\dfrac{\text{Total net}}{\text{operating capital}} = \left(\begin{array}{c} \text{Net operating} \\ \text{working capital} \end{array} \right) + \left(\begin{array}{c} \text{Operating} \\ \text{long-term assets} \end{array} \right).$

Net cash flow = Net income + Depreciation and amortization.

NOPAT = EBIT(1 − Tax rate).

FCF = NOPAT − Net new investment in operating capital.

MVA = Market value of stock − Equity capital supplied by shareholders
    = (Shares outstanding)(Stock price) − Total common equity.

EVA = NOPAT − (Operating capital)(WACC).

Chapter 8

$$\text{Bond's value} = V_B = \sum_{t=1}^{2N} \frac{\text{INT}/2}{(1 + r_d/2)^t} + \frac{M}{(1 + r_d/2)^{2N}}.$$

$$\text{Price of callable bond} = \sum_{t=1}^{2N} \frac{\text{INT}/2}{(1 + r_d/2)^t} + \frac{\text{Call price}}{(1 + r_d/2)^{2N}}.$$

Chapter 9

$$\text{Expected dividend yield} = \frac{D_1}{P_0}.$$

$$\text{Expected capital gains yield} = \frac{\hat{P}_1 - P_0}{P_0}.$$

$$\text{Stock value} = \hat{P}_0 = \text{PV of expected future dividends}$$

$$= \frac{D_1}{(1 + r_s)^1} + \frac{D_2}{(1 + r_s)^2} + \cdots + \frac{D_\infty}{(1 + r_s)^\infty}$$

$$= \sum_{t=1}^{\infty} \frac{D_t}{(1 + r_s)^t}.$$

$$\text{Constant Growth Stock: } \hat{P}_0 = \frac{D_0(1 + g)^1}{(1 + r_s)^1} + \frac{D_0(1 + g)^2}{(1 + r_s)^2} + \cdots + \frac{D_0(1 + g)^\infty}{(1 + r_s)^\infty}$$

$$= D_0 \sum_{t=1}^{\infty} \frac{(1 + g)^t}{(1 + r_s)^t}$$

$$= \frac{D_0(1 + g)}{r_s - g} = \frac{D_1}{r_s - g}.$$

$$\text{Zero Growth Stock: } \hat{P}_0 = \frac{D}{r_s}.$$

$$\text{Perpetuity} = V_{ps} = \frac{D_{ps}}{r_{ps}}.$$

$$\text{Nonconstant Growth Stock: Terminal value} = TV_N = \frac{D_{N+1}}{r_s - g_n} = \frac{D_N(1 + g_n)}{r_s - g_n}.$$

$$\text{Nonconstant Growth Stock: } \hat{P}_0 = \frac{D_1}{(1 + r_s)^1} + \frac{D_2}{(1 + r_s)^2} + \cdots + \frac{D_N}{(1 + r_s)^N} + \frac{TV_N}{(1 + r_s)^N}.$$

$$\text{Corporate Valuation Model: Value of operations} = V_{OP} = \text{PV of expected FCFs}$$

$$= \sum_{t=1}^{\infty} \frac{\text{FCF}_t}{(1 + \text{WACC})^t}.$$

$$\text{Corporate Valuation Model: Terminal value}_N = \frac{\text{FCF}_{N+1}}{(\text{WACC} - g_n)}.$$

Chapter 10

$$\text{After-tax component cost of debt} = \text{Interest rate} - \text{Tax savings}$$
$$= r_d - r_d T$$
$$= r_d(1 - T).$$

$\Delta FX^e = (FX_t - FX_{t-1})/FX_{t-1}.$

After-tax component cost of foreign-currency-denominated debt = $r_d(1 - T)(1 + \Delta FX^e) + \Delta FX^e.$

$r_{ps} = \dfrac{D_{ps}}{P_n}.$

r_s = Bond yield + Risk premium.

CAPM: $r_s = r_{RF} + (RP_M)b_i.$

Global CAPM: $r_s = r_{RF} + (RP_W)b_{i, W}.$

Global CAPM with Partially Segmented Capital Markets: $r_s = r_{RF} + (RP_W)b_{i, W} + (SRP_j)b_{i, Seg}.$

Country-Spread Approach: $r_s = r_{RF} + (RP_M)[0.6(\sigma_j/\sigma_M)] + $ Country credit spread.

Country-Risk-Rating Approach: $r_{sj}/2 = a + d_{cr}\ln(\text{Country-risk rating}_j).$

Chapter 11

$$\dfrac{\text{Payback}}{\text{period}} = \dfrac{\text{Year before}}{\text{full recovery}} + \dfrac{\text{Unrecovered cost at start of year}}{\text{Cash flow during year}}.$$

$$NPV = \dfrac{CF_0}{(1+r)^0} + \dfrac{CF_1}{(1+r)^1} + \dfrac{CF_2}{(1+r)^2} + \cdots + \dfrac{CF_n}{(1+r)^n}$$

$$= \sum_{t=0}^{n} \dfrac{CF_t}{(1 + WACC)^t}.$$

$$0 = \sum_{t=0}^{n} \dfrac{CF_t}{(1 + IRR)^t}.$$

$$\dfrac{\text{Free}}{\text{cash flow}} = \dfrac{\text{Net operating}}{\text{profit after taxes}} - \dfrac{\text{Net}}{\text{fixed asset}} - \dfrac{\text{Change in}}{\text{net operating}}.$$
$$\text{(NOPAT)} \qquad \text{expenditures} \qquad \text{working capital}$$

$$\begin{pmatrix}\text{Required change} \\ \text{in net operating} \\ \text{working capital}\end{pmatrix} = \begin{pmatrix}\text{Required} \\ \text{additions to} \\ \text{inventory}\end{pmatrix} + \begin{pmatrix}\text{Increase} \\ \text{in accounts} \\ \text{receivable}\end{pmatrix} - \begin{pmatrix}\text{Increase in} \\ \text{accounts payable} \\ \text{and accruals}\end{pmatrix}.$$

Going Concern Concept: $SV_t = \dfrac{NOCF_t(1 + g)}{WACC - g}.$

Chapter 13

MM, No Taxes: $V_L = V_U = S_L + D.$

MM, Corporate Taxes: $V_L = V_U + $ Value of side effects $= V_U + $ PV of interest tax shield
$= V_U + TD.$

Miller, Corporate and Personal Taxes: $V_L = V_U + \left[1 - \dfrac{(1 - T_c)(1 - T_s)}{(1 - T_d)}\right]D.$

$$ROIC = \dfrac{NOPAT}{\text{Invested capital}} = \dfrac{EBIT(1 - T)}{\text{Invested capital}}$$

$$= \dfrac{\dfrac{\text{Net income to}}{\text{common stockholders}} + \dfrac{\text{After-tax}}{\text{interest payments}}}{\text{Invested capital}}.$$

$$\text{Dividends} = \text{Net income} - \begin{array}{c} \text{Retained earnings needed to} \\ \text{finance new investments} \end{array}$$

$$= \text{Net income} - \left[\begin{array}{c} \text{Target equity} \\ \text{ratio} \end{array} \times \begin{array}{c} \text{Total capital} \\ \text{budget} \end{array} \right].$$

Chapter 14

$$\text{Inventory conversion period (DIH)} = \frac{\text{Inventories}}{\text{Cost of goods sold}/365}.$$

$$\text{Receivables collection period (DSO)} = \frac{\text{Accounts receivable}}{\text{Sales}/365}.$$

$$\text{Days payables outstanding (DPO)} = \frac{\text{Accounts payable}}{\text{Cost of goods sold}/365}.$$

$$\text{Cash conversion period} = \text{DIH} + \text{DSO} - \text{DPO}.$$

$$\begin{array}{c} \text{Nominal annual} \\ \text{cost of} \\ \text{trade credit} \end{array} = \frac{\text{Discount percent}}{100 - \begin{array}{c} \text{Discount} \\ \text{percent} \end{array}} \times \frac{365 \text{ days}}{\begin{array}{c} \text{Days credit is} \\ \text{outstanding} \end{array} - \begin{array}{c} \text{Discount} \\ \text{period} \end{array}}.$$

Chapter 15

$$\text{Break-even rate} = \frac{(\text{Spot dollar-equivalent of obligation} - \text{Cost of option})}{\text{Foreign currency obligation}}.$$

Chapter 16

$$\text{FTC} = \frac{\text{Foreign-source taxable income}}{\text{Worldwide taxable income}} \times \text{U.S. tax liability before FTC}.$$

GLOSSARY

A

Abandonment Option The option of discontinuing a project if operating cash flows turn out to be lower than expected. This option can both raise expected profitability and lower project risk.

Absolute Advantage Adam Smith's theory that all countries can gain from specialization and trade, thus resulting in a positive-sum game.

Absolute PPP A PPP theory based on relative prices of similar baskets of goods and services estimating the equilibrium exchange rate at any given point in time.

Accounting Exposure The effect on the firm of the different currency translation methods and resulting translation gains and losses.

Accounting Profit A firm's net income as reported on its income statement.

Active Business Operations Operations in which the net income of the activity rather than the gross income is taxed by the host country.

Actual (Realized) Rate of Return, $\bar{r}_s$ The rate of return on a common stock actually received by stockholders in some past period; $\bar{r}_s$ may be greater or less than $\hat{r}_s$ and/or r_s.

Advance Pricing Agreement (APA) An approach to determining the appropriate cost-plus transfer price through negotiation with tax authorities of both governments of the affiliates involved in the transaction.

After-Tax Cost of Debt, $r_d(1 - T)$ The relevant cost of new debt, taking into account the tax deductibility of interest; used to calculate the WACC.

Agency Problem A potential conflict of interest between the agent (manager) and (1) the outside stockholders, (2) the creditors (debtholders), and (3) stockholders and debtholders in times of financial distress.

Aggressive Financing Strategy With this financing policy, not only is temporary NOWC financed with short-term debt, part of permanent NOWC is also financed with short-term funds.

All-In Cost Literally, total costs explicit and implicit. As the term is used with respect to floating-rate bonds, it is equivalent to the YTM assuming the bond is a fixed-rate bond.

American Depository Receipt (ADR) A negotiable certificate, issued by a bank, denominated in dollars, and traded on an exchange like the NYSE; represents underlying shares of a company and is held in trust by a foreign depository institution.

American Terms The foreign exchange rate quotation that represents the number of American dollars that can be bought with one unit of local currency.

Annual Report Issued annually by a corporation to its stockholders. It contains basic financial statements, management's analysis of the past year's operations, and opinions about the firm's future prospects.

"Arms-Length" Price The theoretically correct transfer price; the amount an unrelated customer would have to pay in a free market for the product.

Around-the-Clock Trading Global financial institutions maintain offices in different time zones around the world and thus offer anytime trading.

Asset Market Approach The hypothesis that investors decide whether to hold monetary assets denominated in a foreign currency by looking at the country's real interest rates and its economic outlook for future growth and profitability. This theory implies that in the short run, exchange rate movements are driven by interest rates, expectations for future growth and profitability, and opportunities in the asset markets.

Assets Management Ratios A set of ratios that measure how effectively a firm is managing its assets.

Asymmetric Information The situation in which managers have different (better) information about firms' prospects than do investors.

Average-Risk Stock A stock with b = 1.0.

B

Balance of Payments (BOP) Report A statistical summary of all transactions during a given time period between the residents of one country and the rest of the world.

Balance Sheet A statement of the firm's financial position at a specific point in time.

Balance Sheet Hedge The situation that occurs when the change in assets value exactly offsets the change in value of the liabilities.

Base Case An analysis in which all of the input variables are set at their most likely values.

Base-Case NPV The NPV when sales and other input variables are set equal to their most likely (or base-case) values.

Basic Earning Power (BEP) Ratio This ratio indicates the ability of the firm's assets to generate operating income; calculated by dividing EBIT by total assets.

Behavioral Finance Incorporates elements of cognitive psychology into finance in an effort to better understand how individuals and entire markets respond to different circumstances.

Benchmark Companies A selection of a small subset of similar companies within the same industry as the company to which comparisons are made.

Benchmarking The process of comparing a particular company with a smaller group of similar companies within the same industry, otherwise known as "benchmark" companies.

Best-Case Scenario An analysis in which all of the input variables are set at their best reasonably forecasted values.

Beta Coefficient, b_i A measure of market risk, which is the extent to which the returns on a given stock move with the stock market.

Bid Rate In a foreign exchange context, the rate at which traders buy currencies.

Bilateral Netting A technique in which receivables and payables entries are "netted out" between pairs of affiliates, and then the sum of the remaining nonzero entries represents the total accounts payable and accounts receivable in the internal market. Payments are now made in only one direction.

Bird-in-the-Hand Theory MM's name for the theory that states a firm's value will be maximized by setting a high dividend payout ratio.

Blockage Government regulations or laws restricting an MNE's ability to transfer funds into or out of an affiliate country.

Bond A long-term debt instrument.

Business Climate Refers to a country's social, political, and economic environment.

Business Ethics A company's attitude and conduct toward its employees, customers, community, and stockholders.

Business Risk (1) The risk of doing business in the new environment. It exists in all countries but varies across countries. (2) The riskiness inherent in the firm's operations if it uses no debt.

C

Call Option An option to buy, or "call," an asset at a certain price within a specified period.

Call Premium The additional amount that must be paid to a bondholder if a bond is called.

Call Provision Gives the issuer the right to redeem the bonds under specified terms prior to the normal maturity date.

Cannibalization A type of externality that occurs when the introduction of a new product causes sales of existing products to decline.

Capital Account (Group B) Includes all capital transfers into and out of a country related to the purchase and sale of fixed assets, including real estate.

Capital Asset Pricing Model (CAPM) A model based on the proposition that any stock's required rate of return is equal to the risk-free rate of return plus a risk premium that reflects only the risk remaining after diversification.

Capital Budgeting The process of planning expenditures on assets whose cash flows are expected to extend beyond one year.

Capital Component One of the types of capital used by firms to raise money.

Capital Export Neutrality (CEN) Suggests that investors should have to pay exactly the same total amount of taxes on income from foreign investments as they do on domestic investments.

Capital Import Neutrality (CIN) Suggests that investments in any country should all be taxed at the same rate no matter where the investor resides.

Capital Markets The financial markets for equity and for intermediate- or long-term debt (one year or longer).

Cash Budget The device used by most companies to forecast cash needs and availability.

Cash Conversion Cycle Focuses on the length of time a dollar is tied up in current assets other than cash.

Cash Conversion Period (CCP) Indicates the extent to which a company must use costly investor-supplied debt to finance its working capital and is equal to the sum of the inventory conversion period and the receivables collection period minus the payables deferral period.

Citizens' (Golden) Shares Class of common stock that may be issued by a company for investors in the company's home country in order to maintain local control of the company.

Classified Stock Common stock given a special designation, such as Class A, Class B, and so forth, to meet special needs of the company.

Clientele Effect The tendency of a firm to attract a set of investors who like its dividend policy.

Clienteles Different groups of stockholders that prefer different dividend payout policies.

Closely Held Corporation Owned by a few individuals who are typically associated with the firm's management.

Coefficient of Variation A standardized measure of the risk per unit of return; calculated as the standard deviation divided by the expected return.

Collaborative Arrangements Arrangements that allow a company to participate in global commerce without incurring the full cost or the total risk of the venture.

Commercial Paper An alternative to bank loans for large, financially stable borrowers that takes the form of short-term, unsecured promissory notes.

Commodity Price Risk The risk that the prices of a company's generic production inputs or outputs (commodities) may change.

Comparative Advantage David Ricardo's theory that all countries could still gain from specialization and trade if they produced those goods in which they were relatively more efficient than others.

Compensating Balances Bank balances that firms must maintain to compensate the bank for services rendered.

Component Cost The required rate of return on each capital component.

Conservative Financing Strategy With this financing policy, part of temporary NOWC is financed from long-term sources and, when it is not needed to support operations, it is parked temporarily in short-term investments.

Consolidated Financial Statements Aggregated financial statements for parent and subsidiary organizations presented in annual reports and required in SEC filings that exclude intracompany transactions.

Constant Growth (Gordon) Model Used to find the value of a constant growth stock.

Consumer Credit Markets Markets that involve loans on autos, appliances, education, vacations, and the like.

Consumption-Based Tax A tax borne only by those who wish to consume specific products or services. This is a primary device for raising revenues by U.S. cities and states.

Continuing Risks Risks that are ongoing and not related to specific transactions.

Contractual Hedges Exist when a formal contractual relationship is established to lock in the exact terms of a future transaction.

Corporate Bonds Bonds issued by corporations.

Corporate Governance System Provides the financial and legal framework for regulating the relationship between a company's management and its shareholders.

Corporate Valuation Model Discounts a firm's free cash flows rather than its dividends in order to value the firm.

Corporate (Within-Firm) Risk Risk not considering the effects of stockholders' diversification; it is measured by a project's effect on uncertainty about the firm's future earnings.

Correlation The tendency of two variables to move together.

Correlation Coefficient, r A measure of the degree of relationship between two variables.

Cost of Common Equity, r_s The rate of return required by stockholders on a firm's common stock.

Cost of Preferred Stock, r_{ps} The rate of return investors require on the firm's preferred stock. It is calculated as the preferred dividend, D_{ps}, divided by the net issuing price, P_n.

Costly Trade Credit Credit taken in excess of free trade credit, whose cost is equal to the discount lost.

Counterparty Risk The risk that the other party to a contractual arrangement will not be able to carry out its obligations as specified in the contract.

Country Attractiveness Scorecard A system used to consolidate information and compare the attractiveness of different countries.

Country Perspective Evaluation of a capital budgeting project that looks at the project's contribution to the host nation and local stakeholders who will be most affected.

Country Risk The additional risk, on top of the usual business risk, when operating in a foreign country. It arises mainly out of indigenous factors.

Country Risk Premium (CRP) A premium that reflects the risk that arises from investing or doing business in a particular country.

Country Credit Spread Calculated as the difference between 10-year yields on dollar-denominated foreign bonds and U.S. Treasury bonds.

Country-Risk-Rating Approach It uses the Institutional Investor's country-risk rating to estimate a regression model of equity returns against corresponding country-risk ratings.

Country-Spread Model This model estimates the emerging-market cost of equity by adding a country credit spread to the U.S. risk-free rate along with an adjusted beta times the U.S. market risk premium.

Coupon Interest Rate The stated annual interest rate on a bond.

Coupon Payment The specified number of dollars of interest paid each period, generally each six months.

Covered Interest Arbitrage A riskless transaction in which an individual earns a profit on borrowed money due to a disequilibrium condition in the forward rate.

Credit Policy A set of decisions that include a firm's credit period, credit standards, collection procedures, and discounts offered.

Credit Risk The risk that relates to the possibility that a borrower will default on its debt.

Cross Rate The exchange rate between any two currencies.

Cross-Listing Occurs when a company lists shares of stock on multiple exchanges to increase its global recognition.

Crossover Rate The cost of capital at which the NPV profiles of two projects cross, and thus at which the projects' NPVs are equal.

Cumulative Translation Adjustment (CTA) The entry made in the equity account to reflect the unrealized gain or loss on the net asset exposure under the current rate translation method.

Currency Board Arrangement Occurs when a country has its own currency but commits to exchange it for a specified foreign money unit at a fixed exchange rate and legislates domestic currency restrictions, unless it has the foreign currency reserves to cover requested exchanges.

Currency Futures Contract Calls for delivery, at a preset location, of a standardized amount of a particular currency, at a specific time in the future, and at a fixed price.

Currency Markets Markets in which transactions for foreign exchange occur.

Currency Swap A contractual agreement to exchange the currency of the debt service for the same notional principal.

Current Account (Group A) Records all inflows and outflows of income derived from exporting and importing goods and services, net income from investment and employee compensation, and net unilateral transfers.

Current Rate Method One of two methods permitted in most countries for translating financial statements. Assets and liabilities are translated at the spot exchange rate on the day the financial statements are prepared, while equity accounts are translated at historical exchange rates in effect on the dates the items were recorded.

Current Ratio This ratio is calculated by dividing current assets by current liabilities. It indicates the extent to which current liabilities are covered by those assets expected to be converted to cash in the near future.

Current Yield The annual interest payment on a bond divided by the bond's current price.

D

Days Inventory Held (DIH) This ratio is calculated by dividing inventories by average cost of goods sold per day; it indicates the average length of time between receipt of raw materials until they are moved into accounts receivable upon being sold.

Days Payables Outstanding (DPO) Represents supplier credit that usually has no explicit cost.

Days Sales Outstanding (DSO) This ratio is calculated by dividing accounts receivable by average sales per day; it indicates the average length of time the firm must wait after making a sale before it receives cash.

Debt Ratio The ratio of total debt to total assets.

Decision Tree A diagram that shows all possible outcomes that might result from a decision. Each possible outcome is shown as a "branch" on the tree. Decision trees are especially useful for analyzing the effects of real options.

Deemed-Paid Credit An indirect credit available if the parent received actual or constructive dividends from the subsidiary. Foreign taxes are deemed paid by the parent shareholder in the same proportion as the dividends actually or constructively received to the total undistributed income of the subsidiary.

Default Risk The risk that an investor will receive less than the promised return on the bond because the issuer fails to make either interest or principal payments.

Default Risk Premium (DRP) A premium that reflects the difference between the interest rate on a U.S. Treasury bond and a corporate bond of equal maturity and marketability.

Deficit (Surplus) Represents a net debit (credit) balance in the overall balance of payments.

Denominated Expressed or designated in nominal money units.

Derivative Security Any asset whose value is derived from the value of some other "underlying" real or financial asset.

Direct Quotation The home currency price of one unit of the foreign currency.

Discount Bond Sells below its par value; occurs whenever the going rate of interest is above the coupon rate.

Discrete Risks Related to specific transactions that lead to economic gains or losses as underlying variables change.

Diversifiable Risk That part of a stock's risk associated with random events; it can be eliminated by proper diversification.

Dividend Growth Rate, g The expected rate of growth in dividends per share.

Dividend Irrelevance Theory States that a firm's dividend policy has no effect on either its value or its cost of capital.

Dollarization Occurs when a country abandons its own currency and adapts the U.S. dollar as its legal tender.

E

EBITDA Earnings before interest, taxes, depreciation, and amortization. It represents a better measure of cash flow than net income.

EBITDA Coverage Ratio A ratio whose numerator includes all cash flows available to meet fixed financial charges and whose denominator includes all fixed financial charges.

Economic (Operating or Strategic) Exposure The impact of changing economic variables on firm value and the reaction of competitors to these variables.

Economic Order Quantity (EOQ) Model A technique for finding the optimal inventory balance.

Economic Value Added (EVA) Value added to shareholders by management during a given year.

Efficient Markets Hypothesis (EMH) The hypotheses that securities are typically in equilibrium—that they are fairly priced in the sense that the price reflects all publicly available information on each security.

Electronic Markets Markets with no physical location, but rather exist as a computerized trading system.

Entity Multiple A multiple based on total value; it is a measure of the entire firm.

Equilibrium The condition under which the expected return on a security is just equal to its required return, $\hat{r}_i = r_i$. Also, $\hat{P}_0 = P_0$, and the price is stable.

Equity Alliances Collaborative arrangements that involve independent companies in related or supporting fields that band together to solidify a collaboration contract and make it harder to break.

Eurobond An international bond underwritten by an international syndicate of banks and sold to investors in countries other than the one in whose money unit the bond is denominated.

Eurocredits Floating-rate bank loans, available in most major trading currencies, that are tied to LIBOR for the issue's currency as the reference rate and issued for a fixed term with no early repayment.

European Terms The foreign-exchange rate quotation that represents the units of local currency that can be bought with one U.S. dollar. "European" is intended as a generic term that applies globally.

Exchange Rate The number of units of a given currency that can be purchased for one unit of another currency.

Exchange Rate Risk The risk that relates to what the foreign currency cash flows will be worth in the parent company's home currency.

Exchange Rate Risk Premium (ERP) A premium that results from the possibility that an exchange rate change will lead to a loss in a bond's value.

Exchange-Traded Currency Derivatives They are standardized, prepackaged instruments used more for speculation than for hedging, although some companies use them to hedge continuing exposures that cannot be neutralized with natural hedges.

Expected Capital Gains Yield The expected increase or decrease in share value during the coming year divided by the beginning stock price.

Expected Dividend Yield The expected dividend divided by the current stock price.

Expected Rate of Inflation The amount by which prices are expected to increase over time.

Expected Rate of Return, $\hat{r}$ The rate of return expected to be realized from an investment; the weighted average of the probability distribution of possible results.

Expected Return on a Portfolio, $\hat{r}_p$ The weighted average of the expected returns of the individual assets held in the portfolio.

Expected Total Rate of Return, $\hat{r}_s$ The rate of return on a common stock that a stockholder expects to receive in the future. It is equal to the sum of the expected dividend yield and the expected capital gains yield.

Exposed Assets Assets that are subject to a change in value if exchange rates change.

Exposed Liabilities Liabilities that are subject to a change in value if exchange rates change.

Externalities Effects of a project on cash flows in other parts of the firm.

Extra-Territorial Income (ETI) Allows U.S. exporters to exclude from U.S. tax a portion of export profits from goods produced domestically in the United States.

F

Financial Account (Group C) Includes all foreign direct investment, portfolio investment, and external flows of other financial assets and liabilities.

Financial Asset Markets Marketplaces that deal with financial instruments such as stocks, bonds, notes, mortgages, currencies, and so on.

Financial Instruments Pieces of paper or electronic entries in account ledgers with contractual provisions that spell out their owners' claims on specific real assets. Their value is defined in terms of a fixed number of money units.

Financial Intermediary A specialized financial firm that facilitates the transfer of funds from savers to demanders of capital.

Financial Leverage The extent to which fixed-income securities (debt and preferred stock) are used in a firm's capital structure.

Financial Risk An increase in stockholders' risk, over and above the firm's basic business risk, resulting from the use of financial leverage.

Fisher Equation Shows how the nominal risk-free rate, r_{RF}, is a function of the real risk-free rate, r^*, and the inflation rate, I.

Fixed Assets Turnover Ratio The ratio of sales to net fixed assets.

Fixed Peg Arrangement Occurs when a country locks its currency to a specific currency or basket of currencies at a fixed exchange rate. The exchange rate is allowed to vary only within $\pm 1\%$ of the target rate.

Flexibility Option The option to modify operations depending on how conditions develop during a project's life, especially the type of output produced or the inputs used.

Floating-Rate Bond Its interest rate payments fluctuate with shifts in the general level of interest rates.

Floating-Rate Notes (FRNs) Eurobonds with floating-rate coupons.

Foreign Bond A type of international bond issued in the domestic capital market of the country in whose currency the bond is denominated, and underwritten by investment banks from the same country.

Foreign Exchange, FX The money of a foreign country.

Foreign Exchange Markets Range from local cab drivers to sophisticated telecommunications and global computer networks that connect banks, professional dealers, brokers, central banks, and the treasury departments of many MNEs.

Forward Contract A contract in which one party agrees to buy or sell an asset or commodity at a specific price on a specific future date from another party, and physical delivery occurs.

Forward Market Hedge Involves a contract to exchange specific amounts of two currencies at an exact time in the future and a source of funds to fulfill the contract.

Forward Rate Agreements (FRAs) Contracts restricted mainly to major markets and currencies that can be tailored to fit specific company situations, much like forward contracts. They allow firms to lock in future interest rates.

Forward-at-the-Money Near the forward rate.

Founders' Shares Stock owned by the firm's founders with sole voting rights but restricted dividends for a specified number of years.

Franchising A collaborative arrangement that involves the transfer of a trademark and its business processes to a foreign entity and the continual infusion of required assets for the franchisee to operate.

Free Cash Flow (FCF) The cash flow actually available for distribution to all investors (stockholders and debtholders) after the company has made all the investments in fixed assets, new products, and working capital necessary to sustain ongoing operations.

Freely Floating Occurs when the exchange rate is determined by supply and demand for the currency.

Fronting Loan A type of lending arrangement structured as an indirect loan from a nonaffiliated bank. It is denominated in local currency to prevent blockage from the local host government.

Functional Currency The currency of the primary economic environment in which the subsidiary operates.

Futures Contract A standardized agreement similar to a forward contract that is traded on exchanges, but no physical delivery occurs.

Futures Markets The markets in which participants agree today to buy or sell an asset at some future date.

G

Global CAPM A model based on the proposition that any stock's required rate of return is equal to the risk-free rate of return plus a risk premium that reflects only the risk remaining after diversification in world markets.

Global CAPM with Partially Segmented Capital Markets A model that estimates the cost of equity in markets that are not perfectly integrated. The cost of equity is determined partly by an integrated market risk premium component and partly by a segmented market component.

Global Registered Share (GRS) Share not held in bearer form that trades electronically on a number of exchanges in the local host currencies.

Globalization The increasing interconnectedness of economies, markets, and people across countries.

Going Public The act of selling stock to the public at large for the first time by a closely held corporation or its principal stockholders.

Greenfield Investment The name given when companies expand internationally by building operations de novo rather than through acquisitions.

Gross World Product (GWP) The aggregate value of all goods and services produced worldwide in a given year.

H

Hedging Refers to creating offsetting assets and liabilities so that gains in one offset losses in the other. It locks in expected losses or gains and protects against unexpected changes.

Historical (Embedded) Rate The interest rate on previously issued, or currently outstanding, debt.

Hyperinflation A situation in which cumulative annual inflation of approximately 100 percent occurs over three years. In this situation, currency no longer functions as a storehouse of value.

I

Income Statement Summarizes the firm's revenues and expenses over an accounting period, generally a quarter or year.

Incremental Cash Flows The cash flows representing the change in the firm's total cash flows that occurs as a direct result of accepting the project.

Independent Projects Projects whose cash flows are not affected by the acceptance or nonacceptance of other projects.

Indirect Quotation The foreign currency price of one unit of the home currency.

Inflation The amount by which prices increase over time.

Inflation Premium (IP) A premium that must be added to the real risk-free rate to adjust for inflation; calculated as $I + r*I$.

Information Content (Signaling) Hypothesis The theory that investors regard dividend changes as signals of management's earnings forecasts.

Initial Public Offering (IPO) Market The market in which firms "go public" by offering shares to the public for the first time.

Integrated Foreign Entity An operating unit located in another country that functions as an extension of the parent and whose cash flows are interrelated with those of the parent.

Interest Rate The price paid to borrow debt capital.

Interest Rate Cap A type of call option that constrains the maximum interest rate value over the life of the loan.

Interest Rate Collar The simultaneous buying and selling of caps and floors. It allows the company to benefit from constraints on the upside or downside, whichever it is concerned with, while having a reduced premium cost.

Interest Rate Floor A type of put option that sets a minimum effective interest rate to be received on an invested notional principal.

Interest Rate Futures Standardized contracts traded on exchanges around the world whose underlying security is a debt obligation.

Interest Rate Parity (IRP) A theory that shows that the forward premium or discount on the foreign currency is equal in magnitude but opposite in sign to the interest rate differential.

Interest Rate Risk The risk of capital losses to which investors are exposed due to rising interest rates.

Interest Rate Swaps Allow a company that has floating-rate debt to switch debt servicing to a fixed-rate basis, or vice versa.

Internal Rate of Return, IRR The discount rate that forces the PV of a project's inflows to equal the PV of its costs.

Internal Rate of Return Method A method of ranking investment proposals using the rate of return on an investment, calculated by finding the discount rate that equates the present value of future cash inflows to the project's cost.

Internalization Advantages Valuable assets usually associated with "know-how," product designs, research skills, and customer lists. Information that the company needs to keep confidential to maintain its competitive advantage.

International Bonds Bonds issued by either foreign governments or foreign corporations.

International Fisher Effect, Fisher-Open The theory that states in equilibrium the expected change in the spot exchange rate should be equal in magnitude but opposite in sign to the interest rate differential.

International Monetary System The framework within which exchange rates are determined. It is the blueprint for international trade and capital flows.

Intrinsic (Fundamental) Value, $\hat{P}_0$ The value of an asset that, in the mind of a particular investor, is justified by the facts; $\hat{P}_0$ may be different from the asset's current market price.

Inventory Conversion Period The average time required to convert raw materials into finished goods and then to sell those goods.

Investment Banking House An organization that underwrites and distributes new investment securities and helps businesses obtain financing.

Investment Risk The likelihood of actually earning a low or negative return on an investment.

Investment Timing Option An option as to when to begin a project. Often, if a firm can delay a decision, it can increase a project's expected NPV.

J

Joint Ventures Business ventures formed by two or more companies to achieve a specific, but limited, objective.

Just-In-Time Inventory Management Suggests that the optimum level of inventory is near zero, with companies holding the minimum levels of raw materials required to avoid production interruption.

L

Lagging Strategy The company alters the timing of intrafirm payments in order to preserve wealth by keeping it in strong currencies for as long as possible.

Leading Strategy The company alters the timing of intrafirm payments in order to preserve wealth by getting it out of weak currencies and into strong currencies as quickly as possible.

Licensing Allows a company to earn a return from an intangible asset by granting permission for another firm to use the asset in its own production and marketing operations.

Liquid Asset An asset that can be converted to cash quickly without having to reduce the asset's price very much.

Liquidity Premium (LP) A premium added to the equilibrium interest rate on a security if that security cannot be converted to cash on short notice and at close to "fair market value."

Location-Specific Advantages Local attributes or resources that can be used by the firm to enhance its global competitiveness.

Low-Regular-Dividend-plus-Extras Policy The policy of announcing a low, regular dividend that can be maintained no matter what and then, when times are good, paying a designated "extra" dividend.

M

Managed Float Occurs when there is significant government intervention to control the exchange rate via manipulation of the currency's supply and demand.

Management Contracts Occur when a foreign company is hired by the owner of the asset to run the operation for a contracted payment; used when the foreign company manages better than the owners.

Marginal Investor A representative investor whose actions reflect the beliefs of those people who are currently lending capital. It is the marginal investor who determines the market interest rate and a firm's stock price and cost of capital.

Market Multiple Analysis A method used for valuing companies that applies market-determined multiples to net income, earnings per share, sales, book value, and so forth.

Market Portfolio A portfolio consisting of all stocks.

Market Price, P_0 The price at which a stock sells in the market.

Market Risk The part of a project's risk that cannot be eliminated by diversification; it is measured by the asset's beta coefficient.

Market Risk Premium, RP_M The additional return over the risk-free rate needed to compensate investors for assuming an average amount of risk.

Market Value Added (MVA) The difference between the market value of the firm's stock and the amount of equity capital investors have supplied.

Market Value Ratios A set of ratios that relate the firm's stock price to its earnings, cash flow, and book value per share.

Market/Book (M/B) Ratio The ratio of a stock's market price to its book value.

Maturity Date A specified date on which the par value of a bond must be repaid.

Maturity Risk Premium (MRP) A premium that reflects interest rate risk.

Mercantilism An economic and military system developed to gain and retain national power and wealth.

Moderate Financing Strategy A financing policy that matches asset and liability maturities. This is a moderate policy.

Monetary Relating to a unit of currency; value defined in terms of a fixed number of money units.

Monetary Balance The situation that occurs when the gains or losses from translation on the assets side exactly match the losses or gains from translation on the liabilities side.

Monetary Item Includes both financial assets and liabilities whose values are based on a fixed number of nominal money units.

Money Market Hedge Similar to forward market hedge, but it involves an investment or loan contract.

Money Markets The financial markets in which funds are borrowed or loaned for short periods (less than one year).

Monte Carlo Simulation A risk analysis technique in which probable future events are simulated on a computer, generating estimated rates of return and risk indices.

Mortgage Markets Markets that deal with loans on residential, commercial, and industrial real estate.

Multilateral Netting Where affiliates make payments for other affiliates to reduce transactions costs even further.

Multinational Enterprise (MNE) A firm that operates in an integrated fashion in a number of countries.

Municipal Bonds Bonds issued by state and local governments.

Mutually Exclusive Projects A set of projects where only one can be accepted.

N

Natural (Operating) Hedges Arise from the firm's operating cash flows. Occur when monetary assets denominated in a particular foreign currency on the balance sheet offset liabilities in the same currency and same maturity. There are no transaction or translation gains or losses.

Natural Trade Barriers Trade barriers that are not governmentally imposed.

Net Asset Exposure The situation that occurs when there are more exposed assets than exposed liabilities.

Net Cash Flow The actual net cash, as opposed to accounting income, that a firm generates during some specified period.

Net Errors and Omissions (Group D) An adjustment made to force total debits to equal total credits.

Net Liability Exposure The situation that occurs when there are more exposed liabilities than exposed assets.

Net Operating Profit After Taxes (NOPAT) The profit a company would generate if it had no debt and held no nonoperating assets.

Net Operating Working Capital (NOWC) Operating working capital less operating current liabilities. It is the working capital acquired with investor-supplied funds.

Net Present Value (NPV) Method A method of ranking investment proposals using the NPV, which is equal to the present value of future net cash flows discounted at the cost of capital.

Net Present Value Profile A graph showing the relationship between a project's NPV and different values for the firm's cost of capital.

Net Working Capital Current assets minus current liabilities.

Netting A technique for minimizing transactions costs by simply "canceling" the obligation of one affiliate with obligations of another.

New (Marginal) Debt Debt that is not already outstanding.

Nominal, Risk-Adjusted Rate of Return (r) The actual rate charged on a loan; it compensates investors for postponing consumption, inflation, and risk.

Nominal, Risk-Free Rate (r_{RF}) The rate of interest that both offsets inflation and provides the required real return on a riskless investment.
Nonconstant (Supernormal) Growth The part of the firm's life cycle in which it grows differently from the economy as a whole.
Nonmonetary Item Items such as inventory and fixed assets whose values are not equilivent to a fixed number of nominal money units.
Nonoperating Assets Cash and marketable securities above the level required for normal operations, investments in subsidiaries, land held for future use, and other nonessential assets.

O

Offer Rate In a foreign exchange context, the rate at which traders sell currencies.
OLI Paradigm A tool used for evaluating foreign direct investments. It considers three dimensions: owner-specific advantages, location-specific advantages, and internalization advantages.
Operating Assets The cash and marketable securities, accounts receivable, inventories, and fixed assets necessary to operate a business.
Operating Leverage The extent to which fixed costs are used in a firm's operations.
Operating Working Capital Current assets used in operations.
Opportunity Cost The return on the best alternative use of an asset, or the highest return that will not be earned if funds are invested in a particular project.
Optimal Capital Structure The mix of debt, preferred stock, and common equity that strikes a balance between risk and return so as to maximize the firm's stock price.
Optimal Dividend Policy The dividend policy that strikes a balance between current dividends and future growth that maximizes the firm's stock price.
Option (1) The right, but not the obligation, to take some action in the future. In finance, we deal with financial and real options. (2) A contract that gives the buyer the right, but not the obligation, to buy or sell an asset at a set price (the "strike" price) on or before a specific date.
Option Value Value that is not accounted for in a conventional NPV analysis. Positive option value expands the firm's opportunities.
Original Maturity The number of years to maturity at the time a bond is issued.
OTC Option Hedge Foreign currency exposure is hedged using an option contract. Currency options are priced relative to the forward rate, but the price of the option is paid immediately.
Overall Balance All debits and credits recorded in Groups A through D are netted out and represent

the net inflow (credit balance) or outflow (debit balance) of private sector transactions.
Owner-Specific Advantages Competitive advantages in its home market that a company can transfer to another country.

P

Par Value The face value of a bond.
Parent Perspective Evaluation of a capital budgeting project from the perspective of the parent company; it is mainly concerned with the cash flows to be realized by the parent.
Parity Conditions Economic theories that interact with each other to determine national interest rates and exchange rates.
Passive Investment Income Consists of such things as dividends, interest, royalty income from securities investments, and the licensing of intangible assets to foreigners. Foreign countries typically apply a withholding tax rate to the gross amount of the transfer of passive investment income.
Payables Deferral Period The average length of time between the purchase of materials and labor and the payment of cash for them.
Payback Period The length of time required for an investment's net revenues to cover its cost.
Pecking Order The idea that firms have a preference order for raising capital, first using retained earnings, then debt, and new stock only as a last resort.
Permanent Establishment Activities of the company in the host country rise beyond a minimal level. These activities include opening a local office, building a factory and starting manufacturing operations, or establishing some other fixed place of business.
Permanent Working Capital Current assets that a firm must carry even at the trough of its cycles.
Perpetuity A stream of equal payments expected to continue forever.
Physical Asset Markets Also known as tangible, or real, asset markets. Capital budgeting decisions are important to these markets.
Physical Markets Formal organizations having tangible physical locations that conduct auction markets in designated ("listed") securities.
Possessions Credit A credit that reduces the effective tax rate meant to encourage U.S. companies to aid in the economic development of U.S. possessions. Domestic corporations can claim a credit for income derived from sources within one of these possessions even when little or no foreign taxes are actually paid on it.
Precautionary Balances Cash balances held in reserve for random, unforeseen fluctuations in cash inflows and outflows.

Preemptive Right A provision in the corporate charter or bylaws that gives common stockholders the right to purchase, on a pro rata basis, new issues of common stock (or convertible securities).

Premium Bond Sells above its par value; occurs whenever the going rate of interest is below the coupon rate.

Price/Cash Flow Ratio The ratio of price per share divided by cash flow per share; shows the dollar amount investors will pay for $1 of cash flow.

Price/Earnings (P/E) Ratio The ratio of the price per share to earnings per share; shows the dollar amount investors will pay for $1 of current earnings.

Primary Markets Markets in which corporations raise capital by issuing new securities.

Private Markets Markets in which transactions are negotiated directly between two parties.

Probability Distribution A listing of all possible outcomes, or events, with a probability (chance of occurrence) assigned to each outcome.

Production Opportunities The returns available within an economy from investments in productive real assets.

Production-Based Tax A tax paid on units produced rather than units consumed.

Profit Margin on Sales This ratio measures net income per dollar of sales.

Profitability Ratios A group of ratios that show the combined effects of liquidity, assets management, and debt on operating results.

Project Perspective Evaluation of a capital budgeting project from the perspective of a local company undertaking a project.

Public Markets Markets in which standardized contracts are traded on organized exchanges.

Publicly Owned Corporation Owned by a relatively large number of individuals who are not actively involved in the firm's management.

Purchasing Power Parity (PPP) Also known as the law of one price. Asserts that in the absence of transactions costs, the ratio of prices of identical products in two countries determines the exchange rate between the two currencies.

Pure Play Method An approach used for estimating the beta of a project in which a firm (1) identifies several companies whose only business is to produce the product in question, (2) calculates the beta for each firm, and then (3) averages the betas to find an approximation to the project's beta.

Put Option Gives the holder the right to sell an asset.

Put Provision Protects investors against an increase in interest rates by permitting a bondholder to "put" bonds back to the issuer, who must redeem them at par.

Q

Quick Ratio This ratio is calculated by deducting inventories from current assets and then dividing the

remainder by current liabilities. It is a measure of the firm's ability to pay off short-term obligations without relying on the sale of inventories.

Quoted (Stated) Rate The nominal, risk-adjusted rate of return, which is actually published in financial publications.

R

Real Option Involves real, rather than financial, assets. Real options exist when managers can influence the size and riskiness of a project's cash flows by taking different actions during or at the end of a project's life.

Real Risk-Free Rate of Return (r*) The interest rate that would exist on default-free U.S. Treasury securities if no inflation were expected.

Realized Rate of Return, r̄ The return that was actually earned during some past period. The actual return (r̄) usually turns out to be different from the expected return (r̂) except for riskless assets.

Receivables Collection Period The average length of time required to convert the firm's receivables into cash, that is, to collect cash following a sale.

Reference Rate The rate to which the coupon rate of a floating-rate bond is adjusted.

Reinvestment Rate Risk The risk that a decline in interest rates will lead to a decline in income from a bond portfolio.

Reinvoicing Center A separate affiliate, often located in a tax haven country, through which intracompany transactions pass.

Relative PPP A PPP theory stating that the spot exchange rate should change in an equal, but opposite, manner to the inflation differential between two countries.

Relevant Cash Flows The specific cash flows that should be considered in a capital budgeting decision.

Relevant Risk The risk of a security that cannot be diversified away, or its market risk. This reflects a security's contribution to the riskiness of a portfolio.

Remeasuring The process of translating financial statements from a local currency into a functional currency using the temporal method.

Reporting Currency The currency into which a subsidiary's financial statements are ultimately recast from its local currency. For U.S. multinationals, and other multinationals required to submit financials to the SEC, the reporting currency is the U.S. dollar.

Repricing (Rollover) Risk The risk that relates to the possibility (1) that a company will have to pay a higher interest rate when renewing maturing credit, or (2) that it will receive a lower interest rate on securities it holds due to changing market rates.

Required Rate of Return, r_s The minimum rate of return on a common stock that a stockholder considers acceptable.

Required Return The minimum rate of return on a common stock that will induce a stockholder to purchase the stock.

Reserve Borrowing Capacity The ability to borrow money at a reasonable cost when good investment opportunities arise. Firms often use less debt than specified by the MM optimal capital structure in "normal" times to ensure that they can obtain debt capital later if necessary.

Reserves and Related Items (Group E) These are changes in official monetary reserves held by the government, including monetary metals, foreign exchange, and the position of the country with the International Monetary Fund (IMF).

Residual Dividend Model The dividend paid is set equal to net income minus the amount of retained earnings necessary to finance the firm's optimal capital budget.

Restating The process of translating financial statements from a functional currency into a reporting currency using the current rate method.

Return on Common Equity (ROE) The ratio of net income to common equity; measures the rate of return on common stockholders' investment.

Return on Total Assets (ROA) The ratio of net income to total assets.

Risk In a financial market context, the chance that an investment will provide a low or negative return.

Risk Analysis An assessment of the uncertainty inherent in projects' cash flows, which should then be reflected in the WACCs used to evaluate the projects.

Risk Aversion Risk-averse investors dislike risk and require higher rates of return as an inducement to buy riskier securities.

Risk Management Refers to various strategies used to manage discrete foreign exchange, interest rate, and commodity price risks.

Risk Premium (RP) A premium that reflects the difference between the expected rate of return on a given risky asset and that on a less risky asset.

Risk-Adjusted Cost of Capital The cost of capital appropriate for a particular project, given the riskiness of that project. The greater the risk, the higher the cost of capital.

S

Scenario Analysis A risk analysis technique in which "bad" and "good" sets of financial circumstances are compared with a most likely, or base-case situation.

Secondary Markets Markets in which existing securities and other financial assets are traded among investors.

Security Market Line (SML) The line on a graph that shows the relationship between risk as measured by beta and the required rate of return for individual securities.

Self-Sustaining Foreign Entity An operating unit located in another country that functions as a separate ongoing concern and is largely independent of the parent.

Sensitivity Analysis A risk analysis technique in which key variables are changed one at a time and the resulting changes in the NPV are observed.

Shell Corporation The situation in which a foreign company raises most of its subsidiary's capital in the local market.

Signal An action taken by a firm's management that provides clues to investors about how management views the firm's prospects.

Sinking Fund Provision Requires the issuer to retire a portion of the bond issue each year. It facilitates the orderly retirement of a bond issue.

Solvency Condition where the firm has sufficient assets to cover all claims of creditors on the assets.

Solvency and Liquidity Ratios Ratios that show the relationship of a firm's cash and other current assets to its current liabilities.

Spot Markets The markets in which assets are bought or sold for "on-the-spot" delivery.

Spread Profit from buying and selling currency.

Stakeholders Include a firm's employees, customers, banks, suppliers, and community, as well as its stockholders.

Stand-Alone Risk The risk an asset would have if it were a firm's only asset and if investors owned only one stock. It is measured by the standard deviation or coefficient of variation of the asset's expected NPV.

Standard Deviation, σ A statistical measure of the variability of a set of observations.

Strike-Out Rules Designations given to critical conditions in the country evaluation process that mean if it is not possible to negotiate acceptable terms, the company will not make the investment.

Sunk Cost A cash outlay that has already been incurred and that cannot be recovered regardless of whether the project is accepted or rejected.

Supply Chain Management An integrated process that coordinates production scheduling and sales development throughout the company and with manufacturers' suppliers and retail customers.

Swap A contractual agreement to exchange a series of cash flows.

Swaption Shorthand for swap option. Gives the firm the right, if it chooses, to enter into a swap on some notional principal at a fixed date and at a designated strike rate.

T

Target Capital Structure The mix of debt, preferred stock, and common equity with which the firm plans to raise capital over the long run and that minimizes the firm's WACC.

Target Payout Ratio The percentage of net income paid out as cash distributions (dividends and/or stock repurchases) as desired by the firm.

Tax Havens Locations with low or no taxes on most transactions and no restrictions on the movement of cash into or out of these locations.

Tax Preference Theory Suggests there are tax-related reasons for investors preferring a low dividend payout to a high payout.

Technical Analysis Involves looking at patterns in price and volume data to assess the likely movements of future exchange rates.

Temporal Method One of two methods permitted in most countries for translating financial statements. This method distinguishes between monetary and nonmonetary items. All monetary asset items and all liabilities are translated at the spot exchange rate on the day the financial statements are prepared. However, nonmonetary items must be translated or remeasured at the historical exchange rates in effect on the dates the items were first recorded.

Temporary Working Capital Current assets that fluctuate with seasonal or cyclical variations in sales.

Terminal (Horizon) Date The date when the growth rate becomes constant. At this date it is no longer necessary to forecast individual dividends.

Terminal (Horizon) Value The value at the horizon date of all dividends expected thereafter.

Time Preferences for Consumption Consumer preferences for current consumption as opposed to saving for future consumption.

Times-Interest-Earned (TIE) Ratio The ratio of earnings before interest and taxes (EBIT) to interest charges; a measure of the firm's ability to meet its annual interest payments.

Total Assets Turnover Ratio This ratio is calculated by dividing sales by total assets.

Trade-Off Theory States that firms trade off the benefits of debt financing against higher interest rates and bankruptcy costs. A levered firm's value is equal to the value of an unlevered firm plus the value of any side effects, including the benefits of the interest tax shield minus the costs associated with potential financial distress.

Traded Option Contract Similar to OTC options, but like traded futures contracts, they are standardized.

Transaction Exposure The risk that arises because accrual accounting rules require that transactions be recorded at a spot rate or price even though the transaction will not be completed until a later date.

Transactions Balances Cash balances associated with payments and collections; the balance necessary for day-to-day operations.

Transfer Price The price charged for a transaction between affiliates.

Treasury Bonds Bonds issued by the U.S. federal government, sometimes referred to as government bonds.

Turnkey Operations Ownership is transferred after the facility is built and tested, so the owner only runs the operations.

U

Unbiased Predictor States that if foreign exchange markets are efficient and reflect all relevant information about future conditions, then the forward rate we observe today is the best unbiased estimate of what the spot rate will be in the future.

V

Value-Added Tax (VAT) The tax paid by an entity on the value added to the product by that particular stage of production.

Variance, σ^2 The square of the standard deviation.

Vertically Integrated Investment Occurs when a firm undertakes investment to secure its input supply at stable prices.

W

Weighted Average Cost of Capital, WACC A weighted average of the component costs of debt, preferred stock, and common equity.

Window Dressing Techniques Techniques employed by firms to make their financial statements look better than they really are.

Working Capital A firm's investment in short-term assets—cash, marketable securities, inventory, and accounts receivable.

Worst-Case Scenario An analysis in which all of the input variables are set at their worst reasonably forecasted values.

Y

Yield to Call (YTC) The rate of return earned on a bond if it is called before its maturity date.

Yield to Maturity (YTM) The rate of return earned on a bond if it is held to maturity.

Z

Zero Coupon Bond Pays no annual interest but is sold at a discount below par, thus providing compensation to investors in the form of capital appreciation.

Zero Growth Stock A common stock whose future dividends are not expected to grow at all; that is, g = 0.

INDEX